MARK TWAIN

The Bachelor Years

MARGARET SANBORN

Doubleday

New York   London   Toronto   Sydney   Auckland

MARK
TWAIN

The
Bachelor Years

A Biography

PUBLISHED BY DOUBLEDAY
a division of Bantam,
Doubleday Dell Publishing Group,
666 Fifth Avenue, New York, New York
10103

DOUBLEDAY and the portrayal of an anchor
with a dolphin are trademarks of Doubleday, a
division of Bantam Doubleday Dell Publishing
Group, Inc.

Library of Congress Cataloging-in-Publication Data
Sanborn, Margaret.
    Mark Twain : the bachelor years : a biography / Margaret Sanborn.
— 1st ed.
        p.   cm.
    Bibliography: p. 488
    Includes index.
    1. Twain, Mark, 1835–1910—Biography.   2. Authors, American—
19th century—Biography.   3. Humorists, American—19th century—
Biography.   I. Title.
PS1331.S17   1989
818′.409—dc19
[B]   88-31287
                                                                              CIP

ISBN 0-385-23702-2
Copyright © 1990 by Margaret Sanborn

DESIGNED BY CHRIS WELCH

ALL RIGHTS RESERVED
PRINTED IN THE UNITED STATES OF AMERICA
APRIL 1990
FIRST EDITION
RRH

To the memory of my father,
historian and scholar,
who introduced me at an early age
to Mark Twain,
by reading aloud The
Adventures of Huckleberry Finn.

Acknowledgments

M Y D E E P E S T G R A T I T U D E goes to Carolyn Blakemore, formerly with Doubleday, for her faith in this concept of Samuel L. Clemens and for her encouragement over the years. I am likewise grateful to Howard Kaplan, who carried on the editorial oriflamme with inexhaustible enthusiasm. The book has profited from his sensitive approach and capable judgment.

I am also greatly indebted to the late Sallie K. Gilbert, oral historian of her people, who lived for generations in the Southern Appalachians under conditions similar to those of Samuel Clemens' forebears. Her birthplace in the Tennessee mountains was perhaps two days travel by horse from the upland hamlet where Clemens' father settled just before moving to Missouri. Invaluable were her narratives (spiced with vernacularisms which seemed to step from the pages of *Huckleberry Finn)* of daily life in those remote coves and hollows, on farms and in villages set along rivers and creeks, drawn from her own experiences (many of which were also Sam Clemens' experiences on his uncle's farm), and from accounts by her parents and other kinsfolk. Apart from Clemens' writings about his childhood, Sallie Gilbert's recitals of events (which revealed attitudes and beliefs, and gave glimpses of the countryside), heard during almost daily meetings for over two years, not only imparted a strong sense of being there, but led to a broader understanding of the Appalachian culture which so markedly affected Clemens.

I want to thank Fred W. Thienes, grandson of Clemens' close friend Stephen E. Gillis, for giving reality to Sam's literarily productive stay with Steve's older brother, James N. Gillis, at his cabin in Jackass Gulch, near Tuttletown, California. Awareness of Sam's presence grew as Mr. Thienes recalled family traditions concerning Clemens, and pointed out sites familiar to Sam: under this tree stood the cabin of Dick Stoker, who appeared in several of Clemens' tales; there was the gold mine whose workings the sagacious cat "Tom Quartz" understood so well; and here near the spring was the place where Jim Gillis' large garden and orchard had been, and there his cabin.

I am equally grateful to Fred Thienes' daughter, Janet McDonald of Rochester, New York, who through correspondence and numerous long conversations enlarged my knowledge of and admiration for the remarkable Gillis family with whom Sam Clemens was intimate. She thoughtfully provided photocopies of her Gillis and Clemens material, and granted permission to quote from it.

I am also most grateful to Eunice E. Reader and Fred Langdon of Shady Creek Ranch, Nevada County, California, for graciously sharing their intimate knowledge of the region—especially of nearby Nevada City and Grass Valley, the gold towns where Sam Clemens lectured in 1866 and again in 1868. This enabled us to locate the hotels where he stayed, the halls where he spoke, the homes where he was entertained, and the mines he inspected and described. With Eunice Reader as guide, I explored the forested country through which Clemens rode his horse (and gave a vivid account of getting lost on the return ride) to lecture at Red Dog, now a ghost camp. Together we followed the Sierra crest route Sam traveled so often by stagecoach over the Henness Pass, between Virginia City, Nevada, and California.

I want to thank Julian C. Smith, Jr., owner of the house Orion and Mollie Clemens built in Carson City, Nevada, for kindly offering to give us a tour of the home. After seeing its interior, it became possible to picture life there when Sam's brother, Orion, was Secretary of Nevada Territory and Acting Governor. Then the

ACKNOWLEDGMENTS

house was the capital's social center, and Sam's presence enlivened those scenes during the months when he reported the legislature's sessions for *The Territorial Enterprise.*

I am very grateful to Dr. Robert H. Hirst, General Editor of the Mark Twain Project, The Bancroft Library, University of California, for granting permission to publish pictures from the Mark Twain Papers, and for his thoughtfulness in many ways. I am also most grateful to Robert Pack Browning, Associate Editor of the Mark Twain Project, for generously giving so much thought and time to answering countless questions, and helping with the collection of pictures to be used for illustrations. I wish to thank Janice Braun, Editorial Assistant, Mark Twain Project, for numerous courtesies.

A special note of appreciation is extended to Edgar Marquess Branch, Editor of the Mark Twain Project, for having written "Fact and Fiction of the Blind Lead Episode of *Roughing It.*"

I am thankful to Lisa Brower, Curator of Rare Books and Manuscripts, The Library, Vassar College, who furnished photocopies of the Samuel L. Clemens letters to his family, in their collection, and to her successor, Nancy MacKechnie, who gave permission to quote from those letters and to publish pictures from the library's archives.

I am likewise grateful to Henry Sweets, Curator, Mark Twain Home & Museum, Hannibal, Missouri, for granting permission to use Clemens family pictures from that collection.

I am highly grateful to Guy Louis Rocha, Nevada State Archivist, for responding so promptly and fully to innumerable inquiries and, most important, for calling attention to little-known and valuable sources.

I greatly appreciate the interest and time given by Dr. Linda A. Mainville, Curator of Photography, Nevada Historical Society, in helping with the selection of pictures from the Society's vast collection. I also want to thank Eslie E. Cann of the staff, for her aid.

For Jane Sheeks, Reference Librarian, Marin County Library, Fairfax Regional Branch, whose enthusiasm for this project nearly matched my own, there is a special note of gratitude. Her help in finding answers to challenging questions, in obtaining rare books and tracking obscure sources, has been invaluable over the years.

ACKNOWLEDGMENTS

There is special note of thanks owed to Walter Provines of the Mill Valley Public Library, for his never failing courtesy and his efficiency in handling the mass of interlibrary-loan material.

To the following people I am also deeply obliged for their helpfulness and interest:

Barbara Hughes, Administrative Librarian, Marin County Library, Civic Center Branch, San Rafael, and at that same library, Jocelyn Moss, Reference Librarian, the California Room; John Gonzales, Reference Librarian, California Section, California State Library, Sacramento; Michael Plunkett, Curator of Manuscripts and University Archivist, University of Virginia, Charlottesville; Fae Sotham, Editorial Secretary, *Missouri Historical Review;* Jeanne T. Newlin, Curator, Harvard Theatre Collection, Harvard College Library; Sara S. Hodson, Associate Curator, Literary Manuscripts, The Huntington Library, San Marino, California; Eric N. Moody, Curator of Manuscripts, Nevada Historical Society; Joan G. Caldwell, Rare Books and Manuscripts, Howard-Tilton Memorial Library, Tulane University, New Orleans; Thelma Percy, Administrative Librarian, Mill Valley Public Library (since retired), and staff; Madelyn Helling, Nevada County Librarian, Nevada City, California; Edwin Tyson, Searles Historical Library, Nevada City; Jacquelyn Mollenkopf, Dominican College Library, San Rafael, California; and Leslie V. Tusup, *The San Francisco Examiner.*

Contents

C O N T E N T S

Author's Note

Mark Twain, the Bachelor Years follows closely the most important and interesting period in the life of Samuel Langhorne Clemens who, as a young journalist, adopted the pen name "Mark Twain." The years from boyhood to marriage in 1870, at age thirty-four, were adventure-filled and saw Sam Clemens, who had been born into a genteel but poor family, change from a sickly, reticent child repressed by his austere father, into a robust, extroverted adolescent and young man. During that time he ran the gamut of experience and emotion at home and abroad as he became, in turn, a roving teenage printer who contributed humorous verses, squibs, and letters to country newspapers; a Mississippi River pilot; a Confederate soldier; a Nevada silver miner; a Far Western journalist; a widely traveled newspaper correspondent; and finally, a popular lecturer and famed bestselling author who became engaged to a beautiful and wealthy girl.

Those significant years also witnessed his development as a literary artist when he amassed the rich fund of knowledge upon which he would draw throughout his long career as a writer. Surely no other renowned author turned so often to his boyhood, adolescence, and young bachelor days for inspiration, ideas, incidents, characters (often his relatives), and settings—usually Hannibal,

Missouri, where he grew up, but occasionally the nearby village of Florida in which he was born.

In *The Adventures of Tom Sawyer* he immortalized his boyhood life along the Mississippi, including in it his mother, his sister, his younger brother, and himself (as Tom); his schoolmates, comrades, teachers, and certain townspeople of Hannibal. In the sequel, *Adventures of Huckleberry Finn,* Clemens' experiences appear again, but the boys are older, and there are more of the darker aspects of life on the river and in the Missouri villages he knew so well. He included more folklore of the blacks, with whom he associated daily, and of the Appalachian culture to which he was exposed constantly because his family had come from the Blue Ridge.

In *Life on the Mississippi,* he recorded in part his cub pilot and piloting days from 1857 into May 1861. His trip by overland stage to Nevada during July and August of 1861, his Far Western adventures, and his experiences in the Hawaiian Islands during 1866 were recounted in *Roughing It.* His travels in Europe, the Holy Land, and Egypt in 1867 appeared in *The Innocents Abroad.* Still, not one of these books can be considered strictly autobiographical, for he invariably took liberties with the facts.

Because no in-depth book which also recreated the scene and the times, and brought Clemens and those close to him alive, had yet been written, in 1982 I decided to undertake such a work.

At the start of my research I formed a kind of fellowship with Sam Clemens as I followed him through the years up to 1870, by way of his autobiography, letters, travel books, novels, sketches, newspaper correspondence, and magazine contributions. I was not rereading these works for pleasure this time, but with the objective of finding clues to personality and character, and of trying to establish which of the many adventures and experiences he claimed as his own were true.

But it was not until I began reading the large collections of his manuscript letters written to his mother, sister, brothers and close friends, that the real Sam Clemens came alive. These letters proved to be the single most valuable source. In them Clemens recorded his innermost thoughts and feelings, made his frank admissions, gave his outspoken opinions, and revealed his quickly changing moods.

The fact that these letters held so much material that was entirely new to me was puzzling until I began comparing them with
the only published collection, edited by Clemens' friend, designated biographer, and literary executor, Albert Bigelow Paine. It
was startling to discover how extensively the letters had been silently deleted by Paine in his anxiety to protect what he called the
"traditional Mark Twain." Not only had Paine left out whatever he
considered objectionable—the offense being all revelations that
might disclose the man as he really was, but he also conflated,
shifted portions of the text, restored contractions, and changed the
order of words. The effect of this heavy editing often deprived a
phrase, sentence or paragraph of its sense, and destroyed its spirit.
Further, he frequently substituted words for propriety's sake. He
followed the same practice in preparing Clemens' autobiographical
writings and dictations for publication. Caution is required when
using those works for without notice Paine would incorporate his
own thoughts or reflections into the text. In 1916 he took the
liberty of fabricating and publishing a version of the "Mysterious
Stranger" manuscripts, reordering, cutting, and enlarging the original material according to his own ideas, and departing signifi-
cantly from Clemens' original intention. Not until 1969 did Paine's
hand in the drastic revision so long accepted as Sam Clemens'
work, become generally known with the publication of *Mark
Twain's Mysterious Stranger Manuscripts.*

In May 1988, five months after this book was finished, the Mark
Twain Project at The Bancroft Library, University of California,
published *Mark Twain's Letters, Volume I: 1853–1866.* This is the
first scholarly edition of the letters, skillfully annotated, to ever be
printed.

It was not alone correspondence with his family that shed light.
Between September 7, 1868 and January 20, 1870, he wrote 184
letters to Olivia Langdon, the young woman he married. They were
withheld from publication as a collection until 1949, when thirty-
three were printed in book form. The remaining ones (some are
missing) are in the Mark Twain Papers at The Bancroft Library.
These letters also revealed a spectrum of moods and vagaries, imposed this time by a consuming passion, and unfolded the story of
his determination in the face of frequent rejections from Olivia and

continual rebuffs from her parents. They disclosed his almost fanatical struggle to become a Christian in order to win her approval and that of her family, and they recounted his final triumph.

There were many roads to follow in search of Sam Clemens and those close to him. One of them led to old photographs and daguerreotypes in archives and private collections. The earliest extant picture of Sam shows him at fifteen, as a printer's devil in Hannibal. Looking at him, it was easy to visualize him in his Cadets of Temperance uniform, with its scarlet sash, as he marched in a Fourth of July parade. At the Nevada Historical Society in Reno, I found a virtually unknown picture of his mother, Jane Lampton Clemens, taken in her fifties. No earlier likeness is known to exist, which is unfortunate, because her famed beauty was gone, but her bright mind, keen wit, and animation were obvious in her eager expression, sparkling eyes, and smile. I saw Sam as a pilot, seriously searching the distance as though on watch for snags and other dangers. Another rare picture is one of his handsome, sweet-natured younger brother, Henry. It is poignant because the daguerreotype was made just before his tragic death at nineteen in a steamboat explosion.

At The Bancroft Library one day, I examined a small marble head of a Greek woman or girl, blackened and eroded by time, and could easily envision Sam Clemens in a red fez, which he told of wearing on this excursion, stooping to pick it up from the court outside the Parthenon, where marble faces fallen from wall sculpture peered at him from the deep grass. It was after midnight in August 1867, the full moon was riding high, and the place seemed haunted. As he stood on the summit of the Acropolis he felt that a spell had been cast. Athens by moonlight was a "vision," he said. In the hope of taking some of that magic with him, he carried away the marble head—a kind of talisman.

In Carson City, Nevada, his brother Orion's house (where ghosts are reportedly seen), still stands. Here was a strong sense of Sam's presence, for in the second-story front bedroom, he wrote much of his correspondence for the Virginia City *Territorial Enterprise.* There is reason to believe that in this room he may have first signed "Mark Twain" (his *"nom de guerre,"* he called it), to a despatch.

At Jackass Hill in California's gold country, I spent a fine spring day with the grandson of Sam's intimate friend, Steve Gillis, of Nevada and San Francisco newspaper days. I listened to recollections of Steve, saw the little cottage where he spent his final years, and visited his grave in the family cemetery on the Hill. We walked over the site in Jackass Gulch, just below, where the cabin of James N. Gillis, Steve's older, scholarly brother, had stood. In the winter of 1864–65, Sam Clemens spent almost two months with Jim. In his cabin, Sam saw "The Tragedy of the Burning Shame," a skit he adapted for *Huckleberry Finn.*

From Jackass Hill I drove on to nearby Angels Camp, where Jim Gillis and Clemens went to prospect for gold. One rainy day the two took shelter in Lake's Hotel, and as they sat by the stove, puffing their pipes, Ross Coon, the bartender, told them about a jumping-frog contest. Shortly, Sam turned Coon's matter-of-fact account into what was finally known as *The Celebrated Jumping Frog of Calaveras County.* It brought Clemens his first fame, and remains one of his best-known tales.

After a careful study of Clemens' eleven notebook-journals (1853 into July 1868, following which there is a lapse of five years) and hundreds of his personal letters, it became apparent that the true story of his early years lay chiefly in those sources. The narrative for that period, it seemed, could be told best in his own words as often as restrictions on the manuscripts and a sense of literary fitness allowed.

Direct quotation from the letters and notebooks has given him the opportunity to reveal his personality and character in many moods, and bring to the telling a vitality and color distinctly his own.

This approach has made it possible to further enrich the story of those bachelor years, broaden its scope, and open the way for a fresh interpretation through the use of little-known material previously withheld, deleted, or overlooked, and published here for the first time in any biography of Samuel Langhorne Clemens / Mark Twain.

—MARGARET SANBORN

1989

I

———————————○———————————

BEGINNINGS

O N A G E N T L E R I D G E that rises between the north and south forks of the Salt River flowing through Monroe County, Missouri, stands the village of Florida, some thirty miles west of the Mississippi. Bounding it closely, in 1835, were fine forests of oak, hickory, maple, and tulip poplar; of pawpaw, persimmon, sweet gum, and dogwood, thickly entwined with the shaggy vines of fox and possum grape whose flowers filled the air with heavy fragrance, and the equally rampant muscadine whose large bunches of dark blue, richly flavored grapes with their strong aroma of wine, were prized, as they are still, for eating, and for jelly, preserves, and wine. The frosts of autumn brought flavor to the persimmon, set the hickory nut, and turned the woods into a blaze of scarlet, crimson, and luminous yellow. The moist banks of the Salt were lined with cottonwood, willow, and sycamore, marking the river's course in spring and summer with a sinuous path of varied green—and in fall by a winding trail of gold. Beneath these trees grew thickets of haw, thimbleberry, and maroon-flowered spice shrub whose aromatic leaves were used for tea, its berries for seasoning.

Beyond forest and highland there are fertile rolling prairies where herds of bison once grazed on the rich herbage. But within the first quarter of the nineteenth century these plains were tamed and planted to thriving orchards of peach, apple, and pear; to fields of corn, oats, wheat, hemp, and tobacco; to sweet and Irish potatoes; to beans, squash, and melons. Where the plantings ended, grassland and wood took up again and spread, untrammelled, north and south and west to meet the horizon. Most of the bison were gone by then, but planter-hunters and their sons, on horseback and afoot, followed instead the trails of deer, pronghorn and bear, while from the tall, sweet-smelling grasses their hounds flushed coveys of grouse, quail, and wild turkey.

Founded in 1831, the town grew slowly, and four years later, when Samuel Clemens was born there, it contained only a hundred persons. By then a scattering of log structures faced its two streets, Main and Mill, the most prominent among them a church with slab benches and puncheon floors which doubled as a schoolhouse on weekdays. There were also two stores, one run by Sam's uncle, John Quarles. Each stocked a few rolls of printed calico, spools of thread, "trimmings," and a small assortment of bonnets, wide-brimmed straw- and beaver hats, and tinware, hung by strings from pegs on the walls. Behind the front counter were several barrels containing salt mackerel, coffee, New Orleans molasses and brown sugar (coffee and sugar were five cents a pound), and native corn whiskey on tap (ten cents a gallon), for there was already a thriving distillery. There were "stacks of brooms, shovels, axes, hoes, rakes and such things here and there"; while on the back counter were bags of shot, a keg of gunpowder, a wheel or two of yellow cheese, shallow baskets of eggs (three cents a dozen), and flat black plugs of tobacco—only a few, for most villagers chewed the natural leaf which they twisted and dried themselves.

Under the white awnings outside were social centers where men in shirt sleeves and wide, yellow straw hats in various stages of delapidation gathered daily to lounge on empty drygoods boxes, puff their corncob pipes, gossip, argue politics, whittle with their large Barlow knives, spit tobacco juice at far-off targets (this usually worked up into a contest), or simply sat back to watch the passers-by—barefoot schoolboys in homespun jeans, blue roundabouts, and slouch or straw hats, shouting, teasing, and chasing one another; sedate schoolgirls in neat braids, bonnets, and white

Beginnings

pinafores; black women and girls going to and from the town pump, balancing full pails of water deftly on their heads; little boys, white and black, dressed in a single garment—a short, tow-linen shirt—bound on some errand; an occasional farmer on horse- or muleback, come in from the country; sows with their litters— and vagrant dogs whose arguments roused the loungers as nothing else did: "There couldn't anything wake them up all over, and make them happy all over, like a dog-fight," Sam Clemens would observe through his character Huckleberry Finn.

At random intervals the unpaved streets—deep dust in dry times, sloughs of black mud sticky as tar in winter—were inter-sected by lanes with cornfields on either side enclosed by rail fences crowded with thickets of fragrant pink pasture rose and yellow honeysuckle. Along one of these lanes, called aspiringly South Mill Street, stood a two-room cottage with lean-to kitchen, conspicious among the log cabins because it was built of clapboard. There, on November 30, 1835, a feeble, seven-months' boy was born to Jane Lampton Clemens, a beautiful young woman with a fair, clear complexion, rosy cheeks, and a wealth of auburn curls. When she looked at the tiny, wrinkled infant (her sixth child), she held little hope for his survival: "I could see no promise in him. But I felt it my duty to do the best I could. To raise him if I could," she wrote later.

Although waning, Halley's comet still glowed luminously that night. It was remarkable during this visit for the size and brilliance of its nucleus. Jane saw at once some mystic link between the comet's presence and this child's premature birth, for she had grown up with the traditions and beliefs of a people who were ruled by the positions of the constellations, and the moon's phases: Plow in Aries, pick apples and pears, and cut timber in the old moon, and hunt in Taurus. To them, a whippoorwill's call, or a stray dog's howl were portents of death. Witches and ghosts were real. In the quiet of the night when old beams or stairs creaked mysteriously, spirits were abroad. The moaning of the night wind was a ghost voice, grieving or trying to tell one something. When a person talked in his sleep, it meant a witch was after him. The dark held real terror, and few people dared venture beyond the candle's gleam. They knew that in every wood, swamp, field, or lane lurked witches, or ghosts, who were jealous of the living, ready to lure astray with flitting lights the lone traveler or the child sent on an errand. Everyone knew that it was bad luck to pick up a snakeskin —worse than looking at the new moon over your left shoulder; that one must not count the things to be cooked for dinner, or shake a tablecloth after sundown.

Jane Lampton was familiar with this lore, and had heard tales of the supernatural, as well—of haunts and witches, and night-riding; of spells and incantations, told about the winter fire. All of her life she found prophetic meaning in dreams, and heeded forewarnings and the promptings of intuition. Once her little boy Samuel took a firmer grip on life she watched him for signs of the unusual. As he was growing up, she so impressed him with the significance of the comet's presence at his birth he came to think of it as symbolically intertwined with his life span: "I came in with the Comet and I shall go out with the Comet," he once said in all seriousness. The prophecy was fulfilled.

Jane Lampton had named her first child Orion*for the constellation under which he was born, but there was nothing celestial in the choice of names this time. The boy was called Samuel after his paternal grandfather, and Langhorne, so tradition holds, for a close "Virginia friend" of his father, John Marshall Clemens, who was also from that state.

"There's a contribution in him from every ancestor he ever had. In him there's atoms of priests, soldiers, crusaders, poets, and sweet and gracious women—all kinds and conditions of folk who trod this earth in old, old centuries," Samuel Clemens observed through Colonel Sellers in *The American Claimant.* Among his own forebears there were Quakers, Indian fighters, militia and army officers, merchants, legislators, prosperous planters and slave holders—and women who were endowed with the force of character and adaptability to cope with poverty, adjust to a wandering existence, and endure the hardships of primitive frontier living. For such a woman he had only to look back as far as his mother.

Of that grandfather, Samuel B. Clemens, planter and public servant, who contributed his name and his atom to Jane Lampton's

* Pronounced "O'-ree-on."

boy, not even the given names of his parents, or his place of birth are known, but he was probably a native of Bedford County, Virginia, in the shadow of the Blue Ridge. That is where he was living at the time of his marriage, before he had begun his wanderings. Of his personal character there is only a family tradition that holds he was a loving husband and father, and enjoyed writing verse.

As to his wife, Pamela Goggin, the little boy's grandmother, her beginnings are less obscure. There are records of her maternal forebears, the Moorman family, who were Quakers, reaching Nansemond County, Virginia, a refuge for that sect, in 1670. The Moormans then spread into Louisa and Albemarle counties, settling not far from Thomas Jefferson's Charlottesville. Her father's line was not established in America until 1742, when Stephen Goggin, an Anglican, left Ireland for Virginia, where he also took up land in Bedford County. Stephen's son, another Stephen, married Rachel Moorman of the Quaker family, whose dowry consisted of "one Horse & Sadle one feather Bed and Furniture"—and, curiously for a member of the Society of Friends, Jude, a black slave girl. Young Stephen built his bride a substantial log house with a cobblestone fireplace, on the green banks of Goose Creek which flowed through his Bedford County farm. There, in October 1775, a daughter was born, whom they named Pamela.

Twenty-two years later, Pamela became the wife of Samuel B. Clemens, of undetermined age. Their first child was called John Marshall in honor of Virginia's foremost lawyer, who would soon become John Adams' Secretary of State, then Chief Justice of the United States Supreme Court. It is said that Samuel Clemens and Pamela knew Marshall through her brother, Pleasant Moorman Goggin, a lawyer active in the Virginia legislature.

Although Samuel B. Clemens was prospering—able to invest one thousand dollars cash in four hundred acres of farmland in the Goose Creek area, to buy two slaves, and household furnishings which included a fine mahogany sideboard—he succumbed to the allure of that part of the West so long praised for its bounty by Daniel Boone.

Late in June 1803, Clemens sold 93 acres to a close friend and neighbor. It is not known when the Clemens family began their westward journey, but by the following summer Samuel was already farming the rich bottoms along the Ohio River six miles above Point Pleasant, where Boone had once lived, and had been appointed the first Commissioner of Revenue in newly organized Mason County, Virginia. The next spring found him able to buy two tracts totalling a hundred and nineteen acres along Ten Mile Creek.

Then one morning during the fall or early winter of 1805, he rode off from home before sunrise to help a neighbor with a house-raising. In the flurry of departure he neglected to kiss his eldest child, seven-year-old John Marshall, who was waiting with the others to say goodbye. The grave, acutely sensitive boy was deeply hurt, and brooding over this departure from custom, concluded it was a deliberate slight.

As it happened, that was the last time he saw his father alive. At the house-raising, while Clemens was pushing a heavy log up a steep incline, it slipped suddenly, knocked him over, and swept him down against a large stump, crushing him fatally. The omitted kiss was never forgotten by the boy, nor was his father ever forgiven. In time the story was repeated, still with bitterness, to his own children.

Four years afterward, Pamela Clemens, who had been left in comfortable circumstances, was sought in marriage by a one-time suitor, Simon Hancock, a prosperous dealer in farmland; she accepted his offer, and settled with him in Adair County, Kentucky. Supported by money drawn from his father's estate, her eldest child, John Marshall lived at home until age fourteen. Considered old enough by then to make his own way, he took a job as clerk in an iron foundry at Lynchburg, Virginia. Industrious and ambitious, after the long hours demanded by his work he studied far into the night, determined to prepare for a career in law. Driving himself with amazing discipline, he paid little attention to proper diet or sufficient sleep, and undermined his constitution. All his adult life he was to suffer from chronic indigestion, and every spring from migraines, which he called "sunpain." He was subject to prolonged attacks of bronchitis which sent him periodically into the mountains for relief, and he was annually prostrated by malarial chills and fever. Very early, his health became one of his major concerns and it was remembered by the family that he doctored himself continually with various patent remedies.

Deciding at length that he was sufficiently grounded to begin regular law studies, he moved to Columbia, Kentucky, the seat of Adair County, where his mother was living, and commenced reading law in the office of Cyrus Walker, the county attorney. On October 29, 1822, young Clemens passed his oral examination, and, after presenting a certificate from the County Court of Adair which attested to his "honesty, probity, and good demeanor," he was granted his license to practice law in Kentucky.

By this time he had received his portion of his father's estate: cash, farm land in Mason County, three slaves, and the mahogony sideboard. As a man of some property, launched upon a promising career, he was able to consider marriage. He had had some close associations, business and personal, with the Lampton family (originally spelled Lambton), scions of English landed gentry who had emigrated to Virginia in the mid-eighteenth century, and who, like the Clemens family had pushed westward into Kentucky.

Among the Lamptons who had settled in and near Columbia, there were several eligible young women. Of them, Jane Lampton was most sought after for she was considered one of the most beautiful girls in the State, as well as the finest dancer. She was also bright and witty. Her father, Benjamin, who claimed kinship with George Lambton, Earl of Durham, was a successful merchant and small planter who was known widely for his sociability and his good singing voice. He was also, like many another forebear of Samuel Langhorne Clemens, active in public affairs. In 1801, he had married a neighbor, pretty Margaret Casey, also of Virginia stock, whose grandfather had been a captain in George Washington's Continental army. Her father, William Casey, was a noted Indian fighter, and a pioneer who led a party of settlers into Adair County. Being civic-minded as well, he hired a traveling tutor for children living in the Kentucky wilderness and helped found several academies. Later, he was elected to the state senate. All of these ancestors were active and energetic achievers.

Jane Lampton, "the great beauty," was the eldest daughter of Benjamin and Margaret Casey Lampton. She was widely admired for her delicate, shapely hands and small feet, for her flawless

complexion and mass of curly dark auburn hair, and for a remarkable grace of movement—attributes passed on to her son, Samuel
Langhorne. She was also an expert rider—a skill he did not in-
herit, for he never went far on horseback without mishap or discomfort. Jane and her favorite sister, Patsy, spent long hours in the
saddle, posting across the wooded Kentucky countryside from one
end of the state to the other, to visit relatives. During Christmas
week they observed the local custom of riding from house to house
(often far-flung) to attend the parties given to celebrate the season.
They would dance jigs, reels, and quadrilles the first night through
to the accompaniment of fiddles and guitars, sleep a few hours, eat
a bite, then ride on to dance all day at the next plantation. No ball
was considered a success unless Jane Lampton was there. She remained a dancer into her eighties when she was delighted to show
family and friends those steps and figures she had learned as a girl.
Whenever dance music was played she could hardly sit still. She
also kept her beauty and agility to the end, and at eighty-five was
said to have "looked the duchess." Whenever she attended the
theater (to which she was devoted), dressed in black velvet and
white lace, with lavender kid gloves and stylish ostrich-tip bonnet,
everyone turned to look and admire.

She was very affable, and made friends easily, but had no use
for people who bored her. She attended church, not because of
strong religious convictions, but for the sociability, the same reason she attended funerals. If the funeral was for some important
person, she enjoyed it for its pageantry, just as she did a parade.
She laughed easily (and also cried easily) for she was emotional,
and her feelings were readily touched. "She was very bright, and
was fond of banter and playful duels of wit; and she had a sort of
ability which is rare . . . the ability to say a humorous thing with
the perfect air of not knowing it to be humorous,"—a key to her
son's later success as a lecturer. Jane's gift was enhanced by a
drawl which made everything she said seem funnier, and by the
fact that she was a clever mimic. It was often told in the family how
she once kept a room full of people at a party in Cyrus Walker's
house "in stitches" with her perfect imitation of the attorney's
notably clumsy dancing. Walker, who had been out of town on
business, arrived late. As he rode up to his place he heard the

sounds of music and "uproarious laughter," but the moment he opened the door there was an instant and uncomfortable silence. Looking about the room he saw Jane Lampton (a cousin of his bride) standing flushed and breathless in the middle of a circle of spectators. What had the fun been about, he wanted to know? But there were only a few titters in reply. He kept up a fire of questions until Jane at last admitted what she had been doing. Not at all displeased, he asked her to repeat the performance but she refused. He begged her, but she was adamant. At length she agreed, but only after he promised to give her the fine silk dress he had brought home for his wife. Walker, it was remembered, joined in the laughter.

Jane Lampton Clemens has often been pictured as a woman of stern morality and rigorous religious observance who warped her son's talents. Her delight in card-playing and dancing, her liveliness and obvious enjoyment of life, and the fact that her intimates never heard her refer to "the retribution of a stern Calvinistic God," contradicts that concept of her as a puritan. Further, during the many years that she lived in St. Louis, her family recalled that she did not attend church at all, but did remember her going several times to the synagogue. She would always retain an inquiring mind.

She was also impulsive and quick-tempered, displaying outbursts that were short-lived because she was naturally of "a sunshiny disposition." She possessed a heart "so large that everybody's grief and everybody's joy found welcome in it and hospitable accommodation," Sam once wrote of her. She was the "natural ally and friend of the friendless," he added. This sympathetic interest included all creatures, particularly cats, who were so often homeless or victims of cruelty. Cats were Sam's favorite animal.

She detested all irksome and boring tasks, particularly housework and cooking. "Don't learn to do anything you don't like to do, because if you don't know how to do it, you'll always find somebody who does," she advised.

This, then, was the joyous and carefree girl who attracted John Marshall Clemens, the austere and humorless young attorney who was still quick to find offense in innocent words or acts. He was her opposite in appearance as well, being sallow with lank black hair which he wore brushed close to his head and held in place by his ears as "one keeps curtains back by brackets." Deep-set gray eyes piercing as an eagle's glinted from under thick black eyebrows. His nose was aquiline, his mouth thin and unsmiling. His dress was fastidious, his manner courtly: he was "always a gentleman."

There was another admirer who had been courting Jane for two years, Richard Ferrel Barrett, who was preparing to become a physician. He lived in Columbia and she in the country, but he rode over almost daily to see her. "I loved him with my whole heart, and I knew he felt the same way toward me, though no words had been spoken. He was too bashful to speak—he could not do it," Jane related.

There came a day when both were invited to a party in a neighboring town. After learning that Jane was going, Barrett wrote her uncle who had arranged to take her, declaring his love for her, and asking permission to drive her home afterward in order to propose. Her uncle was sympathetic, but believing that Jane ought to be prepared, read her the letter. She was overcome by reticence and flatly refused to go or to send Richard any excuse. Weeks passed while both young people waited vainly for some word from the other. Then, without telling her, he went to live in neighboring Green County, Kentucky. They apparently never saw one another again.

Unwilling for the world to know how deeply she was hurt, Jane put on a brave front. Then, "to stop the clacking tongues" (for everyone supposed they were engaged), "and to show him *I* did not care, married in a pet." The man she turned to impulsively in this turmoil of emotions was John Marshall Clemens, whose future seemed the most promising of all her other admirers.

Sometime after Jane's marriage in May 1823, Richard Barrett commenced his medical studies at Transylvania College in Lexington, Kentucky. After graduating, he was for a time professor of materia medica at Kemper College in St. Louis, and was also successful in business, acquiring wealth through land investment.

With remarkable flexibility and self-discipline, the blithe Jane Lampton adjusted to this loveless marriage—John Marshall being incapable of deep affection and Jane in love with another man—

Beginnings

without sacrificing her high spirits and relish of life, although she was forced to suppress these most of the time. In boyhood, their son, Samuel Langhorne, noticed that the attitude of his parents toward one another was like that of friends, always courteous and considerate and respectful, even deferential—but never warmer. This did not surprise him since his father was such a dignified, reserved, and austere man, who rarely smiled and never laughed, who had pleasant relations with a few select friends, but never intimate ones. His mother, he knew, was warm-hearted and affectionate, but it seemed natural to him that she would withhold those qualities in his father's presence.

Their relationship, however, was by no means always placid, for John Marshall was acutely nervous and sensitive, moody and irascible, which often provoked sharp words from Jane. Further, he somehow learned that she had accepted him to spite another man. Still, after nineteen years of marriage and seven children, Jane Lampton was found to be a handsome woman of cheerful disposition—affable and spirited, and a great favorite. Her husband, it was noted, was solemn and taciturn.

Secretly, she had never stopped regretting her rashness in marrying to spite Richard Barrett. Once, in later life, she told the story of her only true love to her son, Orion, and when speaking of the letter in which he had declared his love and requested permission to propose, she observed:

"My uncle should have done as he was asked, without explaining anything to me, but instead, he read me the letter; and then, of course, I could not go."

After their marriage, tradition holds that Jane Lampton and John Marshall Clemens lived in a handsome two-story brick house in Columbia. Although this was an auspicious start, Clemens already had misgivings about his future in that community where there were a number of competent attorneys already well established. Had he been more friendly and sociable he would have found no difficulty in overcoming the competition, for his probity and high principles were widely respected. But that pride, aloofness, and lack of humor left him entirely unfit for dealing with the public, particularly since it was necessary to make friends among all classes in order to build up a clientele.

As his prospects seemed to stagnate, his health declined, and he decided to move to a different climate and a smaller community, which he believed would hold greater opportunities. Lawyers were always in demand on the frontier to settle the endless disputes over land titles, surveys, and boundaries, and the claims of creditors in that era of reckless borrowing and wild speculation in nebulous schemes for quick riches. Shortly before their first child, Orion, was born in July 1825, they had settled near Jane's cousin, Dr. Nathan Montgomery, in the tiny log and frame village of Gainsboro, seat of Jackson County, on the Cumberland River in the highlands of Tennessee, a location presumably beneficial to both John Marshall's chest complaints and his prospects.

But after nearly two years spent in a vain struggle to establish a law practice, the family packed up—although Jane was pregnant again—and traveled north and east to a site just chosen as the seat of Fentress County, which was not yet organized. This practically invisible community on the edge of the great Cumberland Plateau, a district known as the Knobs of Tennessee, was called Jamestown, and consisted simply of a row of several small log cabins beside an old Indian trail leading to a group of springs. But Clemens, who was known as "an energetic dreamer" at times, was filled with hope. By arriving at the virtual opening of the territory, there were chances such as he had never had for becoming a civic leader and prominent lawyer. These bright prospects prompted him to persuade his brother, Hannibal, and Hannibal's wife, Jane, to join him and move his tanning business there.

Anticipating civic prominence, John Marshall proceeded to build the community's first frame house, which was looked upon with disapproval by his less ambitious neighbors: "Common log house ain't good enough for *them*—no indeedy!" was the consensus. As if that were not enough, they "tuck 'n' gaumed the inside . . . all over with some kind of nasty disgustin' truck—some whoop-jamboree notion from Kaintuck which they say is all the go amongst the upper hunky, and which they calls it plarsterin'!" The house boasted not only plastered walls but a window spanned with glass in every room, prompting the villagers to call it the Crystal Palace.

Although Clemens was classed as one of the "upper hunky," things went his way from the start. With the county's organization he was appointed clerk of the circuit court, acting attorney-general, and county commissioner, whose duties included drawing plans and specifications for the courthouse and jail. He also found time to open a law office.

His next act, having important consequences for his family, was the purchase of about seventy-five thousand acres of Tennessee land. After he had paid some four hundred dollars for it, he is said to have turned away, looked toward his vast holdings twenty miles off in the hazy distance, and said: "Whatever befalls me, my heirs are secure; I shall not live to see these acres turn to silver and gold, but my children will."

In the transient and uncertain existence on the Western frontier, land offered the only security. But this land never fulfilled the great promise Jane Lampton's favorite cousin, James, had proclaimed: "There's millions in it—millions!" Mercilessly it kept the Clemens family in a state of expectation for forty years. Whenever times grew hard and the outlook was bleak, there was always the Tennessee land to encourage them: "Do not be afraid—trust in me —wait," it seemed to say.

With the acquisition of this acreage Clemens realized his ambition and became the county's largest landholder and its leading citizen. He dressed accordingly, in a blue tail-coat of twilled worsted, trimmed with brass buttons, and he carried a mahogony cane with a silver handle. He bought a barouche and several throughbreds for riding and harness. Jane wore dimity and lawn in lavender-grey, pale yellow, rose, or "mignonette green," for white was no longer fashionable.

This period marked the high point in Clemens' success and prosperity. Within two years of his settling there, it was easily seen that Jamestown had no future. Its growth came to a halt with the completion of the twenty-fifth log house. These dwellings were scattered among the cornfields and tall pines in such a way that "a man might stand in the midst of the city and not know but that he was in the country if he only depended on his eyes for information."

Contrary to expectation the surrounding territory remained sparsely settled and Clemens' law practice declined. With his waning fortunes he began complaining of poor health, blaming his circuit-court duties which forced him to ride horseback all over the county. Inconsistently, he was to maintain later that nothing benefitted his constitution more than horseback travel.

Meanwhile, Jane Lampton had borne three more children. Two girls—Pamela,* in September 1827, and Margaret in May 1830— separated by a boy, Pleasant Hannibal, who died at three months and was buried in the lonely mountain cemetery, under the pines.

In an effort to better his finances, Clemens opened a small general store, but this also failed to prosper, and he was at length forced to sell many personal possessions. After that, pride kept him from staying on at the scene of his former affluence, to become an object of public pity, and late in 1831 he went on alone to the Three Forks of Wolf River, nine miles east of Jamestown, still deeper in the mountains, where he took up about two hundred acres of rich bottom land, which he planned to farm, even though he had no knowledge of farming or any aptitude for it.

Jane Lampton, with her three young children and a fourth on the way, refused to go with him. In her anger at his announcement of the move she had hurled a book at his head, she told afterward. She stayed on at the comfortable house with plastered walls and glass windows, in the company of her sister- and brother-in-law, until well after June 1832 when Benjamin, the baby she named for her father, was born. By that time John Marshall had taken over a small crossroads store, and was serving as postmaster for the hamlet of Pall Mall, across Wolf River. He had completed a rough log cabin of two rooms, one above the other, connected by an interior ladder. For cooking and heat, there was a rock fireplace chinked with red clay. For nearly three years this cramped dwelling sheltered eight, including Jennie, the black maid-of-all-work and children's mammy.

But not one of John Marshall's undertakings succeeded here, either. Poverty, worry, hard work, poor health, and an overwhelming sense of failure took a toll, and, in the words of a neighbor, he was "all wore out, tore down, used up," and looked far older than thirty-five. Nor was Jane Lampton unscathed. The discomfort, the scrimping, and the demands made upon her by four young children tried her patience and temporarily dampened her spirits. The fine

* Pronounced Pam-ee'-la.

Beginnings

lawn and dimity dresses were of necessity cut up for baby garments, and she wore drab linsey-woolsey.

Then in the summer of 1834, encouraging letters began arriving from her family. Her father, Benjamin Lampton, her dearest sister, Patsy, and Patsy's husband, the jovial John Adams Quarles (still another transplanted Virginian) had followed the siren call of the West, and with babies and older children, some twenty slaves, household furnishings, farming and carpentering tools, and horses and stock, journeyed over mountains and up rivers to the newer territory of Missouri. There in the village of Florida, John Quarles opened a general store. Like most westering Americans, he and Ben Lampton were optimists, and wrote the Clemenses letters filled with enthusiastic praise for the prospects of the village, already containing fifty-four houses. In reality, there were only twenty-one, but in the desire to make the picture rosy and entice them to follow, they had counted roofs—barns, corncribs, stables, and tobacco sheds. They told of the enterprising citizens who had built three mills along the banks of the Salt River, below town—two grist and one sawmill, already working. This was not exaggeration. Large numbers of "Keels, Batteaux, and Flat boats" were plying the river with cargos of lumber, meal, hemp, and whiskey (already there were four distilleries producing about ten thousand gallons of whiskey and three thousand gallons of brandy and gin), marketing this produce in the Mississippi River towns—also fact. The family had nothing but good to say for the fine soil, the healthful climate, the pure spring water, and the fine forests. John Marshall and Jane *must* come at once!

There was only one response to such letters: Clemens began immediate preparations to leave Tennessee. From the sale of his farm, stock and store he realized a few hundred dollars. The seventy-five thousand acres, which held the promise of millions, was left intact.

Early one spring morning in 1835, the Clemens family started off for Missouri, the parents and three younger children riding in the barouche, Orion astride the trotting horse, and Jennie, the slave girl, mounted on the pacer. Hannibal Clemens was to oversee the transportation of such heavier pieces as the mahogany sideboard; then he and his wife would follow them to Missouri.

The travelers crossed the highlands, where in the woods, spring beauty, arbutus, and violets were already blooming. They ferried over the Cumberland River, then followed the trace northward to Louisville. There they boarded a steamboat for the voyage down the Ohio to Cairo, Illinois, then up the Mississippi to St. Louis. They did not linger, for cholera was raging in the city, but hurried on either by riverboat, or overland by way of the old road that led north to St. Charles through Moscow and Troy to New London and Hannibal. There they turned westward toward the village of Florida, where a warm and enthusiastic welcome awaited them.

Late in April, someplace on their journey, Jane Lampton had become pregnant again. This time she carried the child that would be her genius.

II

---○---

"A HEAVENLY PLACE FOR A BOY"

THE CLEMENS FAMILY arrived in the village of Florida about the first of June 1835. Shortly, John Marshall rented the two-room frame house on South Mill Street, just a few doors away from the store of his brother-in-law, John Quarles. Until he could set up a law practice, Clemens went into partnership with him. Then, applying his formula for success, he plunged into the purchase of land, making down-payments on a 120-acre tract of government land east of town, and on eighty acres of timber. In September, he bought a three-acre parcel on North Mill Street and began planning a house that would be in keeping with his social position.

On November 30, Jane Lampton unexpectedly went into labor and Dr. Thomas Jefferson Chowning, yet another Virginian, was called in to deliver the premature boy, whom they named Samuel Langhorne. Nothing was ready. There was not even a shirt to put on the child, but neighbors came to the rescue with used baby clothes.

It is curious that John Marshall agreed to name his son for the father against whom he still held a grudge, but he doubtless thought it mattered little for it seemed obvious the boy would not live long.

Jane succeeded in pulling Sam through that crucial first winter, but he remained a "sickly and precarious and tiresome and uncertain child" until he was eight years old, and always more trouble than the rest of Jane's brood collectively. Once, after he was grown, he was talking with his mother about those early years, and asked, "I suppose that during all that time you were uneasy about me?"

"Yes, the whole time."

"Afraid I wouldn't live?"

Then, after a pause designed to give impact to the kind of remark they both relished, "No—afraid you would."

When "Little Sam," as he was called for years because he remained frail and undersized, began developing he proved an acutely sensitive and excitable child. "I was born excited," he once wrote. He was easily upset and was given to outbursts of hyperactivity when he would throw himself about, wildly flailing his arms and kicking, or rolling over and over on the floor or in the grass, laughing or crying uncontrollably. He was also highly imaginative and impressionable and, young as he was, listened attentively to the adults talk of happenings then or long ago, about such dire subjects as murders, Indian massacres, suicides, and hangings, or death by fire or drowning. He would reconstruct the details so vividly in his mind's eye he came to believe he had witnessed them all.

For many years he was plagued by sleep-walking and by terrifying nightmares in which he relived many of those occurrences he had come to accept as experience. One dream in which robbers came tip-toeing into his room to steal the bedclothes, was annoyingly recurrent. Still asleep, Sam would jump up, hide the covers, then return to bed, only to awaken later shivering with cold and fear, and calling for his mother, who would come in and comfort him. His father had no patience with such doings. He believed that this boy, for whom he felt no attachment, purposely caused annoyance.

One hot August night in 1839, when Sam was going on four he got up from his bed and, fast asleep, walked into the room where his sister Margaret lay ill with what Dr. Chowning called "bilious fever." Standing beside her bed, the boy stretched out his hand

"A Heavenly Place for a Boy"

and picked at the coverlet persistently, just as the dying were known to do. His mother watched his actions with horror, for she knew what was meant. When nine-year-old Margaret, who had promised to be the dark-haired beauty of the family, died a few days later, Jane Lampton decided that this son, whose birth was heralded by Halley's comet, had second sight. Certainly, all of his life he was intuitive, and he often had prophetic dreams. As a child, he apparently gained a local reputation as a mind reader, and his mother sometimes invited neighbors to come in and be entertained by his gift.

Margaret's passing was his first encounter with death. He heard the church bell toll nine times to mark her age, he saw his mother's tears and the sober faces of relatives and friends who came to sit up with the corpse. He looked at Margaret, dressed all in white, lying in the wooden coffin set up on chairs in the parlor of the new house, and listened to the watchers singing hymns softly in the candlelit room—strains of music which wove themselves into his dreams. The next day, the shoemaker who lived next door told Jane Lampton of the vision he had had several weeks before of a coffin and funeral procession filing out the gate and along the winding road to the cemetery. Sam, who heard her repeat the story many times afterward, was deeply impressed.

How often during his first decade he came near to dying himself he could never count, they were so numerous. In fact, his family became so used to the recurring death-watch, they often fell asleep during the ordeal. Being intellectually curious and experimental in all things, Jane Lampton would try out on Sam the latest panaceas she read about in the health journals. Taking no chances, however, she also continued to administer such proven remedies as calomel, jalap, rhubarb, blue mass pills, Epsom salts, mustard plasters, and castor oil—half a dipperful, with an equal measure of New Orleans molasses to help it down. However, if she saw that Sam was not responding, she called in the doctor.

When hydropathy became popular, she used it as a cure and to build him up, subjecting him to cold showers, cold sitz baths, and cold packs, and winding sheets soaked in ice water around his torso. Of this vividly remembered experience he once wrote, "When the chilly rag touches one's warm flesh, it makes him start with sudden violence and gasp for breath just as men do in the death agony. It froze the marrow in my bones and stopped the beating of my heart." Afterward, to bring him to, she rubbed him down with a towel "like a file."

The last death-watch took place when Sam was ten. There was an epidemic of measles in town, a virulent type that had caused seven deaths in one day among the children. All the mothers were terrified, and Jane Clemens took every precaution to keep her children from coming in contact with the disease. Sam remembered how very tired he had grown of being under the constant threat of death, and he made up his mind to end the suspense and settle things one way or the other. His best friend, Will Bowen, was dangerously sick, and Sam decided to catch the measles from him. The first time he slipped into Will's bedroom Mrs. Bowen found him and promptly marched him out of the house. The next time, he managed better and was able to get into bed with Will.

The result was a case of measles which took Sam to "within a shade of death's door." Nothing his mother or the doctor did for him helped. The family gathered in the sickroom to see him off. He recognized them all, and was aware they were crying, which interested him because he was "the center of all this emotional attention and was gratified by it and vain of it." The doctor decided to try one thing more: he placed bags of hot ashes on the boy's chest, wrists, and ankles. To everyone's astonishment, Sam began to improve. The doctor had managed to drag "me back into this world and set me going again."

In recollecting his sickly childhood, he came to believe that he somehow managed to live, not on account of the various remedies —but in spite of them.

During the first two years of Sam's life, his father made those familiar rapid strides toward success. He was chosen to head a board of commissioners from three counties, to form the Salt River Navigation Company, licensed by the state legislature to raise money for dredging the river, as well as building dams and locks to enable Mississippi River steamboats to dock at Florida. He also headed another commission formed to promote the Florida and Paris Railroad (Paris was the county seat), and he shortly began to serve on the board of trustees to found the Florida Academy. As his reputation grew, his law practice kept pace. Then, in November 1837, he was sworn in as judge of the Monroe County court, to serve four years. His pay was a mere two dollars a day when sitting, but the prestige was considerable, and from then on he was always called Judge Clemens.

At this same time, a single-story double house was being built on the North Mill Street site, far less imposing and roomy than originally planned—but a start. Next, with growing confidence, he dissolved his partnership with John Quarles and opened a store of his own across the street, in his optimism installing as his counter clerk his fourteen-year-old son Orion, a dreamy, impractical lad. Remembering his own ambition, self-discipline, and independence at that age, he expected Orion to profit from the experience and metamorphose into a likeness of himself.

Within another year the pattern of blasted hopes and thwarted plans so characteristic of all John Marshall's endeavors had begun to take form. But this time he was not alone, for it had become evident that Florida's future was more promise than substance. The effects of a general economic depression the previous year lingered, and not enough money could be raised from outside sources to launch either the navigation company or the railroad. Production of local products—whiskey, flour, and hemp—was up but business began to stagnate because of inadequate transportation to market. Clemens' law practice and store suffered.

John Quarles met the challenge by selling his business and returning to the land. He bought a large acreage four miles from town, built a roomy, comfortable log house, stocked cattle, and planted fruit trees, wheat, tobacco, and a large subsistence garden to provide for his eight children and thirty slaves.

John Marshall Clemens faced the problem of support for his family by accepting odd jobs. In what spare time he had he experimented with perpetual motion. He hoped to gain considerably from the sale of his land but the acreage east of town proved unfit for farming, and the forest holdings turned out to be too small to lumber profitably. But the new frame house was finished and, clinging to the last shreds of hope, the family moved in not long before Jane's seventh and last child, Henry, was born in June 1838.

At heart, Clemens knew he had made a mistake by settling in Florida, and was soon contemplating another move. Margaret's death decided him. Late that fall he sold what real estate he could in and around Florida and with the proceeds bought a quarter of a city block, which included a row of shops and a small hotel, "The Virginia House," in downtown Hannibal, a growing Mississippi River port with a population of sixty families.

Moving day was never forgotten either by four-year-old Sam or his sensitive brother Orion, who lived in dread of his father's disapproval. The wagon was packed with the final load. Everyone had taken a seat except Orion, who maintained afterward that he was waiting for his father to "invite" him to get in. Instead, Clemens started to drive off. The boy was horrified. "The sense of abandonment caused my heart to ache," he remembered, yet he admitted to hoping secretly that the family would drive the thirty miles to Hannibal without missing him. "Then the world would have seen how I was treated and would have cried 'Shame!' "

With mixed emotions, he watched the wagon slow down a little distance away, and heard the shouts for him to come on—and hurry!

Why had they left him behind? he demanded, when he caught up. He refused to accept his father's explanation that he was so preoccupied he could forget his son. Orion would always believe the act was intentional and hold a lifelong resentment, just as John Marshall had done with his own father for the overlooked kiss. The tense emotion of the scene impressed Sam so deeply he came to think it had happened to him.

The family moved into rooms in the newly acquired Virginia House, and once again Clemens prepared to make his way as a merchant, this time in his own store. He bought two thousand dollars' worth of dry goods and groceries on credit, and borrowed cash to sustain himself until he built up a trade. Then, outfitting Orion in a suit of new clothes, he installed him once again as a sales clerk, and opened his doors for business.

It was here in Hannibal that Sam was to have his first experience with school. When he was four and a half he was sent to a dame school kept by Elizabeth Horr, the cooper's wife, in a small log house at the end of South Main Street. The terms were twenty-five cents a week. Piety, good manners, reading, recitation, long division, and spelling were the subjects taught, through third grade.

Mrs. Horr was a "New England lady of middle age with New England ways and principles." Short, thin, dark-haired, and bespectacled, she had a straight stern mouth but gentle eyes, and wore a white cap, edged with starched ruffles which was tied under her chin.

It was desperation that dictated sending Sam to school, for he was a "backward," uncommunicative child, the least promising of the lot. He was still hyperactive, and if not watched every minute, would run away—invariably toward the river. Whenever that happened, Jane Lampton expected momentarily to have someone bring him home half dead. With Henry now a toddler, Sam was more than she could handle. Further, she hoped that learning might draw him out, and that discipline would curb his antics.

Rules were many and strict at school. Sam never forgot his first day because he broke a rule without knowing it and was warned that a second breach would bring a whipping. Presently, he repeated the offense and Mrs. Horr sent him outside to get a switch. In the mud not far from the door he found a cooper's shaving two inches wide and a quarter-inch thick, old and rotting. He brought it in, placed it on her desk, and waited with an attitude of meekness and resignation which he believed would win her sympathy—the head, crowned with a "dense ruck" of short, auburn curls just like his mother's, slightly bowed, the blue-grey eyes (which sometimes looked green) cast down. Instead, after a few seconds of oppressive silence, she addressed him by his full name—it was the first time he had ever heard Samuel Langhorne Clemens strung together "in one procession"—said she was ashamed of him, and sent an older boy to cut a proper switch. The lesson learned was that when a teacher calls a boy by his entire name, trouble is in store.

Another memory from this period concerned the power of prayer. Mrs. Horr declared that whoever prayed for anything with earnestness and strong desire could be certain it would be answered. This information, new to Sam, was strongly appealing for he had no end of wants which were never satisfied. He decided to experiment by praying for gingerbread. Sam coveted the fresh slabs of gingerbread his classmate Margaret Koeneman, the baker's daughter, brought to school each morning. She always kept them carefully out of sight and harm's way, but one day, when Sam had finished his prayer, on opening his eyes he saw the ginger- bread lying within easy reach, and Margaret looking the other way. He was an immediate convert, and during the next few days did as much earnest praying as anyone in town. But nothing came of it. He discovered that not even the most powerful prayer was "compe- tent to lift that gingerbread again" and decided that "if a person remains faithful to his gingerbread and keeps his eye on it he need not trouble about your prayers." This experience sowed the seeds of his first religious doubts.

The many hours of confinement to the schoolroom were a sore trial for a child as young, frail, and restless as Sam, and learning by rote bored him. His outlet was to disobey rules for the sake of breaking the monotony. On beautiful spring and summer days he tended to sit back and stare out the windows at the woods and hills where he longed to be, and lapse into a dreamworld—also subject to punishment.

A schoolmate, Annie Laurie (Laura) Hawkins, two years his ju- nior, "a little girl in calico dress, sunbonnet and pigtails," remem- bered Sam from his first day at Mrs. Horr's: He was barefooted, and his fingers were stained purple from mulberries, which he divided with her. Sam recalled that she was the very first sweet- heart he ever had. He had an apple, fell in love with her, and gave her the core. He remembered it perfectly—exactly where it hap- pened, and what kind of day it was. Laura was to become the model for Tom Sawyer's sweetheart, Becky Thatcher—"a lovely little blue-eyed creature with yellow hair plaited into two long tails, white summer frock and embroidered pantalettes."

By the end of a long day in school Sam was running on nervous energy, and came home either over-excited and wild, or exhausted and fretful. The only school he did not regard as drawn-out torture was the one he attended a few days a week during the months he spent yearly at his Uncle John Quarles' farm, outside the village of Florida. Jane Lampton had decided that country living in a relaxed atmosphere would improve Sam's health, and made arrangements with her sister Patsy for his care. The first time he went, the entire family planned to accompany him for a few days' stay. Early one

"A Heavenly Place for a Boy"

Saturday morning in June, Jane Lampton set out in the light wagon with Pamela, Benjamin, Henry, and Jennie, the children's mammy; Orion drove. For some reason, Sam, the object of this pilgrimage, was left behind to come on by horseback with his father the next day.

John Marshall wakened early that Sunday, got up, ate breakfast, and was on the road before sunrise. When he reached the farm, Jane Lampton's first question was, "Where is Sam?"

"Why, I never once thought of him," he replied. Jane's young uncle, Wharton Lampton, jumped on a horse and sped back the thirty miles to Hannibal. He found Sam in the house crying softly, trying to amuse himself by encouraging meal to run out of a hole in the sack. Like Orion, he demanded to know why he had been left behind, and he, too, would always hold rancor toward their father. In later years he fused the two incidents of desertion, and wrote graphically of the fear that seized him when he discovered that he had been abandoned at the time the family moved from Florida to Hannibal. He described the "grisly deep silence" that descended upon the empty, locked house, and the eerie black shadows that stole in and engulfed him with the coming of night, which held unseen terrors—ghosts and witches, and those demons who did their bidding. Of his father, he would observe, "Ungentle of manner toward his children." His sister Pamela did not agree, for cold indifference toward their feelings was reserved for his sons.

The log cabin where that country school was held stood in a clearing surrounded by oaks, hickories, and maples, three miles from the Quarles plantation. In the cool of early morning, the children would set off (eight Quarles cousins, and Sam) carrying baskets packed with slices of ham, corn dodgers, dishes of peach cobbler, and containers of buttermilk, which were devoured at noon, picnic-fashion, under the trees. As it neared dusk, they sauntered back over the same forest paths. For Sam, there were lasting memories from those walks—the "solemn twilight and mystery of the deep woods," the rustle of dry fallen leaves underfoot, the sheen of rain-washed foliage and the pleasing smell of damp earth; the exotic fragrance of wildflowers; the distant drumming of ruffed grouse, and far-off tattoo of the flicker.

All of his life he was to learn from experience, observation, and emotion, rather than from schools, text-books, or set courses of study. When he came to write, he was able to call upon this remarkable treasure stored in a memory so retentive of such details that they remained as sharp as if they had been put there yesterday.

From tramps with his cousins, he soon acquired the skill of identifying wild animals from their tracks and birds by their calls, and in the clear night skies to name the stars and constellations. From his Uncle John, he learned the proper time to tap the maples, and just how to place the troughs and boil down the juice. He would not have been Sam Clemens had he not also learned how to "hook" the sugar after it was made, and come to realize how much better maple sugar "acquired by art" tasted than that "honestly come by." He learned to tell without "plugging," which was the ripest watermelon in the field—knowledge gained through experience when he overate of green melons and became so sick he was, again, not expected to live. His mother, who happened to be at the farm, took him in hand and after dosing him with those tried remedies to check cramps, announced confidently, "Sammy will pull through. He wasn't born to die that way."

He became skilled in forecasting the weather: it will rain within three days when birds fly a yard or two and then lighten, if smoke hugs the ground, or if leaves show their undersides. A winter will be hard if hickory nuts have thick shells, or if screech owls are heard in late fall crying like a woman in distress. All this lore found its way into his writings. He also learned to tell time with his nose—whether it "smelt late" or early.

He put by memories of expeditions to pick luscious wild strawberries, "fragrant and fine," in the "fresh crispness" of early morning when "dew beads sparkled upon the grass," and the woods rang with a chorus of birds; and of nutting in autumn when the oaks were "purple," the maples and sumacs "luminous with crimson fires," and the hickories washed with gold. He would always be able to feel the thumping rain of nuts on his head when sudden gusts flung them down in the frosty dawn. The tangy flavor and smell of dark blue fox grapes hanging in clusters among the leaves of saplings remained with him forever, as did the "ripe

"A Heavenly Place for a Boy"

cucumber" taste of pawpaws, and the bitter-sweet of little purple-blushed persimmons picked wild in the groves.

There were solitary rambles over the prairie starred with pinks and walled on all sides by forest, which left lasting impressions. Once, lying on his back among the wildflowers and gazing up into the sky, he watched a huge hawk, hovering motionless, "wings spread wide and the blue of the vault showing through the fringes of their end feathers." This vision came to symbolize the prairie's strength, its peace and loneliness, an emotional sensation that made the throat tighten and tears well.

Days were not devoted entirely to play for it was part of the children's training to help with household and farm chores, requirements which Sam viewed with characteristic distaste, and avoided as much as possible. Within reach of his upstairs bedroom window was a lightning rod—"an adorable and skittish thing to climb up and down, summer nights, when there were duties on hand of a sort to make privacy desirable."

He always looked forward to the first frosty nights of fall, when the cavernous rock fireplace was piled high with flaming hickory logs, and the whole family gathered about it, cats and dogs included. His Aunt Patsy sat in one chimney corner, knitting; his Uncle John sat in the other, smoking his corncob pipe. Sam would never forget that room—the gleaming, carpetless floor "mirroring the dancing flame tongues," pitted with black spots where fire coals had "popped out and died a leisurely death"; the guns resting on deerhorns over the mantlepiece; the trundle bed in one corner and a tall day clock in another; the dining table with leaves; the dozen or so splint-bottomed chairs here and there, some with rockers; a cradle ("out of service, but waiting with confidence"), and a spinning wheel whose "rising and falling wail" was to Sam the "mournfulest of all sounds," which made him feel low-spirited and "filled my atmosphere with the wandering spirits of the dead." Huck Finn is made to say, "I heard the dim hum of a spinning-wheel wailing along up and sinking along down again; and then I knowed for certain that I wished I was dead for that is the lonesomest sound in the whole world."

When the apples were ready to eat, that was the time for story-telling. Some of John Quarles' tales were tall, others were true;

some were scary, and many were humorous. There were bound to be repetitions after awhile, but in such an atmosphere, "how fresh and crisp and enchanting" they all seemed to be, and how funny the jokes no matter how old, Sam felt. He noticed how quickly the evenings passed when compared with those seemingly endless ones at home when John Clemens sat stiffly in his chair and read poetry aloud with the same "inflectionless judicial frigidity" he used in court.

There were other nights memorable for experiences of a different sort, when the children, white and black, crowded into "Uncle Dan'l's" cabin beyond the orchard for stories and songs. "All the negroes were friends of ours," Sam once wrote. The boys played, swam, fished, and explored together. Daniel, of middle age, was the "faithful and affectionate good friend, ally, and advisor" of the cousins. When Clemens came to write *Huckleberry Finn*, he cast Uncle Daniel as that noble character, Jim.

Sam, who had a remarkable eye for detail, ear for vernacular, and sense of drama, was deeply impressed by the setting in which the tales of humor, fantasy, horror, and the supernatural were told. He would always be able to picture how the firelight played upon the faces of the children clustered about the hearth, and piercing the blackness of the room, cast dancing shadows, red and eerie in shape, on the back wall. Ever afterward he would be able to recapture the inflections of the storyteller's voice, his imitative sounds of animals and birds, thunder and wind; the pat-pat-pat of footfalls; the gibber of ghosts and screech of witches. His animals and birds not only sang, whistled, chirped, growled, and barked, but talked as people do. Uncle Daniel's dialect, phrasing, cadences, and the impact of his intentional pauses were all useful in the development of Sam's story-telling art, oral and written.

Years later Sam could still recall the feeling of "creepy joy" which made him tingle all over with anticipation when it came time for the final tale, a ghost story, "The Golden Arm." The children moved back from Uncle Daniel and closer together for he became terrifying when he clenched his teeth and imitated the "wailing and wheezing singsong" of wind in the graveyard and mixed with it the long, piercing, high-pitched cry of the ghost protesting the theft of her golden arm. When, at length, the ghost finds the thief, she stands beside his bed, bends down over him (" 'en he cain't skasely git his breath!'") and wails, "plaintively and accusingly, 'W-h-o—g-o-t—m-y—g-o-l-d-e-n—*arm?*' " Here Uncle Daniel would make one of those important pauses, his hands up in front of his chest, the fingers bent to resemble claws, and look steadily and impressively into the face of first one, then another of his listeners. They would hold their breath and shiver for although they knew what was coming, that made it no less frightening. At exactly the right moment he would jump at that child who appeared most under the spell, grab him or her by the shoulder, and shout, *"You've* got it!"

For many years, this frightening tale was retold with great skill by Clemens from the lecture platform.

Excitement was intense throughout this dramatic recitation, especially for such a volatile child as Sam, and he remembered well the feeling of emptiness which oppressed him when the tale was done, and there was nothing to look forward to but "unwelcome" bed, and restless spirits that would weave themselves into his dreams.

Bed could also be a welcome haven, as on those nights when he looked out his bare window on the "white cold world of snow outside," and the wind whistled about the eaves and shook the house. Then, how "snug and cozy" it was to lie between the feather-ticks. In the morning, he would see the powdery snow, driven between the sashes, lying in little ridges on the floor, making the room cold and uninviting and bed seem ever more warm and comfortable, curbing the "wild desire to get up—in case there was any."

Some nights at Uncle Daniel's were given over to singing, accompanied at times by fiddle or banjo. Sam liked jubilee songs best. He learned them all, and throughout his life they remained his favorite music: "It is utterly beautiful to me & it moves me more than any other music can. . . ." It came straight from the heart and needed no explanation. When he sang those spirituals himself, they were an outlet for his own joys and sorrows, and all who heard him considered it a memorable experience. One night, years later, he was visiting friends in Hartford, Connecticut. They were talked out momentarily and were sitting silently in a room lighted only by the full moon. Suddenly, Sam Clemens stood up and, with his eyes shut, began singing in his clear, tenor voice, very softly at first, "a faint sound, just as if it was wind in the trees," which gradually swelled as, his face alight, he became lost in another world. Those who were in the room sensed he was no longer in Hartford. He sang song after song, all spirituals, all sorrowful. Then he stopped a moment, put both hands up to his head, and began to sing "Nobody knows de trouble I got. . . ." He finished the "Glory Hallelujah!" with a great shout.

There were also lasting memories of predawn expeditions on the farm, with a company of men and boys, black and white, and a pack of hounds, to hunt rabbits, squirrels, prairie chickens, and wild turkeys—cold and dismal affairs at the start, which Sam always regretted ever have consented to join. A blast on a tin horn brought twice as many dogs as were needed, who in their enthusiasm "raced and scampered about, and knocked small people down, and made no end of unnecessary noise." He was one of those small people. Uncommonly sensitive to sounds, Sam, who could not even bear the ticking of a clock in his bedroom, found the barking of dogs intolerable all of his life—"they bark when there is no occasion for it"—and never had any liking for them.

Now, at a word, the hounds loped off toward wood and prairie, and the hunters drifted after them silently in the "melancholy gloom." Presently, the first faint streaks of yellow glowed along the horizon and a few birds piped in the thickets. Then the sun rose and poured "light and comfort all around; everything was fresh and dewy and fragrant," and for Sam, "life was a boon again." After three or four hours, they were back at the farmhouse, laden with game, ravenously hungry, and just in time for breakfast.

Meals there were also memorable—looking back, they made Sam "cry to think of them." In summer, a long trestle table was set on the planked floor of the covered breezeway that connected the big double log house with the kitchen. The sumptuous fare was a welcome novelty for Sam, used to plain meals and small portions dictated by economy and his mother's lack of interest in cooking. He would always be able to picture those huge platters of fried chicken and roast pork from his Aunt Patsy's kitchen; of wild and domestic turkey, of duck, goose, pheasant, rabbit, squirrel, prairie

"A Heavenly Place for a Boy"

chicken, and venison. With what delight he remembered the procession of biscuit, batter cakes, buckwheat cakes, light rolls, corn pone, and wheat bread, all brought from the ovens piping hot; the plates of steaming corn on the cob, succotash, string beans and butter beans, peas, sweet and Irish potatoes, and the watermelons, cantaloupes and musk melons—all just picked in the garden. Then there were the tall pitchers of sweet milk and buttermilk, and the bowls of clabber sprinkled with brown sugar, and finally, the apple, peach and pumpkin pies, the fruit dumplings and cobblers.

Aside from the hunts, and the tramps over the prairies, there were other pleasures found close by. Just down past the barns, corncribs, tobacco-curing houses, and stables (where Sam had a riding horse), was a stream which "sang along over its gravelly bed and curved and frisked in and out and here and there and yonder" in the shade of overhanging trees and luxuriant vines—a "divine" place for wading. It had deep pools as well, perfect for fishing much of the year and for swimming during Dog Star days, that sultry period between mid-July and September, when Sirius rises and sets with the sun. In still another part of the wood were long swings made from the tough bark of hickory saplings. With the help of Mary, a black girl of eleven, who was sent along by Aunt Patsy to keep the younger cousins from harm, the children pumped as high as forty feet, and thrilled to a sense of flying.

The Quarles farm was "a heavenly place for a boy," Sam once reflected, and he had it in mind when he came to write *Huckleberry Finn*, using it as a model for both the Grangerford plantation, with its big double log house, and the Phelps farm (which also appears in the book *Tom Sawyer, Detective*). Each year, he could hardly wait for the time to go there, and his cousin and playmate Tabitha ("Puss") Quarles, who looked forward to his coming with equal eagerness, never forgot his arrival. She remembered that on his earlier visits he was a "pale, sickly boy who did a great deal more thinking than was good for him."

The house was set in the middle of a very large fenced yard, in one corner of which stood a dozen large hickory trees and an equal number of black walnuts, which gave welcome summer shade. Just beyond the front rail lay the road from Hannibal. When the wagon that brought Sam for his long visit pulled up by the stile, Tabitha's father would hurry out to greet him with a hug and carry in his heavy carpet bag. Sam would follow with a covered basket which he allowed no one else to carry. It contained a favorite cat (sometimes two) which he could not bear to leave behind. She was impressed by his great fondness for cats (which remained lifelong), the gentle way in which he played with them, and his patience in training them. She saw, too, how devoted they were to him. He would always believe that they conversed with one another and held many traits and attitudes in common with human beings. Since his mother's sympathies reached out to homeless and unfortunate cats, her house was often overflowing with them (once there were nineteen) so Sam had his pick for adoption. During one of those times when cats and kittens were everywhere underfoot, John Marshall Clemens took his nearly grown daughter, Pamela, aside and urged her to learn to be a good housekeeper, and when that time came, to always keep her husband's comfort in mind—and see that she did not keep too many cats. Those months spent at the Quarles' farm every year, at various seasons, until he was nearly fourteen, were among the happiest of his boyhood. Freed from his father's irascibility, coldness, and undisguised dislike ("my father and I were always on the most distant terms when I was a boy—a sort of armed neutrality, so to speak") Sam was able to gain strength emotionally as well as physically. Most important in this development was the fact that he felt wanted. Of his Uncle John he once said, "I have not come across a better man than he was in his character." His Aunt Patsy was, after all, his mother's favorite sister, and very like her.

At home, Sam's natural fluency, wit, and sense of the comic was sternly suppressed by his father's disapproval of whatever he considered frivolous. His Uncle John encouraged him to talk and tell stories. Sam's cousin, Puss, recalled that most of Sam's early efforts at being funny took the form of teasing the girls, and playing such tricks on her mother as hiding a bat or harmless garden snake in a darning-basket or a coat pocket—"for a surprise." But after a time, his sense of what was truly humorous began to evolve and there came a day when Puss and her sisters and brothers were convulsed with laughter over Sam's delivery of a "comic lecture" on the habits of the garter snake, given in his "slow drawling voice." "Sammy's long talk," Jane Lampton called it, unaware of her own drawl. Once, when someone who had never seen her was sent to meet her at a railroad station, and without hesitation walked right up, she asked how he had done it. "Mrs. Clemens, I would have known you anywhere because you talk exactly like Sam."

"Nonsense," she retorted. "I talk just like anybody else."

There were times after supper when his uncle called on him to give an account of the day's adventures which he did with many embellishments and considerable humor. He carried this practice home and, in his father's absence, entertained Jane Lampton with some astonishing accounts of daily exploits. Some of the best she repeated to her friends, but they only served to gain Sam a local reputation as a teller of tall tales.

"Do you believe *anything* that boy says?" one of them asked.

"Oh, yes," she replied brightly. "Sammy is a wellspring of truth, but you can't bring up the whole well with one bucket.—I know his average. . . . I discount him 90 per cent for embroidery, and what is left is perfect and priceless truth, without a flaw in it anywhere."

But not even at the farm was there unalloyed happiness—for there were Sundays, when attendance at the log church in town was compulsory. For Sam it was a form of punishment. First, the preacher read aloud the hymn in a style much admired at the time, starting on a medium key and rising steadily until he reached a particular height. Then, stressing the "topmost word," he would let his voice plunge as if from a springboard. After the hymn was sung by the entire congregation, he read off the notices of various meetings and of strayed or stolen horses and cattle—a list that seemed to Sam "to stretch out to the crack of doom." Next came the prayer, a "good, generous" one that interceded on behalf of almost everyone in the world, even to the millions "groaning" under the oppressive heel of European kings and Oriental despots. Sam endured it but did not listen, for he knew the ground by heart. He fidgeted, he thought about the contents of his pockets—a piece of chalk, a buckskin thong, two fish hooks, a ball, marbles, a wooden soldier with one leg—and he daydreamed. Then the minister announced his text, and Sam's sufferings at confinement continued.

He generally ignored the droning voice in the pulpit, but occasionally his attention was caught by a more than ordinarily dramatic and vivid depiction of the limitless fire and brimstone in store for transgressors (every boy was one of those). At such times his lively imagination called up clear and terrifying visions of the everlasting torture that lay in wait for him after Judgement Day, and "clammy fears gathered about my heart."

It was not easy for Sam to free himself from nightmares and sleepwalking, even in the relaxed home atmosphere at the Quarles' farm. One morning, long before sunrise, his Uncle John found him in his nightshirt, sitting fast asleep on the back of Old Gray, in his stall. The boy was clinging to the horse's mane and shouting at him to hurry. He was escaping from some terrifying peril which had overtaken him in his dreams.

There were other times when he wakened accidentally on moonless nights to find himself oppressed by the blackness of the little room under the eaves, packed with "ghostly stillness." As he lay there striving to go back to sleep, "forgotten sins" came flooding out of memory's secret chambers and demanded to be heard. How "ill chosen" the time to confront visions of eternal punishment. In an attempt to banish his fears he would turn his thoughts to the dark world outside, but found no compassion there. His keened senses heard only the "dismal" hooting of an owl lamenting someone's death, and the wail of a prairie wolf sent "mourning by" on the wind.

III

"A BOY'S PARADISE"

In LOOKING BACK, Sam Clemens always thought of Hannibal, his home from the time he was four until he was almost eighteen, as "a boy's paradise." It was his ideal of a small country town and became the model for those villages in his fiction. The most famous was St. Petersburg, home of Tom Sawyer and Huckleberry Finn. But Hannibal was also the prototype for Dawson's Landing, Hadleyburg, and even the medieval village of Eseldorf, Austria, the setting for one version of *The Mysterious Stranger.* The youthful narrator in that novel introduces his riverside town by saying, "Eseldorf was a paradise for us boys."

John Quarles' farm was "a heavenly place for a boy," but of the two Edens, Hannibal had the advantage, for past its doors flowed the nation's main artery of commerce: the Mississippi River. Sam never forgot the procession of trim steamboats, the miles of coal barges and mighty timber-rafts—"an acre or so of white, sweet-smelling boards in each one," with a crew of at least two dozen men. Often he and his comrades would swim out a quarter-mile to ride on one of those rafts.

Although when the Clemens family first settled in Hannibal only two steamboats a day called there—one upriver from St. Louis, the other down from Keokuk, there was bustle and excitement enough to satisfy a boy. Their approach was always heralded by John Hannicks, a free black drayman noted for his quick eye and stentorian voice. Invariably the first to sight the far-off film of smoke, he would lift the cry, "S-t-e-a-m-boat a-comin'!"

At this signal, doors flew open and people came hurrying out; carts and drays started rattling over the cobblestones; town loafers roused from their perches; dogs barked and raced along; boys whooped as they ran—all with a common direction. Once at the wharf every eye was fixed upon the approaching vessel as though on a wonder they were seeing for the first time. It *was* a handsome sight, Sam admitted—"long and sharp and slim and pretty," and gleaming white. Its tall twin chimneys, with ornate crowns and a large gilded emblem swung between, belched clouds of black smoke—a dramatic touch achieved by tossing pine pitch on the fires as the boat approached port. Perched on that high deck called the "texas" was the "fanciful" pilot house, all glass and "gingerbread," he wrote. The paddleboxes were "gorgeous" with a picture painted in gold or bright colors, or simply gilded rays, above the boat's name. A flag flew "gallantly" from the jack-staff. The furnace doors stood open and the fires roared and blazed, while pent steam hissed and screamed through the gaugecocks. The captain, calm and imposing, the envy of all, lifted his hand—a bell rang, the wheels stopped, then reversed, beating the water to foam, and the ship came to rest. Sam would always recall the mad scramble that followed, with everyone trying to get aboard and go ashore, take on freight and discharge it at the same time, while the mates yelled and swore mightily to "facilitate" matters.

Ten minutes later she was in the main stream again, the jack-staff bare, and the black smoke gone. By the time Sam was nearing twelve, over a thousand steamboats a year stopped at Hannibal and carried away products from the surrounding country worth one and a quarter million dollars.

In 1819, a group of land speculators drew up plans for the town of Hannibal, which was to be built at the foot of a little valley cut through gentle wooded hills by Bear Creek; and held a sale of lots at St. Louis. Even though it was pointed out to prospective buyers that the community was bound to flourish through river trade and become the metropolis of northern Missouri, lots sold slowly, and

"A Boy's Paradise"

by 1829 only "thirty souls" were living there, according to an early account. However, during the next decade there was a sudden spurt of growth, the population jumped to about a thousand, and the town began spreading up the slopes. By Sam's day, the grandest house in town—a "palace" in his eyes, stood near the summit of the highest knoll, Holliday's Hill, which rose nearly three hundred feet and seemed "to pierce the skies." There lived Mrs. Holliday, who enjoyed entertaining the town's young people with candy, gingerbread, lemonade—and ice cream, the latter attesting to her prosperity. Behind her house stood a grove of mossy oaks and elms, known to Sam and his friends as Sherwood Forest. There in a brush-covered cache, the boys kept bows and arrows, wooden swords, and a tin trumpet, which they used to enact scenes from Robin Hood. This fine, secluded haunt was a favorite one in which to pass a day of truancy from school. Sam remembered stealing along the seldom-used bypaths that led to the hilltop, making sure to cross several times those creeks he came to, as a certain foil to pursuit. As he wound through clumps of trees over grassy stretches, past large outcroppings of rock, and skirted the quarry so as to avoid notice, he thought about which adventures to enact that day, for he was certain of having the company of at least one classmate. He could be ready in a matter of minutes. Pulling out his accouterments from their hiding place, he would fling off his jacket and trousers, convert his suspender into a belt, (cinching his shirt into a semblance of a medieval tunic), thrust his sword in place, sound a blast on the trumpet, and, in the role of Robin, bound off to challenge a comrade with "Hold! Who comes here into Sherwood Forest without my pass?" and hear the answer, "Guy of Gisborne wants no man's pass"—for they talked "by the book."

Beyond this ridge lay forest, and farther off, prairies where farmers grew corn, wheat, hemp, and tobacco which they hauled by wagon over the single road to Hannibal—rough at all times of year. To one side were fields fenced with rails, their angles crowded with hazel bushes and blackberry vines. On the other side were woods where bluebirds sang and village grandmothers gathered their medicines—ginseng, ginger root, May apple, bergamot, pennyroyal, and sassafrass bark to make teas, spring tonics, and poultices—for "every old woman was a doctor," Sam remembered.

Five miles out that way lived Hannibal's faith healer, Mrs. Utterback, a farmer's wife, whose specialty was toothache. Sam rode out to her place twice behind his mother on horseback. Jane was the patient, and the boy watched with interest as the old woman laid her hand on his mother's jaw and said, "Believe!" The cure was prompt.

Hannibal was proud of its setting, for here the mile-wide river, bounded by Holliday's Hill on the north, by the steep bluff—Lover's Leap—below, and by dense forest on the opposite shore, seemed more like a sea, not a turbulent sea, but "a very still and brilliant and lonely one," Sam thought, reflecting the vivid colors of dawn and sunset and catching the shadows of fleeting clouds.

The most extensive view was from the summit of Holliday's Hill (called Cardiff Hill in *Tom Sawyer)*, where one saw miles up and down the Mississippi and far over the wooded expanses of Illinois on the other shore. Sam came to believe, after he had explored the river from Cairo to New Orleans, that this was one of the most beautiful outlooks along the Mississippi.

The other fine vantage point was Lover's Leap, a name derived from a supposed Indian tale of thwarted love and suicide. One fall night when Sam was nine, he watched a group of local Millerites, in their long white ascension robes, assemble on the sloping, grassy summit, ready to meet their God. They had left harvests ungathered and had taken tearful leave of friends, for Adventist William Miller of New York had set October 22, 1844, for the Second Coming, when his disciples would be snatched to Heaven before the world was destroyed. It was eerie to watch the robed figures move about in the wavering red glare of pitch-pine torches, which made their faces glow; to see them fall to their knees in loud prayer, or stretch their arms skyward with ecstatic shouts, impatient for the first trumpet blast to summon them. To the boy it appeared to be a gathering of ghosts in cerecloth shrouds. Many years later when he was considering some further tale about Tom Sawyer and Huck Finn, he recalled that scene and made a note on the possibility of setting a Walpurgis Night on Lover's Leap, and having his boy-characters witness the orgy of witches, demons, and sorcerers.

That same year, Hannibal's future looked bright: It already had two hotels, three saloons (a number that would shortly double), four general stores, two schools, and a cigar manufactory, which was owned by the family of one of Sam's closest friends, John Garth. There were also two churches, one of them Methodist—a brick building beside the square called the Old Ship of Zion, where Sam first attended Sunday school. His teacher was a kindly, patient stonemason named Richmond, who regularly presented the boy with three blue tickets as a reward for his perfect recitation of five Testament verses. Mr. Richmond did not mind that each Sunday Sam gave the same verses about the five foolish virgins. The tickets were valued because they might be exchanged for a book from the Sunday school library. In addition to his patience, Sam remembered Richmond because "at some time or other he had hit his thumb with his hammer and the result was a thumbnail which remained permanently twisted and distorted and curved and pointed like a parrot's beak." The boy was fascinated because it was the only one in town, and he was envious, wishing that he might have been so fortunate.

The second church was Presbyterian. In its slim, white steeple which towered over North Fourth Street, hung a bell from the wreck of the steamboat *Chester.* In one of her experimental moods, Jane Lampton one Sunday attended service in that church, spoke well of it afterward, and shortly the rest of the family, in Sam's words, became "abandoned Presbyterians." This did not include his free-thinking father, for within the family's recall he went to church only once—and never again.

Hannibal also had five physicians, all of whom made their way into Sam's writings. There was Dr. Hugh Meredith, that "gruff old bass-voiced sailorman," who saved Sam's life several times during his sickly years. There was Dr. Humphrey Peake, one of John Marshall Clemens few close friends and, like him, proud of his Virginia ancestry. Peake clung to the fashion of twenty years ago, and still wore knee-breeches, silk hose, and buckled shoes. There was Dr. Cunningham, who brought Sam through the measles, and Dr. Orville Grant, who kept a drugstore, and after the total collapse of the Clemens fortunes, shared his house with the family. There was also Dr. James Radcliff, in whose family madness ran. It had skipped a generation and appeared in his two teenage sons, one of whom, known as "Crazy" Radcliff, lived a hermit's life in a bark hut on the Stillhouse Branch of Bear Creek. His brother, who had suicidal and homicidal tendencies, was kept locked and chained in a small house in the family's yard, and was fed through a hole. Once he mysteriously obtained a hatchet, and in the belief that one hand had committed a mortal sin, hacked it off. Another time, he somehow escaped, entered the kitchen, snatched up a butcher knife, and attempted to kill his mother. The doctor came just in time to save her. All this was of great interest to Sam Clemens, who slowed his steps whenever he passed the Radcliff place, and looked closely at the little prison in the yard. This was fine stuff from which to weave tales, and lunatics appear in a number of his stories.

Hannibal also had a jeweler, T. B. Stevens, whose son, Ed, was another of Sam's comrades, and a tailor, William Kercheval, whose pretty daughter, Helen, was a playmate (she grew up to marry John Garth). There was also the German baker, Koeneman, upon whose gingerbread young Clemens had tested the efficacy of prayer. The numerous branches of Bear Creek contributed to the local economy by powering a gristmill, a whiskey distillery, and three sawmills and two planing mills, which were making rapid inroads on the fine forests nearby. At the Creek's mouth stood two pork houses which, Sam recalled, supplied "free spareribs, livers, hearts, &c.," to the needy, and gave the boys bladders, which they dried and used for balloons. Close by stood the tanyard and in a marshy spot not far away was the little brick calaboose, so seldom used, the town provided no guard.

By the mid-1840s, Hannibal could boast a number of substantial two-story houses of brick and clapboard, some with fashionable Greek pediments and pilasters, uniformly steep-roofed and white-washed, their walls almost hidden by tangles of tea-roses, honey-suckle and jasmine. Dooryards were planted to hollyhocks, mari-golds, touch-me-nots, and fragrant wallflowers. Dark blue morning-glory cascaded over palings, and on windowsills stood clay pots of scarlet geraniums. Along the outer edges of the dirt streets were plantings of red mulberry trees, and honey-locust, sweet-smelling in spring.

Lining Market Street, which was claimed to be one of the widest

"A Boy's Paradise"

thoroughfares in Missouri, were three-story brick mercantile houses and hotels towering above the little frame shops wedged between. On one busy corner was the tinmonger's tall, unpainted pole, encircled from top to bottom with pots, pans, cups, pails, and other samples of his wares, every stir of air noisily proclaiming his trade. On Market Street, Sam watched the parades—Fourth of July, circus, and political—which filled it from side to side with brightly uniformed and costumed marchers and horsemen. There were fire companies, veterans, militia, Masons, Odd Fellows, Temperance Society members, antic clowns, and strident brass bands, all with fluttering banners. There were times when Sam joined these processions.

Just beyond the heart of town lay Draper's Meadow, named for another of John Marshall Clemens' close friends, Judge Zachariah Draper of South Carolina, an early settler in Hannibal who had made a success in his law practice and business career. He joined John Clemens in founding the local Library Institute and in planning the Hannibal & St. Joseph Railroad. On Saturdays, Sam and his friends caught crayfish in the stream that meandered through the Meadow. They feasted on the blackberries, raspberries, and strawberries that grew wild there, and played hi-spy and gulley-keeper, or fox, haste, three-cornered cat, and hide 'n' whoop, choosing sides, or "It" with the old chant:

Eggs, cheese, butter, bread
Stick, stock, stone—dead!

And they took out their marbles to play knucks, ring-taw, and keeps.

In the willow thickets, the boys divided themselves into warring Indian tribes and killed one another again and again from ambush. Or they became highwaymen, members of Murrell's terrible gang, hiding in the roadside groves and charging out to shoot their squirt- and pea-guns at passing hog-drivers and farmwives with their carts of melons, peaches, and garden truck. Recollections of these raids so pleased Clemens that he had Huckleberry Finn describe them. Many a Saturday, Sam recalled, was spent in damming one of Bear Creek's branches to operate watermills of their own making. In less industrious moods they raided orchards and watermelon patches, feasting to surfeit. "The true Southern watermelon is a boon apart, and not to be mentioned with common things," Clemens once wrote. "When one has tasted it, he knows what the angels eat. . . ." There were other times when, in imagination, they converted an empty flatboat moored along the river into a steam packet, and personated captain and pilot, for nearly every youth aspired to be one or the other.

These comrades were all schoolmates save one. There was Will Bowen, whom Sam always considered his *best* friend, and with whom he kept up a lifelong contact. Later, he used Will as one of the three models for the composite Tom Sawyer. There was John Briggs, almost as close and the prototype for Tom Sawyer's companion, Joe Harper. And there was John Garth, and Sam Honeyman, and Clint Levering, and Ed Stevens. There was also Norval Brady, known as "Gull" because his favorite book was *Gulliver's Travels;* and Jimmy McDaniel, envied by all because he was the confectioner's son and was thought to live on candy. The exception in the group was Tom Blankenship, son of Hannibal's current Town Drunkard—an "exceedingly well-defined . . . office," who worked occasionally at the local sawmills but fed his large family mainly by hunting and fishing. Tom's mother also drank, and several of his sisters were suspected of being prostitutes, but this was never proved.

Tom Blankenship, four years Sam Clemens' senior, was unschooled, underfed, and unwashed. His nakedness was covered by the ragged, cast-off clothing of grown men, therefore, the seat of his trousers "bagged low and contained nothing; the fringed legs dragged in the dirt when not rolled up." His coat, when he wore one, hung nearly to his heels; and his hat was "a vast ruin with a wide crescent lopped out of its brim." But he was the only completely independent person in town, coming and going just as he pleased, living by his wits, but neither tough nor cynical, having as good a heart as any boy had. He was continually good-natured and cheerful. No one made him go to school or church. No one prohibited his fighting. "Pa wouldn't allow us to fight," Sam Clemens once reminded his sister, Pamela: and Tom could swear magnificently. Naturally he was admired by every "harrassed, hampered, respectable boy" who yearned to be just like him, and was looked on by parents as a "juvenile pariah." Although everybody in Hannibal knew everybody else, and was affable, there were nevertheless grades of society: people of good family, people of unclassified family, and people of no family, and the lines between them were well defined.

Tom Blankenship's company was therefore forbidden by Sam's parents and those of all his comrades, which made its value quadruple. "We sought and got more of his society than of any other boy's." For Sam, this was easy because the Blankenships lived in a large, rickety house just across the lane behind the Clemenses' Hill Street place. The two boys worked out a code of cat-call signals for night meetings. Sam would respond to Tom's call by slipping out the bedroom window onto the single-story back roof, then steal down through the arbor.

" 'Huckleberry Finn' was Tom Blankenship," Sam Clemens once wrote. He was one character in *Tom Sawyer* so like the original that anyone familiar with Hannibal of the 1840s would recognize him immediately. When Pamela Clemens read the description of Huck Finn, she exclaimed, "Why that is Tom Blankenship!"

As a gang or in smaller numbers, these boys were responsible for some long-remembered pranks. On one occasion, Ed Stevens, the jeweller's son, led a foray to demolish Dick Hardy's stable, Hardy having somehow incurred their wrath. Tom Blankenship masterminded the plot to sneak a wild stray cat, tied up in a hatbox, into every bedroom at the Western Star Hotel. The great joke was to imagine the simultaneous uproar when the guests going to their rooms, after a wedding reception, removed the lids to see what the curious boxes contained.

When Sam was about twelve, he and Will Bowen worked many an afternoon stolen from school to pry loose an immense boulder on the edge of the summit of Holliday's Hill, paying for their truancy with whippings the next mornings. At last, one Saturday afternoon, after three further hours of work, it was poised and ready to go. Before they gave it the final push, they sat down, wiped the sweat from their faces, and waited for a picnic party to get out of the way in the road below. Then they started the boulder: "It was splendid! It went crashing down the hillside, tearing up saplings, mowing bushes down like grass, ripping and crushing and smashing everything in its path—eternally splintered and scattered a pile of wood at the foot of the hill, and then sprang from the high bank clear over a dray in the road . . . and the next instant made infinitesimal mince-meat of a frame cooper-shop, and the coopers swarmed out like bees. Then we said it was perfectly magnificent, and left. Because the coopers were starting up the hill to inquire." The boys escaped suspicion because it was judged to be the work of a gang of forty.

The town and its outskirts offered a variety of opportunities for boys to entertain themselves, but it was the Mississippi's infinite variety and its promise of untold adventure that cast the spell. Skiffs "borrowed" from absent owners took them to Sny Island, near the Illinois shore, where in tramping through its marshy thickets they came on the nests of grebes and rails in the midst of tall reeds, and painted turtles sunning themselves in rows on half-sunken logs. Here they angled for catfish and perch. If it was the season, they went on to the mainland and searched for pecans. It was more fun to row over to the larger Glasscock's Island (Jackson's Island in *Tom Sawyer* and *Huckleberry Finn*), opposite the mouth of Bear Creek. There, completely free, for it was uninhabited, they would throw off all their clothes, being careful when kicking off their trousers not to lose the precious amulet of rattlesnake rattles worn about the ankle to prevent cramps in swimming. Then they would paint stripes all over their bodies with black mud, "from head to heel . . . like so many zebras," and play Indian. They were all chiefs, since no one would consider any lesser rank.

When they grew tired of raiding imaginary pioneer cabins on the frontier, they drew a ring in the sand for a circus, since one of them had perceptively pointed out that their bare skin resembled flesh-colored tights. Each one was a clown, for none would "yield this proudest post." Some days they turned pirate and hunted for chests of gold and jewels, for there were well-founded traditions that Blackbeard and Morgan had buried treasure on the Mississippi islands.

When hunger finally caught up, they looked for turtle eggs in the warm sand and gathering as many as fifty or sixty, had a fried-egg feast. Still easier, since they always had set-lines, was to haul in a catch of perch, bullhead, and sunfish, which they fried crisp with bacon, and devoured with cornpone and coffee, brought from home. Afterward, they would stretch out under the trees to drowse, chat, brag, and puff on their corncob pipes.

At the age of nine Sam started to smoke regularly. He had been shamed into chewing tobacco when a fifteen-year-old girl at the country school near the Quarles farm one day asked him if he "used tobacco." On hearing that he did not, she pointed him out scornfully:

"Here is a boy seven years old who can't chaw tobacco!"

Made to feel that he was a "degraded object," he determined to do better but only succeeded in making himself sick at first. Later, he tried smoking grapevine cigars, which bit his tongue. Then, he turned to the local stogies known as "Garth's damndest," made by the father of his friend John Garth, which "even poverty itself was able to buy."

Age nine seemed to have been the time when Sam left behind the character of the "backward, cautious, unadventurous boy," for he also took to swearing. He had reason to believe that his mother, whose strongest expression when exasperated was "Hang it!" (which she always said with a pleased look, believing she was on the borderline of swearing), would "skin him alive" if she ever heard him. He made sure that she did not.

It was also at nine that he stowed away aboard a large steamboat. It was hard to watch them come in and out of Hannibal, and pass up and down the river, without ever riding on one, he explained later. He slipped on easily with the crowd of boarding passengers and hid himself on the upper deck. When the vessel was in midstream, he crept out cautiously and sat very still to avoid attention, looking at the river from this new vantage point and observing everything that went on aboard, so he could tell about it afterward. Had there not been a rainstorm, he might have gone all the way to St. Louis without being detected, and come back the envy of the other boys because he had traveled; not one of his friends had been more than forty miles from home. When the squall hit, he dashed for shelter but could find nothing to cover him completely. A passing deckhand noticed the feet and legs, called him out, and escorted him to the cabin. At the next stopping place, Louisiana, Missouri, he was put ashore. He had journeyed only thirty miles. In this village lived some of his Lampton kin, who kept him overnight, and the next day delivered him to his anxious mother. She was certain he had drowned, for the last time anyone saw him was at the wharf. After she found that he was whole and well, she dried her tears and, as is not unusual in such cases, suddenly grew angry and punished him for having caused so much worry.

"My mother had a good deal of trouble with me but I think she enjoyed it. She had none at all with my brother Henry, who was two years younger than I, and I think that the unbroken monotony of his goodness and truthfulness and obedience would have been a burden to her but for the relief and variety which I furnished in the other direction. I was a tonic," he liked to believe. Henry was one of the boys Clemens used as a model for Tom Sawyer's half-brother, Sid—but "Henry was a very much finer and better boy than Sid ever was," Clemens explained.

The next year Sam earned the distinction of being a traveler, after he went to St. Louis and back by steamboat, probably with Orion, then twenty, who was working as a journeyman printer there. Orion was feeling degraded and more than ever resentful toward his father, who had insisted he learn a trade rather than enter one of the professions as he had wanted to do.

When Sam stowed away, he did not think of the dangers, but in recalling the later trip he maintained that when he went to sleep his head was filled with "impending snaggings, and explosions and conflagrations, and sudden death." He awakened around ten o'clock with a terrifying dream, and jumping out of bed, burst into the ladies' saloon, where some twenty women were quietly reading and knitting.

"Fire, fire! *jump and run, the boat's afire and there ain't a minute to lose!*" he shouted. "All those ladies looked sweetly up and smiled, nobody stirred." One "sweet, benignant old dame with round spectacles on her nose" pulled them down, looked over them and said gently:

"But you mustn't catch cold, child. Run and put on your breast-pin, and then come and tell us all about it." Sam wrote that he turned and "crept humbly away . . . and never even cared to discover whether I had dreamed the fire or actually seen it."

One Saturday, when Sam was still nine, he attended a boat launching in Bear Creek, that sizable stream that flowed out of the woods and meandered through the lower part of town before joining the river. The affair attracted quite a crowd who went aboard to inspect the craft. When the important moment came, they all filed ashore—save one. As the boat slipped in with a huge splash, the company cheered, and on the deck a boy suddenly stood up, took off his hat, and waved it to the spectators. It was Sam Clemens, obviously enjoying being the focus of attention—freed at last from his confining chrysalis.

Since it was not always convenient to borrow a boat when needed, the boys decided to get one of their own—simply borrow it permanently. John Briggs was responsible for finding and secreting a skiff in a secluded cove off Bear Creek. There, Sam and Tom Blankenship helped him give it a coat of red paint (also "borrowed") to cover the original green. Then Tom fitted it up with a sail, Sam named it *Cecilia,* and they were ready to skim downriver three miles to the pleasant tree-shaded valley called Cave Hollow. Holiday excursionists came there from all around on a little steam ferry to picnic and afterward explore the limestone cave, a tangled wilderness of narrow winding passages, chambers with strange formations, dripping stalactites, deep black pools, streamlets—and a multitude of bats. Sam and his friends considered using one of its unexplored rooms as headquarters for the band of real robbers or pirates they counted on getting together one day—a place to hide their captives and loot. The cave was seven miles in length and its countless hallways were so confusing it was easy to lose one's way in the shadowy twilight of tallow candles, which added considerably to the thrill of being there. "Injun Joe," a local half-breed, got lost there one time and told his whole story to Sam. He would have starved to death before finding his way out if it had not been for the unending supply of bats, he said. "General" Gaines, Hannibal's first Town Drunkard, wandered about the cave for a week before being rescued. Sam also heard this account.

McDowell's Cave was an eerie place which no boy would dare enter alone, for it contained the corpse of a fourteen-year-old girl, preserved in a glass cylinder of alcohol encased in copper, and suspended from a rail. It had been placed there by the girl's father and owner of the cave, "the great Dr. McDowell," a noted, but eccentric, St. Louis surgeon, as an experiment to see whether the limestone would petrify the body.

When they entered the cave, Tom Blankenship reminded them that a person who has not been buried is more likely to "go a-ha'nting around" than one who was "planted and comfortable." They kept constantly alert for signs: a sudden, mysterious flickering of their candles, an unexplained puff of warm air against their cheek (a ghost trying to tell one something), the swish of invisible garments (a wraith passing). Sam felt a tingle of terrible pleasure. The cave fascinated him, and years later when he came to write *Tom Sawyer*, it served as the setting for some of the book's most exciting scenes. For dramatic impact, he had Injun Joe, whose real character he changed markedly, starve to death there. When Tom Sawyer and Becky Thatcher were unable to find their way back to the cave's entrance, Clemens was reliving his own horror:

"I got lost in it myself along with a lady, and our last candle burned down to almost nothing before we glimpsed the search party's lights winding about in the distance."

One of the chief recreations for boys in that watery environment was swimming in the river, especially in the sunny shallows off Glasscock's Island, or diving from empty flatboats moored offshore. But the choice spot was a deep pool in Bear Creek. It was not only close by but was so well-concealed by thickets they could swim naked without getting caught—for Hannibal had an ordinance against bathing, swimming, or washing one's self, "insufficiently clothed," within town limits.

Sam had trouble learning to swim, a difficulty with physical coordination, and would "drown" in Bear Creek "every summer regularly, and be drained out, and inflated and set going again." Not even by the fateful age of nine had he mastered it, for one day, while playing alone on a floating log he thought was attached to a raft, it suddenly rolled over and spilled him into Bear Creek. After he had gone to the bottom twice and was coming up to "make the third and fatal descent," his fingers appeared above water. A slave woman belonging to the tailor, William Kercheval, who happened along just then, seized his hands, and pulled him up. Within a week, he was drowning again, and this time it was the tailor's apprentice who jumped in, "pawed around on the bottom . . . found me . . . dragged me out and emptied the water out of me."

Sam claimed to have drowned seven times after that before learning to swim. One of those times was a day when the boys went to Bear Creek and found their classmate, Reuel Gridley, a tall, strong youth of sixteen, fishing there. He told them to go find some other place to swim. They responded by bombarding him with mudballs and throwing rocks and sticks in the water to scare the fish. Losing his temper Reuel went tearing after them, caught Sam, the smallest one, and tossed him into the middle of the pond. He was saved by some older boys who plunged in and pulled him to shore.

Each time Sam was brought home after such an experience his mother would console herself by saying: "People who are born to be hanged are safe in water." It was spoken in jest, and she earnestly tried, with a variety of contrivances, to keep him from swimming. One was to sew his shirt collar together in front while he was wearing it. But he circumvented this by keeping needles with colored thread to match his mother's under his coat lapel.

Death by drowning plays an important part in *Tom Sawyer* and *Huckleberry Finn*. It appears again in *The Mysterious Stranger,* and among the autobiographical recollections in *Life on the Mississippi,* and in other writings. Its horror was fixed in Sam's mind not only by his own narrow escapes but by having been present when two playmates drowned.

Every accident of its kind was thought to be the result of special orders from on high, as retributive punishment for such unrepented sins as fishing or boating on Sunday, raiding peach orchards, skipping school, saying "bad words," sneaking jam from the pantry—a multitude. A boy could hardly breathe without adding to the list.

Sam wondered why those two comrades had been singled out. The first victim, Clint Levering, was certainly not more "loaded with sin" than other boys in town. The case of the second one, a German lad known simply as "Dutchy," was still more incomprehensible; he was the envy of the Sunday school class and cynosure of the entire village for having recited three thousand Scriptural verses without missing a word. After each of these tragedies, there had been a frightful thunderstorm, and then Sam remembered that those special orders were also sent as warnings. During every storm Sam suffered "agonies of remorse" for sins he had committed and not repented, and for others he was uncertain about, but felt sure had been recorded by some angel who did not "trust such important matters to memory." With all this attention being focused on little Hannibal, he did not see how he could possibly escape notice. He determined to turn over a new leaf instantly and lead "a high and blameless life forever after." Like the boys in those "dreary" books he borrowed from Sunday school, he would visit the sick and the poor, invade the grogshops and warn the drunkards, and instruct other youths in the right way, taking the resulting trouncings "meekly." He would finally drift off to sleep, but in the morning when he awakened, the clear, sunny world looked "so bright and safe" there seemed hardly any need to mend his ways—until the next thunderstorm. In the event he did decide to reform, when the "succeeding days of cheerfulness and sunshine came bothering around," within four weeks he lagged so far behind in good intentions he was back at the starting point, happily "lost and comfortable" again.

Long after he ceased to associate thunderstorms with celestial punishment or admonition, he was awed by their stupendous power and beauty, and still found them fraught with supernatural meaning. He used them effectively in his writings to set the prevailing mood; as portents, or as a highly dramatic climax to some tale of violent death.

IV

━━━━━━━━━━━━━━━━━━━━○━━━━━━━━━━━━━━━━━━━━

EDUCATION

For SAM CLEMENS, school was boyhood's heaviest burden. He coped by absenting himself as much as possible, with or without leave. On those bright, sweet mornings when woods, hills, and river beckoned irresistibly and he knew he could not endure another day of "slow suffering" in the "captivity and fetters" of the classroom, he would carefully canvass his system before getting out of bed in the hope of finding some ailment that would keep him home. If successful he would begin to groan in apparent agony and by the time his mother reached his side, seemed to be dying. As he grew older and his health improved, these chances became slimmer and he was forced to play truant on his own responsibility and take the consequent flogging the next morning—that form of punishment recommended by Solomon and used universally at that time on children, wives, slaves, seamen, soldiers, criminals, and fools.

Of the three dame school teachers Sam had, Miss Torrey was the most patient and agreeable. He remembered well how he had joined an insurrection led by Ed Stevens to force Miss Mary Ann Newcomb, Mrs. Horr's principal, to allow them all to go over to Miss Torrey's side of the room. Nor did he forget how the rebels "sassed" Laura Hawkins when she came out to call them in for the third time, and how they responded by marching "in in threatening and bloodthirsty array" back to class—only to yield meekly, each taking his thrashing and resuming his old seat, entirely "reconstructed." When Clemens came to write *Huckleberry Finn,* Miss Newcomb was drawn on for the character of Miss Watson, "a tolerable slim old maid with goggles on," who helped her sister, the Widow Douglas, with Huck's reformation.

After completing third grade, Sam was enrolled in a school kept by an Irishman of middle years and better than average education. He taught Latin and was the only person in town who knew French. His name was Cross, which Sam considered apt because he was perpetually short-tempered.

"When I was a boy there was not a thing I could do creditably except spell according to the book," Clemens once said. A natural speller, he won the Friday afternoon bee regularly, accepting the schoolmaster's approval, and the medal—a thin, smooth silver disk about the size of a dollar, engraved with the words "Good Speller" in "flowing Italian script," as partial payment for the whippings he got whenever he stumbled through the multiplication tables, parsed incorrectly, or confused mountains with rivers and lakes in geography. He enjoyed being envied by the whole school. There was not a pupil who "wouldn't have given a leg" for the privilege of wearing that medal—or the identical one bearing the word "Amiability," a category which included good behavior. John Robards, a "wee chap" with silky yellow hair that hung straight to his shoulders, had a monopoly on that medal. To vary the "wearisome sameness," he and Sam would occasionally trade medals and find great satisfaction in seeming to be what they were not, for a week.

Only once did Sam fail to win a spelling-down and that was when he purposely "left the first *r* out of February . . . to accommodate a sweetheart" with whom he was competing. "My passion was so strong . . . I would have left out the whole alphabet if the word contained it."

Between times, there were more important lessons to be gained from daily life. Shortly before his eighth birthday, Hannibal had its first murder. Two farmers, James McFarland and Vincent Hudson, neighbors and friends, came to town, marketed some produce, then made the rounds of the rum shops. Before starting home, they stopped at a hardware store on Hill Street, and there commenced arguing over a plow. Words grew hot, Hudson drew an eight-inch cobbler's knife and plunged it nearly to the hilt in McFarland's breast. An hour later he was dead.

That day Sam had skipped school. It was already dark and the moon was just rising as he made his unwilling way homeward. When he came to his father's law office, he decided to climb in through the window and sleep on a lounge, "because I had a delicacy about going home and getting thrashed." As he lay there and his eyes grew accustomed to the darkness, "I fancied I could see a long, dusky, shapeless thing stretched upon the floor. A cold shiver ran through me. I turned my face to the wall. That did not answer. I was afraid that thing would creep over and seize me in the dark. I turned back and stared at it for minutes and minutes—they seemed hours." He hoped the moonlight would finally illuminate the room. But it seemed to lag that night, and when he could no longer stand the waiting, "I turned to the wall and counted twenty, to pass the feverish time away." The suspense grew unbearable and when he looked again, there in a pale square of moonlight he saw a white human hand. His heart sank, he gasped for breath— and covered his eyes. When he summoned the courage to look, there was the naked arm, and as he watched in horror, the palid face was revealed, its eyes "fixed and glassy in death." Sam sat up and saw the moonlight glide down the bare chest—inch by inch— past the nipple, where it disclosed the "ghastly stab."—He had no wish to encounter the ghost of a murdered man, wanting to unburden its mind or seek vengeance.

"I went out at that window, and I carried the sash along with me. I did not need the sash, but it was handier to take it than it was to leave it, so I took it."

He ran all the way home, accepted his punishment, and went to bed. But his sleep was fitful. "It is hard to forget repulsive things." Twenty-four years later, when writing *The Innocents Abroad,* he included an account of this experience with McFarland's corpse, and observed: "I have slept in the same room with him often—in my dreams."

The shooting of old Boggs by the aristocratic Colonel Sherburn, in *Huckleberry Finn*, is an almost verbatim account of Hannibal's first premeditated murder which occurred in January 1845, in Sam's notable ninth year. The site of the actual shooting of Sam Smarr, a farmer, by the proud and prosperous merchant William Owsley, was at the corner of Hill and Main Streets, just down from the Clemens house. The hour was noon, and Sam was on his way home to lunch.

Not only did he witness the murder, but he was aware of what led up to it over the past weeks, when Smarr, drunk, publicly berated Owsley. He called him a "damned pickpocket" for having supposedly cheated Smarr's drinking companion, Tom Davis. Sam also knew of another time when Smarr and Davis, "spreeing around and cutting up smart," shot off their pistols, and Smarr shouted abuse through the open door of Owsley's store—"the whole street packed with people listening and laughing and going on"—while Owsley, attending to customers, turned white and said such behavior was "insufferable."

After Owsley shot Smarr twice through the breast, he fell backward onto the ground, arms outspread (just as Boggs did in the book), and Owsley turned on his heel and walked off (as Colonel Sherburn did). Smarr's friends then carried him into Dr. Grant's drugstore, laying him on his back, as he requested. Grant and a fellow physician tore open the shirt, made a quick examination, and seeing that he was about to faint from loss of blood, simply "stood by to see him die." Meanwhile some "thoughtful idiot" had spread a large family Bible on Smarr's chest. Sam Clemens, who was standing near, observing everything, watched the heavy book rise and fall with each labored breath, and thought of what torture its "leaden weight" must be adding to the dying man's struggles.

Once again Sam recognized the warning from Providence, and when night came he reviewed his sins as he lay in bed, and repented. That "grotesque" closing scene supplied further material for dreams: "In my nightmares I gasped and struggled for breath under the crush of that vast book for many a night." Even during the daytime that picture would often appear to him.

The last school he attended was one kept by J. D. Dawson. By then Sam was twelve, and the stirrings of adolescence made him more restless than ever, more impatient with dull, rote lessons, more resentful of authority and more rebellious against adult tyranny. Dawson, a man of middle age, who was bald, and wore a wig, appears as the schoolmaster Dobbins, in *Tom Sawyer*. He is described there as being always severe, and as taking a "vindictive pleasure in punishing the least shortcomings." His lashings were "very vigorous," and only the biggest boys and older girls escaped. Tom Sawyer and his classmates spent their days "in terror and suffering and their nights in plotting revenge." If this was a true picture of Dawson, then Sam would have likewise spent his days in dread of those "vigorous" whippings, and his nights planning retaliation.

Although Sam knew the price of day-dreaming, he suffered so acutely from boredom and confinement that he took his chances. He let his mind and eye wander as he listened to the "drowsy and inviting summer sounds" which drifted through the open windows from that distant "boy-Paradise," Holliday's Hill, and watched some idle boys whose fathers could not afford schooling, playing on that inviting grassy slope.

Tom Sawyer was made to suffer similarly as his eyes rested on the "soft green sides" of Cardiff Hill, "tinted with the purple of distance," and watched a few birds float "on lazy wing high in the air." Tom's heart ached to be free or have something interesting to do to pass the "dreary time." As Sam Clemens had done so often in church and school, Tom's hand took inventory of his pockets. His spirits lifted as he touched a percussion-cap box that contained a tick. Furtively he released the prisoner on the long flat desk he shared with Joe Harper, who was similarly bored. The two boys entertained themselves "exercising" the creature, making him go in various directions by heading him off with a pin. It was "glorious fun"—until Dobbins, in his "natural mean way," sneaked up and gave each a tremendous whack between the shoulders.

Every detail of that story was true, "as I have excellent reason to remember," Clemens noted after finishing an early version of *Tom Sawyer*. In that account, as in Sam's actual experience, the insect was a louse which, for propriety's sake, was changed to a tick in the book.

There were two boys in that school whom the rest especially envied. One was Arch Fuqua, son of a tobacco merchant, who sold

Will Bowen the louse for one white alley. Arch's great gift was a knack of doubling back his big toe, then letting it "fly" with a snap that could be heard for thirty yards. Sam remembered that trick all his life. The second boy was George Robards, the only pupil who studied Latin. He was pale, slender, and studious and had long, straight black hair hanging below his jaws like a "pair of curtains." It was the heart's desire of everyone in school to have the kind of flexible hair that could be flung clear back with a toss of the head. No one could do that with so much style as George. Certainly not Sam Clemens or his brother, Henry, with their tight curls. Still, they kept hoping, and would soak their heads in water and then comb and brush the hair down tight and flat to the skull, which furnished them only a fleeting satisfaction because, "the first time we gave it a flirt it all shriveled into curls again and our happiness was gone."

There were a number of girls Sam remembered always. He fell in love with Mary Miller, two years his senior, but she ignored his existence and was the first sweetheart to furnish him with a broken heart, making him realize how cold the world could be at times. He believed that for a short while he was as miserable as any grown man could be. Then he transferred his worship to Artemissa Briggs, John's sister, also older. When he revealed his passion to her, she did not make fun of it. She was gentle and kind but also firm, and said she did not want to be "pestered by children." Then there was Jennie Brady, ("Gull's" sister), Lavinia Honeyman, and Mary Moss.

At home, Sam Clemens' manners and speech were under constant scrutiny and correction. He and his brothers learned to be chivalrous toward women (all his life Sam treated them with gallantry) and respectful of adults, especially the elderly; to address gentlemen as "sir" and ladies as "ma'am"; to remove their hats (every boy wore a hat the year around); to bow, rise, sit, or speak at the proper times. At table, the boys stood until their parents were seated, and on first greeting them at breakfast they wished them a good day and good health. It was difficult to maintain these standards in a Western frontier river-town where, through careless habits, even people of good family allowed their grammar to become slovenly and abandoned polite behavior. Although the Clemens

Education

family were unable to live in a style that equalled John Marshall's position as a lawyer and judge, they carried on the traditions. No matter how cramped their quarters, they always found room for the mahogany sideboard on which were displayed Jane Lampton's heirloom English sugar bowl, the silver spoons and forks, and a few other family pieces.

After conditions forced them to sell Jennie, the maid-of-all-work, John Marshall hired from his owner in the country a young black boy named Sandy, to wait on table and help with house and yard chores. Sam would always recall how noisy Sandy was—"singing, whistling, yelling, whooping, laughing" all day long, it seemed— and how "maddening, devastating, unendurable" he found the clamor, and how he went raging to his mother and demanded that she stop the boy. Tears came into her eyes, and she said:

"Think, he is sold away from his mother; she is in Maryland, a thousand miles from here and he will never see her again, poor thing. When he is singing it is a sign he is not remembering and that comforts me. It would break my heart if Sandy should stop singing." Her simple earnest words moved Sam, and Sandy's "noise" no longer bothered him.

Sam could not help but contrast his father's lack of compassion and patience with Sandy, whom he would lash for "trifling little blunders and awkwardnesses." Such acts made him pity the victim and feel "ashamed of the punisher." Those feelings were even stronger when he learned that his father had once whipped Jennie with a bridle for her "impudence" to Jane Lampton.

John Marshall Clemens took no pleasure in his children's company and therefore never participated in any of their home amusements. He could not understand a child's mind and once scolded little Henry severely for planting his marbles and expecting to harvest a "crop." Only for Pamela did he hold some affection, although he never revealed it until the day he died. He did, however, have an interest in furthering their education through reading. For the younger ones, he subscribed to *Peter Parley's Magazine,* one of the first periodicals for young readers that did not stress stories and verses with a moral. When he could afford it, he bought books, but mainly he encouraged them to borrow from Hannibal's Library Institute, which he had helped found. Its four to five hundred volumes were housed in Dr. Meredith's office, and included the works of Scott, Byron, Cooper, Marryat, Dickens, and Goldsmith, which the Clemens children read.

Sam's main interest for some years was in tales of high adventure, of chivalry, and enchantment. He read *The Arabian Nights' Entertainments* (his father owned the only copy in town), knew all the tales by heart, and frequently told his playmates such favorites as "Aladdin and the Wonderful Lamp," and "Ali Baba and the Forty Thieves." He read "Robin Hood and Guy of Gisborne," the best known of the ballads in that cycle, and *Ivanhoe, Robinson Crusoe,* and *Gulliver's Travels.* He read Exquemelin's accounts of the buccaneers and became acquainted early with *Don Quixote,* probably also owned by his father. He read Robert Bird's *Nick of the Woods,* a novel of Indian warfare in the Kentucky wilderness. This would have held special interest for Sam because his maternal great-grandmother, Jane Montgomery, when a girl, had held at bay with a single musket, a band of Indians who had killed her father and surrounded their cabin, while a child-sister, Betsy, clambered out the low chimney and raced over two miles to get help, pursued all the way. This incident became part of Kentucky history, and the name Jane was a traditional one in the family for six generations.

Sam also read what he called "wildcat literature," which included T. B. Thorpe's tall tale, *The Big Bear of Arkansas,* Seba Smith's "Major Jack Downing" letters, Hamilton C. Jones' sketch, "Cousin Sallie Dilliard," and those books credited to Davy Crockett.

Jane Lampton, Pamela, and Sam were the musical members of the family. They all sang well, and Pamela was accomplished enough on the guitar to give lessons. Sometime in 1844, during a brief period of prosperity when Clemens built the house for his family on Hill Street, and invested money in local silk culture, he bought a piano for his daughter. Soon she was teaching that instrument as well. Sam learned to play both guitar and piano, and also banjo, on which he accompanied his singing of jubilee songs. At the Quarles farm, he and his cousins often joined the black people in their dances—shuffles and double-shuffles, breakdowns, cakewalk, and juba. Sam, a born dancer like his mother, learned them all.

Education

It was left to the tender-hearted Jane Lampton to discipline Sam. He has said that his father laid his hand on him in punishment only twice, and then not heavily, and never punished any of the other children at all. This was not necessary, for one look "was enough and more than enough."

In the most serious cases, when Jane's patience with him was sorely tried, she whipped him or set him to work at unpleasant tasks. For lesser offenses she lectured him severely, but often those stern talks were never finished, for Sam would interrupt with some humorous remark that would dissolve her severity and she would break into laughter. At other times—when he was caught "hooking" sugar or jam, she would rap him soundly on the knuckles, or crack him on the skull with her thimble. When he grew older, she sent him to church nights in addition to morning service, as punishment, knowing how much he despised it. She secretly hoped that frequent exposure to those sermons might eventually mend his ways. But he had inherited his father's free-thinking outlook which rejected religious dogma in favor of rational inquiry, and in his mid-teens he began to question the literal concept of hell. With time he grew increasingly skeptical, and would admit one day, "I don't believe in hell—but I'm afraid of it."

To assure herself that Sam had gone to church nights, as soon as he came home she applied her test: he was to give her the Scriptural passage on which the sermon was based. That never caused any trouble; he did not have to go to church to get the text. "I selected one myself." This dodge worked wonderfully until a time when his text and that of a neighbor who had been at church, failed to agree. From then on, Jane Lampton had to think up new methods of checking him, and it became a battle of wits between them. In winter it was the fashion for men and boys to wear long black cloaks lined with bright Scotch plaid. They were the most sensible garment ever made, Sam thought, as well as romantic, for when worn flung back they gave dash to the wearer. One bitterly cold night when he started off to church "to square a crime of some kind committed during the week," he hid his cloak by the front gate and set off in search of his friends. When it was time for the service to be over he went home, picked up his cloak, and in the dark put it on lining-side out. He then walked in and stood ready to be cross-examined. All went well until Jane remarked that it must have been next to impossible to keep warm in church on such a night. Not noticing her drift, he said he had not minded the cold because he kept his cloak on the whole time. And had he worn it all the way home? He stepped into the trap: Yes, he had, he said.

"You wore it with the red Scotch plaid outside and glaring. Didn't that attract any attention?"

In recalling this incident Sam added that to have continued such a dialogue would have been "tedious and unprofitable." He dropped it and accepted the consequences.

Sam's truancies continued, as did the punishments, while his education expanded, for the world would always be his schoolhouse. It was fortunate for the future writer, and for American literature, that this was so. Although during these early years his universe was limited to Hannibal, the Quarles farm, and the river, it was large enough to furnish him with his first lessons in the differences among men—their characters, thoughts, attitudes, and ways—and to offer the chance to collect and store observations, details, and experiences for future use. Certainly no other American writer returned so often and so successfully to his childhood and youth for inspiration and material.

V

THE DARK HOUR

"A BOY'S LIFE IS not all comedy; much of the tragic enters it," Sam Clemens said.

In May of 1842, when Sam was six and a half, his older brother Benjamin, born in the "Crystal Palace" at Jamestown, took sick. He was an amiable child, about to turn ten. In spite of Dr. Meredith's care and Jane Lampton's homeopathic remedies, he was dead within a week. One of Sam's clearest pictures of his mother at this early period was that day when she held his hand and they knelt together at Ben's bedside. The tears were streaming down her cheeks, and she was moaning. He was familiar with her tears but not those sounds of anguish. Also part of that picture was the moment when she placed his hand upon the dead boy's cheek in an effort to make him understand "the calamity that had befallen." He likewise remembered the sight of Ben in his shroud lying in his coffin.

For reasons that will never be known, Sam considered himself responsible for Ben's death. Over half a century later, he made a random note: "Dead brother Ben. My treachery to him." And again, with reference to that brother: "The case of memorable treachery."

Three years later, John Marshall Clemens suffered another of his periodic reversals of fortune and Jane Lampton decided to take in boarders, but by the end of 1846 it was seen that boarders were not the solution. To avoid a writ of attachment in a pending law-suit, they sold all their furniture except the heirloom sideboard, and at the invitation of Dr. Grant (also a Virginian), moved across the street to join him and his wife in a spacious two and a half story white house decorated with pilasters. On the ground floor the doctor had his office and pharmacy. In return for rent-free quar-ters, Jane Lampton, who so detested kitchen duties, agreed to cook the meals. Of the Clemens children there were only two at home now, Sam and Henry, for Pamela, at eighteen, was supporting herself by teaching music in the towns of Florida and Paris. Orion was working as a printer in St. Louis and now able to help support the family. He was more reconciled to his job because of his study of Benjamin Franklin's *Autobiography*. He wrote his mother that he was "closely imitating" the great Franklin, even to living on bread and water. He was amazed to discover how clear his mind had become on that diet. Sam was still spending summers at the Quarles farm, and probably Henry also, for since Ben's death they had become very close.

Accepting charity was gall to John Marshall Clemens, and at this lowest point in his career he worked tirelessly to better his posi-tion. That November, he announced his candidacy for clerk of the circuit court, the election to be held the following August. His chances of winning seemed assured for his legal knowledge, his clerical skills, and his probity were widely recognized, bringing him the support of Hannibal's two newspapers as well as the Whigs and all impartial Democrats. Although Clemens was a Whig himself, the campaign was being kept as non-partisan as possible. At age forty-eight, he looked forward at last to steady employment, for he could keep the office lifelong. The whole family took heart at the prospect of "great prosperity."

One day, early in March 1847, Clemens rode his horse to Pal-myra, the county seat, on business. Upon his return he was caught in a heavy sleet storm, and after traveling twelve miles, was soaked to the skin. He arrived home, Sam remembered, in a half-frozen condition. The result was a chest cold that shortly developed into pleurisy, and then into pneumonia. Jane Lampton sent for Pamela and Orion.

On March 24, aware that he was dying, he looked about the room at the assembled family, and seeing Pamela, beckoned to her. When she came to his side he drew her down, and putting his arms about her neck, kissed her for the first time, Sam was certain. He had never before seen his father display affection.

John Marshall Clemens' mind reverted for a moment to the Tennessee acreage: "Cling to the land and wait; let nothing beguile it away from you," Sam quoted him. Then he said, "Let me die." His arms slipped from Pamela's neck, and he sank back. Sam was deeply impressed that his father did not say goodbye to Jane Lampton, to himself, or to anyone but Pamela.

For some reason, Dr. Meredith performed a post-mortem, and through the keyhole of his surgery door, Sam, just four months past his eleventh birthday, watched the partial dissection of his father's body. There are but two extant references to this macabre experience, both cryptic. Certainly he would have preferred to forget those glimpses which his imagination made even more horrifying, but they were impressed too deeply. Fifty years later, upon finishing a brief sketch of the circumstances of his father's death, he added the underscored words, *"The Autopsy."* The second allusion appeared still later with a note: "1847: Witnessed post mortem of my uncle through the keyhole." Because no uncle died in that year but his father did, it is clear that "uncle" stands for "father."

As soon as he could, Sam relieved his mind by making a confession to the equally sensitive Orion, who remembered every detail. Many years later, Orion included an account of the post-mortem in his autobiography, a work Sam had urged him to write and to make explicit: "tell the straight truth."

Over thirty years later, Sam let his friend and literary mentor, William Dean Howells, editor and novelist, read Orion's autobiography. Howells reacted: "But the writer's soul is laid *too* bare; it is shocking. . . . *Don't* let anyone else *see* those passages about the autopsy. The light on your father's character is most pathetic."

What Howells meant by that final statement will probably never be learned, for sometime after 1906 part of Orion's manuscript, including the account of the post-mortem, was said to have been lost when a satchel containing those papers was stolen in New York's Grand Central Station. Certainly the remaining pages of that autobiography do not contain the "shocking" passages. Possibly they were destroyed (certainly not by Sam) and the theft of the satchel was invented to explain their absence. Clemens had no desire to use the autopsy experience in any of his writings but he certainly must have thought about it when plotting the graveyard scene in *Tom Sawyer*, for young Dr. Robinson had gone there to obtain a cadaver for practice in dissection.

A large crowd of townspeople attended the funeral of John Marshall Clemens. He was buried next to his son Benjamin in the old Baptist cemetery on a hill north of Hannibal. It was surrounded by a "crazy board fence . . . which leaned inward in places, and outward the rest of the time, but stood upright nowhere." Most of the graves were nearly lost in the rank growth of grass and weeds. As the three boys stood together beside the grave, Orion said, "Always remember that brothers should be kind to each other." Sam was in a repentant mood and in tears, for he had been taking inventory of the many times he had acted in defiance of his father's rules, and realized it was now too late to make amends.

Some time during that night, Jane Lampton, who was sleeping fitfully, wakened. In the bright moonlight she was startled to see what appeared to be a tall, white-shrouded figure enter the room and begin to slowly feel its way along the edge of her bed. She watched in terror as it drew near her head, then let out a gasp of relief as she recognized Sam's face, his eyes shut fast, in the folds of a large sheet which had given the illusion of great size. For years, whenever she told of that incident, she shuddered. Sam continued to sleepwalk after that for many nights.

The specter of John Marshall Clemens haunted Sam all of his life, and repeatedly he described his father in random notes, and in sketches, articles, stories, and novels, as if under a compulsion to write him out of his system. He appeared under various names, most often as a judge, and just as he was, or as Sam saw him, in character and physical appearance: proud, austere, unsmiling, silent, a free-thinker; ungentle in manner toward wife and children, but always the gentleman; tall and spare, with a thin, smooth-shaven, intellectual face; a high forehead; long, straight black hair; a hawklike nose, and eyes that seemed to be looking out from caverns.

It was not just John Marshall's failure as a lover, husband, and father that colored Sam's attitude, but the privation and humiliation of poverty and debt which shadowed all his Hannibal years. These left a deep scar, and nearly fifty years later he recalled them in a letter, and told of his own horror of failure and debt.

In his old age, Sam's memory tricked him into believing that right after his father's death he stopped school and became a printer's devil in the office of Joseph Ament, editor and proprietor of the *Missouri Courier;* but it is of record that Ament did not establish his newspaper until 1848. Further, there is a record of Sam attending school into 1849.

Life for him was much the same, with part or all of the next two summers passed at the Quarles farm. Then, in July 1850, his Aunt Patsy died from puerperal fever following the birth of her tenth child, whom she had named Jane Clemens. Jane held John Quarles responsible for the beloved Patsy's death, and never forgave him. Fond as Sam was of his uncle, the farm could never be the same without her.

Huckleberry Finn's staunch loyalty to his fellow fugitive and friend Jim, the slave, had its basis in an event that took place not long after Sam's father died. Tom Blankenship's eighteen-year-old brother, Benson (called "Bence"), who took occasional jobs but lived mainly by hunting and fishing, one day came upon a runaway slave hiding in the marshy thickets of Sny Island. Instead of reporting him and collecting the posted reward, Bence chose to say nothing, and bring him food regularly, trying meanwhile to find a way of getting him up the Ohio River into free territory. But one mid-August day, woodcutters stumbled on the secret camp and chased the fugitive into the boggy shallows known as Bird Slough, where he quickly vanished.

A week or so later, Sam and his friends John Briggs and the Bowen brothers, sailed their boat over to Sny Island to fish. While poling up the slough they pushed aside some snags and, to their horror, the body of the drowned slave rose suddenly to about half his height, head foremost. Although this was another ghastly sight for Sam to cope with, he seems to have been most deeply impressed with Bence's humanity in refusing to betray the man in his trouble and terror.

After finding a prospective buyer for the Tennessee land (which was now the responsibility of Orion, the oldest son), Jane Lampton, with an expansive optimism that was typical of her family, rented a large house, moved in with Sam and Henry, and wrote Pamela to come home. But these expectations were soon dashed when the purchaser decided he wanted only part of the land. Discussing it with Orion, they decided to sell all of the acreage or none. This reversal of fortune necessitated moving to a less expensive house, taking in boarders, and Pamela giving music lessons in Hannibal. "I have never found any difficulty as yet in getting scholars," she wrote assuringly to Orion. There was yet another move, back to the "new" frame house John Marshall had built for them on Hill Street. "That is, some of us lived in the new part, the rest in the old part back of it and attached to it," Sam recalled.

Orion was either not kept abreast of the family's moves or he forgot, but one Saturday evening he took a sudden notion to pay them a surprise visit (he delighted in surprises). He boarded a steamboat at St. Louis and reached Hannibal late at night, "his mind all on fire with his romantic project." (This was one of Sam's favorite stories about his wool-gathering brother.) Walking up to their Hill Street house, unaware that the family had not yet returned to it, he went around to the back door, slipped off his boots, and stole upstairs to his old room. He undressed in the dark and got quietly into bed. He was a little surprised to find an occupant, but presuming it was Henry, nestled against the warm body and prepared to go to sleep, looking forward eagerly to what was going to happen when the family found him there in the morning. After a few minutes the person at Orion's side, half-waking, complained at being crowded, and Orion was paralyzed, for the voice was a woman's. Then the person began to push, and her hands came in contact with Orion's beard.

"A man!" she screamed. This ended Orion's immobility. He shot out of bed, and started to grope in the dark for his clothes. Then a second woman in the bed started to scream. Orion did not wait to get his whole outfit, but raced to the head of the stairs.

The Dark Hour

There he saw a lighted candle coming up, and behind it was Dr. Meredith. "He had no clothes on to speak of, but no matter, he was well enough fixed for an occasion like this, because he had a butcher knife in his hand."

Orion shouted, and the doctor recognized his voice. He then explained that he and his two maiden sisters were renting the house, and told him where to find his own family. According to Sam, Dr. Meredith added some unnecessary advice about Orion informing himself before trying such an adventure again.

Sam went to work as an apprentice for Joseph Ament of the *Courier*, early in 1850. He received lodgings, board, and clothes, but no wages, which was customary. His bed was a straw tick on the floor of Ament's printing office. His meals were taken in the basement kitchen of the Ament house (Sam resented being classed with the servants), and were so scant that to "keep alive" he and his two fellow apprentices had to filch potatoes and onions from the cellar and cook them on the office stove before going to bed. As to clothes—these were Ament's castoffs, and so outsized "his shirts gave me the uncomfortable feeling of living in a circus tent, and I had to turn up his pants to my ears to make them short enough."

Sam was very unhappy during his first months there, his mother and Pamela remembered, for he felt insecure, lonely, and uprooted. They told of coming home late one evening and finding him asleep on the sitting-room floor. After that, he spent an occasional night with them, or had a meal, but actually Jane Lampton was too poor to support and clothe him. He would always look back on that time with aversion and cherish a special dislike for Ament's wife, Sarah, whom he held responsible for the niggardly meals.

Although he would have preferred to live at home, it was not in his nature to mope. Ament's young journeyman, Pet McMurry, whom Sam described as a dandy with oiled, dark red locks, a red goatee, and a mincing gait, who smoked "Cuba sixes," and wore his plug hat tipped so far forward as to rest nearly on the end of his nose, always retained a picture of their short, auburn-haired apprentice standing on a box at the case, puffing away at a huge cigar or a small pipe, and singing over and over the refrain from a comic song about a drunk who had fallen by the wayside: "If I ever get up again, I'll stay up—if I kin. . . ."

Sam found another friend in his fellow apprentice Wales McCormick, a "giant" at seventeen. Ament's old clothes fitted *him* "as the candle mold fits the candle," and he was generally in "a suffocated condition, particularly in the summertime." He was "a reckless, hilarious, admirable creature" who had "no principles and was delightful company," and possessed a secret for cooking those stolen potatoes that made them "noble and wonderful."

During his first year of apprenticeship, Sam joined the Cadets of Temperance, taking a pledge to avoid not only all "connection" with "spiritous liquors," but tobacco as well. Admittedly, it was not through any desire to give up smoking and chewing that Sam was drawn into the organization, but by the power of a gorgeous red merino sash, part of the cadet's uniform. He believed he never could be happy until he wore one of those "stunning" sashes in the funeral procession of a distinguished citizen, or in a May Day or Fourth of July parade. Those parades always ended with a collation in the shade of a large tent set up in the cool woods. The long tables held tubs of lemonade and ice cream, and platters of gingerbread slabs and cookies. Mingling with the crowds there was another fine chance to display the uniform. Sam's brother, Henry, was also a Cadet, as were his friends Tom Nash, the postmaster's son, John Meredith, and Jimmie McDaniel. Sam must have shown promise, for he was given the office of Illustrious Grand Worthy Secretary and Royal Inside Sentinel, privileged to wear a rosette on his sash, and charged with inventing the passwords. After the glory of the May Day and Fourth of July parades, Sam resigned. There were also six or seven other withdrawals. "You can't keep a juvenile moral institution alive on two displays of its sash a year," he objected.

Not thirty steps from the lodge door he was smoking again and "utterly happy," having found a cigar stub in the street.

The frenzy of the California gold rush did not pass Hannibal by. Some eighty of its residents set off across the plains in 1849. On New Year's Day, the husband of Sam's first teacher, Elizabeth Horr, started out. Dr. Hugh Meredith and his son, Charles, and John Briggs' father followed soon after, as did Sam's first cousin, Jim Quarles, who was known as a beau, a dancer, and a flutist. Quarles found only disappointment in California. Having no desire to work hard to get his gold, he died there a "drunken loafer." Captain Archibald Robards organized a party of fifteen, and took his boy, John. Sam and a group of friends watched the Robards cavalcade start, all wishing they were going. More than fifty years later, Sam could still see John "sailing by on a great horse," the boy's long golden hair streaming out behind. Sam was on hand to greet him when he returned, two years later, and heard his story over the weeks to come. Clemens' unfinished tale, "Huck and Tom Among the Indians," which takes the two boys across the Plains as far as the North Fork of the Platte, certainly incorporated some of John Robard's experiences.

Orion may have been tempted strongly to follow the goldseekers but his responsibility for the support of his mother and Henry kept him at his printer's job in St. Louis. Not that he was without dreams of fortune and fame. He had somehow met the noted Virginia lawyer Edward Bates, now practicing in St. Louis, who later served as Lincoln's attorney general. Bates liked the gentle, studious young man with grave expression and "large earnest eyes" that seemed to be always seeking and considering, and advised him to read law and practice oratory in his spare time. He let Orion use his legal books and gave him public-speaking lessons. The best exercise, Bates said, was to read aloud from a book in English and translate it rapidly into French. Since Orion had no knowledge of French, he began studying the language. He accepted every invitation he could get to speak at church or at temperance meetings, for he was now a cold water crusader, but he achieved only moderate success. Once, when asked to give a Fourth of July address in Hannibal, it was remarked that he could not be heard beyond the first row. For this he blamed his father. If he could have had daily practice in the art of speaking as he pursued a course of law, "warmed by the fervor" of his "childish dreams," he was certain he would have become a noted orator, and his life consequently "full of bliss." But that had been forbidden, and he was forced into the "toil of printing."

But Orion was changeable as the weather in his politics, his religion, and his choice of career, Sam once said of him. In January 1850, Jane Lampton wrote him that "Big Joe" Buchanan (to distinguish him from his son, "Little Joe"), a former steamboat engineer turned editor of *The Hannibal Journal*, was preparing to leave for the gold fields (he had already thoughtfully given his piano to Pamela, she interjected). Although his family proposed to run it with a certain "St. Louis swell" named Sam Raymond as editor, she had heard nothing "favorable" about the combination and believed that if Orion will bide his time, they will tire of it. She suggested that meanwhile he get some financial backing in St. Louis. "I could board the hands and you could take Henry."

Orion was captivated by the plan, for to edit a country newspaper had long been another of his ambitions. That summer he quit his job and returned to Hannibal. He never forgot how amazed he was to have his mother and Pamela welcome him home with "kisses and tears." The days of repressing their affection for one another were passed, and Jane Lampton's warmth prevailed.

But Orion's arrival was premature, for the young Buchanans were not ready to make a change, so he bought a press and some type, took on Henry (aged twelve) as his apprentice, and started a Whig weekly called the *Western Union*. Its first issue appeared early in September 1850. He also contracted for job printing. Although Sam told him he wanted to stay on with Ament until he drew wages (revenge for his privations), he finally gave in to Orion's entreaties and his promise of $3.50 a week, but did not leave the *Courier* office until about the first of the new year.

One blustery day that fall, while Sam was walking along the street, a paper fluttered across his path. Picking it up he saw that it was a page from a book, and as he read, discovered that the subject was new to him. It was about the imprisonment and persecution of Joan of Arc. He asked the bookish Henry about her, and he said she was real, and told him a little of her story. It seemed so much like a novel he then asked his mother, who assured him Joan was not fictional. His curiosity aroused, he began reading everything he could find about the girl liberator of France, and her times. This kindled an interest in medieval history and literature that became lifelong and eventually inspired Clemens' *Personal Recollections of Joan of Arc*, a serious although romanticized biography, which was his favorite of all of his books.

Orion took on another apprentice about the same time Sam came to work for him. His name was Jim Wolfe, and he was approaching

The Dark Hour

seventeen—tall, slim, and tow-headed. He came from the village of Shelbyville, forty miles off in the country, and brought with him all "his native sweetness and gentleness and simplicities." He was trusting, and inordinately shy, never able to feel at ease even with Sam's mother, who boarded and lodged him. He immediately became a perfect target for Sam's teasing and practical jokes, and furnished material for his writings.

One Saturday night during that winter of 1850–51, Pamela, now twenty-three, gave a candy-pull for her friends. Sam was too young to be invited and Jim Wolfe too bashful to accept. Sam was sent to bed early, and Jim followed shortly of his own accord. Their shared room was in the new part of the Hill Street house and the window looked out on the pitched roof of the ell annex where stood a squat chimney, a favorite resort on moonlit nights for rival tomcats. That night there was a moon. Around ten o'clock Pamela's party moved out under the arbor to set their plates of boiling-hot taffy in the snow to cool. While waiting, they stood around talking, joking, and laughing—"peal upon peal of it," Sam recalled.

Very shortly a couple of "disreputable" tomcats started arguing noisily on the chimney. Jim began to fume because the yowling kept him awake, and Sam suggested that he go out the window and chase them away. Jim said that for two cents he would go, and Sam egged him on. Finally, thoroughly riled, Jim pulled up the window and climbed out, just as he was, with nothing on but a short shirt. The roof was four inches deep in snow encrusted with ice, and Jim crept along slowly, cautiously, on all fours, a foot and a hand on each side of the slippery ridge—Sam watching him intently, the cats ignoring him, the hilarious company below unaware of him. When at last he was within reaching distance he made "a frantic grab for the nearest cat—and missed it." His heels flew up in the air and down he shot, feet first, through the arbor, landing in "a sitting position" in the midst of two dozen saucers of red-hot candy, and with the party all looking at him intently—"dressed as *he* was—this lad who could not look a girl in the face with his clothes on."

He let out a howl, there was a storm of shrieks and laughter and a mad scramble, and Jim fled up the stairs, "dripping broken crockery all the way." According to a dialect version of that tale

Sam wrote in 1867, Jim was blistered: "Why bless your soul, that poor cretur couldn't reely set down comfortable for as much as four weeks."

In writing squibs for Orion's paper, Sam occasionally made references to him as "our gallant *devil*"; and in giving an account of a fire that broke out in a store next door and threatened their office, Sam told how, in the excitement, Jim snatched up "the broom, an old mallet, the wash-pan and a dirty towel," rushed out the door and carried this "precious burden" to safety "ten squares off." By the time he got back, the fire was out. Nearly thirty years later, Jim Wolfe disguised as Nicodemus Dodge, was sketched in such an unlikely work as Clemens' *A Tramp Abroad.*

About the end of August 1851, Orion, seeing that prospects for the weekly were "gloomy," added to his troubles by borrowing five hundred dollars at ten percent interest from a farmer named Johnson, and buying Buchanan's *Journal.* Shortly he combined the two papers, and according to Sam's recollection, lowered the subscription and advertising rates—paid in drygoods, sugar, coffee, oak and hickory wood, pumpkins, turnips, and watermelons, so that the office resembled a general store much of the time.

So far, Sam had received no wages; in fact, Orion was never able to pay him a single penny as long as Sam was with him. Toward the end of every year Orion had to "scrape and scratch" for the fifty dollars interest due Johnson—never being able to pay on the principal. In desperation, he worked like a slave, and expected his helpers to do likewise.

"I was tyrannical and unjust to Sam. He was as swift and as clean as a good journeyman. I gave him tasks, and if he got through well I begrudged him the time and made him work more." Orion told how once, when he kept Sam until midnight cleaning up Henry's proof ("he always set a very dirty one"), Sam complained with "tears of bitterness."

At such times, Orion would quote some apt maxim from Benjamin Franklin, which succeeded in turning Sam against him, or so he claimed. Those adages, Sam insisted later, were "full of animosity toward boys." "Nowadays a boy cannot follow out a single natural instinct without tumbling over some of those everlasting aphorisms and hearing from Franklin on the spot."

The Dark Hour

Economies at home were even stricter than when John Marshall was alive. Pamela did the housekeeping; Jane Lampton did the cooking and was in charge of finances, keeping a careful record of every penny spent, as her little account books show. Orion supplied the food. "We therefore had a regular diet of bacon, butter, bread and coffee," he wrote. If anyone grumbled about the lack of variety, he promptly heard from Franklin and how he had lived on bread and water.

Pamela was the first to escape. Late in the summer of 1851, about the time Orion was getting more deeply into debt with the purchase of a second newspaper, she traveled to Green County, Kentucky, to visit her Aunt Pamelia. There, on September 20, she married a Virginian, William E. Moffett who, with his brothers and a partner, were successful merchants in Hannibal. Pamela and Will had been secretly engaged for some while, and their meeting in Kentucky was planned, for he would at that time be returning from a stay with his parents in Rockingham County, Virginia. When he called on Pamela at her aunt's house, he had everything arranged to set himself up in business as a commission merchant in St. Louis. He was also prepared to convince her that this was the time for them to marry and take their projected wedding trip to Niagara Falls by railroad. Once Will Moffett was established in St. Louis, he prospered rapidly and was eventually able to afford a fine three-story brick house, and to keep servants. Later, this house became a home for Jane Lampton, and for Henry and Sam intermittantly.

Sam missed Pamela, even though they were so very different— she was quiet, steady, and humorless; intellectual in bent, analytical of mind—and religious. As she grew older she searched for absolute truth, and experimented even more than her mother with various beliefs, which included a study of East Indian philosophies. Although Jane Lampton is always associated with Sam's religious upbringing, it was Pamela who took direct charge from his earliest years, drilling him in his Sunday school lessons and supervising his washing and dressing and combing in preparation for church.—Tom Sawyer had just such a spiritual guardian in his gentle Cousin Mary, who was based on Pamela.

Sam knew exactly what ailed Orion's paper: It lacked local news and humor. He realized that people like to read about themselves and their neighbors. "The idea of publishing local news to interest the general reader never occurred to me," Orion admitted, and those matters received "very slight attention." He was attempting to compete with St. Louis and New Orleans papers and offered his readers the latest telegraphic reports from Washington. The big problem there was that the wire which carried the messages across the river from Illinois was being used by residents for their own needs. In one place, a ferryman cut off enough to make a cable for his boat, so that the ends of the telegraph line lay limply on the ground, useless as "a woolen string." Instead of news from the capital, Orion treated his readers to "Polite Literature," printing Dickens' *Bleak House* in excerpt; and he summoned the courage to invite contributions from Emerson, and Dr. Oliver Wendell Holmes, at five dollars apiece. Foreseeably, neither replied.

Sam was naturally eager to satisfy his yearning to enliven the paper and his grand opportunity came in September of 1852, when Orion left town and charged him with getting out two issues of the weekly. In casting about for material, Sam decided to revive the rabid-dog controversy over which the editor of the rival Whig *Tri-Weekly Messenger* had been exercised ever since July. Orion's *Journal* had contributed its bit with a proposal signed by "A Dog-be-deviled Citizen," that the best solution was to kill all the dogs in town. This facetious remark was certainly from Sam's pen, for he is later found advising, "To prevent Dogs going mad in August: Cut off their heads in July."

The issue of September 16 carried the headline: " 'LOCAL' RE-SOLVES TO COMMIT SUICIDE." The report stated that the *Messenger's* editor, "disconsolate from receiving no further notice from 'A Dog-be-deviled Citizen,' " had resolved, after failing to drink himself to death, to "extinguish his chunk" in Bear Creek. Accompanying the item was a "villainous" cut (engraved by Sam with a jack-knife on the bottom of wooden type, he explained) showing a dog-headed man in tail-coat, sounding the stream with his walking-stick, fearing that he "may get out of his depth," in water nowhere more than two inches deep.

Not content with stirring up one editor, Sam took on his former employer, Joseph Ament of the *Courier*, getting his revenge at last. Going still further, he ran a squib headed "Historical Exhibition—

A No. 1 Ruse," exposing a hoax being perpetrated on his fellow citizens by Hannibal's pioneer, Abram Curtis, who was charging admission to see a panorama of "Bonaparte Crossing the Rhine." It consisted solely of a broken bone laid over a bacon rind.

To Sam's delight, the whole town's attention—"but not its admiration"—was focused on Orion's paper. Never before had it been in such great demand. In the next issue, he printed more of his crude woodcuts in a "Pictur" Department.

In "My First Literary Venture," written twenty years later, Sam told how "very, very angry" his "uncle" was when he got back—"unreasonably so, I thought, considering what an impetus I had given the paper. . . . But he softened when he looked at the accounts and saw that I had . . . booked . . . thirty-three new subscribers, and had the vegetables to show for it"—enough "cabbage, beans, and unsalable turnips . . . to run the family for two years!"

Sam had displayed a certain confidence in preparing those two issues of the *Journal,* for on May 1 of that same year, 1852, there appeared in *The Carpet-Bag,* a humorous weekly published in Boston, a sketch called "The Dandy Frightening the Squatter," signed with the initials "S. L. C." The brief tale about a "spruce young dandy" with "a killing moustache," who for the amusement of his fellow-passengers on a steamboat, tried to scare a squatter, "a brawny woodsman," and got knocked into the river for his pains, was set in Hannibal, when that "now flourishing young city," was but a woodyard. Then, on May 8, the Philadelphia *American Courier* had published a serious piece containing Clemens' reflections on the mutability of human affairs.

Orion was indeed very, very angry upon his return, as Sam had good reason to remember. After giving his young assistant his opinion on mudslinging and hurling clods at hornet's nests, he turned to pacifying the injured parties. Not until November 4 did Sam become a contributor once more.

Not only did Orion continue to make managerial blunders which lost advertisers and subscribers, but misfortune dogged him. A fire had swept through the printing establishment on January 29, doing considerable damage, and forcing him to suspend publication until he could replace destroyed equipment and settle in a new location. Luckily he was able to collect $150 insurance which covered losses. His next problem was to meet the office rent because he was on the delinquent tax list for the Hill Street house. He decided then to move the plant home, which cramped them "cruelly," Sam recalled. During this time, a vagrant cow somehow got into the parlor, tipped over the type-case, and ate two composition rollers. Orion assured his readers when the next issue finally came out, that he would rectify their accounts by extending all subscriptions an extra week. After two months, he made a final move to an upstairs office on Main Street.

"I was walking backward, not seeing where I was going," he observed in retrospect. But, typically, this mood of gloom soon passed, and once again he met his reverses by compounding the problems: he began publication of a daily *Journal* in addition to the weekly.

Orion was highly respected in Hannibal. He was always addressed as Esquire, and was noted for his industry and like his father, for his "perfect probity and high principle." His writing was praised, and it was predicted he would some day gain recognition in that field. He succeeded John Marshall Clemens as a stockholder and trustee of the Hannibal Library Institute, and he lectured ably, although not brilliantly, on various issues. Everyone in town knew that for over ten years he had been the chief support, slim as it was, of his mother and brothers.

Late in January 1853 Sam was to witness another of those dark incidents which impressed him deeply. Walking down the street on a "chilly" Sunday evening, he came upon a stranger, a "harmless, whiskey-sodden tramp," with a pipe in his mouth, asking everyone he saw for a match. He was being followed by a troop of boys who were baiting him. Touched by his "friendless state" Sam furnished him matches, then went home to bed. Later, the tramp was arrested and locked up in the little brick calaboose at the mouth of Bear Creek.

At two in the morning the firebells rang and everyone, including Sam, turned out, to find the jail in flames. The tramp had accidentally set his straw tick on fire, and the oak sheathing of the cell had caught. Sam recognized the face "pleading" through the iron window bars, saw him shake them "frantically," and heard him scream for help. Behind him a "red hell" glowed. The marshal, who had the only key, lived some distance away, so a battering-ram was improvised. But the stout door did not yield and by the time the key was brought, the tramp was long past help. Sam Clemens was no longer there. Heartsick, he had gone home to dream. He maintained that for a hundred nights he had "hideous" visions in which he saw that imploring face at the bars, blaming him for having given the matches. His "trained Presbyterian conscience" bore down on him and he accepted responsibility. Because of his habit of talking in his sleep, he feared that Henry, who shared his bed, would learn the guilty secret. Similarly, Tom Sawyer, who alone knows about Injun Joe's murder of Dr. Robinson, babbles of it in his sleep, and to keep Sid Sawyer from learning more, pretends to have a toothache and ties his jaws together each night.

Clemens had the luckless tramp in mind when he told of Tom and Huck visiting Muff Potter in jail, and passing him "small comforts" through the grated window. Sam told the complete story, with details of its emotional impact upon himself, in *Life on the Mississippi*. In that same book, he was influenced by the experience when he described the horrors of a man imprisoned by debris aboard a burning steamboat. Rescuers worked frantically with axes to cut him free but were driven back by the intense heat. They had to stand helplessly by and listen to the man's screams and supplications. By the time that was written, Sam Clemens had suffered through a similar but far more tragic experience.

Sam made his literary debut on Orion's daily with contributions signed "Rambler." These consisted of bits of local news treated lightly, and sentimental verses addressed to young women, real or imaginary. Then, in the issue of May 6 appeared the announcement: "The Editor left yesterday for St. Louis. This must be our excuse if the paper is lacking in interest." Directly below this statement, the reader found:

TERRIBLE ACCIDENT!
500 MEN KILLED AND MISSING!!!

We had set the above head up, expecting (of course) to use it,
but as the accident hasn't happened, yet, we'll say
(To be Continued.)

On the same page was another set of verses by Rambler, this one
entitled:

LOVE CONCEALED
To Miss Katie of H—l

While setting it up Sam was "suddenly riven from head to heel" by
what he regarded as "a perfect thunderbolt of humor," in apparently addressing lines to a young woman in hell. Pretending that
Rambler was "a gorgeous journeyman tailor from Quincy," Sam
appended a "snappy" footnote from the editor:

> We will let this thing pass, just this once; but we have a character to
> sustain, and from this time forth when he wants to commune with
> his friends in h- -l, he must select some other medium than the
> columns of this journal!

A way was opened for Sam to continue the banter through five
ensuing issues by having an imaginary reader, "Grumbler," spar
with Rambler over the propriety of the whole matter. The following
day, the editorial column contained the first in the series:

> Mr. Editor:
>   In your yesterday's paper I see a piece of poetry addressed "To
> Katie in H—l" (hell). —Now, I've often seen pieces to "Mary in
> Heaven," . . . but "Katie in Hell," is carrying the matter too far.
>   Grumbler.

Rambler expressed a lofty sympathy for anyone so ignorant as
Grumbler who could not see the difference between " 'of' H—l
(Hannibal)" and " 'in' Hell."

One of Sam's most finished contributions printed during Orion's
second week of absence, was a squib entitled, "Oh, She has a Red
Head," a defense not only of red-haired people but of the color red
in general. He pointed out that Thomas Jefferson's hair was red,

The Dark Hour

that Jesus was said to have had auburn hair, and, although "it is not stated in so many words, I have . . . little doubt that Adam's hair was red. . . ." There was a great probability that Eve's was, too, since she was made from Adam's rib. "What gives to the bright flowers of the field . . . the power to charm the eye . . . but the softening touches of the all-admired red! And all children, before their tastes are corrupted, and their judgments perverted, are fond of red." Even Orion admitted after his return that the piece "afforded much comfort to the red-headed portion of the community."

This time, his brother's arrival did not silence Sam. Belatedly, the editor was coming to appreciate his worth, and launched him officially with "Our Assistant's Column." This became a lively miscellany of amusing comments on local affairs, witticisms, and a notably parody of "The Burial of Sir John Moore," in which Sam interred "Sir" Abner Gilstrap, a candidate for the Missouri legislature:

We buried him darkly, at dead of night—
 The dirt with our pitchforks turning;
By the moonbeams' grim and ghastly light,
 And our candles dimly burning.

No useless coffin confined his breast,
 Nor in sheet nor in shirt we bound him;
But he lay like an Editor taking his rest,
 With a Hannibal Journal round him . . .

Few and very short were the prayers we said,
 And we felt not a pang of sorrow;
But we mused, as we gazed on the wretch now defunct—
 Oh! where will he be tomorrow? . . .

Later Clemens claimed, that after reading it Gilstrap "pranced in with a war-whoop," thirsting for blood, but upon seeing the youthfulness of the author, cooled down.

At seventeen-and-a-half, Sam was still dependent upon Orion for support, and had to beg for spending money. Often his brother would refuse, and rebuke him for extravagance. Life was mainly long hours of hard work, with no future. Poverty could be very humiliating, especially if he wanted to invite Mary Bowen or Jennie Brady to see such visiting attractions as the "Floating Palace," a showboat which tied up at Hannibal that May, and then treat her to an ice cream afterward. Fortunately for his restricted social life, there were always free school and church picnics with excursions to Cave Hollow.

Sam could see that the *Journal* was doomed. Not even the loyal Jane Lampton was reading Orion's editorials any more, but turned quickly to Sam's lively contributions. He made up his mind not to follow Orion into his next venture, whatever that might be. He was restless, eager to be on his own, to see something of the world beyond a forty-mile radius, and to escape the oppressive atmosphere of his brother's declining fortunes and his consequent irritability—too reminiscent of John Marshall Clemens.

Orion had failed him personally just as their father had. Forced to submit daily to the will of this indecisive brother fated never to succeed, shaped Sam's lifelong attitude toward him. This would always be a curious mixture of love, condescension, generosity, and impatience mottled with outbursts of raw anger. These years with Orion also matured and made unalterable a resentment of male domination or authority, which had formed during that time when Sam was forced to obey the father he disliked. All of his life he would quarrel and break with men just as soon as they attempted to tell him what to do. Throughout his literary career, he had several male mentors to whose opinions on both his writings and his business affairs he deferred—but he had chosen those men himself, asked for their advice, then taken it voluntarily.

In looking back, Sam seemed to think that Orion's angry refusal to let him have a few dollars for the purchase of a used gun, was the final straw. Angry himself, and feeling he was not appreciated, he made up his mind quickly. He confided to his mother and to Henry his intention of leaving Hannibal for Pamela's house in St. Louis, where he knew he could easily find work as a printer. He kept to himself his intention to go on to New York after he had earned money enough, to see the Crystal Palace Fair. Jane Lampton helped him pack his few belongings and then, it has been said, she took up the Bible, asked him to place his hand beside hers and repeat after her: "I do solemnly swear that I will not throw a card or drink a drop of liquor while I am gone."—By "throwing a card," Jane implied gambling, for she was a card-player herself. This seems a reasonable request for a mother to ask her teen-age son when he is leaving home for the first time, but it has been interpreted by some Clemens students as the initial step in the trammeling of his free spirit and his creative genius, which his wife and one or two literary mentors supposedly completed. But this pledge was in effect only during the time he was away. There is no record of his mother trying to renew it at any later time.

When Sam left the house to catch the night boat to St. Louis, she kissed him goodbye and asked him to be sure he wrote her often. The date was probably May 26, for on the following day Orion ran an advertisement:

"Wanted! An Apprentice to the Printing Business. Apply Soon."

"And so he went wandering in search of that comfort and advancement and those rewards of industry which he had failed to find where I was—gloomy, taciturn, and selfish," Orion observed. "I could have distanced all competitors . . . if I had recognized Sam's ability and let him go ahead, merely keeping him from offending worthy persons."

He was so overwhelmed by Sam's departure that publication of the *Journal* was suspended for an entire month.

VI

―――――――――○―――――――――

JOURNEYMAN PRINTER

S AM WENT DIRECTLY from the steamboat to the boarding-house where Pamela, her husband, Will Moffett, and their one-
year-old daughter, Annie, were living until they could afford their
own home. Since quarters were crowded, Sam took a room with a
Mrs. Pavey of Hannibal, in a "large, cheap place" which attracted
students from a nearby college. He did not share his room with a
student, however, but with a young journeyman chair-maker, Jacob
H. Burrough, who had good taste in books, and a sense of humor.
They became "comrades & close friends," which made separation
from Henry less keen.

Clemens had no trouble finding work in the composing-room of
the St. Louis *Evening News*, a daily, where he was told that his
proofs were the cleanest ever set in that office. There are no details,
but sometime during his two-and-a-half month's stay he had cholera. In looking back several years later, he said that he had been
very sick.

He remained with the paper until about mid-August 1853, and
then, having saved money enough for the trip to New York, he
packed his "duds" and left for that "village" on the nineteenth, he
reported home. It proved to be "an awful trip" by rail and steamboat, which took five days when it ought to have been only three.

Journeyman Printer

Before looking for work, he was going to have to wait a day or two for his "insides to get settled, after the jolting they received."

"I arrived in New York with two or three dollars in pocket change and a ten-dollar bank bill concealed in the lining of my coat." He found an inexpensive room, and after changing his shirt, set off for the Crystal Palace. There the country's first world's fair was being held in a glass and iron building patterned after one built in London's Hyde Park for the Great Exhibition sponsored by Prince Albert in 1851. The site of New York's Crystal Palace was Sixth Avenue between 40th and 42nd streets—almost in the country.

That night, he wrote his mother to tell her where he was:

> You will doubtless be a little surprised, and somewhat angry, when you receive this, and find me so far from home; but you must bear a little with me, for you know I was always the best boy you had, and perhaps you remember that people used to say to their children— "Now don't do like O. and H. C. —but take S. for your guide!"

His excuse for leaving St. Louis was that he was out of work and "didn't fancy loafing in such a dry place."

Knowing that she shared his interest in the extraordinary, he hoped to put her in a good humor by giving an account of the "curiosity" he had watched for two hours that day. Two young white men, found in Borneo, the "only ones of the species ever discovered," were on exhibit. What distinguished them from ordinary men was that their faces resembled the orangutan's, that they possessed more than human strength, and that they lacked the "apple" in their throats and therefore could "scarcely make a sound." They had "bright, intelligent eyes," but no memory. Also strange, was the fact that they could walk on all fours as easily as upright. He devoted so much space to these wonderful creatures that there was none left in which to describe the Crystal Palace, other than to say that it was a "beautiful building." Possibly, he did not reach there in time to go inside. He closed with a promise to tell about the fair.

This letter was the first of Sam's travel letters to be published. It appeared in *The Hannibal Journal* on September 5, with an introductory note from Orion: "The free and easy impudence of the writer of the following . . . will be appreciated by those who recognize him. We should be pleased to have more of his letters."

But it was to Pamela he wrote that the exhibition hall was "a perfect fairy palace—beautiful beyond description." It would take a week to look at every display, he said, so many "departments of art and science" were represented. From the second floor gallery, the sight of the lofty dome, sparkling in the lights, the colorful flags of the countries exhibiting, the glittering jewelry, the "gaudy" tapestries, and the "busy crowd passing to and fro," was "glorious." He was awed by the realization that the average daily attendance was double the population of Hannibal.

On the Monday following his arrival, he obtained full-time work at John A. Gray & Green, 97 Cliff Street, the second largest book and job printers in the city (Harper's was first). He was very fortunate, he wrote home, for there are at least fifty good printers in town with no work at all. Although he must start at the foot of the wage-scale, "I will learn a great deal for they are very particular about spacing, justification, proofs, etc.; . . . Why, you must put exactly the same space between every two words, and *every line must be spaced alike.*" Once again, his was the cleanest of all the proofs.

His boarding-house on Duane Street, more than a mile from the office, was a "villainous" one, and the food was not at all to his liking. He missed Southern cooking, especially fried chicken. "The art cannot be learned north of the Mason-Dixon line," he declared. He missed biscuits and cornbread hot from the oven. "Perhaps no bread in the world is quite so good as Southern corn bread." New Yorkers, he complained, ate only "light-bread," stone cold, and preferably stale.

In his letters home he also expressed impatience with the numbers of dirty children he had to "wade" through in the streets. On his way to lunch, within six or seven squares, he could count at least two hundred "brats" who literally "block up" the narrow streets. It was an experience to "raise the ire" of the most patient man who ever lived—certainly not Sam Clemens. On Broadway, he was "borne, and rubbed, and crowded along" by throngs of adults, scarcely needing to use his legs. When he emerged from the crush, he felt as though he had been "pulled to pieces" and "very badly put together again." In a postscript, he told Jane Lampton that the printers had two libraries in town, free to the craft, and in these he could spend his evenings most pleasantly. "If books are not good company, where will I find it?" This letter was also printed in Orion's paper.

Pamela had forwarded their mother's letters written to him in her care. From them he learned that Henry had been sick. "He ought to go to the country and take more exercise; for he is not half so healthy as Ma thinks he is. If he had my walking to do, he would be another boy entirely. Four times every day I walk a little over one mile; and working hard all day, and walking four miles, *is* exercise—I am used to it now . . ." Pamela must be sure "to tell Ma that my promises are faithfully kept," and that he has been saving his money to take her to Kentucky in the spring. Homesick, he instructed his sister to get a message to Jim Wolfe and all his other friends, that they must write to him, and "give me all the news."

In his next letter to Pamela, he told about having been to the Broadway Theatre to see Edwin Forrest, the noted Shakespearean actor, play "Sparticus" in Robert Bird's *The Gladiator,* another of his famous roles. Sam liked the tragic ending best, for Forrest's "whole soul" seemed totally "absorbed" in the part; it was "startling" to see him.

Pamela must not worry if his letters are infrequent, he wrote, for "if you have a brother nearly eighteen years of age, who is not able to take care of himself a few miles from home, such a brother is not worth one's thoughts: and if I don't manage to take care of $N^{o.}$ *I.*, be assured you will never know it. I am not afraid, however: I shall ask favors from no one, and endeavor to be, (and *shall* be,) as 'independent as a woodsawyer's clerk.' " Just as soon as he can tell her where to direct her letters, she must write him at once—with *news.*

It was from Philadelphia that he was heard from next. He wrote to Orion, complaining that letters from the family were scarce. "It was at least two weeks before I left New York, that I received my last letter from home: and since then, devil take the word have I heard from any of you. And now, since I think of it, it wasn't a

letter, either, but the last number of the 'Daily Journal,' saying that
that paper was sold," to *The Tri-Weekly Messenger.* He supposed
then "that the family had disbanded and taken up winter quarters
in St. Louis."

Sam was "subbing" at the *Philadelphia Inquirer* office, and had
been hired by someone else to work every Sunday until the first of
April, when "I shall return home and take Ma to Ky." He enclosed
a gold dollar, "sparkling . . . fresh from the Mint," for Jane
Lampton; that was what they were paid with every Monday. "You
see it's against the law in Pennsylvania to keep or pass a bill of less
denomination than $5." He apologized for sending such a small
amount, but it was his last dollar. At least "it will buy her a
handkerchief."

". . . I like this Phila amazingly, and the people in it," he
added, and had been spending all of his free daylight hours sightseeing. He knew it would interest Orion to learn that he looked
through the locked iron gates at the graves of Benjamin Franklin
and his wife. A flat marble slab covered both, and as well as he
could see, was inscribed just with their names. The day before, he
had gone to the Exchange, or depot, and "deposited myself in a
Fairmount stage, paid my sixpence, or 'fip,' as these heathen call it,
and started." Soon they were rolling along through the beautiful
suburbs where he saw large houses of polished red granite with
fluted pillars of white marble. They were so imposing they could be
mistaken for public buildings. What a contrast to those "infernal
bogus brick columns, plastered over with mortar," which one saw
in St. Louis and Hannibal.

He explored the park, "rich in natural beauties," and the Water
Works, with its Grecian temples reflected clearly in the lake, its
marble fountains decorated with cupids and naiads, and its fine
waterfall. He saw the noted Wire Bridge, stretching across the
Schuylkill River—the first suspension bridge he had ever seen.
Upriver, he noticed little steamboats which make excursions
through the romantic gorge of the Wissahickon to Germantown, a
trip he intended to make later. He admired handsome Girard College, with its long colonnades of gleaming marble, "took a squint
at the 'House of Refuge,'" about which he had read in Sunday
school and then jumped aboard a returning omnibus to town.

"I must close now. I intend visiting the Navy Yard, Mint, &c. before I write again. You must write often. You see I have nothing to write interesting to you, while you can write no thing that will not interest me. . . . Tell Jim to write. Tell all the boys where I am, and to write, Jim Robinson, particularly. I wrote to him from N.Y. Tell me all that is going on in H- - -l."

Wherever he was, Sam made friends easily. In his Philadelphia boardinghouse, he met a pleasant older man named Sumner, an Englishman, who, as cold weather approached, invited Clemens to sit by his wood fire evenings and talk. At ten o'clock sharp, Sumner rose to prepare his night-cap—a dried herring grilled over the coals. The first time Sam watched this ceremony his mind flashed back to an experience of four years earlier that he could not forget easily.

The family was living in the Hill Street house in Hannibal, and Pamela was giving a party for a large group of friends. The entertainment was to be a "fairy play," in which Sam would take the part of a bear. About ten-thirty, he was told to put on his brown, furry costume and be ready in half an hour. He started upstairs but changed his mind, for he wanted to practice, and his room was small. Taking Sandy, the black boy, with him he ran down the street to a large unoccupied house on the corner of Main, unaware that a dozen other players had also gone there to get into costume. He and Sandy picked out a spacious room on the second floor. "We entered it talking and this gave a couple of half-dressed young ladies an opportunity to take refuge behind a screen undiscovered." Although their street dresses were hanging on hooks behind the door, neither boy noticed, their minds being so preoccupied with the theatrical. The screen was an old one with a number of holes in it, a detail that did not bother Sam since he was unaware there were girls behind it. Had he known, he would have "died of shame" to undress in the flood of moonlight pouring in through the curtainless window. Untroubled, he stripped to the skin and began his practice. "I was determined to make a hit, I was burning to establish a reputation as a bear and get further engagements," and he threw himself into his part with "an abandon that promised great things." He capered on all fours the length of the room and back several times, and walked upright and "growled and snapped and snarled." He flung handsprings, and danced a clumsy dance with paws bent and imaginary snout sniffing from side to side, Sandy meanwhile applauding wildly. Then he stood on his head to take a minute's rest.

Suddenly, Sandy spoke up: "Mars Sam, has you ever seed a dried herring?"

"No. What is that?"

"It's a fish."

"Well, what of it? Anything peculiar about it?"

"Yes, suh, you bet; you bet dey is. *Dey eats 'em guts and all!*"

There was a burst of smothered laughter from behind the screen —girls' laughter. All the strength went out of Sam and he "toppled forward like an undermined tower" and brought the screen down on the girls. They let out a couple of "piercing screams." If there were more Sam did not hear them for, snatching up his clothes, he fled to the dark hall, dressed in half a minute and, swearing Sandy to secrecy, dashed out the back way and hid until the party was over. It was not possible for him to face that "giddy company . . . for there were two performers who knew my secret and would be privately laughing at me all the time." He was hunted for but not found, and the bear was played by "a young gentleman" in his "civilized clothes."

The house was dark and everyone was asleep when Sam slipped in, feeling very downhearted about the whole adventure. What he found pinned to his pillow did not cheer him. On a slip of paper was a line in a "laboriously" disguised hand: "You probably couldn't have played bear but you played bare very well—oh, very *very* well!"

Sam "suffered miserably" the rest of that night, expecting the facts to be spread all over town the next morning—but they were not. Although it was a comfort to know that the secret was being kept, for weeks he was unable to look any of Pamela's girl friends in the face. If one smiled or spoke, he was certain she was one of the two who had been behind the screen and that she was laughing at him, and he would hurry off in confusion. By the time he left Hannibal he still had not found out those two girls.

Sumner's herring was perhaps the first Sam ever saw since they were salt-water fish; Sandy knew them because he came from

Journeyman Printer

Maryland. Sam would have looked at the herring closely and satisfied himself that it was indeed eaten "guts and all." As he reflected on that earlier episode, he wondered how it was that those two girls had never betrayed themselves—or had he been simply too dull to catch any signs? He never expected to learn their identity.

But Sam Clemens' life was filled with curious twists, and in 1896, when he was seventy-one, he was in Calcutta. At the hotel he met one of Pamela's friends who had a part in that fantasy so long ago. He recalled her from that far-off time as being sweet, dainty, "peach-blooming and exquisite." He had stood in awe of her because she "seemed made out of angel clay," and he never thought of suspecting her. Now she was a grandmother, but still handsome and youthful. She and Sam spent hours together, steeping "our thirsty souls in the reviving wine of the past," recalling incident after incident from their Hannibal days, some pathetic, but most of them amusing. They laughed until they were in tears. Then, suddenly, without preamble, she said, "Tell me! What is the special peculiarity of dried herrings?"

Not until November 28, 1853, did Sam finally hear from his family. Orion wrote to tell of his move with their mother and Henry (they had rented out the Hill Street house), to Muscatine, Iowa, where he had bought (on credit) a weekly which he called the *Muscatine Journal.* Although he did not say so, Sam suspected it was another languishing paper he hoped to build up.

Sam replied that same day, to urge that Jane Lampton spend the winter at St. Louis; Muscatine was far too cold for her. He was already becoming disenchanted with Philadelphia. "I always thought the eastern people were patterns of uprightness; but I never before saw so many whisky-swilling, God-despising heathens as I find in this part of the country. I believe that I am the only person in the Inquirer office that does not drink. One young fellow makes $18 for a few weeks, and then gets on a grand 'bender' and spends every cent of it." There was also the question of there being too many "abominable foreigners" who "hate everything American." Just that morning he had been in Franklin's old office, where he published his *Pennsylvania Gazette,* now being used by the *Phil-*

adelphia North American, and was amazed to find at least one foreigner for every American at work there. Foreigners in large numbers were new to the young man from Hannibal. In St. Louis, he was aware of many Germans and French, but he had met none in his trade. Now that he was having to compete with them for wages, he reflected the general resentment among workingmen of the time for all emigrants.

Orion asked him to correspond for the new paper. Sam, in turn, wanted to know how many subscribers it had and what the job-work paid—in fact, "what does the whole concern pay?" He wanted to see a copy. As to writing for it, he would try to do so occasionally but feared his letters would not be very interesting since constant night work "dulls our ideas amazingly."

A week later, he wrote Pamela that if he had the money he would leave for St. Louis at once, while the river was still open, but over the past two or three weeks he had spent some thirty dollars on much-needed clothing, so he supposed he must stay where he was. He disguised his homesickness by telling her that the only reason for leaving would be to avoid night work, which was also injuring his eyes.

Thoughts of his family made him downhearted and he became irritable, complaining to Pamela that the letters from home were not written as they ought to be, so that after reading them he knew "no more about what is going on there than the man in the moon." They lack specific detail. One has only to leave home to learn what the absent person craves in the way of word about family and friends.

After he had bought his new outfit, he had a ferrotype made for his mother. It was a full-face, bust view, showing him dressed in a white shirt with high standing collar that came forward only a little beyond the earlobes, leaving the neck bare in front; a dark cravat tied in a generous stiff bow, a light-colored, double-breasted vest patterned in small contrasting checks and styled with broad lapels, and a dark coat with wide notched collar.

He wrote two letters to the *Muscatine Journal,* one on December 4, which described the city of Philadelphia physically and told of his "awe and reverence" at visiting the old State House, and seeing the Liberty Bell and the "rude bench" upon which Franklin and

Washington had sat. On December 24, with Christmas at hand, he managed a cheerful letter describing the markets and shops crowded with people making their holiday purchases. Turkeys and other fowl were vanishing as if by magic from the stalls. He asked a woman what the best turkeys were selling at, and she told him seven dollars each. "This seems a high figure, but everything else is in proportion." He told also about his excursion by boat to Germantown, where, during the Revolution, the Americans had made their terrible charge upon the British, who were quartered in the Chew mansion. He examined the scars left on the house by musket and cannon balls.

During the long, dark days of mid-February he grew depressed and made what he termed a "flying trip" to Washington for a change of scene and possibly better weather, for Philadelphia was "intensely cold" with sleet and winds of hurricane force. In the way of weather, he found no improvement in the capital, for when he left his room the first morning to start a tour of the city, he walked out into a heavy snowstorm. But his spirits were high, for everywhere he heard the soft accents and drawls of Southern speech, which were welcome to his ears. "A Southerner talks music," he said. He saw black people again, the friendly "old-fashioned" kind he told Orion he was longing to meet again, and he was able to find fried chicken and hot cornbread cooked to his taste. The aversion to hurry and bustle, which gave Washington the air of a small Southern town rather than the national capital, also made him feel comfortable.

Although the city had been building for more than sixty years, it was still unfinished. Sam noted that the Washington Monument was not yet a third of its projected height. As he started to walk toward the park in front of the White House he sank ankle-deep in mud and snow at every step for there were no sidewalks, and only Pennsylvania Avenue had been paved. He stood in the driving snow to admire Clark Mills' equestrian statue of Andrew Jackson, a "great" work, well worth "a long walk on a stormy day to see."

He was well impressed with the grandeur of the public buildings but observed, as every other first-time visitor did, how "sadly out of place" they were in such surroundings. They looked like "so many palaces in a Hottentot village," for flanking them were huddles of dirty shanties and poorly designed and constructed shops, hotels, and boardinghouses of brick and frame. As for the dwellings, they were "strewed about in clusters," with vast spaces between the groups, as though they had been emptied from a sack by some "Brobdingnagian gentleman," and while falling were caught by the winds and scattered.

His experience with the transportation system did not recommend it. After standing fifteen minutes or more in a puddle of water, with the snow driving in his face, an omnibus finally rolled "lazily by," already packed with nineteen passengers inside and fourteen outside. By this time, he had begun to feel like a very wet dishrag, and having no wish to wait until he had to be wrung out, he decided to walk. "And so, driving your fists into the innermost recesses of your breeches pockets, you stride away in despair, with a step and a grimace that would make the fortune of a tragedy actor, while your 'ornery' appearance is greeted with 'screams of laftur' from a pack of vagabond boys over the way."

The Capitol has been described so often he would only say it was "a very fine building." He went in the Senate Chamber to see those men "who give the people the benefit of their wisdom and learning for a little glory and eight dollars a day." He regretted the passing of such giants as Clay, Webster, and Calhoun—"the void is felt." Stephen Douglas "looks like a lawyer's clerk," while William Seward, slim, dark, and bony, appeared likely to be blown out of the country by the first "respectable" wind.

He approved of the senators' plain dress and lack of "display," and the fact that they did not speak unless they had something to say. This was in marked contrast to the Representatives, he found, each of whom seemed to have on his mind some weighty matter he felt compelled to make known. At least half a dozen were on the floor at the same time, shouting for the chairman's attention. Sam noticed Missouri's Thomas Hart Benton sitting "silent and gloomy" in the midst of the clamor, like a "lion imprisoned in a cage of monkeys, who, feeling his superiority, disdains to notice their chattering." Benton had other reasons to feel somber; recently, he had lost his senatorship after serving thirty consecutive years, and had just been elected to the House. He was of special interest to Clemens who had seen him once in Hannibal, addressing a large rally. The boy had been disappointed, just as Tom Sawyer was, that Mr. Benton, "the greatest man in the world," an "actual" United States Senator, was not "twenty-five feet high."

He visited the Smithsonian Institute, a fine, large building, "half-church and half-castle." He inspected the library and extensive art gallery, and heard a lecture by the journalist and poet, Park Benjamin.

Most worthy of interest was the Patent Office Museum, which contained the country's largest collection of "curiosities." Sam spent four hours examining ancient Peruvian mummies. "Their hair was perfect, and remained plaited just as it was centuries ago; but the bodies were black, dry, and crisp." He saw Washington's dress uniform, sword, war-tent, and camp utensils, loaned by his adopted grandson, George Washington Parke Custis of nearby Arlington House; the original Declaration of Independence, Bonaparte's autograph—and the printing press used by Franklin in London about 1734. For Orion's sake, Sam described it in detail. As a relief from sightseeing, he saw Edwin Forrest in *Othello;* the huge National Theatre was crowded, he noted.

Sam's funds determined the length of his stay. When these ran low toward the first of March, he returned to Philadelphia, finding work this time with the *Public Ledger* and the *North American.*

Late that summer of 1854, after a brief return to New York, of which there are no details, he set off for St. Louis. He took the most direct route, by rail, and sat up three days and nights in the smoking car. Although exhausted on his arrival, he was so anxious to see his mother and Henry—and Orion, with whom he had parted fifteen months before—he declined Pamela's invitation to stay over and rest. After a short visit with her, he boarded the red-and-buff-painted side-wheeler *Westerner,* bound for Muscatine, and without bothering to undress, threw himself on his bunk and slept thirty-six hours—the length of the trip.

VII

————————○————————

KEOKUK DAYS

NOT LONG AFTER Sam Clemens reached Muscatine he was drafted into helping Orion with the *Journal*, even though there was not enough work to keep Henry busy full time and he was clerking part of each day at Burnett's bookstore. Orion could not of course pay Sam, but he hoped his contributions to the paper would increase circulation sufficiently to allow him to do so later.

Sam found the family living in a modest one-story cottage on Walnut Street, at the top of a grassy knoll that overlooked the Mississippi. At the rear of the house was a latticed porch and fine grape arbor which offered Jane Lampton a pleasant refuge during Orion's fits of gloom and outbursts of anger. Sam noticed that his brother seemed more preoccupied than usual, and soon learned it was because he was in love, a frequent occurrence, Sam remembered, apparently forgetting that he too was always falling in love. But this time it was different, because Orion had two girls at once. First, he had met a "winning and pretty" young woman from Quincy, Illinois, and they became engaged. Orion had never gone that far before. Then he met a plain and determined girl from Keokuk, Iowa, and fell in love with her (the Clemens family would always believe she talked him into it), and before he knew it he was engaged to her. Sam sympathized with Orion's dilemma:

whether to marry the pretty girl from Quincy or the one from Keokuk, or yet, marry both and satisfy all parties concerned.

But nineteen-year-old Mary Eleanor (Mollie) Stotts of Keokuk, "a master spirit," with a determined jaw, settled it by ordering Orion to write a letter to her rival, breaking off the engagement—which he did.

On December 19, 1854, he and Mollie, whose mother had been a girlhood friend of Jane Lampton's, were married at the Stotts house in Keokuk. Jane was not there. Before the river closed, she packed up and moved to St. Louis to stay with Pamela and her family in a rented house on Pine Street—for from what Jane had heard about Mollie already laying down rules for Orion, Henry, and Sam in Jane's own house, she knew a clash would be inevitable. She had no wish to be confined to that tiny place all winter with the only practical means of escape (the river) frozen over.

At sunrise, the morning after the wedding, Orion and Mollie left by stage for Muscatine. They stopped at Burlington for lunch, and when it came time to board the coach again Orion climbed right in, took his seat, tucked the buffalo robe around himself, leaned his head back, and closed his eyes. He roused just as the driver prepared to start on hearing a man outside ask, "Miss, do you go by this stage?" and Mollie's reply that she did.

"Oh! I forgot!" Orion remembered himself saying as he sprang out and helped Mollie in. "A wife was a new kind of possession to which I had not yet become accustomed; I had forgotten her."

In looking back Sam wrote that after he married the Keokuk girl "they began a struggle for life which turned out to be a difficult enterprise. . . ."

It was obvious to Sam that there was no future in Muscatine, and about the first of February he returned to St. Louis. By March 14, Orion was ready to admit the fact that he was failing, and ran an advertisement offering for sale his half-interest in the printing office. The reason he gave for wanting to sell was "Important business in another State" which made prolonged absence necessary. He offered low terms for cash. At Mollie's urging, he was looking for an opening in Keokuk, which was in the midst of a real estate boom and was prospering. Not only did the future there seem promising, but Mollie would be near her family and friends. Not until June, however, was the move made, when Orion took over the "Ben Franklin Book and Job Office." Henry Clemens went with them.

The permanent ambition of every boy in Hannibal was to be a steamboat captain or pilot. Many of Sam's schoolmates and comrades were already on the river—among these were his friends Will Bowen, and Will's brother, Sam, both of them pilots. There is no record as to how long Sam Clemens had been considering abandoning printing in favor of the river, but that summer he asked his wealthy kinsman, James Clemens, Jr., ("Old Jimmy Clemens, Jr.," he called him privately), for help. Sam told him he wanted to become a cub pilot. The older man urged him to stay with printing but did agree to speak to a friend, a pilot on one of the large steamboats. But when that vessel next came into St. Louis, James Clemens was sick (so he said) and was unable to see his friend. He seems to have made no further effort to carry out his promise. Sam told about going "meekly aboard a few of the boats that lay packed together like sardines at the long St. Louis wharf, and humbly inquired for the pilots, but got only a cold shoulder and short words from mates and clerks."

However, skilled compositor that he was, he had no trouble finding work on any of the city's dozen newspapers, doubtless subbing once more since that gave him his choice of hours. He was lodging again with Mrs. Pavey.

Early in July, Sam took passage (fare two dollars) on the steamboat *Westerner* for the fourteen-hour trip from St. Louis to Hannibal to attend to some business connected with the sale of the Hill Street house, the lease of a lot, and to dispose of the furnishings and possessions left in the care of various persons in town. Orion had sent a list of things to be shipped to Keokuk: his maps, his press, his table and secretary, his law books, the family Bible (containing records of marriages, births and deaths), and, looking to the future, for Mollie's first child was due in September, the "little Red Rocking Chair" which his sisters and brothers had used in turn.

After finishing his business and visiting with former schoolmates and friends, he traveled on to the house of John Quarles, who had sold his farm and was living just outside the village of Florida.

Sam found his uncle still the jovial raconteur, and made brief notes of some of his anecdotes in the little memorandum book he had recently commenced carrying. So far, its pages were filled with vocabularies for seven French lessons, a language he was then studying, and with notes made during this trip, which were interspersed with entries about that branch of phrenology which divided mankind into four predominating temperaments. He decided that his was the "Sanguine Temperament," and Orion's the "Nervous."

His stop in Florida was not just social, for he had business to carry out for his mother there, and at Paris, the county seat, where he collected her share of the proceeds from a court sale of farm land that had belonged to her father, Benjamin Lampton, and to her aunt, Diana Lampton. He then returned to Hannibal to oversee shipment of Orion's goods, and took passage for Keokuk, possibly on the same riverboat. Almost immediately on his arrival, Orion offered him work on his largest project to date: the publication of the *Keokuk City Directory*, an ambitious work for which he was writing a historical sketch.

Sam's sense of responsibility toward his family was strong (one day he would support them all), and he accepted Orion's offer of five dollars a week and board at the Ivins House, the town's best hotel. Henry took his meals with Orion and Mollie but slept at the printing office, in the third story of a red brick building on Main Street. A bookstore was located on the ground floor and a music school run by Professor O. C. Isbell was on the second. Sam was to share Henry's bed.

Many evenings at the printing office were made lively with the addition of Orion's two apprentices, Dick Higham and John Kerr, and Edward Brownell, who clerked in the downstairs bookstore. Sam was the leading spirit, playing guitar and banjo, and singing comic or nonsense songs, some of his own making or adaptation, others heard among the blacks, and still others picked up at minstrel shows. In Hannibal he had entertained his friends with his version of "The Old Gray Mare," and now he sang it again:

> *I had an old horse and he died in the wilderness,*
> *Died in the wilderness,*

Died in the wilderness;
I had an old horse and he died in the wilderness,
Way down in Alabam'.

That song, with a few word changes, remained always a part of his repertoire and he amused audiences with it wherever he went—Nevada, California, and Hawaii. It was his way of singing it—emphasis, facial expression, gestures—and certainly not content which made it so long remembered as being very funny. There was another:

Boston isn't in Bengal,
And flannel drawers ain't made of tripe;
Lobsters don't wear specs at all,
And cows don't smoke the German pipe . . .

And one he accompanied on the banjo. It began:

Grasshopper sittin' on a sweet-potato vine,
Turkey come along and yanked *him from behine . . .*

At the word *"yanked,"* he swept his fingers discordantly across the strings. Occasionally he would jump to his feet and do a shuffle.

These were loud sessions and Professor Isbell, attempting to teach a night class just below, was often frustrated. One day he confronted Sam and demanded in a surly fashion that he stop the noise. Sam ignored him, and the following night organized a game of tenpins, using empty wine bottles for pins and cobblestones for balls. No attention was paid to Isbell's pounding on the bolted door. In the morning the professor threatened Sam—and that evening was forced to listen to the steady tramp and shouted orders of a military company drilling overhead. The music teacher then decided on a radical change in approach and, coming up to Sam the next morning, explained in a pleasant way how the nightly racket disrupted his singing classes and greatly upset his young lady pupils.

Sam said to him in surprise:

"Does it? Why didn't you say so before?" They had no wish to distress any young ladies. The affair ended with an invitation for Sam and his comrades to join a singing class.

Keokuk (named for a chief of the Sauk-Fox confederation, who, in 1832, eloquently persuaded his people not to join Black Hawk in the war against the whites) was built on the top of a group of steep, wooded bluffs overlooking the confluence of the Des Moines and Mississippi rivers, and had a view into three states. It was a pretty little city of neat frame and red-brick dwellings and commercial buildings, its residential streets lined with plantings of locust and chinaberry trees, and its dooryards bright with a profusion of flowers. The College of Physicians and Surgeons, a branch of the state university, was situated there, and gave the town an academic air. But Sam's new friendships were not made on campus, for aside from Higham, Kerr, Brownell, and William Clagett, a law student, his chief social interest was in girls. Through Orion's wife, Mollie, who was close to Sam's age, and her younger sister, Belle, both of whom had grown up in Keokuk, he was able to meet a bevy of them. His high spirits, instinctive gallantry, and skill as a dancer made him popular. It had been said of Jane Lampton that no party was a success without her; now the same was being said of Sam.

In letters, he mentioned those favorites he and Henry admired —Emma Graham, Ella Patterson and Bettie Barrett, and their own Lampton cousin, Ella Creel—"a great belle." But it was Orion's neighbor, "the talented and brilliant" Ann Elizabeth Taylor, in whom Sam became especially interested. She was well read, was musical, liked to draw, and shared his ability to see the comical side of things. He appreciated the fact that she was somewhat a rebel, too, and had received low grades in deportment, for "very irregular" attendance at prayer meetings. She also had ambitions beyond marriage (which Sam would have taken lightly, for he had made fun of feminists in *The Hannibal Journal*) and was now continuing her education at Iowa Wesleyan College in Mt. Pleasant, forty miles north. After completing her studies at Lindenwood College, near St. Louis, she became an instructor in English there, an outstanding achievement for a young woman in that day.

He and Annie spent much time together during her school holidays, and when apart they corresponded regularly. Her letters were described as being "strikingly original and humorous," which inspired Sam to write about subjects he knew she, above others, could appreciate.

One of these, which addressed her as "My Dear Friend Annie," opened with an imaginative tale about all the varieties of insects which had been attracted by the gas light flaring above his head while he worked the previous night at his press until almost two in the morning. At first they came in little social groups of a dozen or so, but their numbers increased so rapidly there was soon a crowd of several million. This great mass meeting was presided over by a "venerable beetle who occupied the most prominent lock of my hair as his chair of state, while innumerable lesser dignitaries of the same tribe were clustered around him, keeping order." It was, perhaps, "a great bug jubilee," commemorating the victory of the locusts over Pharaoh's crops, eons ago. Certainly, good seats with an unobstructed view were in "great demand," and Sam did not doubt that "small fortunes were made by certain delegates from Yankee land by disposing of comfortable places on my shoulders at round premiums."

"The big 'president' beetle (who, when he frowned, closely resembled Isbell when the pupils were out of time) rose and ducked his head and, crossing his arms over his shoulders, stroked them down to the tip of his nose several times, and after thus disposing of the perspiration, stuck his hands under his wings, propped his back against a lock of hair, and then, bobbing his head at the congregation, remarked, 'B-u-z-z!' " Satisfied with his flock's prompt "B-u-z-z!" in response, he led a grand anthem—"three dignified daddy longlegs, perched near the gas burner, beating quadruple time during the performance." A final grand chorus, "Let Every Bug Rejoice and Sing," ended the affair. In the morning, Sam combed 976 beetles out of his hair.

Annie looked forward to his letters (she saved them in a japanned box for sixty years), and scolded him for being slow to reply. Anticipating this, he warned in the bug jubilee letter, "Now, Annie, don't say anything about how long *my* letter was in going, for I didn't receive *yours* until Wednesday—and don't forget that I *tried* to answer it the same day, though I was doomed to fail. I wonder if you will do as much?" Obviously, he was just as eager for her letters.

Keokuk Days

She had sent him a drawing of Mt. *Un*pleasant, as they dubbed the school because it was the cause of their separation, her homesickness, and considerable concern over assignments in essay writing. He proclaimed her sketch both "beautiful" and *"perfect."* Then he told how he had "delighted Henry's little heart" by delivering her message, for his brother was writing her, too, although it was Ann's younger sister, Marie, also enrolled at the college, who had won his affections. Sam then encouraged her, "Ah, Annie, I have a slight horror of writing essays myself; and if I were to write one I should be afraid to do it, knowing that you could do it so much better if you would only get industrious once and try." This suggests that she may have asked him for help and that his insect fantasy was to show her how to expand a simple idea about almost anything.

The year and a half Sam spent in Keokuk was apparently a happy period. It was active socially, and not without benefit to his development. On January 17, 1856, he made his first after-dinner speech at a printer's banquet held at the Ivins House to celebrate the 150th anniversary of Franklin's birth. Orion, who was chairman of the affair, practiced his oratory with an address, after which prominent guests were called on for speeches. After the program was finished, Sam Clemens was "loudly and repeatedly called for." Completely unprepared, he got slowly to his feet, blushing and fumbling for words at first. But suddenly he mastered the situation and gave a talk that combined "pathos and humor," it was reported. It was also said that he "convulsed his hearers," who interrupted with "long and continued bursts of applause." After this success he was invited to join a local debating society.

Sam's friend, Ed Brownell, from the bookshop, remembered seeing him often with a work by Dickens or Poe under his arm, or some book on English history or exploration, to read at odd moments. But most of his reading was done after he went to bed, for he found it relaxing to stretch out with a book and a cigar or pipe, a habit which was lifelong. Sometimes, on his way to his own room on the floor above, Brownell would stop in to see Sam. He recalled that one night when he asked Clemens what he was reading, the reply was, "Oh, nothing much—a so-called funny book. One of these days I'll write a funnier one than this, myself."

"Oh, no you won't!" Brownell countered, "you're too lazy to ever write a book." Sam did not forget that remark, which had been provoked by an incident involving Brownell the night before, but eleven years passed before he was able to get revenge. The episode concerned a hookah Sam had made for himself because it held more tobacco than a briar or corncob, gave a cooler smoke, and, most important, was comfortable to use in bed. Its one disadvantage was a tendency to go out, which meant having to sit up, reach for a match, and lean down to light the bowl on the floor. Therefore, this was usually Henry's task. But that night, as Ed Brownell was coming upstairs to bed he heard Sam call him. When he opened the door, Clemens said, "Come on in. Henry's asleep, and I'm in trouble. I need somebody to light my pipe."

Brownell asked, "Why didn't you get up and light it yourself?"

"Oh, I was going to, only I knew you'd be coming along in a few minutes and save me the trouble." Ed's observation on Sam's laziness followed.

Early in 1856, Clemens became interested in South America, then being talked about widely as the new frontier, a place where a man could make a fortune by working the vast, unexploited natural resources. He was fascinated by Lieutenant William Lewis Herndon's report, *Exploration of the Valley of the Amazon*, printed two years before, and especially by what he had to say about coca. Sam discussed with Henry the possibility of going together to the headwaters of the Amazon where it grew abundantly, and become rich trading in it. Coca was in short supply and in great demand for medical uses as a source of cocaine and related alkaloids. He talked about the idea openly with his mother, guardedly with Orion, and with great enthusiasm to a young friend named Ward and to Dr. J. S. Martin, a lecturer on chemistry and toxicology at the local medical college. Both Ward and Martin were eager to accompany Clemens.

Sam was growing restless again, and was impatient with Orion's methods. Finding it impossible to pay Sam most of the time, he solved the problem by taking him into partnership, which meant no wages and barely enough for living expenses. That June, Sam wrote to his mother and Pamela that the directory was coming along "finely" only because all other work was being neglected. He could no longer count on finishing a promised job on time because Orion was continually taking away his helpers to work on the directory, and insisting that Sam drop everything and help. In July the directory was finished, and in it Samuel L. Clemens was listed as an antiquarian. "Every town should have at least one, and Keokuk had none," he explained.

On August 5, he answered a letter from Henry, who was visiting at Hannibal. He opened with the news, "Annie is well." That was Annie Taylor. He then went on to say that after a long consultation with Ward "us two have determined to start to Brazil in *six weeks* from now, in order to look carefully into matters there (by the way, I forgot to mention that *Annie* is well,) and report to Dr. Martin in time for him to follow on the first of March. We propose going *via.* New York. Now, between you and I and the fence you must say nothing about this to Orion, for he thinks that Ward is to go clear through alone, and that I am to stop at New York or New Orleans until he reports. But that don't suit me. . . . I want to see with my own eyes and form my own opinion. But you know what Orion is. When he gets a notion into his head, and more especially if it is an erroneous one, the Devil can't get out again." Even their mother counseled him "to keep it from Orion. She says I can treat him as I did her when I started to St. Louis and went on to New York—I can start to New York and go to South America! (This reminds me that—Annie *is* well.)" Although Orion "talks grandly" about furnishing Sam with fifty or a hundred dollars in six weeks, "I am not such an ass as to think he will retain the same opinion such an eternity. Though I don't like to attribute selfish motives to him, you could see yourself that his object in favoring my wishes was that I might take all the hell of pioneering in a foreign land, and then when everything was placed on a firm basis, and beyond all risk, he could follow himself. . . . With these facts before my eyes, (I must not forget to say that Annie *is well,)* I could not depend upon Orion for ten dollars, so I have 'feelers' out in several directions, and have already asked for a hundred dollars from one source (keep it to yourself.) I will lay on my oars for a while, and see how the wind sets, when I may probably try to get more."

He then gave Henry the kind of home news he liked to hear when he was away: "Emma Graham has got home, and Bettie

Barrett has gone up the country. I may as well remark that *Annie is well.* " He had spent Sunday afternoon with her, and she had heard nothing from any of the other girls who were out of town. "The report that Belle and Isbell are about to be married, is still going." The subject of marriage reminds him: "Between you and I, I believe that the secret of Ma's willingness to allow me to go to South America lies in the fact that she is afraid I am going to get married. Success to the hallucination." There was a postscript: "I will just add that *Annie* IS WELL."

Sam's attempts to raise money were not successful, so the trip to Brazil was postponed. Then, one blustery morning in early October, as he was walking along Keokuk's nearly deserted main street, he had his second fateful adventure with the wind. Again, a piece of paper blew across his path, just as the page about Joan of Arc had done. This one lodged against the wall of a house. Something about it attracted him, so he went over and picked it up. It proved to be a fifty-dollar bill, the first he had ever seen, "and the largest assemblage of money I had ever seen in one spot." He advertised it in the papers and during the next few days "suffered more than a thousand dollars' worth of . . . fear and distress," lest the owner come and claim it. After four days passed and no applicant appeared, he felt he had better take that money "out of danger." He went to the railway office and bought a ticket for Cincinnati. Before leaving, he made arrangements to write a series of humorous travel letters for George Rees, editor of the Keokuk *Daily Post.* Rees agreed to pay him five dollars each.

The first published letter was dated October 18, 1856 from St. Louis, and written while Sam was visiting his mother and sister. It relied upon backwoods dialect, ignorance, and gullibility for humor, a form of comic writing then very popular. Sam's correspondent, Thomas Jefferson Snodgrass, was a rustic from Keokuk whose first visit to the metropolis of St. Louis opened the way for countless awkward situations, which included being twice removed by the police for causing a near-riot during a performance of *Julius Caesar.* His readers were treated to details of the whole affair, as well as a synopsis of the play about "Mr. Cesar."

The next letter furnished a clue to Sam's movements, for it was written from Cincinnati on November 14. Snodgrass explained that, having seen so "many wonderful things" at St. Louis, he wanted to see more, and "took a notion to go a travelin, so as to see the world, and then write a book about it—a kind o daily journal like—and have all in gold on the back of it, 'Snodgrass' Dierrea', or somethin of that kind, like other authors that visits forren parts." Readers this time were treated to his mishaps on the journey from St. Louis.

There was only one more letter, written four months later, from Cincinnati, where Sam had been working as a printer. By then, Snodgrass supposed, some people must think that "your umble sarvent has 'shuffled off this mortal quile' and bid an eternal adoo to this subloonary atmosphere—nary time. He aint dead," but has "pooty much quit scribblin," for Sam's travels had stopped, and material for Snodgrass' peregrinations became a problem. Now that Sam was about ready to move on, he revived Snodgrass, in this number saddling him with an unwanted foundling, which offered unlimited possibilities for further adventure. In explanation of the fact that the Snodgrass letters ended abruptly, the son of editor George Rees recalled that Sam asked for a raise after each contribution, which was granted until he asked for ten dollars. Since their limit was seven-fifty, and Sam insisted on more, the agreement was cancelled.

In Cincinnati, Sam told of meeting another congenial and interesting fellow-lodger, a tall, lank, scholarly Scotsman named Macfarlane, who was twice his age. He had no humor or any comprehension of it; his smile was simply an expression of his good nature. He had educated himself by reading history, philosophy, science, and the Bible, and his one pride was that he knew the meaning of every word in his dictionary. Sam tried, but never succeeded in finding one Macfarlane could not define. They were exact opposites in most ways but "comrades from the start." Clemens always spent his evenings by the wood fire in his friend's room, with its shelves of "weighty books," listening to Macfarlane's tireless talk about matters "grave and large." Before Darwin, he was expounding his own theory of evolution, which Sam never forgot because it was a revelation to one brought up with Genesis.

At ten o'clock promptly, he also put a dried herring on the coals to grill, as had Sam's English friend, Sumner, in Philadelphia. "His herring was his nightcap and my signal to go."

Except for Macfarlane's company, Clemens had a lonely time (almost four months) in Cincinnati. Letters from home were few, and beyond those there had been only three or four from friends. One was from Annie Taylor, which arrived when Sam was sick, and it "rather 'set me up', for I imagined that as you had got started once more you would continue with your ancient punctuality." Although he replied as soon as he read her letter, she did not respond, and he became homesick and downhearted.

But just as soon as the rivers opened in April, his spirits lifted. He had saved money enough for the passage to New Orleans (sixteen dollars)—and further, for Brazil had not been abandoned. He packed his bag, bid Macfarlane good-bye, and boarded "an ancient tub" named the *Paul Jones,* for the first part of a voyage in quest of a fortune.

VIII

―――――――○―――――――

LEARNING THE RIVER

As soon as the *Paul Jones* got under way and went poking down the broad Ohio, Sam was overcome by a feeling of exultance such as he had never experienced before, realizing that he was starting for "mysterious lands" and "distant climes" which held untold adventure and possible riches. "I became a new being, and the subject of my own admiration." Already he thought of himself as a world traveler, and he wanted everyone to know it. So whenever the little boat put in at towns, villages, or woodyards, he made it a point to loll carelessly on the boiler deck in order to enjoy the envy of young men standing on the riverbank. If they did not seem to notice, he sneezed, and when he was sure they saw him, he yawned and stretched to give the impression of being bored with travel.

"The poor old *Paul Jones* fooled away about two weeks in making the voyage . . . to New Orleans," which gave Sam time to become acquainted with Horace Bixby, one of the pilots, who was ten years his senior. Sam opened their conversation by asking if he knew the Bowen brothers—Will, Sam, and Bart, all pilots in the St. Louis–New Orleans trade—which Bixby did. After that, Sam was in the pilot-house every day, listening to river talk, and it was not long before Bixby let him do some steering during his daylight watches.

As soon as Clemens felt the boat in hand, all his old fascination with piloting seized him, and the Amazon no longer seemed so alluring. Still, when he landed at New Orleans, the first thing he did was to make inquiries about vessels leaving for Pará. There were none, he found, and probably wouldn't be any "during that century." He could easily have found a job as a printer, but he hunted up Horace Bixby instead. At the end of a hard, three-day seige—"cub pilots are more trouble than they're worth!" Bixby said—he agreed to teach Sam the river from New Orleans to St. Louis and back, because it differed in each direction, for five hundred dollars—one hundred in advance, and the rest to be paid after he was licensed and began receiving wages.

Sam returned with the *Paul Jones* to St. Louis, and called on his rich kinsman, James Clemens, Jr., to borrow the hundred-dollar advance. Before he got to the subject, however, James was wailing about having to pay $25,000 taxes in New York City, which "makes a man poor," so Sam never asked him. The only other person he knew who might consent was Pamela's husband, Will Moffett—"a fine man in every way," Sam thought. When asked, Moffett was willing to make the loan.

Pamela's daughter, Annie, then going on five, remembered the excitement over the news that her Uncle Sam was going to become a pilot. It seemed to her that everyone in the house was running up- and downstairs, and in and out of rooms, to talk about it, for it was an esteemed and well-paid profession. It was also a great point of pride to have a pilot in one's family.

It is easy to see why piloting appealed so strongly to Sam Clemens, who had been yearning for total freedom from authority. At this time a Mississippi River pilot was the "only unfettered and entirely independent human being" on earth. He was in sole and unquestioned control of the steamboat from the moment she left the wharf and was under way in the river. "He could do with her exactly as he pleased, run her when and whither he chose, and tie her up to the bank whenever his judgment said that . . . course was best." He consulted no one, "he received commands from nobody. . . ." In fact, federal law prohibited him from listening to orders or suggestions on the grounds that he, the pilot, "necessarily knew better how to handle the boat than anybody could tell him." Here, then, was "the novelty of a king without a keeper, an absolute monarch who was absolute in sober truth and not by a fiction of words." As a boy in Hannibal Sam Clemens had envied kings, and now he was on his way to becoming one.

Had he realized what would be required of his "faculties" in learning thirteen hundred miles of the Mississippi, he would never have had the courage to start, he observed later. But with the "easy confidence" of youth he began the task supposing that all a pilot had to do was keep his boat in the river—not much of a "trick" since the Mississippi was so wide.

Horace Bixby started the lessons just as soon as they set off for St. Louis. It was four o'clock in the afternoon when the *Paul Jones* left the city wharf at New Orleans. Right after he had "straightened her up" and "plowed her along the sterns of the other boats that lay at the Levee," he said to Sam, "Here, take her; and shave those steamboats as close as you'd peel an apple."

It seemed to Clemens that they were already so close he would scrape the side off every one. Holding his breath, he steered away from danger and in half a minute had a wide margin of safety between them. In ten seconds, Bixby had taken back the wheel and was trimming those ships with only inches between them, all the while "flaying" Sam for his cowardice.

After Bixby had cooled, he began calling attention to landmarks: "This is Six-Mile Point." And later, "This is Nine-Mile Point," and then, "This is Twelve-Mile Point." Sam regarded this information as "pleasant enough," but saw no particular reason for it. All the Points looked about alike, and "monotonously unpicturesque." He hoped Bixby would change the subject.

But no, just beyond Twelve-Mile Point, he announced, "The slack water ends here, abreast these China trees; now we cross over." And over he crossed. Sam noticed how he hugged the shore "with affection," a practice which made Clemens nervous. Once or twice, he gave the wheel back to Sam, who in trying to follow the example, came close to "chipping off the edge of a sugar plantation," then in alarm, "yawed too far from shore," and so slipped back into disgrace.

During their second watch that night, Bixby turned to Sam suddenly and asked: "What's the name of the first point above New Orleans?" Sam promptly said he didn't know.

"Don't *know?* Well, you're a smart one. What's the name of the *next* point?" Sam couldn't tell him that one either.

"Well, this beats everything. Tell me the name of *any* point or place I told you." Sam thought awhile, then admitted he was unable to do that either.

"Look here! Where do you start out from, above Twelve-Mile Point, to cross over?"

"I—I—don't know."

"You—you—don't know?" Bixby mimicked Sam's drawl. "What *do* you know?"

"I—I—nothing for certain."

Bixby exploded. "You're the stupidest dunderhead I ever saw or heard of, so help me Moses! The idea of you being a pilot—*you!* Why, you don't know enough to pilot a cow down a lane." Sam remembered that Bixby would "boil awhile to himself, and then overflow and scald me again."

"Look here! What do you suppose I told you the names of those points for?" Sam considered a moment, then unable to resist, replied, "Well to—to—be entertaining, I thought."

This provoked the worst outburst of all. After his fund of expletives was exhausted, he fell silent. Presently he turned to Sam and said in the "gentlest" way, "My boy, you must get a little memorandum-book; and every time I tell you a thing, put it down right away. There's only one way to be a pilot, and that is to get the entire river by heart. You have got to know it like A B C."

Sam took this injunction seriously, and the little notebook, "fairly bristling" with the names and positions of points, islands, towheads, shoals, chutes, bends; landmark buildings and trees, soundings, the height of banks, and minute instructions about troublesome places, still exists. It is a thin ledger which Sam, in need, evidently persuaded one of the clerks on board to surrender, for it contains a few entries in another hand, concerning cargo.

Clemens set his mind to the task in earnest, and by the time the *Paul Jones* had covered seven or eight hundred miles, he had learned to be a "tolerable plucky upstream steersman" in daylight;

Learning the River

and before they reached St. Louis, he had made a "trifle of progress in night-work, but only a trifle." But it made his heart ache to think that he had only half the river set down. Because their watch was four hours on and four hours off, day and night, "there was a long twenty-four hour gap in my book for every time I had slept since the voyage began."

The usual stop-over for a steamboat at St. Louis was three days, and when it was time to start back to New Orleans on that first trip, he had another fit of discouragement when he realized that his notes were useless: "I had got to learn that troublesome river *both ways.*"

After what seemed to him a "tedious while," he managed to fill his head with an enormous amount of miscellaneous but necessary information, and was just beginning to take heart, when one day Bixby challenged him: "What is the shape of Walnut Bend?"

Reflecting a few moments, Sam replied "politely" that he was not aware it had any particular shape. When Bixby had cooled down, he said to him gently, "My boy, you've got to know the *shape* of the river perfectly. It is all there is left to steer by on a very dark night. Everything else is blotted out and gone. But mind you, it hasn't the same shape in the night as it has by day."

This depended upon the kind of a night it was. A clear, starlit one cast such heavy shadows that unless one knew the shape of the shore perfectly, he would "claw" away from every stand of timber, mistaking it for a solid cape. "Stars and shadows ain't good to see by," Clemens' character, Huckleberry Finn, was to say as he rafted down the river. Pitch black nights were another story. Then, all shapes seemed to be straight lines, and dim ones at that. Of necessity, a steamboat would run without lights on such a night, and the pilot would order the skylights and furnaces curtained with tarpaulins, and he would even refrain from smoking a cigar. On such nights a steersman might be tempted to run for the straight lines, only he knew better, and boldly steered his boat right into what appeared to be a solid wall, aware that in reality there was a curve there, and that the "wall" would fall back and make way.

There were other nights of solid white fog when nothing took any particular shape, the kind of night to puzzle the most experienced pilot on the river, and he had to keep alert to catch such sounds as the wash of current against a dead limb, or brush hanging down a bank, which would tell him where he was. Then there were phases of moonlight when nothing looked natural. And in fall, an impenetrable pall of smoke caused by a hundred miles of damp sugar-cane refuse—bagasse—fired and smoldering in huge piles. At such times not even the sugar plantations themselves were recognizable. In addition, there was the season of thaw when, in high water the river topped its banks and at midnight the pilot might find himself in the middle of what appeared to be a shoreless sea that lost itself in the murky distance. He could only hope that he was keeping in the river, but there was no way of telling. On one such night, a large packet from Vicksburg dashed right into the middle of a cane plantation, and had to remain there for a week.

Sam protested, "Have I got to learn the shape of the river according to all these five hundred thousand different ways? If I tried to carry all that cargo in my head it would make me stoop-shouldered."

"*No!*" Bixby said, "you only learn *the* shape of the river; and you learn it with such absolute certainty that you can always steer by the shape that's *in your head,* and never mind the one that's before your eyes."

Sam agreed to try; but then another doubt arose. Will he be able to depend on it keeping that shape and "not go fooling around?"

Before there was time for a reply, the relief pilot came on watch.

"Bixby," he said, "you'll have to look out for President's Island, and all that country . . . above the Old Hen and Chickens. The banks are caving in like everything. Why, you wouldn't know the point above 40. You can go up inside the old sycamore snag, now."

Again Sam's spirits fell as he realized that to be a pilot he would have "to learn more than any one man ought to be allowed to know; . . . and that he must learn it all over again in a different way every twenty-four hours." There were no shortcuts. It was plain he had to master the river "upside down, wrong end first, inside out, fore-and-aft, and 'thort-ships,' in star and moonlight, in pitch dark, and impenetrable fog or smoke.

At this point, Horace Bixby transferred to the big, new steamboat *Pennsylvania,* and Sam packed his bag and went with him. To

Learning the River

encourage himself, he made a tour of the vessel and wondered how he could have ever felt so proud of the little old *Paul Jones,* with its tiny, battered, dingy "rattle-trap" of a pilot-house. This one was a "sumptuous glass temple," with room enough to hold a dance in. It had a costly inlaid wheel as high as Sam's head, shiny brass knobs for the bells, an "imposing" sofa, red and gold window-curtains, and a fine leather-cushioned seat and back to the high bench where, between runs, visiting pilots sat and spun yarns and observed the river closely for changes. There was a big "hospitable" stove for winter, and a neat, white-aproned "texas-tender" to bring up ices, tarts, and coffee during mid-watch, night and day. As Sam explored the rest of the boat, he saw that there was a picture done in oils by some "gifted" sign-painter on every stateroom door. The long, gilded saloon sparkled with prismed chandeliers. He admired the fires glaring "fiercely" from a long line of furnaces, and the row of eight huge boilers above them. This was "something like," he decided, and took heart. When he found that the "regiment" of "natty servants respectfully 'sir'd' " him, his satisfaction was complete.

After considerable time had passed and Sam was beginning to feel some confidence in his knowledge, Horace Bixby was ready for him. "How much water did we have in the middle crossing at Hole-in-the-Wall, trip before last?"

Sam was outraged. How could he be expected to remember, when, on every voyage up and down, the leadsmen were "singing through that tangled place for three quarters of an hour on a stretch." "M-a-r-k three! . . . M-a-r-k three . . . Quarter-less-three! . . . Half twain! . . . Quarter twain! . . . Mark twain! . . . Quarter-less—"

"My boy, you've *got* to remember it. You've got to remember the exact spot and the exact marks the boat lay in when we had the shoalest water, in every one of the five hundred places between St. Louis and New Orleans." And he must remember, they were almost never twice the same.

"When I get so I can do that, I'll be able to raise the dead, and then I won't have to pilot a steamboat to make a living," Sam objected. "I want to retire from this business. I want a slush-bucket and a brush; I'm only fit for a roustabout."

Bixby cut him short. "Now drop that! When I say I'll learn a man the river, I mean it. And you can depend on it, I'll learn him or kill him."

There were a hundred other things he had to learn: the difference between those lines on the water's surface which marked an actual bluff reef from identical lines made by the wind (called a wind reef). When he asked Bixby how he was to tell them apart, the pilot was unable to explain. "It's an instinct. By and by you will just naturally *know* one from the other. . . ." Sam had to learn that a silver streak on the river's face meant a new snag to avoid, that a slick place indicated a spot that was shoaling dangerously while a dimple marked a buried wreck or huge rock that would tear the boat apart. He had to learn to tell the direction of sounds—a raftsman's halloo, for instance—for nearby islands, and tow-heads (sandbars with cottonwoods on them "thick as harrow teeth") soon swallowed them up or made them seem to come from six different points. As Huck Finn observed in such a situation, "You never knowed a sound to dodge around so, and swap places so quick and so much." Then, for weather prediction, there were cloud types and formations to study, and the color of sunsets and sunrises, and the look of the moon—bright, hazy, or encircled— and winds to interpret, and the actions and flight patterns of shore-birds and waterfowl. The very smell of the air told things.

After Sam had this all well in mind, he began to feel that his education was about complete, and at the wheel he got to tilting his cap on the side of his head, and wearing a toothpick in the corner of his mouth. Bixby was waiting for this, and one day asked him the height of "yonder bank at Burgess's." Sam said he could not tell; after all it was three-quarters of a mile away.

"Very poor eye—very poor. Take the glass." Sam looked through it and said presently that he couldn't tell; he supposed it was about a foot and a half high.

"Foot and a half! That's a six-foot bank." How high was it on the last trip?

"I don't know; I never noticed." He was in for it. He must always notice hereafter, "because you'll have to know a good many things that it tells you. For one thing, it tells you the stage of the river—tells you whether there's more water or less in the river along here than there was last trip."

While concentrating on these practical essentials of piloting, Sam was aware of the river's beauty, majesty, and power at every season, under all conditions, and at all times of day or night. There were the miles of majestic forests along the bluffs, blazing with color in autumn, and the glint and rattle of cottonwood leaves rippling in the breeze, the thick groves of willows dipping their branches in the still shallows, and above all, the awesome sights and sounds of a thunderstorm.

The memory of magnolias in bloom at Rifle Point, and the "charm" of their "rich and strenuous fragrance" in the "dreamy twilight" of summer remained with him always, as did the color and musky fragrance of oleander flowers banking the lower river. When he came to write about the Mississippi, he captured all the images, sounds, smells, and feelings with a freshness and intensity that suggested recent experience.

He never forgot, either, a girl he met on the Mississippi.

There were many times during the first months of his apprenticeship when he doubted the wisdom of his choice. He became homesick, and wished himself back in Keokuk with Henry and all the girls they knew there. He had been on the river a little more than a month when one of these moods seized him while he was sightseeing in New Orleans, and the next day he wrote Annie Taylor, chiding her gently for having failed to answer his letter sent from Cincinnati so long ago. The previous day, as he wandered among the stalls in the French Market, he told Annie, "it would have done my very boots good to have met half a dozen Keokuk girls there, as I used to meet them at market in the Gate City." Together they could have admired the pyramids of delicious-looking fresh fruits—"oranges, lemons, pineapples, bananas, figs, plantains, and watermelons; the baskets of raspberries, blackberries, and plums, and everything imaginable in the vegetable line." He spoke of the lobsters, oysters and clams, and the meat and poultry. "Then milk, cheese, cakes, coffee, tea, nuts, apples, hot rolls, butter, etc." He thought he had seen "all kinds of markets before—but that was a great mistake—this being a place such I had never dreamed of." That day, he continued, "I visited one of the cemeteries—a veritable little city, for they *bury* everybody *above* ground here." The tombs resemble three- or four-story houses. "I spent half an hour watching the chameleons—strange animals, to change their clothes so often! I found a dingy looking one, drove him on a black rag, and he turned black as ink—drove him under a fresh leaf, and he turned the brightest green you ever saw.

"I wish you would write me at St. Louis (I'll be there next week) for I don't believe you have forgotten how, yet." He enclosed a pressed orange leaf as a memento, and signed himself formally as, "Your old friend, Sam. L. Clemens."

Although Sam had a reputation for eternally falling in love, he always managed to escape becoming seriously involved. Shortly, however, he was to meet the girl he wanted to take seriously. Her name was Laura M. Wright, and her father was "an honored Judge of a high court in the middle of Missouri," and a rich man, although Sam did not learn that until later. Laura had come down the Mississippi to New Orleans with her uncle, Billy Youngblood, a pilot on the freighter, *John J. Roe,* which was owned by a group of prosperous farmers. Although the boat was not licensed to carry passengers, there were always at least a dozen on board. They were listed as guests of the captain, Mark Leavenworth, a giant of a man, "hospitable and good-natured, which is the way of giants," Sam said. His brother, Zeb, equally large, was one of her pilots, and Beck Jolly, whom Clemens once described as a mighty lion hunter and distinguished Chinese linguist, was still another. Jolly, who was very handsome, very intelligent, and companionable, "had the manners of a duke." Sam was familiar with them all, for he had served a term as steersman on that "love of a steamboat," as he called it. The *Roe* had a very large boiler deck, ideal for "moonlight dancing and daylight frolics," of which there were many. In the cabin, there was a piano which Sam often played.

At this time his "owner," Horace Bixby, had been lured by higher wages to pilot on the Missouri River, and "lent" his apprentice to another pilot for further training—a man named Brown, who had a prodigious memory for detail but a tyrannical disposition. They were on that popular passenger steamboat, the *Pennsylvania,* and on this particular trip she was berthed in New Orleans right beside the *John J. Roe.* All Sam had to do was run aft, climb over the rail of the ladies' cabin, and jump onto the *Roe*'s great boiler-deck. It was like coming home to the farm after a long absence, Sam found, and such a joy to shake hands again with that "dear family of steamboating backwoodsmen."

As usual there was a party of guests aboard, old and young, and from their midst, "floating upon my enchanted vision," came Laura Wright, a comely "slip of a girl" with dark brown hair and eyes, dressed in a ruffled, white summer frock that puffed about in the wind. That "charming child" had never been away from home before and brought with her all the "freshness and fragrance of her own prairies." Frank, simple, and winsome, she became Sam's "instantly elected sweetheart." "I was not four inches from that girl's elbow during our waking hours for the next three days." Within this time he discovered that she was well-educated, had a "great appetite for books," and possessed a large spirit. Her ways were "grave" and she was inclined toward introspection. She was a most "unusual girl."

Sam, in love, was heedless of time and the joyous interlude was ended suddenly by pilot Zeb Leavenworth, who ran aft shouting to him that the *Pennsylvania* was backing into the stream. A final kiss, a promise to write, and Clemens put on his "best speed," executed "a flying leap," and just managed "to make the connection with nothing to spare. My toes found room on the guard; my finger-ends hooked themselves on the guard-rail, and a quarter-master made a snatch for me and hauled me aboard."

That was May 26, 1858, a date Sam would always remember. Twenty-seven years later he entered in his notebook on May 26, 1885: "This date, 1858, parted from L. who said 'We shall meet again 30 years from now.'"

Sam wrote to Laura as he had promised, she replied, and they corresponded for more than two years. There was also at least one visit to her home at Warsaw, Mo. But then a coolness arose.

Early in 1861, the steamboat Sam was piloting (he had received his license on April 9, 1859) lay in New Orleans a week. Having exhausted all possibilities for entertainment, he decided to call on a noted fortuneteller, Madame Caprell. The results of his session he reported in detail to Orion, for some of what she said concerned him and their parents. She told Sam he could distinguish himself as an orator or editor, that he had written a great deal, that he wrote well, and would some day write still more. She said he had excellent health and powers of endurance, but that the upper part of his lungs was "slightly affected," so he must take better care of himself. Although he does not drink, he uses "entirely too much tobacco," and must stop. In some respects, he took after his father, but was much more like his mother "who belongs to the long-lived and energetic side of the house." She urged him to marry: "You can get the girl you have in your eye"—she described Laura exactly—"if you are a better man than her mother . . . the old gentleman is not in the way, but the mother is decidedly *cranky*, and much in the way; *she* caused the trouble and produced the coolness which has existed between yourself and the young lady for so many months past—and you ought to break through this ice; you won't commence, and the girl won't—you are both entirely too proud—a well-matched pair, truly. . . ."

Sam was impressed with Mme. Caprell's powers. "Now isn't she the devil? That is to say, isn't she a right smart little woman?" he observed to Orion. What she had said about "that girl's mother being 'cranky,' and playing the devil with me, *was* about the neatest thing she performed—for although I have never spoken of the matter, I happen to know that she spoke the truth. The young lady has been beaten by the old one, though, through the romantic agency of intercepted letters, and the girl still thinks *I* was in fault —and always will, I reckon, for I don't see how she'll ever find out the contrary."

Mme. Caprell, he continued, had the "impudence to say that although I was eternally falling in love, still, when I went to bed at night, I somehow always happened to think of Miss Laura before I thought of my last new flame—and it would always be the case (which will be devilish comfortable, won't it, when she and I (like one of Dickens' characters,) are Another's?) But drat the woman, she *did* tell the truth, and I won't deny it. But she said *I* would speak to Miss Laura first—and I'll stake my last shirt on it, she missed it there."

Although Sam made no overtures to Laura, he kept abreast of her activities and after he went West in 1861, he learned of her

Learning the River

marriage to someone named Dake. From San Francisco, he wrote his mother and Pamela in September 1864, and asked, "What has become of that girl of mine that got married? I mean Laura Wright." Less than four months later he had a vivid dream about her, while staying at Angels Camp, a California gold-mining town. Mme. Caprell was right; Laura would always be with him.

Then, in March 1880, he had a welcome contact with her through one of her students (she was then teaching English at a school in Dallas, Texas), who opened a correspondence with "Mr. Twain" that spanned nearly two years. David Watt Bowser (called "Wattie"), a precocious twelve-year-old, explained in his first letter that their assignment had required them to select from among the living great men one with whom they would like to exchange places, and he had chosen Mark Twain. Wattie and a few of his classmates had thought it would be a "lark" to write their favorites, send their compositions, and ask them if they would willingly become boys again. Wattie enclosed his report card, which he supposed would tell something about him. In a postscript, he said he forgot to mention that their principal (who was also their teacher) had known Mr. Twain when he was a little boy and she a little girl, but expects he has forgotten her, it was so long ago. Wattie did not give her name, but Laura Wright Dake was printed on his report card.

In his reply, Clemens told "Master Bowser" that indeed he had not forgotten the young man's principal, and gave a brief description of the girl he remembered, which she would of course read when Wattie showed her the letter. Recollections of Laura stirred him deeply, and in responding to the question of whether he would want to be a boy again, he said that—under *certain conditions*—he would, but the main condition must be that he emerge from boyhood as a cub pilot on a Mississippi steamboat, and that he become a pilot by and by, and remain one all his days. Minor conditions required that it be eternal summer, with magnolias and oleanders always in fragrant bloom, and that the middle watch be kept only on moonlit nights, a "gracious" time, especially when the boat is steering like a duck and friends are by to keep one company, and smoke, and sing, and spin yarns, and blow the whistle to salute other boats. And he would have the trips long and the port stops short, and the crew select and never change—and his boat must be a "big dignified freight boat." Laura would know he was thinking of the *John J. Roe.*

Wattie wrote him in May about having received a gold medal in mental arithmetic; he was now trying for a prize in composition. His subject was Tennyson's *The Princess,* which of all the works read aloud by Mrs. Dake, he liked best. Some of the boys preferred *Enoch Arden,* but he admires "plucky" heroes, such as the Prince, over martyrs. When the Prince came to woo Princess Ida and she locked him out, Wattie observed wisely that if the Prince had been Romeo he would have poisoned himself; if Othello, he would have "sneaked back and smothered her," while Enoch Arden would simply have gone off and left her to "another fellow." But the Prince behaved sensibly, for he "understood girls." One of his classmates had announced that she was going to be just like Ida and not accept *her* prince until he had asked her three times, and had fought her father and older brother in the bargain.

Here Laura Dake warned that she might get served just as a "romantic girl" she once knew had. That girl held some "wild" notions about being "too lightly won," and when her prince came, she refused him. She thought he would return and "take her in a whirlwind," but he went his way and she never saw him again—those were poignant words for Clemens to read.

Twenty-six years passed, and one day, while visiting with a family member, a chance remark recalled Laura and Sam fell to talking about her. Although he had not seen her in those many years, he found that he remembered her vividly, and that she possessed a lively interest for him in spite of the prodigious interval that had lapsed. He described her as she was in his mind's eye—the comely, charming child. He told about the *John J. Roe,* and how, when aboard, one seemed to be floating around on a farm—there could be no pleasanter feeling. He spoke of the officers, Mark and Zeb Leavenworth, and the handsome pilot, Beck Jolly. He finished his account with the remark that it was now "forty-eight years, one month and twenty-seven days since that parting" with Laura.

When he arrived home there was a letter waiting for him from Laura Wright, now teaching in California. What he read "shook me to the foundations," for it was an appeal for financial help for herself and her disabled son, now a man of thirty-seven. The "peachy young face vanished," and the ruffled white dress with it. In their place, he imagined the "world-worn and trouble-worn widow of sixty-two," dressed in black. She was in need of a thousand dollars—and he sent it to her at once. She had not asked him for money—only for help in arranging a loan from one of his wealthy friends. What an "awful world," what a "fiendish world," Clemens stormed. "What had that girl done . . . that she must be punished with poverty and drudgery in her old age?"

She replied with a charming letter, so characteristic that Clemens visualized her not as sixty-two but once more as the girl nearing fifteen. She took up her adventures on the *Roe,* right after Sam left. In going upriver, they struck a snag in the night, and were "apparently booked" for a trip to the bottom in a few minutes. The vessel hurried to shore, and there was, of course, great excitement and much noise. Everyone was ordered to evacuate instantly, which was done, and for the moment no one seemed to be missing. Then Billy Youngblood, the pilot, discovered that his niece was not there. He and Davis, the mate, rushed aboard and hammered at Laura's door, which was locked, and shouted for her to come out— the boat was sinking, and not a moment to lose!

But Laura replied very calmly that there was something the matter with her hoopskirt, and she couldn't come just yet. They told her to never mind the skirt—come as she was. There was no time to squander on trifles.

She repeated, just as calmly, that she was not going to come until the skirt was fixed and she was in it. She kept her word, and came ashore at her leisure, fully dressed.

Her words carried Sam so far into "the hoary past" that he was for the moment, living it over again and was once more a "heedless, giddy lad." He was therefore astonished when he read her closing passage for it seemed to be addressed to someone else:

"But I must not weary you and take up your valuable time with my chatter. I really forget that I am writing to one of the world's most famous and sought-after men, which shows you that I am still roaming in the Forest of Arden." Arden, that pleasure-grove where simplicity, innocence and joy are perpetual.

IX

---◯---

TRAGEDY ON THE RIVER

W H E N   S A M   C L E M E N S   reached St. Louis in mid-February
1858, he was troubled to find his brother Henry, nearing twenty,
working only at occasional odd jobs. Although he was not wasting
his time, for he spent his hours off at the library, reading widely,
he was making no place for himself in the competitive world. After
Sam's proposal to earn millions in the coca trade failed to material-
ize, Henry, who would have joined him, had no wish to stay on at
Keokuk with the foundering Orion, who was considering a return
to studying law. In June of 1857, Orion sold his printing office and
in September left for the mountains of Tennessee with Mollie and
their two-year-old, Jane (known as Jennie). He was going to try to
sell all or part of that vast acreage which had been their father's
bequest, meanwhile reading law at Jamestown (his birthplace) and
preparing for his examination. He had no success in selling the
land, but was admitted to the Tennessee bar.

It is probable that Henry traveled with them as far as St. Louis,
where they spent ten days at the Moffett house, visiting with Jane
Lampton, and Pamela and her family, and attending "The Great
Fair of the West."

Sam felt that Henry needed direction and encouragement, and
wanted to see him on the river, so he got his brother a place on the

Tragedy on the River

Pennsylvania to work his way for one trip, as a trial, performing such "clerkly duties" as measuring woodpiles and counting coalboxes. Although he would receive no pay, he was in line for promotion to third clerk, then second, and finally chief clerk or purser. Sam was confident he would advance rapidly, for he was serious and earnest, a hard worker, had a retentive memory, and was quick to learn. He also possessed an even temper and a winning personality.

Henry's work was satisfactory on that first trip and at Sam's urging he signed on regularly as a "mud" clerk. He was eager to have Henry's companionship, for they had grown intimate during the months at Keokuk, and Sam was aware that only Henry really knew him, for with no one else was Sam ever in such "entire sympathy." Just then, Henry's company was especially welcome for Sam was having serious problems with the pilot who was training him in Bixby's absence—William Brown, whom he would one day describe as a middle-aged, "long, slim, bony, smooth-shaven, horse-faced . . . malicious, snarling, fault-finding, mote-magnifying tyrant." Brown refused to allow his cubs the pleasure of reading. Sam had a copy of Scott's *The Fortunes of Nigel* which he slipped in his pocket, and then concealed himself behind a barrel. But Brown found him and gave him a lecture upon the ruinous effects of reading. "I've seen it over and over again; . . . if ye're going to be a pilot on this river yer needn't ever think of reading, for it just spiles all. Yer can't remember how high the tides was in Can's Gut three trips before last, I'll wager." "Why no," Sam said, "that was six months ago." "I don't care if 't was; if you hadn't ben spiling yer mind by readin' ye'd have remembered."

After a watch, when Sam left the pilot-house seething with suppressed anger (at such times, he admitted, he wanted to kill Brown), he could divert his thoughts by a game of cribbage with Henry, or in talk about their girls at Keokuk, or by relaxing together as they listened to the second pilot, George Ealer, gentle and kindly, play his flute or read aloud from his favorites—Shakespeare and Goldsmith. Over the ensuing weeks, the brothers became even closer, as though intuitively aware of what lay ahead, and Sam confided his love for Laura Wright.

About seventeen days after parting with Laura at New Orleans, he and Henry were back at St. Louis. By this time the Moffetts had moved into a large house at 168 Locust Street, which had room for Jane Lampton, and for the boys whenever they were in port. Sam was awakened very early on the morning of their vessel's return to New Orleans by a disturbingly vivid dream. "I had seen Henry a corpse. He lay in a metallic burial case," set up on two chairs in the sitting room of Pamela's house. He was wearing one of Sam's suits, "and on his breast lay a large bouquet of flowers, mainly white roses, with a red rose in the center." It was all so real he did not have the courage to go into the parlor and face his mother, so he dressed and took a walk up to the next block to prepare for that ordeal. Then suddenly it occurred to him that it was only a dream, and not true, so he turned and walked back to the house. But as he neared the door he felt some remnants of doubt and realizing he had best learn the truth, rushed up the stairs and into the parlor. He was overcome with relief to find no coffin there. He decided to say nothing about his dream—that was how he recalled the incident nearly fifty years later.

But his mother and Pamela, and his niece Annie, remembered differently. They gave testimony not too long afterward, that they were all up gathered in Pamela's room, Henry included, when Sam, who had slept late, burst in, still in his night-shirt, to tell about his horrifying dream—just as he used to do when he was a little boy. They all listened to his excited account, but only Jane Lampton took the dream seriously, and when Henry left the house she walked with him to the head of the stairs to tell him goodbye a second time. Later, she spoke often about that dream.

One day during this trip downriver, when Sam was steering, Henry came into the pilothouse with a message from Captain John Klinefelter, asking Brown to make a stop at the next plantation. Brown made no response, and Henry, accustomed to Brown's surly ways, went out again. Sam waited for the order to stop but none came, so he went right on by the landing. The captain came hurrying up and said to Brown:

"Let her come around, sir, let her come around. Didn't Henry tell you to land here?"

"*No,* sir!" Brown said.

"I sent him up to do it." Brown admitted that Henry had come,

Tragedy on the River

but maintained he had said nothing. The captain then asked Sam if he had heard him. He had no wish to get involved, but there was no way to avoid it, so he replied, "Yes, sir."

"Shut your mouth! You never heard anything of the kind," Brown said. Sam obeyed. About an hour later, Henry walked into the pilot-house, unaware of what had gone on.

"Here!" Brown snarled, "why didn't you tell me we'd got to land at that plantation?"

"I did tell you, Mr. Brown."

"It's a lie!"

Sam spoke up. "You lie, yourself. He did tell you."

Brown glared at him in surprise. No one dared talk back to a pilot. After a moment, he shouted at Sam:

"I'll attend to your case in a half minute!" Then to Henry: "And you leave this pilot house. Out with you!"

Henry started to go, and Brown "jumped up and collared him—turned him half way around and *struck him in the face!*—and him nearly six feet high—struck my little brother. I was wild from that moment. I left the boat to steer herself, and avenged the insult," he wrote Mollie Clemens.

Sam grabbed a heavy stool and hit Brown a blow that knocked him down. He knew he had committed the crime of crimes in striking a pilot on duty.

"Did you do anything further?" the captain asked Sam later in the privacy of his parlor.

"Yes, sir," Sam replied.

"What did you do?"

"Pounded him, sir."

"Did you pound him much? that is, severely?"

"One might call it that, sir, maybe."

"I'm deucèd glad of it! Hark ye, never mention that I said that. You have been guilty of a great crime; and don't ever be guilty of it again on this boat. *But*—lay for him ashore! . . ."

As soon as Brown went off watch he reported to the captain and demanded that Sam Clemens be put ashore at New Orleans, adding that he would never turn a wheel again as long as "that cub stays. . . . *One* of us has got to go ashore." "Then let it be you," Captain Klinefelter told him.

During the next three days at New Orleans, the captain found no replacement for Brown and proposed to Sam that he stand the daylight watches and leave the night ones to George Ealer. But Sam had never stood any watch alone and was reluctant to try. There was nothing to do but keep Brown and send Sam on another boat. Klinefelter gave him an order on the master of the *A. T. Lacy*, whose pilot was Bart Bowen, brother of Sam's best friend, Will, for a passage to St. Louis.

Sam visited with Henry up to five minutes before the *Pennsylvania* left New Orleans. They would meet again at Pamela's house in St. Louis.

Two days later the *A. T. Lacy* sailed. As they neared the landing at Greenville, Mississippi, Sam heard someone shout, "The *Pennsylvania* is blown up at Ship Island, and a hundred and fifty lives lost!" That evening at Napoleon, Arkansas, they got an extra put out by a Memphis, Tennessee, newspaper which gave some details, for Ship Island was just south of Memphis. Henry Clemens was mentioned and said to be unhurt. Further up the river, they saw a later extra which stated that Henry Clemens had been fatally injured.

It was six o'clock, the morning was hot, and the *Pennsylvania* was creeping along on half steam, Sam reported. George Ealer, on duty in the pilot-house, noticed that the wood-flat they were towing was nearly empty, and rang to "come ahead" full steam and put in to load fuel. The order was obeyed, and the next moment four of the eight boilers exploded, blasting away the whole forward third of the vessel. The sleeping Henry Clemens was blown up, "then fell back on the hot boilers, and I suppose that rubbish fell on him, for he is injured internally. He got in the water and swam to shore," Sam wrote Mollie Clemens. Later, he was told by survivors that Henry, believing himself not seriously hurt (which he may not have been, for Sam never did learn all the particulars), turned back to the boat, which was by then on fire, to help save lives. If true, then Henry most likely sustained his burns and fatal internal injuries aboard the packet when collapsing, flaming superstructure fell on him. In this version, he was carried with the other victims to the flatboat that was later tied up at the head of Ship Island.

Henry had nothing on but his wet shirt, and he lay in the open,

Tragedy on the River

"burning up with a southern sun and freezing in the wind," until picked up finally by the *Kate Frisbee*. His burns and wounds were not tended for fifteen hours after the explosion, when he reached Memphis. "He was senseless and motionless for 12 hours after that."

Sam arrived at Memphis two days after Henry did, and upon approaching his bedside, collapsed at the sight of him. A witness wrote that there was "scarcely a dry eye" in the room, and that even "the poor sufferers shed tears" when Sam sank to the floor.

From Memphis, he telegraphed Pamela's husband, Will Moffett, on June 15: "Henry's recovery is very doubtful." Two days later he poured out his grief to Mollie, the only one in the family to whom he felt he could. He addressed her as

Dear Sister Mollie:

Long before this reaches you, my poor Henry—my darling, my pride, my glory, my *all,* will have finished his blameless career, and the light of my life will have gone out in utter darkness. O, God! this is hard to bear. Hardened, hopeless,—aye, lost—lost—lost and ruined sinner as I am—I, even *I,* have humbled myself to the ground and prayed as never man prayed before, that the great God might let this cup pass from me—that he would strike me to the earth, but spare my brother—that he would pour out the fullness of his just wrath upon my wicked head, but have mercy, mercy, mercy upon that unoffending boy. The horrors of three days have swept over me—they have blasted my youth and have left me an old man before my time. . . . For forty-eight hours I labored at the bedside of my poor burned and bruised, but uncomplaining brother, and then the star of my hope went out and left me in the gloom of despair. Then poor wretched me, that was once so proud, was humbled to the very dust, lower than the dust—for the vilest beggar in the streets of St. Louis could never conceive of a humiliation like mine. Men take me by the hand and *congratulate* me, and call me 'lucky' because I was not on the *Pennsylvania* when she blew up! May God forgive them, for they know not what they say.

Sam went on: "But may God bless Memphis, the noblest city on the face of the earth. She has done her duty by these poor afflicted creatures—especially Henry, for he has had five—aye ten, fifteen,

twenty times the care and attention. . . ." Dr. John Peyton, the
city's leading physician, sat by him thirty-six hours, evidently believing there was hope for his recovery. In that public hall where
Henry lay on a mattress, were thirty-two scalded men, "clothed in
linseed oil and raw cotton," many of them out of their minds,
shrieking and raving. Every doctor and medical student in the area
took a turn working there, and the women came daily with flowers,
fruits, ices, and delicacies of all kinds, and stayed on to nurse. A
Miss Wood devoted all her time to Henry, and tried to comfort
Sam, who was in a frenzy of anguish over his brother's sufferings
and the belief that he was responsible for them. He blamed himself
for having persuaded Henry to take a job on the *Pennsylvania,* and
for his fight with Brown, which had led to Sam's absence when the
vessel blew up. He might have been able to save Henry.

About dawn on Monday, June 21, Henry's "nerveless fingers
'picked at his coverlet.' His hour had struck; we bore him to the
death-room. . . ." Sam, almost crazed with grief, was taken to the
house of a resident to sleep—but not before he had sent a telegram
to Will Moffett:

"Henry died this morning leave tomorrow with the corpse."

In the morning, when he returned to the hall, he found Henry
just as he had seen him in the dream, dressed in one of Sam's
suits, lying in an open casket with a metallic burial case. All the
other coffins were of unpainted pine, but the women of Memphis,
touched by Henry's youth, had collected money to buy the outer
casing. Only one thing was missing, but that was soon supplied
when an older woman came in with a large bouquet of white roses
with a single red rose in the center. She laid it gently on Henry's
breast.

When Sam went north with Henry's body, a young man from
Memphis was sent with him, for he was so distraught it was feared
he would go insane. And it was a "gentleman" from Memphis who
contributed the money which made it possible to bury Henry in the
cemetery at Hannibal, where his brother, Benjamin, and their father lay.

After the funeral, Orion, on his way back to Keokuk from Tennessee, spent a few days at the Moffett house in St. Louis. He
remembered that Sam's nights were tortured by unnerving dreams

and by sleepwalking, and how one night, he heard Sam pacing the floor and moaning. All at once the door to Orion's room opened and Sam came in, wide awake and highly agitated. There was something on his mind, and he had to tell it.

Right after he had written to Mollie on the 18th, Henry had rallied, he said, and Dr. Peyton believed that with the right care, he would recover, although his condition was still so precarious anything might upset the balance. On the night of the 20th, as Peyton was leaving, he told Sam that undisturbed sleep was one of the best remedies, and that if Henry should become restless or wakeful at any time before morning, Sam must ask the doctor in charge to give Henry an eighth of a grain of morphine.

Around midnight, Henry was awakened by the cries of the suffering and dying men in the room and he began to toss fitfully. Sam, unnerved, hastened from Henry's side and gave Dr. Peyton's order to the young physician on duty—"hardly out of medical college," Sam recalled. But he had no way of measuring the morphine, Sam wrote, and was too inexperienced to gauge the amount. He refused to take the risk.

In Sam's judgment, his brother seemed to worsen and frantically he appealed again to the doctor to give Henry just a tiny amount of morphine. In recollecting, Sam thought that they gave him a "vast quantity" heaped up on the end of a rounded knife blade. Shortly, Henry quieted and slipped into a deep sleep, and later into a coma, from which he never wakened.

As Sam told this to Orion, he flayed himself savagely. The responsibility for Henry's death was his entirely. If he had not virtually forced that doctor to give the morphine, Henry would be with them now in Pamela's house. He swore Orion to secrecy: Jane Lampton must never know.

Sam Clemens bore this heavy burden all his days, and not until nearly fifty years afterward could he bear to tell the story again of that tragic night in Memphis, Tennessee.

X

THE PILOT

Sᴀᴍ ᴄʟᴇᴍᴇɴꜱ ᴅɪᴠᴇʀᴛᴇᴅ his mind from the loss of Henry by returning to the river as steersman for the pilot George Ealer, who had survived the explosion of the *Pennsylvania* unhurt. He was so fortunate as to be able to retrieve from the debris his flute and chessmen. Captain Klinefelter had also managed to escape safely, but the pilot, Brown, was killed.

At last there came a day when Sam felt confident enough to be examined by the Inspectors of the District of St. Louis. On April 9, 1859, he was passed by them and granted a pilot's certificate licensing him to navigate the Mississippi River between St. Louis and New Orleans for one year, when he would have to be reexamined. He then began earning $250 a month, a "princely salary," and his first pay since April 1857, when he had started his apprenticeship. Shortly, he could count on banking one hundred of it regularly, as well as send money to his mother and Orion. By the end of 1860, he was able to speculate in the New Orleans produce market for his own and Orion's benefit, and in letters to him quoted current prices for chickens, eggs, and apples, and their fluctuations. He had invested in 3,600 dozen eggs at fifteen cents a dozen, and now they were down to twelve and a half cents; and 18 barrels of apples for which he had expected to get six or seven dollars a barrel, and now "not worth a d-mn." But he had stored the "infernal" produce and would wait for prices to rise. "But in the meantime, *Nil desperandum*—I am deep in another egg purchase, *now.*" When he gets to Memphis, Missouri, where Orion was then practicing law, he will see what can be done about speculating with produce in that part of the country.

Not long after getting his license, Sam was assigned to the *City of Memphis,* which, he was pleased to tell his family, "is the largest boat in the trade and the hardest to pilot, *and* consequently I can get a reputation on her, which is a thing I never could accomplish on a transient boat." He is "also lucky in having a berth, while all other young pilots are idle. . . . Bless me! what a pleasure there is in revenge!—and what vast respect Prosperity commands! Why, six months ago, I could enter the Rooms [Pilot Association rooms] and receive only a nod, but now they say, 'Why how *are* you, old fellow—when did you get in?' And the young pilots who used to tell me patronizingly that I could never learn the river, cannot keep from showing a little of their chagrin at seeing me so far ahead of them. Permit me to 'blow my horn,' for I derive a living pleasure from these things, and when I go to pay my dues, I rather like to let the d---d rascals get a glimpse of a hundred dollar bill peeping out amongst notes of smaller dimensions, whose faces I do not exhibit! You will despise this egotism, but I tell you there is a 'stern joy in it.' "

It becomes obvious after reading his notebook entries on river conditions during each voyage, both up and down the river, that he was a cautious pilot, particularly at night. There are many such notations as:

"Night—didn't run either 77 or 76 towheads"
"Could have run Montezuma (either side,)—slough above Prairie Pt & shore opp Sterling—night—didn't"

However, on November 10, 1860, he started with the steamboat *Alonzo Child* for St. Louis. Some seventy miles above New Orleans, while running in a fog along the coast, in an attempt to beat another boat he grounded the *Child* on the bank. It was nearly flood tide, so they had to remain where they were for twenty-four hours

before she floated off, he wrote Orion from St. Louis. Horace
Bixby, who was again piloting on the Mississippi, was with him
and remembered that since no one was hurt the incident was taken
lightly, for the best of pilots had a little trouble now and then.

Another time, when Clemens was bringing the *Crescent City* into
port at New Orleans, he was expecting orders momently from the
hurricane deck, for he could see Captain Montgomery's hat up
there. (Later, as a commodore, Montgomery commanded the Confederate gunboats in the great battle before Memphis.) But no orders came for Sam. "I had stopped the wheels, and there my
authority and responsibility ceased. . . . The captain was very
strict; therefore I knew better than to touch a bell without orders.
My duty was to hold the boat steadily on her calamitous course,
and leave the consequences to take care of themselves—which I
did. So we went plowing past the sterns of steamboats and getting
closer and closer—the crash was bound to come very soon—." The
truth was, Montgomery was napping in the texas. "Things were
becoming exceedingly nervous and uncomfortable. It seemed to me
that the captain was not going to appear in time to see the entertainment. But he did. Just as we were walking into the stern of a
steamboat, he stepped out on deck, and said with heavenly serenity, 'Set her back on both'—which I did; but a trifle late, . . . for
the next moment we went smashing through that other boat's
flimsy outer works with a most prodigious racket."

Afterward, all the captain said was that Sam had done right, and
he hoped he would not "hesitate to act in the same way again"
under like circumstances.

Clemens was aware that an entire world was compacted on and
along the Mississippi River, and now he had the opportunity to
become "personally and familiarly acquainted" with nearly every
type of person to be met in life. As a boy he had noted the differences and peculiarities of children and adults, white and black,
who lived in Hannibal, in the village of Florida, and on his uncle's
farm. He had been interested in listening to their talk, their stories,
jokes, songs, and music, and had retained much of it. On the river,
he added immeasureably to that fund when he overheard the off-
duty pilots gathered in the wheel-house talk about wrecks, fires,
storms, and steamboat races; about river pirates and smugglers,

and about John Murrell's gang, which had preyed upon rich travelers who went by land up and down the Mississippi. Between watches, he listened to the argot of professional gamblers, confidence men, and prostitutes from New Orleans and Natchez-under-the-Hill, who regularly took passage in order to ply their trades. In the cabin and on deck, he fell into conversation with wealthy cane and cotton planters and their families, with lawyers, land speculators, actors, itinerant portrait painters, and tutors; with fortunetellers, politicians, preachers, and explorers; and with English, French, and German nobility touring the American West. They all, at some time, traveled up or down the river.

From native Southerners, most of them born story-tellers, he heard accounts of young women who passed as men, of premature burials, and cases of mistaken identity which had dire consequences. He heard about local feuds, murders for vengeance, and lynchings. Clemens called on much of this material in his writings, although not everything he used was published.

There were also the people with whom he had contact ashore at those points where the steamboats put in—woodyards, plantation landings, and "one-horse towns." Everywhere, he listened closely to the fine distinctions among regional dialects and became so adept he was able to use in his works the "Missouri negro dialect; the extremest form of the backwoods South-Western dialect; the ordinary 'Pike-County' dialect; and four modified varieties of this last," as he explained in a prefatory statement to *The Adventures of Huckleberry Finn.* The shadings of these dialects were not done haphazardly, or by "guess-work, but pains-takingly, and with the trustworthy guidance and support of personal familiarity with these several forms of speech."

Looking back much later, he realized that his profits from this "brief, sharp schooling" were many and various, and that to have obtained such an education ashore in "average" employment would have required as much as forty years. He came to think of the river as his university. It was certainly the perfect school for the writer of fiction who would draw almost exclusively on personal experiences and observation, and create characters based on those he knew well, or who were mere acquaintances.

Through work he conquered his grief, and his two years as a

pilot proved happy ones. "I loved the profession far better than any I have followed since, and I took measureless pride in it."

He also took pride in his appearance and cut a dashing figure in satin, double-breasted vests, stiff-bosomed white shirts with Byron or standing collars, and silk cravats tied in a wide bow. In winter, he wore blue serge, the sack coat having a velvet collar. His hat was either a dark blue fatigue cap or a round black felt with turned-up brim, known as a "pork pie." For dress ashore, there was the silk top hat. In summer, he wore white linen and a broad-brimmed natural straw hat with a wide ribbon band that hung in short tails at the back.

In his summer white, he and Jane Lampton rode in a carriage with a Miss Castle, not otherwise identified, on a "blazing hot dusty day" in 1861 through the Garden District of New Orleans. He had never been able to make that promised trip with his mother to Kentucky, but now he had brought her down the river to New Orleans. His guests were "hugely delighted" with the fine houses, and the variety of flowers and trees. They were amazed at the topiary displays, for they had never seen such things, and were "hell-bent" upon stealing oranges, ripe and luscious, hanging over the fences. But he had restrained them, he assured Orion by letter. He took them in the horsecars to Lake Pontchartrain, and certainly to the music hall for a variety show or a concert that promised to be lively, for Jane Lampton disliked music that was "low and solemn." She was pleased with the river trip and with the "fuss" made over her as the pilot's mother, but "disgusted," (so Sam claimed), with the girls for allowing him to hug and kiss them. And she was "horrified," Sam said, at the Schottische as performed by Miss Castle and himself, but was perfectly willing for him to dance until midnight at the imminent risk of falling asleep on the after-watch.

This was Jane Lampton's only trip to New Orleans, but Sam took her on shorter voyages frequently, particularly since she was always willing to go and required no advance notice. Because she had a pass on the line, she went to Hannibal whenever she felt inclined to visit friends, and invariably took her granddaughter, Annie Moffett along. They were very close, for Pamela was a semi-invalid at this time, and kept to her bed much of each day. Annie remembered how popular her grandmother was on the boat, especially with the officers and clerks, to whom she was known as "Aunt Jane,"—"Aunt" being a title conferred in the South upon an older woman who was "kind & good & wise & well beloved," Sam explained. Now that he was contributing largely to her support, she could afford to be independent.

Earlier he had been in New Orleans just in time to join the throngs who watched the Mardi Gras parade and revelers, and he described them in a letter to Pamela: "The procession was led by a mounted Knight Crusader in blazing gilt armor from head to foot. . . . Then followed tall, grotesque maskers . . . then the Queen of the Fairies, with a winged troop of beauties, in airy costumes at her heels—then the King & Queen of the Genii, I suppose (eight or ten feet high,) with vast rolls of flaxen curls, bowing majestically to the crowd—followed by . . . other genii, in costumes grotesque, hideous & beautiful in turn—then . . . a big Christmas tree, followed by Santa Claus, with fur cap, short pipe, &c., and surrounded by a great basket filled with toys—and then—well, I don't remember half."

From on board the *Alonzo Child,* at New Orleans, Sam wrote Orion to let him know that since he had become a pilot he could afford to indulge in an occasional epicurean meal. "Yesterday . . . Bixby and I got with the pilots of two other boats and went off dissipating on a ten dollar dinner at a French restaurant—breathe it not unto Ma!—where we ate Sheep-head-fish with mushrooms, shrimps and oysters—birds—coffee with brandy burnt in it, &c &c, —ate, drank & smoked, from 1 P. M. until 5 o'clock, and then— then—the day was too far gone to do anything." Jane Lampton had freed him from his pledge not to drink as soon as he became a licensed pilot, but she would scold him for extravagance.

He wrote his brother in a different mood from St. Louis. He and Pamela had just returned to the house after seeing Frederic Church's huge dramatic picture, *Heart of the Andes,* painted in 1859. They took an "opera glass" with them so as to be able to examine it minutely, "for the naked eye cannot discern the little wayside flowers, and soft shadows and patches of sunshine, and half-hidden bunches of grass and jets of water which form some of its most enchanting features." Sam had seen the painting before, but it was always totally new. "You seem to see nothing the second time which you saw the first."

During these months of piloting he developed a close relationship with his niece, Annie Moffett. She looked forward eagerly to his homecomings not only because he brought her a present each time, but he made the house lively with his stories and songs and jokes and teasing. She never tired of listening to him play the piano and sing; her favorite was that ditty about the old horse who died in the wilderness, " 'way down in Alabam'." Flattered by her appreciation of that number, he began calling her "Old Horse" exclusively, which pleased her immensely for a number of years— or until that day when she suddenly realized that even though it came from her favorite uncle, it was an affront to her developing dignity. After that, she refused to answer his summons or do his errands unless he called her "Annie." She won.

By this time, Will Moffett was prospering in the commission business and had moved his family into a three-story brick house at 1312 Chestnut Street. He had hired a maid, a German girl named Margaret, who stayed with them so many years she came to be counted as a member of the family. Sam had his room on the third floor, and it always delighted Annie to hear his songs drifting down from there first thing in the morning. One she liked especially began:

> *Samuel Clemens! the gray dawn is breaking,*
> *The howl of the housemaid is heard in the hall;*
> *The cow from the back gate her exit is making,—*
> *What, Samuel Clemens? Slumbering still?*

> *Remember how seldom a buckwheat you get,*
> *How long it may be e'er you see one again,*
> *It may be for years, it may be forever!*
> *Then why thus tempt fortune, most reckless of men?*

She also remembered that he once wrote a ghost story while he was at home, and that the family all gathered in Pamela's room at night to hear him read it. It was a chilling tale about a phantom pilot, and it sent shivers up and down Annie's back as she listened and watched him act it out.

The Pilot

One Sunday when she was about nine, it occurred to her that her Uncle Sam needed a little religious instruction, so she took him aside and told him the story of Moses, explaining and simplifying it so that he would be sure to understand. "But I *couldn't*," Sam wrote Jane Lampton later, and Annie said to him that "it was strange that while her ma and her grandma and her uncle Orion could understand any Thing in the world, I was so dull that I couldn't understand the 'ea--siest thing.' And . . . finally a light broke in upon me and I said it was all right—that I knew old Moses himself—and that he kept a clothing store in Market street. And then she went to her ma and said she didn't know what would become of her uncle Sam—he was too dull to learn anything— ever!" Over the years he continued to remind her of Moses and tease her about that lesson, and he used it as an example of his dullness whenever he pretended not to understand some of Annie's letters.

In the opening pages of *Huckleberry Finn,* the Widow Douglas, in her attempt to "sivilize" Huck, "learned me about Moses and the Bulrushers; and I was in a sweat to find out all about him; but by and by she let out that Moses had been dead a considerable long time; so then I didn't care no more about him; because I don't take no stock in dead people."

Beyond the phantom pilot story, Sam certainly wrote other sketches or squibs during his days on the river, because Horace Bixby remembered that he was "scribbling" much of the time when he was not in the wheel-house. On May 17, 1859, there appeared in the New Orleans *Daily Crescent,* under the heading "River Intelligence," Sam's parody of a report on river conditions written by Captain Isaiah Sellers. Sellers was the patriarch of rivermen, having been born about 1803 and navigated the Ohio and the Mississippi first in keelboats, and then under steam, since 1825. He was active yet. He had a remarkable memory, was proud of his long span of service, and was fond of mentioning both in conversation with other pilots (Clemens among them) and in his regular reports to the newspapers. There was exceptionally high water during 1859, and from Vicksburg, on May 4, Sellers sent the following to the New Orleans *True Delta:*

The river from your city up to this point is higher than it has been since the high water of 1815, and my opinion is that *the water will be in Canal Street* before the 1st day of June. Mrs. Turner's plantation, which has not been affected by the river since 1815, is now under water.

Yours, &c.

Isaiah Sellers

Clemens, posing as "Sergeant Fathom," aboard the steamer *Trombone,* also at Vicksburg, dated his report four days later. An introduction by the editor of the *Daily Crescent* noted that Fathom was "one of the oldest cub pilots on the river," and had made 1,450 trips in the New Orleans–St. Louis trade. In his piece, Sam wrote that the river from New Orleans up to Natchez was higher than it had been since the fall of 1813, "and my opinion is, that if the rise continues at this rate *the water will be on the roof of the St. Charles Hotel* before the middle of January," which was eight months away. "The point at Cairo, which has not even been moistened by the river since 1813, is now entirely under water." However, residents of the Mississippi Valley should not act hastily and sell their plantations at a sacrifice on account of this prophecy. He proceeded to show that the river's high water levels had been getting progressively lower ever since the summer of 1763, when he had first come down it in the old *Jubilee,* "a single engine boat, with a Chinese captain and a Choctaw crew, forecastle on her stern, wheels in the center . . ." At that time, the only dry land in sight was the high wooded bluff above Selma, where they had tied up and waited three weeks for the river to fall a hundred feet, passing the time by "swapping knives" and playing seven-up with the Indians. Because of the constant widening and deepening of the river's channel through erosion, the high water mark in 1775 was thirty feet lower; in 1790 it missed the original height by sixty-five feet, and by 1806, it was nearly 250 feet lower.

As soon as Sam showed the squib to his fellow pilots they urged him to submit it to the newspaper. Years later, he claimed that when Captain Sellers read it in print, he was very angry; that he detested Sam from that day on, and never submitted another river report. Looking back, Sam regretted ever having printed it.

The Pilot

Although preparations for war were evident everywhere along the Mississippi—volunteers mustering, militia drilling, existing fortifications being strengthened or replaced—Sam made no mention of any of this in his letters home, or in his notebook, where he continued to record river navigation; keep addresses and laundry lists, write out melodies, and French vocabularies, and copy passages from Voltaire's *Dialogues.*

Then things began happening swiftly. On April 21, 1861, Clemens arrived at St. Louis. According to family tradition, his was the last vessel to get through before the Mississippi was closed to steamboat traffic. Fort Sumter, in Charleston harbor, had been seized by South Carolina on April 12. The Civil War—the War Between the States—had started, and Sam Clemens's occupation was gone.

"I supposed—and hoped—that I was going to follow the river the rest of my days, and die at the wheel when my mission ended."

He was now faced with a difficult choice that was not helped by the stands taken by his family and friends. His brother-in-law, Will Moffett, was strongly Southern in his sympathy but would go to jail rather than fight. Orion had become a Republican and an enthusiastic supporter of Abraham Lincoln. Jane Lampton, typical of most Southern women, was outspoken in her hatred of Yankees. Horace Bixby, from New York, went with his state, and eventually served on the Union flagship *Benton.* Will and Sam Bowen were all for secession and joined the Confederate army. (Sam Bowen was captured, and later piloted the Union boat *J. C. Swon,* on the Mississippi, simultaneously assisting in the secret transportation of Confederate spies.)

Sam Clemens' family remembered that he was obsessed with the fear of being impressed by the federal government and forced at pistol point to pilot their steamboats on the river. In fact, he went into hiding, first at the St. Louis house of his cousin, the visionary James Lampton (he had foreseen millions in the Tennessee acreage, and became the model for Colonel Sellers in Clemens' novel, *The Gilded Age).* Sam insisted that during his stay with James, he was served the turnip and water dinner described in the book. Shortly he was with the Moffetts again, but spending his days in concealment at the home of Will Moffett's partner, George Schroeter, who lived next door. Jane Lampton gave strict orders that if anyone came to Will's house looking for Sam, she was to be called. One day such a young man arrived. He gave the name of Smith and said that he knew Sam. Since he looked familiar, Jane invited him in and sent for Sam. Smith had come to tell Clemens about a company of volunteers being raised in Hannibal; they were planning to attach themselves to Confederate General Sterling Price, recently Missouri's governor. Sam was urged to join.

He still had made no decision about his loyalty. He never did take a firm public stand for either side during the war, for as things turned out, this was impossible. But reading between the lines in some of his personal letters written during that period, it becomes clear that his sympathies were with the South—his own people.

The proposal offered a temporary solution to Sam's dilemma. Beyond that, there was a strong appeal in the thought of associating again with old comrades and schoolmates in what promised to be a lark during the brief period the war was expected to last. Many Confederates "welcomed this opportunity of showing the world how easily one Southerner could take on three or four Yankees, and soundly whip the Northern army in a war that would last no longer than three months."

Within a day, Sam Clemens was "on the wing for Hannibal."

XI

CONFEDERATE SOLDIER

SAM CLEMENS LOOKED forward to "new scenes, new occupations, a new interest. In my thoughts that was as far as I went; I did not go into the details." Arriving at Hannibal, he found about fifteen young men (they called themselves the "Marion Rangers" after their county) who were meeting in secret at night on the hill above Bear Creek. Sam Bowen, Ed Stevens, Arch Fuqua, and John and Clay Robards were among them. They elected "one Tom Lyman, a young fellow of a good deal of spirit but of no military experience," as captain, and Sam Clemens as second lieutenant—he said later there was no *first* lieutenant. Sam Bowen was chosen as an orderly sergeant and Ed Stevens as a corporal—nearly everyone had some rank, and when the election was over it was found there were only three privates. It was like those times when they used to play Indians—they were all chiefs, for no one would consent to being a plain warrior. Their plan of action was to march to New London in Ralls County, ten miles away, and report to Colonel Ralls, a Mexican War veteran, who would swear them in.

They set out toward midnight, in couples and from various directions, for the sake of secrecy and caution, until they were out of town, and then proceeded in a body. "The first hour was all fun, all idle nonsense and laughter." But after that the steady tramping became work, and the stillness of the woods and the somberness of the night cast a pall over the excursion. Presently, the talking died out and during the last half of the second hour no one said a word. "Now we approached a log farmhouse where, according to report, there was a guard of five Union soldiers. Lyman called a halt; and there, in the deep gloom of the overhanging branches, he began to whisper a plan of assault upon that house, which made the gloom more depressing than it was before. It was a crucial moment; we realized, with a cold suddenness, that here was no jest—we were standing face to face with actual war. We were equal to the occasion. In our response there was no hesitation, no indecision: we said that if Lyman wanted to meddle with those soldiers, he could go ahead and do it; but if he waited for us to follow, he would wait a long time."

Lyman "urged, pleaded, tried to shame us, but it had no effect. Our course was plain, our minds were made up: we would flank the farm-house—go out around. And that is what we did."

They struck off into the woods, stumbling in the dark over roots, and getting tangled in vines and torn by briers. Finally, they came out into the open again—a "safe region," and sat down, "blown and hot, to cool off and nurse our scratches and bruises." Lyman was annoyed, and grumbled at them, "but we were cheerful; we had flanked the farm-house, we had made our first military movement, and it was a success. . . . Horse-play and laughter began again; the expedition was become a holiday frolic once more."

Close to dawn, after another two hours of steady trudging, they straggled into New London, completely fagged. Their feet were sore and blistered, their appetites were ravenous, and most of them were in a "sour and raspy humor and privately down on war." They stacked their "shabby old shot-guns" in Colonel Ralls' barn, and then went in a body to breakfast with him. "Afterwards he took us to a distant meadow, where in the shade of a spreading tree we listened to an old-fashioned speech . . . full of gunpowder and glory . . ." He then swore them on the Bible to be faithful to the State of Missouri and drive all invaders from her soil. He closed the ceremonies by buckling around Sam Clemens the sword which Ralls' neighbor had worn at Buena Vista and Molino del Rey.

Confederate Soldier

The company then formed in line of battle and marched four miles to a "shady and pleasant piece of woods on the border of the far-reaching expanses of a flowery prairie. It was an enchanting region for war—our kind of war." They took up a strong position with some low, rocky hills behind them, and a "purling, limpid creek in front." In no time at all, half the company was in swimming and the other half was fishing. They occupied an old maple sugar camp, its half-rotted troughs still propped against the trees. A good-sized corncrib served as the "battalion's" sleeping quarters. They named the position Camp Ralls. Half a mile away, to the left, stood Mason's house and farm; he was a friend to the cause, which added to the comfort.

Shortly after noon, farmers from the region, hearing that there was a military company in their midst, began arriving with mules and horses, which they agreed to lend for use during the war—which they also judged would last about three months. The animals were of all sizes, colors, and breeds, and mainly young and lively. To Sam's lot fell a very small mule, quick and active, with a bobbed tail, which suggested his name—Paint-Brush. Anything Sam required of him was done against the animal's will and under protest—but he was willing enough to do things after his own fashion and after consulting his own judgment. Between Sam and the pillow on the saddle, "there was a Mine of trouble—and between the saddle and the ground there was another Mine of trouble, viz. The Mule." Further, the saddle was always loose and Sam was in constant fear that it would turn; yet he dared not tighten it, for the cinch was old and might break. Therefore, whenever he rode Paint-Brush, it was as though he was astraddle a powder magazine, for if Sam had opposed the mule's wishes to any great extent, he would have retaliated by rolling on the ground, jumping gullies, or running away. Sam's fate would have been of no concern to him.

Late this same day, Lieutenant Clemens ordered Sergeant Bowen to feed Paint-Brush. Bowen replied that if Clemens reckoned he had gone to war to play "dry-nurse to a mule," he would soon discover his mistake. After all, he was a steamboat pilot, too, and pilots took orders from no one—Clemens knew that. Sam thought Bowen's refusal was probably insubordination, but being unsure about all things military, he let it pass and gave the order to one of the privates who simply grinned sarcastically and turned on his heel. Sam then asked Captain Tom Lyman if it was not proper and military for him (Clemens) to have an orderly. Lyman said it was, but since there was but a single orderly in the corps, it was only right that Bowen serve on his (Lyman's) staff. But when they approached Sam Bowen, he refused to serve on anyone's staff, and if they thought they could make him, just try. "So of course, the thing had to be dropped; there was no other way."

The next problem was the cooking. It was considered a degradation for one or two men to have to cook for the rest—so they skipped noon dinner. But by late suppertime they were so famished, the difficulty was met by all hands turning out to gather wood, build fires, and haul water. Then each man cooked for himself.

Afterward, everything was smooth for awhile. Then trouble broke out between the corporal and the sergeant, each claiming to rank the other. No one knew which was the higher office, so Lyman settled the matter by making them both equal in rank.

Camp life proved "idly delicious" for a time. After horsemanship drill every morning they were free to do as they pleased, so "we rode off here and there in squads a few miles, and visited the farmers' girls, and had a youthful good time, and got an honest dinner or supper, and then home again to camp, happy and content."

There was nothing to mar that life until one day some farmers rode in with a rumor that the enemy was advancing their way from over Hyde's prairie. All was sudden consternation and confusion for they could not agree upon which way to retreat. Since it was only a rumor, Captain Tom Lyman was not in favor of retreating at all, but soon found he would fare badly if he clung to that opinion, for the company was in no humor to tolerate insubordination. So he gave in and called a council of war—to consist of himself and his three officers—but the privates made such a fuss at being excluded, he allowed them to stay—for they were already there and doing most of the talking, at that. The question was which way to retreat, "but all were so flurried that nobody seemed to have even a guess to offer. Except Lyman. He explained in a few calm words, that inasmuch as the enemy were approaching from over Hyde's prairie, our course was simple: all we had to do was not to retreat *toward* him; any other direction would answer our needs perfectly. Everybody saw in a moment how true this was, and how wise; so Lyman got a great many compliments." It was decided that they would fall back on Mason's farm, half a mile to their left.

Darkness had come by this time, and since they did not know how soon the enemy might arrive, they decided not to be encumbered with horses and other things but set off at once with only their guns and a keg of powder. The way was rough and rocky, and the night very black. Shortly it began to rain, the leafy slopes of wet clay grew slippery, and men commenced to fall. At one point half the party, including Bowen with the keg of powder in his arms, began stumbling over one another in turn. They went flying down the hill in a body and landed in a stream at the bottom. As they picked themselves up out of the water and fished out their guns, there was a good deal of talk about how they would die before they ever went to war again, and that the invaders might rot for all they cared, and the country with them. "But we got lost presently among the rugged little ravines, and wasted a deal of time finding the way again, so it was after nine when we reached Mason's stile at last; and then before we could open our mouths to give the countersign, several dogs came bounding over the fence, with great riot and noise, and each of them took a soldier by the slack of his trousers and began to back away with him. We could not shoot the dogs without endangering the persons they were attached to; so we had to look on, helpless, at what was perhaps the most mortifying spectacle of the Civil War."

The Masons, father and son, came out with candles, called the dogs off, and asked the company in. As the aspiring soldiers stood around the broad hearth trying to find cheer in the crackling hickory logs, Mr. Mason, his back to the blaze, began plying them with questions. It was soon apparent that they knew nothing whatever about who or what they were running from, so the old man asked why it was they hadn't stationed a picket-guard at the place where the road entered Hyde's prairie, to give warning. Or better yet, send out scouts to spy on the enemy and report his exact number and route, before jumping up and stampeding out of a strong position on a vague rumor. After he learned how much country they had covered before getting to his place, he remarked, "Marion *Rangers!* good name, b'gosh!" They filed off to bed feeling still further humiliated and depressed.

The Rangers stayed several days at Mason's, in hiding, for word had come "that a detachment of Union soldiers was on its way from Hannibal with orders to capture and hang any bands like ours which it could find." Clemens never forgot how the days and nights dragged and how downhearted he became with nothing to do or think about. He was unable to adjust to that "slumberous" farm after the interest and excitement of piloting, of speculating in produce, of taking part in the bright social life of New Orleans. On the farm, the Mason men were away in the fields all day, the women and girls busy and out of sight in the house. The only sound Sam could recall was the "plaintive wailing" of a spinning-wheel "forever moaning out from some distant room." To him it was still the most lonesome sound—"steeped and sodden with homesickness and the emptiness of life." The family went to bed about dark every night, "and as we were not invited to intrude any new customs, we naturally followed theirs. Those nights were a hundred years long to youths accustomed to being up till midnight."

So it was with a feeling very like joy that they received the news that the enemy was on their track again. With a rebirth of martial spirit they sprang to their places in line of battle and fell back on Camp Ralls.

Captain Lyman had taken Mason's advice to heart, and first thing issued orders to post a guard at the place where the road entered Hyde's prairie. It was Clemens' duty to call on Bowen to take the first shift until midnight. He refused, as Sam knew he would, and so did all the others he asked. The same thing was happening in military camps all through the South, for these young men had been brought up to be sturdily independent, and they rebelled at being ordered around by those they had known intimately all of their lives—which explains the existence of the many partisan groups.

Clemens managed to secure his picket that night through diplomacy rather than authority, by temporarily exchanging ranks with Bowen and standing watch with him as his subordinate. They stayed out at the crossroads a couple of hours in a drenching rain, Bowen adding to the dismal monotony by grumbling ceaselessly about both the war and the weather. At length he tired and fell silent. Then they both began to nod and finding it next to impossible to stay in the saddle (Sam was not mounted on Paint-Brush), they turned back to camp, riding in unchallenged, just as the enemy might have done. Everyone was sound asleep in the shelter of the corn-crib, and there were no sentries. They never tried picket-duty at night again, but *usually* kept a guard by day.

Those idle hours continued, but "our scares were frequent. Every few days rumors would come that the enemy were approaching," and the boys went flying off to one of their several well-hidden camps. But as the reports always proved false, increasingly less attention was paid them. One night, a black messenger came to the corn-crib with word that the enemy was "hovering" in the neighborhood. *Let* him hover! They were warm and comfortable and were not going to turn out. So they went on with their talking and joking, but after a while the conversation began to lag, and the jokes and laughter grew forced. Falling silent, they were aware that the atmosphere was tense and apprehensive. Before long, each one had crept noiselessly to the front wall and was peering out through a crack between the logs, staring toward that place near the sugar troughs where the forest path came into the open.

The night was late and very still. A hazy moon gave only light enough to suggest the outline of objects. Presently they caught the rhythmic beat of horse's hoofs, muffled by the thick carpet of damp oak and hickory leaves. Then a dim shape emerged from the forest shadow along that path. It was a man on horseback, and Clemens thought he saw others behind him. He reached for a gun and pushed the muzzle into the crack, so dazed and numb with fright he was hardly aware of what he was doing.

Then somebody said, "Fire!" Without thinking, he pulled the trigger.

"I seemed to see a hundred flashes and hear a hundred reports; then I saw the man fall down out of the saddle." Then someone said, hardly audibly and without conviction: "Good—we've got him!—wait for the rest."

They waited and listened, but the rest did not come. There was perfect stillness—"an uncanny kind of stillness," intensified by the "damp, earthy, late-night smells now rising and pervading it." Realizing that this was a lone horseman, they filed out silently and approached him. The moonlight was just bright enough to reveal his face. No one had ever seen him before. He was a stranger, but not in uniform, and he was unarmed. He lay on his back, gasping for breath, and his white shirt was soaked with blood. Suddenly it came over Clemens that he was a murderer: he had killed a man who had never done him any harm. "I was down by him in a moment, helplessly stroking his forehead; and I would have given anything then—my own life freely—to make him what he had been five minutes before. All the boys seemed to be feeling the same way; they hung over him, full of pitying interest, and tried all they could to help him, and said all sorts of regretful things. . . .

"In a little while the man was dead. He was killed in war; . . . killed in battle, as you may say; and yet he was as sincerely mourned by the opposing force as if he had been their brother. The boys stood there half an hour sorrowing, and recalling the details, and wondering who he might be . . . and saying that if they were to do it again they would not hurt him unless he attacked first."

Then Sam learned that his was not the only shot fired—there had been five others. This division of guilt lightened the burden he was carrying, but thoughts of that lone horseman who had ridden so trustingly out of the shelter of the woods into the open moonlight preyed on his mind, and he could not drive them away. The taking of that life had been such a "wanton thing. And it seemed an epitome of war; that all war must be just that—the killing of strangers against whom you feel no personal animosity; strangers whom, in other circumstances, you would help if you found them in trouble, and who would help you if you needed it."

In the days that followed, the Marion Rangers kept monotonously falling back on one camp or another as the rumors came in. The last warning reached them when they were near the village of Florida. This one seemed to have more substance, and was certainly more uncomfortable to think about: a Union colonel was sweeping down on them with an entire regiment in his wake. "Our boys went apart and consulted; then we went back and told the other companies present that the war was a great disappointment to us and we were going to disband. They were getting ready themselves, to fall back on some place or other, and were only waiting for General Tom Harris," (formerly Hannibal's telegraph operator), who was expected at any moment. They tried to persuade the Marion Rangers to wait, but the majority said no, they were accustomed to falling back, and didn't need any of Tom Harris' advice. Sam Clemens felt that he personally "knew more about retreating than the man that invented retreating." About half the fifteen, including Clemens, mounted and left.

An hour later they met General Harris on the road with two or three men—his staff, probably, but they couldn't tell for no one was in uniform. Harris ordered the Rangers back, "but we told him there was a Union colonel coming with a whole regiment in his wake, and it looked as though there would be a disturbance; so we had concluded to go home." The general stormed a bit, but it was useless, for their minds were made up. They bid him good day and spurred down the road leading to Hannibal.

XII

━━━━━━━━━━━━━━━━━━━━━━━○━━━━━━━━━━━━━━━━━━━━━━━

ACROSS THE PLAINS

LATE IN THE SPRING of 1861, Orion Clemens was appointed Secretary of the newly created Territory of Nevada, with a salary of eighteen hundred dollars a year, the title of "Mr. Secretary," and the duties and dignities of Treasurer, Comptroller, and Acting Governor during James W. Nye's absences (which were frequent and often extended). Edward Bates—in whose office and under whose tutelage Orion, as a young St. Louis printer, had read law and practiced oratory—was now President Lincoln's attorney general, and had secured the office for Clemens. As usual, Orion was "strapped," Sam observed, and therefore could not pay his way to Carson City where he was expected to take up his duties before the end of summer. Unable to borrow money in Memphis, Missouri, where he still had a law office, he decided to try his luck at St. Louis, doubtless intending to ask his kinsman James Clemens, Jr., for an advance. He also wanted to have a final visit with his mother and sister, and to see Sam, who had just reached Pamela's house after his three weeks as a Confederate soldier.

As yet, Sam had no plans for the future. He was still fearful of being drafted to pilot a Union riverboat, or arrested as a possible spy since his departure from the army had been irregular. In many eyes, it was outright desertion. In talking over their problems, it was soon seen that the solution for both lay in Sam going to Nevada as the Secretary's secretary (in the first Nevada *Directory* he was listed as "Assistant Secretary, Nevada Territory"), and paying the expenses with his pilot's savings. There would be no salary, but also probably little or no work, which would allow him time to correspond with the Keokuk and St. Louis newspapers for pay—and to investigate the possibilities of the silver mines which were making fortunes for men daily. Further, he would stay only three months—the war's expected duration—then go back to piloting on the Mississippi. The whole plan was immensely appealing, for beyond providing safety through distance for Sam, there lay the certainty of adventure and the possibility of riches in the midst of new scenes and people in the fabled Far West. Ever since 1849, when he had watched young John Robards ride out of Hannibal for the California goldfields, with his long yellow hair flying in the wind, Sam had yearned to cross the Plains.

On July 18, he and Orion took passage on the steamer *Sioux City* for the seven-day trip up the Missouri River to St. Joseph, the "prairie port." The first thing they did upon landing on the afternoon of the 25th, was to hunt up the overland stage office and buy two tickets, at $150 apiece, for seats in the coach that left the next day for Carson City.

In the morning, they were up before dawn and after a quick breakfast, hurried to the depot. There they learned that each passenger was allowed only twenty-five pounds of baggage, for this stage was carrying three days' delayed mail. Hastily they unlocked their trunks, and made a rapid selection of articles to take—white shirts, underwear, socks, and towels—cramming these into a single valise, shipping the trunks back to St. Louis. "It was a sad parting, for now we had no swallow-tail coats and white kid gloves to wear at Pawnee receptions in the Rocky Mountains, and no stovepipe hats nor patent-leather boots, nor anything else necessary to make life calm and peaceful." Being reduced to a "war-footing," they exchanged their dark suits for blue woolen army shirts, heavy trousers, and "stogy" boots of rough leather. They were also taking two or three wool blankets, for frosty nights in the high mountains, and two large canteens to carry water in between stations on the Plains; and several boxes of "Acetous Extract of Lemons," contributed by Jane Lampton, to be added to the water to prevent scurvy; five pounds of smoking tobacco, several pipes, and a shot bag of silver coin to pay for their meals. Orion "took along about four pounds of United States statutes and six pounds of Webster's Unabridged Dictionary." In his pocket he carried a notebook in which to record the day's events, for he had arranged to correspond with the Keokuk paper, *Gate City*. Sam kept no journal and when, in 1870, he came to write an account of this overland trip in *Roughing It*, he had to borrow Orion's notations to enable him to make a detailed, chronological narrative, instead of "slurring it over and jumping 2,000 miles at a stride." In return, he sent the ever-needy Orion one thousand dollars.

For the journey both men were armed—Sam with "a pitiful little Smith & Wesson seven-shooter, which carried a ball like a homeopathic pill," and Orion with a small "Colt's revolver strapped around him for protection against Indians."

By eight o'clock on that brilliant, sunny morning of July 26, everything was ready. Sam, Orion, and a third passenger, George Bemis, jumped into the Concord coach, an imposing "cradle on wheels," the driver cracked his whip and sang out, "Hi-yi! g'lang!" and the six horses started almost at a run, rapidly leaving the "States" behind. With every mile there was an increasing sense of exhilaration for Sam and Orion at being freed from all uncertainties and responsibilities, and in pleasant anticipation of things to come. Orion, at thirty-six, was unwittingly on the way to achieving the apex of his career; Sam, approaching twenty-six, was literally on the road to fame in a field he had never once considered his true calling.

Every ten to fifteen miles, day and night, the horses were changed, and unless it was storming or they were asleep, Sam and Orion jumped out, stretched their legs, and inhaled the fresh air deeply during the five minutes exactly that was allowed for exchanging the teams. Most stations consisted simply of a cluster of buildings that included a hut used for an eating-room, and express and post office. To one side stood the barn, and the corrals and stables to accommodate about fifteen horses and mules. Mules were used over more difficult terrain, and were especially safe for mountain travel. Accommodations for travelers varied greatly, depending upon location. In Kansas, they stopped at John E. Smith's hotel, which was considered the finest between Atchison and Denver—a handsome, two-storied building with vine-covered verandas and a large flower garden. It also served excellent meals. But once on the unpopulated plains, there was no pretense at quality. The buildings were adobe, with dirt floors. Their flat roofs were covered with wattle and earth in which flourished prairie wildflowers and grasses, giving them the appearance of a misplaced front garden, Sam thought. Only a child could enter the doorway of the station-keeper's hut without stooping. It consisted of one smoke-blackened room which served as a bedroom for himself and the hostlers (there were bunks), and as dining room and parlor for passengers. The fireplace was the cooking center, where in a corner was an open sack of flour, a bag of salt, and a side of rusty bacon, along with battered tin coffeepots and kettles. In another corner of the room stood three or four rifles and muskets, and powder horns and bullet pouches. The dining table was simply a greasy bare board on stilts; at each man's place, Sam noted, was an old tin plate, fork, knife, and pint cup.

At these stage stops, Sam began seeing his first Westerners—ranchmen and cowboys, driving horses and cattle to army posts. He noticed that their trousers were made of coarse, country-woven cloth (held up by *belts* and not suspenders, Missouri fashion) and had the seat and inner side of the legs reinforced with buckskin—"so the pants were half dull blue and half yellow, and unspeakably picturesque. The pants were stuffed into the tops of high boots, the heels whereof were armed with great Spanish spurs, whose little iron clogs and chains jingled with every step." They all wore large mustachios and full, untrimmed beards. On their heads were broad slouch hats with the crowns worn high. Their shirts were of blue wool, and they owned neither coat nor vest. A leather sheath at the belt held a long "navy" revolver slung on the right side, hammer forward; from the right boot-top projected the horn handle of a bowie knife.

Some of these men took seats at the table, where there were a couple of three-legged stools, a four-foot-long pine bench, and two empty candle-boxes. The station-keeper carved off a slice of raw bacon apiece, then sawed slabs from a large disk of last week's bread and piled them on a platter. He next filled their cups with something known locally as "slumgullion." It was supposed to be tea, but Sam found "too much dish-rag, and sand, and old bacon-rind" in it to fool anyone.

"Our breakfast was before us, but our teeth were idle," Sam spoke for Orion and himself. "I tasted and smelt." The bacon was rancid and the bread had the consistency of cement. He simply sat, listening—not to the conversation at table, for there was none, but to the occasional terse remarks and hurried requests for more to eat or drink. Accustomed to the volubility of his own people, Sam was amazed at the Westerner's thrifty use of words. Always interested in vernacular, he was impressed by its vigor and "freshness." Their demands for service never varied:

"Pass the bread, you son-of-a-bitch!"

Sam was startled, even though the tone was "gruffly friendly." He had yet to learn that in the West, "son-of-a-bitch" was a common form of address between friends, a term of affection even, particularly among cowboys and cattlemen. There were times, however, when the manner and tone of voice indicated that the epithet was to be interpreted as originally intended, and the man so addressed "dug for his cannon."

That morning, Sam and Orion gave up on breakfast, paid their dollar, returned to the coach, and found comfort in their "old rank, delicious" pipes. Sam liked to think that breakfast was the rule, and claimed later to remember only one meal between the States and Salt Lake City that they were ever really thankful for. This one was at the Green River station, on the morning of their tenth day out, when they were served fresh antelope steaks, tender and delicious, hot biscuits, and good coffee. Not until they reached Salt Lake City were they able to stock up on emergency rations, for there was never time to do so during those five-minute stops to change teams or the twenty minutes allowed for meals. A two-day layover in Salt Lake enabled them to buy ham, fresh bread, and hard-boiled eggs, enough to last the remainder of the trip. Nor was there ever time for bathing. Only once, before coming to Independence Rock and Devil's Gate, was there a delay which gave them a chance to swim in Horse Creek—"a (previously) limpid, sparkling stream."

Across the Plains

Sam remembered vividly the "gladness and wild sense of freedom" he experienced on those fine fresh mornings when they sat on the top of the flying coach, legs dangling over the side, hats tied on, and searched the vast expanse of green prairie in all directions for things new. The sky was a deep blue, and so clear, the atmosphere possessed that quality which seemed to make it possible to see forever into the distance. The solitude was magnificent and impressive—not a sign of human beings anywhere. It was from this perch that he saw his first "jackass" rabbit, whose "majestic" ears topped the low shrubbery, saw the first antelope and watched them rapidly leave the stage far behind, and saw the first coyote threading its way through the sagebrush. He saw his first snowbanks in summer (something he had heard about as a boy but refused to believe) and viewed his first glaciers among the rugged peaks of the Wind River Range, which truly pierced the skies. In Hannibal, he had thought Holliday's Hill did that.

On the Continental Divide, the driver pointed out the stream that was starting its journey westward to the Pacific Ocean and the other that flowed eastward and eventually made its way into the Missouri River and then the Mississippi. In that one, Sam dropped a leaf freighted with a mental message for a girl in St. Louis. There was a "vague possibility that *she* might take it out of the water as it drifted by the old city, & by the unerring instinct of love know the tender freight it bore." Tears came into his eyes as he reflected on that possibility.

Since the start of the trip Sam had been hoping to catch sight of a pony express rider, one of those mail messengers who sped the 1,966 miles from St. Joseph to Sacramento in an average of eight days, changing horses every ten to twelve miles. The rider covered two hundred miles a day; the stagecoach, in comparison, traveled 125 miles. Only the most important business letters and newspaper despatches written on the thinnest onion skin or tissue paper, were carried, at five dollars a half-ounce in addition to regular government postage. Still, many a letter carried $25 in "pony" stamps. Of the eighty riders employed, at times forty were in the saddle going west, while forty rode east. But the travelers had yet not seen any. Then, one day, the driver shouted: "HERE HE COMES!"

Away across the prairie, a black speck appeared against the sky.

In only a second or two it took shape as horse and rider, "rising and falling, rising and falling—sweeping toward us nearer and nearer" until finally the "flutter" of hoofs came faintly to ear. Another instant, it seemed, and "a whoop and a hurrah from our upper deck, a wave of the rider's hand, but no reply, and man and horse burst past our excited faces," and went "winging away like a belated fragment of a storm."

Although Sam's attitude toward Orion would always remain ambivalent, it was during the spell of these carefree days of shared adventure that he first became "acquainted" with his brother, he told him later. Most often he thought of Orion as a "queer & heedless bird," seemingly doomed never to succeed. But now with his appointment to federal office Sam saw him in a new and more respectful light, and watched for those qualities which had impressed Lincoln's attorney general. For the first time in their lives, perhaps, they were on an equal footing as comrades. Prior to this, he had been Orion's subordinate, his employee, and obliged to take orders from him.

Fortunately Orion possessed a good sense of humor (more quiet than Sam's), which eased the tension of confinement and close contact in the stagecoach for twenty days and nights. However, with Sam's short patience there was bound to be friction. One provocation that arose almost daily was Orion's whistling and "warbling" in which he indulged without restraint whenever he was happy, which was often, now. Sam would have gladly joined him, but with his "diabolical notions of time and tune he is worse than the itch when he begins," he complained to Jane Lampton. He had no choice but to sit still and be "tortured with his eternal discords, and fag-ends of tunes," worn out and discarded years ago, which he gathered and strung together without regard to "taste, time, melody, or the eternal fitness of things." Sam knew Orion prided himself on those medleys and variations, so if he was "to boil over and say I wish his music would bust him, there'd be a row, you know." One day, unable to stand it a moment longer, he did blurt out that if Orion didn't stop his "cursed din," worse than a "rusty wheelbarrow," he would jump out of the stage. Although Orion did not say, "Get out and be damned!" Sam knew he thought it. He therefore urged Jane to "just touch him up a little, and give him some advice about profane swearing. . . . You're his mother, you know, and consequently, it is your right and your business and comes within the line of your duties, as laid down in the Articles of War."

Sam, and surely Orion, arrived at Salt Lake City holding all the popular prejudices against Mormons and Mormonism, and with a consuming curiosity regarding polygamy. Since there was to be a layover, they took a room at the Salt Lake House where that first night they were served a welcome and memorable supper consisting of "the freshest meats and fowls and vegetables—a great variety and as great abundance." Early the next morning they set out to explore the city, enjoying the pleasing novelty of broad, clean, smooth streets with sparkling snow water rippling along in the gutters, in the place of filth. They enjoyed the absence of undernourished waifs, loafers, drunkards, and unruly people. They admired block after block of neat frame and brick houses, with thriving orchards and vegetable gardens behind every one and dooryards planted to flowers. They were impressed with the general air of industry, thrift, and comfort in this city of fifteen thousand, and the obvious good health of its citizens. It was reported there was only one physician to tend them all. Sam admitted to experiencing a thrill every time a house door opened as they passed, and a glimpse was caught of those inside, for he longed to have a good look at a Mormon family in "all its comprehensive ampleness."

Orion, as Secretary of Nevada Territory, was entertained widely by prominent Gentiles who resided there, and was introduced to Mormon elders. Orion's secretary was also invited. They held a long talk with Heber Chase Kimball, one of the Church's Twelve Apostles, and, after putting on white shirts, they were taken to pay a state call on the "King," Brigham Young. He impressed Sam as "a quiet, kindly, easy-mannered, dignified, self-possessed old gentleman," who dressed very simply—in fact, he was just in the act of taking off a plain straw hat as they entered—not the crown someone had said he wore. But there was no chance during their audience for even a brief sight of Young's harem, rumored at twenty to thirty wives, or any of his fifty children, so Sam's curiosity went unsatisfied.

At the end of two days, he and Orion left the city with their bundles of ham, bread, and hard-boiled eggs. They were feeling rested, well-fed, and pleased, but were no wiser regarding the controversial "Mormon question." They heard a great many things new about these people, but since they were invariably presented in at least three versions, it was impossible to know which to believe. Sam gave up trying. Certainly his personal experience had not shown them to be the cold-blooded murderers he had expected. He actually found much to admire in the Mormons and their industrious ways. A few years later, he warned that before passing judgment on the Mormons it must be remembered that for forty years they were persecuted—"mobbed, beaten, and shot down; cursed, despised, expatriated; banished to a remote desert"—only because they were trying to live, and worship God, in a way they believed to be the true one.

Unfortunately, he was unable to apply this same tolerance toward the Indians beyond the Rocky Mountains, whom he now began seeing for the first time, and who had likewise been shot down, beaten, cursed, despised, misunderstood—and driven, in this case, from a domain that had been theirs for more than twelve thousand years, at least. To Sam, they were the "wretchedest type of mankind" he had ever seen, "inferior to all races of savages on our continent." They were "sneaking, treacherous, filthy, and repulsive." They were "prideless beggars," always hungry, yet having no higher ambition than to kill and eat jack-rabbits, crickets, and grasshoppers. The preponderance of settlers and travelers in the Far West took this same short-sighted view. Clemens never took the time to look deeply and thoughtfully into the "Indian question." Therefore he never did revise or qualify his original opinions.

At noon on August 24, 1861, twenty days out from St. Joseph, the overland stage drew up at the depot in Carson City. Sam and Orion were sorry to come to the end of what had proved a fine pleasure excursion. They had grown very fond of that life, with its infinite variety and freedom, and the thought of settling down to routine once more was a depressing anticlimax.

Across the Plains

Looking around, they saw nothing to lift their spirits. The capital of Nevada Territory was a "wooden" town nestled on the edge
of a vast desert, and walled in on the west by the rugged, snow-
capped Sierra Nevada. The main street consisted of four or five
blocks of small white frame stores, packed side by side, as though
cramped for space on that great plain. In the middle of town,
opposite the stores, was the plaza—a large, level vacancy, with a
flagpole in the center. It was used for mass meetings, horse trades,
public auctions, and band concerts. At either end of the plaza were
offices, livery stables, and more shops. Beyond this concentration,
Carson City was decidedly scattered.

The daily wind of gale proportions had now come up and roiled
the dust in such thick clouds the town was almost totally obscured.
Sam and Orion picked up their baggage and resignedly trudged off
to find a place to stay.

XIII

---○---

MINING FEVER

Sam and orion clemens took a room at the boardinghouse of Mrs. Margret Murphy, "a camp follower of his Excellency the Governor," who had known him in his prosperity as New York's Police Commissioner and refused to desert him "in his adversity as Governor of Nevada." Their room was on the ground floor, facing the plaza, and when they had got their bed, a small table, two chairs, a government fire-proof safe, and the unabridged dictionary into it, there was space for one visitor, possibly two, but not without straining the walls. But the walls could stand it because they were made simply of one thickness of "cotton domestic," stretched from corner to corner. This was the rule for partitions in Carson; very often they were just flour sacks basted together.

Rather shortly, to relieve the congestion, Sam moved upstairs and took quarters with the "untitled plebians" in one of the fourteen white cot-bedsteads that stood in two long rows in the single room that comprised the second story. "It was jolly company." They were known as the "Irish Brigade," although there were only four or five Irish among them. They were younger camp followers of Governor Nye who believed that in "the scuffle for little territorial crumbs and offices," they might reasonably expect to pick up something and better themselves.

Mining Fever

It did not take Sam long to discover that he was admirably suited for Western life. It made him feel "rowdyish" to wear a battered slouch hat, trousers crammed into boot-tops, and over-sized Spanish spurs, and he "gloried" in the absence of coat, vest, and suspenders. A few months later, he was carrying a navy revolver at his side, and had started to grow a moustache and beard. "Nothing could be so fine and so romantic," he said of his outfit, and he banished all thoughts of returning to the States.

By mid-September, Orion still had nothing for Sam to do, which left him free to explore the fascinating new country and investigate mining possibilities. He had heard a great deal about the beauty of Lake Bigler, which was being called "Tahoe"—a name Clemens would always object to, claiming that it was Indian for "grasshopper soup," and therefore unfitting. He had also heard from members of the Irish Brigade about the riches to be made through timber claims along the lakeshore. Some of the boys had already taken up claims, and urged Sam to do the same, offering him the use of their headquarters cabin and their stock of rations and tools.

The weather was perfect and the distance only eleven miles, so he decided to make the trip. He had found someone with the same object in view, John Kinney, a "shrewd, ingenious, capital comrade" who was "wonderfully companionable" and amusing. His father was a Cincinnati "nabob" who had sent him West for the experience, under the aegis of Judge George Turner, another of Governor Nye's retainers. They set off afoot, carrying only an axe and two woolen blankets apiece. They had not considered that those eleven miles stretched across valleys and up and down mountains. They tramped a long while over desert, then "toiled laboriously" up the first mountain, about a "thousand miles high," reached the summit, and looked over expectantly. No lake. They descended the other side, crossed a valley, and labored up another mountain, "three to four thousand miles high." Still no lake in view. Hot and tired, they sat and rested awhile, then refreshed, plodded on two or three hours more. Suddenly from a height, the lake "burst upon us"—a vast oval sheet of dark blue water tinged in places with green, lying six thousand feet above the sea, a ring of towering Sierran peaks reflected upon its still surface. Sam thought it must be the fairest sight on earth. "It throws Como in the shade," he wrote Pamela. "Whenever I think of it I want to go there and *die,* the place is so beautiful." He expected to build a country seat by the shore, some day. Then Pamela must come and stay. The air is so pure and invigorating, he predicted that within three months she would be strong enough to "knock a bull down" with her fist.

Clemens and Kinney spent four days hiking along the lake's north shore, its most scenic part, exploring its many bays and small coves in a dugout borrowed from an absent owner. They fished, swam in the sunny shallows (but only a little for the water was icy), and tramped through the fragrant connifer forests to select their timber claims. They saw no other people, and heard no sounds but the wind in the pines, the waves lapping the shore, and the distant thunder of an occasional rock-fall. They made their beds in the warm sand between two large boulders which sheltered them from the night winds.

Sam pictured their life for his mother and sister: "After supper we got out our pipes—built a rousing camp fire in the open air—established a faro bank (an institution of this country,) on our huge flat granite dining table, and bet white beans till one o'clock, when John went to bed. We were up before the sun next morning, went out on the Lake and caught a fine trout for breakfast. But unfortunately, I spoilt part of the breakfast." Both coffee and tea were boiling on the fire in identical pots. Fearing they might not be strong enough, Sam added more tea and more ground coffee— "but—you know mistakes will happen. —I put the tea in the coffee-pot, and the coffee in the tea-pot—and if you imagine they were not villainous mixtures, just try the effect once."

After the timber land was decided on, about two miles in length and one in width, they cleared an area, built a brush cabin, and fenced it in—all requisite for holding the claim in the names of Samuel L. Clemens, William A. Moffett, Thomas Nye (the Governor's nephew), and John Kinney. It was located on what was entered in the records as "Sam Clemens' Bay."

On the evening of the fourth day at the lake, they came back to their cabin, which they never used, for "We did not wish to strain it." They were hungry and to hasten the production of dinner Sam built and lighted the campfire, then turned back to the boat to get the frying pan. He heard a sudden shout, and looking around, saw that the fire was out of control. The flames had caught on the heavy carpet of dry pine needles, raced to a thicket of manzanita and huckleberry oak, then leaped high into the tall, resinous conifers. The heat was so intense it drove them into the boat. Although the roaring of the fire and the loud explosions of ignited pitch were terrifying, it was a fascinating spectacle. He described it for his family: "The level ranks of flame were relieved at intervals by the standard-bearers, as we called the tall dead trees, wrapped in fire, and waving their blazing banners a hundred feet in the air." Turning to look at the lake, they could see "every branch, and leaf, and cataract of flame . . . perfectly reflected as in a gleaming, fiery mirror." Far across the water the cliffs and domes were lighted with a ruddy glare, while the sky above "was a reflected hell."

After the nearby flames had died down, they watched the fire webbing the far-off mountain fronts with a "tangled network" of what appeared to be red lava streams. Around midnight they went to bed with "many misgivings," for embers were still glowing. When they got up in the morning, they found that the fire had burned small pieces of driftwood within six feet of their boat, and had crept to within four or five steps of their bed. Then they took inventory and found themselves homeless wanderers without property—not even a coffeepot—and no insurance. The cabin, the fence, and much of their timber claim were in ashes.

Beggared, they were forced to go back to Carson City, Sam continued, but they planned to return to the lake shortly, select another claim, build a cabin, and get everything in order before November first when Sam planned to leave for the Esmeralda mining district, of which the town of Aurora was the hub.

There was a touch of homesickness in the last paragraph of this letter, which he devoted to messages for his Keokuk and St. Louis friends. ". . . tell Challie and Hallie Benson that I heard a military band play 'What are the Wild Waves Saying?' the other night, and it reminded me very forcibly of them. It brought Ella Creel and Belle across the Desert too in an instant, for they sang that song in Orion's yard the first time I ever heard it. It was like meeting an old friend. I tell you I could have swallowed that whole band, trombone and all, if such a compliment would have been any gratification to them." He asked what had become of Sam Bowen. "I would give my last shirt to have him out here."

As to the timber claim at Lake Tahoe, nothing further is heard about it in extant correspondence, nor did Sam wait until November to go to Aurora, for he had caught silver fever. How could he avoid it when he heard talk everywhere about how the great Gould & Curry had leaped from four to eight hundred dollars a foot in two months; how the Ophir, worth only a trifle last year, was now selling at nearly four thousand dollars a foot; "how Tom So-and-So had sold out of the Amanda Smith for $40,000—hadn't a cent when he 'took up' the ledge six months ago." And how "the Widow Brewster had 'struck it rich' in the 'Golden Fleece' and sold her ten feet for $18,000 . . ." To give substance to the wild talk, Sam saw cartloads of solid silver bricks, as large as pigs of lead, arriving from the mills daily. "I succumbed and grew as frenzied as the rest."

By October 25, when he wrote to Pamela, he was back from his first trip to Aurora, and with Orion, now owned some 1,650 feet of mining ground. If it proves *good,* Will Moffett's name will be added; if not, then Sam can get feet for him in the spring. There is plenty of mining ground; the trouble lies in raising the money to work it. He has plans to lay a claim for little Sammy Moffett—for to everyone's astonishment Pamela, the confirmed invalid, had had a baby in the late fall of 1860, a boy she named Samuel after her brother. Clemens, who was still piloting then, had the opportunity to see the "unexpected but not unwelcome stranger," and report his arrival to Orion and Mollie.

In this letter to his sister, he included a message for Mrs. Benson, mother of two of his girlfriends, Challie and Hallie, that he has no intention of becoming a lawyer. He has been a slave several times in his life and he will not be one again. "I always intend to be so situated *(unless* I marry,) that I can 'pull up stakes' and clear out whenever I feel like it." He wanted Pamela to know that he and Orion are grateful for the newspapers she has been sending them; next to letters, they are the most welcome visitors they have.

After returning from that strenuous trip to Lake Tahoe, Sam decided he needed a riding horse. In *Roughing It,* he devoted a chapter to his purchase at auction of a black, Genuine Mexican

Mining Fever

Plug, which in his innocence he believed to be some very special kind of fine Western horse. He told how that horse bucked him off immediately and how everyone to whom he loaned him always walked home, for the animal had either thrown the rider or run away. Actually, Sam did buy a black horse with a white face, but his character was quite different: "I feel . . . sometimes, as if he were a blood relation of our family—he is so infernally lazy," he wrote Jane Lampton. On December first of that year he sold the horse for $45 to his close friend of Keokuk days, William H. Clagett, then a law student, now an attorney. Clagett had been lured to Carson City by the prospect of a successful practice in the new Territory's capital, and by reports of riches from the great silver lodes.

Every few days word would come of some newly discovered silver mining region, the newspapers would be filled with accounts of its richness, and away the "surplus" population would rush, singly and in parties, to take possession. Just now, "Humboldt!" was the cry and "Hurry!" was the word. Sam Clemens wasted no time in getting away. With him went William Clagett, a second lawyer, A. W. (Gus) Oliver, and Cornbury S. Tillou, a sixty-year-old blacksmith who was the only experienced miner in the group. They invested in a horse, and a wagon which they loaded with 1,800 pounds of provisions and blankets—the "necessaries of life —to which the following luxuries were added, viz." Ten pounds of what Sam called "killikinick," for smoking, fourteen decks of cards, a cribbage board, a keg of lager beer, a copy of *Dombey and Son,* Watts' *Hymns,* and two dogs—not Clemens' idea.

They started out on the two hundred-mile trip northeast through the desert on a cold December morning, with Billy Clagett driving and Sam, Gus Oliver, and Mr. Tillou trudging behind, pushing, for whenever they came to a hard stretch of road, "Bunker," the " 'near' horse on the larboard side" (named after Nevada's attorney general, Benjamin Bunker, toward whom Clemens held ambivalent feelings), would come to a dead stop, and Sam's horse, also in harness, was of no help. It took "a vast amount of black-snaking and shoving and profanity" to start Bunker again, and once on his way "he would take up the thread of his reflections where he left off, and go on thinking and pondering, and getting himself more and more mixed up and tangled in his subject, until he would get regularly stuck again, and stop to review the question. . . . In fact, Ma, that horse had something on his mind," on the entire trip. Sam was taking obvious pleasure in endowing the horse with the attorney general's shortcomings.

It seemed to Clemens that they pushed that wagon nearly all the way to Unionville, in the Buena Vista District of Humboldt. Some parties they met hailed them with the facetious suggestion that they put the horses *in* the wagon, and pull it themselves. It proved to be a "hard, wearing, toilsome journey," in Sam's opinion, but it did have some bright moments. The ones remembered best were those filling meals of fried bacon, hot bread, molasses, and coffee, which satisfied their ravenous appetites at the end of an arduous day, he told his mother. After the meal they would draw close to the campfire, light up their pipes, spin yarns, sing, tell "lies," and quote Scripture—Jane Lampton knew when to believe Sam.

They entered Unionville in a driving snowstorm. The settlement consisted of eleven cabins (one was the assay office) and a liberty pole. Six of the cabins were in a row at the base of a high, steep canyon wall; the others faced them. The settlement appeared to lie in the bottom of a deep narrow crevice which was still dark long after daylight spread over the mountain tops. Sam never forgot how cold it was there, and how scarce fuel was, for the only source was sagebrush which Indians brought in on their backs. "When we could catch a laden Indian it was well—and when we could not (which was the rule, not the exception), we shivered and bore it."

They inquired around and were told that there were any number of "immensely rich" leads in which they could get feet enough to make their fortunes. Mills, however, would not be operating until about June first, so they decided to prospect on their own, until that time, with Tillou as their guide. Every night they returned with pockets full of sample rock. Tillou's experience had been in the gold mines of California, where work went on all year, and he was soon to learn that in the dead of winter at Unionville the ground was frozen solid, and no one could possibly uncover ledges or sink shafts. All they could do was wait for spring, so they got busy and built a three-sided cabin (the fourth side was formed by the steep canyon wall) out of willow, rock, and packed earth. Sam

soon discovered that he possessed a "shining talent" for constructing rock and willow houses.

When the cabin was finished, Clagett hung out his shingle as a
notary public, and Oliver put up his as probate judge and wrote
poetry while he waited for clients. As for Sam, ever restless, he
clapped on his Spanish spurs, mounted his horse, and with three
companions (one of them "Major General BBBunker, L.L.D.,
Esq."), started out in a snowstorm for Carson City, intending to go
from there to Esmeralda to look after his mining interests. About
sixty miles northeast of Carson, the party stopped for the night at
Honey Lake Smith's, a two-story log tavern set on a knoll above
the placid North Fork of the Carson River. It was an overland
coach station with ample hay-barns, stables for teams, and smaller
outbuildings for travelers on their own. Toward sunset, about
twenty hay-wagons came in and camped around the house, and half
a dozen "vagabonds and stragglers," all a "very, very rough sort."
The house was filled that night and every available bit of space on
the floors and in chairs was taken for sleeping. Sam and his companions had secured a bed on the second story.

They had been asleep a little more than an hour when they were
awakened by a great sound of rushing and roaring outside, and by
the shouts of men and neighing of horses. Hurrying to the window,
Sam saw by moonlight that the river was raging and nearly overflowing. A heavy storm in the mountains had started this flash
flood. In a few minutes the water was coursing through the stable
where Sam and his companions had their animals. They ran down,
waded knee-deep into the building, untied their horses, and led
them out through water that was already nearly waist-high. Within
an hour or two the tavern was standing on top of an island in a
vast, muddy sea.

Clemens and his party were waterbound eight days, "cooped up
. . . with that curious crew," who passed their time drinking and
gambling at cards, with "an occasional fight thrown in for variety."
In *Roughing It*, he described this experience (which was not imaginary, for Orion wrote about it in a letter to Mollie), and started to
tell of the "dirt and vermin" but cut it short by saying, "their
profusion" was "simply inconceivable." But in his letter to Jane

Lampton, which described the entire trip, he said he could tell her how he and his two companions got "fearfully and desperately lousy; and how I got used to it and didn't mind . . . and slept with the Attorney General, who wasn't used to it, and *did* mind it; but I fear my letter is already too long. Therefore—*sic transit gloria mundi, e pluribus unum forever! Amen.*"

After reaching Carson City, Sam was delayed until early April 1862 by the unprecedented storms which made the roads to Aurora almost impassable. This was the memorable winter when all the rivers in California overflowed. The capital city of Sacramento was transformed into an American Venice, and boats were the only form of transportation. The great interior valleys were turned into seas which were navigated by steam riverboats. Sam was fretting at his confinement and swearing like a trooper at his foolishness in having left the Humboldt District so hurriedly, he wrote Billy Clagett. He wished he was back in Unionville to give Billy a hand with building his house and construct his fireplace and chimney for him. To help pass time, he renewed his affiliation with the Freemasons, whose Polar Star Lodge No. 76 he had joined at St. Louis the previous year.

But he was not without news of his Esmeralda holdings, for Robert M. Howland, his partner there in the Horatio and Derby ledge, was in Carson. He was staying at Mrs. Margret Murphy's "ranch," as Sam liked to call it. Bob Howland, tall, well-built, and handsome, was a "jolly, cordial 'don't-care-a-cent' young man, ready for any lark, afraid of nothing in the world." Sam had met him when he first took up quarters with the "Irish Brigade." He was Governor Nye's nephew, and had been appointed marshal of Aurora. Sam never forgot the night Howland came into the "corral" drunk, knocked down a shelf of glass jars containing scorpions and tarantulas collected by the Brigade, and set them free— causing an uproar among the sleeping occupants in the dark dormitory when he shouted, "Turn out, boys—the tarantulas is loose!"

Clemens worked that incident into a memorable scene in *Roughing It.* Instead of picturing him drunk, he had Howland awaken suddenly, jump up and knock over the shelf with his head when a stable roof was slammed into the side of Mrs. Murphy's house by the violent local wind known facetiously as the "Washoe Zephyr." Sam credited that daily wind with bringing new and interesting sights to the upper air of Carson City—"hats, chickens, and parasols sailing in the remote heavens; blankets, tin signs, sage-brush, and shingles a shade lower; door-mats and buffalo robes lower still; shovels and coal scuttles on the next grade; glass doors, cats, and little children on the next," and down at only thirty or forty feet above the ground, "a scurrying storm of emigrating roofs and vacant lots."

Now he and Howland discussed their prospects. "He says our tunnel is in 52 feet, and a small stream of water has been struck, which bids fair to become a 'big thing' by the time the ledge is reached," because water is of immense value in this arid country for working the ore mills, he explained to his mother and Pamela. "If the ledge should prove worthless, we'd *sell the water* for money enough to give us quite a lift." Then *"we* wouldn't care whether school kept or not." But they feel confident, and "if nothing goes wrong, we'll strike the ledge in June—and if we do, I'll be home in July, you know.

"So, just keep your shirt on, Pamela, until I come," he urged, for she had inquired about the best routes to the West for herself and Will Moffett, and he was aware that she had taken his certainty of gaining riches too seriously. "Don't you know that I have only *talked,* as yet, but proved nothing? . . . Don't you know that I have never held in my hands a gold or silver bar that belonged to me? Don't you know that its all talk and no cider so far? Don't you know that people who always feel jolly, no matter where they are or what happens to them—who have the organ of Hope preposterously developed—who are endowed with an uncongealable sanguine temperament—who never feel concerned about the price of corn—and who cannot, by any possibility, discover any but the *bright* side of the picture—are *very* apt to go to extremes, and exaggerate, with 40-horse microscopic power?" He hadn't tried to raise her expectations—"but then your knowledge of the fact that some people's poor frail human nature is a sort of crazy institution anyhow, ought to have suggested them to you." Still, he has unlimited confidence in his own ability to make a fortune here for,

THE BACHELOR YEARS

"In the bright lexicon of youth,
There's no such word as Fail"—
and I'll prove it!

He had convinced Orion (so he thought) that he (Orion) hadn't enough "business talent" to operate a peanut stand, Sam informed the family, and had made him promise to meddle no more with mining. "So you see, if mines are to be bought or sold, or tunnels run, or shafts sunk, parties have to come to me—and me only. I'm the 'firm,' you know." What he failed to tell them was that Orion had become the all-important financial partner in the *firm*.

"Send me $40 or $50—by mail, immediately," Sam's letters to him ran. "I want . . . anywhere from $20 to $150, as soon as possible." He was "strapped" and hadn't three days rations on hand: "If you can spare $100 conveniently, let me have it—or $50." Or "Send me whatever you can spare. . . . I want it to work the 'Flyaway' with."

Orion seems always to have supplied the money but he paid no attention to Sam's injunction not to meddle in their mining affairs, provoking Sam to a long, angry letter.

You have promised me that you would leave all mining matters, and everything involving an outlay of money, in my hands. Now it may be a matter of no consequence at all to *you*, to keep your word with me, but I assure you *I* look upon it in a very different light. Indeed I fully expect you to deal as conscientiously with me as you would with any other man. Moreover, you know as well as I do, that the very best course that you and I can pursue will be, to keep on good terms with each other—notwithstanding which fact, we shall certainly split inside of six months if you go on this way. You see I talk plainly. . . .

Now, Orion, I have given you a piece of my mind—you have it in full, and you deserved it—for you would be ashamed to acknowledge that you ever broke faith with another man as you have with me. I shall never look upon Ma's face again, or Pamela's, or get married, or revisit the "Banner State," until I am a rich man—so you can easily see that when you stand between me and my fortune (the one which I shall make, as surely as Fate itself,) you stand between me and *home*, friends, and all that I care for—and by the Lord God! you must clear the track, you know!

Family and friends were particularly meaningful to him now and never far from his thoughts. Jane Lampton kept him informed of their activities in long letters reporting local news. What he did not learn from her he read about in the St. Louis, Keokuk, Hannibal, and New Orleans papers Pamela forwarded. It was there that he discovered that Horace Bixby was serving on the Union flagship. "He always was the best pilot on the Mississippi, and deserves his 'posish,' " Sam observed. Sometimes his mother was careless or vague, and in one instance he had to ask, "O, say, Ma, *who was* that girl—That sweetheart of mine you say got married, and her father gave her husband $100 (so you said, but I suppose you meant $100,000)?" He suspected she was referring to Emma Roe, whose family owned the riverboat *John J. Roe.* —"What in thunder did I want with *her?* I mean, since she wouldn't have had me if I had asked her to. Let her slide. . . ." The girl he would have liked to hear about was Laura Wright.

As preoccupied as he was with striking it rich, he let no opportunity pass to tease his mother. The born speller could never refrain from chiding those not so gifted. In one letter, she had reported that a certain Mr. Axtell "was 'above suspition'—but I have searched through Webster's Unabridged and can't find the word. However, it's of no consequence—I hope he got down safely."

She had observed that "it looks like a man can't hold public office and be honest." He commented:

Why, certainly not, Madam. . . . Lord bless you, it is a common practice with Orion to go about town stealing little things that happen to be lying around loose. And I don't remember having heard him speak the truth since we have been in Nevada. He even tried to prevail upon *me* to do these things, Ma, but I wasn't brought up that way, you know. You showed the public what *you* could do in that line when you raised me, Madam. But you ought to have raised me first, so that Orion could have had the benefit of my example. Do you know that he stole all the stamps out of an 8-stamp quartz mill one night, and brought them home under his overcoat and hid them in the back room?

Sam took immense pleasure in imagining her rising to the bait, for although she was humorous and witty she sometimes took things more seriously than intended. Sam remembered the time she told him that Annie Moffett had said that goobers (peanuts) grew on trees. "Isn't that silly," Sam replied, "everyone knows they grow on bushes." "Bushes!" Jane cried, "why of course they don't grow on bushes!"—and she was off, with Sam adding just enough fuel to keep the argument blazing.

During these busy days, Sam worried about the upbringing of Pamela's young son, his namesake. Just as soon as Sammy was old enough to understand, he urged that Pamela must say to him, "Now, my boy, every time that you allow another boy to lam you, I'll lam you myself; and whenever a boy lams you, and you fail to pitch into that boy the very next time you see him and lam *him*, I'll lam you *twice.*" She would never regret it, nor would he. "Pa wouldn't allow us to fight, and next month Orion will be Governor, in the Governor's absence, and then he'll be sorry that his education was so much neglected."

He corresponded with Annie, and fell into disfavor when he corrected her errors in construction and spelling—she spelled with "a fearful latitude." By way of apology, he reminded her of the day when she tried to teach him about Moses, and he proved so dull: "I'm just as dull yet." He supposed her last letter was really just as it ought to be, only he read it according to his lights, and these being "inferior," she must overlook his criticism, "especially, as it is not *my* fault that I wasn't born with good sense." He suspected she might "detect an encouraging ray of intelligence" in *that* statement.

By April 13, Sam was in Aurora, living with another friend he had made in Carson City, Horatio (Raish) Phillips, in a ten- by twelve-foot clapboard "mansion" with a dirt floor and canvas roof. Shortly they were joined by Aurora's marshal, Bob Howland, and by Calvin H. Higbie, a civil engineer who had considerable experience mining in California. Higbie was a handsome man, genial, large, and strong, and endowed with the "perseverence of the

devil." Sam was to see him climb 7,000 feet out of Yosemite Valley, carrying sixty pounds of gear on his back, a shotgun in one
hand, and a rifle in the other, when the two made a walking trip
there in June.

When the partners first acquired the cabin it stood on the town's
outskirts, but wanting to be in the heart of things they decided one
day to move it to some vacant land on Pine Street, the main thor-
oughfare. Fifteen or so acquaintances agreed to help them carry it
there. When they got as far as the Bank Exchange Saloon on Pine,
they set down their load and filed in for drinks. As they ranged
themselves at the bar, the partners congratulated themselves on
how little it was going to cost to relocate the cabin. Soon the word
spread, and a crowd began pouring in, each man coming up to
display a bruised or blistered hand in proof of having been a
helper. Suddenly it came over the partners that at "two-bits" a
drink it would have been almost as cheap to buy a new house with
"a mansard roof and an observatory."

Aurora, set in a sagebrush-covered valley between mountains
barren of all vegetation except scattered dwarf junipers, was on its
way to reaching a peak population of five thousand the next year.
Typical of all new mining regions, one saw in its streets a hundred
men to one woman or child. Although ranked second in importance
to Virginia City, Nevada, it had no hotel, one visitor noted, but
dozens of lodging-houses, restaurants, and "saloons—saloons—saloons, everywhere!" By actual count, there were twenty-five.

Sam's mood was petulent when he reported to Orion on April
13. Nothing was happening in the entire district, he wrote. He
could not even *see* the Horatio and Derby, for it was still deep in
snow. It would be another three or four weeks before work could
be continued on the tunnel. "Guess it is good—worth from $30 to
$50 a foot in California. . . . Guess the 'Red Bird' is probably
good. . . . The 'Pugh' I have thrown away," for he doubts if
there is a ledge. Clayton's mill was the only one worth a damn.
And—*"why* didn't you send the 'Live Yankee' deed—the very one
I wanted . . . Send it along—by mail—d—n the Express—have
to pay three times for all express matter; once in Carson and twice
here. . . . Stint yourself as much as possible, and lay up $100 or
$150, subject to my call. I go to work to-morrow, with pick and

shovel. Something's got to come, by G--, before I let go here. . . . Don't buy *anything*. . . . Don't send any money home. I shall have your next quarter's salary spent before you get it, I think. I mean to make or break here within the next two or three months."

He also told Orion, "Man named Gebhart shot here yesterday while trying to defend a claim on Last Chance Hill. Expect he will die."

By May 11, Sam owned a one-eighth interest in the new Monitor mine, and will not part with even a foot "because I *know* it to contain our fortune. The ledge is six feet wide, and one needs no glass to see the gold & silver in it."

Six days later, Sam had startling news for Orion. On reaching the Monitor the morning before, they had found three men with revolvers already there. "We went up and demanded possession, but they refused. Said they were in the hole, armed, and meant to die in it, if necessary. I got in with them, and again demanded possession. They said I might stay in it as long as I pleased, and work—but they would do the same. I asked one of our company to take my place in the hole, while I went to consult a lawyer. He did so. The lawyer said it was no go. They must offer some 'force'. Our boys will try to be there first in the morning—in which case they may get possession and keep it. Now you understand the shooting scrape in which Gebhart was killed the other day. The Clemens Company—all of us—hate to resort to arms . . . and it will not be done until it becomes a forced hand—" They did get possession, but no work could be done until the end of June, the interval of time allowed by mining law for the opposition to appeal.

Sam did not delay getting to work on his other holdings, belying the reputation he enjoyed encouraging—that he was physically lazy. "The pick and shovel are the only claims I have confidence in now. My back is sore and my hands blistered with handling them to-day. . . . If I can dig pay rock out of a ledge here *myself*, I will buy—not otherwise. . . . Well, things are so gloomy I begin to feel really jolly and comfortable again. I enjoy myself hugely now." Although he was pretending to react to the disappointments as the indomitably cheerful Mark Tapley would have in *Martin Chuzzlewit* (a novel Sam had been reading), one day he was to write: "Everything human is pathetic. The secret source of Humor itself is not joy but sorrow. There is no humor in heaven."

A month later he reported to Orion: "The cards are on the Flyaway and the Monitor—and we will stake the whole pile on them. If they win, we are alright—if I lose, I am busted."

In April he had asked Orion to send Raish "one of those black portfolios," and slip into it a couple of penholders and a dozen steel pens. Several of Sam's letters home had been printed in the Keokuk *Gate City,* and he now decided to write some humorous accounts about Nevada life for the Virginia City *Territorial Enterprise.* With Raish, he will also "drop a line" occasionally to the Carson City *Silver Age.*

Some six weeks later, he asked Orion to put all of his *Enterprise* letters (which he had signed "Josh") into his scrapbook since he might have use for them some day. —"Those Enterprise fellows make perfect nonsense of my letters—like all d--d fool printers, they can't follow the punctuation as it is in the manuscript. They have . . . made a mass of senseless, d--d stupidity out of my last letter."

Nonsense or no, the staff and readers found them clever and amusing. One squib that set the whole Territory chuckling and brought Sam an offer from the *Enterprise,* concerned Professor Personal Pronoun, who was immediately recognized as Judge George Turner, recently appointed Chief Justice of the territorial supreme court. Although young, he was pompous, and his habit of referring to himself in laudatory fashion in both conversation and speeches furnished an ideal subject for a lampoon. He had recently made an oration, and even though Clemens did not hear it, he knew just what Turner would say and how. He would scatter through it all his pet quotations, such as "Whom the gods would destroy they first make mad," along with countless allusions to himself. In the piece, Sam gravely regretted that it had been impossible to reprint the Professor's address in full because the type case was out of capital I's.

His letters to Orion now showed him to be in no "high good humor," as he admitted. He was brusque and contradictory. He berated his brother and issued him peremptory orders. He even failed to acknowledge Orion's contributions of money. "Yes, I have received the $100—much obliged," he responded after prodding. He was completely out of patience because riches were not coming his way faster. Nearly every day he heard of some "common loafer" who fell asleep in the gutter and woke up to find himself worth a hundred thousand dollars. Yet, after devoting all his thought and effort to getting rich, he has gained nothing. The next most irksome feature of this venture has been that he was forced to stay in one place for six months. He reminded Orion he had not done that since 1853, and it was not in his nature to remain put for so long. He would leave that very day if he could, but his sense of duty dictated that he be on the spot to oversee their holdings and make decisions. Meanwhile, he must find some way of supporting himself.

He naturally thought about newspaper correspondence, for pay. A Carson friend, William M. Gillespie, who became chief clerk of the first Territorial Legislature, was talking about starting a daily newspaper. If he planned on a large one, Sam wanted to correspond with it at four or five dollars a week, and also with the *Silver Age* on those same terms. He expected Orion to make the arrangements, he wrote him. When Gillespie's paper seemed certain, Clemens asked his brother to tell him not to find a San Francisco correspondent, for he would like that job himself for the winter. Since snow suspended all work in Esmeralda, he wanted to pass those months in California.

His partner, Bob Howland, arranged to have Sam appointed a deputy sheriff, and he now asked Orion to find out why in "the devil" his commission hadn't been sent to him. —Everything in this infernal country is vexatious—except that pretty little "Miss P- —she with the long curls, out there under the hill." He instructed that his "dear love" be given her.

By mid-June, when flour had reached a dollar a pound, Sam was without credit. He therefore went to work in Clayton's six-stamp quartz mill for ten dollars a week and board, to learn the business in case he ever had to oversee his own ore, and to make money. He took his turn breaking up masses of silver-bearing rock with a sledge-hammer and shoveling it into the battery of stamps, at screening tailings, at feeding quicksilver and sulphate of copper into the amalgamating pans, and at scooping pulp out of those pans and tediously washing it with a horn spoon. At the end of the first week he had to quit for, as he wrote Orion, he came near "getting salivated, working in the quicksilver and chemicals." On top of that he caught a "violent cold" which settled in his chest and lasted two weeks.

When Clemens wrote *Roughing It,* he dedicated the book to Calvin H. Higbie, "an honest man, a genial comrade, and a steadfast friend, . . . in memory of the curious time when we two were millionaires for ten days."

By the time Sam sent Orion word of his experience in the mill and his heavy cold, he and Higbie had already been millionaires. Higbie had discovered a potentially rich blind lead while inspecting the Wide West mine, which was already producing heavily. A blind lead or cross vein is a ledge that does not appear above the surface of the ground but is usually struck accidentally when driving a shaft or tunnel. Higbie noticed that this lead ran diagonally across the chimney and entered the walls at both sides, making him certain that it was a permanent and distinct vein from the Wide West, the Dimes, Annipolitan, and Pride of Utah, all running close together. "Accordingly I made a mining location on this cross vein, as the mining laws permitted me to do, and put Sam L. Clemens' name on the location notice."

"It's a blind lead for a million!" he told Sam. "Well, it *does* seem like a dead sure thing," Sam wrote Orion, and sent him a detailed sketch of the location.

For more than a century, Sam's dramatic account in *Roughing It* of the discovery of the blind lead, of the heady experience of being millionaires for ten days, and of the trauma of losing the claim, has been discounted as fiction based on the jumping of the Monitor mine. It has been looked upon as a tale of "what *might* have happened," as "a possibility rather than an actuality," and as "a quintessential recording of Washoe lusts in which the whole era is compressed."

However, in dismissing the tale as imaginary, it is necessary to discredit Clemens' statement in the book that although the incident reads "like a wild fancy sketch . . . the evidence of many witnesses, and likewise that of official records of Esmeralda District, is easily obtainable in proof that it is a true history." To this reader these words seemed to have been written in all seriousness, and a search of those records was undertaken. This led to the discovery that the story of those exciting events was indeed founded on their actual experience (further supported by Higbie's narrative), and that in the telling Clemens departed from fact only in a few details.

For simplification, Clemens identified the blind lead as a spur of the Wide West rather than involve the Annipolitan, Pride of Utah, and Dimes-Wide West. Further, the Wide West was famed and remembered for heavy production of rich ore, which heightened the drama of their forfeiture of millions of dollars. Other instances of literary license were taken by Clemens for dramatic effect, as, having the partners miss the chance of saving their claim by minutes when it was actually days. Even that most improbable situation, which found both Calvin and Sam away when one or the other ought to have been doing the work required to hold the blind lead, is true. Higbie was indeed far away on California's Owens River, where he had an interest in some cement mines. He had been called away to give important advice and to take supplies to his partner. And Sam Clemens, just as he said in *Roughing It*, was at M. C. Gardner's Nine-Mile Ranch on the Walker River, nursing his friend Captain John Nye, the governor's brother, who lay "dangerously ill." He was back in Aurora by July 9, after giving almost constant attention, night and day, to Nye—who made no effort to hire anyone to relieve him, Sam complained to Orion. Then Nye grew so demanding and abusive they quarreled—"I was what the Yankees call 'ugly'," Sam said, and he left the ranch.

In the book, Clemens had the responsibility for the loss of the blind lead shared, through a failure in communication, each having left the other a note he never found until it was too late. At this point in the account Higbie differs: When he received the summons to the cement mines, he had "a long serious talk with Sam," reminding him that the assessment work on the claim had to be done soon, probably before Higbie could get back.

"Don't you fear, man, I'll do it," he remembered Clemens saying. In *Roughing It*, Sam told of meeting Gardner and learning from him that John Nye was near death. "I said if he would wait for me a moment, I would go with him and help in the sickroom. I ran to the cabin to tell Higbie. He was not there, but I left a note on the table for him. A few minutes later I left town in Gardiner's wagon."

In an autobiographical sketch written several years later, Clemens stated that he was really worth millions for ten days, "but lost it through my own indolent heedlessness."

Nearly everything in that account of their lost fortune is true. Even the snatches of conversation they shot back and forth from their bunks that first sleepless night after recording the claim, if not the exact words, were in character for men almost delirious in anticipation of a fortune. Calvin Higbie also recalled their grand plans for a mansion on San Francisco's Russian Hill, with two acres of "grass plat," a billiard room, statuary and paintings, a landau with matched gray horses and coachman in livery, a steam yacht which Sam would steer himself, and trips to Europe and Egypt in the spring. Calvin was intrigued with Samoa as an alternative paradise in which to settle.

In his reminiscences, Higbie tells that no social gathering in Aurora was complete without Sam Clemens, whose songs, quips, and amusing stories kept spirits high. But Sam was not partial to large formal celebrations because he was inherently shy, Calvin thought, and it took a great deal of persuasion to get him to go. He did attend the dedication of Sam Davis' new saloon and dance hall. The five respectable women in the area came, and close to a thousand men, mainly miners in red or blue woolen shirts, wearing their knives and revolvers. Since this was a formal occasion, their jeans were not tucked into their boots. There was, as well a sprinkling of merchants, lawyers, and mine superintendents in conventional black, frock-coated suits.

The women were of course constantly engaged but Sam did finally manage to get a partner and join a quadrille, "which is very simple and easy," he wrote not long afterward. "All you have to do is stand up in the middle of the floor, being careful to get your lady on your right hand side, and yourself on the left hand side of your lady. Then you are all right, you know. When you hear a blast of music . . . you lay your hand on your stomach and bow to the lady of your choice—then you turn around and bow to the fiddlers. The first order is, 'First couple fore and aft'—or words to that effect. This is very easy. You have only to march straight across the house—keeping out of the way of advancing couples, who very seldom know where they are going to—and when you get over, if you find your partner there, swing her; if you don't, hunt her up— for it is very handy to have a partner. . . . The next order is, 'Ladies change.' This is an exceedingly difficult figure, and requires great presence of mind. . . . At this point order and regularity cease—the dancers get excited—the musicians become insane— turmoil and confusion ensue. . . ."

It was during one of those states of confusion that Higbie noticed Sam rushing off into another set without a partner, as though he considered it useless to try to get things right. Then, with a "maybe-you-think-I-can't-dance-air," he suddenly launched into a solo shuffle in a clear space on the floor. His eyes were half-closed and he was saying softly to himself that he "never dreamed there was so much pleasure to be had at a ball." Higbie felt that this "was no attempt at affectation: he was natural as a child." Shortly everyone was laughing so hard at Sam's antics and the quizzical expression on his face, the sets broke up.

Clemens tells of going to a ball at Gold Hill that same year in a "ramshackle . . . dismal old barn of a place" that was lighted from end to end by "tallow-candle chandeliers made of barrel hoops suspended from the ceiling." He remembered that the grease "dripped all over us." There were two to three hundred "stalwart men" present, dancing with "cordial energy." Half of them represented women, each with a handkerchief tied around his left arm to distinguish him from the men. "I was a lady myself. I wore a revolver in my belt, and so did all the other ladies—like- wise the gentlemen."

By June 22, Clemens had received a letter from William Bar- stow, business manager of the *Territorial Enterprise.* Joseph T. Goodman, editor and proprietor of the *Enterprise,* recalled that Sam's "voluntary contributions . . . struck us as so funny we sent him word to come to Virginia City and take a job on the paper." Instead of accepting at once, Sam sent Barstow's letter to Orion, and warned him not to say anything about the offer to William Gillespie since he did not want to ruin his chances with Gillespie's paper.

Shortly he was writing his brother, "My debts are greater than I thought for I bought $25 worth of clothing, and sent $25 to Higbie, in the cement diggings. I owe about 45 or $50, and have got about $45 in my pocket. But how in the h--l I am going to live on something over $100 until October or November, is singular. The fact is, I must have something to do; and that *shortly*, too." He asked Orion to write to the *Sacramento Union* "folks" and tell them he will contribute as many letters a week as they might want, for ten dollars—"my board must be paid." California was full of people who had investments in Nevada and it was seldom they heard anything from there. "Who'll run from morning till night collecting materials cheaper." He has decided to write a short letter twice a week for the *Silver Age*, for five dollars.

On July 30, he told Orion he hoped that the *Union* would answer promptly because Barstow had offered him the post of local reporter for the *Enterprise* at $25 a week, and "I have written him that I will let him know next mail if possible, whether I can take it or not." If Gillespie is not *sure* about getting his paper started within a month, perhaps he had better close with Barstow.

Six days later, Sam was still stalling. Barstow wrote that if he wanted the place he could have it, and Clemens replied that he "guessed" he would take it, "and asked him how long before I must come up there. I have not heard from him since," Sam told Orion.

"Now I shall leave at midnight to-night, alone and on foot for a walk of 60 or 70 miles through a totally uninhabited country, and it is barely possible that mail facilities may prove infernally 'slow' during the few weeks I expect to spend out there." Therefore, Orion must write Barstow that Sam has left for "a week or so, and in case he should want me he must write me here, or let me know through you. You see I want to know something about that country yonder." Obviously, he was going to join Higbie at the cement mines, and look over the prospects. He had planned this trip before July 9, when he wrote to Orion about starting off then. Now it was July 30. But, on August 15, he wrote Pamela from Esmeralda, telling her he must answer her letter that had just come, "right away, else I may leave town without doing it at all." This strongly suggests that he still had not left on that long walk. For some reason, Clemens' first biographer, Albert Bigelow Paine, attached great spiritual significance to that trip, seeing it as a kind of vision quest which took Sam into the wilderness for guidance in deciding about taking the *Enterprise*'s offer, an interpretation that has been generally accepted ever since.

Sam opened his letter to Pamela with a blast at Orion for writing home everything he ought to keep to himself. He had told the family that Sam would like to be on the river again. "I never have *once* thought of returning home to go on the river again, and I never expect to do any more piloting at any price. My livelihood must be made in this country—and if I have to wait longer than I expected, let it be so—I have no fear of failure. . . . This country suits me, and—it *shall* suit me, whether or no."

He made no mention of the *Enterprise* offer, but told her, "I will spend the winter in San Francisco, if possible." Apparently, he was still hopeful that Gillespie's paper would be launched and that he could act as the California correspondent.

Less than a month later, the mystery of Sam's soul-searching expedition was solved when he wrote Billy Clagett that for more than two weeks he had been "sloshing around" in California's White Mountain District, east of Bishop, partly for pleasure and partly for other reasons (these being to examine the cement mines). A Mr. Van Horn of Keokuk, who knew Billy's "daddy," Judge Clagett, and "used to go with your father when he stumped the district, and sing campaign songs," was one of their party. "He is a comical old cuss, and can keep a camp alive with fun when he chooses. We had rare good times out there fishing for trout and hunting. I mean to go out there again before long." He added, "Billy, I can't stand another winter in this climate, unless I am obliged to. I have a sneaking notion of going down to the Colorado mines 2 months from now."

Just what prompted Clemens to accept the *Enterprise* offer, instead of slipping off to Colorado, he never explained, but it was doubtless economic. He must have made his decision not long after writing to Clagett, for he arrived in Virginia City about the end of September.

XIV

―――――――――――○―――――――――――

SAM CLEMENS/MARK TWAIN

O N E D A Y L A T E I N September 1862, Sam Clemens, foot-
sore and dusty, came into the office of the Virginia City *Territorial
Enterprise,* slipped his blanket roll from his shoulders, and dropped
wearily into the nearest chair. According to a late-life recollection,
he had walked the 130 miles from Aurora.

Denis McCarthy, the newspaper's co-owner who superintended
the pressroom, looked up and spoke, and Sam, gazing at him with
a faraway look, returned his greeting and said, "My starboard leg
seems to be unshipped. I'd like about one hundred yards of line; I
think I am falling to pieces." After a moment he added, "I want to
see Mr. Barstow or Mr. Goodman. My name is Clemens, and I've
come to write for the paper."

When he got in to see Goodman, he asked for instructions regarding his duties, and was told to go all over town and ask all
sorts of questions of all kinds of people; to make notes on the
information gathered, and then put them together for publication.
But, he cautioned, "Never say 'We learn' so-and-so, or 'It is reported,' or 'It is rumored,' or 'We understand' so-and-so, but go to
headquarters and get the absolute facts, and then speak out and
say 'It *is* so-and-so.' —Unassailable certainty is the thing that gives
a newspaper the firmest and most valuable reputation." Further, it

did not pay to make mistakes in a country where every man "was his own judge as to whether his dignity had been offended."

Joseph Thompson Goodman, brilliant, handsome, affable, and gracious, with the reputation of a bon vivant, had just turned twenty-four that September. At eighteen, he had left his birthplace in Masonville, New York, and come to California with his father. Shortly he found a job as a typesetter on a San Francisco literary journal, *The Golden Era,* owned and edited by Rollin M. Daggett— a poet of considerable local fame who eventually moved on to Virginia City and to the *Enterprise* staff.

In March 1861, Goodman and Denis McCarthy, a friend and fellow journeyman printer, borrowed forty dollars and set out to try their fortunes in Virginia City. There they found that the weekly *Territorial Enterprise* was foundering and bought it—fixtures, type, and goodwill—for one thousand dollars, on time, and turned it into a daily. It was Nevada's oldest newspaper, which had been launched in December 1858 at the village of Genoa (population 200), a Pony Express stop. A year later, the paper was moved to Carson City, and then, within another twelve months, to Virginia City.

When Goodman and McCarthy took over the *Enterprise,* it was housed in a small, one-story frame building on A Street. "The editorial sanctum, news-room, press-room, and publication office . . . were all compressed into one apartment." A lean-to at one side was fitted up as a bedroom, parlor, kitchen, and dining-room. A Chinese, known as Old Joe, did the cooking.

Joseph Goodman took on the editorial duties since he had a clear prose style and, as a newspaper writer, had "few equals." He also had considerable talent as a poet and playwright. Dan De Quille (the pen name of William Wright), was hired to report locals, and mining news. In less than a year and a half the *Enterprise* had gained a national reputation; it was the biggest daily between Chicago and San Francisco, and the *New York Herald,* which refused to exchange with country editors, subscribed to it yearly. Prosperity went along with fame and the paper was able to move into more spacious quarters on North C Street, which was where Clemens joined it. Not quite a year later, the *Enterprise* was established in its own building of fireproof brick at 24 South C, opposite the International Hotel, the city's finest, its dining and smoking rooms, ladies' parlor, bar, and billiard room furnished with rare, costly mirrors, pictures, and crystal chandeliers. By then the paper had five editors, a corps of talented reporters, twenty-three compositors, and presses run by steam. It was clearing a thousand dollars a day. It was said that Goodman and McCarthy kept no books, but conducted their business on a strictly cash basis, and that at the end of each week, carried their profits home in water buckets, for there was no "rag" (paper) currency in Nevada yet.

The *Enterprise's* success was born of Goodman's belief that it was the paper's duty to "keep the universe thoroughly posted concerning murders, street fights, balls, theatres, packtrains, church doings, lectures, city military affairs, highway robberies, Bible societies, hay wagons, and the thousand other things which it is in the province of local reporters to keep track of and magnify into undue importance for the instruction of the readers of a great daily newspaper." Sam was well aware of this fundamental truth when he was attempting to increase the circulation of Orion's *Hannibal Journal.*

But often even so lively a town as Virginia City failed to provide news enough to fill those long columns on page three, devoted to locals. Goodman therefore allowed his reporters almost unlimited freedom in providing copy, and readers were treated to poetry, humor, the baiting of rival editors and newsmen, lampoons, and scientific hoaxes.

Clemens never forgot his first day as a reporter. He wandered about the streets, according to order, asking questions of everyone but finding no one who knew anything. At the end of five hours his notebook was still empty and he went back to consult with Goodman. Joe said that when Dan De Quille (whose place Sam was to fill while Dan visited his family in Iowa), was starting, he often made a good thing out of hay wagons in those dry times when there were no fires, shootings, or inquests. He asked Clemens if there had been any hay wagons in from Truckee. If so, he might tell of the renewed activity in the hay business.

Sam went out again and discovered one "wretched old hay truck dragging in from the country," which, with license, he multiplied by sixteen, brought into town from sixteen directions, and "got up such another sweat about hay as Virginia City had never seen in the world before." In the morning when he read over his piece he knew that he had found his "legitimate occupation" at last. "I reasoned within myself that news, and stirring news too, was what a paper needed, and I felt that I was peculiarly endowed with the ability to furnish it." Joe Goodman told him he was as good a reporter as Dan. "I desired no higher commendation."

While in Humboldt, Clemens had somehow incurred the enmity of the coroner and justice of the peace, one G. T. Sewall. After Sam returned to Carson and was waiting for the opening of the road to Aurora, he wrote Billy Clagett that he had heard from several reliable sources that Sewall will be in town shortly and has sworn to whip him on sight. He asked for legal advice: should he, Clemens, take a thrashing from that "son-of-a-bitch," or bind him over to keep the peace? He has no idea why the judge should dislike him. Sewall is a Yankee—and "I naturally love a Yankee."

Now, early in October, *Enterprise* readers were interested to learn about the discovery of a petrified man at Gravelly Ford, an old emigrant crossing on the Humboldt River. The "stone mummy" was described in all seriousness as having every "limb and feature . . . perfect, not excepting the left leg, which had evidently been a wooden one during the lifetime of the owner— which lifetime, by the way, came to a close about a century ago," in the opinion of a local savant who had examined the "defunct." (There was not a living creature within fifty miles of the place). The body was in a sitting position, the back against a mass of rock outcropping. The attitude was "pensive."—The right thumb rested against the side of the nose, the fingers of that same hand were spread apart, and the right eye was closed. In other words the man was thumbing his nose and winking. Upon hearing of the discovery, Coroner Sewall had summoned a jury, mounted his mule, and with a "noble reverence for duty," proceeded at once to the spot and held an inquest on the body. The verdict of the jury was that death came from "protracted exposure." The people of the neighborhood then volunteered to bury the "poor unfortunate," but found when they attempted to remove him that water dripping down the limestone had cemented him firmly. They then proposed to blast him loose, but Judge Sewall refused to allow them to on grounds that it would be little less than sacrilege. "Everybody goes to see the stone man, as many as 300 persons having visited the hardened creature during the past five or six weeks."

In a letter written on *Enterprise* stationery and dated October 21, Sam asked Orion if he had seen his squib headed "Petrified Man." It was "an unmitigated lie, made from whole cloth. I got it up to worry Sewall. Every day I send him some California paper containing it; moreover, I am getting things so arranged that he will soon begin to receive letters from all parts of the country, purporting to come from scientific men, asking for further information concerning the wonderful stone man. If I had plenty of time, I would worry the life out of the poor cuss."

Sam fitted well into the uninhibited, youthful atmosphere of the *Enterprise* office, where nearly everyone was in his twenties. He was soon intimate with Joe Goodman, Denis McCarthy, Dan De Quille, and an incorrigible prankster, Stephen E. Gillis, a compositor from Mississippi, who weighed ninety-five pounds. Clemens was most often the butt of Gillis' practical jokes, for he was quick to anger and therefore satisfying. The former pilot, who had taken such delight in dropping a watermelon shell on the head of his mate aboard a riverboat, saw no humor in tricks played upon himself. One certain way to get him worked up was to hide things from his desk. Not having the patience to keep a kerosene lamp clean, Sam wrote by candlelight. Often the candle was missing when he sat down to work. He would look for it a little, then get up and start to walk slowly in a circle, all the while cursing the thieves. The staff enjoyed listening to him swear, for he had developed it into a fine art—rich, profuse, colorful, and apt. At the height of his anger, the office-boy would appear with a replacement.

Scissors also had a way of disappearing with mysterious regularity. In those cases he would take out his knife, fiercely stab the newspaper from which he wanted to cut columns, swearing all the while, and slash deeply through the green baize table cover. He and Dan De Quille shared a table and Dan recalled that at Sam's end little was left of the cloth; in its place was something that resembled a "representation of the polar star, spiritedly dashing forth a thousand rays."

As they worked, they smoked cigars and pipes—Sam's pipe was so strong it was known as "The Remains"—drank beer and ate

Limburger cheese, a favorite combination, with newsmen. There always seemed to be time for a few stories or songs, when Sam would entertain the group with his favorite about the old horse, and Steve Gillis would pick up his violin. It was said he "could fiddle a man's shirt off."

The newspaperman's life was a carefree, bohemian existence. Every night after the theater (to which he always had passes) he would escort his young woman companion home, then cruise the town, usually with another reporter on his own or a rival paper, in search of news and pleasure, stopping in at all the popular resorts. A midnight oyster supper at Chauvel's fine French restaurant might be in order first, then a game of billiards at the International Hotel, and drinks. Then, a stop at the shooting gallery next door, with its lifelike figure standing outside in blue coat, yellow pants, high black boots and "fancy hat, just lifted from his head," that once "riveted" Clemens to the pavement in the belief he had met a phantom as he was "plodding home at the ghostly hour." They would call in at one of the hurdy-gurdy houses which provided live entertainment and a well-stocked bar. There were seats for viewing the line of dancing girls (not prostitutes, as has often been said) dressed discreetly in crinoline ballgowns, who also sang—chiefly those popular "regrets for bygone days and vanished joys," which often dissolved homesick miners in tears. The girls accompanied themselves with tamborine, castanets, and that medieval, lute-shaped instrument, the hurdy-gurdy.

Another regular stop was the Delta Saloon, for an order of "Reporter's Cobbler,"—a refreshing iced drink made from wine or liqueur, sugar, and citrus juice—accompanied perhaps by a game of cribbage. They would then move on to Tom Peasley's Sazerac Saloon for more drinks and news, for Peasley was the recognized leader of one of the rough elements in town, although always "on the side of the law." The Sazerac was the resort for political aspirants because Peasley was "a very Warwick" in such matters. The night usually ended with a run through Chinatown, and a visit to Bow Windows and The Brick, which were first-class bordellos. Then back to the office to write their stories. This itinerary, with a few variations, was typical of Dan De Quille's cruising. After he returned from Iowa, Clemens ran with him almost nightly.

He and Dan worked well together, for it was soon obvious to the older man (Dan was six years his senior) that Sam "hated" solid fact, figures, and measurements, which were required for reports on mining, and would give them a "lick and a promise" when they came his way, while Dan enjoyed such detail. He considered Clemens an "earnest and enthusiastic" reporter, "really industrious" in those realms that interested him. So he let Sam concentrate on human interest features—accidents, street fights, barroom shootings, murders, social activities, and entertainment, which allowed him freedom in working with his copy.

One night very late, Sam was in his room writing a letter to his mother and Pamela. He had just finished when something happened which caused him to put a postscript at the top of the first page. "I have just heard five pistol shots down the street—as such things are in my line, I will go and see about it." Several hours later he added: "P. S. N° 2—5 A. M.— The pistol did its work well—one man—a Jackson County Missourian, shot two of my friends (police officers,) through the heart—both died within three minutes. Murderer's name is John Campbell."

In the margin of this same letter he added, "Ma, write on *whole* letter sheets—is paper scarce in St. Louis?" To add effectiveness to his order, his next letter was written on paper of every size, kind, and color, including wrapping paper, the scraps all jumbled and stuffed into an envelope. Jane Lampton reportedly spent several "indignant" hours sorting all the pieces.

Newspapermen received invitations to all important social events—weddings, balls, receptions for visiting celebrities, and house-warmings at the mansions of the newly rich. By his own admission, Sam drank too much champagne at these affairs, but still managed to make the acquaintance of the prettiest and most interesting young women present, who were charmed with his gallantry, intrigued by his humor, and found him an ideal dancing partner. Shortly, he was writing home about his wide acquaintance among the daughters of Virginia City's best families.

With the discovery of new ore bodies and the expansion of the great Comstock Lode, which stretched its "opulent length" under the town from north to south, flush times came to Virginia City in 1863 and reporters found no dearth of local news. In fact, the

problem became a lack of space to accommodate each day's happenings. Sam wrote that the plank sidewalks along the main streets
had become so crowded with men from around the world—Germans, Englishmen, Irish, Welsh, Chinese, Spaniards, and Mexi-
cans—it was often nearly impossible to push through. The streets
themselves were jammed with an endless procession of wagons,
carts, and drays hauling hay, freight, and quartz, and Wells, Fargo
Express stages with their passengers, mail, and bullion. Buggies
frequently had to wait half an hour for a chance to cross C Street.
Adding to the din, and the babble of many tongues, were the
raucous cries of fruit peddlers, and auctioneers, who were "shouting off the stocks of delinquent investors"; the pounding of quartz-
batteries; and thunderous subterranean blasts in the mines, which
shook the ground, rattling windows, and throwing up great piles of
earth on all sides.

Viewed from a distance, the entire town, built halfway up the
steep, barren slopes of Mt. Davidson (rising 7,200 feet above the
sea), had a slant like a great roof. Each street was a terrace, with a
drop of forty or fifty feet to the one below. Since cross-streets were
infrequent, a person on foot and in a hurry to get from an upper to
a lower level would simply make his way down over the house tops,
saving a half-mile detour. With the boom times, the thoroughfares
were being extended to accommodate the mansions of mining millionaires, while in town the old wooden structures were being replaced by fireproof buildings of red brick.

Money was plentiful as dust, Sam remembered. Every face was
joyous, for every man in town owned feet in at least fifty different
claims, and considered his fortune made. "Think of a city with not
one solitary poor man in it!" Even the streets, surfaced with mine-
tailings, were in a sense paved with silver and gold.

Reporting became lucrative, for every day new claims were
taken up—and it was the custom to run straight to the newspaper
offices, give the reporter forty or fifty feet, get him to go out and
look at the property, and then print something favorable about it.
Sam admitted to getting feet "for lying about somebody's mine."
He claimed to have a trunk almost half full of mining stock, and
whenever he needed a hundred dollars or so, he sold some. Be-

tween times he "hoarded" it, satisfied that the shares would eventually be worth a thousand dollars a foot.

One evening toward the end of October, Clemens and Joe Goodman were having a quiet dinner together at Chauvel's, something they did occasionally. These were times when foolery was set aside and they had serious talks and recited poetry—sometimes their own. Clemens expressed his deepest emotions in poetry, about which little is ever heard. Goodman was already recognized as a poet, and was also an inherent scholar. Later he discovered the key to the Maya glyphs after a seven-year study, enabling him to reconstruct a chronological compilation of the principal events found in the ancient inscriptions. He then wrote a book about his findings, *The Archaic Maya Inscriptions.*

For the rest of his life, Goodman retained a mental picture of Sam reciting some dramatic or moving poem or stanza, his "noble head" thrust back, his blue-gray eyes half-closed, his voice vibrant and soaring with feeling, a lighted cigar held between the fingers of a hand as delicate as a girl's—completely lost in the imagery and rhythm of the lines. These meetings with Goodman revealed a Sam Clemens most of his friends never saw or even suspected was there. The sensitive boy who never forgot the delicate, exotic fragrance of wildflowers on the Missouri prairies, the smell of lichen and rain-washed leaves in the woods, or the dawn chorus of birds—the boy to whom the wail of a spinning-wheel gave such a keen stab of longing it brought tears—had not been left behind. Now there was the equally impressionable and sensitive man capable of writing unfeigned pathos in verse and prose and such sensitive fantasies as the unsung "My Platonic Sweetheart," in which Laura Wright appears as his dream-lover. These qualities were hidden behind a deceptive but genuine delight in burlesque, Rabelaisian humor, and bawdy speech and play.

On that October night, when it was nearly time to go, Joe Goodman spoke of sending Clemens to Carson City to report the proceedings of the second Territorial Legislature, which would convene on November 11. There was an opening, for William Gillespie, who had covered the first legislature for the *Enterprise,* had other commitments. Sam believed he could compensate for his lack of parliamentary knowledge by finding interesting things to tell about the members. Goodman was agreeable, and about November first Sam packed his "carpet-sack," and boarded "Messrs. Carpenter & Hoag's stage" for Carson City.

As always, he welcomed the change. Further, he was eager for a reunion with Mollie Clemens, of whom he was very fond—she was the only member of his family to whom he sent "slathers of love." —In later life, he would reject her just as he did almost everyone but his mother. But now, he chose Mollie as his confessor and confidante, although they were nearly the same age. She apparently never betrayed his trust.

On October 2, Orion had gone to San Francisco to meet the steamer that brought her and their eight-year-old daughter, Jennie, up the coast from the Isthmus, and now they were in Carson. Mollie had arrived at just the right time, for Governor Nye would be absent nearly all the coming year. Orion was then Acting Governor and she was Mrs. Governor Clemens.

"No one on this planet ever enjoyed a distinction more than she enjoyed that one," Sam wrote. Since this placed her at the head of society in the capital, she looked about for a house "commensurate with these dignities." Finding none she persuaded Orion to build. The following year he bought land and put up a two-story clapboard house, "at a cost of twelve thousand dollars," which still stands on North Division Street. When it was finished, "there was no other house in town that could approach this property for style and cost," Sam observed. It became his headquarters whenever he was in Carson, and at such times he was one of the capital's most popular guests.

His first daily reports on legislative proceedings drew sharp criticism in print from Clement T. Rice, whom Sam had known as a miner in Esmeralda. Rice was now local reporter for the rival Virginia City *Daily Union,* and was covering the Legislature's actions for the second time. Experienced, he was quick to point out Sam's ignorance. Although the two were close friends privately and sometimes cruised in company for news, they enjoyed baiting one another in their columns. In his next weekly letter to the *Enterprise* (Sam wrote a daily, unsigned letter reporting on the Legislature, and a weekly signed one, devoted to personalities), he stated that Rice's reports might be technically correct but they were totally untrustworthy, and nicknamed Rice "The Unreliable," signing himself "Reliable." However, he took Rice's censure seriously, and applied to his friend, William Gillespie, who had been chief clerk of the House, for coaching. In evidence that Clemens learned his lesson well, at the end of the session he and Rice received a vote of thanks from the Council for their "full and accurate reports of the proceedings."

"The Unreliable" now began appearing regularly in Clemens' weekly letter, first with only a brief mention: Sam had attended "The Grand Bull Driver's Convention" (fictitious), in Washoe City, and "The Unreliable went also—for the purpose of distorting the facts."

Soon he was featured. Sam attended a party at the house of former California governor J. Neely Johnson, now a Carson City lawyer. "Around nine o'clock the Unreliable came. . . . He had on my fine kid boots, and my plug hat and my white kid gloves (with slices of his prodigious hands grinning through the bursted seams), and my heavy gold repeater, which I had been offered thousands and thousands of dollars for. He took these articles out of my trunk, at Washoe City, about a month ago." The reader was then given a glimpse of the Unreliable at the supper table draining the great bowl of hot whiskey punch (Sam admitted to helping with that), and gorging himself: "First, he ate a plate of sandwiches; then he ate a handsomely iced poundcake; then he ate a roast pig; after that a quantity of blancmange . . . Dishes of brandy-grapes, and jellies . . . and pyramids of fruits, melted away before him. . . ." Next he "planted himself at the piano," and began singing. But "there was no more sense in it, and no more music, than his ordinary conversation. . . . After the Unreliable had finished squawking, I sat down at the piano and sang—however, what I sang is of no consequence to anybody. It was only a graceful little gem from the horse opera"—meaning, of course, the old horse in the wilderness.

This letter to the *Enterprise* is historically important because as soon as the Unreliable walked into the room he "intruded himself" upon Clemens "in his cordial way and said, 'How are you, Mark, old boy?' "—and because Sam closed with the following:

I went to bed at four o'clock. So, having been awake forty-eight
hours, I slept forty-eight, in order to get even again. . . .

> Yours, dreamily,
> *Mark Twain*

In the absence of complete *Territorial Enterprise* files (destroyed
over the years by fire), this appears to be the first of Clemens'
letters to the paper signed with the pen name that was to become
the most famous in American literature.

This letter, headed only "Carson, Saturday night," can be said
with assurance to have been written on January 31, 1863 (a Saturday), for it was published on Tuesday February 3. Since the despatch had to go to Virginia City by the stage, it could not have
arrived in time for the Sunday *Enterprise;* and no paper appeared
on Mondays.

The choice of the Mississippi leadsman's call, "mark twain!"
(two fathoms, or twelve feet), signifying safe water, was both eu-
phonious and fitting for the former pilot. Shortly most of his local
friends were calling him Mark rather than Sam, and he was signing
some of his letters home with his new name. There would come a
time when Mark Twain was known universally, but few had ever
heard of Sam Clemens.

Years later, he invented an elaborate fiction as to how he
adopted Mark Twain, insisting that it was the pen name of Captain
Isaiah Sellers, one of whose river reports he had burlesqued in
May 1859. Clemens wrote that when the news of Sellers' death
reached him, he was in the West, "a fresh, new journalist," in need
of "a *nom de guerre,* so I confiscated the ancient mariner's discarded one. . . ."

A careful search through the New Orleans newspapers for the
period when Sellers was contributing his river reports, and reference to his logbooks, reveal nothing about any pseudonym. Nor
was there any mention of a pen name in the numerous obituary
articles. The captain invariably signed his observations on river
conditions "Isaiah Sellers."

Further, when Sam Clemens adopted "Mark Twain" in January
1863, Captain Sellers was still living.

XV

———○———

WILD OATS

SAM CLEMENS ADMITTED he was not in very good
humor when he wrote his mother and sister on February 16, 1863,
for he wanted "to rush down and take some comfort for a few days,
in San Francisco," but there was no one to substitute for him on
the paper. "I am very well satisfied here. They pay me six dollars a
day, and I make 50 per cent. profit by doing only three dollars'
worth of work." He asked why his family insisted upon showing
his letters to others. "Can't you let me tell a lie occasionally to
keep my hand in for the public, without exposing me?"

But his desire for a change was not satisfied until early May,
when he and Rice, the Unreliable, started by stagecoach over the
mountains, by way of Henness Pass, for San Francisco. It was
Sam's first visit to the Pacific Coast metropolis, where he was already well known through his columns. He and Rice put up at the
Lick House, California's first palatial hotel, which boasted flagged
marble floors, paneling of rare, imported wood, thousand-dollar
chandeliers, and luxurious rooms. Sam (and presumably Rice) had
sold "wild cat" mining ground that had been given him, to finance
the trip. He was getting his salary as well, for he was to correspond
with the *Enterprise.*

He had no sooner arrived than he saw a familiar face: Neil Moss, the son of Hannibal's rich pork-packer. Moss had been a school-mate at Dawson's, although not a member of the gang. He had gone to Yale—"an incomparable distinction"—and had come back with Eastern clothes and Eastern ways, of which the hometown young men made merciless fun. Sam spent every day with Neil for two weeks, but now Moss had gone to the mines of Coso (later Inyo) County, California, to get rich. "He has done everything to make a living, including teaching in a country school," Sam wrote home. By age thirty, however, he had become a drifter in Nevada, "living by mendicancy and borrowed money." Later he disappeared. In Clemens' novel *Pudd'nhead Wilson,* some of Neil's qualities and experiences were given to the supposed "Tom Driscoll," who attended Yale and affected New England manners and dress.

There was also another Hannibal boy in town whom Sam met every day on Montgomery Street—Bill Briggs, his comrade John's oldest brother. Bill is known as the "handsomest & finest looking man in California," Sam told his mother and sister. Unlike Neil Moss, Briggs had been outstandingly successful, for he owned a large "gambling hell" opposite the Russ House, a first-class hotel popular with prosperous miners from Washoe. "I went up with him once to see it." Bill also kept a mistress.

He and Rice were planning to stay ten days to two weeks longer and then return to Virginia City, but they were by no means eager. Sam had already made a wide acquaintance—"at least a thousand people"—many of them San Franciscans but most of them from Nevada, for the California capital was financing the Virginia City and Gold Hill mines. So, as he walked each day down Montgomery Street, the Wall Street of the West, shaking hands with this man and that, it was just like going down Main Street in Hannibal. He reported home:

"We fag ourselves out every day, and go to sleep without rocking, every night. We dine out, & lunch out, and we eat, drink and are happy—as it were. After breakfast, I don't often see the hotel again until midnight—or after. I am going to the Dickens mighty fast. . . . We take trips across the Bay to Oakland, and down to San Leandro, and Alameda, and those places . . . and Hayes Park, and Fort Point, and up to Benicia; and yesterday we were invited out on a yachting excursion, & had a sail in the fastest yacht on the Pacific Coast." Sundays they often took the Mission Railroad out to the "Willows," a popular resort in the city, which had lawns, flowers, a dancing pavilion, merry-go-round, aviary, sea-lion pond, and a zoo, all set amongst shady groves along a winding stream. There was also a hotel which served fine refreshments. "Ah me! Summer girls and summer dresses, and summer scenes at the 'Willows'," Sam sighed. "Rice says: 'Oh, no—*we* are not having any fun, Mark—Oh, no, I reckon not—it's somebody else—it's probably the 'gentleman in the wagon!' (popular slang phrase)."

He and a "gentleman" rode the horse-drawn omnibus from Portsmouth Square to Ocean House, at Seal Point. From the balcony they looked down on the breakers, and gazed through binoculars at the sea lions on the rocks and at ships on the horizon. The specialty of the House was fried Eastern oysters, and its bar was famous for mixed drinks. After lunch, Clemens removed his shoes and walked along the beach, letting the surf flow over his feet. It reminded him of that time ten years ago in New York, when he had done the same thing on the Atlantic shore; "& then I had a proper appreciation of the vastness of this country —for I had traveled from ocean to ocean. . . ."

One night, Rice insisted they go to the Bella Union Melodeon on Washington Street, just off Portsmouth Square, the old city's hub, to see the variety show. It was supported entirely by Washoe patronage, he told his *Enterprise* readers. On stage were several "gentlemen" and half a dozen "lovely and blooming damsels with the largest ankles you ever saw," dressed "like so many parasols." The songs, dances, jokes, and conundrums were received with "rapturous applause."

Already, the daily *Call* had asked him to correspond from Virginia City, which he intended to do if it will pay enough. But then, "the pay is only a 'blind'—I'll correspond anyhow. If I don't know how to make such a thing pay me—if I don't know how to levy black-mail on the mining companies,—who does, I should like to know?" he wrote home.

"Ma, I have got five twenty-dollar greenbacks—the first of that kind of money I ever had. I'll send them to you—one at a time," in case of loss in the mail. "I have been mighty neglectful about remittances heretofore, Ma, but when I return to Virginia, I'll do better. I'll sell some wildcat every now & then, & send you some money. Enclosed you will find one of the rags I spoke of—a ratty-looking animal . . ." Each letter afterward, through August 5, contained a notation on the first page: "$20 enclosed."

In his June 4 letter, he regretted that the visit to San Francisco, although far longer than expected, was gradually drawing to a close. The thought of returning to the "snows and deserts of Washoe after living in this Paradise," would be like going back to prison. During these weeks "I have lived like a lord—to make up for two years of privation." He had written only two letters to the *Enterprise,* for there was always something "more agreeable on hand"—for instance, Frank Mayo in *Romeo and Juliet,* Lotta Crabtree, the blackface minstrels, and Italian opera—where just that night he was sure he had seen Bill Nash of the Hannibal family. Although Sam had not seen him in a long while, he recalled, "I never forget faces."

He still had not torn himself away from the city by June 20. That day, he wrote Orion about his mining speculations, indicating he was not staying in the city solely for pleasure. He told about trading his Emma stock for Echo which was on the main Gold Hill lead, at the rate of five feet for one. "I have played my cards with a stiff upper lip since my arrival here—sometimes flush, sometimes dead broke & in debt—have spent eight hundred dollars, & sent Ma two hundred—was strapped day before yesterday, but I'm on the upper side of the wheel again to-day, with twelve hundred dollars in the bank & out of debt—nine-tenths of it will be invested to-morrow." Through it all, he had kept a strict watch on Echo, and whenever "money was to be spent in order to get into anybody's good graces or gain a point in the way of information, I have spent it, like a lord, & trusted to get even again. Oh, I tell you I'm *on it.* . . ."

He was back in Virginia City by July 5, the date of his first letter to the San Francisco *Call,* which described the journey home. Shortly, a letter came from his mother, questioning him closely about his accounts of high living and of going rapidly to the deuce in the city. He replied, "Ma, you are slinging insinuations at me again. Such as 'where did I get the money,' and 'The company I

Wild Oats

kept' in San Francisco." Why, he had sold feet that had been given him, "& my credit was always good at the bank for two or three thousand dollars, & is yet. I *never* gamble in any shape or manner, and I never drink anything stronger than claret or lager beer, which conduct is regarded as miraculously temperate in this country. As for my company, Ma, I went into the very best society to be found in San Francisco, & to do that I had to keep myself pretty straight." Mrs. John B. Winters, of Virginia City, whose husband was a congressman, was a good friend while he was in San Francisco. He liked her because she reminded him of Pamela, and had taken her regularly to church. In Virginia City, "I also move in the best Society, & actually have a *reputation* to preserve. . . .

"I manage to make a living, but if I had any business tact, the office of reporter would be worth $30,000 a year." He was referring to those mining stocks given to him in return for favorable publicity, or to prevent unsavory disclosures. However, he was counting on getting no more than four to five thousand by this system, for he was careless and either tossed the stock into his trunk and forgot it was there when the price had risen, or else he misplaced it. The memory of one such instance was vexing: if he had paid attention and sold the stock when it was first given to him, he would have netted ten thousand dollars; now, it had dropped to nothing. "I don't think I am any account, anyhow. . . . I don't care a straw for myself, but I ought to have had more thought for you. Never mind, though, Ma—I will be more careful in the future. I will take care that your expenses are paid—SURE." He signed this letter, "Mark."

On August 5, he wrote home that he had been burned out ten days before in a disastrous fire. He had saved nothing but the clothes he was wearing, and had lost a "couple of handsome suits" he had had made in San Francisco. But he was fortunate in other ways, for Mrs. Leonard Ferris, wife of the probate judge, had offered him the use of her spare rooms, free of charge. She normally rented them for $250 a month. Sam was looking forward to living in considerable style for a time. He had had another stroke of good luck when a man he had never seen before came up to him on the street, and presented him with some "feet," which he promptly sold for two hundred dollars and "fitted myself out again half as good as new."

He worked no more than two hours a day, he wrote, "but then I am busy all the time, gadding about, you know,—consequently I don't expect to write you very often. You can hear from me by the paper," for the *Enterprise* was being sent to them regularly.

That very evening Sam had seen Orion at Maguire's New Opera House. With typical forgetfulness, his brother had left letters from home at Carson. The theater had just opened with a performance of Bulwer-Lytton's comedy *Money*. The "Beautiful Miss Julia Dean" had the lead. During the play, there was "considerable agitation visible in the fairer portions of the audience, and among the cast," the *Enterprise* reported, when a "Washoe Zephyr," sweeping up the canyon, "rained a shower of gravel stones upon the rear of the new building which creaked in the tempest like a ship at sea." Many feared that the opening and closing of Maguire's would occur the same evening.

Mention of Orion reminded Sam of the "fearful lecture" on the subject of "dissipation" his brother had delivered by letter. Sam mentioned it only because he knew Orion would have already alerted the family. By protesting to Jane Lampton and Pamela, "I don't dissipate & never expect to," he hoped to forestall the inevitable cross-examination by his mother. "He will learn after a while, perhaps, that I am not an infant, that I know the value of a good name as well as he does, & stop writing such childish nonsense to me."

Sam admittedly subscribed to the practice of sowing wild oats as the surest way to make the future man "steady, reliable, *wise*, thoroughly fitted for this life," and equal to its "emergencies."

Not long after he arrived in Carson City from across the Plains, he gave his views on a woman's role in marriage. For himself he wanted a wife who would be a companion, and he would not consider marriage until he could afford servants to free her from all other demands on her time. "I don't want to sleep with a three-fold Being who is cook, chambermaid and washerwoman all in one. I don't mind sleeping with female servants as long as I am a bachelor—by *no* means—but *after* I marry, that sort of thing will be 'played out,' you know."

Wild Oats

These words come as no surprise from such a normal, virile young man as Sam Clemens, who was strongly attracted to girls and young women (and they to him) ever since he was in first grade at Mrs. Horr's school, and that "lovely little blue-eyed creature," Laura Hawkins, became the first in a long procession of sweethearts. His admission, however, becomes extremely important in view of the long-held belief by many Clemens students that he was virgin when he married at age thirty-four.

The mores of his social group forbid sexual relations with any of those young women he met through family and friends, until marriage. Servant girls and chambermaids were always at hand in the lodging houses and hotels where Clemens stayed during his years as a roving journeyman printer, and as pilot. There were no servants except possibly Indians, in such mining camps as Aurora and Unionville, but prostitutes "abounded," according to first-hand accounts. What Clemens' personal experience with them may have been can only be conjectured because he left no record. However, circumstances, sexual drive, and the fact that he was drinking heavily after he became a reporter and his better judgment was often blurred, and that most of the newsmen with whom he cruised nightly were regular customers of the whorehouses, suggest that Sam was familiar with them as places one went not just to get items for the local column.

The greatest significance of his admission to sleeping with servant girls is the knowledge that he did not enter marriage with inhibitions or any abnormality, which abstention from sexual activity all those years would imply.

On July 31, Nevada's first steam press went into operation in the *Enterprise*'s own building. This called for a round-the-clock celebration by editors, reporters, compositors, and friends, while the work of putting the paper together went on. For Sam, the result of overwork and over-indulgence in food and drink was a "desperate" cold, which settled in his head and then in his chest. He went to bed, and Clement Rice, the Unreliable, offered to write his local items for him. The first morning Clemens' suspicions were aroused when he saw his column headed "Apologetic." He read:

"It is said, 'an open confession is good for the soul.' We have been on the stool of repentance for a long time, but have not before had the moral courage to acknowledge our manifold sins and wickedness. We confess to this weakness." Upon "our bended marrowbones—we ask forgiveness" of the host ridiculed "from behind the shelter of our reportorial position." Among those victims were the two *Daily Union* reporters, one of them the Unreliable. "We feel that no apology we can make begins to atone for the many insults we have given them. Towards these gentlemen we have been as mean as a man could be—and we have always prided ourself on this base quality." If tomorrow "we . . . get in the same old way again . . . this confession stands."

Sam found the strength to send off a prompt reply: "We are to blame for giving 'the Unreliable' an opportunity to misrepresent us, and therefore refrain from repining to any great extent at the result. We simply claim the right *to deny the truth* of every statement made by him in yesterday's paper, to annul all apologies he coined as coming from us, and to hold him up to the public commiseration as a reptile endowed with no more intellect, no more cultivation, no more Christian principle than animates and adorns the sportive jackass rabbit of the Sierras. We have done."

He returned to work, but the cold was stubborn. He coughed "incessantly," and had a "voice like a bullfrog." Reminiscent of his father's searches for relief from his chronic chest disorders, Sam decided on a change of climate. He "seduced" Adair Wilson, a Missouri boy who reported for the *Daily Union,* from his labors and together they boarded a Pioneer coach and "flew up" to Lake Tahoe, "alongside of Hank Monk, the king of stage drivers." But Sam failed to improve, he wrote his mother and sister, for the Lake House at Hobart, on the east shore, was crowded with the "wealth and fashion of Virginia," and he could not resist "the temptation to take a hand in all the fun going. Those Virginians—men & women both—are a stirring set. . . . We sailed and hunted and fished and danced all day, and I doctored my cold all night . . . I found if I went with them on all their eternal excursions, I should bring the consumption home with me—so I left." By that time, he had succeeded in "toning down" his voice from a croak to an "impalpable whisper." A number of those "stirring" Virginians had pooled resources and bought acreage for a town beside the lake, and before Sam left they gave him a lot. When Jane Lampton and Pamela come West, he told them, he will build them a house on it. Tahoe seemed to him "more supernaturally beautiful" than ever. "It is the masterpiece of the Creator."

This letter was being written from Steamboat Springs, a health resort located ten miles from Virginia City, where Sam went to cure his resistant cold with a regimen of scalding steam, icy showers, and rub-downs which left one's "hide" glowing "like a parlor carpet." "The hot, white steam puffs up out of fissures in the earth like the jets that come from a steamboat's 'scape pipes, & it makes a boiling, surging noise like a steamboat, too—hence the name." Sam put eggs in a handkerchief and dipped them in the springs: in two minutes they were soft boiled, and were hard as a rock in four. Baths, board, and lodging were to be had for twenty-five dollars a week, which was cheaper than living in Virginia City without baths.

In his *Enterprise* letter written from the Springs, Sam undertook (doubtless at the proprietor's request), to correct the mistaken impression that the spa, with its hospital, was created solely for the "salvation of persons suffering from venereal diseases." True, the fame of the baths rested chiefly on the "miracles" worked on such patients, but it had been shown that all other ailments, except "consumption," had been treated successfully. He made specific mention of cures for people with rheumatism and erysipelas.

When he spoke of erysipelas, it certainly revived memories of the time when he was six, and his four-year-old brother, Henry, was recovering from that disease, for there was an incident connected with it that assumed increasing importance with passing years. Henry's skin was peeling, and the dead tissue from one of his heels came off in a single piece, the shape of a cup. For some reason, Sam wanted it, but it clung by a single shred, and Henry complained whenever he tried to pull it. But one day, Sam boldly gave it a jerk, it came off, and Henry cried loudly. This, of course, called attention to the act, and Sam was punished. When he was seventy, he placed that occurrence at the head of a list of "accidents" he was compiling which he considered responsible for the important steps in his life. "Accident is a word which I constantly make use of when I am talking to myself about the chain of incidents which has constituted my life."

Sam's cold furnished material for a sketch entitled "How to Cure a Cold," published first in the *Enterprise,* and reprinted on September 20 in San Francisco's *Golden Era,* that sprightly literary journal on which Joe Goodman had taken his first job as a typesetter. In the squib Sam claimed that nearly everyone he met suggested some infallible remedy: plain gin, gin with molasses, gin with onions, hot foot-baths, cold showers, wet sheets, a quart of warm water, taken internally; and a wine glass of molasses, aquafortis, turpentine, "and various other things," to be drunk every fifteen minutes. Finally, there was application of the old adage—"feed a cold and starve a fever." Since Sam had both, he stuffed himself, then "kept dark" and let the fever starve. Twelve years later, he thought well enough of this piece to include it in his collection, *Sketches New and Old.*

His mother had written him that if he worked hard and attended closely to his business, he might aspire to a place on a big San Francisco daily some day. He replied, "Ma, you have given my vanity a deadly thrust. Behold, I am prone to boast of having the widest reputation as a local editor, of any man on the Pacific coast. . . . There's a comment on human vanity for you! Why, blast it, I was under the impression that I could get such a situation as that any time I asked for it. But I don't want it. No paper in the United States can afford to pay me what my place on the 'Enterprise' is worth. If I were not naturally a lazy, idle, good for nothing vagabond, I would make it pay me $29,000 a year. But I don't . . . care a cent whether school keeps or not. Everybody knows me, & I fare like a prince wherever I go, be it on this side of the mountains or the other. And I am proud to say I am the most conceited ass in the Territory."

He had sent her a picture he had had made in San Francisco. "You think that picture looks old? Well, I can't help it—in reality I am not as old as I was when I was eighteen."

He left the Springs for Virginia City on August 23, 1863, but was back in "paradise" (San Francisco) less than two weeks later. On his departure, Dan De Quille, who would now have the locals all to himself, announced that "the moral tone of this column will be much improved."

Clemens' first letter to the *Enterprise* from San Francisco opened with a lively account of his trip as an outside passenger seated next to the stage-driver, who kept him awake with chilling tales of death for those who on past trips had gone to sleep and fallen overboard, breaking their necks.

This was followed by a review of *Mazeppa,* a play based on Byron's poem, in which the leading role was taken by the actress-poet, Adah Isaacs Menken. Male audiences were going "crazy" over her performance as a young Polish nobleman who, detected in an affair with the wife of a politically powerful citizen, was punished by being stripped naked and bound to the back of a wild horse, which was then lashed into madness and sent racing off into mountain wilderness. Everyone in town was talking about that one sensational scene; in fact, Clemens found, they were talking about little else. Descriptions of her beautiful body, her "matchless grace, her supple gestures, her charming attitudes," were on every man's tongue, and had traveled over the Sierras to Washoe. But they would have to wait until "la Menken" had played the part sixty times at $500 a performance before she appeared in Nevada, Sam warned.

Knowing how eager his readers were for details, he titled his piece provocatively, "The Menken—Written Especially for Gentlemen." He then took perverse delight in exasperating them by being vague and devoting almost as much space to the horse as to the naked woman. He had been *told* that she was not really nude, but was dressed in thin, flesh-colored tights from head to toe, but he could not *vouch* for this because he had no opera glass. On the other hand, so far as he could see, she seemed to be wearing only one garment—"a thin, tight white linen one, of unimportant dimensions . . . indispensable to infants of tender age. I suppose any young mother can tell you what it is, if you have the moral courage to ask. . . ." After this circumlocution to avoid the word "diaper," he similarly shunned using "naked" by saying that the Menken "dresses like the Greek Slave," an allusion to Hiram Powers' famous and controversial statue of a naked woman.

He did at length get around to saying that she was "finely formed." Only her legs did not satisfy him. Down to the knees, she was "an exceptional Venus." And her acclaimed "suppleness" was true, for he had seen her bend herself back like a bow, and pitch headlong at the atmosphere like a battering-ram, and work her arms, legs, and whole body like a "dancing jack."

He next described at length the "fiery untamed steed . . . the fierce old circus horse," led on stage by "a subordinate Pole," who stirred him up "occasionally to run away," and then hung on to him "like death to keep him from doing so." Mazeppa was strapped to his back, "fore and aft, and face uppermost, and the horse goes cantering up-stairs over the painted mountains, through the tinted clouds of theatrical mist, in a brisk and exciting way, with the wretched victim unconsciously digging her heels into his hams to make him go faster. Then a tempest of applause bursts forth, and the curtain falls." When it rises again, the "noble old steed . . . has made his way at last to his dear old home in Tartary down by the footlights, and beholds once more, O gods! the familiar faces of the fiddlers in the orchestra. . . . But poor Mazeppa is insensible—'ginned out' by his trip, as it were. . . . The next day, without taking time to dress—without even borrowing a shirt, or stealing a horse, he starts forth on the fiery untamed, at the head of the Tartar nation, to exterminate the Poles. . . ."

The actor in Clemens was critical of Menken's "vocal delivery" and "extravagant gestures." He believed her reputation rested on her "shape" more than anything else.

He had promised a young woman in Washoe to furnish her and other readers with an account of the latest fashions to be seen at the Lick House. This resulted in four articles written in the best style of the metropolitan society editor, who identified the women mentioned by initials only and who also made lavish use of stilted speech, overworked adjectives, and French phrases to describe materials and parts of dress. The women of Nevada learned that at the recent Lick House ball their own Mrs. A. W. B. (Baldwin), was "arrayed in a sorrel organdy trimmed with fustians and figaros, and canzou fichus, so disposed as to give a splendid effect without disturbing the general harmony of the dress. The body of the robe was of zero velvet, goffered, with a square of pelerine of solferino *poil de chevre* amidships. Her headdress was . . . surmounted by . . . a tasteful tarantula done in jet."

During his stay at the Lick House, he was forced to endure an invasion of unruly children who shouted and raced up and down the halls outside his door at the time of day when he was at work. "Hi, Johnny! look through the keyhole! here's that feller with the long nose, writing again—less stir him up!" Sam quoted them. Born of this experience was a squib, "Those Blasted Children," which he wrote at Carson City on January 9, 1864, and sent to the *New York Sunday Mercury*. However, he must have written about them earlier, while still in San Francisco, for one of his fashion reports written from there was interrupted with—"but there come the children again. —When that last invoice of fifteen-hundred infants come around and get to romping about my door with the others . . . I cannot write with such serene comfort as I do when they are asleep. . . ." Obviously, readers of this piece in *The Golden Era* were already familiar with those "blasted children."

On his return to Virginia City in October 1863, he and Dan De Quille rented two rooms, a bedroom-parlor combination, for which they paid thirty dollars a month, on the third floor of a large brick building at 25 North B Street. Joe Goodman saw to it that the suite was furnished comfortably with a table, chairs, sofa, "splendid carpets," a "huge, elaborately carved black walnut four-hundred dollar" bedstead, and "piles of bedding." Sam said to Dan that since Goodman had been "so keen to do the ordering, just let him foot the bill." So whenever the furniture man came for his money they referred him to Joe.

"Mark and I agreed well as room-mates," Dan recalled. "Both wanted to read and smoke about the same length of time after getting into bed, and when one got hungry and got up to go down town for oysters the other also became hungry and turned out." Shortly he was writing for *The Golden Era*, "We (Mark and I) have the 'sweetest' little parlor and the snuggest little bedroom . . . all to ourselves. Here we come every night and live—breathe, move and have our being, also our toddies."

They usually found waiting for them on their table, "a fine spread of pie, cake, milk and the like," courtesy of Anna M. Fitch, a writer who lived across the hall. Her husband, Thomas Fitch, was a lawyer, journalist, and politician noted for oratory, who had been wounded in a duel with Joe Goodman. Dan added that "Mrs. Fitch's mince pies were perfection." He then told about the good "dodge" he and Sam had for getting wood to burn. All they had to do when they went out was to leave their door open, and "the fellows that are hired to carry up wood . . . make a mistake nearly every day and pile a lot in our parlor. I never have seen the fellow making these mistakes, but Mark assures me that the wood all gets into our parlor that way. I suppose he was right—it looks very plausible, but lately I've been thinking that it was rather strange that the fellow quit making these mistakes the very day Mark went down to Carson to report the proceedings of the Constitutional Convention . . . and hasn't made a single mistake since."

After a time the menage became noted and the *Gold Hill Daily News* ran an announcement: *"To Be Married.* —Dan De Quille and Mark Twain are to be married shortly. About time."

Domestically they were compatible. Their sense of humor was a strong bond. Even some of the squibs they wrote were remarkably similar in style. Professionally, however, they feuded, and Joe Goodman encouraged them because it enlivened the paper.

The French restaurateur, O. V. Chauvel, was also a proficient swordsman, and gave lessons in fencing and the use of the broadsword at his gymnasium on North C Street. He likewise kept a supply of boxing gloves for those who wanted to practice. It was a very popular place with newspapermen, and every afternoon they took over the gymnasium for an hour or two. Clemens, Joe Goodman, and Dan De Quille were interested only in fencing, and went at once for the foils, whereas Denis McCarthy and Steve Gillis immediately took up the gloves. For Sam the appeal of the sword was a romantic one, having associations with Robin Hood, Ivanhoe, and other tales of chivalry—as well as with pirates.

A rival paper commented that it was "highly amusing" to watch Mark Twain and Dan De Quille in action, for they "sometimes get so terribly in earnest. Then do their blades describe wicked circles, and their nostrils breathe forth wrath. We understand that Dan came out of one of these conflicts minus several buttons and one shirt-sleeve, and that Twain was in an almost equally dilapidated state."

Dan said that Clemens became quite expert with the foils. "In attack he was fiery and particularly dangerous for the reason that one could not watch his eyes," which he habitually kept half-closed. He was not as good in defense, and would always give ground when "hotly pressed."

One afternoon Sam decided to try the gloves and started shadow-boxing with "all the airs of a knight of the prize ring." George Dawson, an English journalist who had recently joined the *Enterprise* staff, prided himself on his own skill as a boxer. He was noted as a hard hitter and few cared to face him. Now, as Clemens started capering around the hall, a perfect mimic, Dawson stopped punching the bag to watch him. Sam seeing that he had an audience, danced up to within a short distance of him, and with eyes narrowed, began working his right arm with the rapidity of a steam piston, aiming his blows at Dawson. Interpreting these gestures as a serious challenge, the Englishman closed the gap and "let one fly straight from the shoulder and 'busted' Mr. Twain on the 'snoot,' sending him reeling—not exactly to grass, but across a bench—with two bountiful streams of 'claret' spouting from his nostrils."

Dawson, "flushed with victory, ran up and against all rules, began pounding him in the head." Steve Gillis and Denis McCarthy rushed over, hauled the Englishman off, and "sternly rebuked him." Sam was raging, and with a string of oaths staggered to his feet and began searching the hall for a club with which to kill Dawson. Persuaded to give up the hunt, Clemens left for home, leaving a trail of blood all the way, according to Dan. An hour later he found Sam in their little parlor sitting before a mirror, applying towels and sponges soaked in "sugar of lead and other cooling lotions." In spite of constant attention, the nose remained red and swollen for many days, and Sam, always sensitive about his nose because of its length, ventured out only after dark to take his place at the office. Dan recalled that he was "quite unamiable" during that period.

He therefore welcomed an assignment from Joe Goodman to report on the mines which were attracting attention around Silver Mountain on Ebbetts Pass. This area was actually in Alpine County, California, but was thought at the time to be located in Nevada. Shortly, Dan treated *Enterprise* readers to a fictitious account of Sam's reception at Silver Mountain: As soon as the stage rolled into town, Clemens looked out the window, and the alert inhabitants catching sight of him raised the cry that a "freak" show had come. The Man with the Big Nose was in the coach. People dropped whatever they were doing and flocked about the vehicle trying to peek inside. At the hotel a great crowd was waiting, and gave three cheers as the Nose stepped out.

By the time Clemens had returned to Virginia City, his nose had about healed, but he was still fuming over Dan's squib. "It wasn't a damned bit smart!" Sam told him. By the time he reached Carson, all the "bums" in town had read the piece and teased him unmercifully, and he was forced to stand treat at the bars to shut them up. He could hardly wait to get his revenge.

That opportunity came within a few days when Dan was thrown from a "vicious Spanish horse" (Clemens); "a fiery steed of Spanish extraction—a very strong extract, too" (De Quille). Dan sprained his knee, and had to spend several days in bed, leaving Sam to do all the locals.

Heading his piece "FRIGHTFUL ACCIDENT TO DAN DE QUILLE," he told how "our time-honored confrere," when coming down the road from American City at the rate of a hundred miles an hour (as stated in the will Dan had made shortly after the accident) he turned a sharp corner and suddenly "hove in sight of a horse standing square across the channel; he signaled for the starboard, and put his helm down instantly, but too late . . . he was swept like an avalanche against the . . . strange craft, . . . wrenched from his saddle and thrown some three hundred yards . . . alighting upon solid ground and bursting himself open from the chin to the pit of his stomach; his head was caved in out of sight. . . . One leg was . . . so torn and mutilated . . . it pulled out when they attempted to lift him into the hearse" sent for him "under the general impression that he might need it."

Aside from these injuries, "he sustained no other damage. They brought some of him home in the hearse, and the balance of him on a dray. . . . Our noble friend is recovering fast, and what is left of him will be around the breweries again today, as usual." The breweries also were favorite places of rendezvous for all newsmen.

Sam's story called for a rejoinder from Dan: "Mark Twain, our confrere and room-mate, a man in whom we trusted . . . wrote such an account of our accident as would lead the public to believe that we were injured beyond all hope of recovery. The next day he tied a small piece of second-hand crape about his hat, and putting on a lugubrious look, went to the Probate Court, and getting down on his knees commenced praying—it was the first time he ever prayed for anything or to anybody—for letters of administration to our estate . . . He had on our only clean shirt and best socks, also was sporting our cane and smoking our meerschaum. . . ."

In the midst of this professional feuding Clemens' social conscience prodded him to inveigh against the practice of mining companies and others, who declared "cooked" dividends when in financial trouble, thereby increasing the value of their stock and allowing their directors the chance to sell out at a profit. The San Francisco papers, the *Bulletin* in particular, were clamoring about Nevada's Daney Mining Company, which had recently declared a false dividend, and were urging the public to sell all Nevada silver stocks and to invest in such safe concerns as the local Spring Valley Water Company. But in the very midst of the outcry, Spring Valley cooked several dividends themselves, and Sam seized the opportunity to write a "scathing satire" on the practice.

He put the piece in the form of a straight news story about a mass murder and a suicide, naming actual persons and places to give it a semblance of truth. The particulars came from Abraham Curry, one of the two original locators of the fabulously rich Gould & Curry mine; a principal founder of Carson City, and a pillar of the community. Everyone respected his word. (He amused Sam by invariably introducing himself to strangers as, "Curry—*Old* Curry —Old *Abe* Curry").

About ten o'clock on Monday evening, October 26, a man known as P. Hopkins, who lived with his wife and nine children in an old log house on the edge of the great pine forest between Empire City and Dutch Nick's, dashed into Carson City on horseback, Sam's story read. His throat was "cut from ear to ear," and in his hand was a "reeking scalp from which the warm, smoking blood was still dripping." He fell in a "dying condition in front of the Magnolia Saloon," and within five minutes had expired without speaking. The long red hair of the scalp identified it as belonging to Mrs. Hopkins. A group of citizens led by Sheriff Gasherie (he who had withheld Sam's commission as deputy in the Aurora days), rode their horses to the Hopkins place, "where a ghastly scene met their gaze."

With evident relish Clemens launched into even more grisly details. "The scalpless corpse of Mrs. Hopkins lay across the threshold, with her head split open and her right hand almost severed from her wrist." Near her lay the weapon—an axe. Six of the children were found in the bedroom, their brains evidently dashed out with a club. Julia and Emma, aged 14 and 17, were discovered in the kitchen, "bruised and insensible, but it is thought their recovery is possible." The oldest girl, Mary, had fled to the garret where she had died from multiple knife wounds, the weapon still sticking in her side.

"Curry says Hopkins was about 42 years of age, and a native of Western Pennsylvania; he was always affable and polite, and . . . we never heard of his ill-treating his family."

The crux had been reached: Hopkins had been "a heavy owner in the best mines of Virginia and Gold Hill, but when the San Francisco papers exposed the game of cooking dividends . . . he grew afraid," sold out and invested an immense sum in the Spring Valley Water Company, having been so advised by one of the editors of the San Francisco *Bulletin*. Then Spring Valley cooked its dividends, its stock fell to nothing, and Hopkins lost his entire investment. Presumably "this misfortune drove him mad and resulted in his killing himself and the greater portion of his family."

The San Francisco newspapers "permitted this water company to go on borrowing money and cooking dividends . . . leaving the crash to come upon poor and unsuspecting stockholders, without offering to expose the villainy at work. We hope the fearful massacre detailed above may prove the saddest result of their silence."

The story struck like a thunderbolt. It was the talk of the entire Territory and was copied in every paper there and all over California. Washoe readers were so fascinated by the gruesome details they failed to notice the discrepancies in fact and the "tell-tale absurdities" which Sam had inserted purposely to mark it as fiction. It did not strike Carson or Virginia City readers as ridiculous to speak of the murderer's family,—when it was common knowledge that the well-known P. (Pete) Hopkins, proprietor of Carson's Magnolia Saloon, was a bachelor—or to locate the murder site on the edge of a great pine forest *between* Empire City and Dutch Nick's, when those were two names for the same place. Further, there was not a single tree within fifteen miles, let alone a forest. The physical impossibility of a man being able to ride his horse four miles with his throat cut from ear to ear failed to impress anyone either. The reader ought to have known that such a wound "would kill an elephant in the twinkling of an eye," Clemens defended himself later.

Anger is the most common reaction of those who have been completely fooled. The San Francisco papers which had printed the report in good faith, were especially angry when they learned it was a hoax. Some threatened to make no more exchanges with the *Enterprise* as long as that fellow Mark Twain remained on the staff. Others berated him for "bringing the high mission of journalism into disrepute," and demanded his immediate discharge. Locally he was in trouble with Pete Hopkins, for having given his name to the murderer, and with "Old *Abe* Curry," for citing him as the story's source.

Sam was so distressed he could not sleep nights. "I am being burned alive on both sides of the mountains," he told Dan, who assured him, "Never mind this bit of a gale; it will soon blow itself out." A week later Clemens' letter from Carson City to the *Enterprise* (he had gone there to cover the Constitutional Convention) mentioned:

"Messrs. Pete Hopkins and A. Curry have compromised with me, and there is no longer any animosity existing on either side. They were a little worried at first, you recollect, about that thing that appeared recently (I think it was in the Gold Hill News), concerning an occurrence . . . in the great pine forest down there at Empire." The *News*, failing to notice the incongruities, had rushed it into print.

On the night of December 11, 1863, the Constitutional Convention adjourned. Directly afterward, at eleven o'clock, in the same hall, what was known as the "Third House," which had been organized the previous year as a travesty on the regular legislature and included many of its members, "met in solemn grandeur." They elected Mr. Mark Twain President of the Convention and Governor of the Third House. He was conducted to the Chair "amid a dense and respectful silence" by James Small, who stepped grandly "over" the desks, and William Hickock, who walked "under them." The President then addressed the house, "taking his remarks down in short-hand as he proceeded: 'Gentlemen—This is the proudest moment of my life. I shall always think so. I think so still. I shall ponder over it with unspeakable emotion down to the latest syllable of recorded time. It shall be my earnest endeavor to give entire satisfaction in the high and bully position to which you have elevated me.' [Applause.]"

He then turned to selecting and swearing officers, among them James Small as Secretary and Peter Hopkins of the Magnolia Saloon as Chief Page. They were called upon to take the oath. "We do solemnly affirm that we have never seen a duel, never been connected with a duel, never heard of a duel, never sent or received a challenge, never fought a duel, and don't want to. . . ." This was a parody of the oath included in the proposed state constitution: ". . . I do . . . solemnly swear . . . that I have never fought a duel, nor sent or accepted a challenge to fight a duel, nor been a second. . . ."

The meeting as reported by Clemens, consisted almost entirely of irrelevant suggestions, comments, and actions by members, and reproofs from the Chair. To Samuel Youngs who was warbling, "For the lady I love will soon be a bride, with a diadem on her brow-ow-ow": "Order, you snuffling old granny! Take—your—seat!"

And, "Mr. Chapin, will you stop catching flies while the Chair is considering the subject of religious toleration. . . ." And, "I observe that Messrs. Wasson and Gibson and Noteware and Kennedy have their feet on their desks. The chief page will proceed to remove those relics of ancient conventional barbarism from sight. . . ."

Sam closed the meeting: "Gentlemen, your proceedings have been exactly similar to those of the convention which preceded you. You have . . . spoken on every subject but the one before the house, and voted without knowing what you were voting for or having any idea what would be the general result of your action. I will adjourn the Convention."

Chief Page Hopkins was then instructed to provide "a spoonful of molasses and a gallon of gin, for the use of the President," who had another heavy cold. He planned to recuperate at the new Logan Hotel on the eastern shore of Lake Tahoe. "I take with me a broken spirit, blighted hopes and a busted constitution. Also some gin." He was "weary of the gay world," and pined for solitude. "I shall return again, after many days, restored to vigorous health; restored to original purity; free from sin, and prepared to accept any lucrative office the people can be induced to force upon me."

His *Enterprise* readers learned that the Logan "stands within fifty feet of the water's edge, and commands a view of all the grand scenery thereabout. It is new, handsomely furnished, and commodious;" its table provides "the best the market affords, and behold they eat trout there every day." It is very accessible—only fifteen miles from Carson by way of the new King's Canyon road—"after which the worn pilgrim may rest in peace in the bosom of Logan & Stewart. That is as good a thing as I want, as long as I am not married." Such a recommendation was certainly rewarded by free room and board.

But his stay was brief, for he was back in Virginia City in time to greet the then-famous Maine humorist, Artemus Ward (the pen name of Charles Farrar Browne), who arrived on December 18 to give his lecture, "Babes in the Wood," which had not the slightest connection with its title. For humor and comic situations in his writings and lectures, Ward depended upon the traits and dialects of Down East and backwoods characters; and on misspellings, mispronounciation, and malapropisms, a style Clemens had experimented with in his Snodgrass letters and had discarded. In his "Greeting to Artemus Ward," Sam gave a sample of Ward's writing. "In his last letter to us he appeared particularly anxious to 'sekure' a kupple ov horned todes; alsowe, a lizard which it may be persessed of 2 tales, or any komical snaix. . . . Could you alsowe manage to gobbel up the skulp of the layte Missus Hopkins? I adore sich footprints of atrocity as it were, muchly. I was roominatin on gittin a bust of mark Twain. . . ."

Clemens added, "We shall assist Mr. Ward in every possible way about making his Washoe collection and have no doubt but he will pick up many curious things during his sojourn."

Ward pretended to be a traveling showman; he intended to remain only a few days, for he was at the peak of his fame and was booked for lectures across the country. But he was so drawn to Clemens, Joe Goodman, Dan De Quille, and the rest of the staff, that he stayed twelve days and made the *Enterprise* office his headquarters. "He would pull off his coat and help them fill the local columns in order that there might be a longer session about the convivial board," Joe Goodman wrote. Dan De Quille remembered that Ward was an entertaining companion, for "everything he saw called forth a joke or quaint saying. His drollery was without effort. . . . He teemed with waggery. . . ." He was fond of delivering in "a solemn and impressive manner," long, involved, and meaningless definitions of such subjects as genius. He tried this on Clemens at a dinner given for Ward by the town's leading citizens at the International Hotel. Ward had made all of Sam's friends party to his intent. After finishing his vague discourse he turned brightly to Sam and asked, "Does my definition not hit the nail squarely on the head, Mr. Clemens?" Fumbling a bit, Sam admitted that he did not fully grasp his meaning. Pityingly, Ward shook his head and began again. When he had finished, Clemens told him, "I am almost ashamed to say it, but to tell the truth, I was not able to catch your exact meaning."

"Well, perhaps I was not sufficiently explicit. What I wished to say was simply that genius is a sort of illuminating quality of the mind inherent in those of constitutionally inflammable natures whose conceptions are not of that ambiguous and disputable kind which may be said—"

"Hold on, Artemus," Sam interrupted, "it is useless for you to repeat your definition. The wine, or the brandy, or the whisky . . . has gone to my head. Tell it to me some other time; or, better still, write it down . . . and I'll study it at my leisure." Dan De Quille recalled that at this point Sam's friends were ready to explode with suppressed laughter. This experience furnished Clemens with the subject for a sketch, "First Interview with Artemus Ward."

It devolved upon Sam and Dan to show Artemus the town. They

took him on an underground tour of the Comstock mines, and to a celebration in Chinatown where they drank plentifully of "fiery" rice brandy and narrowly missed being shot when trouble broke out between rival tongs. They went to hear the Cornish singers, and afterward took Ward along when they "ran" after news, stopping for drinks at all their favorite saloons, for Ward had an unquenchable thirst. They went into one of the hurdy-gurdy houses, a new experience for Ward, and after he had been there a few minutes, he said to them, "Now, we three have got to have a dance together. It'll be a thing our offspring to the furthest generation will be proud of!"

Selecting three of the handsomest girls as partners, they danced to the "unbounded admiration of a large and enthusiastic audience." When they left, Ward threw a twenty-dollar gold piece on the bar to pay for the girls and for drinks. Close to dawn they wove their unsteady way back to the rooms Sam and Dan shared, all three tumbling into the huge carved bed: "Three saints—Mark, Luke and John," Ward mumbled hazily.

He and Clemens also had some serious talks over glasses (or bottles) of sparkling Moselle, Sam's favorite wine, times when Ward encouraged him to seek an audience in the East. Sam knew he was right, for as he wrote his mother and sister immediately after Artemus had left, "I sometimes throw a pearl before these swine here (there's no self-conceit about that, I beg you to observe) which ought, for the eternal welfare of my race to have a more extensive circulation than is offered by a local daily paper."

Fitzhugh Ludlow, who had won acclaim and notoriety for his book *The Hasheesh Eaters,* based on his own experiences as an addict, had published in *The Golden Era* "a high encomium of Mark Twain (the same being eminently just and truthful, I beseech you to believe)" Sam continued in his letter home. Ludlow had said: "In funny literature, that Irrepressible Washoe Giant, Mark Twain, takes a unique position. . . . He imitates nobody. He is in a school by himself."

Ward had pointed out that when Sam's "gorgeous talents" were publicly acknowledged by such a high authority as Ludlow, he ought to appreciate them himself, "leave sage-brush obscurity," and accompany him (Artemus) to New York. But Sam was reluctant to burst too suddenly upon the New York public, and decided to remain where he was. In that case, Ward told him, he would write "a powerfully convincing note" to his friends on the New York *Sunday Mercury*. Clemens did agree, however, to accompany Ward to Europe the following May or June.

In spite of claims to the contrary, the extent of Ward's influence on Sam Clemens was to appreciate his own talents more and to broaden his horizon, which was important. But stylistically, he had nothing to offer the man who was soon to become a master of timeless humor of almost universal appeal. Few today have even heard of Artemus Ward.

Ward spent his final days at Virginia City in feverish activity and celebration with those congenial souls he had found there. As though in an awareness of the brief time left him in life he was attempting to fill every hour with exhilarating experiences. (Three years later, he died of tuberculosis and alcohol addiction, in London. He was just thirty-three.)

On Christmas Eve, Ward lectured in Silver City, five miles from Virginia City. About midnight, he came to the *Enterprise* office and invited everyone present to an oyster supper after the paper was put together. It was about two o'clock when he piloted them to Chauvel's—Joe Goodman, Sam, Dan, and Denis McCarthy. "Course succeeded course and wine followed wine, until day began to break." Goodman remembered that the mountain peaks were touched with a pale light as they came out into the street. Ward was animated: "I can't walk on the earth; I want to walk in the skies— but as I can't, I'll walk on the roofs."

Unsteadily he climbed to the top of a shed, then onto the steeply pitched roof of the first house, with Sam and Dan following. Up one side they clambered over frosty shingles, and down the other they slid. If houses were close enough, they jumped from one to another—a "noisy wild scramble from roof to roof." Suddenly, there was a shouted command:

"Halt there or I shoot!" They saw the watchman with his pistol aimed in their direction. He kept them covered until they climbed down and marched up to him as ordered. Explanations followed and as soon as he learned their names, he put down his gun and advised them to go home. Gratefully Ward handed him a fistful of tickets to his next lecture.

Just as the sun rose above the desert range and gilded the slopes of Mt. Davidson, it illuminated a scene in front of Fred Goetzler's saloon on C Street. There astride a recumbent wine barrel sat Sam Clemens. Artemus Ward was feeding him mustard with a spoon and asking bystanders if they had "ever seen a more perfect presentation of a subjugated idiot."

A night or two later, as the final dinner party drew to a close, farewells were said in the form of toasts, and parting gifts given, for Artemus was leaving town after that night's lecture. One of the presents was "a toy rabbit of the jackass persuasion—swathed in sage-brush," to be preserved as a specimen of Washoe's resources. Another was a sizable demijohn filled with liquid comfort. His friends left Ward to go and give his talk. He tried to persuade Clemens to come with him, but Sam was drunk. Instead of going directly to the theater, Artemus stopped for drinks along the way and "got drunker, beating, I may say, Alexander the Great in his most drinkinest days." He then proceeded to the Melodeon, blackened his face, and made a "gibbering, idiotic speech. God-damit!," he told Sam in a letter (he greeted Sam as "My Dearest Love") written on New Year's Day from Austin, Nevada, where he was to speak that night. He supposed the Virginia City Daily *Union* would make a big thing out of his fiasco—but let it slide. "I shall remember Virginia as a bright spot in my existence." Soon, he would write the promised letter to his friends on the *Sunday Mercury*. He then inserted one of the irrelevant paranthetical remarks for which he was noted. "[Why would you make a good artillery man? Because you are familiar with Gonorrhea (gunnery.) How's that?]"

He hoped to see Sam in New York. "My mother—my sweet mother—she, thank God, is too far advanced in life to be affected by your hellish wiles. My aunt—she, might fall. But didn't Warren fall at Bunker Hill?" He sent his love to Joe Goodman and Dan. For Clemens it was "Goodbye, old boy—and God bless you!" He signed himself, "Faithfully, gratefully yours."

Early in January Sam wrote and asked his mother to be sure to invite Ward to the house when he reached St. Louis, and "treat him well, for behold, he is a good fellow. But don't ask him too many questions about me & Christmas Eve, because he might tell tales out of school."

XVI

FAREWELL TO WASHOE

On February 7, 1864, Sam Clemens made his debut as Mark Twain in the New York *Sunday Mercury*. Artemus Ward had sent a "flattering letter" to the editors, Sam told his mother, and he was going to write for the paper "semi-occasionally." His first piece, "Doings in Nevada," was a lighthearted treatment of the political scene in the Territorial capital where a constitution for the future State had just been framed. "It was an excellent piece of work in some respects, but it had one or two unfortunate defects which debarred it from assuming to be an immaculate conception. . . .

"We do not fool away much time in this country." No sooner was the constitution framed, than a convention had met at Carson City to nominate candidates for State offices. "Now, that ticket will be elected, but the constitution won't. In that case, what are we to do with those fellows. We cannot let them starve. They are on our hands and are entitled to our charity and protection."

He proposed that the *Mercury* "put in a little advertisement for me . . . and it would be a real kindness to me if you would be so good as to call attention to it in your editorial columns. You see I am a sort of orphan away out here, struggling along on my own hook, as it were. My mother lives in St. Louis. She is sixty years of age, and a member of the Presbyterian Church. She . . . don't rush around much in society, now. However I do not ask any man's sympathy on that account. . . ."

Among the candidates he listed as being "For Sale Or Rent" was Orion Clemens, who was on the slate for Secretary of State: "An old, experienced hand at the business. Has edited a newspaper, and been Secretary and Governor of Nevada Territory—consequently, is capable; and also consequently, will bear watching; is not bigoted—has no particular set of religious principles—nor any other kind." Sam enjoyed imagining his mother's reaction to these statements. The advertisement concluded: "Also, a large and well-selected assortment of State Legislators, Supreme Judges, Comptrollers, and such gimcracks, handy to have about a State Government, all of which are for sale or rent on the mildest possible terms. . . . For further particulars, address Mark Twain, Carson, N.T."

On January 9, he wrote to his mother and sister from Carson City. It was two in the afternoon and he had only just gotten up, he said, but then, he had not gone to bed until seven that morning, for he was finishing another story for the *Mercury*. They must watch for it on a Sunday soon after his letter arrived, and be sure to tell Beck Jolly to get copies and "stick them around everywhere there is any one acquainted with Zeb Leavenworth," for the article contained a testimonial letter purportedly from Leavenworth. This at once identifies the sketch as "Those Blasted Children," which contains just such a letter from Zeb attesting to the effectiveness of "Mr. Mark Twain's . . . sovereign remedy" to cure a child of stuttering by removing the lower jaw. The very day the pilot learned of it, "I sawed off my Johnny's under-jaw. May Heaven bless you, noble Sir. It afforded instant relief; and my Johnny has never stuttered since." The piece was printed in the *Mercury* on February 21.

As Governor of the Third House, Sam was expected to deliver his annual message before the assembled members. The date was set for Wednesday evening, January 27, in the District Courtroom. Clement T. Rice, the Unreliable, reported the affair for the *Daily Union*. "Last night a large and fashionable audience was called out to hear a message delivered by the Mark Two—otherwise called

Twain. Indeed, this was the resuscitation of the celebrated Third House, or rip-snorting gymnasium, prepared for the benefit of outsiders who must orate or bust. Hal. Clayton assumed the chair, and the levities spread spontaneously. . . .''

Sam reported on it himself in the *Enterprise:* "I delivered that message last night, but I didn't talk loud enough. . . . I had never talked to a crowd before, and knew nothing of the tactics of the public speaker. . . . Some folks heard the entire document, though—there is some comfort in that. Hon. Mr. Clagett, Speaker Simmons of the inferior House, Hon. Hal Clayton, . . . Judge Haydon, Dr. Alban, and others whose opinions are entitled to weight, said they would travel several miles to hear that message again. It affords me a good deal of satisfaction to mention it. It serves to show that if the audience could have heard me distinctly, they would have appreciated the wisdom thus conferred upon them. They seemed to appreciate what they did hear though, pretty thoroughly. After the first quarter of an hour I ceased to whisper, and became audible. . . .''

In a letter to Pamela Sam told her that he could not send her his Message for "it was written to be *spoken*—to write it so it would *read* well, would be too much trouble, & I shall probably never publish it. It was terribly severe on Gov. Nye, too, & since he has conferred on me one of the coveted Notarial appointments (without the formality of a *petition* from the people,) it would be a mean return to print it now." He had had his satisfaction out of it, however, for there was a larger audience than Artemus Ward had drawn. "The comfort of knowing that the slow-going, careless population of Carson could be induced to fill a house *once,*—The gratification of hearing good judges say it was the best thing of the kind they had ever listened to—& finally, a present of a handsome $225⁰⁰ gold watch, &c &c. I am ahead on the Message, anyhow."

In this letter Sam enclosed for his niece Annie (now twelve), a full-length picture showing his "excellency Gov. Mark Twain, of the Third House, Hon. Wᵐ H. Clagett of the House of Representatives [Billy had been sent by the Humboldt district], and Hon. A. J. Simmons, Speaker of the same. Ma will know Clagett by his frowsy hair & slovenly dress. He is the ablest speaker in the Territory."

The photograph shows Clagett wearing a shirt several sizes too

large, with a turndown collar and a generous cravat knotted and
flowing in streams down an expanse of vestless shirt-front stuffed
with many folds into his jeans. The trouser cuffs are turned up,
revealing his heavy mining boots.

Sam had mentioned to Pamela his appointment as a notary. In
January, the legislature was considering an act to limit the number
of notaries a governor could appoint, for those lucrative positions
(every mining transaction had to be notarized, for a fee) were much
coveted and sought after. Many had been granted indiscriminately,
most often as political rewards. Consequently, there were many
abuses, and countless errors owing to ignorance. Representative
Billy Clagett reported that there was hardly a valid deed on record
in his district. He supposed that mining property worth millions
had already been lost or was in jeopardy. The bill proposed to
remove all present notaries and appoint seventy-two new ones for
the Territory's ten counties, and six more for each county that
might be created. This, Clemens informed his *Enterprise* readers in
a report on the situation, would leave Storey County, where the
capital was, twelve notaries in place of the "fifteen hundred" there
presently.

As a journalist active on the political front, Sam Clemens had
become an influential figure. He was perceptive, fearless, and outspoken. When he saw a bill that must be defeated he attacked it
mercilessly; to those measures he knew must be passed because
they offered universal benefits to the people, he gave unqualified
support. In either case he relied on ridicule and burlesque.

"I was a mighty heavy wire-puller at the last Legislature," he
wrote home. "I passed every bill I worked for. . . ." He favored
the bill to limit notaries and define their duties, and not only
supported it in his daily legislative reports but wrote a piece, "Concerning Notaries," which appeared in the *Enterprise* on February 9
and was reprinted in *The Golden Era*. With the appointment of all
new notaries, there was naturally a mad rush of office-seekers, but
in his report from Carson he affected amazement:

A strange, strange thing occurred here yesterday, to wit:
A MAN APPLIED FOR A NOTARY'S COMMISSION.
Think of it. Ponder over it. He wanted a notarial commission—

he said so himself. . . . He brought his little petition along with him. He brought it on two stages. It is voluminous. The County Surveyor is chaining it off. Three shifts of clerks will be employed night and day on it, deciphering the signatures and testing their genuineness. . . .

Since writing the above, I have discovered that the foregoing does not amount to much as a sensation item, after all. The reason is because there are seventeen hundred and forty-two applications for notaryships already on file in the Governor's office. I was not aware of it, you know. There are also as much as eleven cords of petitions stacked up in his back yard. A watchman stands guard over this combustible material—the back yard is not insured.

—He was not exaggerating excessively, for there were more than a thousand petitions.

In his account he told of going downtown and being accosted first by strangers who recognized him and, knowing his influence, asked him to sign their petitions, then by people he knew—Chief Justice Turner on his way to the governor's office with a petition in his hand; and William Stewart, council for all the big mining companies; and A. W. (Sandy) Baldwin, Stewart's partner; and Representative John B. Winters; and Rufus Arrick, Mayor of Virginia City; and Ah Foo and Hong Wo; and Wells, Fargo. Sam examined their documents and promised to use his influence. "I also drank with them."

Toward the end of the afternoon, Sam fell victim to the "fatal distemper," wrote out his application in "frantic haste," attaching to it in place of signatures a copy of the Nevada Directory, and fled down the deserted streets to join the throng pressing toward the governor's house.

Sam had written Pamela that the notarial appointment was conferred on him by the governor without the formality of a petition. It is probable that the idea originated with Orion, for he signed the application. Possibly this was one of those surprises in which he delighted. Whatever Sam's opinion of the office may have been (he received it about March 1), he sent in his resignation to Acting Governor Orion Clemens on April 14, having kept it only a little more than a month.

Five days after Clemens gave his Third House address, Jennie, the only child of Orion and Mollie, died at the age of eight. She became sick on Thursday morning, January 28, with what was diagnosed as "Spotted Fever." She died at sundown on February first. Sam was at Orion's house during the crisis and was the first to write of it to their mother. Jane Lampton replied with a letter addressed "To my dear children," and said of her namesake: "Jennie was an uncommon smart child, she was a very handsome child, but I never thought you would raise her, she was a heaven-born child. She was two [sic] good for this world."

The legislature adjourned to attend Jennie's funeral at ten o'clock on the morning of February third. As Sam climbed the bleak, sagebrush-covered hill to Lone Mountain Cemetery, his thoughts must have flashed back to Hannibal's equally forlorn and desolate burying-ground, when he had trudged up that hill first to his brother Benjamin's grave, then to his father's, and finally to the beloved Henry's.

In his *Enterprise* letter, dated two days after Jennie's funeral, Sam blasted the one local undertaker, who had a monopoly because he also owned the only respectable cemetery. He was therefore able to take unfair advantage of those who lost a husband, wife, child, or mother, and "extort ten-fold more than his labors are worth," particularly now, "when his ghastly services are required at least seven days a week." To support the truth of his statements, Sam appealed to those whose "firesides death has made desolate during the few fatal weeks just past." Apparently there was an epidemic in Carson of one of the often fatal infectious diseases of the past century, such as typhus or spinal meningitis (known commonly as "spotted fever"), and Jennie had been one of the victims.

After Artemus Ward, the next celebrity to reach Virginia City was Adah Isaacs Menken. It was doubtless the Unreliable who had hinted in the *Union* that Mark Twain had been at work "writing a bloody tragedy for her . . . which will excel *Mazeppa* in many respects. It is to be called 'Pete Hopkins, or the Gory Scalp'."

She arrived close to noon on Saturday, February 27, bringing with her the poet, novelist, actress, and famous beauty, Ada Clare (who had been born Jane McElheney). She was a "petite blonde, with a wealth of fluffy golden hair," who was known as the "Queen of the Bohemians" at Pfaff's Cellar, the New York—rendezvous for such other celebrities as Walt Whitman, Louis Gottschalk, Bayard Taylor, and—the Menken. It was noted that Adah's husband (her third), Orpheus C. Kerr, wrapped in a heavy gray blanket against the cold, was occupying "a decidedly lively and conspicious position on the top of the stage's hind boot." Orpheus C. Kerr (a play on "Office Seeker") was the pen name of Robert H. Newell, a New York journalist whose political lampoons and comic interpretations of current events had gained him recognition. Under his own name, he had published a continuation of Dickens' unfinished novel, *The Mystery of Edwin Drood.* He and Menken had been married less than a year and a half but he was already in disfavor; three months later they separated.

The party, which included nineteen dogs of as many breeds, filed into the International Hotel, where a large banner proclaimed "WELCOME TO THE MENKEN AND ORPHEUS!"

During her stay in Virginia City she was squired almost everywhere by Tom Peasley, owner of the "sumptuous" Sazerac Saloon, fire chief, and "representative citizen," as Clemens called him, because he had "killed his man." He and the Menken danced together at the Melodeon; rode horseback (she, daringly, astride); went down through the Comstock Mines; and met after each of her performances for a midnight supper. Peasley saw to it that she was elected an honorary member of the Young America Engine Company No. 2, and he presented her with a belt bearing the unit's name in large letters of solid bullion. When Clemens wrote *Roughing It,* Tom Peasley became the model for the character, Buck Fanshaw. Sam's description of Fanshaw's funeral, "that marvel of pomp," is classic.

In a mid-March letter to Pamela, Sam explained: "(I will not write to Ma, this time, because in a day or two I shall write to her through the columns of the N. Y. Sunday Mercury.) I would have finished it to-day, but I took it over to show it to Miss Menken, the actress . . . she is a literary cuss herself. Although I was acquainted with Orpheus, I didn't know her from the devil, & the other day (I am acting in place of *both* the chief editors, now, & Dan has the local all to himself,) she sent a brief note, couched in stately terms & full of frozen dignity, addressed to 'Mr Mark Twain,' asking if we would publish a sketch from her pen." Dan De Quille recalled that they printed two or three of her poems, "long ones in the blankest of blank verse."

"Now you ought to have seen my answer—(3 pages of 'legal cap,') because I took a great deal of pride in it. It was extravagantly sociable & familiar, but I swear it had humor in it, because I laughed at it myself. It was bad enough as it was when first finished —but I took it out of the envelop & added an extra atrocity. She has a beautiful white hand—but her handwriting is infamous; she writes very fast, and her chirography is of the doorplate order— her letters are immense. I gave her a conundrum—thus: 'My Dear Madam—Why ought your hand to retain its present grace & beauty always? Because you fool devilish little of it on your manuscript.'

"I think I can safely say that woman was furious for a few days. But that wasn't a matter of much consequence to me, & finally she got over it of her own accord, & wrote another note. She is friendly, now."

The Menken decided to give an elaborate dinner party in her suite for just four persons. She chose a Sunday afternoon when Clemens and Dan De Quille were free. With Ada Clare and herself there would be the right number. Orpheus Kerr was stationed in the hall to guard against intruders. There were so many courses, it took a procession of waiters three hours to bring the dishes up three flights of stairs from the kitchen. Some courses were hardly tasted before they were removed, Dan recalled. Adah was dressed in a free-flowing garment of yellow, her favorite color for off-stage wear.

The purpose of the gathering was to discuss a "realistic" novel Menken was planning, for she was considering leaving the stage and devoting full time to writing. The other object was to choose a play suited to Ada Clare, who was hoping to abandon writing and return to acting. To Sam and Dan, the party seemed "rather dull," and an effort was made to try to enliven things by singing. "But Menken was no nightingale, Clare was a sort of wren, and I was a screech owl," Dan told. "Mark enchanted us with his one and only song of

'There was an old horse and his name was Jerusalem. . . .' "

Throughout dinner the nineteen dogs, some of them Ada Clare's, were fed sugar cubes soaked in brandy or champagne. By the end of the meal, the animals were tight, and their antics were "howlingly hilarious" in the opinion of their mistresses. But Clemens, who sat on Menken's side of the table, "where the canine carnival was most rampant," was disgusted. Then one of the dogs bit Clemens' leg. Guessing at its whereabouts under the table, "Mark undertook to avenge the nip . . . with a sly kick." He missed the culprit and hit Menken's slippered foot. She sprang from her chair with a cry, threw herself on a lounge, and tossed and groaned as if in agony.

Annoyed, Sam grew sulky and even when she came limping back to her seat and begged him not to mind, he refused to be "conciliated."

This mishap threw a further damper on the party, and Sam shortly remembered he had important business at the office and begged to be excused. Dan did likewise. As they walked into the hall they found Orpheus still on duty, and not in good humor. He "scowled and muttered in reply to our salutations."

At this time, as Clemens mentioned to Pamela, he was acting in the place of both chief editors, for Joe Goodman had gone to the Sandwich (Hawaiian) Islands. Sam had wanted to accompany him, but the news editor was on the verge of a serious illness, so he was forced to stay behind. When he agreed to take Goodman's place, he stipulated that he not be expected to write editorials about either politics or Eastern news. "I take no sort of interest in those matters." In addition to these further responsibilities, he continued his coverage of the legislature and other doings at the capital, making the thirty-two-mile round trip to Carson sometimes daily. Dan De Quille meanwhile took care of the locals.

In his weekly letter from Carson, dated April 25, Sam told about the "extraordinary preparations" being made by the capital's women (Mollie Clemens among them), for a "grand fancy-dress

ball" to be held in the county buildings there on May 5. It was for
the benefit of the great St. Louis Fair, a fund-raiser for the Sanitary
Commission, an organization formed for the relief of sick and
wounded Union soldiers. Declining government support, the Commission depended on private funding.

Whatever Pamela's sympathies may have been at the start of the
war, she was now at work to raise money for the St. Louis Sanitary
Fair. She had written to Orion and Sam asking them to see if they
could arouse interest for the cause locally. Sam immediately "went
after" A. B. Paul, president of the Storey County Sanitary Commission, who in turn sent out calls to the other counties. The women of
Gold Hill were the first to respond, and gave a ball, an elaborate
supper, and a concert which netted a silver brick worth more than
three thousand dollars.

When Sam wrote his mother and sister at midnight on May 17,
to post them on the progress of the fund-raising, he had no idea
that a few hours earlier he had unwittingly and irrevocably determined his own future. He told his family that the women of Virginia City were the next to act but they only raised about $1,800—
"and that made us sick." They tried again, but the results were
even more disappointing. They had just about decided to give up
when "along came RUEL GRIDLEY (you remember him), whom I
hadn't seen for 15 years, and he brought help." Gridley was the
"elderly pupil" in Sam's school at Hannibal, who had one day
nearly drowned young Clemens by throwing him into the deepest
part of the Bear Creek swimming hole. Gridley was now keeping a
general store in Austin, Nevada. He admitted to being Union to the
core, "but a Copperhead in sympathies." He had recently made an
"eccentric" wager, so his townsmen thought, with Dr. H. S. Herrick, a Republican, that if the Republican candidate was elected
mayor of Austin, Gridley would give the doctor a fifty-pound sack
of flour, carrying it to him on his shoulder a mile and a quarter,
with a brass band at his heels playing "John Brown's Body." If the
Democrat was elected, Herrick was to carry the flour to the tune of
"Dixie." Gridley lost the bet, and carried the flour, with the band
and the entire town following. The doctor gave the flour back to
Reuel. About that time, one of A. B. Paul's letters arrived, and

Farewell to Washoe

Gridley, responding to the plea for money, put the flour up for auction and sold it at $5,300 for the benefit of the St. Louis Fair.

The idea of auctioning the sack of flour appealed to Gridley and he went on with it by carriage to Virginia City, reaching there on Sunday, May 15. An impromptu auction was held, but it only brought five or six hundred dollars. The next morning at eleven, Paul had two open barouches waiting. One was for Gridley with his sack of flour, now decorated with red, white, and blue ribbons and miniature Stars and Stripes, and for the speakers. The other carriage was for reporters, editors, and "other people of imposing consequence." With a brass band in the lead, the procession filed down C Street and out of town on the road to Gold Hill, a telegram having been sent ahead. Within half an hour "we descended into Gold Hill with drums beating and colors flying, and enveloped in imposing clouds of dust. The whole population—men, women, children, Chinese and Indians, were massed in the main street, all the flags in town were at the masthead, and the blare of the bands was drowned in cheers."

The Gold Hill *Evening News* observed that "Tone was given to the Procession by the presence of Governor Twain and his staff of bibulous reporters, who came down in a free carriage ostensibly to take notes but in reality in pursuit of whiskey." Clemens spoke of nothing stronger than "new lager beer and plenty of it—for the people brought it to the carriages without waiting to measure it."

At Gold Hill, Gridley stood up and gave the history of the flour sack, and said that from what he could see people outside of Austin didn't care much for flour. "But they soon made him sing small," for Gold Hill "raised Austin out of her boots, and paid nearly seven thousand dollars in gold for the sack of flour," Sam told his mother and Pamela in the same long letter.

Presently the party moved on to little Silver City, where the flour sold for $1,700, then to the village of Dayton, where it brought in around two thousand.

It was four in the afternoon when the procession rolled into Gold Hill again. It had grown so large along its line of march, by volunteers joining in "to see the fun," it was styled "The Lord's Army." The crowds were out once more, waving flags and shouting: "Virginia's boomin'!" "Virginia's mad!" "Virginia's got her back up!"

"You'd better go 'long to Virginia; they say they'll be d---d if the whole Territory combined shall beat them!" Sam wrote. So they hurried on with still more people following, and didn't reach Virginia until after dark. There they found all the buildings near the opera house illuminated and the surrounding streets completely blocked with people.

"Then the fun commenced, and I wished Pamela could have been there to see her own private project bringing forth its fruit and culminating in such a sweeping excitement away out here among the barren mountains, while she herself, . . . unaware of the row she was kicking up, was probably sitting quietly at home and thinking it a dreary sort of world, full of disappointments, and labors unrequited. . . ." He spoke of the "row" as hers, for if she had not written, the St. Louis Fair would have doubtless never heard from Washoe. "In two hours and a half Virginia cleaned out the Territory and paid nearly $13,000 for the sack of flour! How's that?"

Sam seemed sober when he penned this letter at midnight, yet by his own admission he was drunk earlier, when he went to the *Enterprise* office and laid an editorial he had just written in front of Dan De Quille. It explained how it happened that Gridley and the sack of flour had not gone on to Carson City from Dayton. It had been stated that the money raised by the Fancy Dress Ball recently held at Carson for the benefit of the St. Louis Fair had been "diverted from its legitimate course, and was to be sent to aid a Miscegenation Society somewhere in the East; and it was feared the proceeds of the sack might be similarly disposed of." Sam qualified the statement by saying that it was "a hoax, but not all a hoax, for an effort is being made to divert those funds from their proper course."

These remarks had not originated with Clemens but had been said in "drunken jest" by some of his companions during the day's tour with Gridley. Still, the notion had appealed to Sam in his cups, and he wrote it up.

After Dan read it he asked, "Is this a joke?" Sam told him it was. Dan said he would not like such a joke "perpetrated upon him, & that it would wound the feelings of the ladies of Carson. He asked me if I wanted to do that, & I said 'No, of course not.' " The manuscript lay on the table while they were talking, and a little later when the two went off to the theatre, it was left there, and they thought no more about it.

When Clemens went to the *Enterprise* office on the evening of May 20, he found a letter addressed to the editor. It was dated May 18 at Carson City, and opened with a direct quote from the discarded editorial about the diversion of funds from the ball to a miscegenation society. It was signed by the four women who had headed the ball's committee.

"Let us say that the whole statement is a *tissue of falsehoods,* made for *malicious* purposes, and we demand the name of the author. . . ."

Until that moment, Sam was not aware that the rejected piece had been printed, for he was too busy in Goodman's absence to read the paper, and had not looked at it for a week. Dan had not seen it either. How did this mistake happen, they wondered. The only explanation Sam could offer was that the foreman, "prospecting for copy," had seen it on the table, and recognizing Sam's handwriting, presumed it was meant to be published, and carried it off.

Greatly perturbed, he unburdened himself that very night to his confessor, Mollie Clemens. He has had nothing but trouble and vexation since the Sanitary trip, "& now this letter comes to aggravate me a thousand times worse." If it had come from a man he would answer it with a challenge "as the easiest way of getting out of a bad scrape, although I know I am in the wrong & would not be justified in doing such a thing. I wrote the squib the ladies' letter refers to, & although I could give the names of those parties who made the offensive remarks, I shall not do it, because they were said in drunken jest and no harm was meant by them. . . . We kept that sanitary spree up for several days & I wrote & laid the item before Dan when I was not sober (I shall not get drunk again, Mollie). . . ."

"Now, Mollie, whatever blame there is rests with me alone, for if I had not just sense enough to submit the article to Dan's better judgment, it would have been published all the same, & not by any mistake, either. Since I have made the ladies angry, I am sorry the thing occurred, & that is all I can do . . . for their communication is unanswerable, I cannot publish that, & explain it by saying the affair was a silly joke, & that I & all concerned were drunk. No— I'll die first. . . . I cannot submit to the humiliation of publishing myself as a liar (according to the terms of their letter)."

He can do one of two things: either satisfy the women that he dealt with them honorably when he consented to let Dan suppress the article on grounds that its publication would hurt their feelings, "or else make them appoint a man to avenge the wrong done them with weapons in fair & open field. . . . Mollie, the Sanitary expedition has been very disastrous to me. Aside from this trouble, (which I feel deepest,) I have two other quarrels on my hands engendered on that day, & as yet I cannot tell how either . . . is to end.

"Mollie, I shall say nothing about this business until I hear from you."

In an editorial written directly after the Virginia City auction, the *Union* praised the generosity of the merchants, miners, mechanics, and professional men. However, "the great companies, which could easily have afforded to donate a quarter of a million from their coffers, were generally most shamefully indifferent." Clemens seized upon that statement, and in an editorial headed "How is it?—How it is." accused the *Union*'s publishers and employees of having failed to fulfill their pledges, and stressed the *Enterprise*'s generosity and honorableness. His timing was unwittingly poor, for that same day the *Union* printed the names of all those connected with the paper who had donated, along with a facsimile of the receipt from the treasurer of the Sanitary Fund, showing that $515 had been paid in gold. Sam was quick to point out in a squib that if it had not been for the *Enterprise*'s promptings, the *Union* people would have never paid.

On May 21 two reprisals appeared in the *Union.* An editorial headed "The 'How Is It' Issue," accused the *Territorial Enterprise* of having only pretended to contribute. "Never before, in a long period of newspaper intercourse . . . have we found an opponent in statement or in discussion . . . who conceived in every word . . . such a groveling disregard for truth, decency, and courtesy, as to seem to court the distinction only of being understood as a vulgar liar."

Farewell to Washoe

In a second piece, "How It Is.", a printer for the *Union* took umbrage at the *Enterprise*'s "cowardly slander." "We can only view his blackguardism as an attack upon members of our craft. . . . He has endeavored to misinterpret the generous, patriotic promptings of laboring men who gave their little mite willingly; and in so doing proved himself an unmitigated *liar, a poltroon, and a puppy.*"

The battle was on, and Sam seemed to relish it. He looked forward to taking on both antagonists in the next day's paper, and would have if the fiery Steve Gillis had not insisted that such insults could be avenged only by blood. It was not easy to convince Clemens that this was the proper course, for he had no taste for duels except in fiction. But Gillis argued convincingly, and other staff members supported him. Reluctantly Sam agreed, and that same morning he wrote to James Laird, editor and proprietor of the *Union*.

Sir: In your paper of the present date appeared two anonymous articles, in which a series of insults were leveled at the writer of an editorial in Thursday's *Enterprise*, headed "How is it?—How it is." I wrote that editorial.

Some time since it was stated in the Virginia *Union* that its proprietors were alone responsible for all articles published in its columns. You being the proper person, by seniority, to apply to, . . . I demand of you a public retraction of the insulting articles I have mentioned, or satisfaction. I require an immediate answer to this note. The bearer of this—Mr. Stephen Gillis—will receive any communication you may see fit to make.

Sam. L. Clemens

It was now time for Sam to retrieve the navy revolver he had discarded soon after taking the job as reporter.

Gillis returned shortly with a reply:

Samuel Clemens, Esq. —Mr. James Laird has just handed me your note of this date. Permit me to say that I am the *author* of the *article* appearing in this morning's *Union*. I am responsible for it. I have nothing to retract.

Respectfully,
J. W. Wilmington

Back flew a letter to Laird accusing him of shirking the responsibility which a newspaper owner assumes for all articles published, and for making Wilmington, "a person entirely unknown to me in the matter," answerable. Another attempt "to make a catspaw of any other individual . . . will show that *you* are a cowardly sneak. I now *peremptorily* demand of you the satisfaction due to a gentleman—without alternative."

Laird was obliged to reply. Obviously he was no more eager than Clemens to fight a duel, for he carefully clarified the point that the *Union* proprietors were responsible for all editorials, but not for "communications" appearing in their pages. He said nothing about the editorial, but insisted that the controversy had grown out of the attack upon the printers. Since this was replied to by a printer and a representative of the printers, "I have no right under the rulings of the code you have invoked, to step in and assume Mr. Wilmington's position, nor would he allow me to do so." Wilmington was a gentleman, he assured Clemens; before fighting gallantly at Shiloh, he had been proprietor of the Cinncinnati *Enquirer.*

Laird continued: "In short, Mr. Wilmington has a prior claim upon your attention. When he is through with you, I shall be at your service. If you decline to meet him after challenging him, you will prove yourself to be what he has charged you with being: 'a liar, a poltroon and a puppy,' and as such, cannot of course be entitled to the consideration of a gentleman."

At nine o'clock that same night Sam fired off his reply: "To my utter astonishment you still endeavor to shield your craven carcass behind the person of an individual who in spite of *your* introduction is entirely unknown to me, and upon whose shoulders you *cannot* throw the whole responsibility. . . . You assume in your last note, that I 'have challenged Mr. Wilmington,' and that he has informed me 'over his own signature,' that he is quite ready to afford me 'satisfaction.' Both assumptions are utterly false. I have twice challenged *you,* and you have twice attempted to shirk responsibility. . . . In the meantime, if you do not wish yourself to be posted as a coward, you will *at once accept my peremptory challenge, which I now reiterate.*"

Steve Gillis, whom Clemens had appointed as his second in the affair, was aching for a fight. It seemed to him that the question of responsibility was going to keep the two principals from the field. Therefore, this same Saturday night Gillis, unknown to Clemens, sent off a note to the printer, Wilmington, hoping to provoke him to action by insult: "I take the liberty of suggesting that you are getting out of your sphere. A *contemptible ass and coward* like yourself should only meddle in the affairs of *gentlemen* when called upon to do so. I approve and endorse the course of my principal in this matter, and if your sensitive disposition is aroused by any proceeding of his, I have only to say that I can be found at the ENTERPRISE office, and always at your service."

But Steve was disappointed. Wilmington's verbal reply, sent by reporter Bailey Millard (who had delivered Gillis' note), stated simply that he had no quarrel with Mr. Gillis, that he had written his communication as a defense of printers only, and that he had no desire for a dispute with any member of that craft.

The next day, Sunday, was possibly spent in the target practice with Steve Gillis, which Clemens described in his autobiography, over forty years later. He recalled he was such a poor marksman he constantly missed the barn door they were using as a target, and lost heart when he heard pistol shots in the next ravine and suspected that Laird was also practicing. "I knew that if Laird came over that ridge and saw my barn door without a scratch on it," he would be anxious to fight. Just at that moment, a bird no larger than a sparrow flew by and lighted on a sage bush. Steve whipped out his revolver and shot its head off. "We ran down there to pick up the bird and just then, sure enough, Mr. Laird and his people came over the ridge, and they joined us." When Laird's second saw the bird, he was interested, and asked who had shot it. Before Sam could answer, Steve spoke up and said in a matter-of-fact way, that Clemens had. The second asked how far off the bird had been, and Steve said about thirty yards. The second then asked how often Clemens could do that, and Steve said languidly, "Oh, about four times out of five!"

"Well, they said good morning. The second took Mr. Laird home, a little tottery on his legs, and Laird sent back a note in his own hand declining to fight a duel with me on any terms."

Actually, in the sequence of events, the following morning (Monday), a note came from Laird stating once again that Clemens' quarrel was with the printer, Wilmington, and not with him. Any attempt by Clemens to avoid a meeting with Wilmington and force one upon Laird "will utterly fail, as I have no right under the rulings of the code to meet or hold communication with you in this connection." The threat of being posted as a coward cannot have the slightest effect upon his position. "If you think this long correspondence reflects any credit upon *you*, I advise you by all means publish it. . . ." Meanwhile, he asked to be excused from receiving any more lengthy "epistles" from Clemens. The following morning, the correspondence appeared in the *Enterprise*, accompanied by a statement from Clemens, denouncing Laird as "an unmitigated liar," "an abject coward," and a "fool," giving reasons for each epithet.

An editorial was printed in the *Gold Hill Evening News* this same day, reflecting the general attitude toward "the cross-firing that has been going on for a week past between the *Union* and the *Enterprise*. . . . In the first place the cause of the quarrel was not one to enlist public sympathy; neither did the discussion of the question demand the use of the language resorted to. If the matter results in bloodshed, the victim will not be mourned as a martyr in a holy cause, nor the victor crowned with laurel as a champion of right."

Sam had decided he must try to mollify the women of Carson City, whose communication he had so far ignored. He had learned that Mollie Clemens was being humiliated on his account and that she was deeply hurt. He therefore wrote a personal letter to Mrs. W. K. Cutler, who had served as president of the ball committee: "I address a lady in every sense of the term. Mrs. Clemens has informed me of everything that has occurred in Carson in connection with that unfortunate item of mine about the Sanitary Funds accruing from the ball, and from what I understand, you are almost the only lady in your city who has understood the circumstances under which my fault was committed, or who has shown any disposition to be lenient with me."

His chief object in writing her (he asked her pardon for taking the liberty) was to thank her "very kindly and sincerely," not only for her consideration of him but for her "continued friendship for Mollie while others are disposed to withdraw theirs on account of a fault for which I alone was responsible." The next morning he printed a public apology. And on the following day, May 25—the day Joe Goodman returned—he begged Orion: "Don't stump for the Sanitary Fund—Billy Clagett says he certainly will not. If I have been so unlucky as to rob you of some of your popularity by that unfortunate item, I claim at your hands that you neither increase nor diminish it by so fruitless a proceeding as making speeches for the Fund. I am mighty sick of that fund—it has caused me all my d---d troubles—& I shall leave the Territory when your first speech is announced, & leave it for good."

As to the women of Carson, "they have seduced from me what I consider was a sufficient apology, coming from a man open to a challenge from three persons & already awaiting the issue of such a message to another—They got out of me what no man would ever have got. . . ."

Much to his surprise, he wrote Orion, that morning's *Union* said nothing about the Laird feud. However, "I still have a quarrel or two on hand—so that this flour sack business may rest as far as Carson is concerned. I shall take no notice of it at all except to mash Mr. Laird over the head with my revolver for publishing it if I meet him to-day—otherwise, I do nothing. I consider that I have triumphed over those ladies at last, & I am quits with them now."

He included a message to his sister-in-law, who was concerned for his safety. "I have no intention of hunting for the puppy Laird, Mollie, but he had better let me have 24 hours unmolested to get cool in."

At this point Joe Goodman offered Clemens and Gillis some advice based on personal experience. The previous August, Goodman and Tom Fitch, then editor of the *Union*, had met in Six-Mile Canyon at nine in the morning to fight a duel. Clemens and Adair Wilson, reporter for the *Union*, had ridden their horses "at the rate of a mile a minute," on the trail of the principals, Sam wrote, "but we lost our bloody item—for Marshal Perry arrived with a detachment of Constables, and Deputy Sheriff Blodgett came with a lot of blarsted Sheriffs, and these miserable meddling whelps arrested the whole party and marched them back to town." Although Goodman and Fitch had been placed under a five thousand dollar bond to keep the peace, they had met again, secretly, on Ingraham's

Ranch in Stampede Valley at nine o'clock on the morning of September 28. This time Joe "tumbled his man down with a bullet through the lower leg," just below the knee, which left Fitch with a permanent limp.

Although the first Territorial Legislature of 1861 had passed a law making dueling or the sending of a challenge a criminal offense, it was not often enforced, so Clemens and Gillis had little to fear there. But Goodman certainly suggested that they leave the Territory for a few weeks until things quieted down, especially since Sam had so many other quarrels on his hands. Mrs. Cutler's husband had just expressed himself publicly as being dissatisfied with Sam's apology to his wife, and Dr. H. H. Ross, husband of the Ball committee's secretary, was being belligerent. Sam suspected Ross was "at the bottom of the whole business."

On Thursday morning, May 26, Sam wrote Orion: "Send me two hundred dollars *if you can spare it comfortably.* However, never mind—you can send it to San Francisco if you prefer. Steve & I are going to the States. We leave Sunday morning per Henness Pass. Say nothing about it, of course. We are not afraid of the grand jury, but Washoe has long since grown irksome to us, & we want to leave it anyhow." He and Gillis "thoroughly canvassed the Carson business, & concluded we dare not do anything, either to Laird or Carson men without spoiling our chances of getting away. However, if there is any chance of the husbands of those women challenging *me,* I don't want a straw in the way of it. I'll wait for them a month, if necessary, & fight them with any weapon they choose." He had thought of challenging one of them, and then crossing the state line to await results, but "Steve says it would not be safe, situated as we are."

The next morning an abusive letter from W. K. Cutler changed his mind with regard to ignoring those Carson men. He replied immediately: "Sir—To-day, I have received a letter from you, in which you assume that you have been offended by certain acts of mine. Having apologized once for that offensive conduct, I shall not do it again. Your recourse is a challenge, I am ready to accept it.

"Having made my arrangements—before I received your note—

to leave for California, & having no time to fool away on a common bummer like you, I want an immediate reply to this."

He left this first draft on Dan De Quille's desk. According to Dan, Clemens wrote and sent a second version. But before a reply could come from Cutler, Sam and Steve Gillis were on their way to San Francisco over a route that by-passed Carson City.

This affair was as close as Sam Clemens ever came to fighting a duel.

On May 30, the Gold Hill *Evening News* commented: "Among the few immortal names of the departed—that is, those who departed yesterday morning per California stage—we notice that of Mark Twain. We don't wonder. Mark Twain's beard is full of dirt, and his face is black before the people of Washoe. Giving way to the idiosyncratic eccentricities of an erratic mind, Mark has indulged in the game infernal—in short, 'played hell.' . . . He has *vamosed,* cut stick, absquatulated; and among the pine forests of the Sierras, or amid the purlieus of the city of earthquakes, he will tarry awhile, and the office of the *Enterprise* will become purified, and by the united efforts of Goodman and Dan De Quille once more merit the sweet smiles of the ladies of Carson."

However, that other colorful Washoe journalist, John K. Lovejoy, editor of the *Daily Old Piute,* lamented sincerely. "The world is blank—the universe worth but 57½, and we are childless. We shall miss Mark . . . to know him was to love him. . . . We can't dwell on this subject; we can only say—God bless you, Mark! be virtuous and happy."

XVII

─────────○─────────

EXILE

S A M C L E M E N S I N T E N D E D to stay in San Francisco no
more than a month. During that time he expected to sell his and
Orion's mining stocks at a profit, and "fix" their most valuable
holdings, Hale & Norcross, "in a safe shape." With the proceeds,
Orion would be able to pay his debts and Sam would take that
long-projected trip home, stopping at St. Louis to see his family,
then proceeding to New York, where he hoped to join Artemus
Ward and try writing for Eastern publications.

But his careless attitude toward his investments, of which he had
once boasted, caught him again, this time when he desperately
needed the gains to carry through his plans. The Virginia City
mines were no longer working at peak production and the market
had been declining all year, a fact Sam ought to have known,
situated as he was in their midst. Now when he came to sell, he
discovered that he had waited too long. It was a repetition of that
"indolent heedlessness" which had lost him and Higby the rich
blind lead. He therefore put the Hale & Norcross stock (they were
one of the big producers on the Comstock Lode) in Orion's name so
that if fortune suddenly favored Sam, "and I want to leave here at
any time, there'll be no bother about it." He sent the certificates to

Carson, with strict orders for Orion to put them in the safe. Then he went to look for a job.

He had written occasionally from Washoe for the *Morning Call,* and it was that paper which now hired him as the local reporter (there was only one). Steve Gillis found work as a typographer on the *Evening Bulletin.* On June 8, right after he started with the *Call,* Sam registered at the city's newly opened luxury hotel, the Occidental; Steve doubtless shared the room. Shortly Clemens sent off a letter to the *Enterprise:*

"To a Christian who has toiled months and months in Washoe; whose hair bristles from a bed of sand, and whose soul is caked with a cement of alkali dust, . . . whose eyes know no landscape but barren mountains and desolate plains; where the winds blow, and the sun blisters, and the broken spirit of the contrite heart finds joy and peace only in Limberger cheese and lager beer—unto such a Christian, verily the Occidental Hotel is Heaven on the half shell. He may even secretly consider it to be Heaven on the entire shell, but his religion teaches a sound Washoe Christian that it would be sacrilege to say it."

Within a few weeks they moved into less expensive quarters, but continued to take their meals at the Occidental because of the excellent cuisine, and the select company at table. The most interesting to Clemens were Martha Hunter Hitchcock, a Virginian, wife of Dr. Charles McPhail Hitchcock, medical director for the Army of the Pacific, and their twenty-one-year-old daughter, Eliza, always called "Lillie," who were residents of the hotel. Mrs. Hitchcock, whom Sam once characterized as "a rare gem of a woman," contributed regularly to the *Alta California.* She was also an active member of the local literary circle that included the beautiful Ina Coolbrith, who would become California's poet laureate, Bret Harte, Ambrose Bierce, Fitzhugh Ludlow, the former hasheesh eater and admirer of Clemens' work, Joe Lawrence, editor of *The Golden Era,* Charles H. Webb, founder of *The Californian,* and Charles Warren Stoddard, the twenty-two-year-old musician, poet, and friend of Robert Louis Stevenson. She introduced Sam to them all. He greatly admired Stoddard whom he once described as "the purest male I have ever known in mind and speech." At the height of Clemens' fame, when he was living in London, he hired Stoddard as his secretary simply because he delighted in his companionship and enjoyed hearing him play the piano.

When Lillie Hitchcock was eight, she became the mascot of San Francisco's Knickerbocker Fire Engine Company No. 5, and rode to nearly every fire, wearing her own monogrammed helmet. She had been made an honorary member of the company by the time Sam met her, wore her number 5 gold badge at all times, and never failed to answer the fire-bell signaling her company, even if it meant leaving a ball.

Lillie was also a crack marksman, and skilled in handling horses. She would often race her men friends to the Cliff House, daring them to follow her hazardous shortcuts. She always rode astride, in trousers, and at times bareback. She had learned from a stagecoach driver to handle a four-in-hand as well as he. Once, disguised as a man, she attended a cock-fight. She was present at all the important horse races at Bay View Park on Hunter's Point, and often beat the city's best poker players. Sam Clemens wrote that she also liked to sail, fish, swim, hunt, and box.

Although not beautiful, she had a host of admirers, and was said to have been engaged fifteen times before she was twenty. One of her women friends remarked that she had never seen Lillie enter a ballroom. When asked why, the friend replied, "I would see a crowd of men walking into the room, and another following; then you knew Lillie Hitchcock was in the center."

She and her mother were ardent Confederate sympathizers, and Lillie managed to help a suspected Secessionist steal out of San Francisco by buying him a red wig and getting him a job aboard a ship bound for China. Although Dr. Hitchcock was also a Southerner, he had declared himself for the Union when the Civil War broke out. He could not afford to jeopardize his post by Lillie's impulsive acts, so he sent mother and daughter to live for a time in Paris. There Lillie was presented to the Empress Eugénie and, because of the girl's fluency in French, she was requested by Napoleon III to translate Confederate state papers. She also became the San Francisco *Evening Bulletin*'s Paris correspondent.

Lillie had not been home from Paris for long when Sam Clemens met her. Although his ideal woman was not a hoyden, they were attracted to one another. "That girl, many & many a time, has waited till nearly noon to breakfast with me," for he seldom got to bed before three in the morning. "She was a brilliant talker. . . . It always seemed funny to me that she & I could be friends, but we *were*—I suppose because under all her wild & repulsive foolery, that *warm* heart of hers would show." Later he spoke of her heart as "tropically" warm. He thought of her as being "stored to the eyelids" with energy and enthusiasm, her mind, hands, feet, and body in a state of tireless activity, not unlike his own.

He did not forget Lillie, and when he was sixty-two, he commenced writing a story about just such a girl, Rachael Hotchkiss, who was nicknamed "Hellfire". In the tale, set in Dawson's Landing (patterned after Hannibal), she is first seen on her black horse, riding astride and bareback, her hair flowing free, as she races to rescue a boy stranded on a cake of ice in the Mississippi. No one in town except "Hellfire" has the courage to venture onto the treacherous floe and save Oscar Carpenter, a character Sam based on Orion Clemens.

Just as with Lillie Hitchcock, the local fire company conferred honorary membership on Hellfire. Wearing her official belt and helmet she appears in another dramatic scene in the midst of smoke billows and leaping flames, climbing over the roof of a house to rescue its inhabitants. But the tale Lillie Hitchcock inspired was never finished. Clemens evidently had her in mind again when he created the character of Shirley Tempest, "A San Francisco Belle and Heiress of adventurous spirit," for the play, *Ah Sin,* on which he collaborated with Bret Harte in 1877.

Sam wrote his mother and Pamela that although he and Steve Gillis had been in the city only four months, they have changed their lodgings five times and their hotel twice. At the time of writing, they were "very comfortably fixed" in a house on Minna Street, and had no fault to find with either the rooms or the people —a well-to-do private family with one grown daughter, and a piano in the parlor. "But I need a change, & must move again. I have taken rooms further down the street," this time possibly with Steve Gillis' family who kept a quiet lodging house at 44 Minna. Steve's father, Major Angus Gillis, was a veteran of William Walker's filibustering expedition to Nicaragua. (He had lost an eye in the fighting and his son Philip, twenty-two, had been killed.)

Sam's restlessness during this prolonged, enforced stay was in part responsible for his many changes of residence, but there is also evidence that he and Steve were not always welcome lodgers. In July he wrote Dan De Quille about what was probably their first move. Steve failed to tell his parents, and his father went to their rooms, found the door locked, and hunted up the landlady to ask where the young men were. Not knowing who he was, she said, "They are gone, thank God!—and I hope I may never see them again." Had she known they were such desperate characters—they were gamblers and murderers of the very worst description, from Washoe, she would have never let them enter her house. "I never saw such a countenance as the smallest one had on him. They just took the premises, & lorded it over everything—they didn't care a snap for the rules of the house. One night when they were carrying on in their room with some more roughs, my husband went up to remonstrate with them, & that small man told him to take his head out of the door (pointing a revolver,) because he wanted to shoot in that direction. O, I never saw such creatures. Their room was never vacant long enough to be cleaned up—one of them always went to bed at dark & got up at sunrise, & the other went to bed at sunrise & got up at dark—& if the chamber-man disturbed them they would just set up in bed & level a pistol at him & tell him to get scarce! They used to bring loads of beer bottles up at midnight, & get drunk, & shout & fire off their pistols in the room, & throw their empty bottles out of the windows at the Chinamen below. You'd hear them count 'One—two—three—fire!' & then you'd hear the bottles crash on the China roofs & see the poor Chinamen scatter like flies. O it was dreadful! They kept . . . any number of revolvers & bowie knives in their room, & I know that small one must have murdered lots of people."

And, they always had women running to their room—"sometimes in broad daylight—bless you, *they* didn't care. They had no respect for God, man, or the devil."

In closing the letter Sam told Dan that their actor-friend Walter Leman "sails for the Sandwich Islands tomorrow—just going for recreation . . . But don't I want to go to Asia, or somewhere—Oh no, I guess not. I have got the 'Gypsy' only in a mild form. It will kill me yet, though."

Exile

To satisfy his wanderlust in some measure, he and Steve frequently took day-long excursions into the country. One trip that he described was typical: On a pleasant Sunday morning in mid-August, he and Gillis, with six other newspapermen, boarded the eight-thirty train for San Jose. The route was a scenic one through a valley bounded by rolling hills, some covered only with dark gold grass, others with stands of live oak and California laurel. There were vast fields, too, threaded by little willow-lined streams, where huge herds of horses and cattle from the ranchos grazed.

The party arrived at eleven, and after refreshing themselves at the well-stocked bar in the Continental Hotel, strolled along the shady, tree-lined streets of this town, which was about the size of Hannibal. It was charming, Sam wrote home, because it was "buried" in lush gardens of fragrant and colorful flowers and blooming shrubs. Following lunch at the hotel, they hired buggies for the twelve-mile drive to Warm Springs, where fashionable San Franciscans vacationed, drinking the mineral waters and taking the baths. Indians had been the first to discover the water's medicinal properties.

Sam and his companions wandered about the oak-shaded grounds, socialized with those San Franciscans they knew; bathed, sampled the water, and had dinner. If any reliance can be placed in the squib Sam wrote afterward for the *Call*, considerable time was spent in the bar room as well. Heading his piece, "Inexplicable News from San José," it purported to be a letter to Mr. Mark Twain from a special correspondent. It opened: "Sarrozay's beauriful place. Flowers—or maybe it's me—smells delishs. . . . Full of newsper men—re porters . . . And all drunk—all drunk but me. By Georshe!"

Toward the end of September, he announced to his family that Steve Gillis, his comrade of two years, was to be married on October 24 to a Miss Emeline Russ, a very pretty young woman who is worth $130,000 in her own right. "And what is much better, is a good, sensible girl and will make Steve an excellent wife." After a bridal tour of one week (Sam was included), he will be alone—but only until they build a house, which will be shortly, for he is expected to live with them. Because of his "contract" to stand up as "chief mourner or groomsman" at the wedding (he wrote "funeral," but lined it out), he has had to refuse an invitation to go to San Luis Obispo (near which there were copper and cinnabar discoveries), and then travel on to Mexico City, no doubt to look at silver mines.

There was a strong bond of affection between Sam and Steve, perhaps very similar to the earlier ties between Clemens and his brother, Henry. Steve was also three years Sam's junior. Clemens was soon "intimate" with the whole Gillis family, admiring the "dauntless spirit" of Major Angus (all the Gillises were "made of grit"), his humor, and his "dry, unsmiling way" of recounting a funny story. Sam was drawn by the charm and warm-heartedness of Steve's mother, Margaret Alston, of South Carolina, related to Joseph Alston, husband of Theodosia Burr. An added attraction in this surrogate family was the presence of Steve's sisters, Francina (Fanny), sixteen, and eighteen-year-old Mary Elizabeth (Maim), in whose album Sam wrote a parody of Poe's "The Raven," calling it "The Mysterious Chinaman."

Once upon a morning dreary, while I pondered, weak and weary,
Over many a quaint and curious shirt that me and Steve has wore,*
While I was stretching, yawning, gaping, suddenly there came a tapping,
As of some one gently rapping, rapping at my chamber door—
"I guess it's Maim," I muttered, "tapping at the chamber door—
 At least it's she, if nothing more.

 x x x x x x x x x x x x x

Presently my soul grew stronger—hesitating then no longer,
"Maim," said I, "or Fannie, truly your forgiveness I implore;
But the fact is, I was washing, and so gently you came sloshing . . .
That I scarce was sure I heard you—here I opened wide the door—
 Chung was there—and nothing more!— . . .

*The sacrifice of grammar to rhyme, in the second line, is a "poetic license" which was imperatively demanded by the exigencies of the case.—m.t.

By September 28, Sam was no longer working nights for the *Call*, having persuaded George Barnes, editor and proprietor, to hire someone part-time. As sole reporter, Clemens' day had been starting at nine in the morning when, wearing his silk hat and

Exile

frock-coated black suit, he stopped at the police court to take notes on the previous night's happenings. An hour later, he moved on to the higher courts to learn the latest decisions there. The rest of the day was spent raking the town "from end to end" for news to fill his column, "and if there were no fires to report we started some." In the evening, there were six theaters to cover, which made his working day end long after midnight. This left him no time in which to carry out an ambitious literary plan—a book. He had already spoken of it to Orion and cautioned him to say nothing, since it was a "secret." He would like to begin right away, he told his brother, but he and Steve were so busy with wedding preparations, he will have to wait until that "business" is all over before he can ask Orion to send him the "files." This suggests that Sam was intending to write the story of their overland journey to Nevada, of which only Orion had kept any record, and to make use also of the scrapbooks in which his brother had pasted Sam's newspaper contributions. This was the seed of *Roughing It,* although circumstances kept him from working on it seriously until September 1870.

In his new leisure, he told his family, he has found time to contribute a weekly article (for which he received twelve dollars) to *The Californian,* a local literary paper which Bret Harte was then editing. Sam had stopped writing for *The Golden Era* because he no longer considered it "high-toned" enough. By contrast, *The Californian* circulated among only the "highest class" in the community. Further, it had an "exalted reputation" in the East, where it was copied from "liberally" by all the best papers. That will help familiarize Eastern readers with "Mark Twain."

Sam's involvement in the progress of Steve's love affair, house-building plans, and wedding arrangements—subjects he could not keep apart from with such a close friend—turned his own thoughts to a wife and home of his own. He was "resolved" on marriage or "on suicide—perhaps," he told Mollie. No doubt he was in love again, but unless the young woman was independently wealthy, as was Emeline Russ, he could not hope to support her on his income. At such times, and in his daily association with what he termed "the upper crust of society," he was made depressingly aware that he was barely holding his own financially, and that the gap between them was wide. His mind reverted to the rank and dignity of piloting, and the high pay, and he seriously considered returning to the Mississippi as a government pilot, in spite of earlier protests to the contrary. He also thought about his ideal, Laura Wright, and asked his mother for news of her.

This was an emotionally stressful time for Clemens. When he left Virginia City, he was admittedly tired of the scene and was eager to go East. Presently, he began to feel that his prolonged stay even in the city he had once called "paradise," amounted to forced exile. Now that all his plans for financial independence had gone awry, he saw little hope for escape. Further, it was a blow to his self-esteem to be still working as a reporter on what was known as "the washerwoman's paper," the cheapest in California, after having edited one of the country's most distinguished newspapers. As a veteran journalist at Carson City, he had grown politically powerful, and had at least a speaking acquaintance with every important man in Washoe, which gave him the chance to include items about individuals in his columns. The majority of people in San Francisco were total strangers, and he realized that big city happenings lacked the dramatic impact of events in the roaring mining camps. Nothing here could compare with the robust energy of frontier life, and the inspiration it provided him.

He tried reporting local items with the same originality of style that had made him so popular in Nevada. He even initiated a feud with a rival reporter, Albert S. Evans of the *Alta California,* but the good-natured ridicule such as he had heaped upon Clement T. Rice, the Unreliable, was not accepted in the same spirit, and Evans' returns were malicious. Sam came to despise him. He also attacked another coroner, this time for withholding information from reporters. He won his case by publishing "the wickedest article . . . I ever wrote in my life." But he was not inspired to produce another such imaginative and controversial piece as "The Petrified Man," aimed at the coroner in Humboldt.

However, he could still boast to Orion and Mollie of a local following. He knew the women in his family would be pleased to learn that one of these was the Reverend Dr. Henry Bellows, a popular Unitarian minister who was filling the vacancy left by the death of young Thomas Starr King, who had been noted for his charisma, eloquence, and perceptive writings about nature. Bellows told Sam that he never failed to read his locals and that he went into "convulsions of laughter" over a squib called "What a Sky-Rocket Did."

Frustration made Clemens irritable, and at such times, writing to his mother and sister became a burden. He wrote to Jane Lampton soon after he and Steve Gillis reached San Francisco, and not again until August 12, when he sent what his mother called a "scolding" letter, evidently in response to one from her or Pamela urging him to mend his ways. In defense, he cited his friendship with Dr. Bellows, and Jane wrote back in a long communication, "To My Dear Children: Sam tell Dr. B. if he is a good friend of yours I wish he would give you good advice." If they can get Sam to write only by making him mad, "we will have to try that for we would rather have a scolding letter than none." She begged Mollie to write and give all the news, for both Orion and Sam "write like they thought they must write and they don't know anything."

Interestingly, Jane Lampton failed to mention a "valuable letter" Sam had written her in a different mood a short while before.

My Dear Mother—You have portrayed to me so often & earnestly the benefits of taking exercise, that I know it will please you to learn that I belong to the San F. Olympic Club, whose gymnasium is one of the largest & best appointed in the United States. I am glad now that you put me in the notion of it, Ma, because if you had not, I would never have thought of it myself. I think it is nothing but right to give you the whole credit. . . . I feel like a new man. I sleep better, I have a healthier appetite, my intellect is clearer, and I have become so strong & hearty that I fully believe twenty years have been added to my life. I feel as if I ought to be very well satisfied with this result, when I reflect that I was never in that gymnasium but once in my life & that was over three months ago.

He sent a copy to Orion and observed:

I think I can see the old lady pluming herself as she reads the first page aloud, [and saying to her listeners,] "Thar, now, I always told Sam it would be so, & in those very words, I expect, but he was always so headstrong he never would listen to me before. I guess he's found out that I know some things worth knowing." . . . Oh, no—I guess she won't snort, though, when she turns the page over, it ain't likely. It takes *me* to make her life interesting for her.

After Clemens began working a shorter day he was able to spend time with Bret Harte, whose office was on the second floor of the *Call* building. Harte supported a wife and child by acting as secretary to the superintendent of the United States Mint. Since that job was not demanding, he was able to do much of his writing in the office. Harte recalled that George Barnes introduced them. Clemens' "head was striking. He had the curly hair, the aquiline nose, and even the aquiline eye—an eye so eagle-like that a second lid would not have surprised me—of an unusual and dominant nature." To a man whose clothes were ultra-fashionable, Sam's dress seemed a little "careless." Harte noted the "slow, rather satirical drawl, which was in itself irresistible." When Clemens told a story, he "half unconsciously dropped into the lazy tone and manner of the original narrator." They had many long talks, and he urged Sam, just as Artemus Ward had done, to break away from routine newspaper reporting and write creatively for a wider audience. At the time, and for thirteen years to come, Clemens considered Harte "one of the pleasantest men I have ever known." In 1877, however, an estrangement resulted from the failure of the play, *Ah Sin*, on which they had collaborated. Then Sam added to his earlier characterization of Harte: "He was also one of the unpleasantest men I have ever known." Harte might well have applied the same words to Clemens.

The Democratic State Convention to nominate candidates for Congress and presidential electors pledged to General George B. McClellan, met in San Francisco on September 7–8, 1864. James Norman Gillis, Steve's older brother, was one of the delegates from Tuolumne County, a gold mining region in the Sierra foothills (it includes the northern half of Yosemite National Park). Clemens reported all the sessions.

He was drawn at once to Jim Gillis, five years his senior, by his "lovable nature," his "bright and smart imagination," and the fact that he was a "born humorist," possessing the Southerner's unique gift for building a good story as he went along—on any subject. He soon discovered how widely read Jim was, and that he was university educated and trained as a physician. He observed how at times, Jim "unconsciously interjected" Greek and Latin quotations into his discussions and soliloquies. As Clemens grew better acquainted with him over the next two months, he came to believe that Jim Gillis "was a much more remarkable person than his family and his intimates ever suspected," and that as a writer he would have been "a star performer" if he had been "subjected to a few years training with a pen."

By mid-September, Clemens' writings for the *Call* began to give evidence of his growing discontent. It was time for another change because all his plans for a home with Steve Gillis and his wife, and a literary career in San Francisco, were frustrated by the breaking of Steve's engagement. This was surely the time when Sam wrote "The Doleful Ballad of the Rejected Lover," which Joe Goodman remembered hearing him and Gillis sing in duet at San Francisco. The words were bawdy—and angry, and directed at women in general and at one in particular. Goodman could always picture the two men standing side by side, shaking their fists furiously, their eyes flashing and their whole manner menacing.

Then, early in October, the *Call* dismissed him. George Barnes did not show Sam rudely to the door—"it was not in his nature to do that. . . . He took me privately aside and advised me to resign. It was like a father advising his son for his good, and I obeyed." Barnes softened the blow by telling him he was out of his element in routine reporting. "You are capable of better things in literature."

Sam had never been discharged before, and recalling it at the age of seventy, he said, "it hurts yet—although I am in my grave."

He insisted that for two months following his dismissal, his sole occupation was "avoiding acquaintances," for during that time he did not earn a penny, buy a single article, or pay for his board. "I became very adept at 'slinking.' I slunk from back street to back street, I slunk away from approaching faces that looked familiar." During all this time he had but one piece of money, a silver ten cent piece, which he would not spend on any account, "lest the consciousness coming strong upon me that I was entirely penniless, might suggest suicide. I pawned everything but the clothes I had on. . . ."

Actually between October first and December third of that year, he wrote ten articles at twelve dollars each for *The Californian.* There appeared on November 6 a piece entitled "Daniel In The Lion's Den—And Out Again All Right." In it he stated, "Now for several days I have been visiting the Board of Brokers, and associating with brokers, and drinking with them, and swapping lies with them . . ."

In a letter to Orion six days later, the inspiration for the piece becomes clear: Sam was watching the Hale & Norcross stock with an eagle eye, in the hope it will go up enough for him to sell some and set up his brother in a law practice, with a new house, "debt-free." By fraternizing with brokers he was hoping also to get tips which would help him dispose profitably of other mining shares. In addition, he had been attempting to borrow money for Orion, but without credit he was "pretty certain" it could not be done. Instead of slinking from alley to alley, he had been very much in evidence along Montgomery Street.

This letter to Orion is the last extant communication to his family until October 19 of the following year, 1865. In his November 11, 1864, letter there is no hint that about three weeks later he would abandon everything and set off with James Gillis for the cabin he shared with his younger brother, Billy Gillis, in Jackass Gulch, where they supported themselves by pocket-mining for gold.

The reason for Sam's seemingly sudden departure was supplied by his first, and designated, biographer, Albert Bigelow Paine. Paine stated that one night that fall, as Steve Gillis was walking by himself past a saloon, he heard sounds of an altercation and, walking in, found five men brawling—three, including the burly bartender, against two. Gillis immediately jumped into the fight on the side of the two, pitched into the barkeeper, and beat him so badly he had to be sent to the hospital. Small as Steve was, "with his fists he could whip anybody that walked on two legs, let his weight and science be what they might." Gillis was arrested and charged with assault with intent to kill, and Clemens went his bond. Then Gillis skipped off to Virginia City, and when the case was called, and he failed to appear, action was instituted against Sam Clemens, "with an execution against his loose property." According to Paine, this was the opportunity the city's police chief, Martin J. Burke, had been waiting for to avenge the attacks made on him and his force by Clemens in the *Territorial Enterprise*. Just at that moment, Jim Gillis appeared opportunely from Tuolumne County and rushed Sam off to the "far seclusion" of his Sierra cabin.

The problem with this tale, which has been accepted generally since 1912 and repeated countless times, is that there are no facts to support it. Most important, a careful search of the San Francisco newspapers during those weeks has disclosed no record of Steve Gillis' arrest and indictment, or of any court action against Clemens. Anything that happened to Sam Clemens/Mark Twain was newsworthy, no matter how trivial. This incident, involving a barroom brawl, bail-jumping, and Clemens' imminent arrest, would have been relished by reporters, especially his enemy Albert S. Evans, of *The Alta California*, who watched all Sam's doings closely in order to write them up in his locals with animosity and innuendo. But in this case, Evans was silent.

Further, there is no evidence that Clemens, before he left San Francisco, did anything to incur the enmity of Police Chief Burke, or that their relations were anything other than friendly.

Now, at November's end, Jim Gillis was ready to go back to the mountains and invited Sam to go with him. Steve Gillis, finding there was no hope of reconciliation with Emeline Russ, had already returned to Virginia City and his job on the *Enterprise*. Just now, mining stock prices were still low, Sam had some debts, marriage was out of the question, and Steve was gone. There was nothing to keep him in San Francisco, so he decided to leave. He had never given up the hope of striking it rich, and from what Jim Gillis told him about pocket mines, he believed there was a chance.

Dan De Quille was aware that Clemens had been chafing at the demands of "literary drudgery," and he knew the Gillis cabin as "a friendly place of retreat" where one could "rusticate and rejuvenate." Many a California writer had gone there for that purpose and was made welcome, for "the latch-string is always on the outside." Gillis' cabin was "a sort of Bohemian infirmary. There the sick are made well, and the well made better," mentally and physically.

On December 4, he and Jim Gillis boarded a San Joaquin River steamer for Stockton, and from there went on by stagecoach to "that serene and reposeful and dreamy and delicious sylvan paradise"—Jackass Gulch.

XVIII

———○———

THE JUMPING FROG

O N E O F T H E F I R S T things Sam Clemens noticed when he walked into Jim Gillis' cabin at Jackass Gulch was the collection of books—Shakespeare, Byron, Dickens, Bacon, "only first class Literature," and many works of other kinds—metaphysics, science, the ancient philosophers. About once a year, Jim went to San Francisco to visit his family and buy books. A friend remembered that Gillis was "bold enough to dispute any proposition he found in them where he thought the author had failed in either principal, consistency or logic," and that he and Jim often held long and earnest discussions. Gillis was interested in contemporary thought as well, and when Clemens went East at a later time, he offered to send him Darwin's work.

Just after Christmas, Sam, wearing his old blue flannel shirt, slouch hat, trousers stuffed into high boots, and revolver, set off with Jim on foot over the pine- and oak-covered hills to Vallecito, an old mining town. New Year's Day, found them inspecting a 480-foot tunnel being driven into an ancient river deposit of gold-bearing Eocene quartz gravels, which was already proving rich. At eight o'clock that night, with the moon in the first quarter and a light drizzling rain, they saw a rare and "magnificent" lunar rainbow, a fact which Clemens jotted in the notebook-journal he had started keeping again after a four-year lapse. He also put down that this night he had dreamed about Jim Townsend—James W. E. Townsend, a California and Nevada journalist and editor of great originality and humor, who was known as "Lying Jim" because of his fanciful imagination and utter disregard for truth in whatever he said or wrote.

Everything about Jim Gillis interested Clemens, from a personal and literary viewpoint, and the notebook contains frequent entries recording his opinions, attitudes, actions, stories, and snatches of his conversation, gained during their daily association in prospecting, or at relaxed times when they sat and smoked. But every so often, Jim would get an inspiration and stand up before the log fire, with his back to it and his hands crossed behind him, and "deliver himself of an . . . extravagant romance," most often featuring his mining partner, Dick Stoker, as the hero. Jim pretended that what he was telling was strictly true, and Dick, who had a cabin on Jackass Hill but spent most of his evenings at Jim's, would sit there puffing on his pipe and listening with "a gentle serenity to those monstrous fabrications" without a word of protest. Jacob Richard Stoker, of Kentucky, forty-five, "gray as a rat, earnest, thoughtful, slenderly educated, slouchily dressed, and clay-soiled," possessed a heart of "finer metal than any gold . . . that was ever mined or minted," Sam wrote. He was a Mexican War veteran who had joined the gold rush of 1849, and had stayed on after the boom, as Jim Gillis had done, because he enjoyed the way of life and was successful in finding gold enough to keep him comfortable.

One of Jim's stories was about Tom Quartz, a sagacious cat Dick Stoker was supposed to have owned, a cat who had "more hard, natchral sense than any man in this camp—'n' a *power* of dignity— he wouldn't let the Gov'ner of Californy be familiar with him. He never ketched a rat in his life—'peared to be above it. He never cared for nothing but mining. He knowed more about mining, that cat did, than any man *I* ever, ever see. You couldn't tell *him* noth'n' 'bout placer diggin's—'n' as for pocket-mining, why he was just born for it. . . ." Five years later, Clemens found a place for that tale in *Roughing It.*

By this time, Sam was aware of Jim Gillis' rapport with the wild creatures of the surrounding woods and fields. When he spoke to the quail or the rabbits he came upon in his three-acre garden, planted just below a big spring, his intentions were understood and they did not run away. Birds and squirrels being loquacious, they always responded whenever he talked with them, and he claimed to know just what they were saying. Some animals have large vocabularies and a fine command of language; therefore they talk a great deal. After long and careful observation, Jim had reached the conclusion that blue jays were the best talkers among both birds and beasts. "There's more to a bluejay. . . . He has got more moods, and more different kinds of feelings than other creatures; and, mind you, whatever a bluejay feels, he can put into language. And no mere commonplace language . . . but rattling, out-and-out book-talk—and bristling with metaphor, too. . . . Yes, sir, a jay is everything that a man is. A jay can cry, a jay can laugh, a jay can feel shame, a jay can reason and plan and discuss, . . . a jay has got a sense of humor, a jay knows when he is an ass just as well as you do—maybe better. . . . Now I'm going to tell you a perfectly true fact about some bluejays."

Jim then went on to tell about a blue jay he saw flying about with an acorn, looking for a place to store it; how he spotted a knothole in the roof of a one-story vacant cabin, and decided that was just the place, how the jay dropped in the one acorn, then flew off to get others; and how at length he became concerned at being unable to see the bottom of the hole or hear the acorn fall, and called in other jays for consultation; and how they all examined the hole, and discussed it, and "got off as many leather-headed opinions about it as the average crowd of humans could have done. . . ." Fourteen years after listening to Jim's tale, Clemens worked what he called "Baker's Bluejay Yarn," into *A Tramp Abroad.* Literarily, Sam's stay proved fruitful.

There is an entry in his notebook made soon after he and Gillis returned from Vallecito. It reads: "The 'Tragedian' & the Burning Shame. No women admitted." In looking back after forty-two years, Clemens thought that what Jim Gillis called "The Tragedy of the Burning Shame" was one of his "impromptu tales." However, in a letter written to Jim just five years later, when the memory was fresh, he said: "And wouldn't I love to take old Stoker by the hand, and wouldn't I love to see him in his great specialty, his wonderful rendition of 'Rinaldo' in the 'Burning Shame!' " It was a skit rather than a story, then. Doubtless Jim Gillis was the narrator, and Dick Stoker worked in pantomime.

Clemens adapted it for a performance given by the king and the duke in *Huckleberry Finn*. "I had to modify it considerably to make it fit for print and this was a great damage." In 1907, he recalled it as being "one of the most outrageously funny things I have ever listened to."

In the manuscript of *Huckleberry Finn*, it is seen that he originally intended to call the king's performance "The Burning Shame," but changed it in the final revision to the "Thrilling Tragedy of THE KING'S CAMELOPARD or THE ROYAL NONESUCH!!!" The bottom line of the handbills announcing the show was in the biggest print of all: "LADIES AND CHILDREN NOT ADMITTED."

In the book, Huck Finn tells how, after the curtain was rolled up, the king came "a-prancing out on all fours, naked; and he was painted all over, ring-streaked-and-striped, all sorts of colors, as splendid as a rainbow. And—never mind the rest of his outfit, it was just as wild, but it was awful funny. The people most killed themselves laughing; and when the king done capering, and capered off behind the scenes, they roared and clapped and stormed and haw-hawed till he come back and done it over again. . . ."

"How mild it is in the book and how pale; how extravagant and how gorgeous in its unprintable form!" Clemens regretted.

In the early 1930s, an account of just such a skit, also called "The Tragedy of the Burning Shame," was heard in Seattle. It was said to have been performed in a small town in Sweden, implying folk origin. However, when the description of the Swedish piece is compared with Huck Finn's, they are so alike in every detail but one, the reader is forced to suspect that Samuel Clemens was the original source. The Seattle version even includes the preparation of the stage, the one actor collecting admissions at the door, then making a curtain speech praising the tragedy—and afterward, the angry audience feeling cheated and clamoring, "What, is it over? Is that *all?*", just as Huck's does. The only particular missing from the boy's description of the king's "outfit," but present in the

The Jumping Frog

Swedish account, was a lighted candle inserted between his buttocks. The candle's presence explains the title "The Burning Shame," a candle having phallic significance which Clemens used later in *Letters from the Earth,* long suppressed.

Although he never published the unexpurgated story, Clemens would have relished telling it to an appreciative and select male audience in this country or abroad. He told it to his friend and literary mentor, William Dean Howells, who had read *Huckleberry Finn* in typescript, so that he would know "how extravagant and how gorgeous" Jim Gillis' skit was in its unprintable form. He regretted to Howells the existence of that "sad, sad false delicacy" which deprived modern literature of one of its most valuable sources—"obscene stories." And he certainly told it to his clerical friend, Joseph Hopkins Twichell of Hartford, for whom he wrote the letter, "1601: Fireside Conversation in the Time of Queen Elizabeth." Its object was to reveal "the picturesqueness of parlor conversation in Elizabeth's time . . . therefore if there was a decent or delicate word findable in it, it is because I overlooked it." He recalled that he and Twichell would lie in the grass upon a carpet of golden hickory leaves, read "1601" aloud, and "laugh ourselves lame and sore" over it.

In 1899, Clemens spent the summer in Sweden, where he would have found opportunities to give an account of "The Tragedy of the Burning Shame" just as he had seen it in Jackass Gulch. Over the ensuing thirty-odd years, the original identification with Clemens might easily have been lost in its many retellings on the road to Seattle.

Jim Gillis may have come upon "The Burning Shame" in his wide and unorthodox reading, for its Rabelaisian humor was not limited to any age, or he might have seen it performed, or heard it described. However, the presence of the character "Rinaldo," Dick Stoker's "great speciality," suggests that Gillis added to the cast— or gave a classical touch to an otherwise bald skit—by borrowing Orlando's cousin Rinaldo from the fifteenth century poem, *Orlando Innamorta,* in which the frantic pursuit of Rinaldo by the lovesick Angelica would have presented further opportunities for bawdy humor.

At French Flat, not far from Tuttletown, the village nearest Jackass Hill and Jackass Gulch, lived the Daniels family. Their two daughters, Nelly and Molly, were of an age to provide romantic interest and dancing partners for Sam Clemens and Billy Gillis. The girls boasted of having "the slimmest waists, the largest bustles, and the stiffest starched petticoats" in the entire area. They were known locally as the "Chaparral Quails." Clemens described them as "lovely" and "peerless" and thought it important enough to jot in his notebook that Jim Gillis imagined him married to Nelly.

By January 22, he and Jim were at Angels Camp in Calaveras County, another early gold town, intending to start pocket-mining, but the following day it began to rain and storm, forcing them to take refuge in a hotel run by a Frenchman. Their stay was memorable for the wretched food. The first time the waiter served coffee, Jim told him he had made a mistake: he had ordered *coffee*—this was day-before-yesterday's dishwater. Delighted with the description, Sam put down in his notebook: "Beans & dishwater for breakfast . . . dishwater & beans for dinner, & both articles warmed over for supper." His entries for eight days recorded the monotony: "Rained all day—meals as before." "Same as above." "Same old diet." Variety was introduced twice—a beefsteak tough as Mexican leather, which was of "no use," for they couldn't even bite into it, and a kind of "slum" which the Frenchman insisted was hash. "Hash be d--d."

Sam's notes were once more interspersed with French words, for he had his grammar with him and was studying the language again. It was recalled that Jim sometimes lost patience with him for working on his French lessons when there was wood to be chopped and brought in, and other chores to be done around the cabin at Jackass. The notebook contained those snatches of conversation he jotted down for possible literary use, as well as random items from his own experience or told to him by Jim.

One of these he turned into "The Californian's Tale," almost thirty years later, while living in Florence. His original note made at Angels read: "Boden crazy, asking after his wife, who had been dead thirteen years—first knowledge of his being deranged."

The story spun from that jotting opened: "Thirty-five years ago, I was out prospecting on the Stanislaus, tramping all day with pick and pan and horn. . . . It was a lovely region, woodsy, balmy, delicious. . . ." In his wanderings he came across a rose-clad cottage, and a man standing by the gate who greeted him and invited him in. It was "Boden," of course, who showed him through the rooms of the neat house with wall-paper and rag carpets, framed lithographs, and "bright-colored tidies and lamp-mats, and Windsor chairs, and varnished what-nots, with seashells and books and china vases on them. . . ." Seeing his look of approval, Boden said: "All her work; she did it all herself—every bit. Nothing here that hasn't felt the touch of her hand." Where was she? Away visiting her parents. But she would be coming home in three days. Only later, when friends stopped by, did the narrator learn that she had been dead all those years.

After a week of the Frenchman's cooking, Jim Gillis said to Sam that they *had* to stand the weather but "we *won't* stand this dishwater & beans any longer, by God!", and the following day they moved to Lake's, a new hotel which had just opened. The genial Ross Coon, one of the best-known chess-players and bartenders in the Southern Mines, was the proprietor and host. The hotel offered good food, and coffee that "a Christian may drink without jeopardizing his eternal soul."

At this point in the journal is the first mention of "Bilgewater" as a name. Its appeal was strong and Clemens used it often in his works—in an unpublished sketch about Angels Camp, in an 1866 letter to the *Alta California,* in *Roughing It,* in *Huckleberry Finn,* and even in "1601," where the Duchess of Bilgewater takes part in the conversation between Queen Elizabeth, Shakespeare, Ben Jonson, Bacon, Beaumont, and Sir Walter Raleigh.

On the night of February first Sam saw Laura Wright in a dream. It was morning, and she was seated in a carriage; they shook hands and said good-bye. This entry was made not in the body of the notebook but on the last page, facing the back cover, in a special place by itself.

By this time, Dick Stoker had joined them, and the stormy days and nights were spent mainly in the hotel bar room where Ross Coon presided, smoking and drinking, playing cards, billiards, and chess, or sitting around the stove telling stories and jokes, or listening to the townspeople gossiping and recounting their life stories. Once or twice, Sam and Jim Gillis entertained themselves and others by talking like men eighty-years-old and toothless. Sam noted that the popular drink was whiskey of a kind that "will throw a man a double somerset and limber him up like boiled maccaroni before he can set his glass down. . . . Marvelous and incomprehensible is the straight whisky of Angels' Camp."

One stormy day as they sat about the tavern stove, Ross Coon told a story which Sam condensed: "Coleman and his jumping frog —bet stranger $50—stranger had no frog, & C got him one—in the meantime stranger filled C's frog full of shot & he couldn't jump—the stranger's frog won."

Shortly, Clemens was to write "Jim Smiley and His Jumping Frog," which, with revisions, became "The Celebrated Jumping Frog of Calaveras County"—the story that brought him his first wide recognition.

At last the weather cleared and the days became "blazing" hot, according to Sam's notes, and the three men turned at last to pocket-mining, Jim and Dick digging and washing, and Clemens carrying the water, for the complicated process was not for the novice. But they had no success, and went on to tour the groves of rare Big Trees northeast of Angels, and then south to Yosemite.

After almost two weeks of tramping, the weather grew stormy again, and on February 20, the three men walked back over the mountains to Jackass Gulch in a snowstorm—the first Sam had ever seen in California. From the heights, the view across the expanses of whitened forests was magnificent.

They found Jackass Hill deep in snow and buzzing with excitement over the birth of a baby to Mrs. Carrington, wife of Jim Gillis' partner in what was perhaps the richest mining property there. In Sam's eyes, there was nothing remarkable about the week-old infant, and he believed that if the lady had given birth to a cast-iron dog of a size to ornament the State House steps, the event would not have created more of a stir. But then, that "sparse community" was always in "dire commotion" about some thing of small importance. Of more consequence to him was the discovery that he had left his knife, his meerschaum, and his toothbrush at Angels Camp.

Clemens was preparing to return to San Francisco. Although Jim Gillis certainly urged him to stay longer, and the "old philosopher," as Sam called him, had won his lifelong admiration and affection, he was restless again. Perhaps he thought he could make a start on the planned book about his Nevada experiences, for his most recent notebook reminders contained references to Billy Clagett, Benjamin Bunker, Honey Lake Smith's, and Bob Howland. But another heavy snowstorm kept him at the cabin two days more. On February 23, he started by horseback for Copperopolis, a settlement of one thousand, twelve miles distant, to connect with the morning stage for Stockton. He found to his disgust that the stage would not be leaving until the morning after. He spent his time vainly hunting in that "hell-fired" town for another pipe, and took a tour of the great Union Copper Mine, the largest producer in California. He walked through all the branches of its six galleries and countless drifts, noticing that in places the vein was eighteen feet wide. A week or so earlier, one of the partners had sold his half for $650,000. That was the kind of fortune Sam was always hoping for.

The Stockton riverboat docked at San Francisco on the twenty-sixth. "Home again—home again at the Occidental Hotel," he recorded the same day. After Jackass Gulch and Angels Camp, here was "Heaven on the half-shell."

In his accumulated mail, he found letters from Artemus Ward urging him to contribute a sketch for Ward's new book of travels, to be published shortly. Sam thought of working up that jumping frog story but when he saw that the letters were dated early in November, he concluded it was too late.

XIX

<hr>

TASTE OF FAME

I N T H E A B S E N C E O F any record, life for Sam Clemens was presumably much the same as it had been during those months before he went to Jackass Gulch. Soon after he returned he discontinued his notebook, and although he corresponded with his family, no letters have been found for the period up to October 19, 1865, when he wrote to Orion and Mollie. That letter was in response to a sermon from his brother; in it Orion had exhibited "true, unmistakable *genius*. . . . It is one of the few sermons that I have read with pleasure—I do not say profit, because I am beyond the reach of argument now. . . .

"And now let me preach *you* a sermon. I never had but two *powerful* ambitions in my life. One was to be a pilot, & the other a preacher of the gospel. I accomplished the one & failed in the other, *because* I could not supply myself with the necessary stock in trade—i.e. religion. . . . But I *have* had a 'call' to literature, of a low order—i.e. humorous. It is nothing to be proud of, but it is my strongest suit. . . .

"Now *you* aspire to be a *lawyer*, when the voice of God is thundering in your ears, & you are wilfully deaf & will not hear. *You* were *intended* for a preacher, & lo! you would be a scheming, groveling mud-cat of a *lawyer*. A man *never is* willing to do what his

Taste of Fame

Creator intended him to do . . . *You* see in me a talent for humorous writing, & urge me to cultivate it. But I always regarded it as brotherly partiality . . . & attached no value to it. It is only now, when editors of standard literary papers in the distant East give me high praise, & who do not know me . . . that I really begin to believe there must be something in it. . . .

"But . . . I will toss up with you. I will drop all trifling . . . & strive for a fame . . . if you will record your promise to go hence to the States & preach the gospel. . . . I am in earnest. Shall it be so?"

Orion had mentioned his debts. "I am also in debt. But I have gone to work in dead earnest to get out. Joe Goodman pays me $100 a month for a daily letter, and the Dramatic Chronicle pays me $—or rather *will* begin to pay me, next week—$40 a month for dramatic criticism. Same wages I got on the *Call,* & more agreeable & less laborious work.

"Mollie, my Dear, I send you slathers of love. Write to me to-night."

After additional urging from Artemus Ward to contribute a sketch to his book, Sam wrote what he called "Jim Smiley and His Jumping Frog," and mailed it to Ward's New York publisher, G. W. Carleton. It arrived after the book was in proof and might have been included if Carleton had wanted to delay publication. But he did not think highly of the squib, and using the excuse that it had come too late, sent it on to Henry Clapp, Jr., editor of the expiring *Saturday Press,* a New York weekly which had published Walt Whitman, Ada Clare, Adah Isaacs Menken, and other frequenters of Pfaff's Cellar. Clapp liked it, and the story appeared on November 18, introduced by a complimentary note:

We give up the principal portion of our editorial space to-day, to an exquisitely humorous sketch—"Jim Smiley and his Jumping Frog" —by Mark Twain, who will shortly become a regular contributor to our columns. Mark Twain is the assumed name of a writer in California who has long been a favorite contributor to the San Francisco press, from which his articles have been so extensively copied as to make him nearly as well known as Artemus Ward.

Sam was not to learn for another six weeks that "Mark Twain's story . . . called 'Jim Smiley and His Jumping Frog,' has set all New York in a roar, and he may be said to have made his mark . . . the papers are copying it far and near. It is voted the best thing of the day."

Uncertain as to the tale's fate after Carleton received it, Clemens showed Bret Harte a version that differed in having the leading character named Greeley rather than Smiley, and the "ancient mining camp," scene of the incident, called by its rightful name, Angels, instead of Noomerang, as it appeared in the manuscript sent East. Harte liked the story and printed it in *The Californian* on December 16.

On October 20, Sam wrote to Mollie on the back of his letter dated the previous day. "Friday—Have just got your letter . . . I read all your sermons—and I shall continue to read them, but of course as unsympathetically as a man of stone. I have a religion— but you will call it blasphemy. It is that there is a God for the rich man but none for the poor.

"You are in trouble, & in debt—so am I. I am utterly miserable —so are you. Perhaps your religion will sustain you, will feed you —I place no dependence in mine. Our religions are alike, though, in one respect—neither can make a man happy when he is out of luck. If I do not get out of debt in 3 months,—pistols or poison for one—exit *me*. [There's a text for a sermon on Self-Murder—Proceed.]"

He was determined to get money enough to pay his debts and Orion's, and take him home better off financially than when he had left four years ago,—a point of pride that had kept him in the West. He approached an old friend, Herman Camp, who was a "rustler," a man of untiring energy, large capital, and influential business connections in New York, about selling the Tennessee acreage. Although oil had been recently discovered on the land, Camp said the acres were valuable even without oil, now that there was peace and no slavery. Camp was leaving for the East in five days, and Clemens told him that if he would send him five hundred dollars from New York to travel on, and another five hundred afterward, and pay all his expenses while he helped sell the land, Sam would give him one-half of the entire proceeds of the sale.

"I am tired of being a beggar—tired of being chained to this accursed homeless desert,—I want to go back to a Christian land once more," he wrote Orion, who must send *immediately* all pertinent papers and memoranda which will help Camp understand the conditions and resources of the acreage.

Sam's pent-up frustration at being a beggar in exile found outlet in a campaign of biting sarcasm launched against the San Francisco police in his letters to the *Territorial Enterprise*. The best were reprinted in the *Golden Era* and did not pass unnoticed by the chief of police, the mayor, and the supervisors. One piece, "What Have the Police Been Doing?" opened:

"Ain't they virtuous? Don't they take good care of the city? Is not their constant vigilance and efficiency shown in the fact that . . . ladies even on the back streets are safe from insult in the daytime, when . . . under the protection of a regiment of soldiers?" He pointed out that while many "offenders of importance" went unpunished, the police "infallibly snaffle every Chinese chicken-thief that attempts to drive his trade, and are duly glorified by name in the papers for it."

He cited the case of a citizen who had recently broken a man's skull with a club for supposedly stealing "six bits" worth of flour sacks, and who had taken him to the station house, where he was "jammed into one of the cells in the most humorous way. . . . And why shouldn't they shove that half-senseless wounded man into a cell without getting a doctor to examine and see how badly he was hurt, and consider that next day would be time enough, if he chanced to live that long? And why shouldn't the jailor let him alone when he found him in a dead stupor two hours after—let him alone because he couldn't wake him—couldn't wake a man who was sleeping . . . with that calm serenity which is peculiar to men whose heads have been caved in with a club. . . . Why certainly—why shouldn't he?—the man was an infernal stranger. He had no vote." Besides, had he not put himself outside the pale of humanity and Christian sympathy by the "hellish act" of stealing the flour sacks? "I think so. The Department think so. Therefore when the stranger died at 7 in the morning, after four hours refreshing slumber in that cell, . . . what the very devil do you want to go and find fault with the prison officers for? . . . It takes all my time to defend them from the people's attacks. . . ."

It is not surprising then that the police had orders to watch Clemens, and that some time after mid-January 1866, he was arrested for being drunk in public, and jailed overnight. Here was an item to delight Albert Evans of the *Alta California,* who, in writing on January 22 of the relocation of the city's slaughter houses, objected to removing them to North Beach near the Presidio since the prevailing winds coming through the Golden Gate would give the entire city the full benefit of "a stench which is only second in horrible density to that which prevails in the Police Court when the Bohemian of the Sage-Brush is in the dock for being drunk over night."

Two days before Evans' reference to his jailing, Clemens wrote to his mother and Pamela: "I don't know what to write—my life is so uneventful. I wish I was back there piloting up & down the river again. Verily, all is vanity and little worth—save piloting. To think that after writing many an article a man might be excused for thinking tolerably good, those New York people should single out a villainous backwood sketch to compliment me on!—'Jim Smiley and His Jumping Frog'—a squib which would never have been written except to please Artemus Ward, & then it reached New York too late to appear in his book. But no matter—his book was a wretchedly poor one, generally speaking, & it could be no credit to either of us to appear between its covers." Here Sam pasted in the clipping about the sketch having set all New York in a roar.

He and Bret Harte have quit *The Californian,* Sam continued. Harte will contribute regularly to the *Christian Register* of Boston, and he will write for the New York *Weekly Review,* and possibly the *Saturday Press.* "I sent a sketch to the *Review* by yesterday's steamer, which will probably appear . . . about the middle or latter part of February." It was called "An Open Letter to the American People."

There is, he wrote in the article, "only one brief, solitary law for letter-writing. . . . Write only about things and people your correspondent takes a living interest in." Yet how do they write? He quoted a letter from his fictitious "Aunt Nancy" as an example: she talked about people he had never heard of before; and urged him to mend his ways, suggesting he read "II. Kings, from chap. 2 to chap. 24 inclusive. It would be so gratifying to me if you would experience a change of heart." She gave war news: "I could never drive it into those numskulls that the overland telegraph enabled me to know here in San Francisco every day all that transpired in the United States the day before. . . ." And, " 'Read twenty-two chapters of Second Kings' is a nice shell to fall in the camp of a man who is not studying for the ministry." There is not a word about his girlfriends, or about Zeb Leavenworth, or Sam Bowen, "or anybody else I care a straw for. . . . My venerable mother is a tolerably good correspondent—she is above the average, at any rate. She puts on her spectacles and takes her scissors and wades into a pile of newspapers and slashes out column after column— editorials, hotel arrivals, poetry, telegraph news, advertisements, novelettes, old jokes, recipes for making pies, cures for 'biles'— anything that comes handy . . . she is entirely impartial," just so it comes from a St. Louis paper. Then she "jams it into the envelope along with her letter," which includes news about everyone Sam ever knew or heard of, the only problem being that she identifies them solely by their initials, forgetting, when she tells him that W. L. is going to marry T. D., or that B. K. has died, that some of the once familiar names are no longer remembered.

"The most useful and interesting letters . . . from home are from children seven or eight years old. This is petrified truth. Happily they have got nothing to talk about but home, and neighbors, and family—things their betters think unworthy of transmission thousands of miles. They write simply and naturally, . . . tell all they know, and then stop. They seldom deal in abstractions or moral homilies. . . . Therefore, if you would learn the art of letter-writing, let a little child teach you." He then quotes a letter attributed to his niece Annie, "the only letter I ever got from the States that had any information in it." It runs thus:

St. Louis, 1865. Uncle Mark, if you was here I could tell you about Moses in the Bulrushers again. I know it better, now. Mr. Sowerberry has got his leg broke off a horse. He was riding it on Sunday. Margaret, that's the maid, Margaret has took all the spittoons, and slop-buckets, and old jugs out of your room, because she says she don't think you're ever coming back any more, you been gone so long. Sissy McElroy's mother has got another little baby. She has them all the time. It has got little blue eyes, like Mr. Swimley that boards there, and looks just like him. . . . Miss Doosenberry was here today; I give her your picture, but she said she didn't want it. My cat has got more kittens. . . . And there's one such a sweet little buff one with a short tail, and I named it for you.

In his letter home, telling his family to watch for this piece, he said, "If it makes Annie mad I can't help it." No offense was meant to any of them. The aunt he mentions is neither Aunt Ella nor Aunt Betsy Smith; they will see she has no resemblance to them. He was only using these people as types of a class.

"Though I am generally placed at the head of my breed of scribblers in this part of the country, the place properly belongs to Bret Harte, I think . . . though he denies it, along with the rest. He wants me to club a lot of old sketches together with his, & publish a book. . . ." Sam was interested only if some money could be made from it. Harte had already written to a New York publisher, and if they offer enough money to pay "for a month's labor, we will go to work. . . . My labor will not occupy more than 24 hours, because I will only have to take the scissors & slash my old sketches out of the Enterprise & the Californian—I burned up a small cart-load of them lately—so *they* are forever ruled out of any book—but they were not worth publishing.

"Understand—all this I am telling you is in confidence—we want it to go no further. . . ."

Sam was brimming with literary plans. He and Harte had another secret: They are going to parody a book of poetry which will be published in the spring. "We know all the tribe of California poets, & understand their different styles, & I think we can just make them howl."

At this point he pasted in a clipping from the San Francisco *Examiner,* which read:

"That rare humorist, 'Mark Twain,' whose fame is rapidly extending all over the country, informs us that he has commenced the work of writing a book. He says it will treat on an entirely new subject, one that has not been written about heretofore. We predict that it will be a very popular book, and make fame and fortune for the gifted author."

The book referred to was a "pet notion" of his. No one, not even Orion, knew what it was going to be about. "I am slow & lazy, you know, & the bulk of it will not be finished under a year. I expect it to make about three hundred pages, and the last hundred will have to be written in St. Louis, because the materials for them can only be got there." This suggests the subject may have had to do with piloting on the Mississippi, his own experiences included—an idea which he developed later for the semi-autobiographical *Life on the Mississippi,* published in 1883. "If I do not write it to suit me at first I will write it all over again, & so, who knows?—I may be an old man before I finish it. I have not written a line for three weeks, & may not for three more. I shall write only when the spirit moves me. I am the Genius of Indolence."

He enclosed one of his *Enterprise* letters, to be given to pilot Zeb Leavenworth. It described the ship *Ajax,* "the finest ocean steamer in America, & one of the fastest." Sam was among the fifty-two guests invited on her maiden voyage to the Sandwich Islands—one month, round-trip. The "cream of the town—gentlemen & ladies both" made up the party, and there was to be "a splendid brass band" besides. He knew most of the people going, but could not leave because there was no one to write his daily letter to the *Enterprise.* "If the Ajax were back I would go—quick!—and throw up the correspondence. Where could a man catch another such crowd together?"

This was the second time that work for the *Territorial Enterprise* had kept him from visiting the Islands. Previously, he had had to sacrifice making the trip with Joe Goodman because there was no one to edit the paper. Now the "vagabond instinct was strong" upon him, and he was determined to find some way of going without losing the needed pay. His *Enterprise* letter of February 25 was written from Sacramento, where he had arrived by the riverboat *Antelope* at three that morning. His business was to call on the editors of the Sacramento *Daily Union,* whom he already knew, and discuss with them the possibility of becoming their special correspondent for a few months. He told his old schoolmate, Will

Bowen, that it was with the understanding he was to go anywhere they chose, and that they decided on the Sandwich Islands. Certainly, he must have suggested the possibility, for it was there he wanted to go. Back in San Francisco, he booked passage on the *Ajax.*

A few days before Clemens went to Sacramento, his nemesis, Albert S. Evans of the *Alta,* wrote his vale. Mark Twain was "played out," he announced. "I understand that the individual aforesaid, who used to run as a deck-hand on a stern wheeler . . . is disgusted with San Francisco. Well, my boy, the disgust is mutual. . . . He has been a little out of health lately and is now endeavoring to get a chance to go to Honolulu, where he expects to get rid of one disease by catching another; the last being more severe for the time being, but more readily yielding to medical treatment. If he can get a chance to correspond for some respectable newspaper, the new steamer line will carry him free, and he will make a desperate effort to retrieve his waning fortunes. . . . If he goes he will be sadly missed by the police, but then they can stand it. . . ." Later, Goodman recalled Clemens saying that one of his main objects in life was to make enough money to stand trial, then go and kill Evans.

Sam was confident his friend, Herman Camp, would manage to sell the Tennessee land eventually, and was counting on the proceeds after his return. But things happened more rapidly than he anticipated. After looking over the property, and getting some advice, Camp decided to buy it himself and plant the acres to grapes, importing skilled growers and wine-makers from Europe's most famous wine-producing districts. He sent a telegram to Sam offering $200,000, and Clemens immediately wired back his acceptance. Almost in disbelief he telegraphed Orion the news of their great good fortune that would solve all their financial problems forever.

Herman Camp then authorized his San Francisco agent to prepare the contract. Sam signed it and sent it on immediately to Orion at Carson City. He urged his brother to put his name to it right away, before anything could possibly interfere.

But Orion, as Sam once wrote, "changed his principles with the moon, his politics with the weather, and his religion with his shirt." Just at this moment he was a strong temperance advocate. He refused to sign the contract and become party to "debauching the country with wine." Further, in the role of Christian and humanitarian, how could he be sure Mr. Camp was going to deal fairly with those poor people he would import from Europe?

Sam was appalled and furious, and blasted his brother for his selfishness in refusing to consider what the sale would mean for the entire family. Could Orion not sacrifice his objections to drinking just this once for the sake of their mother (Sam alone was contributing to her support), and now Pamela and her two children—for Will Moffett had died suddenly the previous year, leaving many debts because the war had ruined his business. There was Mollie, "utterly miserable" in her poverty, and Sam, an exile, barely making his way. It was Orion's *duty* to let the land be sold. But in his replies Orion turned the other cheek and quoted scripture, which infuriated Sam still more, provoking additional angry letters and finally a break with his brother. He tried to prod Orion's conscience to a realization that after ruining the family's opportunity for wealth, he was obliged to go East and sell the land himself.

At first, after he had signed the contract, Sam was undecided about his assignment for the Sacramento *Union*. Perhaps he ought to give it up and simply wait in San Francisco until his share of the money came, then start for the East. But when he found that Orion could not be reasoned, shamed, or badgered into approving the sale, there was no question as to Sam's course. He felt utterly hopeless about his future, and deeply bitter toward his brother. A change of scene and activity was the proper solution. His friends encouraged him and supplied him with introductory letters to everyone worth knowing in the Islands, the king included. And they furnished him with a case of wine, several boxes of cigars, and a "small assortment of medicinal liquors and brandy."

On March 5, two days before the *Ajax* sailed, he sent news of his departure to his mother and Pamela. Sam was still staggering from Orion's blow; the note was perfunctory, and closed not with the usual affectionate words, but simply with, "Goodbye for the present." He planned to remain a month, he told them, "ransack" the Islands, and write twenty or thirty letters, for which he will earn the same amount he would have if he had stayed at home. He is to arrive at Honolulu in about twelve days. *If* he returns to San Francisco—he has been thinking of a trip around the world, starting from the Islands—he will set off at once across the continent, going by way of the Columbia River, Pend O'reille Lake, over the Rockies, through Montana, and down the Missouri River to St. Louis. The journey would be almost entirely by water, he noted. It is curious that he should have considered this wilderness route which so closely paralleled the one taken by Lewis and Clark. Possibly it was a reflection of his mood of disillusionment.

The *Ajax* sailed about four o'clock on the afternoon of March 7, the tides and winds being compatible. It was a pleasant breezy day, and Sam was quickly caught up in the strange new sense of "perfect emancipation from labor and responsibility," and went up to the hurricane deck where he could have "room to enjoy it."

The first of three writer's notebooks was started again, and on the second night out from San Francisco he made one of his few personal entries. Sam had just finished reading those letters from home he had not had time to open before sailing. They contained accounts of further oil discoveries on the Tennessee land, provoking him to observe, "& that worthless worthless [cancelled twice] brother of mine, with his eternal cant about law & religion, getting ready in his slow, stupid way, to go to Excelsior, instead of the States," to market the acreage. "He sends me some prayers as usual." Excelsior was a mining district in Nevada's Esmeralda County, where Orion intended to open a law office which was naturally doomed to failure.

During the voyage his entries concentrated on the weather, which was stormy for three days, prompting him to take Balboa, that "foreign person," to task for having named this ocean the Pacific, "thus uttering a lie which will go on deceiving generation after generation." In his notebook, he jotted down what information he could glean about the islands through talk with those passengers who were resident. This resulted in a miscellany of bits about the king, the royal family, the missionaries, statistics on the sugar industry, and the government, and customs and superstitions. The practice of secretly obtaining some personal possession of an enemy, and then attempting to pray him to death, had its counterpart in parts of the American South. As always, he recorded

Taste of Fame

reminders of anecdotes, bits of conversation, regional dialect, and occupational vernacular. He listened to three whaling captains playing euchre: "Who hove that ace on there?" "Here goes for a euchre—by G--; I'll make a point or break a rope-yarn." "Now what'd you trump that for?—You're sailin' too close to the wind— there, I know'd it—royals, stuns'ls—everything, gone to h--l." From these notes he built a scene which included himself in a game of euchre with the whalers, having a little trouble because of their seafaring terminology. He included it in his first letter to the Sacramento *Union*.

When the *Ajax* docked at Honolulu, about noon on Sunday, March 18, there was a crowd of some four or five hundred to greet it. It was not unlike the event of the day at Carson City, when the whole town turned out for the arrival of the overland stage—only here it was more colorful and novel. Sam's eye was immediately drawn to the bright yellow, orange, and crimson robes, "voluminous as a balloon, with full sleeves," worn by the native women. Their "jaunty" little hats were trimmed with fresh flowers, and about their throats were necklaces of vermillion ohia blossoms. He saw that many of the younger ones had very pretty faces, splendid black eyes, and heavy masses of long black hair. Some were afoot (they wore no shoes), others on horseback, "astraddle," which he acknowledged must be the best way to ride, for he learned there were no more accomplished horsewomen in the world. Out of the throng he picked Chinese in native dress, affluent Hawaiians in bright colors, and foreigners wearing cool summer white. And children—scores of "half-naked" bright-eyed boys and girls—chattering happily and laughing.

Sam's alter ego, "Mr. Brown," an imaginary companion, uncouth and irrepressible, whom readers of his later contributions to *The Californian* and the *Enterprise* had met briefly, appeared in his first letter to the *Union,* and then with growing frequency and importance. Clemens was obviously intrigued by Brown through whom he expressed earthy, skeptical, and irreverent thoughts as they came to mind, and he quickly developed the character. This ancient literary device was possibly suggested to Sam by Sancho Panza in *Don Quixote*. He had already experimented with it in

Nevada, by having "the Unreliable" display ignorance, atrocious manners, and prejudices through crude remarks.

Sam soon found quarters in Honolulu—a room in a neat white cottage with green window-shutters, surrounded by a large grassy yard. The house was shaded by "noble" tamarind trees covered with striking red-striped yellow flowers, by the fragrant Pride of India, whose purple blossoms resembled the lilac, he thought, and by mangos. He then set off on foot to explore, leaving Mr. Brown in bed to recover his land legs.

Clemens quickly fell under the spell of this city where, instead of the eternal geranium languishing in a pot on the doorstep, as in San Francisco, he saw "luxurious banks and thickets of flowers," rich with glowing colors, in every yard. He was particularly attracted to those blooms which perfumed the air—jasmine, ginger, nicotiana, and balsam. "In the place of roughs and rowdies staring and blackguarding on the corners," it was pleasing to see pretty, long-haired native girls in flower-colored dresses, sitting on the ground in the shade, speaking softly in musical voices. And to his delight, he saw cats—"individual cats, groups of cats, platoons of cats, companies of cats, regiments of cats, armies of cats, multitudes of cats, millions of cats," of every color and kind—orange, grey, black, white, striped, spotted, long-tailed, bob-tailed, one-eyed, cross-eyed—and all of them "sleek, fat, lazy, and sound asleep."

The absence of care-worn, anxious faces impressed him. "God! what a contrast with California & Washoe." Here they *live*—"d--n San F. style of wearing out life." He relaxed and quickly recovered from the mumps, which he had developed four days before landing. He feared he would take "a new disease to the Islands & depopulate them, as all white men have done heretofore."

Although claiming that he preferred to "idle," in reality Sam enjoyed the demands of his assignment, which kept him constantly on the move. During the first two weeks at Honolulu he acquired another quirky horse, similar in disposition to "Bunker" of his Nevada mining days, and toured the entire island of Oahu, chiefly in the company of newly made friends who acted as his guides.

On the day set for the first excursion, Sam arranged to inspect the government prison in the morning and join his party later at

Taste of Fame

Diamond Head. He was hardly out of sight of the livery stable that afternoon when his new horse exhibited the first of many eccentricities—that of entering every gate they came to. "I had neither whip nor spur, and so I simply argued the case with him," but the horse resisted firmly: "Within the next six hundred yards he crossed the street fourteen times and attempted thirteen gates." Ultimately yielding to "insult and abuse," the animal proceeded to take a straight course and after further persuasion, to break into "a convulsive sort of canter, which had three short steps in it and one long one—a cross between the last big clattering earthquake Sam had experienced at San Francisco, and the rolling pitch of the steamer *Ajax.*

A mile and a half from the city was Waikiki, where the king went frequently to spend quiet days in a modest white cottage nestled in the heart of a large coconut grove. As he passed, Sam noticed that the royal flag was on the staff. Not far away was the ruin of an ancient temple built of rough lava blocks, which he stopped to see. As he walked about in the roofless enclosure, he reflected on those times long past, centuries before the missionaries arrived and made the native people "permanently miserable by telling them how beautiful and blissful a place heaven is, and how nearly impossible it is to get there; and showed the poor native how dreary a place perdition is and what unnecessarily liberal facilities there are for going to it . . . showed him what a rapture it is to work all day long for fifty cents to buy food for the next day with, as compared with fishing for pastime and lolling in the shade through eternal summer, and eating the bounty that nobody labored to provide but nature. How sad it is to think of the multitude who have gone to their graves in this beautiful island and never knew there was a hell! . . ."

Clemens was thirty when he wrote this. Plainly, his skepticism was already well formed and was not the product of his later years, as is often claimed.

He caught up with his party just beyond Diamond Head. Although it was growing dark, instead of turning back they went "on —on—on—a great deal too far, I thought, for people who were not accustomed to riding on horseback, and who must expect to suffer on the morrow." He was speaking of himself, for he hit the saddle hard. Then night fell, the moon rose, and a cool yet balmy breeze, "with its odor of countless flowers," sprang up. "Moonlight here is fine, but nowhere so fine as Washoe," he observed. It was time then to start home. The high tide, they soon discovered, had cut off the regular route, but their leader, young Henry McFarlane, said not to worry because he knew a "nice, comfortable" short-cut, so they all dropped into his wake. But his "chart was at fault," for he led them into a vale surrounded by precipices, and with apparently no way out in the right direction. Ultimately, they were rescued by a native who took them to a "first-rate" road, and "gaily laughing and talking, the party galloped on; and with set teeth and bounding body I clung to the pommel and cantered after."

At length they came to a broad, sandy plain, an old battle-ground, where the bleached bones of warriors gleamed silvery in the moonlight. The party stopped to walk over it, and picked up a good many mementoes, mainly arm and leg bones. At this point the conversation took "a unique and ghastly turn." One man said, "You haven't got enough bones, Mrs. Blank; here's a good shinbone, if you want it." And another said, "Give me some of your bones, Miss Blank; I'll carry them for you," while "from the lips of the ladies" came: "Mr. Smith, you have got some of my bones; and you have got . . . my spine, Mr. Twain. . . ." Sam, who liked to believe the bones he picked up belonged to some great chiefs who fought there fiercely and died bravely, intended to take them home to his mother and sister.

"Very considerably fagged out," the party reached town about nine that night, with Sam in the lead, for when his horse discovered he was homeward bound he "threw his legs wildly out before and behind him, depressed his head, laid his ears back, and flew by the admiring crowd like a telegram."

Clemens (and the imaginary Brown) pulled up in front of the McFarlane house to wait for the others. Henry's sister, "a comely young girl," came out. Sam thought she looked at him admiringly. Perhaps it was his horsemanship that attracted her, so he made a "savage jerk" on the bridle and cried out, "Ho! will you!" to show how "fierce and unmanagable the beast was," although he was actually leaning peaceably against the hitching post at the time. Sam "stirred" him up and went to look for the others, then loped "gallantly" back, pretending that he was unaware of being the object of attention. He next addressed a few "pert" remarks to Brown, "to give the young lady a chance to admire my style of conversation, and was gratified to see her step up and whisper to Brown and glance furtively at me at the same time. I could see that her face bore an expression of the most kindly and earnest solicitude." He was shocked and angered to hear Brown burst into a fit of "brutal laughter."

Later, with a show of indifference, Sam asked what Miss McFarlane had said, and Brown told him: "She thought from the slouchy way you rode and the way you drawled out your words, that you was drunk! She said, 'Why don't you take the poor creature home. . . . It makes me nervous to see him galloping that horse and just hanging on that way, and he so drunk.' "

This anecdote, which was included in one of his *Union* letters, was built around the terse notebook entry: "Miss McFarlane thought I was drunk because I talked so long."

In the same letter he described himself as being "probably the most sensitive man in the kingdom of Hawaii that night—especially about sitting down in the presence of my betters. I have ridden fifteen or twenty miles on horseback . . . and to tell the honest truth, I have a delicacy about sitting down at all." He admitted to being one of the "poorest horsemen in the world."

Early in April he wrote his mother and Pamela about his social triumphs. That very evening, he and the United States minister resident, James McBride, had dined with the king's Grand Chamberlain, David Kalakaua, a member of the royal family. The Chamberlain had an excellent English education, Sam found, and a fine presence, and "would not do discredit to the kingly office." (In 1874 he became the last king of Hawaii). "The dinner was as ceremonious as any I ever attended in California—five regular courses, & *five* kinds of *wine* and one of brandy . . . After dinner . . . they called in the 'singing girls' & we had some beautiful music, sung in the native tongue." Their voices were clear and melodic. In the morning, the Chamberlain will call in his carriage and accompany Sam to the palace to meet King Kamehameha V. "Both are good Masons—the King is a Royal Arch Mason." Sam was having his first experience with a society where brown-skinned people ruled and white men obeyed.

A high point during his visit with the king was seeing the magnificent war cloak worn by Kamehameha the Great. It was made entirely of bright yellow feathers from the bird called locally 'Ō'ō (*Moho nobilis*). Several generations were required to collect the feathers from at least 80,000 birds, because each one had only four yellow feathers. At the time of Sam's visit, there was just one old man who knew the art of weaving the feathers closely into a netting of grass. The practice of killing such great numbers of the 'Ō'ō led to its extinction.

Clemens attended sessions of the legislature, which were exactly like all others. "A woodenhead gets up and proposes an utterly absurd something or other, and he and half a dozen other woodenheads discuss it with windy vehemence for an hour, the remainder of the house sitting in silent patience the while, and then a sensible man—a man of weight . . . gets up and shows the foolishness of the matter in five minutes; a vote is taken and the thing is tabled."

But time did not drag for Sam, who was greatly interested in watching and listening to William Ragsdale, the official interpreter, who turned "every Kanaka speech into English and every English speech into Kanaka, with a readiness and felicity of language" that was amazing, and "a volubility that was calculated to make a slow-spoken person like me distressingly nervous." Ragsdale's fluency in both languages was explained by his having a Polynesian mother and an English father. Sam came to know him well, was greatly impressed with his personality and character, and described him as "a brilliant young fellow." He was very popular, and a distinguished political career seemed certain. Later, the prophecy was fulfilled, but the discovery that he had leprosy led to his committing himself to Hawaii's leper colony. In 1884, Clemens wrote the first draft of a novel about Bill Ragsdale, set in that "peacefulest, restfulest, sunniest, balmiest, dreamiest haven . . . the earth can offer," but the work was never revised.

In mid-April, Sam reached Maui by interisland schooner, to investigate the sugar plantations there, and visit the famed extinct volcano, Haleakala. He was welcomed by the planters and their families, urged to stay at their houses for as long as he liked, and

Taste of Fame

invited to participate in their quiet social activities—chiefly card parties and picnics. He was particularly happy in this warm family environment, with fathers, mothers, aunts, and grandparents in every house; and daughters and nieces, many of whom were accomplished and pretty. So it was that his intended week on Maui stretched easily into five.

At eleven o'clock on the night of May 4, he wrote home from Wailuku Plantation. He had been invited to take tea there with the Peck family, who were Honolulu friends. Afterward, he was urged to spend the evening playing seven-up and whist ("plenty of ladies" in the house, he wrote). When he left to ride on to Waihee Plantation where he was expected to pass the night, it was so pitch-black outside—"this is the infernalest darkest country, when the moon don't shine"—he could not even see his picketed horse, and in searching, stumbled over the lariat, fell and hurt his leg. Now he would have to spend the night here—which would not be a hardship. The fall might not have been so painful if he had not hurt the same leg the previous week, when a "spirited colt" (something he always tried to avoid), urged on him by one of the planters, "let out with his left & kicked me across a ten-acre lot." He had been in the act of tightening the cinch, preparatory to calling for a girl and escorting her to a card party. A native man, witnessing the accident, rubbed his leg and "doctored" him so well Sam was able to stand up within half an hour. By then it was four-thirty, the party was at five, and the girl lived seven miles away. "If I hadn't had a considerable weakness for her she might have gone to the devil under the circumstances." But he climbed into the saddle, and arrived at her house at five minutes after five, satisfied at having "got even with the colt," since the road was extremely rough. But by then his leg was hurting badly again. Although the young woman was ready and her horse saddled, it was decided Sam had better not try to ride further. So he was invited in, became the object of concerned attention, and was waited on by the girl. "But I had a jolly time—played cribbage nearly all night. If I were worth even $5,000 I would try to marry that plantation—but as it is, I resign myself to a long & useful bachelordom as cheerfully as I may." If he were *really* affluent, he would try for the Ulupalakua Plantation, with *two* "pretty and accomplished girls in the family," and an annual "income of $60,000—chance for some enterprising scrub." He had had a "pleasant time of it" when he stayed there. It was, of course, Orion's refusal to sell the Tennessee land that was responsible for Sam's poverty and his single state.

Sam dreamed of marriage, and talked about it, but in reality, he was not ready to settle down. On May 7, still with the Peck family, still nursing his leg, purposely prolonging recovery (as he would do some three years later, at the home of the young woman he was determined to marry), he wrote to Will Bowen. Since Bowen was piloting as yet, he talked to him about ships and travel. Sam has a wide acquaintance among sea captains, especially whalers, who put in at Honolulu, he said, and has had invitations from them to go practically "every blamed place" on the globe. The latest was from the master of a fine vessel that was going around the world. He was strongly tempted to throw up his berth on the paper and go. If Will had been there, he would have. Although he has had a "gorgeous" time of it so far, he is restless after two months in the Islands and ready to move on, even though he has "done" only Oahu and part of Maui. The possibilities for interesting experiences in new places, and the wealth of subjects for articles and travel letters afforded by long voyages, intrigue him, and he has begun to think seriously about how this can be accomplished.

By May 22, he was back in Honolulu after a "perfect jubilee" of pleasure on Maui. Never before had he "bade any place good-bye so regretfully." He had not fooled away any of his precious time there writing letters for the paper, either. He had given himself up totally to enjoyment, thinking not once about business or "care, or human toil or trouble or sorrow or weariness. Few such months come in a lifetime."

A letter from Mollie was waiting for him at Honolulu. She said that Orion had already abandoned his law practice in Excelsior, Nevada, and that they were preparing to start for Keokuk by way of San Francisco. Ought they to wait there for him and go home together? Orion was the last person Sam wanted to see, and he replied at once,

"I shall not reach San Francisco before the latter part of July—so it is no use to wait for me, to go home. Go on yourselves. It is Orion's duty to attend to that land, after shutting me out of my attempt to sell it (for which I shall never entirely forgive him,) if he lets it be sold for taxes, all his religion will not wipe out the sin. It is no use to quote scripture to me, Mollie—I am in poverty & exile now because of Orion's religious scruples. Religion & poverty cannot go together. I am satisfied Orion will eventually save himself, but in doing it he will damn the balance of the family. I want no such religion. He has got a duty to perform by us—will he perform it?

"I have crept into the old subject again, & opened the old sore afresh that cankers within me. It has got into many letters to you & I have burned them. But it is no use disguising it—I always feel bitter & malignant when I think of Ma & Pamela grieving at our absence & the land going to the dogs when I could have sold it & been home now, instead of drifting about the outskirts of the world battling for bread."

Then a letter came from Orion ordering Sam to go home and sell the land. In his reply Sam told his brother to go to "thunder," and take care of it himself.

But his time was running out and, putting Orion out of his mind for the present, he made plans to sail for the island of Hawaii, explore it, and see Kilauea, the active volcano. He left on May 26 for the 150-mile voyage aboard the little schooner *Boomerang*. He landed at Kilau Bay and hired a horse to ride through the coffee and orange district of Kona. He was delighted with the trail that led along a high mesa about a mile from the ocean, for it afforded him an ever-changing panorama of alternate open country, dense tropical forests ("haunted with invisible birds" and the perfume of unseen flowers), and vast orange groves laden with ripe fruit.

He planned to rejoin the *Boomerang* at Kealakekua Bay, where Captain Cook had been killed in 1779—an act Clemens justified. The natives had believed him to be Lono, a deity whose return was long anticipated, and therefore welcomed him with religious enthusiasm and veneration, and lavished kindness on him and his men. In return, Cook desecrated their temples, insulted their priests and chiefs, and punished indiscriminately and without provocation. Three inhabitants had been killed before resistance was offered.

At sunset on the day Clemens arrived at the bay, he walked down to the water's edge and stood on the flat lava rock where

Cook had stood (at the same hour) when he was stabbed to death with an iron dagger obtained in trade from one of his sailors. Sam tried to imagine the wild scene.

There were other sites of interest he wanted to see, some of them accessible only by canoe—the ruins of the ancient City of Refuge, sacred caves, more temples, another battlefield, and a "petrified" waterfall. In returning from one of these excursions, he saw at a distance a "bevy" of young women swimming naked in the shallows, and went down to take a closer look. "But with a prudery which seems to be characteristic of that sex everywhere, they all plunged in with a lying scream, and when they rose to the surface, they only just poked their heads out and showed no disposition to proceed any further in that direction." Irritated, he picked up their clothes, piled them on a rock close to the surf, and sat on them. "I had them in the door, as the missionaries say. I was comfortable, and I just let them beg." He hoped to "freeze" them out, but his patience was exhausted before that happened. He therefore went off, undressed, and plunged in himself, intending to swim out to them, but the girls raced for shore, snatched up their dresses, and ran. "I never saw such perversity." Brown, who was standing by, observed that they were "very handsomely formed." Sam agreed, but had one objection, which he classed as a "peculiarity": they were nearly as narrow through the hips as men.

It was the schooner *Emeline* that came in to pick him up (the *Boomerang* was just an idle speck becalmed on the horizon), and take him on to Kau, for the ascent of Kilauea.

One moonless night during his week's stay at the newly opened hotel, Volcano House, which was made entirely of thatch, he joined a party of six, with native guides, for a walk across the floor of the crater to North Lake, a body of fiery lava. Soon after they started, however, it was discovered that a nearby cauldron of molten matter was threatening to overflow and everyone deserted except a stranger whom Clemens called Marlette. He said he had walked over the floor a dozen times by day and believed he could find his way with a lantern. He offered to lead them, but only Sam consented to follow. "His pluck gave me backbone." They then began their run over the hot floor, skipping across "the red crevices with brisk dispatch and reached the cold lava safely but with pretty warm feet. Then we took things leisurely and comfortably, jumping tolerably wide and probably bottomless chasms, and threading our way through picturesque lava upheavals.

"By and by Marlette shouted 'Stop!' I never stopped quicker in my life. I asked what the matter was. He said we were out of the path. He said we must not try to go on till we found it again, for we were surrounded with beds of rotten lava through which we could easily break and plunge down a thousand feet. I thought eight hundred would answer for me, and was about to say so when Marlette proved his statement by accidentally crushing through and disappearing to his armpits. He got out and we hunted for the path with the lantern." Eventually, they found it.

It proved a long tramp but "an exciting one." They reached North Lake between ten and eleven o'clock, and sat down on a large overhanging lava shelf, "tired but satisfied." Below them stretched a heaving sea of molten fire of "seemingly limitless extent." All around its shores, at unequal distances, stood nearly white-hot chimneys of lava, four to five feet high, "and up through them were bursting gorgeous sprays of lava-gouts and gem spangles, some white, some red, and some golden." "Now and then the surging bosom of the lake under our noses would calm down ominously and seem to be gathering strength for an enterprise." Then suddenly a red dome of lava the size "of an ordinary dwelling would heave itself aloft like an escaping balloon, then burst asunder. . . . The crashing plunge of the ruined dome into the lake again would send out a world of seething billows," which shook the foundations of their perch. "By and by, a loosened mass of the hanging shelf we sat on tumbled into the lake, jarring the surroundings like an earthquake and delivering a suggestion that may have been intended as a hint, and may not. We did not wait to see."

On the way back they lost the trail again, and spent more than an hour searching for it. It was two in the morning when they finally reached the hotel, "pretty well fagged out."

A few days later he witnessed the greatest eruption that had occurred in several years; it was the kind that belched a colossal pillar of fire, but did not overflow.

A two-hundred-mile horseback ride over the mountains to Hilo lay ahead. Afterward, he declared that the route led over the hardest mountain roads in the world. Feeling pressed for time, he pushed himself to include all the important scenic and historic sites. At Hilo, he rested three days at the home of a Mr. Cony ("he lives like a prince"), who apparently had Missouri beginnings for he was acquainted with everyone Sam knew in Hannibal and Palmyra. He was now the King's Deputy Marshal. The two men sat up all the first night reminiscing.

On the return voyage to Honolulu, Clemens succumbed to exhaustion and severe saddle boils, and went to bed as soon as he reached his room, on June 18. He was "too badly used up" by the trip to write an account of it then, he explained to his *Union* readers.

"I shall not be strong again for several weeks yet," he wrote home three days after his arrival. "I rushed too fast. I ought to have taken five or six weeks on that trip. . . . Confound that Island, I had a streak of fat & a streak of lean all over it—got lost several times & had to sleep in huts with the natives and live like a dog." These experiences were not recorded in the surviving notebooks or in his newspaper correspondence. "Take it altogether, . . . it was a mighty hard trip." He was not discouraged, however, and planned to sail for Kaui on June 28, to be gone three weeks. After that, he expected to return to San Francisco.

The reason he was out of bed, writing this letter (while sitting in a splint-bottom chair, "deep-sunk, like a basket"), was that Anson Burlingame, United States Minister to China, and Robert Van Valkenburgh, Minister to Japan, had sent word they would call on him that morning. Both had just arrived in the *Swallow,* en route to their posts.

"You know the condition my room is always in when you are not around," Sam continued, "so I climbed out of bed & dressed & shaved pretty quick, & went up to the residence of the American Minister & called on *them. "* He found Burlingame to be a man of great personal charm and, although well-educated and urbane, also possessed a marked freedom and directness of manner gained during a childhood and youth spent on the Ohio frontier. Clemens knew his mother would be interested in hearing that Burlingame told him "a good deal" about Senator Jere Clemens of Alabama, lawyer, politician, and novelist, and about "that Virginia Clemens who was wounded in a duel." This was Sherrard Clemens. Burlingame was associated with both men in the United States Senate. Then eighteen-year-old Edward Livermore Burlingame was called in to meet Sam. His father said he could tell that jumping-frog story as well as anyone. Clemens remarked that he was glad, because whenever he tried he always seemed to make a botch of it. He was immediately drawn to the young man—"handsome . . . overflowing with animation, activity, energy, and the pure joy of being alive." There was a studious and literary side to him which Sam also appreciated. He had been attending Harvard, and shortly would work at Heidelburg for his Ph.D. (At twenty-three, he joined the editorial staff of the *New-York Tribune,* then went on to become literary advisor to the publisher, Charles Scribner, and finally the editor of *Scribner's Magazine.* He and Clemens remained friends for years.)

On the same day, word was received at Honolulu that an open boat carrying fifteen men in "a helpless and starving condition" had drifted ashore on the island of Hawaii. They had been afloat forty-three days—ever since the burning of their vessel, the clipper *Hornet,* about 130 miles north of the equator. Then, on June 25, it was learned that the third mate and ten sailors had been brought to the hospital in Honolulu. Although Clemens realized the importance of being the first to get their story, he was still too weak and uncomfortable to make the necessary arrangements for an interview. Anson Burlingame, also aware of the importance of an exclusive news story, volunteered to get the required permissions to talk with the men, and accompany Sam to the hospital (he was carried there on a cot). He stayed with Clemens the whole time and helped question the survivors, at the sacrifice of "invitations to dinner with princes & foreign dignitaries, & neglecting all sorts of things to accommodate me," Sam told his mother, "& you know I appreciate that kind of thing—especially from such a man, who is acknowledged to have no superior in the diplomatic circles of the world." Because of his generosity, Sam was able to get the survivors' whole story.

Back at his room, seated in the basket chair, he began at once to write, racing against time to get the story off to San Francisco in the morning. He worked right through the night, and just as the bark *Milton Badger* was casting off the next day, the envelope containing what would be Clemens' most significant news story, was tossed on board.

"If my account gets to the Sacramento Union first, it will be *published* first all over the United States, France, England, Russia, and Germany—all over the world, I may say," he wrote happily. "You will see it." He spoke of still further indebtedness to Anson Burlingame, who had done him "a hundred favors" since he arrived. "He says if I will come to China . . . next January & make his house in Pekin my home, he will afford me facilities that few men can have there for seeing & learning." From China Sam intends to go on to Paris for the World's Fair. "I expect to do all this, but I expect to go to the States first. . . ."

In one postscript he cautioned, *"Don't show this letter."* In a second one, he enlarged: "Now *please* don't read this to anybody— I am always *afraid* to write to you—you always show my letters." Jane Lampton took him so literally, this letter now consists of carefully cut out fragments with several pages missing.

His story reached Sacramento in time for the *Union* to be the first newspaper to give details of the *Hornet* disaster and the ordeal of the survivors. On July 19, Clemens' signed article appeared on the front page. It was forceful reporting, depicting in simple words the men's physical and mental sufferings, almost day by day. The piece was widely reprinted, adding materially to his growing reputation.

He did not leave for Kaui as planned, for he had decided to give variety to his newspaper correspondence by describing the month-long mourning ceremonies then being held for the twenty-seven-year-old Crown Princess Victoria, sister of the king, and the "grand funeral pageant" set for June 30. In his notebook he recorded the well-founded rumor that she had died during a forced abortion, that she had already had seven, and that she kept a "harem" of half a dozen "bucks." In his *Union* account he prudently made no mention of the cause of her early death, but stressed her careful upbringing and education under the direction of Dr. Gerrit Judd, an American missionary-physician and powerful political figure in the Hawaiian government.

Sam's readers were given a full account, continued in several despatches, of the princess' "funeral orgies," a term he had the king in *Huckleberry Finn* use in the place of "obsequies." Clemens apologized to the *Union* for the employment of "orgies," and justified it exactly as the fictional king would: because it was exact. For more than thirty days, troops of natives from the several islands had been thronging past his door on their way to the palace, where the princess lay in state. All night they burned their candlenut torches, sang their dirges to the thud of drums, and "wailed their harrowing wail for the dead." For the "grand finale," held the night before the funeral, a few foreigners, Clemens included, were allowed to enter the grounds and watch the ceremonies. This was the night, he wrote, they would see the famous hula-hula of which they had heard so much and had longed to see—that "lascivious dance that was wont to set the passions of men ablaze in the old heathen days, a century ago."

In deference to the missionary influence, some thirty "buxom young Kanaka women were gaily attired in white bodices and pink skirts" that covered the ankles, rather than appearing barebreasted, and in grass skirts which hung just below the knees. On their heads were wreaths of pink and white flowers and garlands of green leaves. They formed themselves into half a dozen rows, "shook the reefs out of their skirts, tightened their girdles and began the most unearthly caterwauling," which did, however, have a marked and regular beat. To this they kept strict time with "writhing bodies," and head and arm movements, all in unison. Then came "a mingling together of the performers—quicker time, faster and more violently excited motions—and more and more complicated gestures—(the words of their fierce chant meantime treating in the broadest terms, and in detail, of things which may be vaguely hinted at in a respectable newspaper, but not distinctly mentioned)—then a convulsive writhing of the person, continued for a few moments and ending in a sudden stop and a grand caterwaul in chorus. . . ."

In describing the Princess Victoria's funeral procession, he certainly had his mother in mind, for he included the kind of detail which she, as a connoisseur of funerals, would relish. From horseback, he watched it form. Exactly at eleven that morning, the parade began to move to the toll of bells and the boom of minute guns. Sam was fascinated by the pageantry. A glance down the line revealed large groups of women dressed in "melancholy black," and horses draped from head to hoof in "sable velvet." In strong contrast were the crimson tunics of Zouaves, nobles in royal yellow, mounted lancers with red and white penants fluttering from their spears and palace troops in blue, white, and scarlet uniforms heavily trimmed with flashing gold braid. In the middle was the catafalque, flanked by rows of kahilis, symbols of mourning, in rich purple, red, orange, and yellow, forming a varicolored wall "brilliant as a rainbow." The coffin could be glimpsed, covered with the famous yellow feather war cloak. He listed all the groups and individuals in the procession, from the undertaker in the lead to the police force bringing up the rear. There was even a place for the princess' five poodles.

Sam spent his last eighteen days on Oahu, in further sightseeing on horseback, and in social activities. At one affair, he sang about the old "hoss" in the wilderness: And "didn't I make those solemn missionaries' eyes bug out with it? I think so," he wrote Will Bowen. He danced half the night away at a Fourth of July ball given by the retiring American Minister, and attended a "great luau" held at Waikiki by David Kalakaua to honor Burlingame and Van Valkenburg, soon to sail for their posts. He went with Ed Burlingame to some of those "balls and fandangos, and *hula hulas* . . . anybody's, brown, half-white, white," at which the young man was present nightly. He accompanied the convivial ministers to China and Japan to some official function where they "just made Honolulu howl. I only got tight once, though. I know better than to get tight oftener than once in 3 months. It sets a man back in the esteem of people whose opinions are worth having."

He was reluctant to leave the Islands when faced with the prospect, and he might have delayed his departure if Josiah Mitchell, the *Hornet*'s captain, and two of her passengers, the brothers Henry and Samuel Ferguson, were not leaving for San Francisco on July 19. The captain had kept a log every day he was adrift, and the Fergusons had journals covering the entire trip from the date the *Hornet* had left New York. Sam had their permission to copy the log and the diaries. Further, he wanted to talk with all three, for he had plans to submit this material in some form to *Harper's Monthly*. He therefore took passage on the same vessel, the sailing ship *Smyrniote*.

At two o'clock in the afternoon the ship *Comet,* with several notables on board, left Honolulu with a great salute of cannon. At four-thirty, the *Smyrniote* departed "peaceably" in the same direction. "Now we shall see who beats to San Francisco."

XX

―――――○―――――

"THE TROUBLE BEGINS AT 8"

At THREE O'CLOCK on the afternoon of August 13, 1866, the *Symrniote* (on which Sam Clemens was a passenger), and the *Comet* came through the Golden Gate side-by-side. They were twenty-five days out from Honolulu. A gale was blowing up the channel and both vessels, under full sail, swept into the Bay at a "magnificent gait," three hundred yards apart. Sam had wondered, when they left Hawaii only two and a half hours after the *Comet,* which would win the race to San Francisco. But weather conditions had not favored a race, because there were long periods when both ships lay becalmed. These delays delighted Clemens, who was not at all eager to return.

On the day of his arrival he jotted: "Ashore again, & devilish sorry for it." He admitted to feeling as though he was "in prison again—and all the wild sense of freedom gone. The city seems so cramped, & so dreary with toil & care & business anxiety. God help me, I wish I were at sea again!" Part of his initial depression can be explained by the presence of Orion and Mollie, who were in San Francisco. Sam's anger with Orion over the lost fortune was still at white heat. Happily for him, Orion and Mollie were leaving for Santa Cruz, and a projected tour of other parts of California.

But Sam had no time for unprofitable regrets because he had to finish his letters to the *Sacramento Union*. Taking a room at the Occidental he went right to work, for he had telegraphed the paper of his arrival. On August 20, in concluding a long journal-letter to his mother and sister, begun at sea on July 30, he told them he had just returned from Sacramento where he had delivered his correspondence and "squared accounts." He was pleased, because they had paid him more than they had agreed to; and they gave him a local assignment to report on the livestock entries and horse races at the State Fair.

While coming down from Sacramento on the steamboat *Capital*, he picked up a pamphlet issued by an accident insurance company describing the various risks upon which one could get a policy. This afforded subject matter for a letter to the *Enterprise*. It took the form of a series of questions to the company: "Do you allow the same money on a dog bite that you do on an earthquake? . . . and supposing I got insured against earthquakes, would you charge any more for San Francisco earthquakes than for those that prevail in places that are better anchored down? And if I had a policy on earthquakes alone, I couldn't collect on a dog-bite, may be, could I?" And so on. The squib, "How, For Instance?" was reprinted in the *New York Weekly Review*.

He sent Captain Mitchell's log by overland mail to the *New York Times*, and asked that his own name not be connected with it. If he had time, he hoped to write a full account of the *Hornet* disaster for *Harper's*. He managed that as well. The article was accepted, and appeared in the December 1866 issue of the monthly. He looked forward to the January number when his name would appear in the annual list of contributors. Then he would be famous, and he planned to give a banquet in celebration. "I did not give the banquet. I had not written 'Mark Twain' distinctly, it was a fresh name to *Harper's* printers," who turned it into "Mark Swain." This blow was still six months away.

He turned next to revising his *Union* correspondence for an illustrated book on the Islands. He even made a rough draft of its dedication to his mother. He was also giving thought to a lecture tour, for upon his return he had found himself to be "about the best known honest man on the Pacific coast," and his friend Tom Maguire, impresario and theater-owner, had suggested that now was the time to make his fortune by breaking into the lecture field. "In a fever of hopeful anticipation," Sam wrote out a talk. Then he had second thoughts, for he was actually terrified by the entire prospect. He might break down in the middle of it and make a "humiliating failure." Then he asked one of his editor friends, John McComb of the *Argus,* who slapped him on the back and told him to go ahead: Take the largest house in town, and charge one dollar a ticket.

"The audacity of the proposal was charming," and courageously he went off to talk with Tom Maguire, who offered him the use of his handsome new Academy of Music on Pine Street at half price —fifty dollars. "In sheer desperation I took it—on credit," for the evening of October second. He then spent a hundred and fifty dollars on printing and advertising, and became "the most distressed and frightened creature on the Pacific coast. I could not sleep—who could, under such circumstances? For other people there was facetiousness in the last line of my posters, but to me it was plaintive with a pang when I wrote it:

'Doors open at 7 o'clock. The Trouble will begin at 8.' "

The poster reminded the public that Mark Twain was "Honolulu Correspondent" for the *Sacramento Union,* and stated that the lecture would cover a variety of topics: well-known personalities in the Islands, American missionaries, Hawaiian royalty, native customs, scenic wonders, and the eruption of Kilauea. Below this were announcements that "A SPLENDID ORCHESTRA is in town, but has not been engaged"; that "A DEN OF FEROCIOUS BEASTS WILL BE ON EXHIBITION in the next block"; and that a "GRAND TORCHLIGHT PROCESSION may be expected; in fact the public are privileged to expect whatever they please."

Denis McCarthy, his friend and associate on the *Territorial Enterprise,* agreed to act as Sam's manager. The previous year (1865), McCarthy, then twenty-four, having made a "snug" fortune, had sold his interest in the paper to his partner, Joe Goodman. Presently, he was living in San Francisco, speculating in mining stock, and was now about to lose everything.

On the day of the lecture Clemens was so nervous he ate nothing. "I only suffered." At four o'clock that afternoon, he "crept down" to the theater to see if any tickets had been sold. But the ticket-seller was gone and the box-office locked up. "I had to swallow suddenly, or my heart would have got out. 'No sales,' I said to myself; 'I might have known it.' I thought of suicide, pretended illness, flight. I thought of these things in earnest. . . . But of course I had to drive them away, and prepare to meet my fate." He could not wait until the doors opened, so at six he went to the theater, entered by the back door, stumbled in the dark among the rows of painted scenery, and stepped out on the stage. "The house was gloomy and silent, its emptiness depressing." He returned back stage and sat in the dark for an hour and a half, with the feeling of a man doomed to hang.

Then suddenly he heard a murmur: "It rose higher and higher, and ended in a crash, mingled with cheers. It made my hair raise, it was so close to me, and so loud." Then it was repeated, and before he knew what he was about, he was in the middle of the stage, staring at "a sea of faces, bewildered by the fierce glare of lights, and quaking in every limb. . . . The house was full, aisles and all!"

It was a minute before he could gain command over "the tumult in my heart and brain and legs." Confidence came as soon as he grew aware of the "charity and friendliness" in the faces before him. Then he began to talk, and within three or four minutes was "comfortable, and even content."

All of the newspapers were "kind" the next day. One of them, under the heading, "The Trouble Is Over," wrote, "The inimitable 'Mark Twain' delivered himself last night of his first lecture on the Sandwich Islands, or anything else." Long before the appointed hour the Academy of Music was "densely crowded with one of the most fashionable audiences it was ever my privilege to witness during my long residence in this city. The élite of the town were there, and so was the Governor of the State, occupying one of the boxes. . . . The audience promptly notified Mark by the usual sign—stamping—that the auspicious hour had arrived, and presently the lecturer came sidling and swinging out from the left of stage," with that "half-skipping, half-shambling gait" Joe Goodman once described. Under his arm was a sheaf of notes written on manila paper in a large hand so as to be legible in dim light, and bunched together in such a way they resembled a ruffled hen. His appearance alone brought laughter.

He opened with an apology: He had "partly succeeded" in hiring a band, but at the last moment they had backed out. Then he had engaged a trombone player, but he, learning that he was to solo, said he wasn't going to make a fool of himself sitting up there on the stage all alone, "just blowing his horn." After the house had quieted, Clemens "assumed a very grave countenance, and began: "When, in the course of human events. . . ." He talked for about an hour and a quarter, interspersing his serious commentary (he stressed the importance of United States proprietorship of the Islands, which was a new idea) with just the right proportion of humor. In picturing the scenery and the drama of the volcano in eruption, he soared "to the pinnacle of descriptive power."

The talk had been a resounding success. The gross returns were well over twelve hundred dollars, and Sam Clemens was launched as a lecturer, a calling he would follow nearly to the end of his life. Promptly he and McCarthy mapped out an itinerary for a tour. Logically, Sacramento, the capital and home of the *Daily Union,* would be the first stop. He was amazed to discover how widely the paper was read and how well-known Mark Twain had become through his Sandwich Islands letters. Towns of all sizes were clamoring to hear him talk.

"Off for Washoe.—'Mark Twain' has started for Sage Brush Land, the alkali of which nourished his humor and gave his wit the pungency which it now possesses," the daily *Dramatic Chronicle* reported on October 10. "We know there will be a jollification when 'Mark Twain' reaches Virginia City; we hope he won't get so fond of his old home as to be unwilling to return to San Francisco." Before leaving, Sam arranged to correspond with the local *Evening Bulletin* during his coming tour.

Sacramento's Metropolitan Theater "contained a liberal share of the beauty, intelligence and fine clothes of the capital last evening," the *Daily Union* reported on October 12. "The object of the assemblage was to listen to a lecture by the distinguished humorist, traveler, correspondent and missionary, Mark Twain. . . . The lecturer entertained the audience for about an hour, discoursing in an easy, colloquial style . . . seasoning a large dish of genuine information with spicy anecdotes, depicting the lights and shades of Kanaka society. . . . Mark goes hence to cultivate an acquaintance with the people of the up-country towns."

From Sacramento, Clemens and McCarthy—whom he now styled "the Orphan" in his newspaper correspondence—traveled by riverboat to Marysville (named for young Mary Murphy, a survivor of the ill-fated Donner Party). Sam found it a "sociable, cheerful-spirited community," composed mainly of men who had made money in Washoe and had built for themselves and their families, handsome red-brick houses surrounded by spreading trees and fine gardens. After a successful lecture at Maguire's New Theatre, he and the Orphan continued by stagecoach, rapidly covering miles over the level valley floor, and passing through the once-populous gold towns of Timbuctoo, Smartsville, and Rough and Ready, then slowing as they began climbing into the pine-forested foothills. Grass Valley, their immediate destination, was a still-flourishing community whose Eureka Mine had at that September's end brought its owners a net profit of nearly $370,000, and was paying its shareholders "princely dividends." Still richer was the Empire Mine on Ophir Hill, a mile south of town. It was one of the world's major gold producers. On his visit to the Empire, Sam was shown "chunks of quartz as large as a child's head . . . plastered nearly all over with gleaming leaves and plates of purest gold. . . ." Grass Valley was noted, as well, for having been the home of Lola Montez, Countess of Landsfeldt and mistress of King Ludwig I of Bavaria, and of her neighbor, the famed child actress Lotta Crabtree, a friend of Clemens.

The *Grass Valley Union* reported on the evening of October 20: "Crowds are flocking into Hamilton Hall, as we write, to hear Mark Twain's lecture. . . . But a moment ago we saw the lecturer preparing himself for a clear voice with a copious dose of gin and gam, after which he started for the Hall with the irregular movement of a stern-wheel boat in a heavy wind. . . ."

He followed this successful performance with another at adjoining Nevada City, so close he could have easily walked. Although there were many rich mines there, "I enjoyed myself rather too well to bother much about statistics," he informed *Bulletin* readers. Collected in that pretty community of attractive houses and large gardens, he discovered "a notably refined and intelligent society," to some of whom he carried introductions, and was hospitably entertained. Here he found another hotel as good as Grass Valley's Exchange. This was the National Exchange.

He spoke at the Nevada Theatre before a crowded house. A reporter for the local *Transcript* wrote: "Everybody was delighted with the lecture. . . . We think that 'Mark Twain' as a lecturer is far superior to 'Artemus Ward' or any of that class. . . . We bespeak for him large audiences wherever he goes."

The following day, he and McCarthy rode horseback to the old mining camps of Red Dog and You Bet. Sam was scheduled to perform that night at the Odd Fellows Hall in Red Dog, the center for a number of other gold diggings with such names as Gouge Eye. Throughout the tour so far, Clemens had considered it necessary to be introduced to his audience before each talk, and it was McCarthy's task to recruit some prominent man. At Red Dog he found such a person who agreed to be at the hall early. But as the hour set for the lecture drew near and he did not arrive, Sam grew nervous, and Denis had to go into the audience and ask for a volunteer. Since no one offered he was forced to impress a likely older man, a miner.

However, no sooner had the man climbed up on the platform than he was overcome with stagefright. When, after some minutes, he finally recovered his voice, he said, "I don't know anything about this man. At least I know only two things; one is, he hasn't been in the penitentiary, and the other is [after a pause, and almost sadly] I don't know why."

Since the business district of Red Dog had recently been destroyed by fire, Sam and Denis started back after the talk, to the comforts of the Exchange Hotel. Clemens almost never rode a horse without meeting with some misadventure, and this time proved no exception. Their way led through a heavy forest of incense cedars and pines, and a dense undergrowth of manzanita, buck-brush, and scrub oak, cut up into innumerable side-roads and trails, which proved very confusing in the dark. "In our simplicity we depended upon the horses to choose the route for themselves, because by many romantic books we had been taught a wild and absurd admiration for the instinct of that species. . . ." The in-

"The Trouble Begins at 8"

stinct of their animals, unerring, was to hunt out places where no roads or trails existed, and to wander about in the wilderness until dawn. Sam was grateful for one thing: neither horse went lame. "It was very singular. My experience of horses is that they never throw away a chance to go lame, and that in all respects they are well meaning and unreliable animals."

On their way east over the mountains, Clemens and McCarthy stopped to see the projected metropolis of Meadow Lake City, also called Summit City, for it was almost on top of the Sierra crest. At 7,100 feet, it was the highest of the gold mining districts. Sam was especially eager to visit it, for that March Orion had opened a law office there, intending to spend the summer. He was also acting as mining agent for absentee stockholders, which he expected would bring him some money, he wrote Pamela. Meanwhile, Mollie was going to pass her time in San Francisco and in sightseeing around the State. Summit City had been laid out on a grand scale, with streets eighty feet wide, and a huge plaza dedicated for public use. At the time Sam was there, the residents numbered only about a hundred (Orion not among them, for he had already failed), yet there was a post office, a bank, and a stock exchange, thirteen hotels, two theaters, several printing establishments, doctors' and lawyers' offices, and restaurants, saloons, and billiard parlors in number. "A bright, new, pretty town, all melancholy and deserted, and yet showing not one sign of decay or delapidation! I never saw the like before," Sam observed. Three years later, the post office closed, and by 1872 the town was abandoned. How typical of Orion, Sam thought, to have chosen Meadow Lake City as the place to make money.

From there they set off by stagecoach for Virginia City. "We had 14 passengers, (there was comfortable room for 9,) and baggage for 150. That is a little extravagant—but we did have the hind boot full of trunks (and a cooking stove,) and the forward boot full of carpet sacks and rolls of blankets, and on the roof a stack of valises, several chairs, and a few joints of stovepipe. . . ." He and Denis walked much of the way, to escape the crowding and relieve the horses.

When they arrived at Virginia City, about ten on Saturday night, October 27, Sam was sick. Before going to bed he sent a telegram to his former mining partner Bob Howland, now warden of the State Prison at Carson City, telling him of his arrival, and that he was not well. When he replied to Howland's return despatch on Monday, he said he was by then "all right," and expected to be able to lecture in Virginia City on Wednesday. He would like to speak in Carson on the following Saturday, but after all the furor over the Sanitary Ball proceeds, he was not sure if anyone would come to hear him. Would Bob ask Abe Curry what *he* thought?

In announcing his Virginia City talk, the *Enterprise* commented:

> The enthusiasm with which his lecture was everywhere greeted is still ringing through California, and now that his foot is in his native heath, we expect to see the very mountains shake with a tempest of applause.
>
> Our state can justly claim Mark Twain as its own peculiar production. It was while a resident here and associated with the *Enterprise* that he assumed the name Mark Twain and developed that rich and inexhaustible vein of humor which has made the title famous. . . .
>
> From present appearances he will receive an ovation seldom if ever equalled in our city. . . .

Alfred Doten, who worked on the *Enterprise* as one of its locals, noted in his diary that he attended Clemens' lecture on the night of October 31: "Crammed house—at Opera House—I heard it all—mighty good." In writing it up for the paper Doten considered it an "immense success." The audience was one of the "largest and most fashionable that ever graced the Opera House. . . . The entire dress circle and the greater portion of the parquette were filled with ladies while all available space for extra seats and standing room was occupied. It was a magnificent tribute to the lecturer from his old friends." It was an entertainment of "rare excellence and intelligence."

In a letter dated November 1, at Virginia City, and addressed exuberantly to "All the Folks, Affectionate Greeting," Sam reminded them, "You know the flush times are past, & it has long been impossible to more than half fill the Theatre here with any sort of attraction—but they filled it for me . . . full—dollar all over the house." He had been "mighty dubious" about Carson City, but Howland, Old Curry, and politician J. Neely Johnson "set that all right," and he received a "call" from the governor and a committee of other prominent citizens to lecture there. He responded the same day: "I shall gladly accept your invitation, and shall appear on the stage of the Carson Theatre on Saturday evening November 3d, and disgorge a few lies and as much truth as I can pump out without damaging my constitution." He signed himself, "Ex-Gov. Third House, and late Independent Missionary to the Sandwich Islands."

In this letter to the "Folks," he also said: "They offer me a full house and no expenses at Dayton—go there next." He added that Alexander (Sandy) Baldwin, Washoe's leading mining attorney, "says I have made the most sweeping success of any man he knows of." There will be lectures also at Gold Hill, Silver City, Washoe City, and then Virginia again, "if I have time to re-hash my talk." If not, then he will return to San Francisco, speak there once more, and then start for New York by steamer, about December first. "But I'll telegraph you." In this jubilant mood he sent "love to all," and signed himself, "Yrs Mark."

His spirits were high at being with his close friends Joe Goodman, Dan De Quille, and Steve Gillis (now foreman of the composing room), and at finding things almost unchanged. When they all met in the office, after the paper was put to bed, it seemed as though he had never been away. A closer look at the town showed it to be enjoying "a fair degree of prosperity" after the collapse brought on by reckless mining speculation.

Fame had not spoiled Sam Clemens, his friends found; he was just the same. They were eager for him to stay longer and urged him to lecture again. Steve Gillis believed he could fill the Opera House every night for a week, but Sam was reluctant to repeat himself in the same town. He would only consider it if he had time to revise his talk, as he had told his family.

Then Steve had what seemed to him a brilliant idea that would keep Sam a few days longer and also provide him with a fresh topic, and he commenced working out the details. He planned to stage a hold-up after Clemens' lecture at Gold Hill, his final one before returning to San Francisco, when Sam and Denis would be walking the few miles up to Virginia City, carrying the night's profits. It was a complex plot, for nearly all of Sam's friends were to be involved, and the police advised.

The night of November 10 was cloudy and cold, with a high wind and icy rain. Gillis and six confederates stationed themselves on the "Divide," that high ground between the two towns—a desolate spot which had been the scene of "twenty midnight murders and a hundred robberies," Sam maintained. Ordinarily, he and Denis would have stayed overnight at Gold Hill, but they had promised to meet Virginia friends for an all-night farewell party, in order to start Clemens off in good shape for San Francisco in the morning. Therefore, at ten o'clock, he and McCarthy started back to Virginia, walking briskly to keep warm. When they topped the Divide, the lights of Gold Hill vanished from sight behind them. "The night closed down gloomy and dismal," and the cutting wind, which swept the summit, "chilled our perspiring bodies."

Then, suddenly, they heard a police whistle just ahead, and McCarthy (in league with Gillis) said, "Thunder! this is an improvement—they didn't used to keep policemen on the divide." Within half a minute "a small man emerged from some ambuscade or other and crowded close up to me," Clemens wrote that same night in a notice addressed to the robbers.

> I was smoking and supposed he wanted a light. But this humorist instead . . . thrust a horrible six-shooter in my face and simply said, "Stand and deliver!" I said, "My son, your arguments are powerful—take what I have, but uncock that infamous pistol." The young man uncocked the pistol (but he requested three other gentlemen to present theirs at my head) and then he took all the money I had ($20 or $25), and my watch. Then he said to one of his party, "Beauregard, go through that man!" meaning Mac—and the distinguished rebel did go through Mac. Then the little captain said, "Stonewall Jackson, seat these men at the roadside, and hide yourself; if they move within five minutes, blow their brains out!" Stonewall said, "All right, sire." Then the party (six in number) started toward Virginia and disappeared.
>
> Now I want to say to you road agents as follows: My watch was given to me by Judge Sandy Baldwin and Theodore Winters, and I value it above everything else I own. If you will send it to me (to the

Enterprise office, or to any prominent man in San Francisco) you may keep the money and welcome. You know you got all the money Mac had—and Mac is an orphan—besides the money he had belonged to me.

Adieu, my romantic young friends.
Mark Twain.

McCarthy had about $125 in cash. The watch had been presented when Clemens was Governor of the Third House.

The wording of this "CARD TO THE HIGHWAYMEN," which appeared in the *Enterprise* the next morning, suggests that Clemens suspected a practical joke, and that he recognized the "small man," the "little Captain," to be Steve Gillis, although he could not be certain because all the robbers wore masks, and Steve would have disguised his voice.

On the Divide, when the five minutes were up, the victims, chilled to the bone, hurried on to the appointed meeting place at one of the saloons on C Street. All their friends, including Gillis, were waiting. Steve had expected Sam to be furious, but he was not, and calmly told the story. Then he asked Gillis to lend him some money and ordered drinks for the company. Later they went on to the *Enterprise* office, and Dan De Quille wrote up an account, "MARK TWAIN ROBBED," and sent it by telegraph to key papers in cities across the country. "This is no joke, but . . . down-right sober earnest," he wrote. "There should be a little hanging done among these rascals. This is the boldest robbery yet." Sam sat down at the old table opposite Dan and composed his "Card to the Highwaymen." He agreed to the suggestion that he give another lecture, perhaps telling the story of the holdup, and so recoup his losses. The next day the Opera House was engaged.

By this time Joe Goodman, who was Sam's host, had become an unwilling accomplice for Steve had given him Sam's valuables for safekeeping. Goodman remembered how "terribly guilty" he felt when Clemens said to him the following morning, "You know, Joe, those damned thieves took my keys and I can't get into my trunk." Maybe Goodman might have a key that would unlock it. He agreed to look.

The next evening, Sam had dinner with Sandy Baldwin, and

when he returned Joe thought he looked grim. Steve Gillis was
there, but Clemens ignored him. Suspecting that during the past
twenty-four hours Sam might have learned more about the holdup
than he was supposed to, Gillis excused himself and left. Sam then
turned to Joe and said, "Let's play cards; I don't feel sleepy." They
played until one o'clock, and then two, Sam saying hardly a word,
and Goodman on edge in expectation of the inevitable eruption.
Finally, Clemens slapped down his cards, and looked at him directly.

"Joe," he said, "Sandy Baldwin told me *all about* the robbery
tonight." Baldwin who was a party to the hoax, had decided after a
few drinks that Sam ought to know. "Now, Joe," he went on, "I
have found out that the law doesn't recognize a joke, and I am
going to send every one of those fellows to the penitentiary." He
said this with "such solemn gravity, and such vindictiveness,"
Goodman believed he was in earnest. "I know that I put in two
hours of the hardest work I ever did, trying to talk him out of that
resolution. . . . I pleaded with him, begged him to reconsider."
He reminded Sam that Steve was one of his closest friends. Then
he went and got the money, watch, and keys and laid them on the
table, but Sam remained unmoved. Just as Goodman began to
think the situation was hopeless, Clemens said, "Well, Joe, I'll let
it pass—this time but if *I should see* Denis McCarthy and Steve
Gillis *mounting the scaffold to-morrow,* and I could save them by
turning over my hand, I *wouldn't do it!*"

The elaborate plan to keep Clemens with them in Virginia City
had backfired. In the morning he canceled the second lecture, and
on the following day left by the Pioneer Stage for San Francisco.
Everyone had expected him to get angry—that was typical—but no
one had thought he would hold a grudge for so long. One reason
was that he was sick again, with that same illness he had when he
arrived in Virginia City, and which kept recurring over the next
three months. In addition, he had caught a heavy cold the night of
the robbery, which settled in his chest. All of this certainly warped
his view of the affair. He spent "quite a sum in doctor's bills" after
he reached San Francisco, he reported. "Since then I play no practical jokes on people and generally lose my temper when one is
played on me."

He was now asked to give another lecture in San Francisco, and decided to prepare a new one. He chose his overland journey with Orion as a subject, but when he read it over he realized that the first fifteen minutes were entirely too serious. He had to open with something that would "break up the house with a laugh and get me on pleasant and friendly terms with it at the start." The idea that occurred to him was so daring he wondered afterward how he had ever had the courage to attempt it. In the West there was a popular anecdote about the famous editor Horace Greeley, who had experienced a wild ride over the Sierra with the noted stagedriver Hank Monk. But the story had been told so many times it had become as much as a man's life was worth to tell it again. However, Sam resolved to begin his lecture with it.

On the evening of November 16, he stood before an audience of fifteen hundred, nearly half of whom were friends, and commenced with a description of his first day in the overland coach. Then he said: "At a little 'dobie station out on the plains, next day, a man got in and after chatting along pleasantly for a while, he said 'I can tell you a most laughable incident indeed, if you would like to listen to it. Horace Greeley went over this road once. When he was leaving Carson City he told the driver, Hank Monk, that he had an engagement to lecture in Placerville and was very anxious to go through quick. Hank Monk cracked his whip and started at an awful pace. The coach jolted up and down in such a terrific way that it jolted the buttons all off of Horace's coat, and finally shot his head clean through the roof of the stage, and then he yelled at Hank Monk and begged him to go easier—said he warn't in as much of a hurry as he was awhile ago. But Hank Monk said, 'Keep your seat, Horace, and I'll get you there on time'—and you bet he did, too, what was left of him!"

Clemens told this in a "level voice, and in a colorless monotonous way. . . . Then I paused and looked very much pleased with myself and as if I expected a burst of laughter." There was only dead silence. "As far as the eye could reach that sea of faces was a sorrow to look upon; some bore an insulted look . . . my friends and acquaintances looked ashamed. . . .

I tried to look embarrassed and did it very well. For a while I said nothing, but stood fumbling with my hands in a sort of mute appeal to the audience for compassion." Presently he commenced again, and "stammered along" with more details of the overland journey. Then he began to work himself into that anecdote, with "the air of a person who thinks he did not tell it well the first time and who feels the house will like it the next time," if told more skilfully. As soon as the audience perceived what he was up to, its indignation was "very apparent." Bravely he went on, not varying a word. At the end he stopped, evidently satisfied and expectant, but the house was "as still as a tomb." Again he feigned embarrassment; again he fumbled, and tried to seem "ready to cry." After a considerable silence, he repeated the whole act, and paused expectantly once more. This time the front ranks suddenly recognized "the sell and broke into a laugh. It spread back, and back, and back, and at the end of a minute the laughter was as universal and as thunderously noisy as a tempest." For Sam, it was a "heavenly sound," for he was nearly exhausted with apprehension, fearing he might have to stay there all night until "the monotonous repetition . . . would infallibly fetch them." He used this anecdote about Horace Greeley's ride effectively in *Roughing It.*

The *Alta California* commented the next day that the enthusiasm with which his talk had been received was "a deserving testimonial to a humorist who has made his fame among us and is now about to take his departure." Sam had already been commissioned by that paper to act as roving correspondent on a proposed world tour that would take him to the Paris "Universal Exposition," through Italy and the Mediterranean, and on to India, China, Japan, and then back to San Francisco by the new China Mail Line. He was not to be "stinted as to time, place or direction—writing his weekly letters on such subjects and from such places as will best suit him." Although recognized primarily as a humorist, "he has no superior as a descriptive writer—a keen observer of men and their surroundings—and we feel confident his letters to the *Alta,* from his new field of observation, will give him a world-wide reputation."

When news of the robbery of Mark Twain appeared in the New York papers, Asa Nudd, "a warm-hearted and impulsive friend" who lived there immediately sent a telegram to Clemens in San Francisco. It read:

Go to Nudd, Lord & Co., Front street, collect amount equal to what highwaymen took from you.
(Signed.) A.D.N.

Nudd and Lord were importers and wholesale dealers in wines and liquors.

Sam was pleased at having the final word with regard to the holdup, which still rankled, and he sat down and wrote a letter to the editors of the *Alta.* It was titled "SO-LONG." Now that he was about to leave, he wanted to say goodbye to his highway-robber friends "of the Gold Hill and Virginia Divide, and convince them that I have got ahead of them. They had their joke in robbing me and returning the money, and I had mine in the satisfaction of knowing that they came near freezing to death while they were waiting two hours for me to come along. . . . so far from bearing them any ill will, I want to thank them for their rascality. I am pecuniarily ahead on the transaction." He then quoted Asa Nudd's telegram, which he took to the store. "I . . . called for a thousand dollars, with my customary modesty; but when I found they were going to pay it, my conscience smote me and I reduced the demand to a hundred. It was promptly paid in coin, and now if the robbers think *they* have got the best end of the joke, they are welcome—they have my free consent to go on thinking so. . . .

"Good-bye, felons—good-bye. I bear you no malice. . . ."

As soon as it became generally known that he would be leaving San Francisco for an undetermined length of time, the public called for a farewell lecture. He spoke at the city's Congress Hall on Saturday night, December 15. After keeping the audience listening in "rapt attention to his gorgeous imagery, in describing scenes at the Sandwich Islands, or convulsed with laughter at the humorous sallies interspersed through the lecture, he seemed to come reluctantly to the promised 'good-bye,' and then his whole manner changed—the words were evidently the language of the heart, and the convictions of his judgment," the *Alta* commented.

"I have been treated with extreme kindness and cordiality by San Francisco, and I wish to return my sincerest thanks and acknowledgments," he began. After enlarging upon this theme and speaking of the prospects of California and the city for a bright future, he closed:

"I am bidding the old city and my old friends a kind, but not a sad farewell, for I know that when I see this home again, the changes that will have been wrought upon it will suggest no sentiment of sadness; its estate will be brighter, happier and prouder a hundred fold than it is this day. This is its destiny, and in all sincerity I can say, So mote it be!"

XXI

―――――○―――――

NEW YORK DEBUT

A BOUT EIGHT O'CLOCK on the morning of January 12, 1867, Sam Clemens stood on the upper deck of the steamship *San Francisco,* watching the stately snow-covered mansions of Staten Island slip by. He picked out Castle Garden in Battery Park, and saw the panorama of New York City unfold with its hundreds of steeples and its foreground palisade of masts. As they pushed past the river he observed tugs and ferryboats swarming through the masses of floating ice. In a short while he was ashore, and "safe housed" at the Metropolitan Hotel, familiar to his Western readers, for it was a favorite stopping-place for Californians, and for mining men from Washoe.

The trip from San Francisco, by way of the Isthmus of Nicaragua, had taken twenty-seven and a half days, and had been hard and at times harrowing. The first night out, the steamer *America,* whose captain was Edgar Wakeman, nearly went to the bottom in one of the worst tempests ever known off the Pacific Coast. Although Clemens was not seasick, as nearly all the other passengers were for many days, he was again attacked by the mysterious illness which had first appeared in Nevada, and would recur intermittently through most of the voyage. It was painful and debilitating, kept him *in* bed and *out* of humor, and caused him to take exception to more people and things than usual. The discomfort was relieved by ice and ice water, but irritated by liquor. His long list of grievances, and of people he disliked intensely was given to the imaginary Mr. Brown, who expressed Sam's annoyance and contempt bluntly in the *Alta* letters.

The single positive note on the first half of this trip was his meeting with Captain Wakeman, who captured his fancy immediately. Not only was he a strikingly handsome man, but he had a genuine talent for creating an effective story out of the most unpromising material. "With his strong, cheery voice, animated countenance, quaint phraseology, defiance of grammar, and extraordinary vim in the matter of gesture and emphasis," he was "inexhaustibly interesting." Wakeman knew the Bible thoroughly, and believed he was the only person on the globe who really understood the secret of Biblical miracles; it delighted him to explain them in his matchless way for the benefit of the less fortunate. Clemens recorded many of Wakeman's tales almost verbatim in his notebook, and made countless one-line reminders of some yarn or adventure of his for future use. As Captain Waxman, he appeared frequently as a storyteller in the *Alta* letters. In *Roughing It,* he was presented as Captain Ned Blakely, and as Captain Hurricane Jones in "Some Rambling Notes of an Idle Excursion." One week into the voyage Sam noted, "I had rather travel with that . . . hearty, jolly, boisterous, good-natured old sailor, Capt. Ned Wakeman than any other man I ever came across." ("Old" Wakeman was fifty.)

On December 30, the first part of the journey was completed with the *America*'s arrival at San Juan del Sur, but the sea-weary travelers were not allowed ashore because cholera was said to be raging among a group of six hundred passengers awaiting transportation to San Francisco. The death toll was set at 250. Careful inquiry proved the report hugely exaggerated; thirty-five had died, and the plague had now subsided. In the morning, it was considered safe to transport the *America*'s passengers over the isthmus on horses and mules and by mud wagon, to Virgin Bay on Lake Nicaragua, a three-hour trip. Since Clemens had a choice, he went by wagon (a faded red one) with a party of eight and a half-clad native driver armed with a wicked-looking long knife. The road was level and hard, and was lined on both sides with fragrant flowering trees and shrubs. The air was cool from a recent shower. Sam observed how pretty the young women were who tended the roadside stands, made of boughs, where oranges, bananas, pineapples, hot corn, chocolate, and native liquors were sold. They wore brightly-colored flowing dresses which did not disguise the fact that they were "singularly" full-breasted. Two were exceptionally beautiful. "Such liquid, languishing eyes, such pouting lips! such glossy, luxuriant hair! such ravishing, incendiary expression! such grace, such voluptuous forms, and such precious little drapery about them!" He was told they were "virtuous according to their lights, but I guess their lights are a little dim."

At Virgin Bay the party boarded a small steamer that would carry them over the lake. Under the shade of an awning, they ate a lunch of ham sandwiches, tea, and coffee, and compared notes on their "jolly little scamper" across the isthmus. Afterward, they simply sat and enjoyed the scenery and the cool lake breeze. Clemens' thoughts turned to Angus Gillis, Steve's father, who had told him about the battle of Virgin Bay, in which he and his sixteen-year-old son, Philip, had fought on September 3, 1855; it had been William Walker's first victory in his filibustering campaign to seize Nicaragua.

The next morning they arrived at San Carlos and were shifted to a long, double-decked shell of a stern-wheeler for the trip down the San Juan River to the sea. Rounding a bend, they came upon another reminder of the Gillises, for one of Walker's privateers stood near shore. The shifting sands had built a little oval island about her, and birds and winds had carried the seeds of grasses, vines, and trees which now covered everything but the two great fore-and-aft braces. Ten miles beyond was another of Walker's ships, also completely shrouded in vines. Both were rapidly-vanishing monuments to Walker's grandiose dreams of conquest, which ended before a firing squad in 1860.

At dawn the following day they arrived at San Juan del Norte, on the Caribbean, and welcomed the sight of the steamer *San Francisco* that would take them on to New York. At noon on New Year's Day the ship sailed, and on January second Sam entered in his notebook, "I am in bed all to-day—same old thing . . . All right now, on this ship—got plenty of ice & ice water—." He also made an ominous entry: "Two cases of cholera reported in the steerage to-day." At four that afternoon the ship's surgeon told the captain in Clemens' hearing, that two of the cases were "mighty" bad, and that a third one had developed that was even worse. At nine o'clock that night, one of the men was dead and, an hour later, he was wrapped in a sheet and slipped overboard. At one in the morning, another victim was gone.

Then, three days into the voyage, a bolt-head (a vital part of the engine) broke, and two hours were spent repairing it. The next day it broke again, and nearly four hours were lost. The same thing happened the following afternoon, and they lay like a log on the water for another four hours. There were fears that the ship might break up in the heavy seas ahead.

Then came worse news: there were at least eight cases of cholera. The dread disease had spread into second class—and one case had been reported in the first cabin. The ship's doctor did all he could to prevent panic by telling everyone the sickness was only severe diarrhea brought on by eating fruit in Nicaragua, and assured them he had all the necessary remedies. Learning that he was a fellow Mason, Sam took him aside, and pledging secrecy, asked for the truth. The doctor said that the scourge was Asiatic cholera, the worst form, and that he could do nothing, for the medicine cabinet was empty. With luck, Key West was a day away, and he hoped to get a stock of medicine there. "I realize that I myself may be dead to-morrow," Sam reflected.

At Key West the vessel was allowed to dock and the passengers to land. Obviously, health officers had been deceived or bribed. On the morning of January 7, well-supplied with drugs, coal, bolts and other spare parts, the *San Francisco* headed for New York. Sam was taking with him from Florida seven hundred of the "noblest cigars," smuggled from Havana, at six dollars a hundred, and forty dollars worth of fine brandy, for future use. Those hours spent ashore boosted morale, and although there were still thirteen passengers sick, two of them dangerously, fear of the cholera spreading, subsided.

Reflecting the more relaxed atmosphere, Clemens' thoughts turned to Nevada, and in his notebook he reminded himself of the man in Humboldt who refused to go out and hunt Indians because, he said, he hadn't lost any. He made notes on regional expressions, and he recalled what Jim Gillis had told him about the California gold miners' reaction to anyone who turned up in the diggings in a white shirt and plug hat. He remembered that Jim was thought by some as an "aristocrat," putting on airs, because he often wore a white shirt. Sam also recorded two more deaths. The final one occurred within full view of Highland Light in New York harbor; the cause was recorded as dropsy, to avert quarantine.

Although the journey had been anything but ideal, Sam wrote his family from New York that he found peace only in excitement and restless moving from place to place, and that ocean travel fulfilled his needs best. At sea he always felt "tranquil & satisfied." However, there was the inevitable end to every voyage. The unhappiness he experienced when he had to go ashore again—never home, for he was a waif—and face the uncertainties of his future and the drudgery of making a living, was pure misery.

Now, however, he knew what lay immediately ahead: completion of those travel letters to the *Alta,* a task that occupied him until February second. Beyond that there was the nebulous plan of traveling around the world as a roving correspondent. In an attempt to raise his spirits and at the same time provide subjects for future letters to San Francisco, he decided to "test" all the entertainments in the city. He chose first the most popular and most talked about performance in town—"The Black Crook!" playing at Niblo's Garden on Broadway. It was said to have already earned over three-quarters of a million dollars, and to have set a record for performances and attendance.

He found the scenic effects—"cascades, fountains, oceans, fairies, devils, hells, angels . . . gorgeous beyond anything witnessed in America;" these captivated the women and girls. Men and boys were entranced by the "splendid tableaux" starring seventy "beautiful clipper-built girls," clad in "dazzling half-costumes; and displaying all possible compromises between nakedness and decency. . . . The scenery and the legs are everything. . . . Beautiful bare-legged girls hanging in flower-baskets, . . . girls—nothing but a wilderness of girls—stacked up, pile on pile, away aloft to the dome of the theatre, diminishing in size and clothing." Viewed through a curtain of gauze to simulate a silver mist, it seemed to him the "wonder of the Arabian Nights realized."

By invitation, he visited the celebrated Century Association, a club whose membership was limited to "authors, artists, and amateurs of letters and the fine arts."—"This has a tendency to exclude parties who have bank accounts and pedigree, but no brains." There was a long waiting list because membership was limited to five hundred. He considered putting in his application—"I won't need to belong till I get old," he told the *Alta.* He found the conversation entertaining and instructive, and enjoyed the food and the brandy punches.

On Sundays all of the city's shops, restaurants, saloons, and theaters closed. Not even a newsboy or a bootblack plied his trade. What was there left to do, Sam asked himself on a Sunday morning when the thermometer stood at "180 degrees below zero," but follow the fashion and attend church. He decided to go to hear the famed Henry Ward Beecher. Sam was advised to get to his church early, for he was immensely popular. When Clemens arrived at ten which seemed early to be out on such a morning, he found the pavement thronged. When his turn came, he was sent up to the gallery, already packed. Capturing a stool from the usher, he crammed himself into a space "about large enough to accommodate a small spittoon."

Looking down, he saw that the altar was simply an elevated, carpeted platform without a rail—more like a stage, with a little pedestal at its front edge for a pulpit. After the choir had sung "charmingly," Beecher preached one of the "liveliest and most sensible sermons" Clemens had ever listened to. He was gauging Beecher as a fellow-performer: "He has a rich resonant voice, and a distinct enunciation, and makes himself heard all over the house without . . . apparent effort." Whenever he abandoned his notes, he went marching up and down the stage, "sawing his arms in the air, hurling sarcasms this way and that, discharging rockets of poetry, and exploding mines of eloquence." He would stop now and then to stamp his foot three times in succession for emphasis. "I could have started the audience with a single clap of the hands and brought down the house," Sam said. "I had a suffocating desire to do it."

New York Debut

In action, when Beecher's eyes flashed and his face was alight with animation, he might pass for handsome, but in repose he was "as homely as a singed cat."

Having inherited his father's interest in labor-saving devices, Clemens was intrigued by a stereotyping machine he saw on exhibit. "With its single alphabet of type arranged around a wheel, the most elaborate book may be impressed, letter after letter, in plaster plates . . . faster than a printer could compose the matter," he wrote. "It works with a treadle and a bank of keys, like a melodeon." It did away with type cases and all the paraphernalia of a printing office. With it, a man might set up business on a large scale for as little as two hundred dollars. It was tempting. Years later, it was an enchanting typesetting machine that would capture his imagination and his fortune, and bankrupt him.

A "calamitous" head cold and a case of the "blues" caused his thoughts to "persistently run on funerals and suicide," and put him in a frame of mind for any kind of "desperate enterprise." With a "recklessness" that surprised himself, he decided to try the Russian Bath. In Washoe, he would have taken a stagecoach over the desert to Steamboat Springs. Here, he set off on foot, "breasting the frosty wind, and ploughing through soft new snow." In the luxurious baths, he submitted to a similar regimen of hot steam and cold showers, a rub-down, and massage—only here, there was a drink afterward, on the house. If the world had seemed dismal earlier, he was no longer aware of it as he strode happily up the street to his hotel.

Actually, there were a number of cheering prospects. When Sam first landed in New York he was overcome by a sense of loneliness in the midst of millions of his fellows. He had more friends in the city than he may have realized, or admitted, for there was a large colony of Californians, and a good many men from Nevada. One of the first San Franciscans he called upon was the witty Charles Webb, founder and editor of *The Californian,* which had published a version of "The Jumping Frog" in December 1865, when Bret Harte was editor. When they met now, Webb proposed collecting a group of Sam's sketches for a book, using the frog story as the lead piece and also for the title. Clemens admitted to being "charmed and excited" by the suggestion. They decided to submit the work to Carleton & Company, so Webb made an appointment for Sam to see him. But Carleton refused the jumping frog tale a second time, and Webb bravely undertook to publish it himself. He agreed to pay Sam a ten percent royalty.

In an undated letter to Mollie Clemens, written in February, he said that "the Californians in town have almost induced me to lecture, but . . . I am not going to rush headlong in & make a fiasco of the thing, when I may possibly make a success of it by going a little slow." He had been warned that New York audiences might not appreciate his brand of humor. He also told her that several newspapers had made him good offers, "a little above what they pay any body else in my line—but I have not closed with any of them yet."

Before and during the Civil War, abolitionist leaders promised to support women's rights: "After the slave, then the Woman," Wendell Phillips had pledged. Now the blacks were free, but women were forgotten. Feminists were bitter about the broken promises, and were aroused to action. Twenty-four-year-old Anna Elizabeth Dickinson, a Quaker girl, who at nineteen had made her first speech, (in support of abolition) was one of the most forceful and convincing advocates of women's rights. She drew huge crowds and was paid in "very high figures" for her talks, Clemens observed. Known now as the Queen of the Lyceum, she was speaking at Cooper Institute in February.

Since Sam was considering a lecture in New York, he decided to hear her and observe her methods of holding and swaying an audience. She was escorted on stage by Peter Cooper and introduced by Horace Greeley. Clemens saw that she wore her thick, straight hair cut short (it just touched her collar), and was dressed in a plain, cherry-colored silk with lace cravat and cuffs—a style he considered much too old for her. The fact that she used no notes, that she never hesitated for a word, and always put the right word in the right place, impressed him greatly. "Her vim, her energy, her tremendous earnestness, could compel the respect and attention of an audience, even if she spoke in Chinese."

Her subject was "the drudging, unintellectual character" of the majority of jobs open to women—chiefly menial tasks in factories, or work as household servants. She demanded that opportunities be created in fields where women could achieve recognition.

Shortly after mid-February Clemens learned that a group of prominent Brooklyn residents (all members of Beecher's Plymouth Church) were organizing a "grand European pleasure trip" for the coming summer. It promised "a vast amount of enjoyment for a very reasonable rate," he reported to the *Alta*. The fare was set at $1,250. The passenger list, limited to 110 to avoid crowding, was filling up fairly fast since the announcement that Henry Ward Beecher (who planned to write a life of Jesus, and wanted to explore the Holy Land), and General William T. Sherman, with his daughter and a party, were going. In his *Alta* letter Sam included the itinerary and explained that in any or all of the ports listed the ship would tie up to give passengers an opportunity to travel overland to places of special interest. "Private caprice will be allowed full scope. . . . Isn't it a most attractive scheme? Five months of utter freedom from care and anxiety . . . in company with a set of people who will go only to enjoy themselves." Nothing like it had been tried before. It was a novelty in the way of excursions. He visualized it as a picnic on "a gigantic scale," where the party would "scamper" about the decks by day, filling the ship with shouts and laughter, and dance the night away on the after-deck, with only the stars and moon for light. They would be able to "hobnob" with kings, queens, princes, "grand Moguls, and the anointed lords of mighty empires!"

Here lay the realization of that dream to sail around the world—provided he could persuade the *Alta* to pay his way. He wrote to Fred MacCrellish at once, and while waiting for his answer, decided to make inquiries about the trip, and possibly enter his name and pay something down. He could always cancel. He took with him a new friend (introduced by Charles Webb), Edward (Ned) House, the distinguished Civil War correspondent for Greeley's *New-York Tribune*. Along the way they met an acquaintance who, upon learning where they were bound, warned that the cruise was a "very stylish affair," and that the standing and character of every applicant must undergo the strictest screening by a committee before being accepted. At this alarming news, Clemens and House stopped at a saloon for drinks.

At his Wall Street office, Captain Charles Duncan, co-promoter of the excursion, greeted them with "distant politeness." House, hoping to thaw him, introduced his companion as the Reverend Mark Twain, "a clergyman of some distinction, lately come from San Francisco." For part of the previous year he had been working as a missionary in the Sandwich Islands, but "officiating in the open air has injured his health, and—"

"And my congregation concluded to start me traveling for my health," Clemens interrupted. "I would like to take some stock—I mean I would like to ship—that is, book my name for this pleasure trip. I hear that Mr. Beecher is going—is that so?" On being told that it was true, House said they had been wondering if the Reverend Mr. Twain might be allowed "to take part in the services on board." Duncan replied: "I have no doubt he would be sincerely glad to have Mr. Twain assist him in the vessel's pulpit at all times —no doubt in the world about that."

The next day, Sam went back and told Duncan who he really was, paid a deposit, and left character references, listing all the people of high standing in the community who would be least likely to know him. "They have got about all they can attend to for the next six weeks to get up a spotless character of me. If they succeed, I will get a copy and have it framed."

The grand *Bal d'Opera*, celebrating the opening of the spring season, was held on the evening of March first at the new Academy of Music. Sam was invited and got himself up in "flowing robes, and purported to be a king of some country or other"—a role he enjoyed until called upon to swing into schottisches and waltzes, when he found he was in danger of "tripping in my petticoats and breaking my neck." He then deserted the dance floor in favor of promenading in the halls, where he mingled "with queens and fairies," and imagined he was in a land of enchantment—until he overheard Joan of Arc say she would give the world for a mess of raw oysters; and the Fairy Queen remark that she wished she had some cheese.

On the snowy night of March 3, Clemens left on the eight o'clock night train for St. Louis, arriving a little more than two days later after a journey beset with annoyances that made him "peevish and fretful." He was obliged to sit up two nights because the sleeping cars were full, and to shiver in the hours after midnight, because the door of the stove that heated the car was locked to keep passengers from using up the coal.

He was returning home after six years and four months, not with the fortune he had vowed to make, but standing firmly on the threshold of fame, with a pen name that was already well known from coast to coast, and a wealth of experience in life and in his profession. He went directly from the depot to Pamela's house at 12 Chestnut Street, and "sat up till breakfast time, talking and telling other lies." His niece, Annie, nearly fifteen, always remembered the excitement over his arrival—and the presents he brought her: a beautiful crystal necklace and matching earrings from San Francisco, and a Bible from Hawaii, inscribed from her "venerable Uncle." It was very like his piloting days. There were books and toys for his nephew and namesake (now going on seven), whom he encouraged half-seriously to become "a great minister of the gospel, because there ought to be one in every family." (Sam Moffett became a distinguished journalist and editor instead, but his career was cut short tragically by accidental drowning in the surf off New Jersey.) He had been eight months old when his uncle left for Carson City, and they had to get acquainted again. Interest in Sam Clemens rose markedly when he produced those arm and leg bones picked up on Oahu's ancient battlefield.

Sam observed that the greatest changes were not in the adults but the young children. It had not occurred to him that during his absence they would grow up to be women and men, and he kept asking about this one or that: "How is little Johnny; does he eat as much candy as ever?" To which the reply was "No, little Johnny is married now and is Captain of a steamboat." When he learned that one of the sweethearts he had been dreaming about for so long had a husband and five children, "it was a great blow to me. If she had had fifty I couldn't have stood it at all."

Jane Lampton and Pamela noticed changes in him. He was thinner, and he had grown a large moustache that covered his upper lip and the corners of his mouth, making less noticeable the length and curve of his nose—which was the effect he wanted. His eyes seemed more deeply set and more piercing, and he appeared much older. They were aware of his restlessness and underlying dissatisfaction and anger, which they could not explain. Pamela, as always, urged him to turn to religion. But then he would relax and become the familiar fun-loving, mischievous boy who joked and teased. Annie was reminded often about Moses and the "bulrushers."

Shortly he was participating in Pamela's church affairs. "I went to church twice last Sunday, and to Sunday School three times. All my folks live here, and I have to go mighty slow," he told his *Alta* readers. "I infest all the prayer meetings . . . and conduct myself in a manner which is as utterly unexceptionable as it is outrageously irksome. . . . I don't think I can stand it much longer. I never could bear to be respectable long at a stretch."

One morning the Sunday School superintendent came up to Clemens after class and asked if he had any experience in instructing the young. He replied that it was his "strong suit," so he was called on for a few remarks. He stood up and told that "admiring multitude" all about Jim Smiley's Jumping Frog, and his efforts were received "with the most rapturous applause." He had intended to "draw an instructive moral from that story, but when I got to the end of it I couldn't discover that there was any particular moral sticking out of it anywhere, and so I just let it slide."

Missouri women were stumping for the right to vote, and had petitioned the legislature for an amendment to the constitution. One week after his arrival at St. Louis, Sam attacked "the monster" with an article, "Views on Female Suffrage," which was printed in the *Missouri Democrat*. He claimed to be reporting on a legislative session at some future time when women members were in the majority. Issues under debate included the regulation of husbands, and whether skirts should or should not have hoops. Mrs. Mark Twain already held office in "sixteen different infernal female associations," making dreadful inroads on her housekeeping. If given the vote, she would surely run for political office. Then she would have time for nothing at home, and "the one solitary thing I have shirked up to the present time would fall on me, and my family would go to destruction; for I am *not* qualified for a wet nurse." This called for a rejoinder from Mrs. Mark Twain. "The old woman states a case well, don't she?" he observed parenthetically. The third piece was a purported attack on him by

Mrs. Zeb Leavenworth, wife of the pilot. She called him an "atrocious scoundrel," among other epithets.

After having "raised a small female storm, . . . it occurred to me that it might get uncommon warm for one poor devil against all the crinoline in camp, and so I antied up and passed out, as the Sabbath School children say." He made another contribution to the press during his stay, a piece entitled "Cruelty to Strangers," protesting signs in St. Louis' Lafayette Park, warning visitors not to *lie* on the grass, the verb being interpreted as telling an untruth. This squib appeared in the *Missouri Republican.*

He was asked to give a lecture on the Sandwich Islands for the benefit of the South St. Louis Mission School. Before accepting he wrote to Charles Webb, asking whether the frog book would be out before the end of March. If so, he must telegraph him, and Sam will refuse this call in favor of an appearance in New York, to coincide with the book's publication. But Webb replied that he was unable to get it out before April 25. Sam therefore went ahead with plans for the St. Louis talk, publicizing it with announcements which offered such "splendid" prizes as a "beautiful elephant" for the best conundrum, and eighteen auger holes for the best poem on "Summer or Summer Complaint (option with author)."

As a prelude to the lecture, he was asked to speak at a Sunday school in Carondelet, grown into a city whose outskirts now bordered St. Louis. This time he determined to include a moral. As an example of mean and miserable behavior he told about one John James Godfrey, who had been hired by the Hayblossom Mining Company of California to do some blasting for them. "Well, one day he drilled a hole about four feet deep and put in an awful blast of powder, and was standing over it ramming it down with an iron crowbar . . . when the cussed thing struck a spark and fired the powder, and scat! away John Godfrey whizzed like a sky-rocket, him and his crowbar! Well, sir, he kept on going up in the air higher and higher, till he didn't look any bigger than a boy—" And he went still higher, looking no bigger than a doll, and then still higher, "till he didn't look any bigger than a little small bee—and then he went out of sight." Presently he came into view again, looking like a bee, then a doll, growing in size until as a man he and his crowbar came "a wh-izzing down," landed in the same place, and went to "r-ramming down again just the same as if nothing had happened!" He had been gone exactly sixteen minutes, but that "incorporated company of mean men DOCKED HIM FOR THE LOST TIME!" That tale, also received with "rapturous applause," was included in *Roughing It.*

He gave his lecture twice before full houses at the Mercantile Library Hall on the evenings of March 25 and 26. The *Missouri Republican* commented that the entertainment was a "complete success. In fact, Mark Twain achieved a very decided success. He succeeded in doing what we have seen Emerson and other literary magnates fail in attempting—he interested a large and promiscuous audience."

Sam escaped the domination of his women at home by "gadding about" among old friends—pilots Beck Jolly and Zeb Leavenworth, and old sweethearts, Essie and Lou Conrad, and he attended meetings of the Euchre Horns Club, stag affairs where "you haven't got to be kept under the tiresome restraints of proper conduct all the time."

Although the levee was lined with steamboats its entire length, just as he remembered it, he was aware that railroads were starting to take away freight and passengers. He observed that the political bitterness which divided St. Louis families and friends during the Civil War, was as strong as ever. These people had never forgiven one another for the sides they took, and still held no communication. Guest lists for every social event were composed of either all Democrats or all Republicans. Even church congregations were based on political party.

One of the pleasant things he noticed was that "those old-fashioned twilights still remain, and enrich all the landscape with a dreamy vagueness for two hours after the sun has gone down. It is such a pity they forgot to put in twilight when they made the Pacific Coast."

After passing nearly a month at St. Louis, he said goodbye to his family and friends, and to the "happy, cheerful, contented old town . . . where people are kind and polite, even to strangers"— something he had not found in New York, that "domed and steepled solitude."

He boarded the steamboat for Hannibal, noticing that passengers were fewer and meals not as good as formerly, but the officers were still all "princes." He was welcomed as a visiting celebrity in his hometown, and invited to lecture, which he did on April 2. Among old schoolmates and familiar surroundings, his thoughts naturally turned to boyhood. Hannibal was said to be suffering from post-war depression and railroad competition with its steamboat trade, but as he remembered, the town had always had hard times. "First, it had me for a citizen, but I was really too young to hurt the place. Next Jimmy Finn, the town drunkard, reformed, and that broke up the only saloon in the village. But the temperance people liked it; they were willing enough to sacrifice public prosperity to public morality. And so they made much of Jimmy Finn—dressed him up in new clothes, and had him out to breakfast and to dinner . . . and showed him off as . . . a shining example of the power of temperance doctrines when . . . eloquently set forth." But Jimmy Finn could not stand it. "He got remorseful about the loss of his liberty; then he got melancholy from thinking about it so much; and after that he got drunk."

This was the first time Clemens had written for print a description of the man who furnished the surname and some of the characteristics of Huck Finn's "Pap." In this letter to the *Alta* he went on to tell how the outraged temperance people rallied and effected a second reform, and how in "an evil hour temptation came upon Finn, and he sold his body to a doctor for a quart of whiskey." He drank it at one sitting, and "his soul went to its long account and his body went to Dr. Grant"—the Hannibal physician who had taken the Clemens family into his home in their hour of desperate poverty.

He told next about joining the Cadets of Temperance, this account differing from the one in his *Autobiography* in the reasons for joining and withdrawing. He said that even though members were not allowed to smoke, drink, or swear, he thought he could never be "truly happy till I wore one of those stunning red scarfs and walked in a procession when a distinguished citizen died. I stood it four months, but never an infernal distinguished citizen died; and when they pronounced old Dr. Norton convalescent (a man I had been depending on for seven or eight weeks,) I just drew out in disgust." And then, within the next three weeks nearly "all the distinguished citizens in camp died. . . ."

On April 4 Sam moved on by boat to Keokuk, which he found prospering again. He did not stay with Orion and Mollie, but at the Heming House—for only one night. "It used to be a good hotel, but that proves nothing—I used to be a good boy, for that matter. Both of us have lost character of late years." In the morning he moved to the Tepfer House, "well furnished, well conducted.

He was among friends again, and his days passed pleasantly. When he was working for Orion here, he had made his first after-dinner talk at a printer's banquet. And it was from the *Keokuk Post* that he had received his first pay as a traveling correspondent, having contributed the Thomas Jefferson Snodgrass letters. Now he was being hailed as "the celebrated California humorist, and most extraordinary delineator of human character in America or upon the Continent of Europe." Chatham Square Methodist Episcopal Church was filled for his April 8 lecture on the Sandwich Islands.

"It has been many a day since our 'ribs were tickled' so much as listening to Sam Clemens last evening," the local *Constitution* wrote. His humor is "original, quaint and irresistible." Those who did not come, "missed one of the treats of their lives." As he was talking, Sam noticed his old friend Ed Brownell in the audience; he was the bookstore clerk who had roomed above him in other days and had laughed at Sam's statement that he would write a funnier book than the one he was trying to read. Now Sam got his revenge. Touching on the unreliability of the native Islanders (from the white man's viewpoint), he said that the King was possibly the greatest liar on earth—save one, "and I am sorry to locate that one right here in Keokuk, in the person of Ed Brownell." The audience laughed, but the point was private. The *Jumping Frog*, Sam's "funnier book" would be issued in a little more than two weeks.

The following night he spoke to a full house in Quincy and left directly afterward for New York by train. He did not want to miss the publication date. Charles Webb was putting the book out in an "elegant style," and pricing it at $1.50. It was being bound in blue, with "a truly gorgeous gold frog on the back of it, and that frog alone will be worth the money. I don't know but what it would be well to publish the frog and leave the book out. . . ." Two weeks later he reported that it was selling "rapidly," and that "a lot of copies will go to San Francisco per this steamer. I hope my friends will all buy a few copies each, and more especially am I anxious to see the book in all the Sunday School Libraries in the land."

After looking at the work more carefully he was dismayed at finding it "full of damnable errors of grammar and deadly inconsistencies of spelling . . . because I was away and did not read the proofs," he explained to Bret Harte; "but be a friend and say nothing about these things."

The mistakes were not obvious to those like James Russell Lowell, who were less familiar with the vernacular. He read it and proclaimed the story "the finest piece of humorous writing ever produced in America," Sam was proud to tell his mother and sister. This letter home was written on Westminster Hotel stationery. "Direct my letters to this hotel in the future," he instructed. "I am fixed, now. This is the gem of all hotels. . . . Full of 'bloated aristocrats' too & I'm just one of *them* kind myself."

Three days earlier he had written his family that the first man he had met after his return from St. Louis was John Murphy, chief of the *Alta*'s New York bureau. Murphy was carrying a check for $1,250 and a telegram from San Francisco instructing him: "Ship Mark Twain in the Holy Land Pleasure Excursion & pay his passage." Together they went to Captain Duncan's Wall Street office, and while they were waiting for him, a reporter came in and asked what notables were going on the cruise. The clerk listed General Sherman, Henry Ward Beecher, Mark Twain, and probably General Banks, in that order. Sam was pleased. Later he and Murphy went to look at the ship—the 1,800-ton side-wheel steamer *Quaker City*. She was "stately-looking," Clemens thought, and had been all newly painted and fitted up. He saw that there was a piano and a parlor organ in the cabin, and learned that a snare drummer, base drummer, and fifer had been recruited. He was also told that there would be a good many young ladies aboard.

After coming back from St. Louis he discovered that during his absence the "boys" had gotten up a call for him to lecture; it was signed by some two hundred Californians living in New York. Frank Fuller, who as acting-governor of Utah Territory in 1861, had entertained Orion and Sam at Salt Lake City, was head of the committee and was prepared to act as his manager. Sam had gone to see him in January when he (Clemens) first came to New York. Fuller had welcomed him and taken him home to meet his wife and daughters. His advice now was to take the biggest hall in the city, for people were "wild" to hear him. He predicted fame and fortune. They hired Cooper Institute, set the date for May 6, and began advertising.

Later they discovered that the date was an unfortunate choice, for Clemens would have competition from Speaker of the House Schuyler Colfax, talking about his cross-country trip, from Adelaide Ristori, the great Italian tragedienne, and also from the Imperial Troupe of Japanese acrobats, jugglers, and magicians, under the sponsorship of Sam's San Francisco friend, the impresario Tom Maguire.

Sam wrote home on May 1 that "everything looks shady, at least, if not dark." Already expenses had reached five hundred dollars. At this point "I cannot back water. Let her slide!" Fuller reacted by advertising more energetically. Posters and notices were placed conspicuously all over the city and in the omnibuses. These announced that tickets were priced at fifty cents, and that the doors would open at 7 o'clock. "The Wisdom will begin to flow at 8." Former Territorial Governor James Nye of Nevada was to introduce the speaker.

"There is not going to be anybody in the Cooper Institute that night but you and me," Sam said to Fuller. "It will be a dead loss, for we shall both have free tickets. Something must be done. I am on the verge of suicide. I would commit suicide if I had the pluck and the outfit." The only solution, he believed, was to paper the house—send out thousands of complimentary tickets. Fuller complied by despatching "basketsful" to teachers all over the area.

Clemens had intended to wear his sack suit for the lecture but Fuller insisted he appear in evening dress for his New York debut, and had a tailor outfit him. Sam was in Fuller's office when he tried on the claw-hammer coat. Never having worn one before, he attempted to button it, and finding the buttonholes sewn together commenced swearing at the tailor for having carelessly left in the stitches. Fuller explained that it was not customary to button a dress coat. Sam pointed to an engraving of Daniel Webster on the wall, which showed his coat buttoned, and asked sarcastically who knew best—Webster, or "a scrub of a tailor." He then took out his knife, cut the stitches, and buttoned the coat.

He was as nervous as he had been before his first talk in San Francisco and, as he had done then, he went to the hall early. "I wanted to see that vast Mammoth Cave and die." But as he neared the building "I found that all the streets for a quarter of a mile around were blocked with people, and traffic was stopped." He could not believe they were all going to Cooper Institute, yet that was just what they were doing. He entered by the stage door, and saw that the seats, the aisles, even the huge stage itself were filled.

He was relieved, but still another problem remained: Governor Nye did not come. When it was nearly time for the lecture to begin and he had still not arrived, Sam begged Fuller to take the governor's place. But Fuller refused, insisting there was no need to have anyone introduce him.

Promptly at eight o'clock, Clemens appeared on stage and the California contingent and their friends stamped and cheered. But Sam was in deep concentration. He walked forward slowly with his head bent, and peered down at the cracks in the floor as if hunting for something. He went up to the very edge of the platform and looked over into the pit, right and left. Then he stepped back, stared at his audience, and explained wistfully:

"I am looking for Governor Nye who promised to introduce me, but I don't see him anywhere. Well, since there are no other governors in town right now we'll just worry along without him."

These words were greeted with "shouts of laughter and bursts of applause . . . far beyond anything I have ever witnessed," Fuller said afterward. The audience was in Sam's hands from the start, and "I poured the Sandwich Islands out to those people with a free hand and they laughed and shouted to my entire content. For an hour and fifteen minutes I was in Paradise." If he did not make the fortune Frank Fuller had predicted, he got "a working quantity of fame" from the appearance. The New York papers all praised his lecture, the country newspapers copied those praises, and Clemens was soon receiving invitations to join lyceum lecture circuits around the country.

"Make your mark in New York, and you are a made man," he wrote the *Alta*. He gave publicity in that letter to the fact that Nye had defected after promising "to introduce me to my audience . . . and I had published it; but he was not at his hotel when the carriage went for him, has not been seen since, and has never sent a word of explanation. However, it is a matter of no consequence. I introduced myself as well as he could have done it—that is, without straining himself."

"I have refused all invitations to lecture in the interior towns of this and neighboring States," for he was eighteen *Alta* letters behind, and "must catch up or bust," he told his family. Therefore, "don't, *don't* ask me to write for a week or two." He did, however, accept a request to talk in Brooklyn. Still lacking confidence in his ability to introduce himself, he asked Corry O'Lanns if he would be "so obliging to a brother member of the press" as to present him. However, he did lecture again in New York City, at Irving Hall this time, and with better financial success. By then, he had placed the manuscript of his Sandwich Islands book in the hands of the publishers, Dick & Fitzgerald. If they do accept it (which he seemed to doubt), he will make arrangements for them to send his mother what money accrues from sales as he had done with the Jumping Frog.

In May, with sailing day just three weeks off, he set to work in earnest to catch up with the *Alta* letters, and sometimes wrote as much as one long article in a day. He covered a variety of subjects: reflections on the mutability of fame written after he had observed Jefferson Davis, "head, and heart, and soul of the mightiest rebellion of modern times," arrive at the New York Hotel, "as unheralded and unobserved as any country merchant from the far West." He commented on a series of photographs taken in Paris of Alexandre Dumas père, and Adah Isaacs Menken, "the poor woman who has so much money, but not any clothes." The poses were amorous—her head on his chest, her arms clasping his neck, his head pressed againt her breast, his arms about her. They were signed in French: "To my dearest love, A. Dumas." Thousands of these pictures had been sold in France and now they would be reproduced in the United States. "She knows the value of keeping herself before the world in new and startling situations."

In one of his letters, he was pleased to tell Californians about the great success of the San Francisco Minstrels. The group was unchanged, and played nightly to packed houses in New York—"I have good reason to know, because I have been there pretty often." Their shows "made life a pleasure," to him. In looking back years later, he said that the genuine minstrel show had no peer in those early days, and in his experience none yet.

He told his readers that he had talked with California's own "Little Miss Lotta"—Lotta Crabtree, from Grass Valley. As a child, she had delighted miners by dancing jigs and flings and singing ballads to her own accompaniment on a miniature banjo, and they had showered the stage with nuggets and bags of gold dust. Now she was twenty, and was playing Little Nell and the Marchioness in a dramatization of *The Old Curiosity Shop,* and had become a star. She looked as pretty as ever, and was just as charming.

In another letter he admitted to having spent a night in jail. "I don't mind mentioning it, because anybody can get into the Station House here without committing an offense of any kind." As he told it, he and a friend were on their way home about midnight, when they came upon two men fighting in the street. "We interfered like a couple of idiots, and tried to separate them, and a brace of policemen came up and took all of us to the Station House. We offered the officers two or three prices to let us go, (policemen generally charge $5 in assault and battery cases, and $25 for murder in the first degree, I believe,) but there were too many witnesses present, and they actually refused."

Sam had amused himself for an hour or so by looking through the bars of his cell at "the dilapidated old hags, and battered and ragged bummers, sorrowing and swearing in the stone-paved halls." Close to three o'clock he went to sleep on his bench, and at dawn was wakened and marched into court with a "vile policeman" at each elbow, "just as if I had been robbing a church, or saying a complimentary word about the police, or doing some other supernaturally mean thing." There was a four-hour wait for the hearing. Meanwhile he observed his companions and later described some of them for the *Alta.* He opened a conversation with "a bloated" old crone who had "a wholesome black eye" and "a drunken leer in the sound one." She gave him her life history, then asked for a chew of tobacco and a cigar. He gave her a cigar and borrowed the tobacco. In return she offered him a pull from the flask of gin she had secreted in the folds of her shawl. He did not accept. Two "flashgirls" of sixteen and seventeen stood by. They had been picked up for soliciting, but insisted the men had made the first advances. They were in tears, and Clemens felt sorry for them. All at once he noticed some handwriting on a wall. He was startled to read: "The Trouble will begin at 8 o'clock!" How well he remembered thinking up that line when he was writing the posters for his first lecture in San Francisco.

When he stood up (under guard) before the judge, he asked about contesting his case on a plea of unjust imprisonment, but was told it was not worth the bother; no one would ever know he had been in jail unless he spoke of it himself. He was then dismissed.

The remaining weeks were spent in searching the city from end to end for items to fill his newspaper letters. He gathered facts and figures on the popularity of California wines in the East, on New York weather, and on its leading hotels. He visited the Bible House, the Blind Asylum, and the Midnight Mission, which took prostitutes off the streets and tried to find them other employment. He went through those "dens of poverty, crime and degradation that hide from the light of day in the Five Points." He attended a horse race and saw the famous "Dexter" run. He contracted to go up in a balloon—only the balloon never went up. He spent an evening at Harry Hill's Club House, whose attractions were a well-stocked bar, music, dancing, "waiter girls," and bawdy skits; also an occasional prize fight. He went under the impression (so he maintained) that it was a place where "the *savants* were in the habit of meeting to commune upon abstruse matters of science and philosophy—men like Agassiz . . . and Professor Morse." He was therefore surprised when he observed the famed "Morse" take his lady on his lap, and the still more renowned "Agassiz" lead his to the bar and call for drinks to treat the crowd.

He visited Barnum's Museum—"nothing in the place worth seeing"—and went to the National Academy of Design's forty-second annual exhibition. Out of three hundred paintings, he liked only thirty or forty. He admired all the marine and mountain views, and the quiet woodland scenes, "and I just reveled in the storms."

New York Debut

There was a painting by an "old master" which he knew he was supposed to admire, but could not. "I am glad the old masters are all dead, and I only wish they had died sooner." Probably he had never seen the work of an old master before, so this was doubtless the first time that often repeated opinion appeared in print. He objected strongly to the commonplace—pictures of playful kittens and wistful puppies, and "the same old detachment of cows wading across a branch at sunset, and the same old naked libels marked 'Eve'; and the same old stupid looking wenches marked 'Autumn' and 'Summer' . . . loafing around in the woods, or toting flowers, and all of them out of shirts." A little later, he went to see Albert Bierstadt's huge oil painting (15 feet long and 9 1/2 feet high) titled "Domes of Yosemite." Most of the critics had been abusing the picture. Sam admitted he was not "cultivated enough" to recognize those glaring faults reviewers had picked out, but to someone as familiar with Yosemite as he was, it seemed "very beautiful" and well worth seeing.

He recommended the newly published *Sut Lovingood Yarns,* a collection of racy sketches by George Washington Harris, a Tennessee River steamboat captain. Ever since they had appeared serially, Sam had relished those tales about an uncouth mountaineer from the Great Smokies, whose two favorite things in life were corn whiskey and a boisterous prank. Eight of his old favorites were included among sixteen new stories. "The book abounds in humor," he said, and he commended Harris for his accurate use of regional dialect.

In one letter Sam mentioned that the body of "poor Artemus Ward" had just arrived by steamer from England, on its way home for burial at Waterford, Maine. Just three years ago, Ward, Joe Goodman, Dan De Quille, and Sam had spent a week skylarking in Virginia City. Ward's recognition of the value of the printer's trade pleased Sam. In his will, Artemus stipulated that his "little valet" be apprenticed to the best printer in the United States, to "learn the value of learning," and then be sent on to college.

After five months in New York City, Clemens found it no more friendly than he had at first. He felt "something lacking, something wanting," in everything he did there. He surmised that "something" was the "provincial quietness I am used to," he said to his readers. "I have had enough of sights and shows, and noise and bustle, and confusion, and now I want to disperse. I am ready to go."

In writing to his mother and sister, he was outspoken. "All I do know or feel is, that I am wild with impatience to move—move— *move!* Half a dozen times I have wished I had sailed long ago in some ship that wasn't going to keep me chained here to chafe for lagging ages while she got ready to go. Curse the endless delays! They always kill me—they make me neglect every duty & then I have a conscience that tears me like a wild beast. I wish I never had to stop *any*where a month. I do more mean things, the moment I get a chance to fold my hands & sit down than ever I can get forgiveness for." They have scolded him for not writing oftener and telling more about himself. They are right, but he has been unable to conquer his reluctance to talk about what he is doing or expects to do. "Manifestly nothing" is left to write about, then. He cannot discuss the voyage, for who can tell whether the ship will ever sail.

His confidence in the entire venture began to wane early in May, when Beecher, and then forty of his parishioners, withdrew. Three weeks later General Sherman announced publicly that he would be unable to go because of what Clemens called the "Indian Row." This applied also to General Nathaniel Banks. Then Maggie Mitchell, the New York actress famed for her interpretation of Jane Eyre, canceled. "Mark Twain" was the only celebrity left. This decline in the tour's prestige had a financial impact, and with only a short time left before the fixed sailing date the passenger list stood far below the anticipated number. Sam therefore made no preparations whatever—"bought no cigars, no sea-going clothing"—and put off packing his trunk until the morning they sailed. Still, he did continue "rubbing up" his rusty French, writing out conjugations in his notebook, reading books of history and travel, and Irving's works on Spain.

He had expected to associate with a group of sophisticated, even stimulating companions, but began to have doubts after he met a social climber who had looked forward to attaching himself to the Sherman party by requesting a seat next to the General at table and, for his wife, a chair beside Miss Sherman. When the man learned that "Sherman was going to remain in the States, he howled fearfully," almost shed tears, and considered staying behind himself. There was another passenger, "a solemn, unsmiling, sanctimonious old iceberg" who asked Captain Duncan if the excursion would come to a halt on Sundays. Duncan replied that he hardly expected to anchor the vessel in the middle of the Atlantic, but when passengers were ashore they might do as they pleased.

Sam tried to believe these were exceptions, and encouraged himself with thoughts about that "brick," Dan Slote, his "splendid, immoral, tobacco-smoking, wine-drinking, godless room-mate," a bachelor, fifteen years his senior, who was bringing with him a "passel" of shirts, three thousand cigars, a cribbage-board, and a history of the Holy Land. "I will not have to carry any baggage at all." He had visited Dan's home and found his mother and sisters the best and most likeable people he had found yet "in a brownstone front. There is no style about them except in the house & furniture." He hoped this would reassure Jane Lampton and Pamela, who were worrying about the company he would keep, although his next words were likely to undermine confidence. An importing house had sent Sam two cases of "exquisite" champagne —Veuve Cliquot and Lac d'Or. He and Dan "have set apart every Saturday as a solemn fast-day, wherein we will entertain no light matters or frivolous conversation, but only get drunk." He added in a parenthetical aside, "(That is a joke)".

When last at Hannibal, Sam had told Will Bowen about the coming excursion, and the day before sailing he wrote him: "We leave tomorrow at 3:00 P.M. Everything is ready but my trunks. I will pack them first thing in the morning." He will be sailing with "a crowd of tiptop people, and shall have a jolly, sociable, homelike trip for the next five or six months." He is going on this trip "for fun only," even though he has to keep up his *Alta* correspondence, and write two letters a month for Horace Greeley's paper. He did not mention that he had also agreed to contribute a few unsigned letters to the rival *Herald,* founded and edited by James Gordon Bennett. If, after all the months of freedom and jollity, they should all go to the bottom, "I think we shall be fortunate. There is no unhappiness like the misery of sighting land (and work) again after a cheerful, careless voyage." Since he has a roving commission, if he finds the prospect of landing at New York unbearable, he will simply shift his trunks to some other vessel and sail away again.

On this same day he wrote to his family, but his mood was dark as he succumbed to feelings of guilt. "I have just written myself clear out in letters to the *Alta,* & I think they are the stupidest letters that were ever written from New York. Corresponding has been a perfect drag ever since I got back to the States. If it continues abroad, I don't know what the Tribune & Alta folks will think.

"I have withdrawn the Sandwich Islands book—it would be useless to publish it in these dull publishing times. As for the Frog book, I don't believe that will ever pay anything worth a cent. I published it simply to advertise myself. . . ."

With regard to Orion: "I wish I had gone to Washington in the winter instead of going West, I could have gouged an office out of Bill Stewart for him, & that would have atoned for the loss of my home visit." When he last saw Orion his law practice was dull. "I wish Orion were going on this voyage, for I believe with so many months of freedom from business cares he could not help but be cheerful & jolly." But then, "I am so worthless that it seems to me I never do anything or accomplish anything that lingers in my mind as a pleasant memory. My mind is stored full of unworthy conduct toward Orion & toward you all, & an accusing conscience gives me peace only in excitement & restless moving from place to place. If I could say I had done one thing for any of you that entitled me to your good opinions (I say nothing of your love, for I am sure of *that,* no matter how unworthy of it I may make myself, —from Orion down, you have always given me that, all the days of my life, when God Almighty knows I have seldom deserved it,) I believe I could go home & stay there—& I know I would care little for the world's praise or blame. There is no satisfaction in the world's praise, anyhow, & it has no worth to me save in the way of business. I tried to gather up its compliments to send to you, but the work was distasteful & I dropped it."

He closed: "You observe that under a cheerful exterior I have got a spirit that is angry with me & gives me freely its contempt. I can get away from that at sea, & be tranquil & satisfied—& so, with my parting love & benediction for Orion & all of you, I say goodbye & God bless you all—& welcome the wind that wafts a weary soul to the sunny lands of the Mediterranean!

Yrs forever——Sam."

XXII

―――――――――――○―――――――――――

THE GRAND PLEASURE
EXCURSION

For the first time, Sam Clemens was starting a voyage with some knowledge of what the future held for him after his return. Just before sailing, he received a letter from Senator William M. Stewart of Nevada, in response to Sam's written inquiry of several months before regarding a post for himself at Washington. He offered Clemens a job as his private secretary during the coming winter. Sam did not accept until August 9, from Naples. Writing home that same day he said, "I believe it can be made one of the best paying berths in Washington." He foresaw ample time beyond his duties, for his newspaper correspondence, and to also write the book about his Western experiences. "Say nothing of this," he cautioned. "At least I can get an office for Orion, if he or the President will modify their politics."

In a letter to his friend John McComb, the San Francisco journalist, written on sailing day, June 8, he gave an account of his previous nine hours. He went to dinner at three o'clock with John Russell Young, managing editor of the *Tribune*, and the Irish humorist, Charles Graham Halpine—"drank wine; dined from 6 to 9 at Jno Murphy's (*God* made *him*, you know, and Mrs. M. too.)—drank several breeds of wine there . . ." From nine until midnight he had his third dinner at Dan Slote's, and "drank much wine there." It was about two o'clock in the morning, then, and he was back at his hotel writing McComb.

Shortly after noon, on this same day, he was standing on the deck of the *Quaker City*, watching the passengers come aboard. It was raining hard, and everyone appeared as "droopy and woe-begone as so many molting chickens. The gallant flag was up, but it was under a spell, too, and hung limp and disheartened at the mast. Altogether it was the bluest, bluest spectacle!"

At two o'clock, just before the tide turned, the order came to cast off, and the steamer backed into the stream. "The picnic had begun! Two very mild cheers went up from the dripping crowd on the pier." Henry Ward Beecher was among the well-wishers. From the slippery decks the passengers responded "gently." Slowly the *Quaker City* steamed to the foot of the harbor and anchored. "It was not only raining, but storming. 'Outside' we could see, ourselves, that there was a tremendous sea on." There they remained until Monday, when clear skies and calmer water allowed them to set off in earnest. As Sam watched the Atlantic coastline fade from view, he felt so jubilant he wanted to sing.

As usual he looked over the passengers carefully and took note of those who might make good characters to develop in his newspaper correspondence. There was Frederick Greer of Boston, a thin, long-legged fellow who made "witless" remarks and then laughed uproariously. Greer considered himself an authority on ocean travel because he had once made a trip to Fort Monroe, Virginia. "He quotes eternally from his experiences on that voyage." He became "young William Blucher" in the *Alta* letters, and gradually replaced Mr. Brown.

There was a small, prosperous farmer from Long Island, Bloodgood H. Cutter, who dressed unpretentiously in homespun. He, unfortunately, possessed a mania for writing "execrable" verses for every occasion. He had brought with him a sheaf of his productions which he had had printed as broadsides with his portrait at the head. He gave them away freely to all who came along— "whether he has anything against them or not," Sam quipped. He became the ship's poet laureate, and also its chief embarrassment when he insisted upon presenting his poems to consuls, governors, and potentates, as the vessel's representative.

For Dr. Edward Andrews, Clemens' nickname was "the Oracle" because he posed as an authority on every subject. He "looks wiser than the whole Academy of France would have any right to look, and never uses a one-syllable word when he could go 'two better', and never by any possible chance knows the meaning of any long word he uses, or ever gets it in the right place." He was a veritable encyclopedia of misinformation, for he read at random in the guidebooks and histories, then jumbled the facts. But Sam was ready to forgive him much after his New York accent distorted the title "poet laureate" into "poet *lariat.*"

There was another character, a young man who was pleasant and well meaning, "but fearfully slow." To him an idea was "a new & dangerous guest to have about his premises." Because his questions were endless, he became known about the ship as the "Interrogation Point, and Sam used the symbol "?" to identify him in his notebook. Although "not bright, not learned and not wise," he will be "some day, if he recollects the answers to all his questions."

Unwittingly, Sam was ridiculing his future brother-in-law, Charles Langdon, not quite eighteen, the only son of Jervis Langdon, a coal magnate of Elmira, New York. Charlie had been sent on this excursion as a substitute for sowing wild oats, a course upon which he had already started. It was also hoped the trip would broaden his education and discipline him, for he had been badly spoiled by a doting mother. His "deadly training," as Sam characterized it later, had made him conceited, arrogant, and overbearing, traits he would have difficulty conquering. His parents believed he was safe in that decorous company bound for the Holy Land. Later, Clemens modified his original opinion to a degree and introduced Langdon into the "smoking-room crowd," or "Quaker City nighthawks," composed of Dan Slote, Jack Van Nostrand, Julius Moulton, and Sam, who drank, smoked, and played cards until late in the men's lounge or in Room 10—the Clemens–Slote cabin. But young Langdon was never a regular member, nor did the Nighthawks meet regularly, for Sam took an active part in enlivening shipboard life. He was a leader in the organization of a mock trial, and with Captain Duncan acted as counsel for the defendant—the purser, Robert Vail, charged with stealing Clemens' overcoat. The verdict was guilty, with recommendation for mercy.

The sentence, surely Sam's idea, was solitary confinement on straight whiskey for one hour in Room 10.

Sam also helped found a social club which met each evening after prayers, to read aloud from the guidebooks and discuss those places they would be seeing. He took a prominent role in the debating society, and in his notebook jotted down possible questions. "Is or is not Captain Duncan responsible for the head winds?" And, "Is a tail absolutely necessary to the comfort & convenience of a dog?" If so, then would a multiplicity of tails enlarge that convenience and comfort by a constantly increasing ratio?

He took part in charades, enacted evenings in the after cabin, and pronounced them a "distinguished success." He encouraged the organization of dancing parties on the upper deck—not under the stars or moon as he had envisioned, but beneath awnings to keep out the spray, and brilliantly lighted with lanterns to simulate a ballroom. Music was provided by a melodeon, a trifle wheezy, a clarinet that was a "little unreliable" on the high notes, and an accordion. But the seas were not always cooperative and when the ship rolled to starboard the whole "platoon" of dancers in a quadrille went charging down in that direction "and brought up in mass at the rail." The Virginia reel had "more genuine reel about it" than any he had ever seen before, and was full of "desperate chances and hairbreadth escapes," which compounded the fun.

Sam's favorite among the girls (a scarce commodity on board) was seventeen-year-old Emma Beach, traveling with her father, Moses S. Beach, the wealthy proprietor of the *New York Sun,* and member of Henry Ward Beecher's Plymouth Church. Clemens played chess with her, danced with her, acted as her gallant, and invited her to "polish" him. He won her lasting admiration when he rescued a boy passenger from a group of men who were bullying him. "Heroism came natural to him," she believed.

Of the young married couples, Sam was drawn to Emily and Solon Severance from Cleveland, and among the slightly more mature women, he admired Mrs. Mary Mason Fairbanks, whom he described as the "most refined, intelligent, & cultivated lady in the ship, & altogether the kindest & best."

Most of the passengers hardly knew what to make of him. The

opinion of Miss Julia Newell, correspondent for the Janesville, Wisconsin newspaper, was typical: "He is a rather handsome fellow but talks to you with an abominable drawl that is exasperating. Whether he intends to be funny for the amusement of the party I have not yet ascertained."

At the start of the voyage, even Mary Fairbanks, who became a lifelong friend, was uncertain whether he was being humorous for their sake or making fun of them. As a correspondent for her husband's newspaper, the *Cleveland Herald,* she contributed her first impression of their most famous and unusual fellow passenger: "We have D.D.'s and M.D.'s—we have men of wisdom and men of wit. There is one table from which is sure to come a peal of laughter, and all eyes are turned toward Mark Twain, whose face is perfectly mirth-provoking. Sitting lazily at the table, scarcely genteel in his appearance, there is something, I know not what, that interests and attracts. I saw to-day at dinner venerable divines and sage-looking men convulsed with laughter at his drolleries and quaint, odd manners."

They were interested, attracted, and amused, and laughed at his humor as they would have if they had attended one of his paid lectures. But few of the passengers accepted him as their equal, because he was "odd," "quaint," and "hardly genteel." In his turn, he took the majority on sufferance; he and they had little in common. Besides, he enjoyed shocking people.

Mary Fairbanks had graduated from Emma Willard's Seminary at Troy, New York, which offered women college level courses in philosophy, mathematics, the sciences, and history, subjects previously denied them at other schools. Emily Severance told how fortunate the party was to have her with them at Marseilles and Paris because of her fluency in French. She had far more experience in journalism than Clemens, not alone because she was older (thirty-nine), but because she had started writing for newspapers when just a girl. After they grew better acquainted, she was strongly drawn to Sam because she perceived his talents, and was seized by an ambition to direct and polish him, and push him further into fame. During their talks she urged him to work harder, to eschew *slang* in his writings and speech—a term they used to cover dialect, indelicacies, and ribaldry—and to stop swearing. "I was the worst swearer, & the most reckless, that sailed out of New York in the *Quaker City.*" He agreed to curb his swearing, but did not promise *never* to swear.

Her maternal instincts were touched by this "waif," and she "sewed my buttons on, kept my clothes in presentable trim, fed me Egyptian jam (when I behaved,) lectured me awfully on the quarter-deck on moonlit promenading evenings, & cured me of several bad habits," his family learned. Although she was not quite seven years his senior, he was soon calling her "Mother," obviously enjoying her attentions, and encouraging her efforts to improve him. He did not, however, always appreciate her attempts to refine his prose. It has been said that he submitted all his copy for her criticism, and that she became a major influence in changing his style. One day Solon Severance noticed him tearing up a number of manuscript pages and throwing the fragments overboard. When he asked Sam why, he replied, "Well, Mrs. Fairbanks thinks it oughtn't to be printed, and, like as not, she is right." And another day he said to Emma Beach as he crumpled some pages, "Well, Mrs. Fairbanks has just destroyed another four hours' work for me."

However, his *Alta* letters prove that he did not show her everything he wrote, for numbers of them contain material that would never have escaped her blue-pencil. There were times when he followed her advice simply to be fed Egyptian jam, and other times when he escaped her civilizing influences entirely and followed his own instincts for humor. Without Mary Fairbanks' knowledge his readers learned that there were no water-closets on French trains, but plenty of them at the stations, "with signs on them, and this made trouble for Brown. He . . . complained that there was a remarkable similarity between the names painted on all the French railway stations. Poor devil, he had them all down in his notebook: 'Cote des Hommes.' " Sam's readers also heard about the young women of Odessa who, when swimming wore only a single loose garment of transparent white material, which always floated up around their necks "in the most scandalous way, and the water is clear. . . . I was never so outraged in my life. . . . Why, those young ladies thought no more of turning somersaults, when I was

The Grand Pleasure Excursion

not looking, than nothing in the world. Incensed as I was I had to look."

Although he recognized the validity of some of Mary Fairbanks' advice, he was not yet ready to accept it. He was still writing mainly for Western readers. The later "refining" of Clemens' writing was due to his own desire to develop a literary style acceptable to Eastern audiences and to young people. When that time came he acknowledged the need himself, and was ready to make the change; he did not have to have it pointed out.

Mary Fairbanks took on two other charges: Charles Langdon and young Julius Moulton, both of whom also called her "Mother"; she called them her "Cubs." She "regularly drummed us up for prayer meeting with her monitory 'Seven bells, my boys—you know what it is time for.' " Sam maintained that he always went, and a record does exist of his leading devotions at least once.

After ten days of head winds and heavy seas, the *Quaker City* dropped anchor at Horta, on the island of Fayal. Sam thought it one of the loveliest towns he had ever been in, with its clean streets and snowy, neat houses half-buried in luxuriant trees and shrubbery, nestled in the lap of hills cultivated to their summits. He joined a party from the ship and called on the American consul, Charles Dabney, and his family who had been on Fayal for sixty years; Dabney's father had served there before him. Notebook in hand, Clemens walked over much of the fifteen acres of garden with Clara Dabney, the consul's sister, enjoying the singing of chaffinches and wild canaries, and the color and fragrance of rampant verbenas and oleanders. He feasted on apricots, figs, and oranges, and then took lunch with the others at the Dabney house.

During the afternoon he visited the cathedral, and with an intolerance that was typical of his time declared that the altars were "a perfect mass of gilt gimcracks and gingerbread," reminding him of the "tawdry trumpery" of the Chinese Temple in San Francisco.

The day ashore had given inspiration to the dozen or so hometown newspaper correspondents on board, and that night, in Sam's words, "the cabin looked like a reporter's congress," pens and pencils scratching busily in notebooks. Head winds kept them over another day and a half, and at ten the second morning, Sam joined a party of men on a sightseeing jaunt—Dan Slote, Judge Jacob

Haldeman, former United States minister to Sweden, and Colonel J. Heron Foster. The unworldly Emily Severance had taken the Judge for a professional gambler because he wore a red flannel shirt printed with hunting figures, a new flashy tie daily, and sported the "tightest" and glossiest of patent leather boots. Shipboard gossip, of which there was plenty, had it that he went on the voyage to cure himself of alcoholism, and that he took morphine to relieve withdrawal symptoms.

Sam rode ten miles on a jackass, with a mattress placed over a saw-buck for a saddle, up hills and through wooded ravines. The scenery was beautiful, but the women they saw were, in his opinion, possibly the "infernalest homeliest tribe" in the world. He was told they were not virtuous, a subject in which he was always interested, but was unable to believe they could be anything but virtuous because "fornication" with such "cattle" would qualify as "a crime without a name."

An accident to the sightseers gave Sam an opportunity to have fun in his notebook with double entendre, safe from Mother Fairbanks' eyes. Their guide was Captain Bursley, sailing master of the *Quaker City*. Suddenly, on going around a corner, a most dreadful and unexpected noise came from Bursley's ass, which threw the entire party into confusion. At that very moment, one of the troop of noisy boys who acted as drivers stuck his goad into Colonel Foster's ass, which ran against Dan Slote, in the lead. Dan fell (on his ass), and all of those following stumbled over the two, and "each & every one of them fell on his ass." This incident so delighted him he included it, in modified form, in his *Alta* letter, and repeated it in the book he wrote about the cruise, *The Innocents Abroad*.

The following day, the ship set off for Gibraltar and a week later sailed through the Straits. The water was green and the weather springlike. Clemens looked at the sand-spotted hills of Africa on one hand and Spain's equally barren, granite-topped knobs on the other. He was attracted to Tangier, gleaming white on a knoll, and decided he must go there. Shortly there loomed out of the sea the enormous mass of lonely rock no one could mistake. That afternoon when he wrote his family a brief six lines on a page torn from his notebook, he said he was "clear worn out" from riding a donkey and clambering on foot "in & over & about" Gibraltar and its fortifications. During his tour he had, with practiced eye, spotted many beautiful girls, Spanish and English. Their virtue was not questioned.

In a matter of hours, he was rested enough to join Dan and a party of six men, with an English merchant as guide, for the four-and-a-half-hour trip by steamer to Tangier. He carried no baggage other than five bottles (contents not recorded) and seventy-five cigars. He had a strong desire to visit some place that was "thoroughly and uncompromisingly foreign," with nothing to remind one of any other people or land. "And lo! in Tangier we have found it," *Alta* readers learned. The marketplace was lively and picturesque, and smelled just like the San Francisco Police Court, he thought they might like to know.

"I would not give this experience for all the balance of the trip combined," he wrote Jane Lampton and Pamela from Tangier on July first. The architecture and the dress were "strange beyond all description." Here "is not the slightest thing that we have seen save in pictures—and we always mistrusted the pictures before. We cannot any more. The pictures used to seem . . . too fanciful for reality. But behold, they were not wild enough," he informed his *Alta* readers. The "true spirit" of Tangier "can never be found in any book save the *Arabian Nights.*" Here Sam was seeing Moors in long, sweeping robes of blue and white stripes, white "trowsers that come only a little below the knee, and yet have twenty yards of stuff in them"; "prodigious" turbans, "curiously-embroidered" jackets, and crimson sashes wrapped around and around the waist (far finer than those worn by Hannibal's Cadets of Temperance), yellow slippers, and jewel-encrusted scimitars. Sam was impressed, as well, by the city's antiquity: Phoenicians, Carthaginians, and Romans had all battled for it, and had won or lost it at some ancient time. Outside the city wall, he inspected the ruins of a Roman town—which he had been warned against doing because of the danger of robbers.

In the morning, they had a brush with strict religious observance. It would have been very embarrassing, and possibly dangerous, for Major James Barry of St. Louis, a Clemens family acquaintance, if Sam had not acted quickly and kept him from riding his donkey through the doorway of a large mosque. A short time before, an English officer, who had only stepped inside, was chased out, and up the street, by angry worshippers, who bombarded him with shoes.

The party called on the American consul, Jesse McMath of Ohio, who furnished Clemens a wealth of information about Tangier's history, and its people, religious groups, government, and customs. Sam took copious notes which he worked into two long letters to the *Alta*. He noticed that the consul's "center-tables" were covered with every kind of parlor game. This suggested boredom. He was right. McMath had almost no official duties, and his was the only American family in Tangier. Although there were many foreign consuls, each family kept to itself. "Tangier is full of interest for one day," he said, "but after that it becomes a weary prison." After one day, Clemens was ready to leave.

They returned to the *Quaker City* that same afternoon of July first, laden with purchases from the bazaars—pounds of fresh dates, little Turkish pipes and tobacco, Moorish robes and baggy trousers, and red fezzes. All they left behind were their white shoes. The whole party was "gorgeous" in bright yellow, pointed slippers. Still under the spell some days later, Sam donned his flowing costume, and wearing a fez and mask, danced in his yellow slippers at the next shipboard ball. One day he was to write: "I would like to dress in a loose and flowing costume made all of silks and velvets, resplendent with all the stunning dyes of the rainbow. . . ."

On July 5, they were at Marseilles, and Sam, Dan Slote, and Dr. Abraham Jackson (known to his readers as "The Doctor") prepared to leave in the morning for Paris. During the hours spent in Marseilles, "we had no disposition to examine carefully into anything at all—we only wanted to glance and go—to move and keep moving!"—an attitude and pace Clemens maintained throughout the voyage. At a late hour that first night on French soil, they sat down to rest in the great casino, its walls "papered" entirely with huge sparkling mirrors, and called for "unstinted" champagne, a fact that might account for his admission—"I can not think of half the places we went to, or what we particularly saw."

On the 500-mile rail trip to Paris, they bowled along through the most "bewitching" countryside. Everything was orderly and beautiful, like one great, carefully tended garden. He could not help but compare this journey with the dismal fifty-four-hour ride between New York and St. Louis, and kept noting the pleasing absence of hog-wallows, muddy cow-lots, tumbledown houses and fences, and yards littered with rubbish. He compared those "five-minute boltings of flabby rolls, muddy coffee, questionable eggs, and gutta-percha beef" American travelers had to accept as dinner, and the full half-hour allowed in France to munch "calmly" through a delicious full-course meal. He was learning that not everything American was necessarily superior.

They lost little time in Paris. Nearly two hours were spent at the International Exposition, to which Clemens had been looking forward since his days in Hawaii, and had been willing to travel half way around the world to see. Now that he was there, he found the visitors from different countries more interesting than the inanimate displays, which he realized would take months to absorb. They "loitered" through the aisles of Notre Dame Cathedral, staring at the stained glass windows, and trying to "admire" the countless "great" paintings in the chapels. They visited the morgue, then spent a few hours at the celebrated *Jardin Mabille*. There they took chairs in a saloon set up in a "domed and filagreed white temple," and ordered drinks. On a circular platform, twenty sets of men and women took their places, the band struck up with lively music, and—Sam put his hands up before his face "for very shame. But I looked through my fingers. They were doing the renowned *'Can-Can.'* " He moved aside, he said, to take "a general view" of the dance. It became a kaleidoscope: "Shouts, laughter, furious music, a bewildering chaos of darting and intermingling forms, stormy jerking and snatching of gay dresses, bobbing heads, flying arms, lightning-flashes of white-stockinged calves and dainty slippers in the air, and then a grand final rush, riot, a terrific hubbub and a wild stampede! . . ."

They viewed "miles" of old masters in the Louvre. His opinion was, of course, unchanged. Versailles was "wonderfully beautiful!" If he lives a thousand years he would never again see anything half so lovely. He lavished praise on its statues, fountains, pools, trees, and flower gardens. He saw the Grand Trianon and the Petit Trianon, those "monuments to royal prodigality." Back in Paris, he sought their exact opposites in the Faubourg St. Antoine, where filth, poverty, misery, vice, and crime, "go hand in hand. . . . Here the people live who start the revolutions."

At the Grand Hotel du Louvre he met old friends—Lillie Hitchcock of San Francisco, living in Paris again; Mrs. John B. Winters of Carson and San Francisco; Mrs. Leonard Ferris, who had given him a room in her house after he was burned out at Virginia City; and Etta Booth, whom he had first seen as a little girl with long braids, dancing in a bright red dress, at a miners' ball in Nevada. He never forgot that vision of her. All except Lillie had come for the Exposition. Sam spent time with them during his last day in Paris, and that evening promised to meet them all in the hotel at nine in the morning, knowing when he made the date that he would be already on the train for Marseilles. "How the world is given to lying," he observed to his family, when he wrote them about leaving his friends in the lurch.

From Marseilles, he started a letter to Lillie, putting her on the defensive. "I should think you would feel mighty rascally now to let me go without that picture. All right, my dear. I am coming back to Paris before long & when I do the Grand Hotel du Louvre will not be big enough to hold both of—"

He ran lines through those sentences and started to write another letter at the bottom of the page, to "My Dear Folks—" He explained that he had started a letter to Lily (as he spelled her name), "but this hotel is out of paper—I shall have to let her go by till some other time. . . .

"We had a gorgeous time in Paris. It isn't any use to try to say anything about it—I am only writing to let you know I am well.

"Oh, confound it. I can't write—I am full of Excitement—have to make a trip in the harbor—haven't slept for 24 hours." He sent love to all.

Two days later he was in Genoa, apologizing to his family for the brevity of his letters from Paris and Marseilles, but he and his companion were "rushing constantly." They get to bed at midnight and start another day of sightseeing at seven the next morning. "I cannot even get a chance to write newspaper letters—but such as they are you must take them as home letters." He was enchanted by the beauty and grace of Genoese women. "They are very fair, and many of them have blue eyes." Most "are robed in a cloud of white from head to foot," and wear on their heads only "a filmy sort of veil, which falls down their backs like a white mist." Seated in the park, Sam watched them promenade. "I never saw such a perfect freshet of loveliness before . . . I fell in love with a hundred and eighty . . . on Sunday evening, and yet I am not of a susceptible nature. Still, I would like to camp here." To his mother he said: "I am just on the eve of starting on a month's trip to Milan, Padua, Verona, Venice & Rome, & shall rejoin the ship at Naples on the 9th of August. . . . We may possibly leave here at daylight tomorrow. . . ."

He continued the grueling pace and still managed to retain his energy and enthusiasm, his humor, his sense of the grotesque and the ridiculous, his irreverence, his cynicism, and vituperative powers, and above all, his appreciation of things fitting and beautiful.

"What a wonder it is! So grand, so solemn, so vast! And yet so delicate, so airy, so graceful! A very world of solid weight, and yet it seems in the soft moonlight only a fair delusion of frost-work that might vanish with a breath," he described Milan's cathedral. It was in this church that the guide led them to the statue of a man without skin, every "vein, artery, muscle, every fibre and tendon and tissue . . . represented in minute detail. It looked natural, because somehow it looked as if it were in pain." It was so perfect, only the famous Phidias could have sculpted it, he was told. But to Sam it was "a hideous thing, and . . . I am very sorry I saw it, because I shall always see it, now. I shall dream of it. . . . I shall dream that it is resting its corded arms on the bed's head and looking down on me with its dead eyes. . . ." The sight of it took him back to Hannibal the night he discovered the body of the stabbed man in his father's law office.

He became exercised over the "mournful wreck of the most celebrated painting in the world—'The Last Supper,' " a miracle of art three hundred years ago, but now battered, scarred, stained, and discolored by time. There was not enough left of it to be called a picture, and yet crowds of people came from all parts of the world to stand before it with "bated breath and parted lips." If they said

anything, their comments were always those "catchy ejaculations
of rapture" he suspected of being insincere.

On first sight, Venice made him think of an "overflowed Sacramento," and it was hard for him not to believe that this was only
the result of a spring freshet and that within a few weeks the river
would fall, leaving dirty highwater marks on the house walls, and
streets full of rubbish and mud. But Sam's dreamworld was moonlit, and on such a night he found it easy to fancy the canals peopled
with "plumed gallants and fair ladies—with . . . Othellos and
Desdemonas, with Iagos and Roderigos," the lanterns of their gon-
dolas darting by like myriad fireflies, and to imagine the shabby
palaces become pristine and gleaming white under a "charitable
moon."

The same applied to Lake Como, which by day had been disappointing. "I thought Lake Tahoe was much finer." But under a full
moon Como was transformed for Sam into a sight that was "striking and picturesque."

It was at Florence that he launched his most savage tirade, this
one aimed at the government and the church, blaming both for the
extreme poverty of the Italian people. "And now that I have got my
temper up, I might as well go on and abuse everybody I can think
of," he wrote the *Alta*. He proceeded to attack the "dead and
damned Medici villains," the curse of Florence for over two hundred years, who had had all their "trivial, forgotten exploits on
land and sea pictured out in grand frescoes . . . with the Savior
and the Virgin Mary throwing bouquets to them out of the clouds,
and the Deity himself applauding from his throne in Heaven! And
who painted these things? Why, Titian, Tintoretto, Paul Veronese,
Raphael—none other than the world's idols, the 'old masters'
. . . and people abuse me because I am so bitterly prejudiced
against the old masters that I cannot see beauty in their productions. It makes me perfectly savage to look at one of those pictures." Such statements Emma Beach urged him to modify. "I
cannot help but see beauty in one of their pictures now and then,
but I keep on despising the groveling spirit that could persuade
those masters to prostitute their grand talents to the disgusting
adulation of such monsters as the French, Venetian and Florentine
princes. . . ." He seethed when he looked at the Medici mauso-

leum, as large as a church, and noticed in front of a statue of one member of that family, "a royal crown that blazed with diamonds and emeralds enough to buy a city, almost." Thoroughly worked up, he promised another column of vituperation soon—"My experiences of Florence were chiefly unpleasant," he wrote later, but gave no details.

He and his party traveled on to Pisa where, naturally, they climbed to the top of the famous tower, and then toured the cathedral and baptistry. Next, they hastened on to Leghorn, where they found the *Quaker City* waiting. Since it was rumored that the ship would be quarantined at Naples, Sam and his friends decided to take a French steamer to Civita Vecchia; go from there to Rome, and then by train to Naples.

There were no newspaper letters until he reached Civita Vecchia. He was by then surfeited with churches, holy relics, palaces, and art galleries—and still irritable. The promised vituperative column was written, but sent to the *New-York Tribune* instead of the *Alta*. "This is the vilest nest of dirt, vermin, and ignorance we have got into yet, except that African perdition they call Tangier," he opened his blast. The people of Civita Vecchia "live in alleys two yards wide. It is lucky the alleys are not wide, because they hold as much smell now as a person can stand, and if they were wider, they would hold more, and then the people would die. These alleys are paved with stone, and carpeted with slush, and decayed rags, and decomposed vegetable tops, and remnants of old boots, all soaked with dishwater, and the people sit around on stools and enjoy it. . . . They do not have any schools here, and only one billiard table. . . . They haven't even a cathedral with . . . a petrified saint in the cellar; and they don't show you . . . any ratty, smoke-dried, old fire-screens, which are the splendid *chef d'oeuvres* of Titian, or Simpson, or Reubens, or Ferguson, or any of those parties. I am going to Rome—there's nothing to see here. This town is the worst swindle yet."

Presumably the correspondence from Rome was lost in the mail. His next newspaper letter was dated August 2 at Naples, and was addressed to the editor of the local *Observer*, an English-language journal, protesting the quarantining of their ship. This had not happened to them before, "but here you have gone and done a thing which will give us a reputation for peddling cholera around the world, and we may never get rid of it. We want to go to Athens, Constantinople, Thebes, the Pyramids and the Holy Land. . . . How can we go . . . if the people in these countries gather the impression that we are a gigantic extermination expedition?" In a postscript, he asked, "If you cannot let us out I wish you would at least suspend the rule that forbids profanity here. Let us have a little comfort."

But Clemens was not suffering from confinement; he was ashore, sightseeing. He went to Pompeii and was fascinated by the curious experience of wandering through that silent city of the dead—not haunted or eerie, he found, because he could feel the presence of those thousands who had once made the place throb with life. It seemed as though they had only just left, for there were the baker's round loaves in the pan, and the merchant's wares on the shelf. Sitting on a stone seat in the great horseshoe-shaped theater, he tried to recreate the life: he imagined the crowds thronging in, the players on stage, and the musicians with their double-flutes and tamborines. As he walked down Merchant Street, he stopped in shop after shop and called for wares from Rome, Egypt, and the East—but the tradesmen were gone, the marts silent. He admired the light and airy Pompeiian houses which contrasted so sharply with the dark, cluttered Victorian interiors he knew. The bright mosaic floors were a great improvement over drab carpets. Above all, he liked the murals—portraits, and mythological subjects, still fresh in color after eighteen centuries, and far more satisfying to the eye and the spirit than "the celebrated rubbish of the old masters of three centuries or so"—those "ghastly old nightmares done in lampblack and lightning."

He went into the ancient brothel, saw the rows of tiny cubicles, each furnished with a masonry couch, and observed how short the beds were. He looked at the wall paintings above the doorways, depicting half-clad couples, kissing, embracing, and drinking wine. These pictures "no pen could have the hardihood to describe," his readers were told.

He spent two days "resting," on the beautiful volcanic island of Ischia, at the entrance to Naples harbor. The island was noted for white wine, delightful climate, and exquisite scenery. A most attractive feature for Clemens was that "there were no antiquities seven thousand years old, and no paintings by the old masters." Upon his return to Naples he had time for only "a word" to his mother and Pamela: "Slept none last night & sailed on return to Naples at daylight, thinking I would go to bed when I got here— got to talking, then went to see the King's palace—lost time in one way or another till now it is night & I learn for the first time that our party have decided to start for Vesuvius at midnight. I have some little preparation to make."

At some time during this crowded day he had written to Senator Stewart, "accepting his private Secretaryship in Washington next winter."

Although Sam headed his next *Alta* letter, "Ascent of Mount Vesuvius" and labeled five paragraphs "Ascent of Vesuvius—Continued," he ignored the subject. His next letter was titled "More on Ascent of Mount Vesuvius," but still told nothing about the climb. "This subject will keep till my next, I suppose" was his final line. He opened his third letter, "Descent of Mount Vesuvius," with an account of the ascent. "The path led straight up a rugged sweep of loose chunks of pumice stone. . . . It was so excessively steep that we had to stop every fifty or sixty steps, and rest a moment. To see our comrades, we had to look very nearly straight up at those above us. . . . The ladies wore no hoops, which was well. They would have looked like so many umbrellas." The view from the top might have been rewarding if there had not been a fog and mist. The crater was only a circular ditch, with no fire visible but plenty of evil-smelling fumes. "The Vesuvius of to-day is a very slow affair compared to the mighty volcano of Kilauea. . . ."

Under a paragraph headed "The Descent," he wrote, "The descent . . . was a labor of only four minutes." They had taken a path knee-deep in loose ashes. His next communication came from Greece and contained an account of what proved to be the second-most satisfying experience of the trip. On August 14, the *Quaker City* dropped anchor in the ancient harbor of Piraeus, and was promptly quarantined for eleven days. A guard was set to keep watch, and if anyone was caught stealing ashore he would be dealt with severely—even harshly. Captain Duncan decided to stay where he was for twenty-four hours, take on supplies, and then sail

THE BACHELOR YEARS

directly for Constantinople. Sam recorded that a stock of honey from Mt. Hymettus was brought on board, honey famed for its excellent flavor since the second century A.D., when Pausanias mentioned its qualities in his guide to Greece.

It was a bitter disappointment to lie so near Athens and not be permitted to visit it. With the naked eye one could see the ruins on the Acropolis, and with a spyglass, count the columns in the Parthenon.

That night at eleven o'clock, when most of the ship's company were in bed, Clemens (wearing his fez), Dr. Jackson, Colonel Denny, and Dr. George Birch of Hannibal, slipped away in a small boat and were set ashore by the quartermaster on a rocky point beyond the quarantine limit; he had orders to keep awake and listen for their signal—a distinctive whistle. Sam and his companions then picked their way quietly over the hills, "serenaded by a hundred dogs," skirted Piraeus under a clouded moon, and within half an hour were safely on the way to Athens. They walked fast because time was short, and at close to one o'clock stopped to quench their thirst at a vineyard. Just as they were about to pick one more bunch of luscious grapes, a dark figure armed with a gun rose up mysteriously out of the shadows and shouted, "Ho!" They hurried on and soon were standing under the huge, towering walls of the ancient citadel of Athens. All was utterly silent, and the gates were shut. Colonel Denny attempted to climb over a ruined wall but several loose stones fell with a crash. Someone shouted from within, and he dropped to the ground. There followed a banging of doors, and the garrison turned out: four Greeks. "We clamored at the gate and they admitted us," Clemens wrote cryptically.

The four Americans crossed a large court, entered a great door, and "stood upon a pavement of purest white marble, deeply worn by footprints." The sky was now clear, and "before us, in the flooding moonlight, rose the noblest ruins we ever looked upon. . . ." Excitedly, Sam began taking notes—on the beauty of the fluted columns of white marble in the gateway to the temples, on the Acropolis, on the size of the Parthenon's columns, on the presence of marble armchairs, entablatures, and bas-reliefs. He remarked, "here and there, in lavish profusion, were gleaming white statues of men and women, propped against fallen blocks of marble, some of them armless, some without legs, others headless —but all looking mournful and sentient, and startlingly human. They rose up and confronted the midnight intruder on every side —they stared at him with stony eyes from unlooked-for nooks and recesses; . . . and through the roofless temple the moon looked down, and banded its floor and darkened its scattered fragments and its broken statues with the slanting shadows of its columns."

He walked out into the overgrown, fragment-strewn courtyard beyond the Parthenon and was startled to see marble faces peering at him out of the deep grass. The place seemed ghost-ridden. "The full moon was riding high in the cloudless heavens" as they walked to the edge of the battlements and looked down. For Clemens, this was the magical setting, and what he saw was "a vision!. . . . All the beauty in the world combined could not rival it!—Athens by moonlight!"

He turned back and walked through the temple again. In crossing the court he stooped down, picked up from the grass a small marble head of a girl or woman (about five inches by four), and slipped it into his pocket. He later presented it to his mother and Pamela, who long treasured it.

Their return to the waiting boat was undisturbed except by several grape-guards who shouted at them, and "seventeen million dogs" that followed them, barking, through Piraeus. They reached the *Quaker City* at four-thirty, just at dawn. Sam sat up an hour or two longer to watch the sun rise and suffuse the sky behind the Acropolis a rich carmine and spread a rosy glow over the temples.

He was still under the spell of ancient Athens when they reached Constantinople, where everything displeased him. It was a veritable circus. People were "thicker than bees" in the narrow streets, and the men were "dressed in all the outrageous, outlandish, idolatrous, extravagant, infernal costumes that ever a tailor with the delirium tremens and seven devils could conceive of"—attire, which in another mood, he would have admired extravagantly. There was nothing remarkable about the famous mosque of St. Sophia: the marble pillars were chipped and stained, the filagree work was only "curious," the mosaics were "gaudy." He had to enter barefoot and not only caught a cold but got his feet all stuck up with the "abominations that besmear" all the paved floors in these cities.

The whirling dervishes, of which he had heard so much, were but "a pack of lunatics in long robes who spin round, and round, and round," emitting a "different odor every time, and a meaner one." Turkish coffee was another "swindle"—thick, black, "unsavory of smell, and execrable in taste." A Turkish bath was one more "poor, miserable fraud."

The women were "rather" pretty, with their veiled faces and flowing gowns. Still, seen flitting about in the distance, they reminded him of "the shrouded dead abroad in the earth." He recorded that Circassian girls were still sold as slaves but that the auctions were no longer public.

His spirits rose just as soon as their vessel sailed for Crimea, and when they stopped at Sebastopol he was pleased to report that no country yet had received them so "kindly." Governor-General Kotzebue—a man of letters—put himself at their service and invited them to feel at home. He came on board with a large party and spent the afternoon. There were many very "handsome" young Russian and English women among them, and all were as "jolly & sociable" as old friends. Sam thought it would have been a great addition to the ship's company if they could have taken the whole group on to Odessa. Several government officers suggested that the ship call by Yalta, where Czar Alexander II and his family were "rusticating" at their summer palace. The officials assured the travelers of a cordial reception. If they accepted, a telegram as well as a courier would be despatched to announce their coming. Sam told his family that it was fear of a rebuff that made them decline the invitation, for they had heard of a large English excursion party recently being refused an audience.

Clemens felt "mighty sorry about this because I never got a chance to take a drink with the King of the Sandwich Islands, and now that I have got a show at an Emperor, I don't like to lose it. It would do me proud to clink glasses with him just once and say, 'Here's luck!' "

The *Quaker City* sailed on to Odessa for coal. Consulting his guidebook, Sam was relieved to find it contained no sights that were obligatory. He prowled through the markets with some of his clique (Dan Slote and Jack Van Nostrand had chosen to remain at Constantinople); watched the girls swim naked in the harbor; looked at the fine houses, admired the pretty, fashionably dressed women, and "closed the entertainment with an ice-cream debauch. We do not get ice-cream everywhere, and if we do, we are apt to dissipate to excess."

Odessa's governor-general also urged the party to visit the czar and, without waiting for their response, sent a telegram. The answer was prompt and gracious, so back they sailed to Yalta. Then what a holding of important meetings and appointing of solemn committees, and what a furbishing-up of claw-hammer coats and white silk neckties. And for the women, similar duties toward their light-colored summer silks.

Sam was appointed chairman of a committee to draft an address to the czar on behalf of the passengers. In his notebook he expressed relief at getting it finished, for addresses to emperors were not his "strong suit." To his mother and Pamela, he said he did not mind writing the address because "I have no modesty & would as soon write to an Emperor as to anybody else. They wanted me to *read* it to him too, but I declined that honor—not because I hadn't cheek enough (& some to spare,) but because our Consul at Odessa was along, & also the Secretary of our Legation at St. Petersburgh," and it was up to one of them to read it. He sent the original draught home, to be put in alcohol and "preserved forever like a curious reptile."

The partners who owned the *Quaker City* (Captain Duncan and Daniel Leary), were anxious to meet with the czar for a reason of their own. They had a secret objective in planning this voyage—to sell the ship. They hoped the Russian ruler might be tempted to buy it.

At noon on the day set for the meeting, the entire party rode to the summer palace in carriages sent by the czar. They felt at ease on one score: the Poet Lariat had been made to swear "a dreadful oath that he would not issue a line of his vile poetry while he was in the Czar's dominions, or else remain under guard on board ship until we were safe at Constantinople again. He fought the dilemma long, but yielded at last, with a heavy heart."

The guests entered the grounds and formed a circle under the trees outside the door, for there was not room for all seventy-seven inside. Within five minutes the royal family appeared and welcomed them. The Emperor said, "Good morning—I am glad to see you—I am gratified—I am delighted—I am happy to receive you!" in perfect English, punctuating each sentence with a bow. Sam made note that he was very tall and slender, and that he had a "determined" appearance, yet it was easy to see that he was "kind and affectionate." He was dressed simply in a cap, frock coat, and trousers all made of plain white linen or cotton twill, and "sported" no jewelry or insignia of rank. For the interest of his women readers, Sam mentioned that the Empress and the Grand Duchess Marie ("fourteen years old, light-haired, blue-eyed, unassuming and pretty") wore simple suits of silk foulard, with a blue dot in it, and trimmed with blue. "Both ladies wore broad blue sashes, linen collars and clerical ties of muslin; low-crowned straw hats trimmed with blue velvet; parasols and flesh colored gloves." Sam's experience in reporting San Francisco fashions for Washoe served him well. "The little Grand Duke [he was ten] wore a red calico blouse and a straw hat, and his pantaloons were tucked into his boots."

The American consul for Odessa then "inflicted" Clemens' address, and the czar commented frequently throughout, "Good—very good indeed," and at its close said, "I am very, very grateful." After a few minutes of general conversation the Emperor and his family led the party into the palace for a tour, about half at a time. Although Sam saw that the appointments were "very rich and very elegant," the atmosphere was "cosy" and "home-like." This was followed by a visit to the young Crown Prince's palace, and an invitation to take lunch with the czar's brother, the Grand Duke Michael, at *his* palace. The royal family accompanied them. Duke Michael appealed to Clemens particularly for "he bears himself like one of those gorgeous knights we read about in the romances of chivalry." Michael was, in his opinion, "a rare brick!"

Lunch was served buffet-style on tables in the reception room and on the verandas—in fact, "anywhere that was convenient; there was no ceremony. It was sort of a free blow-out, like a picnic." Refreshments were simple: bread, a variety of cheese and cold meat, two kinds of wine, and tea. The tea was "delicious,"

Sam found. It was brought overland from China, for to transport it by sea damages the flavor, he was told. It was the first time he had ever been served a lemon to squeeze into tea. There was iced milk, too, but he preferred the lemon.

He had spent nearly half a day in the palaces of royalty, and had felt comfortable and at ease the whole time. He had always supposed Emperors to be terrible people. "I thought they never did anything but wear magnificent crowns and red velvet dressing-gowns, with dabs of wool sewed on them in spots, and sit on a throne and scowl at flunkies . . . and order Dukes and Duchesses off to execution. I find, however, when one is so fortunate as to get behind the scenes and see them at home and in the privacy of their firesides, they are strangely like common mortals."

Early the next morning carpets were spread on the pier in anticipation of a visit from the Czar and his family, who had asked to come aboard, see the ship, and possibly take a sail, provided the weather was calm. "I can entertain them. My hand is in now, and if you want any more Emperors feted in style, trot them out," Sam wrote home the night before.

But the sea remained unusually rough all day, so the royal family did not come (and the ship was therefore not sold), but a steady stream of other distinguished visitors arrived—princes, dukes, barons, counts, admirals, generals, civil officers, and a host of titled and untitled women. Even when they did not speak English, they made themselves "pleasant company," but "our tribe can't think of anything to do or say when they get hold of a subject of the Czar who knows only his own language." The notable exception was Mary Fairbanks, who escorted the Russian women about the ship, talked and laughed with them and made them feel at home. Although they did not understand a word, they were aware of the goodwill and friendliness evident in her voice. The second exception was Sam Clemens.

The shipboard reception ended with a "shampagne blow-out" and a ball. Their guests introduced them to Russian dances, and Sam took part in "an astonishing sort of dance, an hour long." There were twenty people in the set, and the steps were lively and intricate. "It was complicated enough without me—with me it was an astonisher. I just carelessly threw in a figure now and then that made those Russians ashamed of themselves." His partner was "the most beautiful girl that ever lived, and we talked incessantly, and laughed exhaustingly," yet neither knew the other's language. How he wished he could speak Russian—and yet from her responses, the expression on her face and in her eyes, her smiles and laughter, he knew she understood *something* of what he was saying. Thoughts of that bewitching "little devil" ran in his head for days.

XXIII

———◯———

JOURNEY'S END

THE NIGHT SKY BLAZED with fireworks and cannon thundered in salute as the *Quaker City* steamed out of Yalta and headed back to Constantinople. They dropped anchor just after daylight and Sam Clemens was soon ashore to hunt up Dan Slote and Jack Van Nostrand, and tell them what they had missed in the way of hobnobbing with royalty. Their reunion called for a round of visits to the beer-gardens, and further combing of the markets and bazaars to satisfy Slote, the collector. "I thought Dan had got the stateroom pretty full of rubbish at last, but a while ago his dragoman arrived with a bran new, ghastly tombstone of the Oriental pattern, with his name handsomely carved & gilded on it in Turkish characters. That fellow will buy a Circassian slave next," Sam wrote his mother and sister. He told them that he had sat for a portrait in the studio of Abdullah Frères. "They take the finest photographs in the world here. I have ordered some." The print he sent home was a full-face bust that showed him thinner, his curls unruly, his mustache untrimmed, his expression serious, his eyes piercing. He included in his letter a list of his newspaper articles—forty-four to date, all of them long. It was an amazing production, considering how much of his time was spent in strenuous activity and how little he allowed himself for his work.

The vessel moved next to Smyrna, where Sam marveled at the sight of camel trains "laden with the spices of Arabia and the rare fabrics of Persia come marching through the narrow alleys of the bazaar, among porters with their burdens, money-changers, lamp-merchants . . . portly cross-legged Turks smoking the famous narghili, and crowds drifting to and fro in . . . fanciful costumes. . . ." In Constantinople just such a scene had displeased him, but here he wrote, "The picture . . . casts you back at once into your forgotten boyhood, and again you dream over the wonders of the Arabian Nights; again your companions are princes, your lord is the Caliph Haroun Al Raschid, and your servants . . . giants and genii that come with smoke, and lightning, and thunder, and go as a storm goes when they depart."

He was amazed at the ease with which he became acquainted with girls in the Armenian quarter. In the cool of the evening they dressed in their best and sat with their mothers and grandmothers just inside their open doorways. "They are all comely . . . every angel of them, and exceedingly neat in dress and cleanly, . . . many of them, I may say—are even very beautiful; they average better than American girls." Further, they were very sociable and would smile when a stranger smiled, and bow when he bowed, and talk when he spoke. "No introduction is required. An hour's chat at the door with a pretty girl one never saw before, is easily obtained, and is very pleasant. I have tried it." The fact that there was a language barrier wasn't "much of a drawback" in Smyrna either.

At some time during the two days the ship lay at anchor, Sam was in Charlie Langdon's stateroom and saw (so he wrote in 1906) an "ivory miniature" of the young man's only sister, Olivia, then twenty-two. That portrait of Olivia Langdon has never been positively identified. So far, three different pictures have been designated. In his notebook Sam made no mention of seeing the miniature, but in his *Alta* letter about Smyrna he described himself as "fading" for love of that Russian beauty at Yalta.

Soon the pilgrimage to the Holy Land, the object of this excursion for the majority of passengers, began in earnest. Clemens wrote home from the United States Consul's office at Beirut on September 11. "We are here, eight of us, making a contract with a

dragoman to take us to Baalbek, then to Damascus, Nazareth &c."
—to all the celebrated Scriptural areas by pack train. They would
be in the saddle for three weeks. The party included Slote,
Moulton, Van Nostrand, Colonel Denny, and Dr. Birch, the only
real "religious enthusiast" among them. Interestingly, young
Langdon's name was never mentioned as a member of any of Sam's
land expeditions.

Although Clemens was assured that they would be living as well
as at a hotel, he had doubts. He had camped in the West, and was
prepared to rough it. Therefore "I . . . just packed up a blanket
and a shawl to sleep in, pipes and tobacco, two or three woollen
shirts, a portfolio, a guide-book (the same being a Bible), a deck of
cards and a toothbrush. I also brought along a towel and a cake of
soap, to inspire respect in the Arabs, who would take me for a king
in disguise."

The first night on the road, the caravan came to a halt at six
o'clock "on the breezy summit of a beautiful mountain." A few
minutes later the pack train arrived. "I had not seen it before, and
a good right I had to be astonished. We had nineteen serving men
and twenty-six pack mules! . . . I wondered what in the very mischief we wanted such a vast turn-out as that, for eight men. I
wondered awhile, but soon I began to hanker for a tin plate, and
some bacon and beans." He therefore went off to unsaddle, and to
wash. "When I came back, behold five stately circus tents were up
—tents that were brilliant within, with blue, and gold, and crimson, and all manner of splendid adornment." Inside the tent assigned to him and Dan was an iron bedstead already made up with
a soft mattress and pillows, good blankets, and snowy sheets. On a
table around the center pole stood "pewter pitchers, basins, soap,
and the whitest of towels—one set for each . . ." The finishing
touch came when gaily patterned rugs were brought in and spread
on the floor.

Very soon there came the welcome sound of the dinner bell. In a
tent "high enough for a family of giraffes to live in" stood a table
for eight laid with fine linen and service and large silver candle-
sticks, that would shame the *Quaker City*. Shortly a procession of
"stately fellows in baggy trowsers" began filing in with platters of
roast goose, chicken, and mutton; potatoes, bread, pudding, tea,

and bowls of delicious grapes and apples—"They call this camping out. At this rate it is a glorious privilege to be a pilgrim in the Holy Land."

As always, Clemens had problems with his horses. The first one soon showed a disposition to shy. He also had a strange habit of "kicking" flies "off the top of his head with his hind foot. . . . He is going to get himself into trouble that way, some day. He reaches around and bites my legs, too." Sam turned him in at Damascus for one that proved "a magnificent ruin"—half blind, and with two game legs.

Along the way they visited the tomb of Noah—"the party who built the ark," and after a tiresome, five-hour ride in the blazing sun, reached Baalbek. It dated from Roman times, and as Sam wandered over its acropolis and through its great ruined temples, he imagined what a "noble" picture those wonders of architecture would make by moonlight. He became thoroughly incensed over the "pitiful nobodies between Kingdom Come and Baalbek" who wrote their "poor little names" and their towns and states and countries on the walls of the stately relics. "It is a pity some great ruin does not fall and flatten out some of these cattle and scare their tribe out of ever giving their name to fame upon any walls again, save those of the water-closets where they were wont to inscribe them before they wandered from their native land."

At Damascus, their next stop, they stayed in a hotel. At four o'clock in the morning after their arrival, Clemens was taken violently ill with what was diagnosed as cholera morbus—gastroenteritis, characterized by severe abdominal cramps, fever, and vomiting. Dr. Birch said it came from having bathed the previous noonday in the icy mountain torrent at Figia, where they had stopped to look at the fountain from which Baalam's ass ("the patron saint of all pilgrims like us") supposedly drank. Sam was forced to lie in bed all that day, take opium, which he promptly threw up, and listen to the monotonous patter and splash of fountains in the court outside his door. Still, it was "pleasanter" than traveling in Syria. Feeling better in the morning, he got up early, hired a donkey and guide, and with amazing stamina, visited all the historic sites. After that, he had had enough of Damascus, and wanted to move on, he wrote. If he should ever come there again he would camp on Mahomet's hill outside the city, admire it from a distance, and then go away. Traditionally, Damascus was built in the former Garden of Eden. Perhaps—but there was no semblance of it now. The Paradise had become "the very sink of pollution and uncomeliness," cramped and filthy. It was not the illness that warped his view, for some ten days later he wrote that the one pleasant recollection of his Palestine excursion was when he had cholera at Damascus.

He was disenchanted from the moment he discovered the discrepancy between reality and the enthusiastic descriptions of the Biblical lands, people, and events recounted in travel and guide books, in histories, and in the Scriptures. Nowhere between Damascus and the Holy Land did he see any country capable of supporting such large populations as the Bible suggested. The villages he had pictured as clean and flourishing, embowered in flowers and orchards of figs and pomegranates, and surrounded by lush planted fields, were actually tiny hives of squalid one-story, windowless mud huts built near some poor little scummy waterhole in the midst of a vast dreary desert of sand and gravel. In those places he saw "melancholy," starving dogs, naked boys begging, and children "in all stages of mutilation and decay," every one of whom had sore eyes, with a thousand flies "roosting" upon them. "It makes my flesh creep." Sitting humbly in the dust were the deformed, the maimed, and the blind, "fringed in filthy rags."

As soon as he rode into Palestine, concepts and feelings he held for things sacred also began to crumble. He found it difficult to comprehend that he was standing on ground that was once "actually pressed by the feet of the Savior;" that he was surrounded by people whose ancestors had seen and even talked with Jesus, "carelessly, just as they would have done with any other stranger." He added, "The situation is suggestive of reality and tangibility that seem at variance with the vagueness, and mystery, and ghostliness that one naturally attaches to the character of a God. . . . the gods of my understanding have always been hidden in clouds and very far away."

In the grotto of the Annunciation at Nazareth, it was "not easy to bring myself up to the magnitude of the situation. I could sit off several thousand miles and imagine the angel appearing, with shadowy wings and lustrous countenance, and note the glory that streamed downward upon the Virgin's head while the message from the Throne of God fell upon her ears—any one can do that, but few can do it here." He examined the little recess from which the angel stepped, "but could not fill its void. The angels that I know are creatures of unstable fancy—they will not fit in niches of substantial stone. Imagination labors best in distant fields."

In Sunday school he had always considered the Prodigal the "stupidest youth that ever lived" for leaving his father's palace— where he wore fine clothes, had a dozen courses at dinner, fast horses to ride, and money to spend on the circus whenever he wanted to go, and travel to some far-off land where he got "swamped" and had to feed the hogs for a living. Now Sam visited Deburich, where the Prodigal was born, and found its mud hovels "reeking" with filth and "seven kinds of lice." He knew it was exactly as it had always been: "My dream is over. . . . It was just about an even matter between the Prodigal's two homes."

While trotting across the plain of Jezreel they came upon a half dozen Bedouins. The party had been eager all along to see what the guide books called the "wild, free sons of the desert," who wore picturesque costumes and sped like the wind on their sleek Arabian mares. To Clemens, they appeared to be just so many "tatterdemalion vagrants," cavorting about on "old crowbait horses," spearing imaginary enemies with long lances, whooping, fluttering their rags in the wind, and "carrying on . . . like a pack of hopeless lunatics." "Thus, one by one, the splendid attractions of Palestine are passing away—gradually, but surely, the paint and the gilding are pealing from its cheap theatrical scenery and exposing the unsightly boards beneath."

At Jerusalem they camped just outside the walls, near the Damascus Gate, part of which had been repaired by the Crusaders—a fact that pleased Clemens, who had admired their romantic expeditions since boyhood. He stayed at the Mediterranean Hotel in the city, enabling him to walk easily to all the sacred sites "which swarm about you at every step; no single foot of ground in all Jerusalem . . . seems to be without a stirring and important history of its own."

He started off early one morning with a guide and missed nothing. The Church of the Holy Sepulchre was the most significant of all the sites and the only one he visited a second time, except the Pool of Bethesda. On entering, he wrote, the sepulchre was the first thing a person desired to see. "One is grave and thoughtful when he stands in the little Tomb of the Savior—he could not well be otherwise in such a place—but he has not the slightest possible belief that the Lord lay there," for only half a dozen persons knew where he was buried. Credibility is "very, very greatly diluted by that reflection." The same was true of those spots pointed out where Mary stood, and John, and where the angel sat, and where the crown of thorns was found. These, he considered "imaginary holy places."

But the site of the crucifixion was another matter. Jesus was very celebrated before coming to Jerusalem, Sam reflected, and his entry was a remarkable event. His reception became an ovation because many believed him to be the true son of God. To publicly execute such a distinguished person created a great sensation and fixed without doubt the Hill of Calvary as the location.

With these thoughts, he climbed to the top of that pinnacle of rock and "gazed upon the place where the true cross once stood, with a far more absorbing interest than I ever felt in anything earthly before." In this mood he went to a shop and selected for Jane Lampton a little Bible which had inlay covers of fragrant balsam wood from the Jordan, oak from Abraham's tree at Hebron, olive from the Mount of Olives, and ebony, although he did not buy it then.

That night he felt completely "surfeited with sights," his brain so "worn and racked with the day's accumulation of knowledge," it felt like an overloaded stomach. It would have been an immense relief to have taken a "mental emetic" and vomited everything learned that day. But this state did not discourage him from seeking new things to see, and he made preparations to leave in the morning at eight for Bethany, Jericho, the Dead Sea, the Jordan River, and Bethlehem. Before going, he sent a note to the shopkeeper about the little Bible. He asked him to inscribe it to "Mrs. Jane Clemens—from her Son—Mount Calvary, Sept. 24, 1867." Also, he would like to have "Jerusalem" put "around it loose, somewhere, in Hebrew, just by a flyer." Then send it to his tent near the Damascus Gate.

Two days later he was back from that grueling journey. "Such roasting heat, such oppressive solitude, and such dismal desolation cannot surely exist elsewhere on earth." He was disappointed to find that the "manger," covered by the Church of the Nativity, was another below-ground grotto cut in living rock, as was that of the Annunciation. The manger was "tricked out in the usual tasteless style observable in all the holy places of Palestine."

At the Milk Grotto "we took many little fragments of stone . . . because it is well known in all the East that a barren woman hath need only to touch her lips to one of these and her failing will depart. . . . Let the distressed apply to me, postage paid, and a stamp extra, for my sands of life are well nigh run out, and I would do good to my fellow man while I yet can."

One day after his return he was off again, trotting across the Valley of Hinnom, to climb the Hill of Evil Counsel, sit under the tree where according to tradition Judas had hanged himself; see Solomon's Temple and the Wailing Wall; drink at Joseph's Well; look at the Virgin Mary's Tomb, and ascend the Mount of Olives. When abreast of the Damascus Gate, he came upon the "stateliest" tree in Palestine—the Lebanon cedar said to have been planted in 1099 by Godfrey de Bouillon, first Christian king of Jerusalem. Sam cut a small branch, which he later had made into a handle for a gavel. The following year he presented it to the Worshipful Master of the masonic lodge at St. Louis. Although he chided his fellow pilgrims for taking mementoes, as seen, he was not innocent. In his notebook he jotted that he took bits of stone from Solomon's Temple.

He made a final tour of the Church of the Holy Sepulchre and Calvary, and visited the Pool of Bethesda again to fill a bottle with water as he had done at the Dead Sea and the Jordan River. It was time to depart, and he joined his companions for the trip to Jaffa, where the *Quaker City* was waiting. On October 1 they set sail for Alexandria, Clemens finding "ineffable happiness" in the realization that they had somehow "worried through" Palestine, the land of disappointments.

It was good to be "home" once more, he thought as he looked

around the cluttered stateroom, and shed his Western blue woolen shirt, heavy boots, spurs, and "sanguinary" revolver, and shaved off his beard. But he was ready to leave again as soon as the ship anchored the next day at sunset, and he saw the sparkling gilded domes and spires of Alexandria. He and Jack Van Nostrand hailed a small boat and went ashore, took rooms at the Hotel d'Europe, and then set out to walk through the tree-lined streets, passing the great fountain and the rows of handsome dwellings. Jack's discovery of an ice-cream parlor ended the night's explorations, and they sat there eating until the shop closed.

In the morning they went by donkey to see Pompey's Pillar, Cleopatra's Needle, the great groves of date palms, and other attractions. But one day in this European-like city was enough for Sam. He craved something more novel, so he and Jack boarded the train to Cairo. It was just like any other train except that for fuel, so they were told, they used not wood or coal but "mummies three thousand years old, purchased by the ton or by the graveyard for that purpose." It was not unusual, their informant added, to hear "some profane engineer call out pettishly,—'D--n these plebians, they don't burn worth a cent—pass out a King.'"

The narrow streets of Cairo and its honeycombed bazaars crowded with Egyptians, Turks, and Ethopians—"turbaned, sashed, and blazing in a rich variety" of brightly colored costumes —were very like others he had seen. What was different and pleasing were the handsome, shapely girls one saw walking along with no clothing at all.

By this time a large party from the *Quaker City* had caught up, and they all went by dhow across the Nile—muddy, swift and turbid at this point, and nearly as wide as the Mississippi. Sam thought of his niece, Annie, when he saw the spot where Pharaoh's daughter had found Moses in the bulrushes. The Great Pyramid of Cheops was their destination, and Clemens climbed to the top.

"Each step being as high as a dinner table; there being many of the steps; an Arab having hold of each of our arms and springing upward from step to step and snatching us with them, forcing us to lift our feet as high as our breasts every time, and do it rapidly and keep it up till we were ready to faint, who shall say it is not a lively, exhilarating, . . . lacerating, muscle-straining, bone-wrenching and perfectly excruciating, exhausting pastime, climbing the Pyramids?"

At the bottom there were crowds of photographers clamoring to take pictures of the conquerors. Dr. William Gibson, one of their party, carried the title, "Commissioner of the United States of America to Europe, Asia, and Africa, thundering after his name in one awful blast!" Clemens had stood in awe of him until he learned that he was only "a common mortal," and that his function was nothing more than "the collecting of seeds, and uncommon yams and extraordinary cabbages and peculiar bullfrogs for that poor, useless, innocent, mildewed old fossil, the Smithsonian Institute." In his role as official collector he became, in Sam's opinion, their chief vandal.

Dr. Gibson and his wife had just come down the pyramid, and decided to pose for a picture. With unbelievable speed and secrecy, Sam hired a group of ragged Bedouins standing nearby to slip in behind the Gibsons and grimmace and gesture just as the cameraman made the exposures. The doctor and his wife were reported to have been highly incensed when they saw the prints and learned the story behind them. However, after Clemens became famous, the pictures were prized, and his part in them told often.

On October 7 Sam reluctantly said goodbye to Dan Slote, who was leaving the ship and taking an extended tour of Europe. Five days later he began a letter to his mother and sister. It was headed "Cagliari, Sardinia."

They "have just dropped anchor before this handsome city and . . ." He continued directly below, on October 15 from Algiers, to say they had not been allowed to land at Cagliari on account of cholera. "Nothing to write." Just beneath that, he began again from Malaga. He and Captain Duncan were on shore, waiting to learn the health officer's decision. "I am a little anxious, because I want to go inland to Granada & see the Alhambra—I can go on down, by Seville & Cordova & be picked up at Cadiz. Later—We cannot anchor—must go on. We shall be at Gibraltar before midnight & I think I will go horseback (2 long days) & thence by rail & diligence to Cadiz."

Sam stated that he traveled through Spain with three others, but named only one—Julia Newell, the Wisconsin newspaper corre-

spondent, whom he disliked. The second was certainly a woman
friend of Miss Newell, since it would not have been acceptable for
her to travel alone with Sam. The third member of the party was
surely Jack Van Nostrand. From Cadiz Clemens wrote his family,
on October 24:

"We left Gibraltar at noon & rode to Alciras, (4 hours) thus
dodging the quarantine,)—took dinner, & then rode horseback all
night in a swinging trot, & at daylight took a calash (2-wheeled
vehicle) & rode 5 hours—then took cars & traveled till twelve at
night. That landed us at Seville & we were over the hardest part of
our trip & somewhat tired.— Since then we have taken things
comparatively easy, drifting around from one town to another, &
attracting a good deal of attention—for I guess strangers do not
wander through Andalusia & the other Southern provinces of Spain
often. The country is precisely as it was when Don Quixote &
Sancho Panza were possible characters.

"But I see now what the glory of Spain must have been when it
was under Moorish domination. No, I will not say that—but then
when one is carried away, infatuated, entranced, with the wonders
of the Alhambra & the supernatural beauty of the Alcazar, he is apt
to overflow with admiration for the splendid intellect that created
them."

In black ink he added, probably at a later time on this same day:
"I cannot write now. I am only dropping a line to let you know I
am well. The ship will call here for us tomorrow. We may stop at
Lisbon, & shall at the Bermudas, & will arrive in New York ten
days after this letter gets there." This account of his travels in
Spain is the fullest he seems to have given.

That night he wrote another letter—not to the *Alta California,*
or the New York papers, for this side trip was never included in his
correspondence with them, but to Joe Goodman. After reading it,
Goodman published excerpts, with comments, in the *Territorial Enterprise.*

"It seems that the Holy Land excursion, about which so much
has been written, has not been a perfect success in every respect.
In a private letter to the editor of this paper . . . 'Mark Twain'
says: 'Between you and I, (I haven't let it out yet, but am going to,)
this pleasure party of ours is composed of the d--dest, rustiest,

ignorant, vulgar, slimy, psalm-singing cattle that could be scraped
up in seventeen States. They wanted Holy Land, and they got it. It
was a stunner. It is an awful trial to a man's religion to waltz
through the Holy Land.' The most of the excursionists were probably a little too straight-laced for 'Mark'—hence, the rough manner
in which he sums up the general characteristics of the crowd." It
was evident from his newspaper letters, Goodman went on, that
"he has not been especially pleased with his fellow-travelers as a
body. . . . He seems to have been in a state of exasperation the
most of the time, and, with the exception of the Emperor of Russia
and family, has scarcely written a pleasant word of any one. He is
strangely intolerant and irritable, and it is under the inspiration of
some real or imaginary grievance of a trifling character that he
gives vent to his most comical conceits. 'Europe in a hurry,' and
'Europe on foot' have been contributed to our literature. It remains
for 'Mark Twain' to furnish us with a volume or two of 'Europe in a
rage.' "

Sam told Joe about his visit that evening to a four-story billiard
saloon, "filled with gold-laced bilks with crowns on their hat bands
—because, you know, five men out of every six in Spain wear
gorgeous uniforms." For some reason, perhaps secret envy, he was
infuriated by this display of gold lace, and "prayed for two or three
Virginia 'roughs' to 'clear out' the crowd." Goodman added that
Clemens would soon be in New York and then the capital, and has
been engaged as a Washington correspondent for the *Enterprise.*

Back at sea again, on the homeward voyage, the passengers
settled once more into the old routine of deck and cabin games,
prayer meetings, balls, and charades. Then one fair morning Bermuda was sighted, the ship entered the winding channel, steamed
here and there among the "bright summer islands," and dropped
anchor. The party was welcomed warmly by the British. The several days passed there in that equable climate, wandering on foot
through luxuriant groves and gardens, and skimming by small boat
over the deep blue water to peer into coral caves and grottoes, was
Clemens' introduction to the Eden he would return to again and
again in old age, to find relief from chronic bronchitis and angina
pain, and to revive his spirits when he was overburdened by personal tragedy.

On the morning of November 19, the *Quaker City* steamed into New York harbor after an absence of five and a half months. All were on deck, dressed in "Christian garb—by special order," for there was reason to believe that some would astound the public with Moorish *haiks,* Turkish fezzes, and scarlet, blue, and purple sashes from Persia. At ten o'clock a shiver of the decks told the pilgrims that ship and pier had met.

"The long, strange cruise was over. Amen."

XXIV

---○---

ON THE WING

S A M C L E M E N S W A S the first passenger ashore. One of the ship's officers introduced him to the head customs inspector, who passed his trunks without opening them, so he was soon on his way to see John Murphy of the *Alta*. Before leaving the ship, he entrusted a package for his family containing some of his gifts and mementoes—the Bible from Jerusalem, a necklace of olivewood beads, an ancient tear jug, and the small Grecian head—to "Nighthawk" Julius Moulton, who lived in St. Louis. Sam had no idea how long it would be before he could get home.

He spent most of that first day "bumming around" the *Alta* office, he said in a letter announcing his safe arrival to Jane Lampton and Pamela. He had avoided the *Tribune* people because he felt embarrassed after they had treated him so well and he had failed to write a third of the letters he had promised. Nor did he get to see James Gordon Bennett at the *Herald* until six that evening, when they sent Samuel R. Glen, their chief of foreign correspondence, to look for him. Sam was not in his room at the Westminster Hotel, but Glen found him just as he was entering the St. Nicholas, where he was to have dinner with Mary Fairbanks and some other ladies and, afterward, escort them to the theater. Glen persuaded him to write an exclusive for the morning paper—a summary of the

On the Wing

Quaker City excursion. He agreed, because he was a "busted community" and this was a quick way to earn fifty dollars.

Leaving a note for Mrs. Fairbanks, he returned with Glen to the editorial rooms, and wrote until ten o'clock. The article, he predicted, would make "the Quakers get up & howl in the morning"—which it did. Once he started writing, all of his repressed feelings were unleashed: disgust and anger with the concept and fulfillment of the excursion; with the religious hypocrisy of many of its members, along with their shallowness and "muddy intellects," and his special bitterness toward those who said "atrocious things" about him behind his back. In many of his sweeping statements he included himself, as when he reproved his fellow passengers for taking relics from every historic and sacred spot, and bottles of water from all the holy pools, springs, wells, and rivers to the extent of bringing on a drought; for "galloping" through the art galleries and cathedrals; for being critical of the old masters, and intolerant of other races and cultures.

"We failed to sell the ship. I mention this because to sell the ship seemed to be as much an object of the excursion as anything else, and so . . . must necessarily be of interest to the public. We were to sell the ship and then walk home, I suppose. That would have given variety to the pleasure excursion at any rate."

He had used amazing restraint, considering that he insisted his true opinion of them was so "mean" and so "vicious" he could not collect the terms to express it in less than sixteen or seventeen languages.

In the morning he had a "fine row" with the *Herald* people for leaving his signature off the letter. At first he suspected a "shabby" act, but at a dinner with the entire editorial corps the matter was explained and settled "without bloodshed." It turned out that a foreman was innocently to blame, not the editors. Few who read the piece had any doubt as to its authorship, but to rectify the oversight and fully appease Clemens, an editorial appeared the next morning: "In yesterday's *Herald* we published a most amusing letter from the pen of that most amusing American genius, Mark Twain, giving an account of that most amusing of all modern pilgrimages—the pilgrimage of the *Quaker City*. . . ."

On this day, his second in New York, he had expected to leave for Washington, and report to Senator Stewart, but first there had been his confrontation with the *Herald.* Next Dan Slote's mother sent her carriage, and "I went up & kissed the whole family for Dan from his mother straight through aunts, cousins, sisters-in-law & everything, down to his youngest sister. I guess they think I am a sociable cuss." There were other meetings with "a lot of old friends & new acquaintances," and then that dinner with the *Herald* staff which lasted late. "In consequence . . . I did not get off for Washington today, but I think I shall tomorrow," he told his mother and sister. "I will move Heaven & earth for Orion," he promised. He acted promptly, for in his next letter, dated November 25, 1867, he said: "Stewart is to look up a clerkship in the Patent Office for Orion—things necessarily move slowly where there is so much business & such armies of office-seekers to be attended to," he warned. "I guess it will be all right. I *intend* it shall be all right." He was at this moment "tired & sleepy—been in Congress all day & making newspaper acquaintances. . . . Belong on the Tribune staff, & shall write occasionally. Am offered the same berth to-day on the Herald by letter. Shall write Mr. Bennett & accept. . . . Am pretty well known, now—intend to be better known. Am hob-nobbing with these old Generals & Senators, & other humbugs for no good purpose. Don't have any more trouble making friends than I did in California. . . . Shall continue on the 'Alta.' "

He mentioned, "I have 18 invitations to lecture, at $100 each, in various parts of the Union—have declined them all. I am for business, now." In a postscript he noted, "I room with Bill Stewart & board at Willard's Hotel." His address: "224 F. cor. 14th."

He was far better known than he realized. On November 21, Elisha Bliss, Jr., of the American Publishing Company, a subscription house, wrote him: "We are desirous of obtaining from you a work of some kind, perhaps compiled from your letters. . . . If you have any thought of writing a book, or could be induced to do so, we should be pleased to see you. . . ." They have published A. D. Richardson's works, sold 100,000 copies of his last book, and are presently printing 41,000 of his newest, *Beyond the Mississippi,* "with large orders ahead."

Sam replied that he had written fifty-two letters for the *Alta*

California during the *Quaker City* excursion, "about half of which
. . . have been printed thus far . . . and I suppose scarcely any
of these letters have been copied on this side of the Rocky Mountains. I could weed them of their chief faults of construction and
inelegancies of expression, and make a volume that would be more
acceptable in many respects than any I could now write. When
those letters were written my impressions were fresh, but now they
have lost that freshness. . . . If you think such a book would suit
your purpose, please drop me a line, specifying the size and general style of the volume; when the matter ought to be ready . . .
and particularly what your terms with me would be, and what
amount of money I might possibly make out of it. The latter clause
has a degree of importance for me which is almost beyond my own
comprehension."

On the same day, December 2, 1867, he replied to a letter from
Mary Fairbanks, who scolded him for that piece in the *Herald,*
which *he* had considered "the best-natured squib that was ever
written." True, he had promised her that he would deal lightly with
the pilgrims when he came to write about them; but then, he never
could keep a promise. In Sunday school he only learned about the
wise and foolish virgins. Nothing was ever said about keeping
promises. He knows that when he gets married he will say, " 'I
take this woman to be my lawfully wedded wife, & *propose* to look
out for her in a sort of a general way, &c. &c.' It would be dangerous to go beyond that."

The following morning he called on Orville H. Browning, Secretary of the Interior, with regard to a post for Orion, although he
said nothing about it at the first meeting. "If it were *myself,*" Sam
reported home, "I could get a place pretty easily, because I have
friends in high places who offer me such things—but it is hard to
get them interested in one's relatives." A case in point is Supreme
Court Justice Stephen Field: "He wanted to make me Postmaster of
San Francisco, but the place had just been filled when he spoke to
the President about it." Clemens assured Field he wanted no office,
but the judge told him he must have one with a good salary and
nothing to do: "*You* are no common scrub of a newspaper man. You
have written the best letter about Pompeii that was ever written
. . . & if you had an easy berth you could write *more.* Say what

office you want in San Francisco, & the President shall give it to you." Sam admitted, "I like compliments from people who take an interest in me—newspaper compliments I don't care anything about beyond their market value." If he could only turn Field's good offices over to Orion, "it would suit exactly. . . .

"I am writing a lecture—have half promised to deliver it for the Newspaper Correspondents' Club here after the holidays—may be I may & I may not." He remembered to tell them that "Dr. Birch, of Hannibal, has got a bottle of water he & I took from the Pool of Bethesda . . . one Sunday morning when the angel wasn't around. I'll give it to you . . . if you want it and will send for it. You can get Essie or Lou Conrad, or some other angel to stir it, & you can start a hospital & cure all the cripples in your camp."

In Mary Fairbanks' reply to his last letter, she suggested that "a good wife would be a perpetual incentive to progress."

In responding, Sam agreed about the progress, which would be "from house to house because I couldn't pay the rent. However, "the idea is good. I wish I had a chance to try it . . . I want a good wife—I want a couple of them if they are particularly good—but where is the wherewithal? It costs nearly two letters a week to keep *me.*" Double that. "Manifestly you haven't looked into this thing. I am as good an economist as anybody, but I can't turn an inkstand into an Aladdin's lamp. . . . But seriously . . . if I were settled I would quit all nonsense & swindle some [poor] girl into marrying me. But I wouldn't expect to be 'worthy' of her. I wouldn't *have* a girl that *I* was worthy of. *She* wouldn't do. She wouldn't be respectable enough."

"But at the same time, I am worthier of anybody than I was—because, as duly reported in my last, I *still* never think of swearing, now, & consequently never *do* it." In that letter he had said, "I am as perfectly & permanently cured of the habit as I am of chewing tobacco." Now, in closing, he asked her for another sermon.

After one month, he was anxiously looking forward to his "release" from Washington. On December 24 he came close to leaving for the Sandwich Islands with the United States Minister, E. M. McCook, with whom he had been working closely on a reciprocity treaty between the two countries, Sam wrote to Emily Severance. He was anxious to witness its ratification, but when he learned that "troublesome delays westward might be anticipated" on account of weather, he stayed behind. How he wished he were in the Islands or in California then, for the harsh weather "takes all the life out of me . . . I could just as well have been at sea in the Pacific for China now as not, & visited home besides, but for making engagements that tie me here for the season. I am in a fidget to move. It isn't a novel sensation, though—I never was any other way." But it makes "a fellow feel . . . mean & discontented. . . ."

He was able to escape briefly when he left on Christmas Eve to spend the holidays with Dan Slote, who had just returned. The Quaker City Nighthawks, "the unholiest gang that ever cavorted through Palestine," held a "blow-out" at Dan's house, Clemens told his family. All were there except Julius Moulton of St. Louis, and "We needed Moulton badly. . . . I just laughed till my sides ached, over some of our reminiscences."

On New Year's Day he started to make calls (he continued in his letter), but "anchored for the day" at the first house he went to, Mr. and Mrs. Berry's, for "Charlie Langdon's sister was there (beautiful girl,) & Miss Alice Hooker, another beautiful girl, a niece of Henry Ward Beecher's. We sent the old folks home early with instructions not to send the carriage till midnight, & then I just staid there & deviled the life out of those girls. I am going to spend a few days with the Langdons, in Elmira, New York, as soon as I get time, & a few days at Mrs. Hooker's in Hartford, Conn., shortly."

According to family tradition, Charlie Langdon, eager to have his parents and his sister, Olivia (Livy), meet his friend Sam Clemens—the celebrity "Mark Twain"—brought them together at the St. Nicholas Hotel on December 23, two days before Christmas. The Langdons had come to New York to spend the holidays and to hear Charles Dickens read his works at Steinway Hall. If true, Sam's meeting with Livy Langdon on New Year's Day, would have been his second one.

The chief difficulty with that sequence is the fact that Clemens was still in Washington on December 24 and did not leave for New York until that night. His first meeting with Livy was the one described in his letter home, as his own words testify. A year later, on January 6, 1869, he wrote Livy that he had naturally thought about her all day on January first, and a dozen times "recalled our New Year at Mr. Berry's. . . . And I remembered perfectly well that I didn't rightly know where the charm was, that night, until you were gone." Sam was, of course, commemorating the anniversary of their first meeting. That they first met on New Year's Day has also been substantiated by the recollection of a longtime family intimate. Their *second* meeting was at the St. Nicholas Hotel, on the evening of either January 2 or 3, when Sam had been invited by the Langdons to accompany them to a Dickens reading.

Upon meeting Livy at the Berry house, Clemens was surprised to find her far prettier than the picture he had seen in Charlie's stateroom. Her features were delicate, and her expression gentle and winning. Her eyes were large and blue, and she had a wealth of brown hair which she wore parted in the middle and pulled back simply into a large knot, or in a braid coiled around her head. He found her naive, and rather grave, with little to say, for she was shy in the presence of unmarried men. She was tiny, with dainty feet and hands, and girlish figure. He noticed also that she appeared to be frail, and the reason for that he learned shortly.

At sixteen she had fallen on the ice, and became partially paralyzed. For two years she lay in bed, on her back, in a darkened room. When all hope for her recovery seemed to be gone, someone suggested to her parents that they call in Dr. James Rogers Newton, a healer famed for miraculous cures, although he was considered a charlatan by some. He was called, and when he came into Livy's room he pulled back the heavy drapes to let in the sunlight, flung open the windows for fresh air, said "a short fervent prayer," then put his arm firmly behind her shoulders and said to her, "Now, we will sit up, my child." After she had sat for some minutes without discomfort, he told her, "Now, we will walk a few steps, my child"—which she did while he supported her.

This was the limit of his art, he informed her family. He did not claim to have cured her, but he predicted that with determination and daily practice she would eventually be able to walk two or three hundred yards without pain or fatigue, and she could "depend on being able to do *that* for the rest of her life." She had progressed over the four years since then, but not as far as she might have, had her family's attitude been more positive, and had she been allowed to lead a normal, active life. But they had pampered her, restricted her, cautioned her, and filled her mind with fears about overdoing, and with doubts as to her capacity. She had been convinced that she ought not to consider marriage because she could never be a "healthy wife."

Sam was greatly interested in her case, for he had confidence in some faith healers. Many times he had watched old Mrs. Utterback of Hannibal cure his mother's toothache. Years later he met Dr. Newton and asked him what his secret was. Newton said he did not know, but suspected it was some subtle form of electricity which passed from his body into the patient's. Over the years Clemens tried or recommended to others (most often his sister, Pamela) various forms of mind cures and faith healing, although he was well aware that many were frauds. When he came to write *Huckleberry Finn*, he had that supreme imposter, the king, tell his confederate, the duke: "I've done considerable in the doctoring way. . . . Layin' on o' hands is my best holt—for cancer and paralysis, and sich things."

In her cloistered life, Livy had never seen anyone so remarkable and unusual as Sam Clemens (few had) and during his twelve-hour stay at the Berry house she certainly studied him curiously; and wondered at the laughter he provoked, because she was unable to see the point of a funny story or a witticism unless it was explained.

The choice of dates for the Dickens reading was unfortunate because the novelist was suffering from a heavy cold. It had affected his heart, and after one reading he had been "laid upon a bed, in a very faint and shady state," he wrote. On New Year's Eve he was so sick he called in a doctor who tried to forbid his readings until he recovered entirely; but Dickens would not listen, and was "dead beat" after a subsequent performance. At Steinway Hall, he made it a practice to take an egg beaten up in sherry before going on stage, and another during intermission: "I think that pulls me up."

This, then, explains why Sam, in his report to the *Alta*, spoke of Dickens' voice as being "husky," and pronounced him a "bad reader" because he failed to "enunciate his words sharply and distinctly," so that many of them "fell dead before they reached our part of the house. . . . [I say 'our' because I am proud to observe that there was a beautiful young lady with me—a highly respectable young white woman.]"

Clemens felt that in his readings from *David Copperfield*, Dickens ought to have made the "bright, intelligent audience . . . laugh, or cry, or shout at his own good will or pleasure—but he did not." There was "no heart, no feeling" there, and Sam was "greatly disappointed." —He did admire the flawless attire, noting that he was outfitted "regardless of expense." Diamond studs twinkled on his shirt front. Clemens observed critically that he wore a bright red flower in his buttonhole.

Although Sam was obviously pleased to be able to speak of a beautiful young woman seated beside him, after this allusion to Livy Langdon, there is no mention of her for eight months in any of his extant writings. He had found it hard to keep from loving her with all his heart that night, he wrote later, but knew that she was so far beyond his reach, economically and socially, he could not consider her seriously. So it was that after his return to Washington he accepted the invitation of his longtime friend, the gifted J. Ross Browne, writer, artist, and diplomat, whose post as Minister to China was soon to be confirmed, to take a "lucrative position on his staff." Present commitments, he told the *Alta*, will keep him in the East several months more, but no matter: "I shall follow him out there as soon as I am free." Eight weeks later he was working out further plans to spend at least a year in Europe, following the assignment in China. There was no room in any of these schemes for Livy Langdon.

In Clemens' view, Alice Hooker's talented and colorful relatives were far more interesting than Olivia's conservative and reserved parents, who admittedly did not know what to make of him. On January 5, Alice's uncle, Henry Ward Beecher, "sent for me . . . to come over & dine (he lives in Brooklyn, you know,) & I went," Sam wrote his mother and sister. "Harriet Beecher Stowe was there; & Mrs. & Miss Beecher, Mrs. Hooker & my old Quaker City favorite, Emma Beach.

"We had a very gay time, if it *was* Sunday. I expect I told more lies than I have told before in a month. We had a tip-top dinner, but nothing to drink but cider. I told Mr. Beecher that no dinner could be perfect without champaign, or at least some kind of Burgundy, & he said that privately he was a good deal of the same opinion, but it wouldn't do to say it aloud." Such a concession he never could have extracted from Livy's father, Jervis Langdon, who stood inflexible in his prejudice against drinking and the use of tobacco.

While Sam had been away from Washington during the holidays, a friend, whom he accused of not being sober when he did it, made an engagement for him to lecture at the capital on January 9, and again the next evening, but forgot to advise Clemens. He had only learned about it "at 10 oclock, last night . . . & so you must be aware that I have been working like sin all night to get a lecture written," he continued to his family. He drew on *Quaker City* impressions and anecdotes, and called it "Frozen Truth," but considered it "top-heavy."

Directly after the lecture he wrote home again. The talk had come close to being a "villainous failure," for it was not advertised at all, and the manager was taken sick at the last minute. By then, it was too late to cancel, so Sam "scared up" a doorkeeper, and by pure good luck the house was "tolerably good," and he was saved. However, he was so nervous at first, "I hardly knew what to talk about, but it went off in splendid style." A close friend observed that Clemens never failed with a talk, for "some burst or spurt" of inspiration always came to his rescue.

He was hard at work catching up on his newspaper correspondence after his New York holiday, "and I have to get up that confounded book, too," for the publisher had reacted favorably to his suggestion, and they were discussing terms. He asked his mother to cut out his *Alta* letters and send them to him for future use. "A movement is on foot to keep the present Patent Office man in his place. If it succeeds, I think it will be very well for Orion.

"I have got a thousand things to do, & am not doing *any* of them.—I feel perfectly savage."

Two nights later he had a resounding success at the Washington Correspondents' Club annual banquet, with his racy response to the toast, "Woman—the pride of any profession, and the jewel of ours." The banquet was "altogether the most brilliant affair of the kind I ever participated in." Guests included the illustrator Ed-

ward Jump, noted for his political cartoons and caricatures of famous people; Speaker of the House Schuyler Colfax; the Marquis
Adolphe de Chambrun, author and legal adviser to the French
Legation at Washington (he was married to a granddaughter of
Lafayette); and a sprinkling of cabinet officers and senators. Clemens was number twelve on the list of speakers. Midnight arrived,
but his turn had not yet come. The fun was at its height when the
Chair announced that "the Sabbath was come, and that a due
regard for the Christian character of our country demanded that
the festivities" cease. It was then "gravely moved" and as gravely
seconded and carried, "That we do now discontinue the use of
Washington time, and adopt the time of San Francisco"—thereby
gaining about three and a half hours. "When we had used up all
the San Francisco time, and got to crowding Sunday again, we took
another vote and adopted Hong Kong time. I suppose we would
have been going west yet, if the champagne had not given out."

When Sam's turn came he thanked the president for the honor,
"because, sir, I love the sex; I love *all* the women, sir, irrespective
of age or color. Human intelligence cannot estimate what we owe to
woman, sir. She sews on our buttons; she mends our clothes; she
ropes us in at church fairs; she confides in us; . . . she gives us
good advice, and plenty of it; she soothes our aching brows; she
bears our children—ours as a general thing." In whatever position
or estate she may find herself, "she is an ornament to the place she
occupies, and a treasure to the world." Here he paused, looked
inquiringly at the audience, and remarked that applause should
come in at this point. It came, and with it an explosion of laughter,
the reporter who was recording the speech noted.

Sam resumed: "Look at Cleopatra!—look at Desdemona!—look
at Florence Nightingale!—look at Joan of Arc!—look at Lucretia
Borgia!" He was interrupted here by cries of "No, no!" "Well," he
said, scratching his head doubtfully, "suppose we let Lucretia
slide. . . . Look at Mother Eve!" Cries this time of "Oh! oh!" and
renewed laughter. "You need not look at her unless you want to,"
he continued after a reflective pause, "but Eve was ornamental, sir
—particularly before the fashions changed."

Then: "Look at Lucy Stone!—look at Elizabeth Cady Stanton!—
look at Frances—Frances—George Francis Train!" His words were

drowned in laughter, for Train, an exceedingly eccentric shipping and railroad magnate, was a vocal supporter of women's rights and had just published a controversial book on the subject.

As a sweetheart (Clemens continued when there was quiet), woman has few equals and no superiors. As a wet nurse, for example, she has no equal among men. "What, sir, would the people of the earth do without woman? They would be scarce, sir, almighty scarce. Then let us cherish her; let us . . . give her our support, our encouragement, our sympathy, ourselves—if we get a chance."

He closed with a call to the colors: "But jesting aside, Mr. President, woman is lovable, gracious, kind of heart, beautiful—worthy of all respect, of all esteem, of all deference. Not any here will refuse to drink to her health in this bumper of wine, for each and every one has personally known and loved, and honored the very best one of them all—his own mother." The applause, cheers, and stamping were thunderous.

In his next letter to the *Alta* he said, "I think the women of San Francisco ought to send me a medal, or a doughnut, or something, because I had them chiefly in mind in this eulogy."

Twenty-four hours after his talk, Sam slipped a newspaper clipping into an envelope along with a covering note: "Dear Folks—I thought you might like to read my speech, which Speaker Colfax said was the best dinner-table speech he ever heard at a banquet./ Yrs. affly/ Sam."

The *Washington Star* had printed the text taken down by their reporter during the talk. Clemens knew it would be widely copied all over the country, and before Mary Fairbanks could even take aim, he sent his defense. She must not "abuse" him on account of that dinner-speech, in case she happens to see it "floating around" in some paper. It did have *slang* in it, but they had no business reporting it "so *verbatimly.*" They ought to have "left out the slang . . . it was all their fault." When she did see it she wrote him what he called a "scorcher." In his reply he admitted, "I deserve all you have said, & promise that I will rigidly eschew slang & vulgarity . . . even in foolish dinner speeches, when on my guard"—meaning sober.

By January 24 he was at Hartford to meet with Elisha Bliss, because no progress was being made on the book contract through correspondence. He was the guest of Alice Hooker's family at Nook Farm, an exclusive residential development financed in part by John Hooker, Alice's father. Sam was obliged to "walk mighty straight," and was not allowed to smoke. In his *Alta* letter, he claimed to smoke "surreptitiously when all are in bed, to save my reputation, and then draw suspicion upon the cat when the family detect the unfamiliar odor. So far, I am safe, but I am sorry to say that the cat has lost caste. . . . She has achieved a reputation for smoking, and may justly be regarded as a degraded, a dishonored, a ruined cat." He admitted to Mother Fairbanks that he dared not do *anything* that was comfortable and natural. "It comes a little hard to lead such a sinless life," but he has been bearing it because "I desire to have the respect of this sterling old Puritan community, for their respect is well worth having." Three years later he was a member of that select society.

On his way from the capital to Hartford he stopped a day or two with Dan Slote ("his house is my home always in New York," he told his family) and called one morning at the *Herald* office to see the staff. Young James Gordon Bennett asked him to write twice a week for the paper and said he might have "full swing, & abuse anybody & everybody" he had a mind to. Sam told him he must have "the very fullest possible swing," and Bennett agreed. Sam then said, "It's a contract—and let's take a drink on it." In Washington "there are lots of folks . . . who need villifying." He went on to his mother and Pamela that he was especially anxious to "waltz into" those Patent Office people who were constantly changing commissioners and policies, and who procrastinated infuriatingly with regard to that clerkship for Orion.

While still staying at Dan Slote's he went to Niblo's Garden with a group of newspapermen to see the "White Fawn," successor to the "Black Crook!" He reported: "Everybody agrees that it is much more magnificent than the Crook. The fairy scenes are more wonderfully dazzling and beautiful, and the legs of the young women reach higher up." The costumes were "perfectly gorgeous," and the final scene, a vast tropical world of tangled vines and giant flowers—in every flower a beautiful sleeping girl, "apparently naked, for the most part—was a vision of magnificence "no man could imagine unless he had eaten a barrel of hasheesh."

Sam also took the ferry to Brooklyn to call on Henry Ward Beecher, and while there brought up the subject of the contract with Bliss. Beecher said, "Now here—you are one of the talented men of the age—nobody is going to deny that—but in matters of business, I don't suppose you know more than enough to come in when it rains. I'll tell you what to do & how to do it! And he did, and I listened well." Sam followed the advice when he met with Bliss and reported, "I have made a splendid contract," although only verbal and subject to approval by the partners. Sam's percentage was to be a little more than they gave the popular A. D. Richardson. In fact, it was the largest amount they had paid any author except Horace Greeley. "Beecher will be surprised, I guess, when he hears this. But I had made up my mind to *one* thing—I wasn't going to touch a book unless there was *money* in it, & a good deal of it. I told them so," he informed Jane Lampton and Pamela.

"I shall write to the Enterprise & Alta every week as usual, I guess, & to the Herald twice a week— & occasionally to the Tribune & the magazines (I have a stupid article in the Galaxy just issued) but I am not going to write to this, that & the other paper, any more. The Chicago Tribune wants letters, but I hope & pray I have charged them so much they will not close the contract. I am gradually getting out of debt, but these trips to New York cost like sin." His contributions were bringing him close to eight hundred dollars a month, but they would have to be curtailed to allow him time to write his book.

"Now *don't* go & read this letter to *any body* outside the family circle—I am sensitive on this point. If you have to talk, *talk*—but don't *read* my letters," he warned, and at the top of the first page added a note, "Read this only to the family & then burn it—I do *hate* to have anybody know anything about my business. Don't mention the *terms,* herein, on your life. It is a business secret."

Without waiting to hear further from Bliss, he fled the restraints of the Hooker house and returned to Slote's. From there he wrote jubilantly to Will Bowen about the "tip-top" contract he had just made for a five-to-six-hundred-page book with illustrations—the manuscript to be delivered by mid-July. "It is with the heaviest publishing house in America, & I get the best terms they have ever offered any man save one." Sam knew this news would not make

Bowen envious for he had been aware of Clemens' straits during all the years when he was prospering as a pilot.

Sam went on to tell him that he had been thinking about their school days together at Dawson's. He recalled the time when Will bought the louse from Arch Fuqua. "I told about that at a Congressional dinner . . . the other day, & Lord, how those thieves laughed! . . . I just expect I shall publish it yet, some day." That "gorgeous old reminiscence" found a prominent place in *Tom Sawyer*.

Still at Dan Slote's on January 27, 1868, Sam used his friend's business stationery (Slote, Woodman & Co., Blank Book Manufacturers) to answer a letter from Bliss informing him of the publisher's acceptance of his terms. He signed at once and closed the contract.

Back at the capital, he was again offered the coveted postmastership in San Francisco, the previous nominee not having been approved, Sam wrote home. This time Justice Field pledged the President's appointment, and Senator John Conness of California guaranteed the Senate's confirmation. If that position did not suit him, Conness offered a choice of five "influential" offices in California. He admitted that it was "a great temptation," but would make it impossible to "fill" his book contract. "I have to spend August & September in Hartford—which isn't San Francisco. . . .

"They want to send me abroad, as a Consul or a Minister. I said I didn't want any of the pie. God knows I am mean enough & lazy enough, now, without being a foreign consul.

"Sometime in the course of the present century I think they will create a Commissioner of Patents, & then I hope to get a berth for Orion."

Because he would now have to reduce his newspaper letters to one or two a week, he asked Bliss for a thousand-dollar advance to support him while he finished the manuscript. At this point he was gathering all his printed letters about the cruise, and had written to Mary Fairbanks, asking for her correspondence with the *Cleveland Herald*. He had already applied to Dr. Gibson for his letters, and had received them, and Colonel Foster had agreed to collect and forward his. Both men had shared most of Sam's land excursions, and each had corresponded with a hometown paper. "I only want to steal the *ideas*," not the language, he told Mary.

February 9 found him at a new address in Washington—76 Indiana Avenue. "I am sick in bed, & *have* been, for four or five days," he wrote Mother Fairbanks. He was now lodging with James Henry Riley, political correspondent for the *Alta California*, who became his closest friend during his stay at the capital. "Riley is full of humor and has an unfailing vein of irony, which makes his conversation to the last degree entertaining," Sam wrote of him. In a letter to Jane Lampton and Pamela, Sam mentioned that he had already moved five times since he roomed with Senator Stewart, and that he was planning to move again. "Shabby furniture & shabby food—*that* is Washn—I mean to keep moving." Four years ago in San Francisco, he and Steve Gillis had shifted their lodgings five times and their hotel twice within four months. It was doubtless Sam's restlessness more than the conditions which determined his course now.

He had already resigned as Stewart's secretary when he moved to Indiana Avenue, and wrote an amusing account, "The Facts Concerning the Recent Important Resignation," for the *New-York Tribune*. This was followed by an article, "My Late Senatorial Secretaryship," for *The Galaxy*, a New York literary magazine founded recently to offset the supposed provincialism of the *Atlantic Monthly*. In the piece he identified his employer as James W. N——, U. S. Senator, easily recognized as James W. Nye, territorial governor of Nevada during Sam's stay there, and now that state's second senator. Possibly this was Clemens' way of repaying Nye for having failed to introduce him at the Cooper Institute lecture or to apologize. Sam described his methods of satisfying the senator's constituents. For instance, there were the residents of Baldwin's Ranch, Nevada, who asked for a post office. Sam was told to write them convincingly but tactfully that there was no real need for a post office there. In his letter Clemens said: "What the mischief do you suppose you want with a post-office at Baldwin's Ranch. It would not do you any good. If any letters came . . . you couldn't read them, you know; and, besides, such letters as ought to pass through, with money in them, for other localities, would not be likely to get through . . . and that would make trouble for us all. No, don't bother about a post-office in your camp. . . . What you need is a nice jail, you know—a nice, substantial jail and a free school. These will be a lasting benefit to you, . . . I will move in the matter at once."

Four similar letters were quoted and "Nye's" anger described. Then came the dictum: "Leave the house! Leave it forever and forever, too."

He and Stewart did not part in rancor, as has been assumed after reading Sam's sketch or Stewart's *Reminiscences,* written when the senator was old and forgetful. Of Clemens he said: "One morning a very disreputable-looking person slouched into the room." He was wearing a "seedy suit, which hung upon his lean frame in bunches. . . . A sheaf of scraggy black hair leaked out of a battered old slouch hat, like stuffing from an ancient . . . sofa. . . . He had a very sinister appearance. . . . I was confident that he would come to no good end, but I have heard of him from time to time since then, and I understand that he has settled down and become respectable."

Stewart's description is at variance with a Philadelphia newsman's report on Clemens' "faultless taste" in dress, at this time; his "snowy vest . . . suggestive of endless quarrels with Washington washerwomen; his lavender kid gloves" which, it was noted, "might have been stolen from some Turkish harem, so delicate were they in size."

After the publication of *Roughing It,* ill feeling did arise when Stewart claimed he had been portrayed unfairly in the book.

As soon as Sam recovered from that most recent illness which had kept him in bed, he set up "a regular system of working all day long & taking the whole night for recreation—*and* sleep. I don't write *any*thing at night, now. I can write about ten pages of the book a day, pretty comfortably—fifteen if necessary." He was certain of finishing on time.

Then, unexpectedly, a telegram came from Joe Goodman to inform him that the *Alta* proprietors were planning to publish his letters in book form. Having learned that Clemens was at work on a book that would use material to which they held the rights, without asking their permission, they had decided not only to print the correspondence but to refuse to let him use it. A wire to Mac-Crellish confirmed this.

Bliss advised him to write the book all over, and not mind what the *Alta* did, but he refused. His protests by telegram and letter got nowhere, so he decided to leave for San Francisco at once, if Bliss would advance him the money. Bliss did. "I *must* go. If the *Alta*'s book were to come out with those wretched, slangy letters unrevised, I should be utterly ruined." On March 11 he sailed from New York on the steamer *Henry Chauncey*, overjoyed at his escape from Washington and at the prospect of being at sea.

Four days later he wrote his mother from "Latitude 25," to tell her "that the weather is fearfully hot—that the Henry Chauncey is a magnificent ship—that we have twelve hundred passengers on board—that I have two staterooms, and so am not crowded—that I have many pleasant friends here, & the people are not so stupid as on the Quaker City—that we . . . expect to meet the upward bound vessel in Latitude 23, & this is why I am writing now.

"We shall reach Aspinwall Thursday at 6 o'clock, & reach San Francisco less than two weeks later. I worry a great deal about being obliged to go without seeing you all, but it could not be helped."

On April 2 he was home again at the Occidental Hotel. The next morning the *Alta* welcomed "the genial and jolly humorist, (who proposes to lecture in a few days)."

Frederick MacCrellish was no more amenable in person than he had been through telegrams and letters. Obviously two works by Clemens on the same subject, coming out almost simultaneously, could not compete successfully. Still, he refused to give up his book concept or let Sam use the letters. At length he offered a compromise: ten percent royalty to Clemens on the published work. But Sam refused to agree, and decided at this point to let the matter rest while he made some needed money by lecturing. On April 14 he gave a talk titled "Pilgrim Life," based on the cruise. His posters announced that "The Doors will be beseiged at 7 o'clock; the Insurrection will begin at 8." Every seat in San Francisco's Platt Hall on Montgomery Street was quickly bought, and Clemens stopped the sale of tickets because "I didn't want them standing up & bothering me." The proceeds were a little over sixteen hundred dollars in gold and silver. But for some reason he thought the lecture was "miserably poor." Possibly it was his mood, for the audience was delighted and the reviews were favorable. He probably revised the talk but kept the title, for he lectured on "Pilgrim Life" throughout his tour.

He took the evening steamer to Sacramento, where he spoke to a full house. He found the weather there as balmy as summer, and saw roses and peach trees in bloom. On the night of April 21 he gave his talk at Grass Valley. There in the foothills it was still spring, with lilac buds just opening. He went on by rail to Donner Summit, where snow lay thirty feet deep on level ground and one hundred feet in drifts. He was experiencing all the seasons but autumn in a matter of hours. At the summit the passengers boarded a mail coach with four horses, bound for Coburn's Station. From there Sam sent a telegram to the *Territorial Enterprise* (he was to be Joe Goodman's guest): "I am doing well, having crossed one divide without getting robbed anyway. Mark Twain."

On Friday, April 24, the *Enterprise* printed under the heading, "MARK TWAIN: This celebrated humorist, after having visited the Holy Land and all the principal cities of the world, will again once more press his foot upon his native sagebrush this morning." A change has been made in the date and place of the lecture. Instead of speaking Saturday night at the Athletic Hall, as advertised, the Opera House has been booked for the following Monday and Tuesday nights, because of its greater seating capacity. Meanwhile, "he will have enough to do for three or four days to shake hands and swap yarns with his old friends."

The stagecoach from Coburn's Station pulled into Virginia City at five o'clock that morning. The streets were already bustling, and streams of people on horseback and afoot were pouring into town. This was the day that John Milleain (also known as Jean Millian), convicted of having murdered and robbed the popular (and elite) prostitute Julia Bulette, was to be hanged. After months spent in the civilized cities of Europe and America, Clemens, in crossing the Sierra Nevada, had stepped back into a scene from the Old West. Toward mid-morning, he was seen standing on B Street in front of the Court House, where a large crowd had already gathered.

By eleven-thirty, when the carriage for the prisoner drove up to the door of the sheriff's office, the crowd had grown into an immense throng. Twenty-four specials from the sheriff's posse, armed with Henry rifles, and some sixty members of the National Guard in full uniform surrounded the vehicle. At exactly twelve noon, the prisoner and two attending Catholic priests stepped into the carriage; the procession then formed and moved off. Second in line was a vehicle carrying two officiating doctors, and the reporters from Virginia City and Gold Hill newspapers. Behind them came a wagon draped in black, with the coffin and undertaker. On either side of the road marched the posse and the National Guard, and bringing up the rear was an army of people on foot, on horseback, in buggies and carriages. Sam Clemens was in one of the carriages.

The gallows had been built in a sloping ravine about a mile north of Virginia City, near the Jewish cemetery, just below the Geiger Grade. About five thousand people, among them many women and children, covered the encircling hillsides. The prisoner read his farewell as it was written, in French. He said he had been guilty of many "bad deeds" during his life, but of this one he was innocent. A great injustice had been done him during his trial and conviction, for the chief of police had perjured himself, and "abandoned women" had been brought to the witness stand to "swear his life away." Not understanding or speaking English well, he had been unable to refute the accusations. It was claimed that he had confessed; that was not true. What he was reading now was his only confession. He then knelt on the trap, and after a short prayer with Father Manogue, stood up, embraced the priests and shook hands with the officers. Then he waited imperturbably while the noose was fitted around his neck. "Just as the black cap was drawn down over his head, the spring was touched, the trap dropped, and John Milleain dangled in the air," wrote the *Gold Hill News*. His manner and voice had been so sincere in his address, many wondered if this was another miscarriage of justice; another case where advantage was taken of a foreigner lacking knowledge of English.

The following day was so warm and springlike in Virginia City, the ice cream man with his donkey cart and tin horn came out to peddle for the first time that year. Clemens visited with his friends at the *Enterprise* office, and seated at the old table, worked on his letters for the Eastern papers.

On Monday, April 27, the day set for his lecture, Virginia was celebrating the forty-ninth anniversary of the Odd Fellows with a parade through the principal streets to the Opera House, where there was to be an oration, followed by the reading of odes, and the recitation of a poem by Joe Goodman. That evening Clemens had to compete with two large balls in honor of the same event, and did not get a full house.

He tried to persuade Goodman to introduce him but he refused, saying that this was the last place in the world Sam would need an introduction. At eight-thirty on the night of the performance, a piano was heard behind the curtain, and as it rose the audience saw Clemens seated at it, playing. Then, as though completely unaware of where he was, he commenced singing, "There was an old hoss, and his name was Jerusalem. . . ." At the explosion of laughter he stopped, looked about in feigned surprise and embarrassment, got up, came to the front of the stage, and apologized by saying that if any of them had been waiting behind the curtain as long as he had, he guessed they would welcome some such relief, too. He then plunged into the lecture. It was very humorous, a diarist wrote that night, "as well as pleasing & instructive—much applauded. . . ." He enjoyed it so well he attended again the next evening.

Sam spoke in Carson City on April 29, and by May first was back at Virginia, where he started a letter to Mary Fairbanks. "I CANNOT GO A-MAYING today, because it is snowing so hard—& so I have been writing some newspaper letters &" He left the sentence unfinished—continuing it four days later from San Francisco, shortly after getting to his hotel room and reading a letter that had come from her. "I have had the *hardest* trip over the Sierras." There had been a heavy snowstorm, but he had enjoyed "the two & a half hours' sleighing. . . . we made ten miles an hour straight along. We had no such thrilling fun in Palestine." After the clouds parted, the moon spread a magical glow over the glittering white landscape. It was "magnificent."

But "I am utterly & completely worn out. I intended to sleep on the boat—they gave me the bridal chamber as usual—(a ghastly sarcasm on my lonely state, but intended as a compliment) but I knew so many people on board that I staid up to talk—& now I cannot write—I can hardly see, for that matter." His main reason for writing was to tell her, "the *Alta* has given me permission to use the printed letters. It is all right, now."

Not exactly all right, for he will be unable to accompany Anson Burlingame to Europe, which "I wanted to do . . . badly." Burlingame was then in San Francisco and about to start off on a new assignment. The Chinese government had appointed him head of an official delegation, with two high-ranking Chinese colleagues, whose purpose was to visit foreign powers, observe their ways, and negotiate favorable treaties with China. Sam had talked with him in early April and the diplomat had asked him to join his staff, on a mission that was expected to last several years. If the *Alta* refused to agree to Sam's demands (and the outlook was very unpromising then) he would go. Now that the picture had changed, he and Burlingame discussed the matter for several hours, trying to work out possible ways for Clemens to travel with him and still manage to write his book. He will not be going to Europe yet, he explained to Mary, for that would be impractical and inexpedient, but as soon as the book is finished, he will sail. Further enticements, in the form of invitations, have come from "splendid friends" in China and Japan, offering him "princely hospitalities" for months. "Can't go, now—" but surely, later.

"What did I ever write about the Holy Land that was so peculiarly lacerating?" Clemens asked Mary Fairbanks after he had settled in San Francisco to write his book. Local ministers, it seems, cannot get through a sermon without turning aside to give him a "blast." One of them had just called him "this son of the Devil, Mark Twain." If Sam can find the time to write the article he has in mind, he will "make that parson climb a tree." But then, he reflected, it was only the "small-fry" preachers who attack him. All those of influence and high standing he still visits, and swaps lies with, the same as ever.

He renewed his friendship with Steve Gillis, who had married and was living in a house on Bush Street, and he spent time with Bret Harte, now editing the newly founded literary magazine, *Overland Monthly*. Harte was about to publish his own local-color stories which would make him and the magazine famous. Sam showed him some of the chapters he was working on and asked for an opinion.

Once again Clemens limited his daytime social activities, and kept to a regular writing schedule. By doing so he made amazing progress, for in revising he was having to bear in mind his promise to Pamela not to "scoff" at sacred things, to Mary, to eliminate "slang" and polish his style, and to Emma Beach, not to disparage the old masters. He had a further problem in the shortage of material. This he solved by padding the manuscript with recollections of boyhood and mining, and with invented situations and experiences which supposedly took place during the tour. In making these changes and additions he lost much of the freshness, spontaneity, vigor, and raciness of the original letters. On June 17, when he stopped work to reply to Mary, he was on page 2343, was describing the Sphinx, and expected to wind up the sights of Egypt that day. The next day he intended to have the ship sail for Alexandria, homeward bound. *"Then,* it was the most regretful day to me, of the whole voyage—*now,* it is the happiest. Cuss the cussed book. . . . I wish I were a profane young man—how I would let fly the adjectives sometimes. . . .

"I mean to only *glance* at Spain. . . . If I talked much about the week in Spain I should be sure to caricature Miss Newell."

He admitted to Mary that he had been unable to keep from touching the pilgrims "on the raw" occasionally. Considering what they had said about him at Gilbraltar, when he was absent, remarks which Mary heard, "O, I could have said *such* savage things about *them.* . . ." The publisher had asked him to include "that N. Y. *Herald* valedictory squib which worried you so much—but that is all right." He has just read it over and found the article "so mild, so gentle, that I can hardly understand how I ever wrote such literary gruel." Although he revised the piece, he failed to make it stronger.

He was restless. The new steamer *Japan* had come into port: "Oh, such a perfect palace of a ship. I do want to sail in her so badly," he told Mary. She was to leave shortly for China with J. Ross Browne as a passenger, and Sam had to master an overwhelming desire to abandon everything and go with him.

On the Wing

The manuscript was finished by June 23, and he reserved a stateroom on the Pacific Mail steamship *Sacramento,* scheduled to sail on June 30 for the Isthmus of Panama. But at the urging of friends, he agreed to stay over in order to give one more lecture in San Francisco, and "so persecute the public for their lasting benefit & my profit." He wrote a new talk, "The Oldest of the Republics: Venice, Past and Present."

His advance advertising took the form of a handbill purporting to be a series of protests to him in letter form, imploring him not to speak, for "there is a limit to human endurance." The first protest was signed by fifty-eight distinguished citizens and a large number of prominent organizations. The final objection came from the chief of police, who said, "Mr. Mark Twain—Dear Sir, —You had better go."

On Thursday evening, July 2, he lectured at the New Mercantile Library, on Bush Street. As usual, the audience was large and fashionable, and was so enthusiastic, that afterward he felt "some inches taller."

The following day he called at the steamship office to buy his ticket but the company refused to let him pay for it. On July 6, he sailed on the steamer *Montana.* At the dock he said goodbye to many friends whom he would never see again—for this was to be his last trip to the city he called home, and to the Far West, which had been responsible for the making of "Mark Twain."

XXV

---○---

THE SIEGE OF ELMIRA

"I THINK THE MIDDLE of summer must be the pleasantest season of the year to come East by sea," Sam Clemens wrote
the *Alta*. "Going down to the Isthmus . . . we had smooth water
and cool breezes all the time." In addition, the meals were all well-
cooked and served, and from among the 185 "quiet, orderly passengers," ten or fifteen "were willing to be cheerful." Allying himself with those, they jointly contrived an entertainment, a "thrilling
tragedy" called "Country School Exhibition." Sam's hand was obvious throughout. It was presented by the Port Guard Theatre on
the evening of July 10, 1868, and the announcements read:

> New Bill. New Scenery. New Cast.
> Powerful Combination.
> Dazzling Array of Talent.

With the exception of the man who took the part of the teacher,
the rest wore boys' costumes. The program opened with an oration:
"You'd scarce expect one of my age. . . ." followed by a recitation
of "Casabianca," that Felicia Hemens poem Clemens never failed
to include in any account of a school exhibition. Here it was paro-
died as "The Boy Stood on the Burning Deck, with his Baggage
Checked for Troy." Sam read an original composition called "The

Cow," and sang with the chorus, "Old John Brown Had One Little
Injun." There was a definite Clemens touch in the program note:

> Any pupil detected in catching flies or throwing spit-balls at the
> Dominie during the solemnities will be punished. . . . No pupil
> will be allowed to "go out," unless he shall state what he wants to
> go out for.

To his *Alta* readers he said, "I have seen many theatrical exhibi-
tions, but none that equalled the above."

His spirits remained high throughout this trip, and he experimented with some literary ideas. He wrote a draft of "The Story of
Mamie Grant, Child-Missionary," burlesquing one of those righ-
teous children who appeared as the heroes of Sunday school books.
He had already explored the area with "The Story of the Good
Little Boy Who Did Not Prosper," a tale about young Jacob
Blivens, whose ambition it was to be put into such a work, with
pictures showing him in acts of piety and benevolence. But nothing
ever went right with Jacob and in the end one of his good deeds led
to his being blown up and "apportioned among four townships.
. . . You never saw a boy scattered so." It was also Mamie Grant's
desire to see her "poor little name" in a beautiful Sunday school
book. Clemens, however, never completed the sketch.

He worked on a story about a Frenchman who, wrongly con-
demned to the galleys, escaped by slipping away from his guard
while in Paris. He commandeered a balloon and sailed over India,
China, and the Pacific Ocean, to land finally on a farm in Illinois.
Sam went so far as to write a first version, but then abandoned the
tale because, as he explained later, a translation of Jules Verne's
Five Weeks in a Balloon was published in the United States the
following spring. Twenty-five years later he revived the subject of
balloon travel in a short book entitled *Tom Sawyer Abroad.* In that
work Tom, Huck, and Jim were carried off from St. Louis by a
crazed inventor of "a noble big balloon" that had "wings and fans
and all sorts of things."

When the steamship *Montana* reached Panama, Clemens went
into the Grand Hotel to get a drink. While standing at the bar he
heard a voice he recognized at once as that of Captain Ned Wake-

man of the *America*. The unexcelled raconteur was at that moment in the midst of one of his wonderful tales. He and Clemens spent some hours together, and the Captain entertained him with the account of a remarkable dream he had had about making a trip to heaven. Sam was fascinated and decided to turn what he called "A Journey to Heaven" into a parody of Elizabeth Ward's book, *The Gates Ajar,* in which the author imagined "a mean little ten per cent heaven about the size of Rhode Island." Sam worked on this concept sporadically through the 1870s, and took it up again in the next decade, repeatedly revising it. He finally published it as a small book, *Extract from Captain Stormfield's Visit to Heaven,* in 1909, not long before his death.

Clemens arrived in New York aboard the steamer *Henry Chauncey,* on Wednesday, July 29. Five days later he was still in the city, finishing an article for the *Tribune* on the new China treaty sponsored by Anson Burlingame. On August 4, he took the train for Hartford, to work with Bliss on the book. After he had been there about ten days, he found time to write to the *Alta.* He dated the letter "August, Recently, 1868." It read: "I never saw any place before where morality and huckleberries flourished as they do here—I do not know which has the ascendancy. Possibly the huckleberries, in their season, but the morality holds out the longest. The huckleberries are in season, now. They are a new beverage to me. . . . They are excellent. I had always thought a huckleberry was something like a turnip. On the contrary, they are no larger than buckshot. They are better than buckshot, though, and more digestible." During the ten days he has been in Hartford, "I have heard only one man swear and seen only one man drunk. . . . And the same man that did the swearing was the man that contained the drunk. It was after midnight. Everybody was in bed —otherwise they would have hanged him, no doubt. This sample gives you the complexion of male morality in Hartford. Young ladies walk the streets alone as late as ten o'clock at night, and are not insulted. That is a specimen of both male and female morality, and of good order." On his own nightly walks he meets dozens of pretty girls marching cheerfully along in the "loneliest" places, where the darkness was made denser by the somber shadows of great overhanging elms. "I don't dare to speak to them. I should be scalped, sure." Only a little over a year ago, the city had repealed its law prohibiting "the harboring of sinful playing-cards in dwelling houses." What did his Western readers think of *that*, he asked.

For months Mary Fairbanks had been urging him to bring Charlie Langdon and visit her in Cleveland, but up until now there had not been time. His book was at a point where he could leave it for a few weeks, so he planned to go to Dan Slote's in New York on August 18, stay about five days, then take a train to Elmira, and pay his long-deferred visit to the Langdons. After a day or two he and Charlie would go on to Cleveland. But for some reason those plans were changed, and he went directly to Elmira, arriving there late at night on the eighteenth.

In the dark he was unable to see how opulent the Langdons' three-storied mansion was, with its balconies and columned porticoes, its glassed cupola for viewing the countryside, and attached conservatory, set in a full city block. The formal garden was planted with lawn, specimen trees, and flowering shrubs. An ornate tiered fountain stood near the front entrance. The whole was enclosed within an iron picket fence whose wide gates clanged authoritatively behind the visitor, one of Clemens' daughters never forgot.

The next morning Sam was amazed to find what an immense place it was, filled with unexpected stairways and halls leading to remote and mysterious regions. It was also somber, for heavily draped windows let in little light, and fashionably drab furnishings made the rooms still darker.

Clemens went there as Charlie's friend, to pay a brief courtesy call. But the day or so he had planned on staying stretched to two weeks, and he left Elmira as Olivia Langdon's rejected lover. The extension of time was not Sam's doing, but was one of those "accidents" which he maintained made up his life. Charlie had been drafted into helping his father during the absence of the coal company's business manager and was obliged to wait for his return. Since a visit to Mary Fairbanks would lose half its pleasure for her if Charlie were not along, Clemens remained. He did not fret at the delay, for, as he wrote his mother and sister, "I am most comfortably situated here. This is the pleasantest family I ever knew."

There was only one trouble—they gave too much time, thought, and invention to making his visit pass "delightfully."

Because Charlie was at work most of the day, Sam passed time mainly with Mrs. Langdon, Livy, and her houseguest and cousin, the vivacious Hattie Lewis who possessed a good sense of humor, appreciated Sam's, and explained his jokes to Livy. Because Livy tired easily, they occupied themselves with leisurely carriage rides around the countryside, strolls in the garden, cribbage, and singing around the piano, times when Hattie noted Clemens' "very sweet tenor voice." In the evenings there were prayers, and selections from the same *Plymouth Collection of Hymns* the pilgrims had used aboard the *Quaker City.* There was no drink stronger than cider, and no smoking, for the Langdons were founders of the local Congregational Church, and were prejudiced against the use of alcohol and tobacco. Sunday dinner guests always included at least two ministers, a regular being their own pastor, Thomas Beecher, a brother of Henry Ward Beecher. Except for the presence of Livy and Hattie, this might have been an extension of the Holy Land cruise. It can easily be seen why Charlie Langdon had rebelled and attached himself to the worldly, hard-drinking, chain-smoking, profane skeptic, Sam Clemens.

Sam had had trouble keeping himself from falling in love with Livy the night they heard Charles Dickens read. Now that he was in her company daily, he found it impossible to control his feelings, especially when she reminded him of Laura Wright.

He told himself he was unworthy of such a girl. He had explained the problem to Mary Fairbanks when she urged him to find a wife. He knew he was unable to support one, for his only source of income was from his limited newspaper correspondence. He did look forward to making money from his book, and more certainly as one of James Redpath's speakers on the lyceum circuit, for he had recently signed with him. Still, not long before he left Elmira he impetuously proposed marriage, and Livy refused him, gently but firmly. Time would change her feelings, he told her. No, she could never love him, she replied. Pitying him at length, she did consent to be his "sister," and allowed him to write to her occasionally, as her "brother." But she declined flatly to give him her picture.

The Siege of Elmira

Taking advantage of her permission to write, he composed a letter at midnight on August 31, addressing her as "My Honored 'Sister.' " He was grateful to her and the others for having shown patience, consideration, and unfailing kindness during his stay. "I accept the situation, uncomplainingly, hard as it is. Of old I am acquainted with grief, disaster & disappointment, & have borne these troubles as became a man. So, also, I shall bear this last & bitterest, even though it break my heart." He will continue to love her—"worship" is the exact word. "But no more of this. I have said it only from that impulse which *drives* men to speak of great calamities which have befallen them, & so seek relief. . . .

"And so, hence forward, I claim only that you will let me freight my speeches to you with . . . the sacred love a brother bears to a sister." As her brother, he felt free to declare: "My honored sister, you are *so* good & so beautiful. . . . Give me a little room in that great heart of yours—." If she and Mrs. Fairbanks "will only scold & upbraid me now & then, I shall fight my way through the world, never fear." He begged her to write him *"something* from time to time," if only texts from the New Testament, excerpts from her "Book of Sermons" (he had discovered that she was pious), or write a discourse on the sin of smoking—anything. Just knowing it was from the hand of his "matchless" sister will comfort him. In closing, he commended her to the care of "ministering angels." After reading the letter, Livy endorsed it "Sept. 1868/1st.," and put it away in what came to be known in the family as the "sacred green box," which had a lock. She kept his proposal a secret from her parents, but certainly shared it with Hattie Lewis.

On September 4, after he and Charlie were on the road to Cleveland, Mrs. Langdon wrote Mary Fairbanks, having learned how highly she regarded Sam. They had enjoyed Mr. Clemens, and felt that he in turn had enjoyed his quiet stay. She believed he was destined to make his "mark" in the world, and prayed that he might live "to good purpose." (She apparently held doubts.) He and Charlie were looking forward to their visit, she went on, but warned, "I fear they will 'turn the house out of the windows' if they are not watched." Obviously Mr. Clemens' behavior did not always meet the approval of this strong-minded woman whose dignity once prompted Sam to remark that she "was born for a countess." To understand him, she reminded herself that he was a *humorist.*

Sam left the Langdons with the single satisfaction that he had been at least "quite a pleasant addition to the family circle" during that time. Later he was to learn (inadvertently through Livy) that a two-week stay by a stranger on a first visit was a breach of etiquette which only the most brazen would attempt, and that he had *not* been excused just because he was Charlie's friend. He was appalled to think how often he must have annoyed them all by his presence, and how they must have wished he would go, and what they must have said about him in private. And then, to think he had had the effrontery to propose marriage to Olivia. The revelation haunted him for a long while, and he dreamed about Livy barring him forever from her presence. In attempting an apology, he gently shifted the blame to the beautiful little sorceress who had kept him there under her spell.

He also left Elmira determined not to lose the prize, for he was aware of the formidable opposition her protective parents would present, because they did not consider him a fit match for their only daughter. Her father had already declared he would never let any man take her away. Sam had lost Laura Wright through the scheming of her mother, who had not thought him good enough for her daughter either.

He was too despondent to turn Mary Fairbanks' house "out the windows." He managed to play his part passably at a reception she gave for him, but at other times he was moody and irritable. He told her in private about Livy's rejection, and she encouraged him not to give up, for she had visited Elmira while Sam was on his way east from California with his finished manuscript, and had decided that Olivia's peer did not exist on earth. She would make Sam an ideal wife—but he must continue to work at making himself worthy of her.

At Pamela's house in St. Louis, where he went next for a week (without Charlie), he made no effort to control his emotions, and was by his own account, "savage & crazy." His family could not understand what was wrong, because he did not explain until several months later. In his despondency he drank heavily, as he had done at Cleveland, and he suddenly conceived a "deep hatred" for

The Siege of Elmira

St. Louis—"a muddy, smoky, mean city." This feeling would hardly allow him to appear cheerful even at his mother's hearth, he wrote. "Nobody knows what a ghastly infliction it is on me to visit St. Louis. I am afraid I do not always disguise it, either."

Then a letter came from Livy. The fact that she wrote showed that she had relented to a degree. But more hopeful and cheering was the inclusion of her picture and an invitation for him to spend a day and a night at Elmira on his return to Hartford. Further, she said she would pray for him daily, and asked that he pray with her. This offered an opening of which he took fullest advantage in his reply.

After carefully thinking through what she said, he arrived at the conviction that he would be "less than a man" if he went on in his "old careless way" while she was praying for him. He begged her to continue her prayers because "I have a vague, far-away sort of idea that it may not be wholly in vain. In one respect, at least, it *shall* not be in vain—for I will so mend my conduct that I shall grow worthier of your prayers, & your good will & sisterly solicitude, as the days go by." Here was the confessed sinner imploring the zealous missionary to reform him.

If she has not "reconsidered" her "kind invitation," he will "tarry a day & a night in Elmira (Monday 28th)." He did not, however, leave St. Louis as soon as he had intended, so he arrived at the Langdons' on Tuesday night, suffering from a heavy cold. He spent all of Wednesday trying vainly to make progress with Livy, proposing three or four times, and being refused. At eight o'clock that night, after he and Charlie had climbed into the democrat (a light four-wheeled cart) that would take them to catch the train for New York, the horse made a sudden spring forward, broke the seat loose, and threw them out backward. Sam landed on his head in the cobblestone gutter and was knocked insensible for a few minutes. According to his report to Mary Fairbanks, "the seat followed Charlie out & split his head wide open, so that you could look through it just as if you were looking through a gorge in a mountain. There wasn't anything to intercept the view—which was curious, because his brains hadn't been knocked out." This was a reference to Charlie's reputation aboard the *Quaker City* for being empty-headed.

Clemens was brought to by Livy and Hattie pouring water on his head. "They took us into the library & laid us out—& then came the inquest—& so we were already for the funeral in the morning." Seriously, he added, "it came very near to being a fatal mishap . . . I had rather not take the chances on it again."

He could not bring himself to tell Mary about being rejected again and again, but did say there had been no objection to continuing the "friendly" correspondence. He hoped that was a sign worth *something*.

Mary replied at once to his account of the accident, praising him for good timing and excellent selection of place. It must have been a beautiful tableau. Yes, he agreed in his return letter, but "plague take it, there wasn't enough of it," for he had stayed only two days longer. If he had broken his leg, he would have been better satisfied.

Unable to restrain himself, he sent Livy a letter of "hot-blooded heedlessness," which he was certain would "finish" him. As soon as it was mailed, he wished he had it back, to tone it down. He received the anticipated rebuke, a "severe" one, and replied humbly, "I have sinned," but not with deliberate intent. He begged for forgiveness and thanked her for the deserved reproof which had brought him to his senses. He told Mary that her response to his confession was "satisfactory to the subscriber"—except that he had been forced to reaffirm his fraternal role.

This emotional upset caused his cold to worsen after he reached Hartford, and kept him in bed and away from work. He did manage to have a talk with Elisha Bliss (Sam was a guest in his house), and they concluded not to try for December publication but advance the date to March, because the many illustrations they had agreed to include could not be finished earlier. These had to be engraved from photographs, many of them made by Emma Beach's father. This left Sam with time to work on his lecture for the Redpath tour.

He called the new talk "The American Vandal Abroad," and "smouched" a good portion of it from his book. He sent Mary Fairbanks a résumé to prove that, except for one "savage" blast, he had treated the pilgrims "gently & good-naturedly," as she wished. Of course, there would be the "most preposterous yarns" scattered throughout." But I *think* it will *entertain* . . . I *must not* preach to a select few in my audience, lest I have only a select few to listen next time, & so be required to preach no more." He has been asked, he told her, to relieve the heaviness of the other lectures in the series, which are all "didactic."

He continued the siege of Elmira with carefully restrained letters begging for more spiritual and moral guidance, encouraging his naive little mentor with examples of improvement, especially his progress toward becoming a Christian, luring her ever further in the direction he had chosen. In one letter he told of making a friend he was certain she would approve—the Reverend Joseph Hopkins Twichell, pastor of Hartford's Asylum Hill Congregational Church. Sam had known him only a week, but could hardly find words strong enough to tell how much he liked him and his pretty young wife, Harmony. He had met them, appropriately, at a church sociable, and Twichell had invited him to come to tea two days later, and spend the evening. Sam had a "splendid" time, for, he found, they shared many tastes, including authors, and Joe (they were already on a first-name basis) insisted that he "carry off the choicest books in his library."

This was a friendship that developed in only a few weeks to an intimacy, and remained very close and important for the rest of their lives. Joe was soon familiar with the problems of Sam's love affair, and being very much in love with his wife, he was sympathetic. Just thirty, he was tall, handsome, athletic, and genial; tolerant of the ideas and behavior of others (he accepted Clemens without reservations), and gifted with a keen sense of humor. He admired Sam's newspaper writings and had been amused by the *Jumping Frog.* He was therefore eager to meet Clemens. Twichell had graduated from Yale, where he was a member of the crew, and was in New York studying at the Union Theological Seminary, when the Civil War broke out. Although opposed to the war, out of a sense of duty he volunteered as a chaplain in the Excelsior Brigade of New Yorkers. It had been raised by the flamboyant and headstrong lawyer, congressman, and diplomat, Daniel Sickles, who had shot and killed the son of Francis Scott Key because of his attentions to Sickles' pretty, young wife. Twichell worked under fire much of the time, aiding the wounded and dying. He took part in some of the fiercest fighting, including Gettysburg, where he stood by on the field to help Sickles during the hasty amputation of the general's leg.

In a letter to Orion, Sam wrote that the "Rev. Mr. Twichell may be justly described without flattery to be a bully boy with a glass eye (as the lamented Josephus phrases it in his Decline & Fall of the Roman Empire)—so is his wife." In his war experiences Twichell had tasted life much as Clemens had in piloting, mining, and Western journalism.

Sam stayed at Hartford through October, spending much of his time with Twichell, who also shared his enthusiasm for walking. Together they tramped over the green meadows filled with red-violet asters and late goldenrod, down leaf-strewn paths which led through groves of blazing scarlet maples and stands of chestnuts turned deep yellow, and touched here and there with splashes of crimson and purple. Sam thought their colors defied description; they were like the pictures one saw in dreams, he wrote in his letter to the *Alta*. Twichell's interest in sculling took them to Springfield, Massachusetts, to watch an international regatta. Ten years later he was Clemens' companion on a walking trip through the Alps and the Black Forest, and a tour of Europe, which furnished material for *A Tramp Abroad*. In that book, Twichell appeared as "Harris."

From the Everett House in New York City, Sam sent a few lines to Mary Fairbanks to inform her that he will arrive in Cleveland on November 8. He would like to have her write a review of his opening lecture there on the seventeenth, for he knows he can rely on it not being "slurred over carelessly." He realized, he said, how important it was for this first notice to be well done, and favorable, for it will be widely copied by other newspapers, particularly those in cities where he has engagements, and will serve as excellent advance publicity.

He spent part of a week in New York, looking up old friends. He called on John Garth's mother and sisters in Brooklyn (having had dinner first with the Beechers), hoping to see John and his wife (the pretty Helen Kercheval, of Hannibal, who had also been a schoolmate). After graduating from the University of Missouri, John had joined his father in the family's prospering tobacco business, and had later opened a branch in New York. But Sam just missed them, for John and Helen had gone to Baltimore to live. He also visited the Wileys, who had been neighbors and good friends in Hannibal and later in St. Louis. Sam had heard of Clara Wiley through a close friend of Livy's, who was engaged to marry one of the Wiley boys, and that way obtained her address, he reported home. Clara was very pretty and all the boys very handsome, and Mrs. Wiley and husband, George, looked not a day older than when Sam had last seen them, perhaps twelve years ago. He was replying to a letter from his mother that contained a detailed account of a local murder. He had only just glanced over it, but now "it is midnight & I shall go to bed in a minute & read it there. I like murders— especially when I can read them in bed & smoke."

The following evening he called on the Wileys a second time. According to the recollection of a younger daughter, Margaret, who was doing homework in a corner of the sitting-room, but also listening to the talk, Sam told her father that he was desperately in love with a very beautiful girl who was "unfortunately very rich." She was also "quite an invalid." He had proposed and been refused at least a dozen times. What was George's opinion? George replied with a question: "Sam, are you crazy, to think of such a thing?" Clemens said he was afraid that was what he would say. Sam knew he wasn't good enough for her; knew he was too rough, having knocked about the world for so many years in a careless way. Then tears came into his eyes, and Wiley, seeing that he was in earnest, jumped up, ran over to his chair, put an arm around his shoulder, gave him a shake, and told him to brace up: He wasn't rough, he was a perfect gentleman. No girl in the world was too good for him. "Go for her, and get her, and God bless you, Sam!" —Encouraged, he said he would go and see her right away. "I'll harass that girl and harass her till she'll *have* to say yes!"

He gave his new lecture, "The American Vandal Abroad," in Cleveland, as scheduled. The local *Herald* reported the next day that for nearly two hours he had held the audience captive "by the magnetism of his varied talent," and by his "gorgeous word painting"—all proving that "a man may be a humorist without being a clown."

In the morning he wrote home: "Made a *Splendid* hit last night

& am the 'lion' today. Awful rainy, sloppy night, but there were *1900* people present, anyhow—house *full.* I *captured* them, if I *do* say it myself."

The following evening he spoke at Pittsburgh: "I played against the Eastern favorite, Fanny Kemble. . . . She had 200 in her house, & I had upwards of 1,500. *All* seats were sold, (in a driving rain storm, 3 days ago,) as reserved seats at 25 cents extra. . . . When I reached the theatre they were turning people away. . . ." There were 150 or 200 standees. That night, November 20, he would be taking the train to Elmira, he told his family, for he had an engagement to lecture there.

He reached the Langdon house the next morning, and five days later, on Thanksgiving, he wrote joyously to Mary Fairbanks, heading his letter "Paradise," to say that this was also his personal thanksgiving day. The Langdons, after twenty-four hours of "persecution" from him, had yielded a *"conditional"* consent—and Livy told him that she loved him. But they were not *formally* engaged because Livy must have time to prove to herself that her love was permanent, and he will have to settle down and "create a new & better character," and then live up to it.

"I do *wish* you were here. You see it is a grave matter I have so suddenly sprung upon them, & they are bewildered. And yet they are (sensibly) more concerned about what I am likely to be in the future than what I *have* been in the past. They think you could build up their confidence—I *know* that is why they so wish you were here." (He had not yet learned that the Langdons were indeed very concerned about his past. Shortly Olivia's mother would ask him for a list of character references in California and Nevada.)

"I touch no more spiritous liquors after this day (though I have made no promises)—I shall do no act which you or Livy might be pained to hear of—I shall seek the society of the good—I shall be a *Christian.* I shall climb—climb—climb—toward this bright sun that is shining in the heaven of my happiness until all that is gross & *un*worthy is hidden in the mists & the darkness of that lower earth whence *you* first lifted my [ascend] aspiring feet. Have no fears, my mother. I shall be worthy—yet. Livy believes in me. You believe in me, too, whether you say it or not. I believe in *myself.* I believe in God—& through the breaking clouds I see the star of Hope rising in the placid blue beyond.

"I bow my reverent head. Thy blessing, mother."

The following day he added a postscript to this nearly hysterical outpouring. He was going to leave Elmira that night for Dan Slote's because of Livy's health. She had hardly eaten or slept during the past forty-eight hours, and now resembled a "lovely, peerless, radiant ghost." He begged Mary to come right away: "They want so much to question you about me. *Won't* you?" Sam did not escape unscathed from those hours of intense emotions, either, for his lecture in Elmira was, in his opinion, a "botch," a fact he did not forget easily.

From Dan's he wrote a relaxed letter to Joe Twichell, calling on him to "Sound the timbrel! . . . for I have fought the good fight & lo! I have won! Refused three times—warned to quit once— accepted at last!—and beloved!" Livy felt the "first symptoms last *Sunday*—my lecture *Monday* night, brought the disease to the sur- face—Tuesday & Tuesday night she avoided me and would not do more than be simply polite . . . because her parents had said NO absolutely (almost)—Wednesday they capitulated & marched out with their side-arms." That night, "she said over & over & over again that she loved me but was sorry she did & hoped it would pass away." On Thursday she reversed her position and said she was glad and proud she did love him. On Friday night, when he left, the last thing she told him was that he must be sure to write her "immediately," and just as often as possible. He added, "(Hur- ricanes of applause.)"

Twichell sent congratulations and a benediction ("my very choic- est!") at once. It was the sort of news he would celebrate "by a smiting of my thigh, a grand *pas seul* & three cheers with a tiger!" —a thing he somehow could never manage to execute successfully in the pulpit.

Sam wrote Livy as soon as he reached New York, able at last to free himself from restraint and address her as "My Dear, Dear Livy;" to tell her, "I do, love, *love*, LOVE you"; to send her a thousand kisses and ask for hers in return; and to add four post- scripts, stating in each how much he loves her.

But there was a long way yet to go. Since Mary Fairbanks was unable to come to Elmira, Mrs. Langdon wrote to her on December 1, recounting the "utter surprise and almost astonishment" with which she and Mr. Langdon heard Mr. Clemens declare his love for their "precious" child and how they resented the thought of a stranger "mining" in their hearts for that jewel. She has learned from Charlie, and gathered from Mary's conversation when she was at Elmira, that a great change has come over Mr. Clemens, and that he is entering upon a new way of life with higher and better purposes. What she would like to know, to settle her troubling thoughts, is what his conduct and "habitual life" were like *before* the reformation was undertaken. Will this change, "so desirably commenced," make an immoral man into a moral one? And will entry upon a Christian life transform a worldly man into a spiritual one?

At nearly the same time Livy's mother was writing this letter, which caused her head to become "weary" and her thoughts confused, Sam was sending the news to Pamela: "Now—Private— Keep it to yourself . . . do not even *hint* it, to *any* one—I make no exceptions . . . I love—I *worship*—Olivia L. Langdon . . . & she loves me. When I am permanently *settled*—& when I am a Christian—& when I have *demonstrated* that I have a good, steady, reliable character, her parents will withdraw their objections & she *may* marry me—*I* say she *will*—I intend she *shall*— . . . Her parents have refused to permit the attentions of *any body*, before, but I was mean enough to steal a march on them."

Just before his last visit to St. Louis, he explained, she had refused him, which account for his "savage & crazy" conduct. If the family could only see him now, in his *"natural"* character, they would "love" him. "I drink no spirituous liquors any more—I do nothing that is not thoroughly *right*—I am *rising.*"

In an attempt to make amends for his "persecution" of the Langdons, Sam wrote a letter to Livy's father, which for some reason offended him. He joked about being abstracted during his last visit to them, but his head was so full of thoughts about lecturing, newspaper correspondence, and other matters of a *business* nature, he supposed Mr. Langdon noticed that he did not have much time to spend with the family. "Well, that was because I had to get off in the drawing-room by myself, so I could think about

The Siege of Elmira

those lectures & things. I can always think better when I get off in a drawing-room by myself. So you see how it was. I thought I ought to make this explanation. . . ."

Mr. Langdon's reply followed Sam for nearly three weeks during his lecture tour, and finally overtook him at Charlotte, Michigan. In his response, Clemens acknowledged, "I will not deny that the first paragraph hurt me a little—hurt me a good deal—for when you speak of what I said of the drawing-room, I see that you mistook the harmless overflow of a happy frame of mind for criminal frivolity. This was a little unjust—for although what I said may have been unbecoming, it surely was no worse. . . . But I accept the rebuke, freely, & without offer of defence, & I am sorry I offended as if I had intended offense." In closing, he added ten more names to the list of references—one was Joe Goodman, another was Bret Harte.

He also prepared Mr. Langdon for the responses from the West. He believed much of his conduct in Nevada and California was not of a character to recommend him to the respect of a "high eastern civilization," but it was not considered reprehensible there. He felt he had acted just as Charlie would have, "similarly circumstanced, & deprived of home influences." "We go according to our lights." One thing he was sure of: not one of those men could accuse him of owing a cent, or of not always making his own way without asking help of anyone. "I can tell the whole story myself, without mincing it, & will if they refuse." He then added, "Men as lost as I, have found a Savior, & why not I?"

Through Livy, he "pestered" Mrs. Langdon until she "surrendered" and consented to his coming back on December 17 to stay one day and night, and not a moment longer. He planned to arrive early in the morning to make the most of his visit.

As soon as Mrs. Langdon's approval came, he sent Joe Twichell, his "Hip-hip-Hurrah!" Livy, he informed Joe, wrote to him as though everything was settled and did not beat around the bush. She "goes straight at the appalling subject of matrimony with the most amazing effrontery. I am in honor bound to regard her grave, philosophical dissertations as *love letters,* because they probe the very marrow of that passion, but there isn't a bit of romance in them, no poetical repining, no endearments. . . . Nothing but solid chunks of wisdom, my boy—love letters gotten up on the square, flat-footed, cast-iron, inexorable plan of the most approved commercial correspondence, & signed with stately & exasperating decorum. '*Lovingly, Livy L. Langdon*'—*in full. . . .*" But they were more precious to him than "reams of affectionate superlatives" would be from another woman.

He arrived at the Langdon house at seven o'clock on the evening of December 17, breaking a lecture engagement to do so, and stayed until seven the following night. The atmosphere was more relaxed. Mr. Langdon was no longer feeling affronted—in fact, he was in high good humor, and went about playfully interrupting the lovers' confidences and kisses. Mary Fairbanks' reply to Mrs. Langdon's inquiries had come, and Livy read it to Sam, and reread with special delight the passage in which Mary had said she placed "*full* confidence" in him. Livy then turned to her mother and told her, that was exactly what *she* ought to do. Sam felt certain Mrs. Langdon did, "& it is all owing to your cordial, whole-hearted endorsement of me," he wrote Mary. He will be forever grateful to her for that "saving letter."

He was writing her from Lansing, on Christmas Eve. Midnight had come, so it was then Christmas Day, and he spoke of what had happened "eighteen hundred & sixty nine years ago [when] the stars were shedding a purer lustre above the barren hills of Bethlehem." At first he pictured only the city's crumbling walls, the moldy domes and turrets; the noisy mobs, the demanding relic-peddlers, the greasy monks, and leprous beggars. Yet, as he continued to write, these vanished, and he realized that "Jesus *was* born there, & that the angels *did* sing in the still air above, & that the wondering shepherds *did* hold their breath & listen . . . I am glad, a hundred times glad, that I saw Bethlehem," although at the time reality swept away every "pleasant fancy" he had ever held about it.

For several months, Clemens had been thinking about buying into the *Cleveland Herald* and settling in that city after his marriage. Mary Fairbanks favored the plan: Of course they must live in Cleveland. Beyond friendship, there was an economic reason. Mark Twain's association with the paper in which she and her husband held a half interest would increase its reputation and therefore its circulation. Further, it seemed, they hoped to use Clemens as a tool for buying out their partner and gaining complete control.

But the prospect of moving to Cleveland upset Livy. She admitted to being frightened at the thought of leaving her home and those who had always been a part of her life, and living so far away. It made her sad to think of her parents having to grow used to her absence, and ceasing to miss her. She wanted her father to put his arms around her and keep her near him always. In his reply, Sam, the aspiring Christian, recommended that she "turn toward the Cross & be comforted. . . ."

Since Sam's future seemed to be permanently linked with the East, he suggested to his mother and sister that they consider moving to some small, pleasant community where it would be easier for him to visit. In a letter to them at this time, he told of having looked for such a town as he lectured through western New York. A few weeks later he gave a talk at Fredonia, where he had a remarkably responsive audience, and he was happy "as a lord" from the first word to the last. He thought it was about as good a lecture as he had ever listened to. He was so pleased with those people who had inspired him, and with the town itself, he decided it might be the ideal community for Jane Lampton, and for Pamela and her two children. (Directly after his marriage he rented the Episcopal parsonage for them to see whether they liked living in that pretty village surrounded by vineyards, in the heart of New York's famous grape-producing region.)

In this letter home he gave his lecture itinerary, and instructed the family to address their correspondence simply, " 'Mark Twain, Care Lecture Committee'—my *own* [name] is little known." He could have cleared ten thousand dollars this season if he had been able to sign up with Redpath earlier. Now, he will not make more than two thousand.

Arriving at Cleveland, he found Mary Fairbanks about to publish excerpts from his Christmas letter to her. He protested but she repeated Livy's plea: "I want the public, who know you only as 'the wild humorist of the Pacific Slope,' to learn something of your deeper, larger nature." Mary insisted that the Bethlehem passage did him more credit than his "customary productions." Reluctantly he consented.

As soon as Livy learned about the letter she wanted a copy of the *Herald*. "Poor girl, anybody who could convince her that I was not a humorist would secure her eternal gratitude! She thinks a humorist is something perfectly awful. I never put a joke in a letter without feeling a pang."

Sam was so eager to renounce his past, he begged Livy not to read a word of the Jumping Frog book. "I hate to hear that infamous volume mentioned. I would be glad to know that every copy of it was burned, & gone forever. I'll never write another like it."

Had this near-fanatical desire for reformation and acceptance, personal and literary, continued, the influence of Mary Fairbanks and the Langdons could have strangled his distinctive genius. But it was his wild humor, the very thing they were trying to root out, that saved him. Less than a year later he wrote Livy from the road that he had discovered a new way of relating a favorite anecdote. "This teaches me that a man might tell that Jumping Frog story fifty times without knowing *how* to tell it—but between you & I, privately, Livy dear, it is the best humorous sketch America has produced yet, & I must read it in public some day, in order that people may know what there is in it."

He was tired when he reached Mary's home, and looked forward to a quiet stay, but she and her husband were making the most of their friendship with Mark Twain, and held a succession of receptions and dinner parties at which he was the lion, and was expected also to entertain. On January first, he and Solon Severance planned to spend the entire day making calls—going about in Solon's buggy, as a "temperance Phalanx, to shed a beneficent influence far & wide, over this town," a novel role for Clemens. That night his hosts held a large party, but the guest of honor was too "tired & used up" to enjoy its "sparkle & animation." He left the next day, promising to come back on January 22 and lecture for the benefit of the Cleveland Orphan Asylum. However, he stipulated that he not be called upon to drive out or walk out or visit or receive company at all. He wanted to come away rested and rejuvenated— "like a young giant refreshed with new wine. . . ."

Directly after he left, Mary wrote how much they missed him, and that whenever she felt especially blue, she went upstairs and opened the door of his room "to regale my senses with the still lingering perfume of your cigars." He had ignored Livy's sermons against tobacco, continuing to smoke in private at Cleveland and Elmira, but encouraged her in the more important and challenging work of converting him to Christianity. He kept up her interest and enthusiasm for the task by emphasizing his dependence upon her guidance and support. No matter how hard he prayed, or how often —"night & morning, in cars & everywhere, twenty times a day," he found that the "revealing, religious emotion . . . *will not* come." He was "dark," yet. He saw the Savior "dimly" at times, but the intervals were too far apart. It was a hard road to travel for he is bearing upon his head "a deadly weight of sin . . . such as you cannot comprehend—thirty-three years of ill-doing & wrongful speech." He had damned himself from infancy. He has been praying constantly that God will keep him always free from the "taint" of his misshapen, narrow, worldly fancies—"& keep me always pliant to your sweet influence." She must continue to lead him until the "films" are "cleansed" from his eyes and he can see the light.

After such statements, so foreign to his nature and to his thinking as to be almost ludicrous, there arises the question of sincerity. Certainly he was ably playing a part he felt certain would win the woman he loved and gain the respect of her parents and their friends. But because he was a man of intense emotions, and his consuming passion proved deep and abiding, it is safe to conclude that during the first year he was transformed, and truly believed he craved reformation and conversion to Christianity. His feelings and outpourings were therefore genuine, coming directly from the heart. There is no evidence in any of his words or acts then or ever that he regarded this as a practical marriage for him. In fact he and Livy counted on living in a boardinghouse, supported by his income from lecturing and newspaper work.

Often during this struggle to better himself, he was overwhelmed by self-doubt. Late one night he added a postscript to a thirty-page letter he had written Livy in a joyous mood. It had suddenly come over him that he was making no progress toward a better life, worthy of anyone's faith or hope. "And so forth I drift again into the moonless night of despondency." He had done or said nothing for which he could blame himself, yet in his heart there was only bitterness, hatred for his persisting "wickedness," and contempt for having put such easy trust in his aspirations. He now stands on the earth amongst the graves of his hopes and ambitions, he told her, and in the air all about him are their ghosts. Clouds and thick darkness have been closing the gates of heaven against him. He asked her to pray for him, if she can—"for I cannot."—So he closed that letter, "so happily begun, so sadly ended!" There was no play-acting in these declarations. He was genuinely tormented.

Beyond spiritual salvation, he looked to Livy to cure his "rascally irregular ways," once they were married. He hoped that she would *"civilize"* him and make of him a "model husband & an ornament to society." In his opinion she was perfection on a pedestal, and he seems never to have tried to change her. Only her erratic spelling amused the born speller, and he teased her just as he did his mother. Once he wrote, " 'Sicisiors' don't spell *scissors,* you funny little orthographist. But I don't care how you spell, Livy darling—your words are always dear to me. . . ."

In another letter from the road, he told her he was reading *Gulliver's Travels,* and realized for the first time what a "scathing satire" it was upon the English government. When he had read it in boyhood, "I only gloated over its prodigies & marvels. Poor Swift—under the placid surface of this simply-worded book flows the full tide of his venom—the turbid sea of his matchless hate." If Livy would like to read it, he will "mark & tear it until it is fit for your eyes—for portions of it are very coarse & indelicate." He regretted that he had not "prepared" his copy of *Don Quixote* in the same way; it pained him to think of her reading that book, unexpurgated. If she has not finished it, she must not. "You are as pure as snow, & I would have you always so. . . .

"Read nothing that is not perfectly pure. I had rather you read fifty 'Jumping Frogs' than one Don Quixote." Yet Cervantes' work "is one of the most exquisite books" ever written, and to lose it from the world's literature would be "as the wresting of a constellation from the symmetry & perfection of the firmament—but neither it nor Shakespeare are proper books for virgins to read until some hand has culled them of their grossness. No gross speech is ever harmless."

He warned her not to become "discouraged & unsettled" by the "incendiary words" of feminist Anna Dickinson. He liked Anna, and admired her "grand character," and had again and again made her detractors ashamed of themselves. But he was thankful that Livy is not the sort of woman who would be Dickinson's ideal, and grateful that she never can be.

His lecture schedule was strenuous—a new town every night. Akron, Fort Wayne, Indianapolis, Galesburg, Decatur, Iowa City, Toledo—he listed them for Pamela—then back to Cleveland, to raise money for Mary Fairbanks' favorite charity, the Protestant Orphanage.

"Don't be afraid of giving too much to the orphans, for however much you give, you have the easiest end of the bargain," he told the crowded house. "Some persons have to take care of these sixty orphans, and they have to *wash* them. Orphans have to be washed! And it's no small job, either, for they have only one wash tub and it's slow business. They can't wash but one orphan at a time . . . and by the time they get through with the sixty, the original orphan has to be washed again. Orphans won't stay washed. I've been one myself for twenty-five years and I know. . . ."

Replies to Mr. Langdon's letters of inquiry were now starting to come in from the West, and Livy wrote Sam about them, dwelling on one in particular. In responding, he told her he did not mind anything bad those men may have written, provided it was true. But he was ashamed of that one whose friendship was "so weak & so unworthy" he shrank from saying everything he knew, good or bad. There was "nothing generous in his grieving insinuation—it is a covert stab, nothing better. We didn't want innuendoes—we wanted the *truth*."

Sam had made a great mistake in including so many San Francisco clergymen on his list, in the hope of impressing the Langdons. He believed he could rely on their professed friendship of other days. Two years ago he had written his mother and Pamela that he was "as thick as thieves" with the Reverend Horatio Stebbins. But it was Stebbins who now came "within an ace" of breaking off everything by saying, "Clemens is a humbug . . . a man who has talent no doubt, but will make trivial use of it." He offered the opinion (as did other references) that Sam "would fill a drunk-ard's grave."

But it made Sam proud and happy to have Livy tell him how deeply she resented Stebbins' remarks. He was certain that how-ever black they might paint him, she would steadfastly believe he was not so black now, and never would be again. Then came a second letter while he was still at Cleveland, reaffirming her faith in him. Sensing ultimate victory, he asked Mary to help him select an engagement ring.

About the third of February, Sam returned to Elmira. He re-called late in life that not long after he arrived Mr. Langdon took him aside and showed him the letters. After reading them he could think of nothing to say, and neither could Livy's father. Finally fixing his eye on Clemens, he asked, "What kind of people are these? Haven't you a friend in the world?"

"Apparently not."

"I'll be your friend myself. Take the girl. I know you better than they do."

The Langdons gave their consent to a formal engagement on the following day, and Sam prepared to slip the plain gold ring on Livy's finger—but it would do for a bracelet, he found—or even a necklace. "She is small. There isn't much of her, but what there is, assays as high as any bullion that ever I saw," he told Mary. When he leaves he will borrow one of Livy's rings as a guide, and give it to Mother Fairbanks on his way to lecture at Ravenna, Ohio, on the twelfth. He asked her to attend to having the ring made and en-graved with the date, and then shipped express to Elmira.

Even before writing her the news, he sent word to St. Louis with a salutation that included all: Jane Lampton, Pamela, Orion, Mol-lie, Annie, Sammy, and Margaret (the young woman who helped in the house). He announced that the day before, February 4, he was "duly & solemnly, & irrevocably engaged to be married to Miss Olivia Langdon, aged 231/2, only daughter of Jervis and Olivia Langdon, of Elmira, New York. *Amen.* She is the best girl in all the world, & the most sensible, & I am just as proud of her as I can be . . .

"She had said she never could or would love me—but she set herself the task of making a Christian of me. I said she would succeed, but that in the meantime she would unwittingly dig a matrimonial pit & end by tumbling into it—& lo! the prophecy is fulfilled."

It may be a while before they can marry, because he is not yet rich enough to provide her with a comfortable home, and he will not accept help from anyone.

Sam sensed that Mrs. Langdon still held some reservations about him, and after his lecture at Ravenna he wrote a letter he hoped might banish all lingering doubts about his past. He admitted it was not easy to write so freely, but he must. He spoke of those who knew him in the West as a "profane swearer," without religion, as a man of "convivial" ways, never averse to social drinking, as a "wild" young man, although never a dishonorable one in the "trite" acceptance of that term. But what did those men know of him now? "I never swear; I never taste wine or spirits upon *any* occasion . . . I am orderly, & my conduct is above reproach in a worldly sense . . ." Most important, "I now claim that I am a Christian." The only person in all the world who really knows him is Livy. Not even his own mother and sister know him half so well, for only with his brother Henry had he been in entire sympathy. There are no secrets from Livy, "no locked closets, no hidden places, no disguised phases of character or disposition." He asked Mrs. Langdon to apply to Livy with her questions.

He turned next to a point upon which he was sensitive: Livy's wealth—for she was worth a quarter of a million dollars. He was not interested in her money. So far as he was concerned, Mr. Langdon could cut her off with half a shilling. "To use a *homely* phrase, I have paddled my own canoe since I was thirteen, *wholly* without encouragement or assistance from any-one, & am fully competent to so paddle it the rest of the voyage, & take a passenger along, beside." He spoke of his intention to buy into a reputable newspaper, which would afford them a comfortable living. However, if at any time "we get into trouble we will sell our point lace & eat our shucks in a foreign land, & *fight it out,* but we won't come back & billet ourselves on the old home. . . ."

When he stopped this time in Cleveland, to leave the ring with Mary Fairbanks, he decided that he did not want to be associated with the *Herald,* or with Mary's husband, Abel Fairbanks, whom

Sam had always considered her inferior. She was "a Pegasus har-
nessed with a dull brute of the field; mated but not matched," he
wrote. Clemens suddenly saw through the desire to have him associated with the paper, and the next day he wrote Livy that he
looked more and more favorably on the idea of making their home
in Hartford, and felt less and less inclined to "wed" his fortunes to
"a policy-shifting, popularity-hunting, money-grasping paper like
the . . . *Herald.*"

Turning back from the Middle West, he arranged his lectures so
as to have four days at Elmira. The engagement ring had come,
and as he slipped it on Livy's finger he joked that now she was
manacled, and "a hapless prisoner for life."

Engagement to Livy brought Sam a sense of security, for he was
certain he could count on her steady love. He relaxed, and no
longer tortured himself about becoming a Christian. Immediately
his letters to her became freer, and the language less stilted. On
February 22 he started off to lecture again, traveling as far as New
York City with Mr. Langdon, who was going there on business.
Sam stayed with him a day or two, and reported to Livy in a light
vein which he would never have used before when speaking of her
father.

No, he told her, they did not get to see her young married
friend, Mrs. Brooks, and it was all Mr. Langdon's fault, for he had
acted "very badly" in insisting upon getting a shave before they
called, and that was for no other reason than that he wanted to
"show off." He wanted "to appear better looking than me. That
was pure vanity. I cannot approve of such conduct. . . ." Consequently, by the time they reached her house, Mrs. Brooks had gone
out. He didn't get "much of Mr. Langdon's company (except his
Coal company)," he went on. "I hardly like to tell on him—but
Livy you ought to have seen what sort of characters he was associating with. He had his room full of them all the time." He proceeded to describe the company's board members, managers, and
agents as coal-heavers, pirates, and other notorious characters—all
of them dissolute. Nevertheless, it was pleasant. "The subject of
coal is very thrilling. I listened to it for an hour—till my blood
curdled in my veins, I may say."

Obviously, Sam was feeling more at ease with Livy's father, who had come to admire him, for Jervis Langdon was also a self-made man and appreciated Clemens' rise to fame from humble beginnings. As for Mrs. Langdon, her attitude is best understood from her remark, made in a note to Mary Fairbanks, that "Mr. Clemens," her *"child-elect,"* had brought a "strange, new element" into their midst; and through the diary entry of the keenly observant Annie Adams Fields, the Boston poet, who was visiting the Clemens home some six years later. She wrote: "It is a very loving household though Mrs. Clemens's mother, Mrs. Langdon, hardly knows what to make of him sometimes, it is quite evident."

XXVI

CASTING ANCHOR

WHAT WAS THE character of this beautiful girl who captivated Sam Clemens with her charms, and whom he lured into the
matrimonial trap by wile? There are only a few insights furnished
in her letters before marriage, but these indicate far more depth
than met the eye. It was after she was freed from her circumscribed
homelife that she bloomed. But engagement also made her feel
settled and relaxed, and her letters became more revealing. Once,
in writing Sam about having his family come for the marriage, she
instructed: *"Don't* let your sister stay away from our wedding because she fancies her clothes are not fine enough—We want *her,*
and her daughter here we don't mind about their clothing." When
he conveyed this message to Pamela, Sam told her that Livy cared
nothing about luxuries. "Although she has a respectable fortune in
jewels, she wears none of any consequence." She was perfectly
content with the plain gold engagement ring (which also served as
her wedding ring), "when fashion imperatively demands a two-
hundred dollar diamond one," because she understood that "it was
typical of her future lot—namely, that she would have to flourish
on substantials rather than luxuries." In February, when Sam
wrote Mrs. Langdon that if he and Livy ever got into financial
trouble, they would "fight it out" on their own, those were not just

his ideas—he and Livy had discussed the subject. In such matters she revealed an unsuspected forcefulness of character, tempered by kindliness, generosity, and understanding. She developed a special sympathy for Orion and his misfortunes, and soon after she met him Sam reported to Pamela that he believed Livy was about half in love with their brother.

Sam was to discover that she had inherited her father's good business sense, and during their marriage she began keeping three sets of cash books, capably managing their finances. It was Sam, who, having known poverty and debt all his life, yearned for luxury. After he began to prosper he satisfied this desire with costly houses and furnishings, and a staff of liveried servants. During those years, it was the practical Livy who tried to watch the spending closely and declared that if at any time she found them living beyond their means, they would then either board, or rent a cottage close to the horsecars, so that she could manage without a carriage.

She became interested in improving her education through reading, as seen in Sam's recommendation of Swift and Cervantes (expurgated), and took lessons in German and French. Later she tutored her three daughters until they were ready for high school. After she was married, she lost much of her primness, and nearly all her piety. In less than two years she declared that she felt "almost perfectly cold" toward God, and stopped going to church regularly. Under Clemens' tuition, his 'dear little Gravity," as he called her, even developed an appreciation of the comic, although it never matched his. "She had the heart-free laugh of a girl," which she retained always, Sam wrote. "When it broke upon the ear it was as inspiring as music," and he tried to evoke it as often as possible. He must have intuitively sensed her potential as he came to know her better during their courtship, and realized that her attraction for him was not solely physical.

Early in March he finished his lecture season, and about the fifth of that month settled at Hartford to work on his book again. Plans were afoot for another speaking tour of California and Nevada, which he was not looking forward to, because it meant a three-month separation from Livy. He proposed to go overland this time, with political reporter James H. Riley of the *Alta,* and expected to be in San Francisco by the end of that month. But the book was so far behind schedule, the trip was put off until May. The Blisses, beset with sudden doubts about the wisdom of publishing a humorous work, postponed it repeatedly in favor of others on their list.

Now that Sam would be spending considerable time in Hartford, Livy was very anxious for him to cultivate that part of the Beecher clan living in exclusive Nook Farm, a hundred-acre tract of wooded hills east of town. In 1860 Isabella Hooker, her husband John, who was subject to hypochondria and deep fits of melancholy, and their daughter Alice, stayed in Elmira five months to take Gleason's Water Cure. It was then they met the Langdons, and Alice became a close friend of Livy before her accident.

But Clemens was not eager for further acquaintance with the Hookers, because the outspoken Isabella, who was a rabid feminist and unorthodox Christian, had somehow offended and "humiliated" him deeply when he had been their guest the previous year. Nor was he especially drawn to Harriet Beecher Stowe's husband, the learned Professor Calvin Stowe. Since the age of four, Stowe had been seeing animated figures pass through the ceilings, floors, and walls of houses wherever he lived—not just at night, but by day, and even with other people present. He had one favorite whom he called Harvey, who had a "pleasant face" and had been his friend since childhood. Although "neither of us spoke, we perfectly understood, and were entirely devoted to each other," Calvin explained.

Because Livy had reminded Sam of what she considered his duty, he proposed to call on the Hookers that very evening, he wrote her on March 6. Well—not *the* Hookers, for "I am afraid I shall never feel right in that house," but the Burton branch, founded by Isabella's daughter, Mary, who had married Eugene Burton (younger brother of the family's pastor) and settled near her parents. So he went off in a blustery snowstorm, only to find "the depraved & unreliable Burtons" out—and on such a night. Of course he could have called on the "original branch," but turned back instead to the warmth and comfort of his room at the hotel to continue this letter. "Now hold on, Livy dear—don't ruffle your feathers too soon—don't 'fly off the handle,' as we say in Paris— but hear me out. . . ." All of their life together he would take delight in pretending that Livy was something of a tyrant, and that she kept him terrified. "I'll call on the Hookers or die," he assured her.

He soon made the promised call, taking Joe Twichell along for moral support. The following day he reported to Livy: During their visit, Isabella advanced some theology that distressed and troubled poor Twichell exceedingly. She had construed some "vague" words in Peter to mean that Christ preached and continued to preach to souls in purgatory. As proof she quoted the remark to the thief on the cross, about supping with Jesus in Paradise, in one meaning, equivalent to purgatory. Sam did not say, but she may also have advanced her belief that she was destined to become Christ's deputy on earth, and that women were the superior sex, for in childbearing they, like God, were creators.

Interestingly, it was the Hookers' Victorian Gothic mansion, so distasteful to Sam at this time, that he and Livy rented during the autumn of 1871, over a year after their marriage. And it was at Nook Farm that he seemed to feel most comfortable, for it was an intellectual community, albeit quirky and informal. When William Dean Howells first called on Clemens there he observed that the residents kept perpetual open house, going in and out of one another's places without knocking, and that "nobody gets more than the first syllable of his first name—they call their minister *Joe* Twichell." So it was at Nook Farm that Clemens in his initial flush of prosperity, built on five wooded acres the first of his opulent houses which with land and furnishings, cost $122,000—thus satisfying his love of magnificence.

Fellow humorist Petroleum Vesuvius Nasby (David Ross Locke), who lectured in Hartford early in March 1869, called at Sam's hotel room at ten one night, and they talked and smoked until six in the morning. Sam had gone to hear him talk purposely to criticize, but had found the lecture without a flaw, and Nasby a "first rate" person. He also edited the *Toledo Blade,* which had a huge circulation, and he now urged Clemens to join the staff. Sam asked for time to think it over. He did accept Nasby's invitation to go on to Boston and have "a bit of a time" with him and other literary nabobs in the Hub. It was probably during this visit that Clemens was introduced to Dr. Oliver Wendell Holmes, whose *Autocrat of the Breakfast Table* was favorite reading for him and Livy. The easy, genial style of the imaginary conversations around a Boston boardinghouse table appealed to both, and they passed Sam's copy back and forth, each marking passages they especially enjoyed.

Sam's own book was now in page proofs, and most of the 250 illustrations had been engraved. He refused to let Bliss put in a steel portrait of himself as the frontispiece, for he disliked the "effrontery of shoving pictures of nobodies under people's noses that way, after the fashion of quacks and negro minstrels." He asked that they use instead a woodcut of the *Quaker City* weathering a storm—which was done. The illustrator, one of the best, was True Williams, but because of his addiction to alcohol, it was necessary to lock him in a room with nothing stronger than a pitcher of water to get any work from him. Williams had drawn some fine pictures of Dan Slote, Moses Beach, and others, neatly copied from photographs, Clemens reported to Mary Fairbanks. There were also caricatures of Dr. Andrews (the Oracle), Charlie Langdon (the Interrogation Point), and the "Poet Lariat"—only that picture was clearly not Cutter the poetaster, but an easily recognizable wildhaired Sam Clemens, quill-pen in hand, in the throes of composition. Also included were some imaginary old masters, which Sam considered "rich," for he was still "down on them fellers."

He was searching for a title that would be striking and comprehensive, and sent Bliss two titles for his opinion: "The Innocents Abroad; or The Modern (New) Pilgrims' Progress," or "The Exodus of the Innocents," with the same subtitle. Personally, Sam preferred "The Innocents Abroad."

Shortly after mid-March he was back at Elmira, where he counted on staying until he and Livy had corrected some six hundred pages of proofs. He supposed it would take a month, but wished it might be six months, because working with her had become a kind of courtship. He stayed until April's end, finishing the reading, and deciding definitely on "The Innocents Abroad" as a title that could be easily understood "by farmers & everybody." The subtitle, "The New Pilgrims' Progress," was added at the time of publication. He also wrote the dedication to his mother: "My Most Patient Reader and Most Charitable Critic."

In Hartford again by May 12, once more a guest of the Bliss family in their three-story, stark Italianate mansion, he found that what work there was for him to do was not absorbing enough to keep him from longing fiercely for Livy. She was in his mind constantly, and he felt compelled to write daily, though "the very dearest girl in the world has given me strict orders to go to bed early . . . I had rather write to her than sleep—for, writing to her, it is as if I were *talking* to her—& to talk to her so, is in fancy to hold her tiny hand, & look into her dear eyes, & hear her voice that is sweet as an answered prayer to me, & clasp her pigmy foot, & hold her dainty form in my arms, & kiss her lips & cheeks, & hair & eyes for love, & her sacred forehead in honor, in reverent respect, in gratitude & blessing."

In an attempt to assuage these yearnings he had been taking long nightly walks through the silent, empty streets, but they only made it worse, for every step of the way, every flagstone for miles was spread with "an invisible fabric of thoughts" remaining from last fall when he had tramped these same paths for solace, unable to confess to her (then his sister) his consuming passion. Those uneasy phantoms insisted upon rising before him. The very house he was in (he was thankful it was not the same room) was a constant reminder of those three weeks spent "worshipping" her, pouring out his love in letters he was not allowed to send her.

On his walk that May night he told Livy of having heard the voices of millions of frogs "warbling their melancholy dirge" in the still air; and of having detected the distant long-drawn howl of a dog mingled with it. Then the shadows seemed to grow more somber, and the quiet still more solemn, and "the mysterious murmur of the night-wind more freighted with the shrouded wanderers from the tombs. The 'voices of the night' are always eloquent."

Subconsciously he had deep-rooted fears of losing Livy, and the following day he wrote her about a "scary" dream he had the night before, when she came to him in tears, and said farewell. He knew it was final, and that they were never to see one another again. It had made him feel as though the whole world had dropped from under his feet.

His spirits were high when he wrote her next, and he gave an entertaining account of his misadventures in going to the post office in a rainstorm to mail a letter to her. As he left the house he had grabbed a "seedy old umbrella" from the hall stand, which turned out to be shaped like a funnel and poured eighteen tons of water down the back of his neck before he had walked three blocks. "I had my thin shoes on, & I began to soak up, you know. Barrels & barrels. . . ." After posting the letter, "I bought 4 new numbers of Appleton's Journal & went up town & called on Billy Gross a minute, & went away from there & left my Appletons—& went down to the photographers & ordered a lot of pictures, . . . & came away from there & forgot my umbrella—& then rushed back to Gross's & got my Appleton's—& crossed over & started home & got about 3 miles & a half & recollected the umbrella, . . . & so, turned & tramped back again, damp but cheerful—twice three & a half is nine miles—& *got* my umbrella, & started out & a fellow said, 'Oh, good, it's you, is it?—you've got my umbrella—funny I should find you *here*. And it *was* funny. We had unconsciously swapped umbrellas at the post office, or up a tree, or somewhere, & here ever so long afterward & ever so far away, I find him standing unwittingly by his own umbrella looking at . . . pictures, with my old funnel in his hand. But the moment I picked up his property he recognized it. . . ."

Two days later, he wrote Livy that he could not resist the temptation to send her a line even if he sneeze himself to death before he got through—for he had caught a "perfectly *awful*" cold in the rain that day, and was going to stay in bed out of sheer desperation. When, after several days he got up again, he had no idea how long he had been there. Surely a month had dragged by. The ceaseless "miserere" of the rain made him fretful, depressed, weak, savage, and foolish by turns. He was chafing at being a prisoner for so long, and at being in exile.

It was Mary Fairbanks who kept writing him that for propriety's sake he must leave the Langdons' at the end of April, and taking her advice he had "vamosed the rancho" against the wishes of Livy, her father—who had said it was foolish, and "let the world talk if it wanted to"—and Hattie Lewis. Only Mrs. Langdon failed to agree with the others.

When Sam went, Livy ordered him to come back in "fourteen days by the watch!" In his last letter he had brought up the subject and asked her *when,* but he felt that her reply (perhaps imposed by her mother), was not as warm and imperative as it ought to be. He had expected her to name the day, and say "Come!" In his present depressed mood, he believed that her answer contained an "intimation" that he was not to see her again before he left for California. Was this how he was to be rewarded for his fortitude? It was no small sacrifice to be separated from her for two weeks; now she was as good as threatening him with worse punishment. "Why Livy, I can't go without seeing you. I am only flesh & blood. . . ."

He accepted an invitation to visit "The Elms" at East Windsor Hill, the home of novelist Azel Stevens Roe, thinking he might benefit from a change of scene at that "quaint old country house." Sam had known Roe's son in Nevada and California. From "The Elms" he wrote Livy that young Roe had played the piano for hours during the evening, and they had sung, which ought to have been cheering, only the music had filled Sam with longing for her and for their singing about the piano at Elmira. Admittedly his case was hopeless. The only cure was a return to the Langdons', where, with Livy's help, he finished the last of the proofs on June 5. Going over them again after returning to Hartford, nearly every purple ink correction he came upon brought her vividly before him, because as they read together she made suggestions, and if they seemed valid in view of Eastern standards of literary taste or sense of propriety, he accepted them and made changes.

This was a role she was to fill for the rest of their years together. Their daughter, Susy, who at age thirteen began a biography of her father, told in that work about how he read his book manuscripts aloud to her mother while Susy and her younger sister, Clara, listened, and how afterward he would leave certain parts with Livy, who "expurgated" them. He read aloud the manuscript of *Huckleberry Finn*, which enchanted her and Clara. Afterward, the girls watched their mother carefully as she read the pages left with her, and with what "pangs of regret" they saw her turn down the corners, which meant that some "delightfully dreadful part" must be scratched out. There was one "perfectly fascinating" section they liked especially, and "oh with what dispair" they observed her mark that page. They thought the book would be ruined without it.

Livy wrote her suggestions or comments in the margins, and under them Sam put his agreement, his defense, or his refusal to make any changes. This method avoided personal conflict. In one instance, she wanted "hips" substituted for "hams," which she considered a very unpleasant word. His response was, "I've knocked it all out." She objected to the cat of "shady principle" who had a family in every port. Sam answered, "Then I'll modify him just a little." When she disapproved of his use of "stink" and "offal," words which she wanted to take out of the language, his reply was ambiguous. "You are steadily weakening the English tongue, Livy."

Still, he had his own strict standards which allowed no explicit mention of erotic desires or activity to enter any of his works which were intended for general reading. But there were times when he doubted the fitness of some of his words and phrases from the viewpoint of Eastern taste. When Livy (and her mother and aunt who were both "loyal subjects of the kingdom of heaven") let Huckleberry Finn's complaint, "they comb me all to hell," pass uncensored in the manuscript of *Tom Sawyer,* he was glad, for it seemed a most natural remark for Huck to make, and he had been allowed few such privileges in the book. When his friend and literary mentor, William Dean Howells, whom he asked to read the work, also let it go by unprotested, Sam was glad again—but he also feared that he might have missed it. Nothing would do but to write Howells and call his attention to the word. Since *Tom Sawyer* was now "professedly & confessedly" a story for young people rather than adults, as originally intended, the use of "hell" bothered him nights, he told his friend. Naturally, Howells told him to take it out—"it won't do for the children." Clemens changed it to, "they comb me all to thunder."

Sam stayed at Elmira from late June until early August, feeling inclined to do nothing but pass all his time with Livy. The early stages of love were a kind of lunacy, he observed. He did manage each day when she napped, to devote an hour or so to preparing his lecture for the coming season, working in the cupola where it was breezy, cool, and solitary. He had decided to revise his old Sandwich Islands talk.

In July, his tour of California and Nevada was definitely cancelled. Late that month, *The Innocents Abroad* was published, although it was not until fall that it was widely distributed and began to be reviewed. Then it took off, and 30,000 copies were sold within about three months. Sam was so jubilant he predicted that it would beat Harriet Beecher Stowe's record with *Uncle Tom's Cabin,* which had sold 300,000 the first year. *The Innocents* never came near that figure, but it did sell a satisfactory 85,000 in sixteen months.

Clemens announced to his family that he must follow one success with another, but he had no literary plans. He had written almost nothing that year, for his love affair monopolized all his thoughts and consumed all his energies. This realization made him more eager than ever to affiliate with some newspaper of standing, which he might make as distinguished as Joe Goodman had made the *Territorial Enterprise.* He could then let it support him while he wrote best-selling books.

During the first days of August, acting on Mr. Langdon's advice and with his financial help, Clemens bought a one-third interest in the Buffalo *Express.* Jervis Langdon had reasons, it developed, for wanting his prospective son-in-law to edit the paper. His coal company had important connections in Buffalo, after the forming of the Anthracite Coal Association, whose chief purpose was to maintain high prices. The *Express,* along with other local papers, editorialized frequently against coal monopoly, and Langdon was eager for a policy change. A month after Sam joined the staff, he wrote Livy that another of those "anti-monopoly thieves" had sent in a long advertisement concerning "coal for the people" and expected the *Express* to print it free.

"Do they suppose we print a paper for the fun of it?" he stormed, and deposited the notice in the wastebasket. Ordinarily Clemens was for the "people" and strongly opposed to the exploitative practices, greed, and social irresponsibility of big business. That March he had written an "Open Letter to Commodore Vanderbilt," which had been published in *Packard's Monthly.* He had told the Commodore, "Go and surprise the whole country by doing something right. . . . I don't remember reading anything about you which you oughtn't to be ashamed of. . . ." But it was one of the complexities of Clemens' character that loyalty to persons, especially those who had befriended him in time of need, was far stronger than any intellectual commitment to a principle or cause.

When the reviews of his book began appearing, Sam was for

some reason worried about what the *New-York Tribune* would say. On August 15, he wrote Whitelaw Reid, Greeley's assistant, asking if their reviewer would try to praise the "bad passages & feeble places," because the "meritorious parts can get along themselves, of course." The report left Sam much relieved.

The *Cleveland Herald* gave the book a front-page review, probably written by Mary Fairbanks. It praised the author (whom the critic styled "the laughing philosopher") for not stooping to fractured orthography and syntax for his humor. A delighted Oliver Wendell Holmes expressed his warm admiration in a personal letter thanking Clemens for the complimentary copy. He hoped a hundred thousand books would be sold, as the work deserved.

A review in the *Atlantic Monthly* always carried great weight. The favorable one that appeared had been written by a young man whom Sam was soon to meet and find so congenial that a close friendship was formed almost at once. This was William Dean Howells, a novelist and assistant editor of the magazine. Howells observed that *The Innocents Abroad* was no ordinary book of humor but one that contained a good amount of "pure human nature, such as rarely gets into literature." Nor was the author in a class with the ordinary buffoon, but an "original," a genius, "quite worthy of the company of the best."

When Clemens' first cousin and childhood playmate, Tabitha Quarles, read *The Innocents,* she remarked:

> "Shucks, that's just like Sam all over. That's just the way he used to talk and fool about things when he was a boy. Why, that book was the biggest nonsense I ever read. Imagine Sam standing and weeping over Adam's grave, and stuff like that."

Sam was very unhappy in Buffalo, fretting at separation from Livy. He spent as many weekends as possible at Elmira, with the willing cooperation of one of the paper's co-owners, John Larned— who offered to do the work of both from three o'clock on Friday until Monday noon. Between those times Sam wrote her daily, in moods of gloom and self-doubt, or in joyous ones, but always pining to hold her in his arms. In one letter he hated himself for having refused to wear a boutonnière of tuberoses she had made for him when he was home last. In his experience, the only men he had ever seen wearing flowers were such eccentrics as San Francisco's Emperor Norton. He had forgotten that Charles Dickens wore a bright red flower the night Sam and Livy heard him read. But he would *learn* to wear flowers because she wants him to—but only in the house, as yet, for he has "such an invincible repugnance to show or display in a man's dress." These were strange words coming from someone who would shock Boston, and embarrass his friends, just four months later by appearing on the streets in a long sealskin coat and Cossack hat, fur side out.

He now asked James Redpath to free him from lecturing during the coming season.

To Livy he professed disappointment when his manager replied that he could not cancel engagements in Boston and several other New England towns. At heart he was relieved at the prospect of escaping from a job that was already boring and irksome. Reversing himself, he then told Redpath to let him out "to lyceums far & near, & for half the winter or all of it—do with me as he chooses while the lecture season lasts." He justified his contrary stand by telling Livy, "It isn't worth the bother of getting well familiarized with a lecture & then deliver it only half a dozen times." Further, "I ought to have some money to commence married life with."

Livy wanted to wait until spring to be married, but Sam refused to postpone it that long. They discussed it when he was at Elmira at the end of August and decided to set the date for February 4, exactly one year after their engagement. In his next letter he told her, "I am as happy as a king, now that . . . I can count the exact number of days that are to intervene before we are married."

Charlie Langdon, still sowing wild oats, was being sent on another trip, this time around the world. He was leaving on October first, and in telling Mary Fairbanks about the tour, Sam admitted to feeling an itching in his feet. If his life were as aimless as before, his trunk would be already packed. Charlie was traveling this time with Professor Darius Ford, from Elmira's Female College (of which Jervis Langdon was a founder and trustee). For a number of years Ford had been Livy's tutor, and was the villain in a nightmare Sam had earlier at Hartford. In the dream Livy was sitting in the drawing-room, discussing "the properties of light, & heat, &

bugs" with Ford. A maid had brusquely refused Sam admittance: he was not permitted to interrupt the "philosophy" lesson. What had so upset him was that he was told those orders had come directly from Livy. He relived that feeling of hurt and despair many times afterward.

As Charlie started off overland for the Nevada mines, San Francisco, Yosemite, and then the Orient and the Holy Land, Clemens had to content himself with making the trip by proxy. He arranged to run a series of travel letters, "Around the World," in the *Express*, to be written jointly with Ford. The first letter, describing Mono Lake, which he and Calvin Higbie had visited in their Esmeralda days, was entirely Sam's, and was used later in *Roughing It*. Of the dozen letters printed in the paper, only two contained material supplied by the professor.

Sam gave his opening lecture in Pittsburgh at the end of October, and on November 10 he appeared in Boston. The talk was a "handsome success," he wrote Livy and enclosed a clipping from the *Advertiser:* "Boston had a very novel . . . sensation last evening in the shape of a lecture from Mr. Samuel L. Clemens . . . known to fame as the humorist Mark Twain. Known to fame, we say, for who that breathes the vital air of America has not heard of the jumping frog of Calaveras County. . . .

"Mr. Clemens is a very good looking man. He is of medium height and moderately slender build, has light brown hair, a reddish brown moustache, regular features, a fresh complexion; and he has a queer way of wrinkling his nose and half closing his eyes when he speaks. The expression of his face is as calm and imperturbable as that of the sphinx. Looking at him you . . . might suppose him incapable of a joke, if it were not for the merry twinkle in his eyes. His voice is remarkably light and remarkably dry . . . and it seems . . . modulated to only two keys. . . . He delivers his sentences without haste, and in a tone of utter indifference." He used the rising inflection at the start, middle, and end of his sentences. That inflection, the reviewer noted, was not native. Although the text contained a great deal of "genuine and irresistible humor," it would not be "nearly so funny to read as to hear it from Mark Twain's lips."

The following day Sam bought himself a "full wedding outfit" and afterward had not a cent left. The boxes would be coming by express to Elmira, he told Livy, and asked to have her mother unpack them and put the things away. But they must be sure not to let Mr. Langdon go wearing them around. "I tell you they are starchy."

Through the rest of November and all of December he lectured nearly every night with equal acclaim: "Harrington's Opera House was filled last evening with an intelligent and appreciative audience, all of whom had heard of the celebrated Mark Twain and were anxious to see what he was like and whether his tongue held pace with his pen," wrote the Providence *Herald*. His talk was a superb mixture of "sense and nonsense, the dryest humor, bits of fine word painting, and covert satire." It would be impossible "to give the faintest idea of the lecture on paper. Written or spoken by another it would lose half its points and value. We can only congratulate those who heard him, and pity those who did not. . . ."

"Livy my peerless, I had a packed house in New Britain last night," he wrote. At Meridian, he struck upon a new manner of telling a favorite anecdote; without changing a word, it became so absurd he had to laugh, himself. He tried it again at New Britain, and got to one particular point three different times before he could get by it and go on. "Every time I lifted my hand aloft & took up the thread of the narrative in the same old place, the audience exploded & so did I. But I got through it at last, & it was very funny." Now he would try telling the Jumping Frog.

He was still beset by fears of losing Livy and had another *"vivid, vivid"* dream about coming to Elmira and finding a very attentive young man always at her side. She seemed to ignore Sam, who understood that this was a rejected lover who had returned at a time when Clemens was absent, convinced he could regain Livy's affections. The young man was successful, and without a backward glance, she ran off with him, leaving Clemens "prostrate upon the floor."

He stopped in Hartford on November 24 to ask Joe Twichell to stand by and assist the Langdons' pastor, Thomas Beecher, in marrying them. "It's powerful expensive, but then we'll charge him for his board while he is there," he joked. Twichell was to be his representative in the ceremony. Sam loved him, he said, a feeling he could not muster for a Beecher even though he had characterized Henry Ward as a "brick."

While at Hartford he discovered one result of his sudden, sweeping popularity in New England. In June he had approached the *Daily Courant,* Connecticut's leading newspaper, with a proposition to buy into it. His offer had been coldly rejected. Now, when Sam met Charles Dudley Warner, a co-owner and editor, and resident of Nook Farm, he talked himself into a "glow" over what *they* could do with the paper since Clemens had gained so much popularity. A few weeks later, just before a lecture at New Haven, Sam spent two hours in Hartford, "bumming" around with Twichell. While walking down the street, they came on a democrat wagon carrying Isabella Hooker, her daughter Alice (as beautiful as ever), and Mrs. Charles Dudley Warner. They "all assailed me violently on the Courant matter," and insisted it was no longer a private desire but a public demand that he join the paper. In her positive way, Isabella told him that Warner and co-owner Joseph Hawley would do absolutely *anything* to get him there, a statement Mrs. Warner did not deny. Mrs. Hooker added that she had written to Jervis Langdon in an effort to "make" him sell out of the *Buffalo Express.* To sell now, Sam told Livy, he would lose money and incur another large debt. The only gain would be the pleasure of living at Hartford. He admitted that it afforded him a "malicious satisfaction" to have them all begging, and to contrast it with the "insultingly contemptuous indifference" with which the same matter had been treated in June—*"by every one of them."* He knew that revenge was wicked and unbecoming—"but it is powerful sweet anyway."

In mid-December the Langdons went to New York City for a week or so while Livy selected her trousseau, staying as usual at the St. Nicholas. Sam saw her there briefly every day, and learned about the interest Mr. Langdon took in the shopping, going around with her while she tried on dresses and suits. Then, when the purchases were delivered to their rooms, even if late at night, he would not go to bed until he had opened each package and seen that everything was right. This unusual attitude so touched Livy that tears came into her eyes while she was telling Sam. Basking in the devotion of her parents, and in Sam's love, which she knew was likewise "true and steady," she was often so overjoyed she had to express her emotion by dancing about and singing, she said to him. These outlets seemed to her the most sincere and "natural," for one's whole being entered into them.

While lecturing around New England Sam kept his "handsome" room at Young's Hotel, on Court Avenue in Boston, preferring the hour or two train ride after his talk to staying over as a guest in some private home. Unlike the Southern hospitality he knew, the rule for New England hospitality was for the hosts "to make *themselves* comfortable *first*, & leave the guest to get along *if he can*. *No smoking allowed on the premises.*" It was unpleasantly reminiscent of Isabella Hooker. "The next New Englander that receives me into his house will take me as I *am*, not as I ought to be. To curtail a guest's liberties & demand that he . . . come up to the host's peculiar self-righteous ideas of virtue is . . . contemptible." By returning to his Boston hotel, he likewise escaped the customary grand tour of the town, made the next morning in "a freezing open buggy." The sights never varied—the mayor's house, and the ex-mayor's, the home of the state senator, the cemetery, the public school with its "infernal" architecture, the park—or the place where it was going to be, in which case he was obliged to sit and shiver as he stared at "a melancholy grove of skeleton trees," while he listened to a rush of statistics.

On one of his days in Boston, he called on William Dean Howells to thank him for his review of *The Innocents Abroad.* In the *Atlantic Monthly*'s little office above the bookstore of Ticknor & Fields, Sam Clemens loomed imposing in the sealskin coat and hat. Howells never forgot that first sight of him, and admired his courage in defying traditional male attire. With his "crest" of dark red hair, and "the wide sweep of his flaming mustache, Clemens was not discordantly clothed in that sealskin coat." A little later, Howells accompanied the coat down New York's Broadway, and "shared the immense publicity" it won Clemens.

On another day in Boston, he posed for a group portrait with Petroleum V. Nasby and Josh Billings (penname of Henry Wheeler Shaw), who were also Redpath's speakers. Both Nasby and Billings were at their height of fame. Although rivals, all three remained good friends and spent most of their days in Boston at Redpath's office, smoking and talking shop. Then, in the early evening they would scatter out among the towns to speak. Not long before his death, Clemens recalled that during the forty years when he was playing professional humorist before the public, he had for company at least seventy-eight other American humorists, all conspicuous and popular, whose sayings were in everybody's mouth. Each one had vanished by 1906, when he was remembering, and he knew the reason: They were "merely" humorists, and "humorists of a 'mere' sort cannot survive. Humor is only a fragrance, a decoration." Frequently it was just an "odd trick" of speech or spelling, as in the case of Ward, Billings, and Nasby. Then the fashion changed, and their fame passed with it. Explaining his own lasting popularity, he said: "Humor must not professedly teach and it must not professedly preach, but it must do both if it would live forever. By forever, I mean thirty years. . . . I have always preached. That is the reason I have lasted thirty years." If the humor came of its own accord he gave it a place in the "sermon," but "I was not writing the sermon for the sake of the humor. I should have written the sermon just the same. . . . "I am saying these vain things in this frank way because I am a dead person speaking from the grave." He was modest in his estimate of thirty years. His fame remains undiminished, and he has achieved immortality as we know it, by his method.

Shortly before Christmas Sam wrote Livy from Boston that Joe Goodman was in New York, and that he was sending him on to Elmira. He hoped Joe would not get "tight" while in the "States," but would not be surprised if he did. "But he is a splendid fellow, anyhow."

On Christmas Day, he reminded Livy that "it is just a year ago to-day since I quit drinking all manner of tabooed beverages, & I cannot see but that I have fared considerably better in consequence. . . . But all that goes to *your* credit, not mine. I did not originate the idea." But her most recent crusade, to get him to stop smoking for health reasons, he resisted. There are no arguments, he countered, that can convince him that moderate smoking is "deleterious" to him. He has smoked habitually for twenty-six of his thirty-four years, and is the only healthy member of his family. He conveniently ignored those heavy chest colds he contracted regularly. Just a few weeks ago he had cancelled a lecture because he was "killed up" with a cold, and suffered from a sharp pain in his breast. But now he could strengthen his defense with the report of the health insurance doctor, who pronounced him free from all disease and "*remarkably* sound." Yet, he was the supposed victim of this "fearfully destructive habit of smoking." He cited Orion, a teetotaler and non-smoker, whose health has run down instead of *up*. And there is his mother, who smoked a pipe for thirty years and has lived to be sixty-seven. Of course, if Livy desires it, he will give up this habit "so filled with harmless pleasure." He reminded her that he had given up the "mean" habit of chewing tobacco because his mother desired it, that he had stopped swearing because Mary Fairbanks desired it, and that he stopped drinking because she desired it. He has also done what he could to remember to keep his hands out of his pantaloon pockets, to quit "lolling at full length" in easy chairs, and to reduce his slang and his "boisterousness" a good deal, because she wanted him to.

In effecting her reforms, Livy never nagged, Sam said. She had a way of "swindling" him into believing she was doing him a favor rather than curtailing his freedom. Still, those lessons were recalled when he came to write *Huckleberry Finn*. In its opening pages Miss Watson, aiming to "sivilize" the hero, says, "Don't put your feet up there, Huckleberry," and "Don't scrunch up like that, Huckleberry—set up straight. . . ."

Sam was aware that in the use of tobacco and the drinking of even so mild a beverage as ale, Livy was working on behalf of her parents, and the proof came only a few months after their marriage. One evening Mr. Langdon asked him if he and Livy would not like to take a trip to Europe. Sam said he would, if he could afford it. His father-in-law then told him that if he would stop smoking, and stop drinking the glass of ale he was taking before bed to induce sleep, he would give him ten thousand dollars and the European trip beside. Clemens replied, "Thank you, sir, this is very good of you, and I appreciate it, but I can't sell myself. I will do anything I can for you or any of your family, but I can't sell myself."

For a while, he did limit his smoking to Sundays from three to five o'clock, to humor Livy, but as soon as he started to write *Roughing It*, he found he must have a cigar to steady his nerves. "I began to smoke, and I wrote my book; but I couldn't sleep and I had to drink ale to go to sleep," he told Annie Adams Fields. "If I had sold myself, I couldn't have written my book, or I couldn't have gone to sleep, but now everything works perfectly well." From that time on, he kept to his monthly quota of three hundred cigars, limiting himself only by his own rule not to smoke more than one cigar at a time.

He spent four days with Livy at New Year's, and little else was talked about but the coming wedding, which had been moved to February second instead of the fourth. He now sent Pamela a check for one hundred dollars to pay her and Annie's railway fare. Jane Lampton had evidently taken to heart Sam's earlier warning that to cross the country in mid-winter would be equivalent to "murder & arson & everything else," for she decided to stay home. He told Pamela that Mrs. Langdon wanted them to come by January 24 or 25, to enable them to visit. They were not to worry about clothes, he repeated. "*Purchase no outfit.* Come as you are."

On January 20 he wrote the final letter in a correspondence that had lasted seventeen months (daily letters for over a year), because the next night he would be home after his concluding lecture for the season. He was at Hornellsville, sixty miles away. On account of houseguests, he had orders for Livy: If he was not to sleep in his regular room, she must go in there, burrow into those pasteboard boxes stacked in the wardrobe, take out a new shirt, undershirt, and drawers, and lay them on the bed in whichever room he was to occupy. Then she must leave him a note in the newspaper box by the side gate, telling him how to get in and what bedroom to take. He had no desire to repeat Orion's midnight adventure when he mistakenly slipped into bed with Dr. Meredith's two elderly maiden sisters.

"This is the last long correspondence we ever shall have, my Livy—& now on this day it passes forever from its honored place among our daily occupations, & becomes a *memory,*" he closed.

From the Langdon house he wrote to Jim Gillis of Jackass Gulch, on January 26, evidently in reply to a letter from him, for Sam opened:

"I remember that old night just as well! And somewhere among my relics I have your remembrancer stored away. It makes my heart ache yet to call to mind some of those days.—Still, it shouldn't—for right in the depth of their poverty & their pocket-hunting vagabondage lay the germ of my coming good fortune. You remember the one gleam of jollity that shot across our dismal sojourn in the rain & mud of Angel's Camp—I mean that day we sat around the tavern stove & heard that chap tell about the frog & how they filled him with shot. And you remember how we quoted from that yarn & laughed over it out there on the hillside—while you & dear old Stoker panned & washed. I jotted the story down in my note-book that day & would have been glad to get ten or fifteen dollars for it—I was just that blind." But then he published the tale and it became widely known around the world, he told Jim. The reputation it brought him opened the way to make thousands and thousands of dollars since. Having heard the frog story was another of those accidents which made up his life.

Where was Dick Stoker and what was he doing, Sam wanted to know. How he would love to see Stoker again as "Rinaldo." Jim must give him Sam's "fervent love and warm old remembrances."

A week from that day he would be married to a girl even better than Mahala, and lovelier than the "peerless" Chaparral Quails, Nelly and Molly Daniels. Mahala has not been identified, but "mahala" was a California Indian word meaning woman, one of their own. Sam gave the name of his prospective wife, because he knew Jim would like to know. He was aware that Gillis would be unable to come to the wedding, but cordially invited him and Dick anyway, assuring them of a royal welcome if by some chance they would be able to get there.

In a postscript, Sam asked: "Do they continue to name all the young Injuns after me—when you pay them for the compliment?"

He relived those days of complete freedom with Jim and Dick the next year, when he was finishing *Roughing It,* and gave immortality to both. He continued to correspond with Jim, but did not visit Jackass Gulch or Jackass Hill again, except in memory.

Pamela and Annie arrived well ahead of the wedding date, giving them the opportunity to get acquainted with Livy. Then Mary Fairbanks came, and next Joe and Harmony Twichell. Altogether there were about a hundred guests assembled in the Langdons' drawing rooms at seven o'clock on the evening of February second. Blazing chandeliers and arrangements of flowers gave light and cheerfulness to the ordinarily dark parlors. Livy was beautiful in a white satin gown and long white veil. Clemens was elegant in what he called his "trousseau," the outfit that had impoverished him. Mrs. Fairbanks, the only reporter present, covered the wedding for her paper, but was reticent in giving details. She did believe, however, that the public had the right to learn that "Mark Twain" filled "the role of bridegroom with charming grace and dignity."

After the wedding supper, which included boned turkey (the only dish anyone remembered) with cider and other temperance beverages, there was dancing. The following day, Sam and Livy, accompanied by relatives and a small group of wedding guests, boarded a private railroad car for the trip to Buffalo. Before leaving on his last lecture tour, Clemens had arranged with the Langdon Company's Buffalo agent, J. D. F. Slee, to select a suitable boardinghouse for him and Livy, within their means.

On the train, Sam entertained the party by singing an old British folk ballad, learned from Mississippi raftsmen, which had fourteen verses. "I was great in that song," he admitted. It began:

> *There was a woman in our town,*
> *In our town did dwell,*
> *She loved her husband dear-i-lee,*
> *But another man twyste as well.*
>
> *Singing too, riloo, riloo, riloo,*
> *Ri-too, riloo, rilay—e,*
> *She loved her husband dear-i-lee,*
> *But another man twyste as well. . . .*

His niece Annie, tolerant as she was of her Uncle Sam, did not think it was especially appropriate to the occasion. There is no record of what Mrs. Langdon thought.

Clemens had already given Thomas Beecher a generous fee for his services, but during the trip he went up and down the aisle asking for donations in small change. After he had collected one dollar he handed it to Beecher openly, wanting everyone to think this was the extent of his payment. Beecher played his part,

Casting Anchor

thanked Sam profusely, and then turning to his wife, said in a ringing voice, "Mrs. Beecher, until January first you received the salary and I the wedding fees, but since January first you have had the fees and I . . . the salary. Here, Mrs. Beecher, this is yours."

Upon arriving at the Buffalo depot, good-nights were said as the party separated. The Langdons, with Pamela and Annie, climbed into one waiting sleigh, the rest into others, supposedly bound for the hotel. Sam and Livy were the last to be accommodated. The idea of leaving the bride and groom to the very last infuriated Sam. He had never seen anything so badly managed. Then, after what seemed an interminable ride, the driver stopped in front of a three-story brick mansion on fashionable Delaware Avenue. Clemens knew this was the wrong place. People who lived in houses like that didn't take in boarders, he stormed. But Livy assured him that this was the correct address, and while they were climbing the steps to the front door, it opened and there stood Livy's parents, and Pamela and Annie.

It was very hard to make Sam understand what was happening —that this was his house, bought and furnished for him by Jervis Langdon, and decorated in their favorite colors under Livy's direction. It had cost $40,000 cash, and included a stable, a horse and carriage, and three servants, Clemens wrote Will Bowen a few days later. When Mr. Langdon handed Sam a box containing the deed, and a check to help him run the establishment, he announced himself the victim of a "first-class swindle." He was dazed and still somewhat incredulous as Livy showed him the house—their upstairs room dominated by a low, wooden bed, with a canopy and curtains of light blue satin, and bedspread and drapes of the same material and color; and Sam's study, upholstered to his taste in scarlet. She introduced him to the cook, housemaid, and butler-coachman. The drawing room, also done in pale blue satin, was the final surprise. When Sam walked in the rest of the wedding party, who had been secreted there, burst upon him to shake his hand and congratulate him, and to kiss and hug Livy. It was remembered that he was speechless—"for a minute."

All at once they noticed that the Reverend Thomas Beecher was lying on the blue carpet, rolling over and over. "Whatever *are* you doing, Mr. Beecher?'' his wife asked. ''I am trying to take the feather edge off,'' he replied solemnly. While they were all gathered there, Mrs. Beecher suggested that they sing together, ''Heaven is my Home.'' Afterward, they went in to supper.

When Sam came to express gratitude for all Livy's father had done, he was quite overcome. There were tears in his eyes, and he had trouble controlling his voice. At first he could say only a word or two at a time, telling him he didn't know how to thank him and supposed he never would be able to. But after a little he recovered his usual poise and spirit, and said:

''Mr. Langdon, whenever you are passing through Buffalo—it doesn't matter how often or at what time, you can come right here and stay with us as long as you like—and it won't cost you a cent!''

When writing to Dan De Quille about his marriage, he concluded with an account of Mr. Langdon's present. ''I have read those absurd fairy tales in my time, but I never, never, never expected to be the hero of a romance in real life as unlooked for & unexpected as the wildest of them.'' He told the story of ''what happened to Little Sammy in Fairy Land when he was hunting a Boarding House,'' to everyone he took on a tour of what he called the ''palace,'' and he wrote of it to Will Bowen and other longtime friends.

He said to Will that Livy was the ''most beautiful girl I ever saw (I said that before she was anything to me, & so it is worthy of all belief) & she is the *best* girl, & the sweetest, & the gentlest, & the daintiest, & the most modest & unpretentious, & the wisest in all things she should be wise in & the most ignorant in all matters it would not grace her to know, & she is sensible & quick & loving & faithful, forgiving, full of charity. . . . She is the very most perfect gem of womankind that ever I saw in my life—& I will stand by that remark till I die.''

That view of her did not change with the passage of thirty-four years. They managed in spite of declining health, personal tragedies in the death of two children (a son, their first-born, who died before he was two; and their second child, Susy, brilliant and talented, who died at age twenty-four), and financial failure, to keep their love fresh.

Casting Anchor

. . .

The early years of marriage, before the dark clouds gathered, brought Sam Clemens great happiness, and the peace of mind necessary for extended creative work. Seven months after he and Livy were married, he began a major book, *Roughing It,* the long-deferred account of his experiences in the Far West, which he completed the next year. This was followed by *The Gilded Age,* a novel, written with the essayist and editor, Charles Dudley Warner. The idea was Warner's, but Clemens gave the book realism by including many episodes from the Clemens family story, and by the creation of the characters Washington Hawkins, based on Orion Clemens, and Beriah Sellers, whose original was Sam's visionary cousin, James Lampton.

Life with Olivia Langdon wrought no radical changes in Sam, nor did it place unreasonable restraints upon him as has been claimed. It did not suppress that pleasure he derived from ribaldry, and six years after his marriage he wrote *1601* expressly for Joe Twichell, putting into the mouths of his characters "grossness not to be found outside of Rabelais, perhaps," he believed. He remained a skeptic in religious matters after that agonizing effort to become a Christian; and it was not long until he forgot Mother Fairbanks' injunctions and resumed his flow of imaginative swearing at every real or fancied provocation. Within two years he was drinking Scotch whiskey toddies before going to bed; taking wine with his dinner, and ale between times, but with one difference— he did not get drunk. He may have no longer carried his hands in his trouser pockets, or lolled at full length in easy chairs, but he gave no second thought to lying on the floor while he talked with such illustrious guests as Annie and James Fields. Nor did he feel obligated to curb an impulse one night after they had settled at Nook Farm, to come limping into the drawing room, wearing his cowhide slippers with the hair side out, and mimic to perfection, in front of a crowd of guests in evening dress, the speech and actions of an old, black "uncle." He remained a youth to the end of his days, his friend Howells said of him. He had "the heart of a boy with the head of a sage; the heart of a good boy, or a bad boy, but always a wilful boy. . . ."

For nearly three years after his marriage he was free of the restlessness that had tormented him since he was seventeen. But by 1874, he began to find the responsibilities of a celebrity irksome, and at times, overwhelming. Apart from public demands, these included acting as host and entertainer for throngs of houseguests and visitors, invited and uninvited, who flocked to his mansion at Nook Farm. Although it was deeply satisfying after a life of poverty and debt, to be able to live and entertain lavishly (for he was making large sums from his lecturing and his books), his creativity commenced asserting itself and demanding solitude. Then he began yearning for escape (with Livy) to the South Seas, to Europe—any place (preferably rural) that was far from "the rush & roar & discord of the world."

In the summer of 1874, his wish for a spot in the country was granted, and he moved with Livy, Susy, then two, and their new baby, Clara, to Quarry Farm, on the heights above Elmira. It was the home of Livy's older, adopted sister, Susan Crane, who had built for him "the loveliest study . . . you ever saw," Sam wrote Joe Twichell. "It is octagonal, with a peaked roof, each octagon filled with a spacious window." It commanded a view of nearby trees and flowered grasslands; of the Chemung River valley, and the retreating ranges of far-off blue hills. In whichever direction he looked Sam saw something that pleased him. It was a "cosy nest," he told Twichell, with just room enough for a round table, a small sofa, and three or four chairs. It had a fireplace for crisp, fall days. "And when the storms sweep down the remote valley and the lightning flashes above the hills beyond, and the rain beats upon the roof over my head, imagine the luxury of it!" It was a situation to stimulate recollections of Hannibal's woods and meadows; of Holliday's Hill, and the Mississippi.

That summer, perched in complete isolation, and far from all human sounds, he returned to his boyhood, and began writing *The Adventures of Tom Sawyer*. The old life swept by him like a panorama, he said; the old days trooped by in all their glory again. Old faces peered out of "the mists of the past; old footsteps have sounded in my listening ears; old hands have clasped mine, old voices have greeted me, & the songs I loved ages & ages ago have come wailing down the centuries!"

Casting Anchor

For Samuel Langhorne Clemens, marriage marked the end of the most important period in his development as a writer. The genius of "Mark Twain" was at its height after the long apprenticeship, and he was ready to produce two masterpieces—the book about Tom Sawyer, and its sequel, the richer and greater *Adventures of Huckleberry Finn.*

Notes and Sources
Consulted and Quoted

The largest and most important collection of primary source material on Samuel L. Clemens and his immediate family is in the Mark Twain Papers, housed in The Bancroft Library, University of California, Berkeley. This contains original letters to his mother; to his sister; to his brother Orion and his wife, Mollie; and to Olivia Langdon, the young woman who became his wife, both courtship letters and ones written after their marriage. There are, as well, letters to close friends and to Clemens' publishers. Also in the collection are Sam's notebook-journals; literary manuscripts, both published and unfinished; autobiographical writings and dictations; drawings by Clemens; scrapbooks holding clippings of his newspaper correspondence, articles, and squibs; reviews of his lectures; and other related material. There are, as well, daguerreotypes, photographs, and portraits of Sam Clemens and his family, and of those who were a part of his life; and objects associated with him.

Of equal importance to this interpretation of Clemens, was the even larger collection of his letters to his family for the years covering 1853 into 1870, which are held by the Vassar College Library, Poughkeepsie, New York.

Valuable in rounding out the picture of Sam Clemens during his Nevada mining days, particularly in following his activities, is his correspondence with the young attorney William H. Clagett, then also in Nevada. One of Clemens' letters to Clagett contains the highly important solution to the mystery surrounding Sam's sixty-mile walk into the wilderness, just before he went to work for the *Territorial Enterprise.* These letters are in the Clifton Waller Barrett Library, University of Virginia, Charlottesville.

Letters from these three collections can now be read in the new scholarly edition, *Mark Twain's Letters Volume 1: 1853–1866.*

Another valuable source is Clemens' correspondence with Mary Mason Fairbanks. These letters not only furnish insight into personality and character, but follow his activities during late 1867 through the early 1870s. The manuscripts are in the Huntington Library, San Marino, California, but have been published by the Huntington, as *Mark Twain to Mrs. Fairbanks.*

Five of Clemens' letters to his former schoolmate Will Bowen of Hannibal, written from May 1866 to February 1870, show still another facet of Sam's personality. They are part of a collection of sixteen letters in the University of Texas Library, Austin, and can be read in printed form as *Mark Twain's Letters to Will Bowen.*

A rich fund of family recollections, especially those of Sam Clemens' niece Annie Moffett, who had an accurate memory, are contained in the book *Mark Twain, Business Man,* edited by Annie's son, Samuel Charles Webster. This work includes interesting personal letters, a few not found elsewhere.

With regard to Clemens' published autobiography, the reader is referred to Charles Neider's edition because the material has been arranged chronologically and includes parts of the memoirs omitted by Paine. However, Paine's work is arranged as Clemens desired and includes material left out by Neider.

All sources are listed in order of their use in each chapter. Manuscript collections are identified as:

MTP   Mark Twain Papers (University of California)
V   Vassar College
UV   University of Virginia

Printed sources are identified as:

MTBM   *Mark Twain Business Man*

Note: All letters to Will Bowen and to Mary Mason Fairbanks are found in their published forms, cited above.

1. *Beginnings*, pp. 1–16.

Samuel L. Clemens described the village of Florida and its inhabitants in his autobiographical writings found in his published *Autobiography*, in *The Gilded Age*, and in *Adventures of Huckleberry Finn*. In his *Autobiography* he also gave details of his uncle John Quarles' store. Jane Lampton's first impression of the newborn Sam was recalled in her letter of January 7, 1885, to Olivia Clemens (MTP). Planting by signs, a practice still in use in many Southern mountain villages, is covered in *The Foxfire Book 1*. Sallie K. Gilbert, a daugther of Appalachia, enlarged on this subject and also talked about omens and ghosts, in long conversations with the writer. Clemens, through his character Huck Finn, is a further source for "haints," witches, spells, fear of the dark, and acts certain to bring bad luck. This version of Clemens' remark about going out with Halley's Comet is quoted by Dixon Wecter in *Sam Clemens of Hannibal*. "There's a contribution in him from every ancestor . . ." is found in Clemens' *The American Claimant*. Return I. Holcombe, *History of Marion County* was consulted for information about grandfather Samuel B. Clemens, which was supplied Holcombe by Orion Clemens, who obtained it from his mother. C. O. Paullin's "Mark Twain's Virginia Kin," and "The Moorman Family of Virginia" were also referred to. Information about the young John Marshall Clemens, furnished by Jane Lampton, was found in Holcombe. Sam Clemens' account of the Lampton (Lambton) family and their kinship with the Earl of Durham, was based on Jane Lampton's narrative and is found in his *Autobiography*. In a sketch of his mother, written by Orion Clemens right after her death, he spoke of her fame as a beauty and as a dancer, and told about the Christmas balls she attended with her sister. This sketch was published in Walter Blair, *Mark Twain's Hannibal, Huck & Tom*. Doris and Samuel Webster's "Whitewashing Jane Clemens" is a valuable and illuminating study. There we are told about her appearance at the theater; her remaining a dancer into her eighties; her sociability; her pet dislikes; her delight in funerals; and her attitude toward religion. Annie Moffett had still further recollections of her grandmother, who lived with the family for years; these are found in MTBM. Sam Clemens also wrote a sketch of his mother, soon after her death, recalling her bright mind, keen interest in life, her "sunshiny" disposition, and her delight in "playful duels of wit." This sketch is also

in Blair. The story about Jane Lampton mimicking Cyrus Walker's dancing was told by Orion Clemens in his recollection of her. In an unfinished
novel, *Simon Wheeler, Detective,* Clemens based the character Judge Gris-
wold, on his father, and described his appearance (MTP). Jane Lampton's
account of her love for Richard Barrett was told by Sam Clemens in a
letter to William Dean Howells, on May 19, 1886, in Paine, *Mark
Twain's Letters.* Clemens related the story again in a slightly different
form in an autobiographical dictation of December 1906 (MTP), and
spoke there also of his parents' attitude toward each other. In his "Villagers of 1840–3," written in 1897 (included in Blair), he spoke of his
father, disguised this time as Judge Carpenter, as being aware that the
girl who accepted him did so to spite another man. Wecter traced Barrett's later career in *Sam Clemens of Hannibal.* In "Villagers . . . ,"
Clemens described the "Carpenter" family's move to Jamestown. The
plastered house with the glass windows was described by Clemens in *The
Gilded Age.* In his autobiographical dictations (MTP), Clemens discussed
the purchase of the Tennessee acreage and its effect on the family. Rachel M. Varble, *The Story of Mark Twain's Mother,* told about Hannibal
Clemens and his wife, also Jane, joining John Marshall Clemens and Jane
Lampton at Jamestown. She recounted Jane Lampton's firm refusal to
move to Three Forks.

2. *"A Heavenly Place for a Boy,"* pp. 17–34.

The chapter title is taken from Clemens' description of the Quarles
farm and is found in his *Autobiography.* Unless otherwise noted, all material in this chapter is based on the autobiographical writings and dictations, and random notes in MTP, most of which can be found in the
published autobiographies. In MTBM, Annie Moffett recalled stories
about her Uncle Sam sleepwalking as a boy. In *Life on the Mississippi*
Sam Clemens mentioned the belief that the dying person's fingers picked
at his coverlet. The shoemaker's vision of the funeral procession was told
by Albert B. Paine in *Mark Twain, A Biography.* He doubtless heard the
story from Clemens. In his sketch "How to Cure a Cold" Sam described
his own reaction to the sheet soaked in ice water, and recalled the other
hydropathic remedies used on him. Wecter chronicled John Marshall
Clemens' promising start after the move to the village of Florida. He also
told about Orion being installed as clerk in the new store, and about John
Marshall's decline in fortune with the town's depression. Orion, in the
autobiography his brother Sam urged him to write, recalled being left

behind at the time of the family's move to Hannibal. This account is quoted by Paine in *Biography*. Laura Hawkins remembered her first meeting with Sam in an interview held in 1910 and reprinted in the *Hannibal Courier-Post*, December 26, 1928. Sam wrote about falling in love with Laura, and about giving her his apple core, in a letter to Margaret Blackburn, October 9, 1908 (MTP). In "Villagers . . . ," Clemens spoke of his father as being "ungentle." In MTBM, Annie Moffett remembered that her mother, Pamela, did not agree with her brothers about their father's harshness. Through Huck Finn, Sam revealed his own knowledge of weather signs and had Huck express Clemens' feelings about the sound of the spinning wheel. Sam described his father reading aloud in an "inflectionless" voice in memoirs he was writing for *The Galaxy* in 1870. He was then editing a department for that literary magazine. "The Golden Arm" was an example used by Clemens in his sketch "How to Tell a Story." Sam expressed his opinion of spirituals or jubilee songs in a letter to Joseph Twichell, October 22, 1897, found in Paine, *Letters*. Clemens' singing of spirituals was described by Katy Leary in Mary Lawton, *A Lifetime with Mark Twain*. John Marshall Clemens' advice to Pamela is recalled in MTBM. Sam wrote in his *Galaxy* memoirs about being on distant terms with his father. Tabitha Quarles, Sam's cousin and playmate, recalled his visits to her father's farm. She told about him bringing his favorite cats; about his pranks; about his comic manner of telling a story, made more amusing by his drawl; and about his sleepwalking, in an interview of December 10, 1899, reprinted in the *Hannibal Courier-Post*, June 3, 1935.

3. *"A Boy's Paradise,"* pp. 35–50.

The chapter title is Clemens' characterization of Hannibal, in his *Autobiography*. *Life on the Mississippi* furnished recollections of rides on the timber rafts, of John Hannicks, of the excitement in town as soon as his cry was heard, and of the arrival and departure of the steamboats. Minnie M. Brashear, *Mark Twain, Son of Missouri*, told of Hannibal's founding and growth. In *The Innocents Abroad*, Clemens wrote about Holliday's hill, and in *The Adventures of Tom Sawyer*, he described Mrs. Holliday's hospitality; she appears in that work as the "Widow Douglas." In *Tom Sawyer* he told about playing Robin Hood in the grove behind her house, and in a letter of February 6, 1870, to Will Bowen, he recalled their playing Robin Hood together in that wood. In his *Autobiography*, Clemens spoke of his mother's experiences with Mrs. Utterback, the faith healer. In *Life on the Mississippi*, he pictured Hannibal's setting and its views of the river. He wrote about seeing the Millerites on Lover's Leap in *The Innocents Abroad*. In his notes (MTP) for one version of "The Mysterious Stranger," set in Hannibal, he suggested having Huck and Tom witness a Walpurgis Night held on Lover's Leap. Clemens' Sunday school experiences are found in his *Autobiography*. The Radcliffs (Sam spelled the name "Ratcliffe") are described in "Villagers . . . ," as are many other Hannibal residents. A description of Hannibal in the mid-1840s is found in Clemens' *Pudd'nhead Wilson*. Sam wrote about Hannibal's parades, and the collations held afterward, in his "Villagers . . ." The games he and his comrades played are mentioned in "Boy's Manuscript" (MTP) and included by Bernard De Voto in *Mark Twain at Work*. Sam's praise for the "true Southern watermelon," appears in *Pudd'nhead Wilson's Calendar*. Clemens described the Blankenship family in "Villagers . . . ," while Tom Blankenship was pictured in *Tom Sawyer*. In his *Autobiography*, Clemens commented on the grades of society in Hannibal. Sam reminded Will Bowen in a letter of February 6, 1870, of their demolition of Hardy's stable. The prank involving the boxed cats was recalled by Norval L. Brady in the *Hannibal Courier-Post*, March 6, 1935. An account of rolling the boulder down Holliday's Hill appears in *The Innocents Abroad*. The circumstances which forced Sam to use tobacco are recounted in his *Autobiography*. The recollection of Jane Lampton's exasperated "Hang it!" appears in MTBM. In his *Autobiography* Sam contrasted his behavior with Henry's. In *A Tramp Abroad*, he recounted the vivid dream about the riverboat being on fire. Recollections of Sam at the boat launching in Bear Creek appear in MTBM. He described McDowell's Cave in his *Autobiography* and told about getting lost in it himself. In his *Life on the Mississippi*, he described his trouble in learning how to swim and told about his seven "drownings." Jane Lampton's remark "People who are born to be hanged . . ." was quoted by Samuel E. Moffett in "Mark Twain, A Biographical Sketch." The drownings of Clint Levering and "Dutchy" were recounted also in *Life on the Mississippi*, as were Sam's reactions to the thunderstorms which followed each death.

4. *Education*, pp. 51–60.

Tom Sawyer's "slow suffering" in the schoolroom was Sam Clemens'. In Susy Clemens' biography of her father she wrote that she knew it was true that he "played 'Hookey' all the time," and that he would "pretend to be dying so as not to have to go to school!" (MTP). For the recommendation of flogging, see Proverbs 13:24, 26:3, and 29:15. In a letter to Will Bowen, February 6, 1870, Sam recalled the class insurrection in which both took part. The quarrel between Hudson and McFarland is covered in the Palmyra, Missouri, *Whig*, August 8, 1840, and in Marion County Circuit Court Records, No. 3516. Details of the affray in which Sam Smarr was shot fatally, contained in these same records, No. 3873. In his *Autobiography*, Clemens recalled watching the dying man's struggles. "Boy's Manuscript" is the source for the contest with the louse, and the statement that every detail of that story was true. In a letter to Will Bowen, January 25, 1868, he reminded Bowen of the louse incident and mentioned that he had recently told it at a congressional dinner in Washington. In his *Autobiography* he recalled Arch Fuqua's gift; his own and Henry's fruitless attempts to straighten their hair; and recorded memories of various girls. In Sam's sketch of his mother he gave her attitude toward the black boy Sandy. His father's impatience with Sandy was recorded in *Following the Equator*. When Livy Clemens read the manuscript of that work, she objected to Sam's use of the word "lash," in reference to his treatment of Sandy; she suggested that he substitute "cuff," which he did, with the response, "It's out—& my father is whitewashed." In "Villagers . . . ," Sam noted that his father had once whipped Jennie with a bridle. Orion Clemens, in a letter to a Miss Wood of Memphis, Tennessee, October 3, 1858, told of their father scolding little Henry for planting his marbles. This letter appears in Paine, *Biography*, Appendix A. In "Villagers . . . ," Sam listed the books they read. In *Following the Equator*, he stated that his father had punished him only twice, while in "Villagers . . . ," he added there was no need since one stern look from him was more than enough. The letter of Orion to Miss Wood is the source for Sam breaking up his mother's scoldings with some humorous remark. Sam's comment on hell was quoted by Wecter in his "Introduction" to Clemens' *Report from Paradise*. In "Villagers . . . ," Sam described the dashing, plaid-lined cloaks, then in fashion. Sam's experience with his was recounted in his *Autobiography*.

5. *The Dark Hour*, pp. 61–81.

The opening quote is found in Clemens' *Autobiography*. Sam recalled the scene at his brother Ben's bedside, in the sketch of his mother. In "Villagers . . . ," he recalled her placing his hand on the dead boy's cheek. In his Notebook 35, 1902, typescript, MTP, he remembered the sight of Ben in his shroud, lying in his coffin. The random note about his treachery to Ben was written also in 1902; it is likewise in MTP. He spoke of the treachery again in "Villagers . . ." In that same recollection he spoke of Orion imitating Franklin. In MTBM is a letter from Jane Lampton to Orion, telling him about Pamela teaching music. In "Villagers . . . ," Sam noted that the dying John Marshall Clemens showed affection only for Pamela; that he kissed her probably for the first time, and did not say goodbye to his wife or anyone else. John Marshall Clemens' injunction to cling to the Tennessee land appears in the *Autobiography*. Sam mentioned the autopsy in "Villagers . . ." On October 10, 1903, Clemens made the note about witnessing the postmortem of his "uncle" through a keyhole (MTP). William Dean Howells' reaction to Orion's autobiography is found in his letter of June 14, 1880, and in Howells, *Life in Letters of William Dean Howells*. The stolen satchel belonged to A. B. Paine, who so feared Clemens' anger he never told him of its loss. The old Baptist cemetery was described in *Tom Sawyer*. In Orion's letter to Miss Wood, he told her about urging the brothers to be kind to one another. The account of Sam's sleepwalking after his father's funeral appears in MTBM. Annie Moffett never forgot Sam's letter to her concerning his horror of failure and debt, and told Dixon Wecter about it. The recollection of Jane Lampton holding John Quarles responsible for her sister Patsy's death, appears in MTBM. The account of Sam and his friends finding the body of the fugitive slave was told to Paine by both John Briggs and Sam Clemens; it appears in Paine, *Biography*. In his *Autobiography* Clemens recalled the decision to sell all or none of the Tennessee land, and told of the move into the Hill Street house. Sam's favorite anecdote about Orion's "wool-gathering," when he got into bed with Dr. Meredith's sisters, appears in his *Autobiography*. In that same work he recalled his apprenticeship with Ament. His homesickness was recalled in MTBM. Sam described Pet McMurry in a letter of January 23, 1885 (MTP), to Olivia Clemens. His memories of Wales McCormick, and the Cadets of Temperance are in his *Autobiography*. The July Fourth collation recounted in "Villagers . . ." In that same work he made note of his cousin Jim Quarles' misfortunes. The *Autobiography* is the source for Edward Bates befriending Orion. In his own autobiography, Orion blamed his father for forcing him into a trade. Jane Lampton's letter to Orion regarding purchase of the *Hannibal Journal*, is included in MTBM. Sam Raymond was described by Clemens in "Villagers . . ." "Jim Wolfe and the Tom Cats" appeared in the *New York Sunday Mercury*, July 14, 1867, and was reprinted in San Francisco's *Californian*, on September 21, 1867. "I was tyrannical and unjust to Sam," Orion wrote in his autobiography, quoted by Paine, *Biography*. Sam's animosity toward Franklin is expressed in his squib "The Late Benjamin Franklin." An example of Jane Lampton's careful record of expenditures was found on the blank pages of Sam's Notebook 3 (MTP). An account of Pamela's marriage is found in MTBM. Orion's autobiography contains his hindsight admission of what ailed his newspaper, and an account of his fruitless attempts to enliven it. Brashear reprints Sam's contributions to the *Journal.* Milton Meltzer, *Mark Twain Himself,* includes Sam's crude woodcuts. Brashear gave an account of Orion's successes, and the esteem in which he was held by the townspeople. In "My First Literary Venture," Sam told how he was riven with that "perfect thunderbolt of humor" in seeming to address a young woman in hell. In that same piece he described "Sir" Abner Gilstrap's reaction to the verses. The advertisement for the "Floating Palace" appeared in the *Hannibal Journal* on May 6, 1853. The pledge Jane Lampton asked of Sam upon his leaving home is found in Paine, *Biography*. In his autobiography, Orion expressed his regrets at having failed to appreciate Sam's talents.

6. *Journeyman Printer,* pp. 82–93.

Sam's recollections of his roommate Jacob Burrough and of Mrs. Pavey's house are contained in a letter to Jacob's son, Frank E. Burrough. The letter is quoted in Frederick Anderson, Michael B. Frank, and Kenneth Sanderson, *Mark Twain's Notebooks & Journals,* Vol. 1. In a letter of May 29, 1869 (MTP), Clemens told Olivia Langdon about having had cholera at St. Louis. His September 1853 letter to Pamela can be only tentatively dated the third because one or more of its first pages are missing. In a letter to his mother, dated August 3, 1853, and printed in the *Hannibal Journal,* told about his good fortune in getting full-time work. He recalled the "villainous" boarding house and the poor food in his *Autobiography.* The second letter to Pamela (MTP), dated October 8, 1853, spoke of having seen the actor Edwin Forrest. The Philadelphia letter to Orion (V) was dated October 26, 1853. The recollection of Sumner is found in the *Autobiography.* The account of "Playing Bear," is in MTP. Sam's reply to Orion, urging that their mother winter at St. Louis, and expressing his opinion of Easterners and foreigners, was dated November 28, 1853 (V). His homesick letter to Pamela, was written on December 5, 1853 (V). His description of Washington and his experiences there are found in two letters, dated February 18 and 19,

1854, and sent to the *Muscatine Journal*. They appear in Edgar M. Branch, *Mark Twain's Letters in the Muscatine Journal*. Sam recalled the trip to Muscatine, in his *Autobiography*.

7. *Keokuk Days*, pp. 94–106.

Mollie Clemens' Notebook recorded the date and place of her marriage to Orion. Rachel Varble gave the reasons for Jane Lampton leaving before the wedding. In his autobiography, Orion admitted to forgetting Mollie. Sam, in his *Autobiography*, spoke of their troubled marriage. In her Notebook, Mollie also recorded the date of their move to Keokuk, June 9, 1855, and their purchase of the printing office. A letter from James Clemens, Jr., to Orion, dated August 6, 1855, told the story of Sam's application to him for help in becoming a cub pilot. This letter is quoted in part in *Mark Twain's Notebooks & Journals*. Sam recounted his vain attempts to sign on the steamboats, in his *Life on the Mississippi*. In Notebook 1, Sam listed the items to be shipped to Orion. In a letter of April 2, 1862, Sam told his mother and sister about drilling the military company and playing ten pins above Isbell's head (V). Fred W. Lorch, "Mark Twain in Iowa," furnished a sketch of Sam's life at Keokuk, and the lively evenings in the printing office. The song "Boston Isn't Bengal" appears in a letter Sam wrote to the *Keokuk Daily Post*. It is dated March 14, 1857, at Cincinnati, and signed, "Thomas Jefferson Snodgrass." All of the Snodgrass letters are included in Lorch. Both Brashear and Lorch contain biographical sketches of Sam's friend Ann Elizabeth Taylor, and quote Sam's letters to her. Lorch wrote about Sam's first after-dinner speech. In his *Autobiography* Sam tells about reading Lieutenant Herndon's *Report*, and being especially interested in what he had to say about coca, not cocoa, as has so often been stated. Sam wrote about Orion's directory in a letter of June 10 to his mother and sister (V). The letter to Henry Clemens, August 5, 1856, about plans to go to South America, with interjected reports concerning Annie Taylor's health, is also at Vassar. Sam told the story of the fifty-dollar bill in his *Autobiography*. Among his autobiographical sketches is one concerning a man named Macfarlane. Although the sketch has been included in both editions of the *Autobiography*, it has been suggested by Paul Baender, in "Alias Macfarlane: A Revision of Mark Twain's Biography," that the Scotsman may have been fictional, and that his supposed influence on Clemens' thinking was Paine's addition to the story.

8. *Learning the River,* pp. 107–21.

In both "Old Times on the Mississippi," the series of articles which ran in the *Atlantic Monthly* in 1874–75, and in the book *Life on the Mississippi* that followed in 1883, Sam told about poking down the rivers to New Orleans on the old *Paul Jones.* A random note in his autobiographical writings (MTP) told about his calling on James Clemens, Jr., and finding him complaining about his high taxes. Annie Moffett's recollection of the family's excitement about Sam becoming a pilot is found in MTBM. Sam's opinion of piloting and his lessons with Bixby are in "Old Times . . . ," and *Life on the Mississippi.* That "little memorandum book," which Bixby told Sam to get, still exists. Inside the front cover Sam wrote: "[Notes made by me when I was learning to be a Mississippi River pilot in 1856–7.] Found this book among some old rubbish to-day, Dec. 8, 1880. S. L. Clemens." Sam's memory of the "strenuous fragrance" of the magnolia flowers appears in "My Platonic Sweetheart." He recalled the oleanders along the lower river, in a letter of March 20, 1880, to David Watt Bowser. In his *Autobiography,* Clemens described the *John J. Roe,* and told of his meeting with Laura Wright. He spoke of Beck Jolly as the mighty lion hunter and Chinese linguist, in a letter to Will Bowen, August 25, 1866. In a letter of February 6, 1861, to Orion and Mollie (V), he spoke of Laura's dark brown hair and eyes. In his *Autobiography* he told about her being his "instantly elected sweetheart." In the same letter of March 20, 1880, to David Bowser, Laura Wright's pupil, he spoke of her great love for books, and her introspection. This letter is in Pascal Covici, Jr., "Dear Master Wattie." Clemens related the visit to the fortune-teller in great detail in a long letter to Orion and Mollie on February 6, 1861 (V). The letter to Jane Lampton and Pamela, in which Sam inquired about Laura Wright, is dated September 25, 1861, also Vassar. David Watt Bowser's letter to "Mr. Twain," which opened the correspondence with Clemens, was postmarked March 16, 1880. Their entire correspondence is in Covici. In an autobiographical note, as well as his *Autobiography,* there is the story of Laura's appeal for financial help, and quotation from her spirited letter.

9. *Tragedy on the River,* pp. 122–29.

In a letter to Orion and Mollie, dated March 9, 1858 (V), Sam told about finding Henry working at odd jobs. Mollie's Notebook recorded the sale of the printing office; the move to Tennessee, and Orion's admission to the bar. She also mentioned visiting the Moffetts at St. Louis and seeing the fair. In that same letter to Orion and Mollie, Sam told of finding employment for Henry on the *Pennsylvania,* and described the nature of his duties. He spoke of his intimacy with Henry and their total understanding, in a letter to Mrs. Jervis Langdon, February 13, 1869 (MTP). Sam's description of the pilot, Brown, is found in *Life on the Mississippi.* Brown's lecture to him on the ruinous effects of reading, was told by Clemens to Annie Adams Fields, who recorded it in her diary, published by M. A. DeWolfe Howe, as *Memories of A Hostess* . . . Sam's description of his vivid dream about Henry is in the *Autobiography.* His family's remembrance of the circumstances of that dream is found in MTBM. The pilot Brown's quarrel with Henry Clemens is described in *Life on the Mississippi,* and also in a letter of June 18, 1858, to Mollie Clemens (MTP), in which Sam said that Brown "jumped up and collared him . . ." The captain's reaction to the quarrel is recounted in *Life on the Mississippi.* In that June 18 letter to Mollie, Sam told her he had been with Henry up to five minutes before the steamboat sailed from New Orleans. In *Life on the Mississippi,* Sam wrote of receiving the varying reports about Henry after the explosion. Clemens scrapbooks contain many newspaper accounts of the explosion and fire, of Henry's injuries, and of his death. In that same long letter to Mollie, Sam told about Henry lying exposed to the sun for hours before being picked up by the *Kate Frisbie,* and about him being unconscious for twelve hours. The telegram to Will Moffett is in MTP. Sam described the sufferings of Henry, and of the other scalded men, and told of the kind treatment they received from the townspeople of Memphis, in *Life on the Mississippi.* In that same work, he described Henry's death. The second telegram to Will Moffett is also in MTP. In his *Autobiography,* he told of seeing Henry just as he had seen him in the dream at St. Louis. Family recollection of Sam's near insanity is in MTBM. Orion's autobiography gave the account of the overdose of morphine. Not until Sam came to write his recollections in old age did he tell about the morphine. By then Jane Lampton was dead; he had not wanted her to know.

10. *The Pilot,* pp. 130–40.

On Aug. 26, 1896, Sam Clemens wrote Olivia after the death of their daughter, Susy, that when Henry died, "I would not allow myself to think of my loss, lest the burden be too heavy to bear . . ." (MTP). On

November 20, 1860, Sam wrote Orion concerning his investments in produce (MTP). Mollie Clemens' Notebook recorded Orion's opening a law practice in Memphis, Missouri. Sam's pride at being a pilot, and in having a berth on the *City of Memphis*, is contained in a fragmentary letter dated tentatively June 27, 1860 (V). In his letter to Orion, dated November 20, 1860 (V), Sam told about grounding the *Alonzo Child*. His experience while piloting the *Crescent City*, May 22–July 7, 1857, is recounted in *Life on the Mississippi*. In that same work he spoke of becoming "personally and familiarly acquainted" with every type of person, and of recognizing the value of such an education: "I loved the profession . . ." His laundry list contained in Notebook 2; a photograph of him taken in 1858 when he was piloting, and a photograph of Sam Bowen as a pilot, gave clues to the pilot's dress. Works on American costume for those years were consulted for men's summer wear, for the "pork pie" hat and the broad-brimmed straw. Only a seven-line fragment of the letter to Orion dated March 18, 1861, exists. Those lines concern dancing the Schottische with Miss Castle (V). However, Paine had access to the entire letter, which appears in his edition of the letters, but he misdated it 1860. Recollections of Jane Lampton's dislike of "low and solemn" music are in MTBM, as are also Annie Moffett's memories of traveling with her grandmother. Sam told Pamela about watching the Mardi Gras parade in a letter from which the first page (and possibly more) is missing. It has been dated in another hand, March 9–11, 1859, for it was written over several days. The original is in pencil, faded to a degree that makes the words almost illegible in places. Sam told Orion about the epicurean dinner with Horace Bixby and others in a letter dated September 29, 1860 (V). His description of Church's painting, "Heart of the Andes," is contained in that same fragmentary letter of March 18, 1861. Annie Moffett's memories of her relationship with her uncle Sam and his songs and stories are found in MTBM. Sam wrote his mother from Carson City on April 2, 1862 (V), telling her about Annie Moffett and the story of Moses. Clemens' parody of Isaiah Sellers' river report appeared in the *New Orleans Daily Crescent*, May 17, 1859. Sam's stated hope that he would follow the river for the rest of his days appears in *Life on the Mississippi*. Family recollections concerning Sam's fear of being impressed to pilot a federal riverboat are included in MTBM, as is the account of Sam being asked to join the Confederate volunteers. Clemens' letters of February 28, 1862, and May 8, 1862 (UV), to his friend William H. Clagett, when both were in the Nevada silver mines, reveal his sympathy for the South. Confederate belief that the war would last no longer than three months, found in Margaret Sanborn, *Robert E. Lee, A Portrait.* "On the Wing for Hannibal" is taken from Sam's letter of April 26, 1861, to Orion (V).

11. *Confederate Soldier,* pp. 141–49.

Sam Clemens' article, "The Private History Of a Campaign That Failed," *Century Magazine,* December 1885, is the chief source for this chapter. Sam's description of his mule, "Paint-Brush," and the "mine of trouble" he had with the animal, is found in a letter to Mollie Clemens, dated January 21, 1862 (MTP). Sam was replying to a letter from Mollie in which she told him "Paint-Brush" was then, in Sam's words, "doing service for the enemy. *But against his will.*"

12. *Across the Plains,* pp. 150–59.

Mollie Clemens' Notebook gives the date of Orion's appointment as, March 27, 1861; tells that Orion received his papers on April 20; records his visit to St. Louis, the date he and Sam left on the *Sioux City,* and that of their arrival in Carson City, Nevada. Unless otherwise noted, the remainder of this chapter is based on Clemens' account as recorded in *Roughing It.* Frank A. Root, *Overland Stage to California,* gives information about the use of mules on rough terrain, about the various grades of accommodations for travelers, the ranking of Smith's Hotel, and an old photograph of it at its prime. Margaret Sanborn, *The Grand Tetons,* tells about the Western cowboy's different meanings in their use of "son-of-a-bitch." In an unpublished version of *Roughing It* (MTP), Clemens wrote of having dropped a leaf into the eastward-bound stream on the Continental Divide, freighting it with a mental message of love for a St. Louis sweetheart. Sam told Orion that he first came to really know him during their trip across the Plains, in a letter dated October 19, 1865 (MTP). Orion, the "queer & heedless bird," appears in Sam's letter of August 9, 1871, to Livy (MTP). Orion's "diabolical notions of time and tune" appear in a letter to Jane Lampton, April 2, 1862 (V).

13. *Mining Fever,* pp. 160–82.

In *Roughing It* Sam described his and Orion's quarters in Carson City, and told about his joining the "Irish Brigade" and of his delight in Western garb. This book is one source for accounts of his trip with John

Kinney to Lake Tahoe. He described Kinney as a "capital comrade," in a random note in MTP. The other source for the Tahoe adventure is found in a letter of October 25, 1861, to Pamela (V), in which he spoke of the lake's beauty, and his intention to build a country seat there. The awesome fire Clemens accidentally started is described in *Roughing It,* and also in a letter of September 18–21, 1861, to his mother, in which he depicted their camp life. Sam spelled the names of the Benson girls alternately as Hallie and Challie, or Haille and Chaille. In *Roughing It,* he told about getting silver fever. He wrote Orion on November 20, 1860 (MTP), that he had seen Pamela's baby. He described the black horse with the white face in a letter to his mother dated January 20, 1862, and printed in the *Keokuk Gate City,* on March 6, 1862. The bill of sale for that horse, which William Clagett bought, is in the Nevada Historical Society. An account of the trip by wagon to Humboldt is found in the same letter of January 30 to Jane Lampton. Sam pictured the party's arrival at Unionville; described the setting and the bitter cold in *Roughing It.* In that book he also told about building their cabin. Sam mentioned his "shining talent" for constructing rock and rammed earth houses, in a letter to Clagett, February 29, 1862 (UV). The story of being marooned eight days at Honey Lake Smith's is in *Roughing It.* Orion Clemens wrote to Mollie about the flood in a letter of January 3, 1862 (MTP). Sam spoke of being lousy in that same long letter to his mother, January 30, 1862. In a letter to Clagett, dated April 18, 1862 (UV), Sam regretted ever having left Humboldt. Charles Carroll Goodwin, *As I Remember Them,* described Robert Howland. In Notebook 4, Clemens mentioned in February 1865 about Howland coming into their dormitory, drunk and knocking down the jars of tarantulas. Sam's fine description of the "Washoe Zephyr" appears in *Roughing It.* The letter about mining prospects, the value of water, and the expectation of striking ore in June, was written on February 8 and 9, 1862, to Jane Lampton and Pamela (V). In that letter he urged Pamela to wait until he came home. In the phrase "just keep your shirt on, Pamela, until I come," Paine, in his printed version substituted "clothes" for "shirt." Sam's appeals for money in varying amounts were sent to Orion on April 10 (?), fragment; April 13 (V); April 17 and 19 (MTP). The long, angry letter to Orion was written on April 24 and 25, 1862 (V). Sam's comments about Bixby were included in his letter of May 11 and 12, 1862, to Orion (V). His inability to find Jane Lampton's word "suspition" in Webster's is recounted in a letter of February 8, 1862 (V), to his mother and sister. He also told there about Orion's "dishonesty." The discussion about peanuts growing on bushes is found in MTBM. Sam's advice to Pamela about bringing up Sammy is also in the letter of February 8. Mention of his correspondence with Annie Moffett is in a letter to his mother, dated April 2, 1862 (V). Sam's account of Calvin Higbie's prodigious strength, endurance, and perseverence is in a letter to Orion, July 9, 1862 (MTP). Bob Howland wrote about moving their cabin in "An Old Landmark," which appeared in the *Territorial Enterprise,* December 2, 1879. William H. Brewer, a botanist with the Whitney Survey of California, described the Aurora he saw, in his journal, published as *Up and Down California in 1860–1864.* On May 11, 1862, Sam wrote Orion about having an interest in the Monitor mine, and in a letter of May 17 told about finding their claim jumped (V). "Everything human is pathetic . . ." is from "Pudd'nhead Wilson's New Calendar," included in *Following the Equator.* On April 13, 1862, Sam wrote Orion, asking him to send pens and penholders (V); and on June 22, 1862 (UV), he asked his brother to put his (Sam's) *Enterprise* letters into a scrapbook. In an autobiographical dictation, September 4, 1906 (MTP), Clemens recalled what he said in that burlesque of Judge Turner's speech. In a letter of June 22, 1862 (UV), to Orion, Sam spoke of his restlessness. He wrote of his vexation with everything but "Miss P——" with the long curls (referring to Carrie Pixley of Carson City) in a letter of May 17, 1862, to Orion (V). In *Roughing It* he described his duties in the stamp-mill; in a letter to Orion, July 9, 1862 (MTP), he told about getting salivated and catching a "violent cold." Higbie is quoted in Michael J. Phillips, "Mark Twain's Partner." Clemens quoted Higbie in *Roughing It,* and wrote to Orion on June 22, 1862 (UV), "it *does* seem like a dead sure thing," and included a sketch of the ledges. Paine, *Biography,* regarded Sam's account of the blind lead as "what *might* have happened . . ."; Bernard De Voto, *Mark Twain's America,* considered it "a quintessential recording of Wahoe lusts . . ." To this writer Clemens' statement that there were official records to support the truth of the blind lead's existence rang true; my own search for the records led me to the county seats of Esmeralda, Nevada, and Mono, California, then to the Nevada Historical Society, Reno, where I learned that old Nevada mining records had been stored in the State Archives at Carson City. In Clemens' time there was confusion over the California-Nevada boundary, and in 1863 it was found that Aurora, which was county seat of Mono County, California, was actually in Nevada. In Carson City it was the State Archivist, Guy Louis Rocha, who called my attention to Edgar M. Branch's carefully researched and annotated article, "Fact and Fiction in the *Blind Lead* episode of *Roughing It,*" published in the *Nevada Historical Society Quarterly*, Winter 1985. M. C. Gardner's "Nine-Mile Ranch" identified and located in Myron Angel, *History of Nevada*. On July 9, 1862, Sam wrote Orion about his problems in nursing Captain Nye (MTP), and on July 30, 1862, he wrote Orion again about Nye's testiness and their quarrel, admitting that he (Sam) was "what the Yankees call 'ugly' . . ."(V). Higbie recalled what Sam said to him about doing the assessment work, quoted in Michael J. Phillips' article already identified. Clemens' autobiographical sketch was written in 1873 and is found in MTP and the Pierpont Morgan Library. Clemens described the intricacies of a quadrille in the *Territorial Enterprise*, December 12, 1862. He told about the ball at Gold Hill, where he first met Etta Booth, a little girl in a "fiery-red frock," dancing with the miners, in his *Autobiography*. In his letter of June 22 to Orion, Sam told about getting the communication from William Barstow. Joseph T. Goodman recalled how "funny" Clemens' squibs were, in his "Recollections of Mark Twain . . . ," *San Francisco Examiner*, April 22, 1910. In that same July 22 letter Sam warned Orion to say nothing about Barstow's letter. He talked to Orion about his debts being greater than he realized, in a letter of July 23, 1862 (V). On July 30, he told Orion about the *Enterprise*'s definite offer of the post as local reporter (V). Sam's projected walk into the wilderness was first mentioned in the July 9, 1862 letter to Orion, and was spoken of again to Orion on August 7, 1862 (V). His letter of September 9, 1862 (UV), to Clagett, solved the mystery of the walk.

14. *Sam Clemens/Mark Twain*, pp. 183–94.

Recollection of Clemens' arrival at the *Enterprise* office, possibly Joseph T. Goodman's, appears uncited in Paine, *Biography*. In *Roughing It*, Clemens quoted Goodman's instructions to the new reporter and described the editorial sanctum. Dan De Quille in *The Big Bonanza*, the book Dan wrote at Clemens' suggestion, working in Sam's study at Hartford, traced the history of the *Enterprise* and supplied details about Old Joe the cook and general arrangements at the first office. Goodman, *San Francisco Examiner*, April 22, 1910, mentioned the *Enterprise*'s national reputation. Clemens, *Roughing It*, wrote of the number of editors, reporters, compositors, and the press run by steam. Wells Drury, *An Editor on the Comstock Lode*, told about the paper's financial success. In *Roughing It* Sam described his first day as a reporter. He asked lawyer Billy Clagett's advice about how to handle the threats of G. T. Sewell, the coroner, in a letter of March 8, 1862, (UV). Clemens' story, "Petrified Man" was reprinted in the *San Francisco Daily Evening Bulletin*, October 15, 1862, as "A Washoe Joke." Dan De Quille, "Reporting with Mark Twain," told about the tricks played on Sam. Wells Drury spoke of Steve Gillis' talents as a fiddler. The newspaperman's daily routine was based on Alfred Doten, *The Journals of . . .* , and on De Quille. Clemens described the shooting-gallery figure under "More Ghosts," in the *Enterprise*, December 1862–January 1863. J. Ross Browne, *Washoe Revisited*, wrote about the hurdy-gurdy girls. In "Villagers . . ." Clemens recalled the popular, sentimental ballads expressing regrets for vanished joys. He wrote of Tom Peasley's saloon as a political rendezvous, in *Roughing It*. Doten, a conscientious diarist, gave the stopping places during each night's cruising with Dan De Quille; after Clemens and De Quille became close friends and roommates, Sam accompanied him regularly. De Quille, "Reporting . . ." recalled his and Sam's rapport, and Clemens' abilities as a reporter. The postscripts in which Sam reported hearing the pistol shots, going to investigate, and finding that two policemen had been killed, appeared in the left margin and at the top of the first page of a letter to his mother and sister, April 11, 1863 (V). Clemens described Virginia City's flush times in *Roughing It*. J. Ross Browne wrote about the pounding of quartz mills, the underground blasts, the settlement viewed from a distance, and the shortcuts over rooftops. Clemens told his mother and sister, February 16, 1863, about getting feet in return for "lying about somebody's mine." Goodman's book was published in England. In his *Autobiography*, Clemens recalled Mollie's pride in her new station, and told about Orion building the house. Henry Nash Smith, *Mark Twain of the Enterprise*, discussed Clemens' reporting of the legislative sessions. In Sam's correspondence with the *Enterprise*, included in Smith, the growing importance of "the Unreliable" was traced. Sam's account of "The Grand Bull Drivers' Convention," was reprinted from the *Enterprise*, in the *Placer Weekly Courier*, January 17, 1863. Clemens' first letter—signed "Mark Twain," so far as is known, since *Enterprise* files are not complete—is in Smith, who fixes the date. In *Life on the Mississippi*, Clemens told about adopting the late Isaiah Sellers' pen name. Ivan Benson, *Mark Twain's Western Years*, published large portions of Sellers' logbook, where there is no evidence of any pen name. New Orleans newspapers containing Sellers' river reports, as well as those publishing obituary articles at the time of the old captain's death, were read as well. All reports were signed with his own name. In the biographical sketches contained in the obituaries there was no suggestion that he was ever known by any pseudonym.

15. *Wild Oats,* pp. 195–220.

Amelia Neville, *The Fantastic City,* described the Lick House in detail. Neville was an early-day San Franciscan and had first-hand knowledge of her subject. Clemens wrote about Neil Moss' background and his ultimate fate, in "Villagers . . . ." In a letter of mid-May 1863 (MTP), starting with page 3, Sam told his mother and sister about spending two weeks with Neil. In that letter he also spoke about meeting Bill Briggs and mentioned his success. In "Villagers . . . ," he wrote of Briggs' mistress. The account of how Sam and the Unreliable passed their time in San Francisco and environs is taken from Clemens' letters of June 1, 1863 (V), and June 4, 1863 (MTP), both written to his mother and sister. Julia Altrocchi, *The Spectacular San Franciscans,* and Neville gave accounts of the "Willows," definitely locating the famed resort and describing its attractions. Alfred Doten, who also visited the "Willows," noted in his journal the pleasant ride on the Mission Railroad and the good food at the hotel. Neville also described the "Ocean House," predecessor of the "Cliff House," and its specialties. Sam's description of wading in the Pacific is found in his letter of June 1, 1862, to Jane Lampton and Pamela (V). Clemens' letter of May 16, 1863, to the *Enterprise,* described the variety show at the "Bella Union." In the same mid-May letter home, he spoke of having been asked by the *Call* to correspond and remarked upon his ability to levy blackmail. He also enclosed the first of the twenty-dollar greenbacks in that letter. He wrote to Orion in a letter dated June 20, 1863, about mining speculations (MTP). "Ma, you are slinging insinuations . . . ," opens his letter of July 18, 1863, to his mother and sister (MTP). In that letter he also spoke about being careless with his mining stock. In a letter of August 5 (MTP), he told about having been burned out. He was living at the time in a new and "elegantly furnished" boarding house, The White House, on Virginia City's B Street. He also told in that letter about working no more than two hours a day. Walter Leman, *Memories of an Old Actor,* was a member of the company playing at Virginia City; he named the play and the leading actress, and quoted the *Territorial Enterprise's* account of the Washoe Zephyr. In that same August 5 letter, Sam mentioned Orion's lecture on dissipation. In Clemens' letter of January 31, 1862 (MTP), to Mollie Clemens, he admitted to sleeping with "female servants." Angel, *History of Nevada,* wrote about the celebration at the *Enterprise* office when the new steam press went into operation. He also told about Sam's sickness and reprinted the Unreliable's "Apologetic," which appeared under Clemens' name, and Sam's angry response. Sam told about his difficulty in curing his cold in a letter of August 19, 1863 (V), written home. He also told about persuading Adair Wilson to accompany him to Tahoe. His *Enterprise* letter written from Steamboat Springs, and headed, "Never mind the date—I haven't known what day of the month it was since the fourth of July," was in reality written on August 18, 1863. In it he told of flying up to Lake Tahoe alongside Hank Monk. In the letter to his mother and sister, August 19, from Steamboat Springs, he described his active social life at Tahoe, and its adverse effect on his cold, forcing him to try the hot springs, which he pictured. In an autobiographical dictation of October 12, 1906, he talked about Henry having erysipelas, and the incident of the peeling skin which he placed at the head of his list of "accidents." "Ma, you have given my vanity a deadly thrust" opens the letter of August 19, 1863, from Steamboat Springs. Clemens' *Enterprise* letters from San Francisco and his review of *Mazeppa* appeared in Smith. His fashion notes were reprinted from the *Enterprise,* in the *Golden Era,* September 27, 1863, collected in Franklin Walker, ed., *The Washoe Giant in San Francisco.* Those "blasted" children were referred to in the fashion report, "The Lick House Ball." De Quille, "Housekeeping with Mark Twain," appeared in the *Golden Era,* December 6, 1863, and "Salad Days of Mark Twain," is in the *San Francisco Examiner,* March 19, 1893; in each article he described his and Sam's rooms, and Joe Goodman's part in furnishing them. In "Housekeeping . . . ," De Quille told of their compatibility, of Mrs. Fitch's mince pies, and Sam's dodge to get firewood. Benson printed the announcement of the marriage of Sam and Dan from the *Gold Hill Daily News.* De Quille, "Salad Days . . . ," reported the activities at Chauvel's gymnasium. The *Gold Hill Daily News* report on Sam and Dan fencing is in Effie Mona Mack, *Mark Twain in Nevada.*

In "Salad Days" Dan told about Sam half-closing his eyes when fencing; about his encounter with George Dawson; and Clemens' acceptance of Goodman's assignment to look over the Silver Mountain mines. In that article Dan also described Sam's anger at being reminded of his battered nose. Clemens' report of De Quille's accident appeared May 1, 1864, in the *Golden Era,* reprinted from the *Enterprise.* Dan's rejoinder republished in the same issue of the *Golden Era*—both appear in Walker. Clemens gave the background for writing what he called his "scathing satire" on the practice of issuing false dividends, in his *Sketches New and Old*, under the title "My Bloody Massacre." In the *Enterprise* it appeared as "The Empire City Massacre," reprinted in Benson from the *San Francisco Bulletin*, October 31, 1863. In *Roughing It*, Clemens recalled "Old Abe Curry's" introduction. De Quille, "Reporting . . . ," told of Sam's distress over the reaction to his hoax. Clemens' account of the opening of the Third House is in his *Enterprise* letter of December 13, 1863, which appears in Smith, as does his letter of December 12, 1863, describing the Logan Hotel at Tahoe. De Quille, "Artemus Ward in Nevada," *The Californian Illustrated Magazine*, August 1893, gave the date of Ward's arrival at Virginia City and the subject of his lecture. Clemens' "Greeting to Artemus Ward" is in the *Golden Era*, November 29, 1863, reprinted from the *Enterprise*, in Walker. Goodman, "Artemus Ward, His Visit to the Comstock Lode," *San Francisco Chronicle*, January 10, 1892, told of Ward helping to get out the *Enterprise*. De Quille, in his article on Ward, recalled his drollery, his delight in involved and meaningless definitions, and his joke on Sam Clemens. In "Salad Days . . . ," De Quille remembered cruising with Ward and Clemens, and their dancing with the hurdy-gurdy girls. In "Reporting . . . ," Dan said that sparkling Moselle was Clemens' favorite wine. In a letter to Jane Lampton, written possibly around January 2, 1864 (the first two pages are missing), Sam told about Ward's encouragement and Fitzhugh Ludlow's "encomium." When A. B. Paine edited this letter for publication, he omitted "swine" in Clemens' statement that he sometimes throws "a pearl before these swine here"; restored the contraction, and rewrote the sentence. Ward's promise to write "a powerfully convincing note" was repeated in his letter to Clemens of January 1, 1864, from Austin, Nevada (MTP). Sam quoted from this letter quite fully in his *Enterprise* despatch of January 10, 1864, in Smith. Goodman, in "Artemus Ward . . . ," told about the Christmas Eve celebration and the scramble over the roofs of Virginia City. De Quille, in "Salad Days . . . ," recalled the fistful of tickets given the night watchman. Joe Goodman observed Ward feeding Sam Clemens mustard with a spoon and remembered Ward's words. In his January 1 letter, Artemus told the story of what happened to him after their last party. In his letter of around January 2, Sam asked his mother to be sure to invite Artemus to the house.

16. *Farewell to Washoe*, pp. 221–41.

In that same early January letter, from which the first two pages are missing, Sam told his mother about Ward's flattering letter and spoke of writing for the *Mercury* "semi-occasionally." Clemens' "Doings in Nevada," dated January 4, 1864, is included in Smith. Sam's January 9, 1864 letter to Jane Lampton and Pamela (MTP) was written on Orion's official stationery. "Those Blasted Children" was reprinted in the *Golden Era*, March 27, 1864, included in Walker. Clemens reported on his Third House message in a letter to the *Enterprise*, January 28, 1864, in Smith. He told Pamela of his inability to write out his Third House message, in a letter of March 18, 1864 (MTP). In that same letter he mentioned his appointment as a notary. In Clemens' comments on legislative proceedings, January 27, 1864, he wrote of the act providing for the appointment of notaries public, and the defining of their duties; spoke of the bill, which, if passed, would leave Storey County with twelve notaries rather than fifteen hundred; and quoted Clagett. "I was a mighty heavy wirepuller . . ." appears in the letter of August 19, 1863, to his mother and sister. Guy Louis Rocha and Roger Smith, "Mark Twain and the Nevada Notary Stampede," give a contemporary account; state the actual number of applications on file; and give the date of Sam's resignation. Jennie (Jane) Clemens, only child of Orion and Mollie, was born on September 14, 1855. Varble quotes Jane Lampton Clemens' letter about Jennie. Mack tells of the legislature adjourning to attend Jennie's funeral. Sam Clemens' blast at undertakers appeared in his *Enterprise* letter dated at Carson City, February 5, 1864, printed in Smith. Mack quoted the *Union* report that Clemens was working on "a bloody tragedy" for Adah Isaacs Menken. De Quille in "Salad Days . . . ," described Ada Clare; gave the number of dogs with the party; told of the Menken being squired everywhere by Tom Peasley and of his making her an honorary fireman. Sam wrote Pamela about showing his article to Menken and about her note to him; he also described her handwriting and his reply, in a letter of March 18, 1864 (MTP). De Quille, in "Salad Days . . . ," remembered Adah Isaacs' blank verse, provided a detailed account of the dinner party she and Ada Clare gave and told about Clemens being nipped in the leg. Walter Leman recalled Ada Clare's death from rabies at age thirty-eight, following a bite from one of her dogs. Constance Rourke, *Troupers of the Gold Coast*, mentioned Menken liking to wear free-flowing dresses in yellow. Clemens in the March 18 letter to Pamela told her that he was taking the place of both editors while Goodman was in the Sandwich Islands, and had stipulated that he not be expected to write about politics or Eastern news. The *Gold Hill Daily News,* April 26, 1864, told about the value of the silver brick. Angel wrote about Gridley's "eccentric" wager. In *Roughing It,* Clemens described the decorated flour sack and told of joining the procession into Gold Hill. His letter home, May 17, 1864 (MTP), gave a full account of the day's activities with the sack of flour. The contents of his offending editorial were quoted in a letter of May 18, 1864, signed by four Carson City women, and addressed to: "Editors of Enterprise." It is in Smith. Sam wrote to Mollie on May 20, 1864, giving her the history of his editorial and how it came to be printed; he also admitted to having been drunk when he wrote it (MTP). Smith's work contains the entire exchange of letters between Clemens and James Laird, J. W. Wilmington, and other principals in the quarrel. Benson prints "The 'How Is It' Issue," and Clemens' reply, "How It Is." In his *Autobiography,* Sam recalled the Sunday spent in target practice. The *Gold Hill Daily News'* editorial, entitled "HOITY! TOITY!" appears in Smith. Sam's letter to Mrs. Ellen G. Cutler is dated May 23, 1864. "Don't stump for the Sanitary Fund . . . ," Sam's letter of May 25, 1864 (MTP), opens. Sam's account of the aborted duel between Joe Goodman and Tom Fitch was reprinted from the *Enterprise,* in Angel. Both in Smith and in Mack there are accounts of the second meeting at Ingraham's Ranch. In his *Autobiography,* Sam recalled Joe Goodman "tumbling" his man and Fitch's permanent limp. The Henness Pass route was the most popular from Virginia City to Marysville, California. Dan De Quille's note on the back of Clemens' reply to W. K. Cutler, telling that it was not sent, but that a second version was mailed, is found in Smith. John K. Lovejoy's lament at Clemens' departure is in Edgar M. Branch, *Clemens of the 'Call'.*

17. *Exile,* pp. 242–56.

In his letter of May 26, 1864, to Orion (MTP), Sam spoke of staying no longer than a month in San Francisco, and mentioned their Hale & Norcross stock; he sent the certificates to his brother in August, ordering him to put them in the safe (MTP). The San Francisco Directory for 1864 lists Steve Gillis as a typographer for the *Evening Bulletin.* Sam's *Enterprise* letter praising the Occidental Hotel, reprinted in *Golden Era,* June 26, 1864, is in Walker. Clemens characterized Mrs. Hitchcock in a letter of January 13, 1869, to Olivia Langdon (MTP). Altrocchi was consulted for details about Lillie Hitchcock. In that same January letter to Livy, Sam spoke of his and Lillie's attraction to one another. Manuscript of the unfinished "Hellfire Hotchkiss" is in MTP. Sam's letter to his mother and sister, telling them about moving constantly, is dated September 25, 1864 (V). Clemens recalled the dauntless spirit of Angus Gillis, in his *Autobiography*. The Gillis Family History was consulted. On July 15, 1864, Sam wrote Dan De Quille a spirited account of the landlady's recital of their antics (MTP). Sam described San Jose for his mother and Pamela on September 25, 1864 (V). Altrocchi gave a history of Warm Springs. Clemens' squib, "Inexplicable News from San José," is included in Branch, *"Call."* In the September 25 letter to his mother and sister, he told about Steve Gillis' coming marriage to "a very pretty girl worth $130,000 in her own right," but did not name her. He mentioned that he would be alone again, but only until she and Steve built a house. In that letter he told about the invitation to San Luis Obispo and Mexico City. When he wrote to Orion and Mollie on September 28, 1864 (MTP), he spoke of Steve's coming marriage, gave the girl's name, and said she was worth $100,000. She was Emeline (Sam spelled it "Emmelina") Russ, the daughter of Emanuel C. C. Russ, a custom jeweler and large land-holder in San Francisco. "I knew the Gillis family intimately," Clemens said in his *Autobiography* and spoke again of the "grit" which character-ized them. A photocopy of "The Mysterious Chinaman," in manuscript, is from the McDonald Collection. Telling of Steve Gillis' marriage put Laura Wright in Sam's mind, and he asked for news of her in the Sep-tember 25 letter home. In that same letter he told about his attack on another coroner. In a letter to Orion and Mollie, dated September 28, 1864, he talked of making a start on his book. In an earlier letter to his brother, August 13 (MTP), he spoke of Dr. Bellows' delight in his squibs. Jane Lampton's letter of September 28–30, 1864, is included in MTBM. A copy of the letter to his mother extolling the benefits of belonging to the Olympic Club in San Francisco, was enclosed in the August 13 letter to Orion and Mollie. John Howell, *Sketches of the Sixties,* quoted Harte's recollection of his first meeting with Clemens. Sam's conflicting opinions of Harte appear in his *Autobiography*. Branch, *"Call,"* told of James N. Gillis being a delegate to the State Convention, and mentioned that Clem-ens reported all the sessions. Information about James Gillis' training as a physician was furnished by Janet McDonald. In *Roughing It*, Sam told about Gillis, using Greek and Latin quotations, and the fact that he was university educated. He spoke of Jim's outstanding talents, also in his *Autobiography*. Emeline Russ was married in December 1867 to a Frederick Gutzkow ("Marriages," in the *San Francisco Morning Call,* December 31, 1867). In that same month and year, Steve Gillis married Catherine Robinson, a niece of the first Mrs. Joseph T. Goodman, according to the Gillis Family History. According to Alfred Doten, who knew Mrs. Goodman in 1866, she was "formerly 'Maggie Wells'." "The Doleful Ballad of the Rejected Lover" is known only through Joe Goodman's description of hearing Steve Gillis and Sam Clemens sing it and act it out. He told Paine about it, and he mentioned it in his *Biography* of Clemens. In his *Autobiography,* Sam recalled his dismissal by George Barnes. In *Roughing It,* he gave a moving account of his "slinking"; told of holding on to his last ten cents, and of pawning his possessions, an example of exaggeration for impact. De Quille, "Reporting with . . . ," remembered Clemens chafing at his "literary drudgery" in San Francisco. He also knew of Jim Gillis' cabin as a "Bohemian infirmary," where he, too, had gone for rejuvenation. Sam fondly recalled Jackass Gulch as a "sylvan paradise," in his *Autobiography.*

18. *The Jumping Frog,* pp. 257–65.

In Clemens' Notebook 4, he listed some of the authors in Jim Gillis' book collection, and commented that it contained "only first class Literature." Goodwin also wrote about Jim's interest in books, and noted that he was bold enough to dispute any proposition he found in them. In his *Autobiography,* Sam recalled Dick Stoker listening to Jim's tales, and described him further in *Roughing It,* where Clemens retold the story of Dick's sagacious cat, "Tom Quartz." Goodwin, who had also stayed with Gillis, wrote about his rapport with the wild creatures. Clemens retold "Jim Baker's Blue Jay Yarn" in *A Tramp Abroad.* In an autobiographical dictation of May 26, 1907, Sam spoke of "The Tragedy of the Burning Shame" as one of Jim's impromptu tales. Sam recalled in a letter to Jim Gillis, dated January 26, 1870 (McDonald Collection), Dick Stoker playing "Rinaldo." In his dictations, Clemens told of having to modify the skit for use in *Huckleberry Finn.* William Graves, in "Mark Twain's 'Burning Shame,'" wrote about hearing the Swedish version in Seattle. In his *Autobiography,* Sam recalled how he and Joe Twichell laughed themselves "lame and sore" over *1601.* Originally, Clemens called the letter for Twichell, "Fireside Conversation in the Time of Queen Elizabeth"; later he shortened it to *1601* and always referred to it by that title. He wrote that letter in his octagonal study at Quarry Farm. Edna Bryan Buckbee in *The Saga of Old Tuolumne,* described Nelly and Molly Daniels. Buckbee, who grew up in the area, recalled the tradition concerning Jim Gillis wearing a white linen suit in summer. In Notebook 4, Clemens entered one line in French about Gillis being called an "aristocrat" because he wore a white shirt. Gillis family tradition holds that Jim Gillis at times lost patience with Sam over his attention to his French lessons; Janet McDonald is the source. Buckbee described Ross Coon. The qualities of Angels Camp whiskey are enumerated in Clemens' squib, "An Unbiased Criticism," in the *Californian*, March 18, 1865, included in Howells, *Sketches of the Sixties*. In this same piece, Sam expressed admiration for the Calaveras grove of Big Trees. The remainder of the chapter is based on Clemens' Notebook 4.

19. *Taste of Fame*, pp. 266–93.

The fact that no letters from Sam Clemens to his family have been found for an eleven-month period is possibly accounted for because "almost four trunks" of his letters to Jane Lampton Clemens were burned in 1904, by the executor of Mollie Clemens' estate, upon orders from Sam Clemens. This disconcerting information appears in "Description of Provenance," pp. 460–61, in the 1988 edition of *Mark Twain's Letters*, issued by the Mark Twain Project. If this is not the answer for the absence of letters home, then some other disaster befell them, for Jane Lampton never seems to have obeyed Sam's instructions to destroy certain letters, but simply cut away the parts he wanted to be kept secret. The first known letter for this period, October 19, 1865, is in MTP. A clipping from the *Alta Californian* (San Francisco), reprinting their New York correspondent's comment on "Jim Smiley and His Jumping Frog," was pasted on a page of Sam's letter to his mother and sister, dated January 20, 1866 (MTP). In this same letter he said, regarding his piece about correspondents, "If it makes Annie mad I can't help it." On the back of his October 19 letter, to Orion, Sam wrote Mollie about being "utterly miserable" and in debt, and spoke of suicide. On December 13, he wrote Orion about Herman Camp and the almost certain chance of selling the Tennessee land (MTP). "What Have the Police Been Doing?" was printed on January 21, 1866, in the *Golden Era;* in Walker. Albert S. Evans' reference to Clemens being jailed for drunkenness, appeared in the *Gold Hill Evening News*, January 22, 1866. Evans was the *News'* San Francisco correspondent and signed his dispatches "Amigo." Sam's January 20 letter to Jane Lampton and Pamela contained the wish that he was piloting again, and his disgust that his first fame was resting on that "villainous" sketch, the "Jumping Frog." But as he continued with the letter, his mood improved, and he had much to say about his literary plans. Duckett identified the Boston paper Harte would be contributing to. Clemens' letter to Bowen was dated May 7, 1866. Albert Evans' parting gibe appeared in the *Gold Hill Evening News* on February 19, 1866. In his autobiographical dictations, Clemens told about Orion's refusal to sign Camp's contract and his reasons. Although no letter to Orion, blasting him for his selfishness, exists, there are references to Sam's angry correspondence and to Orion's responses, in Sam's ensuing letters. As late as May 22, 1866, in a letter to Mollie (V), Sam was still venting his bitterness toward Orion. His short farewell letter home was dated March 5, 1866 (V). Unless otherwise noted, Clemens' descriptions of the Hawaiian Islands, and his observations and experiences there, are taken from his *Sacramento Union* letters, collected by A. Grove Day, in *Mark Twain's Letters from Hawaii;* and in Walter F. Frear, *Mark Twain and Hawaii.* Sam's comparison of Hawaiian moonlight with that in Washoe, is in his Notebook 6. In his letter of April 3, 1866 (V), to his mother and sister, he mentioned his intention of bringing home the human bones. In his Notebook 6 entry about Miss McFarlane, his use of "long" was the same term his mother used when she spoke of "Sammy's long talk"—meaning his drawl. The April 3 letter told about his social triumphs. Information regarding the bird, 'Ō'ō, and the feather cloak, in Dwight Holing, "The Birds of *Paradise,"* *Pacific Discovery,* July–September 1987. In Sam's letter of June 21, 1866 (V), to his mother and sister, he told about Orion's letter to him, and of his angry reply which he knows had made his brother "mad." In *Roughing It,* Clemens described his adventures during the hazardous walk across the crater floor. In the June 21 letter home, he told about seeing the eruption, of riding over the hardest of mountain roads, of his exhaustion, of his visit with Mr. Cony, and of Anson Burlingame's arrival. He wrote his mother and sister on June 27 about Burlingame's countless acts of kindness to him. Edward Burlingame, Sam described in the autobiographical dictation of February 20, 1906, and spoke of the young man attending all the balls and fandangos. In a letter to Will Bowen, dated August 25, 1866, he told about singing the old hoss song before the missionaries. In Notebook 5, he wrote on July 19, 1866, "Now we shall see who beats to San Francisco."

20. *"The Trouble Begins at 8,"* pp. 294–310.

On August 20, 1866, Sam concluded a thirteen-page letter he had started to his mother and sister on July 30, while still at sea (V). There he told about his ship and the *Comet* entering the Golden Gate together. He also told them he had sent Captain Mitchell's log on the *New York Times.* The *Times* did not accept it. The account of his name appearing as "Mark Swain" in *Harper's* was included in an autobiographical sketch (MTP) written about 1898. A rough draft of his dedication to Jane Lampton appears in his Notebook 5. In *Roughing It,* he wrote about his decision to enter the lecturing field. Angel contains a biographical sketch of Denis McCarthy. Again in *Roughing It* there appears a graphic description of his terrors as time for the first speech approached. He likewise told of its ultimate success. Paine, *Biography,* Appendix D, is the source for "The Trouble Is Over." Joseph T. Goodman recalled Sam as having "always the same slight figure, the same noble head, the same gray eyes, the same delicate hands and feet, and the same half-skipping, half-shambling gait," in Sam P. Davis, *History of Nevada,* quoted in Mack. Clemens described Marysville, and the mines of Grass Valley, in "Interior Notes," written for the *San Francisco Evening Bulletin,* included in Benson. In an autobiographical sketch (MTP), he wrote about his introduction at Red Dog. "Interior Notes" contained a description of the eventful horseback ride back to Grass Valley. Orion wrote a letter to Pamela on March 19, 1866 (UV), telling her about opening a law office at Meadow Lake. Sam described that nearly deserted settlement in his "Interior Notes." Erwin G. Gudde, *California Gold Camps,* was consulted for additional information about Meadow Lake and its subsequent history. Sam told about the overcrowded coach in the "Interior Notes." His letter of October 29, 1866, to Robert M. Howland, is in the Nevada Historical Society. Mack quoted the *Enterprise's* October 21 announcement of Sam's lecture. A letter headed November 1, 1866 (V), to "All the Folks," was misdated by Sam; it was actually November 2. There is a typographical error in the printed version of Sam's response to the "call" for him to lecture in Carson City. He has been made to say, "disgorge a few lines and as much truth as I can pump out . . ." "Lines" must be read as "lies," for the phrase "disgorge a few lies" was a favorite, and he used it on at least four other occasions in reference to his talks. In his *Journal,* Alfred Doten recorded the weather for the night of November 10; he also noted that Steve Gillis had five confederates. In *Roughing It* Clemens said there were six. In that book he described the sharp wind that chilled them through on the Divide. In his "Card to the Highwaymen," written directly after the robbery, Sam told the entire story; the "Card" was included in Benson. Dan De Quille's dispatch, "Mark Twain Robbed," also appears in Benson. Years later Steve Gillis and Joe Goodman gave Paine a joint account of the robbery and the part each played in it. Paine included it in his *Biography*. In *Roughing It*, Clemens recounted the aftermath—the heavy cold, the doctor bills, and the reflection that this prank cured *him* of playing practical jokes. In his *Autobiography*, Sam told about his decision to open his new lecture with the tale of Hank Monk's wild drive with Horace Greeley as his passenger, and how he managed it. Benson reprinted the *Alta California*'s comments on Clemens' lecture, and the announcement of his new assignment. An undated and unidentified clipping in a Clemens scrapbook (MTP), headed "How 'Mark Twain' Got Ahead of the Highwaymen," gave the story of the telegram from Asa Nudd. Sam also told about it in "So-Long," printed in the *Alta*, December 14, 1866. Clemens' farewell lecture in San Francisco, in Benson.

21. *New York Debut*, pp. 311–36.

Unless otherwise noted, all information on Clemens and his activities, and direct quotations from his writings, are found in his Notebook 7, and his letters to the *Alta California*, which appear in Franklin Walker and G. Ezra Dane, *Mark Twain's Travels with Mr. Brown*. Those *Alta* letters not included in this collection were obtained in photocopy from MTP. Clemens' description of Captain Edgar Wakeman are found in the *Autobiography*. In a letter dated June 7, 1867, Sam wrote Will Bowen about the misery he experienced in going ashore after a long ocean voyage. The undated letter to Mollie Clemens is at Vassar. Sam's vision of the long sea trip as a magnificent picnic appears in *The Innocents Abroad*, which is also the source for his having given as references the names of those least likely to know him. His response to Captain Duncan's charge that he came staggering into his office and filled it with the fumes of "bad whiskey," appeared in the *New York World*, February 18, 1877. Recollections of the gifts Sam brought home are found in MTBM. "Keep up your lick & you will become a great minister . . ." appears in a fragmentary letter of November 2 (?), 1866 (V). "Views on Female Suffrage," the defense by "Mrs. Mark Twain," and the attack by Mrs. Zeb Leavenworth were found as clippings in an undated scrapbook (MTP). The March 19,

1867 letter to Charles Webb, about the publication date of "The Jumping Frog," is at UV. In a letter to Charles Warren Stoddard, April 23, 1867, Clemens gave the publication date for the "Frog." Annie Moffett's recollection of Sam's story about John James Godfrey, in MTBM. The Keokuk *Constitution,* April 7, 1867, heralded Clemens as "the celebrated California humorist." The issue of April 8 gave a review of his lecture. Clemens to Harte, May 1, 1867, is in Paine, *Letters.* Sam's "Dear Folks" letter of April 19, 1867 (MTP), gave James Russell Lowell's opinion of the "Jumping Frog." An earlier letter, April 15 (UV), also to "Dear Folks," told about meeting John Murphy with the check from the *Alta,* and his intention to book passage. He also spoke of the "boys" in New York getting up a "call" for him to lecture. In his *Autobiography,* he gave an account of Frank Fuller, and Fuller's enthusiasm in acting as his lecture agent. Sam's letter of May 1, 1867 (V), written on Westminster Hotel paper, told about the gloomy prospects for the lecture. "There is not going to be anybody in the Cooper Institute . . . ," appears in the *Autobiography.* Fuller's recollections of Sam's objections to the claw-hammer coat appeared in the New York *Times,* October 1, 1911. Clemens recollected his feelings of terror at the thought of an empty house, and his later discovery that the streets were thronged and the hall packed, in his *Autobiography.* Fuller, in the same *Times* article, gave an account of the talk and the audience's reaction to it. In a letter home, dated May 20, 1867 (MTP), he told about having placed his Sandwich Islands manuscript in the publisher's hands. In his *Autobiography,* he recalled his enjoyment of the "genuine" minstrel show. His letter expressing his wild impatience to start on the voyage was written on June 1, 1867 (V). His final, dark letter to his family, is dated June 7, 1867 (V).

22. *The Grand Pleasure Excursion,* pp. 337–60.

Clemens to John McComb, by this time an editor and coproprietor of the *Alta California,* is dated June 8, 1867; it was published in the *Boston Sunday Globe,* November 29, 1964. Sam's impressions of sailing day are found in the opening pages of *The Innocents Abroad.* He described certain passengers in his Notebook 8, and in his *Alta* letters, which are on microfilm and have also been published in Daniel Morley McKeithan, *Traveling with the Innocents Abroad.* This work includes six of his letters to the *New York Tribune.* Unless otherwise noted, Clemens' shipboard activities, his travels ashore, and his opinions are based upon his Notebooks 8 and 9, and his letters to the *Alta* and *Tribune.* Personal letters will be cited. His description of the shipboard ball appears in *The Innocents* . . . Sam's characterization of Mary Mason Fairbanks is found in a letter home, December 10, 1867 (V). Julia Newell's opinion of Clemens is quoted in Justin Kaplan, *Mr. Clemens and Mark Twain*. Mary Fairbanks' first impression of Sam appeared in a despatch she sent to the *Cleveland Herald*. It is quoted in Dixon Wecter, *Mark Twain to Mrs. Fairbanks*. In this same work are Emily Severance's remarks on Mrs. Fairbanks' fluency in French. "I was the worst swearer . . . ," appears in Sam's letter to Mary Fairbanks, December 2, 1867. In his December 10, 1867 letter home, he told about Mrs. Fairbanks sewing on his buttons and feeding him Egyptian jam (V). Both Solon Severance and Emma Beach's accounts of Sam tearing up his manuscript because of Mary Fairbanks' criticisms, are found in Paine, *Biography*. A six-line note home from Gibraltar, dated June 30, 1867 (V), told of being "clear worn out"; Sam's letter begun to Lillie Hitchcock and continued to "Dear Folks" is at Vassar. His letter home from Genoa, dated July 14, 1867 (V), was written on lined paper torn from his notebook. In a note home from Naples, August 9, 1867 (MTP), he mentioned sending off his acceptance to Senator Stewart that day. The small Greek head which Clemens carried away from the Acropolis and presented to his family was used by them as a paperweight for years. In a letter to his "Folks," written at Yalta (V), he described the "jolly & sociable" Russians who came on board; mentioned the suggestion that they visit the Czar; spoke of writing the address to the Czar; and assured his family that he was prepared to entertain royalty "in style."

23. *Journey's End*, pp. 361–73.

In Notebook 9, Clemens told about the cannon salute, and the fireworks as the *Quaker City* left Yalta. He described Dan Slote's collections which crowded their cabin in a letter to his mother and sister, September 1, 1867, (V). As with previous chapters, unless otherwise cited, material is found in Clemens' notebook and his newspaper letters. He spoke in his autobiographical dictations about seeing the "ivory miniature" of Olivia Langdon. The letter of instruction to the Bible seller is dated September 24 (actually 25), 1867 (MTP). Alexander E. Jones, "Mark Twain and Freemasonry," told about the gavel. Sam described climbing the Great Pyramid in *Innocents Abroad*, where he also gave Dr. Gibson's credentials and paid his respects to the Smithsonian. Sam's joke on Dr. Gibson appears in Henry F. Pommer, "Mark Twain's 'Commissioner of the

United States.' '" The continued letter begun on October 12, 1867, is at Vassar. It was not until June 17, 1868, after he had started writing *The Innocents Abroad*, that Clemens identified Julia Newell as a member of the group that went up through Spain, in a letter to Mary Fairbanks, June 17, 1868. Sam's fullest account of the excursion to the Alhambra is in his home letter of October 24, 1867 (V). In *The Innocents Abroad* he devoted seven lines to that hurried trip. Clemens' letter to Joe Goodman, from Cadiz, was included in excerpt with Goodman's comments on it, printed in the *Territorial Enterprise* on December 1, 1867 (MTP). In *The Innocents Abroad*, Sam wrote briefly about the visit to Bermuda. "The long, strange cruise was over . . ." is from the final line in that book.

24. *On the Wing*, pp. 374–97.

His "Dear Folks" letter of November 19, 1867 (V), recounted his arrival in New York that morning and followed him throughout the day. In that letter he failed to mention the fact that Charlie Langdon was also to have had dinner with him and Mary Fairbanks, but spoke of it in a note of December 1, 1867, to Mary. Clemens' second day in New York was chronicled in a letter to "Dear Folks" dated November 20 (V), which he ended with a sentence as involved and meaningless as any of Artemus Ward's, done to tease his mother and Annie, surely. After writing, "I will move Heaven & earth for Orion," he began a new paragraph: "The reason I brought nothing from any of these was because it was a bore & when I did, I lost it, which were it not considering to inefficiency of things, notwithstanding in Europe they do & sometimes even in Asia, withal." He left it unsigned. His first letter from Washington was dated November 25 (V). Paine prints in both the *Biography* and *Letters*, Elisha Bliss' letter to Clemens and Sam's reply to Bliss, December 2, 1867 (MTP). In the December 10, 1867 letter to "Dear Folks," he told of calling on the Secretary of the Interior (V). Sam's response to Mary Fairbanks' suggestion of finding a good wife, was written on December 12, 1867. He spoke of his restlessness to Emily Severance on December 24, 1867, in *Fairbanks*. In a letter to his mother and sister, written from Washington on January 8, 1868, he said: "I have just arrived from New York—been there ever since Christmas day, staying at Dan Slote's house . . ."; and told of his meeting on New Year's Day with Olivia Langdon and Alice Hooker. In his *Autobiography* Clemens gave the history of Olivia's accident and her cure by Dr. James Rogers Newton. Charles Dickens described his illness and the sherry eggnog in a letter of

December 22, 1867, included in Norman and Jeanne Mackenzie, *Charles Dickens, A Life*. The January 8 letter to Jane Lampton and Pamela gave an account of his dinner at Henry Ward Beecher's and spoke of his just having learned he is to lecture the next night. It was William Dean Howells who was aware that Clemens never failed in a lecture, and wrote of it in "An Appreciation," included in *Mark Twain's Speeches*. In that same January 9 letter Sam spoke of getting to work on that "confounded book." George Francis Train's book was entitled *Championship of Woman*. For the text of Sam's toast, three sources, all differing, were used: *Mark Twain's Speeches* (no editor acknowledged); Howell, ed., *Sketches of the Sixties;* and Paul Fatout, ed., *Mark Twain Speaking*. Clemens sent the clipping giving his speech and a covering note to "Dear Folks," on January 13, 1868 (V). He defended himself to Mary Fairbanks on January 24; his reply to her "scorcher," January 30, exists only in postscript. On January 24, 1868, he gave Mary Fairbanks an account of his stay with the Hookers, and the restrictions. Clemens wrote his mother and Pamela from Hartford on January 24, 1868 (V) about stopping with Dan Slote and making the contract with James Gordon Bennett. In a letter to Will Bowen, January 25, 1868, from New York, he spoke of taking a drink on the contract. In that same January 24 letter home, he gave an account of his visit with Beecher, Beecher's advice, and the contract with Bliss. In his letter to Bowen he also told about the "tiptop" contract for the book; and he recalled their days together at Dawson's school in Hannibal. Clemens to Bliss is dated January 27 (MTP). Sam told his family about the various posts offered him in a letter of February 6, 1868, (V), written from Washington. Sam to Orion, regarding chasing phantoms, February 21, 1868, is in Paine, *Letters*. Sam asked Mary Fairbanks for her letters to the *Cleveland Herald*, on February 20, 1868. Clemens wrote the sketch, "Riley—Newspaper Correspondent," which he later included in his *Sketches New and Old*. He told "Dear Folks" about moving five times, and the reasons, in a short letter dated February 21, 1868 (V). William M. Stewart, *Reminiscences*, provides faulty recollections of Clemens. A report on Sam's faultless attire appeared in the *Philadelphia Press* (MTP). On February 9, 1868, Sam told Mary Fairbanks about his illness, and gave her the Indiana Street address. On March 10, 1868, he wrote Mary that he *must* go to San Francisco and stop the *Alta*'s publication of those "slangy" letters. Sam's letter to his mother from sea was dated March 15 (V). He wrote Mary Fairbanks on May 5, 1868, about his San Francisco lecture and the proceeds, paid in gold and silver. The telegram to the *Territorial Enter-*

prise is in Mack, as is the *Enterprise*'s announcement of his coming. Alfred Doten, who also witnessed the prologue to John Milleain's execution and the hanging itself, described it in detail in the *Gold Hill Evening News*. In his journal, Doten spoke of the springlike day, April 25, and mentioned the ice cream man; he also recorded that he met Clemens at the *Enterprise* office on that date. Sam told Mary Fairbanks, in a letter commenced on May 1, about working on his correspondence for Eastern newspapers. Doten attended the Odd Fellows celebration and heard Goodman's poetry recited; he also went to hear Clemens speak, listened to Sam playing the piano and singing the old hoss song behind the curtain, and described his apology. Doten was so delighted with the lecture he attended the following evening. He noted that Clemens did not get a full house. In a letter of June 17, 1868, from San Francisco, Sam wondered to Mary Fairbanks why the local ministers were blasting him. He told Mary about the enthusiastic reception to his lecture on Venice, July 5, 1868, and spoke of the steamship company refusing to let him pay for his ticket.

25. *The Siege of Elmira*, pp. 398–423.

Clemens' account of the "Country School Exibition" is included in his *Alta* letter of September 6, 1868. A rough draft of "The Story of Mamie Grant," is in Notebook 11, as is his sketch about a balloon voyage. A note added at a later time, just above the start of the story about the Frenchman and his balloon, states that the sketch was never finished because of the publication of Jules Verne's book. The inventor of the "noble big balloon" in *Tom Sawyer Abroad* was possibly based on Orion Clemens, who in his last years was inventing a flying machine. The meeting with Captain Wakeman was also recounted in his *Alta* letter. His decision to turn Wakeman's account of his dream voyage to heaven into a burlesque of *The Gates Ajar*, a novel by Elizabeth Ward published in 1868 under her maiden name, Elizabeth Stuart Phelps, is in an autobiographical dictation of August 30, 1906, (MTP). He wrote Mary Fairbanks on August 3, 1868, about working on an article for the *Tribune*. Sam Clemens' daughter Clara remembered the authoritative clang of the iron gates, in her book, *My Father, Mark Twain,* and spoke of the unexpected stairways and halls in the Elmira mansion. In a letter started on August 24, 1868 (V), broken off in midsentence and continued the next day, Sam told his family how comfortably he was situated at the Langdons, and the reasons for having to stay so long. Dixon Wecter, *The Love Letters of Mark*

Twain, quoted from an unpublished manuscript, "What I know about Mark Twain," written by Hattie Lewis, Livy's first cousin. Hattie is the source for how she, Sam, and Livy entertained themselves. Clemens' first letter to Livy is included in Wecter, *The Love Letters of Mark Twain,* designated hereafter as L.L. Katy Leary, in Lawton, spoke of the "sacred green box." Mrs. Langdon's letter to Mary Fairbanks, September 4, 1868, is in *Fairbanks.* Sam's letter of March 12, 1869, to Livy (MTP) indicates he had recently learned that his two-week stay at the Langdons' was not appreciated. Sam wrote Mary Fairbanks, in a letter dated September 24, 1868, about his deep hatred for St. Louis. Sam's letter to Livy from St. Louis was dated September 20, 1868 (L.L.). The best account of his and Charlie Langdon's accident is found in a letter to Mary Fairbanks, dated October 5, 1868; it was written just a few days afterward. In his autobiographical recollection of that accident, forty years later, he made a fine story when he told how the extension of time forwarded his suit. Actually during those extra days Livy refused his marriage proposal again and again. He wrote her on October 18, 1868, asking forgiveness for his rash letter. His October letter to Mary Fairbanks, telling her about his new lecture, was undated. In the October 18 letter (MTP), he spoke of having met Joseph Hopkins Twichell and his wife. W. A. Swanberg, *Sickles the Incredible,* was consulted. Sam's characterization of Twichell as a "bully boy," quoted by Wecter in L.L. Clemens' *Alta* letter of October 4, 1868, gives an account of his and Twichell's rambles afoot. His letter to Jane Lampton, from the Everett House, New York, headed only "Election Day," told about his visit with the Wileys and with Mrs. Garth; this letter is only a fragment, and it appears in MTBM, which is also the source for Margaret Wiley's recollection of Sam's talk with her father, George Wiley. His note of November 18, 1868, reporting to "Dear Folks" that he became the "lion" after his lecture, is at Vassar, as is his November 20 letter telling his family about his success in playing against Fanny Kemble. His letter to Mary Fairbanks, from "Paradise," was written on November 26. His jubilant letter to Joe Twichell, November 28, 1868, is found in Clara Clemens. Twichell's reply is quoted in part in L.L. Mrs. Langdon's letter to Mary Fairbanks, is dated December 1, 1868, and is included in *Fairbanks* as well as L.L. Clemens to his sister is also found in L.L. The offending sentences in Sam's letter to Mr. Langdon are discussed by Clemens in his reply to Jervis Langdon, dated December 29, 1868; also in L.L. Sam's "Hip-hip-Hurrah!" to Joe Twichell, written on December 12, 1868, is in L.L. Clemens to Mary Fairbanks, telling about Mr. Langdon's good humor, and about Livy reading Mary's letter aloud, written from Lansing, Michigan, is dated December 24, 1868. Wecter, *Fairbanks*, notes the economic reasons the Fairbankses had for wanting Clemens to buy into the *Cleveland Herald*. The first page of Sam's letter to "Dear Folks," December 10, 1868 (V), in which he told them to address him as Mark Twain, since his own name is little known, was written on a blank page opposite an announcement of an estate sale of "SOLID GOLD JEW-ELRY, Diamonds, Rubies, Emeralds, Pearls, Opals, Stone Cameos of the great artists . . . ," knowing it would interest them. Livy's plea regarding publication of his Christmas letter, written to Mary Fairbanks on January 15, 1869, is quoted in Wecter, *Fairbanks*. "She thinks a humorist is something perfectly awful," is in Sam's January 6, 1869 letter to Mary Fairbanks. The thirty-page letter to Livy was written December 14, 1868, from New York (MTP). His opinion of *Gulliver's Travels* and *Don Quixote*, and their unfitness, along with Shakespeare, for Livy's eyes, unexpurgated, is in a letter from Rochester, dated March 1, 1869. "Mark Twain's Orphanage Lecture," is in Fatout. Clemens quoted the damning words from the Rev. Horatio Stebbins, in a letter to Charles Warren Stoddard, August 25, 1869, adding that Stebbins "came within an ace of breaking off our marriage . . ."; included in L.L. Clemens' *Autobiography* contains his recollections of the letters from the West and Mr. Langdon's talk with him about those character references. At that later time he had forgotten that he gave Joe Goodman's name as a reference in his December 29, 1868 letter to Mr. Langdon, and in reconstructing the scene almost fifty years afterward, he had Langdon asking why he had *not* given Goodman's name. Sam's letter addressed to his entire family, announcing his engagement, dated February 5, 1869, is printed in L.L. Clemens to Mrs. Langdon, February 13, 1869, is also in L.L., as is his February 27 letter to Livy about traveling with her father. Mrs. Langdon to Mary Fairbanks, March 6, 1869, in Wecter, *Fairbanks*.

26. *Casting Anchor*, pp. 424–49.

Livy's letter to Sam, *"Don't* let your sister stay away . . ." was written November 14, 1869. He told his family on February 27, 1869, how unpretentious Livy is (V). On February 13, 1869, he told Mary Fairbanks about Livy keeping three sets of books. Livy to Sam, December 2, 1871, wrote of her decision about how to manage if they ever live beyond their means. In that same letter she spoke of feeling "cold" toward God. He described her "heart-free laugh" in his autobiography. Milton Rugoff,

The Beechers . . . , for information about John Hooker, and Calvin Stowe's imaginary friends. Rugoff enlarges Isabella Hooker's beliefs. Mildred Howells, *Life in Letters of William Dean Howells,* for his report on the informality of life at Nook Farm. The meeting with Nasby was described in Clemens' *Alta* letter, July 25, 1869. Nasby was the pen name of New York-born David Ross Locke. To Mary Fairbanks Sam wrote of his objections to having his picture for the frontispiece; he also listed possible titles. His account of the adventures with the "seedy old umbrella" was written on May 15, 1869. His low-spirited letter expressing his belief that Livy did not wish to see him again before he left for California, was written on May 19. Both letters in L.L. His stay at "The Elms," is described in a letter of May 24, 1869 (MTP). Susy Clemens on their mother's critical reading of *Huckleberry Finn,* is included in Sam's November 19, 1906 autobiographical dictation (MTP). Typical of Livy's suggestions were those she made when reading the manuscript of *Following the Equator* (1896–97); typical also were his responses. On July 4, 1869, while "all the bummers in town" were "busting fire-crackers," he wrote Mary Fairbanks, telling her he did his writing at the top of the house, where it was cool and comfortable. Kaplan and Paine, *Biography,* discuss sales of *The Innocents Abroad.* Sam wrote to Livy about the coal monopoly on September 3, 1869. "Open Letter to Commodore Vanderbilt" (MTP). Clemens' letter to Whitelaw Reid (noted for his Civil War reporting), was dated August 15, 1869 (MTP). Holmes to Clemens, September 26, 1869, is in Paine, *Letters.* The review by Howells, then an assistant editor of the *Atlantic,* appeared in the December issue. Tabitha Quarles (Greening) gave her opinion of *Innocents* in an interview reprinted in the *Hannibal Courier-Post,* March 6, 1935. Sam to Livy, on September 3, 1869, berated himself for refusing to wear flowers in his buttonhole and professed disappointment at not being freed from lecturing. Sam to Livy on November 24 and December 27, told about the Warners and about Isabella Hooker urging him to join the *Courant.* His complaint about New England hospitality was voiced in a letter of November 15, 1869 to Livy, and again on December 21. Howells' distinct recollection of Clemens in the sealskin coat and hat, and the publicity it gained them on New York's Broadway, is in Howells, *My Mark Twain.* Clemens' reflections on the fate of humorists are in his *Autobiography.* In the December 21 letter he spoke of Joe Goodman being in New York. On January 13, 1870, he wrote his defense of smoking. He told Mary Fairbanks that Livy never nagged in a letter of January 6, 1870. Jervis Langdon's attempt to bribe Clemens to stop using tobacco and drinking ale was recounted by Sam to Annie Adams Fields, who recorded it in her diary. His warning to Jane Lampton not to travel across the country in midwinter is included in a letter dated August 20, 1869 (V). He wrote to Pamela, enclosed the check, and told her and Annie to "hurry up," on January 15, 1870, in MTBM. Sam's letter to Jim Gillis is in photocopy in the McDonald collection. The only contemporary account of the wedding that was found after a long search in all possible sources was that written by Mary Fairbanks, "The Wedding of 'Mark Twain,'" for the *Cleveland Daily Herald,* published on February 8, 1870. Annie Moffett's single recollection of the wedding supper was boned turkey, but she remembered vividly the train trip to Buffalo in the private car and Sam's singing of the folk ballad. He used that song in an early version of *Huckleberry Finn,* but changed his mind and put it into *Life on the Mississippi.* In the 1985 edition of *Huckleberry Finn,* issued by the Mark Twain Project, the ballad has been restored to its rightful place. Annie Moffett also remembered her uncle Sam taking up the collection for Beecher, and all other incidents, in MTBM. Katy Leary, in Lawton, told about Clemens being momentarily at a loss for words and recalled what he said to Livy's father, after he had recovered his usual aplomb. "I have read those absurd fairy tales in my time . . . ," taken from Sam's letter to Dan De Quille, is in L.L. In a letter to Livy's parents, written on February 9, 1870, (L.L.), he spoke of telling the Twichells "the story of what happened to Little Sammy in Fairy Land . . ." Katy Leary described the bedroom furnishings and the pale blue satin curtains and spread; she also mentioned the use of the same material and color in the drawing room, and told of the wedding guests hiding there. Sam's letter to Will Bowen was written on February 6, 1870; Katy Leary is the source for the whiskey toddies. Annie Adams Fields wrote in her journal about Sam lying on the floor while he talked to her. William Dean Howells told the story of Clemens mimicking the old black "uncle," in *My Mark Twain.* There also he told about Sam having "the heart of a boy with the head of a sage." Clemens described his study at Quarry Farm in a letter to Twichell dated June 11, 1874.

Bibliography

Primary Sources, Manuscript

Samuel Langhorne Clemens Collection, Clifton Waller Barrett Library, University of Virginia, Charlottesville. Personal correspondence from February 28, 1862 through December 1, 1868.

Mark Twain Collection, The Library, Vassar College, Poughkeepsie, New York. Personal correspondence with family members, October 26, 1853 through June 25, 1870.

Mark Twain Papers, The Bancroft Library, University of California, Berkeley.

Primary Sources, Printed

Clemens, Clara. *My Father, Mark Twain.* Harper & Brothers, New York, 1931. Contains S.L.C. letters not found elsewhere.

Clemens, Mollie. "Molly Clemens's Note Book." Fred W. Lorch, ed. *The Palimpsest,* October 1929.

Clemens, Samuel L. *The Autobiography of Mark Twain.* Charles Neider, ed. Harper & Row, New York, 1959.

————. *The Autobiography of Mark Twain.* 2 vols. Albert Bigelow Paine, ed. Harper & Brothers, New York, 1924.

————. *Mark Twain, Business Man.* Samuel Charles Webster, ed. Little, Brown & Co., Boston, 1946.

————. "Mark Twain's Correspondence with David Watt Bowser." Pascal Covici, Jr., ed. *Southwest Review,* Spring 1960.

————. *Mark Twain's Letters, Vol. I: 1853–1866.* Edgar Marquess Branch, Michael B. Frank, Kenneth M. Sanderson, eds. University of California Press, Berkeley, 1988.

————. *Mark Twain's Letters.* 2 vols. Albert Bigelow Paine, ed. Harper & Brothers, New York, 1927.

————. *Mark Twain's Letters to Will Bowen.* Theodore Hornberger, ed. The University of Texas, Austin, 1941.

————. *Mark Twain to Mrs. Fairbanks.* Dixon Wecter, ed. Huntington Library, San Marino, California, 1949.

————. *Mark Twain-Howells Letters: The Correspondence of Samuel L. Clemens and William Dean Howells, 1872–1910.* 2 vols. Henry Nash Smith and William M. Gibson, eds. Harvard University Press, Cambridge, 1960.

————. *The Love Letters of Mark Twain.* Dixon Wecter, ed. Harper & Brothers, New York, 1949.

————. *Mark Twain's Notebooks & Journals, Vol. I (1855–1873).* Frederick Anderson, Michael B. Frank, and Kenneth M. Sanderson, eds. University of California Press, Berkeley, 1975.

Severance, Emily A. *Journal Letters of Emily A. Severance, "Quaker City" 1867.* Privately printed, Cleveland, 1938. Contains Clemens letter.

Mark Twain's Lectures Collected

Clemens, Samuel L. *Mark Twain on the Lecture Circuit.* Paul Fatout, ed. University of Indiana Press, Bloomington, 1960.

————. *Mark Twain Speaking.* Paul Fatout, ed. University of Iowa Press, Iowa City, 1976.

————. *Mark Twain's Speeches.* Albert Bigelow Paine, ed. Harper & Brothers, New York, 1929.

Mark Twain's Newspaper Correspondence and Sketches Collected

Clemens, Samuel L. *Clemens of the "Call," Mark Twain in San Francisco.*
Edgar M. Branch, ed. University of California Press, Berkeley, 1969.
————. *The Great Landslide Case.* Frederick Anderson and Edgar M.
Branch, eds. The Friends of The Bancroft Library, University of California, Berkeley, 1972.
————. *Mark Twain of the Enterprise: Newspaper Articles & Other Documents 1862–1864.* Henry Nash Smith and Frederick Anderson, eds.
University of California Press, Berkeley, 1957.
————. *Mark Twain's Letters from Hawaii.* A. Grove Day, ed. Appleton-Century, New York, 1966.
————. *Mark Twain and Hawaii.* Walter F. Frear, ed. Lakeside Press,
Chicago, 1947.
————. *Mark Twain's Letters in the Muscatine Journal.* Edgar M. Branch,
ed. The Mark Twain Association of America, Chicago, 1942.
————. *Mark Twain's San Francisco.* Bernard Taper, ed. McGraw-Hill,
New York, 1963.
————. *Mark Twain's Satires & Burlesques.* Franklin R. Rogers, ed. University of California Press, Berkeley, 1967.
————. *Sketches of the Sixties by Bret Harte and Mark Twain.* John
Howell, ed. John Howell, San Francisco, 1926.
————. *Mark Twain's Travels with Mr. Brown.* Franklin Walker & G. Ezra
Dane, eds. Russell & Russell, New York, 1971.
————. *Traveling with the Innocents Abroad. Mark Twain's Original Reports from Europe and the Holy Land.* Daniel Morley McKeithan, ed.
University of Oklahoma Press, Norman, 1958.
————. *The Washoe Giant in San Francisco: Heretofore Uncollected
Sketches by Mark Twain.* Franklin Walker, ed. George Fields, San
Francisco, 1938.

*The Writings of Mark Twain Used
as Sources and Background
in this Work*

Books

Clemens, Samuel L. *Adventures of Huckleberry Finn.* Walter Blair and
Victor Fischer, eds. University of California Press, Berkeley, 1985.

BIBLIOGRAPHY

————. *The Adventures of Tom Sawyer.* Random House, New York, 1952.

————. *Christian Science.* Harper & Brothers, New York, 1907.

————. *Extracts from Adam's Diary.* Harper & Brothers, New York, 1904.

————. *Extract from Captain Stormfield's Visit to Heaven.* Harper & Brothers, New York, 1909.

————. *Following the Equator.* American Publishing Co., Hartford, 1897.

————. *The Gilded Age.* Charles Dudley Warner co-author. American Publishing Co., Hartford, 1873.

————. *The Innocents Abroad; or, The New Pilgrim's Progress.* American Publishing Co., Hartford, 1870.

————. *Life on the Mississippi.* Harper & Brothers, New York, 1928.

————. *Mark Twain in Eruption.* Bernard De Voto, ed. Harper & Brothers, New York, 1940. Previously unpublished writings.

————. *Mark Twain's Hannibal, Huck & Tom.* Walter Blair, ed. University of California Press, Berkeley, 1969. Previously unpublished writings.

————. *Letters from the Earth.* Bernard De Voto, ed. Harper & Row, New York, 1974.

————. *Literary Essays.* Harper and Bros. New York, 1924.

————. *Mark Twain in Three Moods.* Dixon Wecter, ed. Friends of the Huntington Library, San Marino, California, 1948.

————. *My Platonic Sweetheart.* Harper & Brothers, New York, 1912.

————. *The Mysterious Stranger.* Harper & Brothers, New York, 1926.

————. *Personal Recollections of Joan of Arc.* Harper & Brothers, New York, 1896.

————. *The Prince and the Pauper.* Harper & Brothers, New York, 1883.

————. *Pudd'nhead Wilson.* Harper & Brothers, New York, 1899.

————. *Report from Paradise.* Harper & Brothers, New York, 1952.

————. *Roughing It.* 2 vols. Harper & Brothers, New York, 1906.

————. *1601.* Wehman Brothers, Inc. Cedar Knolls, New Jersey, 1968.

————. *Sketches New & Old.* Harper & Brothers, New York, 1907.

————. *A Tramp Abroad.* 2 vols. Harper & Brothers, New York, 1907.

Newspapers
(Signed articles)

Clemens, Samuel L. "Those Blasted Children." *The Golden Era* (San Francisco), March 27, 1864.

BIBLIOGRAPHY

————. "Concerning Notaries." *Daily Territorial Enterprise* (Virginia City, Nevada), February 9, 1864.

————. "Frightful Accident to Dan De Quille." *The Golden Era* (San Francisco), May 1, 1864.

————. "Greeting to Artemus Ward." *The Golden Era* (San Francisco), November 29, 1863.

————. "The Lick House Ball"; "All About the Fashions." *The Golden Era* (San Francisco), September 27, 1863.

————. "Jim Smiley and His Jumping Frog." New York *Saturday Press*, November 18, 1865.

————. "Jim Wolf and the Tom-Cats." New York *Sunday Mercury*, July 14, 1867.

————. "Mark Twain's Farewell." *Alta California* (San Francisco), December 15, 1866.

————. "Mark Twain's Interior Notes." *San Francisco Bulletin*, November 30, 1866–December 7, 1866. Letters covering his lecture tour.

————. "Mark Twain Robbed." "Card To The Highwaymen." *Territorial Enterprise* (Virginia City, Nevada), November 11, 1866.

————. "Mark Twain in Washington." Headed "Washington, December 10th, 1867." Covering the new Hawaiian treaty; postmaster for San Francisco; office seekers. *Alta California* (San Francisco), January 15, 1868.

————. "Letter from 'Mark Twain.'" Headed "Washington, December 14, 1867." Covering "Government Salaries"; "Female Clerks"; "The Sutro Tunnel." Ibid. January 21, 1868.

————. "Mark Twain in Washington." Headed "Washington, January 11th." An account of his hearing Charles Dickens read at Steinway Hall, New York. Ibid. February 5, 1868.

————. "Mark Twain in Washington." Headed "Washington, January 12th, 1868. Account of the Washington Correspondents' Club banquet at which he spoke on "Woman." Ibid. February 19, 1868.

————. "Mark Twain in Washington." Headed "Washington, January 16th." Account of General Grant's reception. Ibid. February 14, 1868.

————. "Mark Twain on His Travels." Headed "Washington, February 1st." Description of "The White Fawn" and of Hartford, Connecticut. Has accepted J. Ross Browne's request to join his staff; expects to follow Browne to China shortly. Ibid. March 3, 1868.

————. "Letter from 'Mark Twain.'" Headed "Hartford, Conn., August Recently, 1868." Account of his voyage from San Francisco to New York via Isthmus of Panama; shipboard entertainment; meeting with

Capt. Ned Wakeman at Panama, and Lotta Crabtree in New York; Hartford morality. Ibid. September 6, 1868.

———. "Letter from 'Mark Twain.' " Headed "Hartford, October 24, 1868." Account of an international boat race. He visits Elmira, Cleveland, Chicago, St. Louis. Ibid. November 15, 1868.

———. "Letter from 'Mark Twain.' " Headed "Hartford, October 28th, 1868." Relates that his book, *The Innocents Abroad*, is ready for engravers and electrotypers. Considering going to China to join J. Ross Browne. Starts lecturing on November 15. Describes fall coloring. Ibid. November 22, 1868.

———. "Letter from 'Mark Twain.' " Headed, "New York, July 1869." First impressions of Boston. Sketch of humorist Petroleum V. Nasby with whom he toured Boston. Ibid. July 25, 1869.

———. "River Intelligence." Signed "Sergeant Fathom." Parody of Captain I. Sellers' report on river conditions. *New Orleans Daily Crescent*, May 17, 1859.

———. "Story of the Bad Little Boy." *The Californian* (San Francisco), December 23, 1865.

———. "What Have The Police Been Doing?" *The Golden Era* (San Francisco), January 21, 1866.

———. "The Whittier Birthday Speech." *Boston Evening Transcript*, December 18, 1877.

Periodicals

Clemens, Samuel L. "Concerning the Jews." *Harper's Magazine*, September 1899.

———. "The Dandy Frightening the Squatter." *The Carpet-Bag*, May 1, 1852.

———. "In Defense of Harriet Shelley." *North American Review*, July 1894.

———. "Eve's Diary." *Harper's Magazine*, December 1905.

———. "Fenimore Cooper's Literary Offenses." *North American Review*, July 1895.

———. "The Man That Corrupted Hadleyburg." *Harper's Magazine*, December 1899.

———. "Old Times on the Mississippi." *Atlantic Monthly*, January–July 1875.

———. "My Literary Debut." *Century Magazine*, December 1899.

———. "The Private History of a Campaign That Failed." *Century Magazine*, December 1885.

————. "Rambling Notes of an Idle Excursion." *Atlantic Monthly*, October–December 1877.

————. "A True Story." *Atlantic Monthly*, November 1874.

————. "The Turning Point of My Life." *Harper's Bazar*, February 1910.

Writings on Mark Twain, Primary Sources, Printed

Newspapers, Magazines

Barnes, George E. "Mark Twain As He Was Known During His Stay on the Pacific Slope." *Daily Morning Call* (San Francisco), April 17, 1887.

Clemens, Clara. "My Father." *The Mentor*, May 1924.

De Quille, Dan. (William Wright). "House-Keeping with Mark Twain." *The Golden Era*, December 6, 1863.

————. "An Infamous Proceeding." and "Mark Twain Takes a Lesson in the Manly Art." *The Golden Era*, May 1, 1864.

————. "Reporting with Mark Twain." *The Californian Illustrated Magazine*, July 1893.

Evans, Albert S. ("Amigo"). San Francisco correspondent for *Gold Hill Daily News* (Nevada). "Mark Twain." Brief, uneventful career as local on *Call.* October 13, 1864. (The nine Evans items following are also from the *Gold Hill Daily News.*)

————. "Professional Jealousy." November 4, 1865. Mark Twain's feud with reporter Young Wilson.

————. "Young Wilson Throws Up the Sponge." November 11, 1865. Also comments on Twain's heavy drinking.

————. "Cold Weather." November 25, 1865. Twain drunk for past two weeks to prevent taking a cold.

————. " 'California literature' " looking up despite Twain's "lamentable failures." December 16, 1865.

————. "Surprisingly, Mark Twain Survives Christmas Day Festivities." December 30, 1865.

————. "Orwell's Execution." January 29, 1866. Twain attends hanging. He is "fearfully down on the police." Evans offers five rules to follow when arrested and jailed for public drunkenness.

————. February 12, 1866. Evans insists nothing personal meant in that advice, but Mark has taken it so. Cites incidents involving the "sage-brush Bohemian" at which he might rightfully take offense.

————. "A Brilliant Idea." January 22, 1866. Relocation of San Francisco slaughterhouses. Compares their stench to that in police court when "sagebrush Bohemian" is in dock for being drunk overnight.

———. "Mark Twain Played Out." February 19, 1866. Comments on Twain's poor health. Twain expects to leave for Honolulu; will be "sadly missed" by police.

Fairbanks, Mary Mason. "The Wedding of 'Mark Twain.' " *Cleveland Daily Herald,* February 8, 1870.

Goodman, Joseph T. "Mark Twain." Comments on personal letter from Clemens, October 4, 1867, Cadiz, Spain. *Territorial Enterprise* (Virginia City, Nevada), December 1, 1867.

———. Recollections of Mark Twain. "Memories of Humorist's Early Days." *The San Francisco Examiner,* April 22, 1910.

Greening, Tabitha Quarles. Interview and recollections of Mark Twain by his cousin. *Hannibal Courier-Post,* March 6, 1935.

Higbie, Calvin H. Reminiscences of Mark Twain in Michael J. Phillips, "Mark Twain's Partner." *The Saturday Evening Post,* September 11, 1920.

Matthews, Brander. "Mark Twain As Speech Maker and Story Teller." *The Mentor,* May 1924.

Twichell, Joseph H. "Mark Twain." *Harper's Magazine,* May 1896.

Webster, Samuel and Doris. "Whitewashing Jane Clemens." *The Bookman,* LXI, 1925.

Unsigned Newspaper Articles

The Daily Dramatic Chronicle (San Francisco), October 10, 1866. "Off for Washoe."

The Era—New Orleans, March 20, 1864. "Death of Capt. Isaiah Sellers."

Grass Valley Daily Union (California), October 19, 1866. "Lecture by Mark Twain." Subject: "The Sandwich Islands."

———. April 21, 1868. "Mark Twain Returns; Insurrection at 8." Lecture on "Pilgrim Life."

Nevada Daily Gazette; Nevada Daily Transcript (Nevada City, California). October 18, through October 24, 1866: Mark Twain's arrival at National Exchange Hotel; announcement of lecture; arrangements to talk at Red Dog.

———. April 20, 1868. Mark Twain's return to lecture on "Pilgrim Life."

Sacramento Daily Union, October 11, 1866. Mark Twain to lecture on Sandwich Islands at Sacramento's Metropolitan Theater.

————. "Mark Twain at the Metropolitan." October 12, 1866. Review of talk.

Primary Sources

Books

Clemens, Clara. *My Father, Mark Twain.* Harper & Brothers, New York, 1931.

Doten, Alfred. *The Journals of Alfred Doten, 1849–1903.* 3 vols. Walter Van Tilburg Clark, ed. University of Nevada Press, Reno, 1973.

Gillis, William R. *Gold Rush Days With Mark Twain.* Albert & Charles Boni, New York, 1930.

Howe, M. A. DeWolfe. *Memories of a Hostess, A Chronicle of Eminent Friendships, Drawn . . . from the Diaries of Mrs. James T. Fields.* The Atlantic Monthly Press, Boston, 1922.

Howells, William Dean. *Life in Letters of William Dean Howells.* Mildred Howells, ed. 2 vols. Doubleday, Doran, Garden City, N.Y., 1928.

————. *My Mark Twain: Reminiscences and Criticism.* Harper & Brothers, New York, 1910.

Lawton, Mary. *A Lifetime with Mark Twain. The Memories of Katy Leary.* Harcourt, Brace & Co., New York, 1925.

Moffett, Samuel E. "Mark Twain: A Biographical Sketch," in Clemens, *Literary Essays.*

Stewart, William M. *Reminiscences.* George Rothwell Brown, ed. Neale Publishing Co., New York, 1908.

Secondary Sources

Books

Studies of Clemens' life and work:

Benson, Ivan. *Mark Twain's Western Years.* Stanford University Press, Stanford, California, 1938.

Brashear, Minnie M. *Mark Twain, Son of Missouri.* University of North Carolina Press, Chapel Hill, 1934.

Brooks, Van Wyck. *The Ordeal of Mark Twain.* Revised ed. E. P. Dutton & Co., New York, 1933.

De Voto, Bernard. *Mark Twain's America,* and *Mark Twain at Work.* Houghton Mifflin, Boston, 1967.

BIBLIOGRAPHY

Duckett, Margaret. *Mark Twain and Bret Harte.* University of Oklahoma Press, Norman, 1964.

Fatout, Paul. *Mark Twain in Virginia City.* Indiana University Press, Bloomington, 1964.

Ferguson, De Lancy. *Mark Twain: Man and Legend.* Bobbs-Merrill Co., Indianapolis, 1943.

Gibson, William M. *The Art of Mark Twain.* Oxford University Press, New York, 1976.

————. ed. *Mark Twain's Mysterious Stranger Manuscripts.* University of California Press, Berkeley, 1969.

Kaplan, Justin. *Mark Twain and His World.* Simon & Schuster, New York, 1974.

————. *Mark Twain, A Profile.* Hill & Wang, New York, 1967.

————. *Mr. Clemens and Mark Twain.* Simon & Schuster. New York, 1966.

Lauber, John. *The Making of Mark Twain: A Biography.* American Heritage, New York, 1985.

Leacock, Stephen. *Mark Twain.* P. Davies, London, 1932.

Lennon, Nigey. *Mark Twain in California.* Chronicle Books, San Francisco, 1982.

Mack, Effie Mona. *Mark Twain in Nevada.* Charles Scribner's Sons, New York, 1947.

Meltzer, Milton. *Mark Twain Himself: A Pictorial Biography.* Bonanza Books, New York, 1960.

O'Connor, Richard. *Bret Harte, A Biography.* Little, Brown & Co., Boston, 1966.

Paine, Albert Bigelow. *Mark Twain, A Biography.* 4 vols. Harper & Brothers, New York, 1912.

Varble, Rachel M. *The Story of Mark Twain's Mother.* Doubleday & Co., Garden City, New York, 1964.

Wagenknecht, Edward. *Mark Twain, The Man and His Work.* University of Oklahoma Press, Norman, 1961.

Wecter, Dixon. *Sam Clemens of Hannibal.* Houghton Mifflin Co., Boston, 1952.

Periodicals

Baender, Paul. "Alias Macfarlane: A Revision of Mark Twain's Biography." *American Literature,* Vol. 38, May 1966.

Branch, Edgar M. "Fact and Fiction in the Blind Lead Episode of *Roughing It.*" *Nevada Historical Society Quarterly,* Winter 1985.

Graves, Wallace. "Mark Twain's 'Burning Shame.' " *Nineteenth-Century Fiction*, June 1968.

Jones, Alexander E. "Mark Twain and Freemasonry." *American Literature*, November 1954.

Leisy, Ernest E. "Mark Twain and Isaiah Sellers." *American Literature*, Vol. 13, 1941–42.

Lorch, Fred W. "Mark Twain in Iowa." *Iowa Journal of History and Politics*, Vol. 29.

———. "Mark Twain's Trip to Humboldt in 1861." *American Literature*, November 1938.

Rocha, Guy Louis, and Roger Smith. "Mark Twain and the Nevada Notary Stampede." *Nevada Historical Society Quarterly*, Summer 1983.

General Background

Altrocchi, Julia Cooley. *The Spectacular San Franciscans*. E. P. Dutton & Co., New York, 1949.

Angel, Myron, ed. *History of Nevada*. Thompson & West, Oakland, California, 1881.

———. *History of Nevada County, California*. Thompson & West, Oakland, California, 1880.

Ayres, James J. *Gold and Sunshine: Reminiscences of Early California*. The Gorham Press, Boston, 1927.

Brady, Norval L. ("Gull"). "Recollections." *Hannibal Courier-Post*, March 6, 1935.

Brewer, William H. *Up and Down California in 1860–1864*. Francis P. Farquhar, ed. Yale University Press, New Haven, 1930.

Browne, J. Ross. *Mining Adventures, California & Nevada, 1863–1865*. Paisano Press, Balboa Island, California, 1961.

———. *A Peep at Washoe and Washoe Revisited*. Paisano Press, Balboa Island, California, 1959.

Buckbee, Edna Bryan. *The Saga of Old Tuolumne*. Press of the Pioneers, New York, 1935.

Chambrun, Adolphe de. *Impressions of Lincoln and the Civil War: Letters to His Wife*. Random House, New York, 1952.

Cummins, Ella Sterling. *The Story of the Files*. Cooperative Printing Co., San Francisco, 1892.

De Quille, Dan. "Artemus Ward in Nevada." *The Californian Illustrated Magazine*, August 1893.

———. *The Big Bonanza.* Alfred A. Knopf, New York, 1947.

Doten, Alfred. "Early Journalism in Nevada." *The Nevada Magazine*, September–November 1899.

Drury, Wells. *An Editor on the Comstock Lode.* Pacific Books, Palo Alto, California, 1948.

Drury, William. *Norton I, Emperor of the United States.* Dodd, Mead & Co., New York, 1986.

Goodman, David Michael. *A Western Panorama, 1840–1875: The Travels, Writings and Influence of J. Ross Browne.* The Arthur H. Clark Co., Glendale, California, 1966.

Goodman, Joseph T. *The Archaic Maya Inscriptions.* Taylor & Francis, London, 1897.

———. "Artemus Ward, His Visit to the Comstock Lode." *The San Francisco Chronicle*, January 10, 1892.

Goodwin, Charles Carroll. *As I Remember Them.* Privately printed, Salt Lake City, 1913.

Gudde, Erwin G. *California Gold Camps.* University of California Press, Berkeley, 1975.

Holcombe, Return Ira. *History of Marion County, Missouri.* n.p. St. Louis, 1884.

Holing, Dwight. "The Birds of *Paradise.*" *Pacific Discovery*, July–September 1987. Hawaiian kings' feather cloak.

House, Homer D. *Wildflowers.* The Macmillan Co., New York, 1934.

Leman, Walter M. *Memories of an Old Actor.* A. Roman Co., San Francisco, 1886.

Martineau, Harriet. *Retrospect of Western Travel.* 2 vols. Saunders & Otley, London, 1838.

McGrath, Roger D. *Gunfighters, Highwaymen & Vigilantes: Violence on the Frontier.* University of California Press, Berkeley, 1984.

Mackenzie, Norman and Jeanne. *Charles Dickens, A Life.* Oxford University Press, New York, 1979.

Neville, Amelia Ransome. *The Fantastic City.* Houghton Mifflin, Boston, 1932.

New York Times, September 15, 1891. "Obituary" for Charles Adolphe, Marquis de Chambrun.

Ornstein, Robert. *Shakespeare's Comedies.* University of Delaware Press, Newark, Delaware, 1986.

Pacific Coast Business Directory for 1867. Henry G. Langly, San Francisco, 1867.

Paullin, C. O. "Mark Twain's Virginia Kin." *William and Mary College Quarterly*, 2d series XV, 1935.

———. "The Moorman Family of Virginia. *William and Mary College Quarterly*, 2d series XII, 1932.

Porter, Eliot. *Appalachian Wilderness.* Ballantine Books, New York, 1979.

Root, Frank S. and William E. Connelley. *The Overland Stage to California.* Privately printed. Topeka, Kansas, 1901.

Rourke, Constance. *Troupers of the Gold Coast or The Rise of Lotta Crabtree.* Harcourt, Brace & Co., New York, 1928.

Royce, Josiah. *California.* Alfred A. Knopf, New York, 1948.

Rugoff, Milton. *The Beechers, An American Family in the Nineteenth Century.* Harper & Row, New York, 1981.

Sanborn, Margaret. *The Grand Tetons.* G. P. Putnam's Sons, New York, 1978.

———. *Robert E. Lee, A Portrait: 1807–1861.* J. B. Lippincott Co., Philadelphia, 1966.

Squires, Monas N. "Henry Lewis and His Mammoth Panorama." *The Missouri Historical Review*, April 1, 1933.

Swanberg, W. A. *Sickles the Incredible.* Charles Scribner's Sons, New York, 1956.

Territorial Enterprise (Virginia City, Nevada), August 23, 1900. "Jim Townsend Dead."

U. S. Federal Writers' Project. "Keokuk, Iowa" in *Lee County History.* Iowa Writers' Program, WPA. n.d.

———. *Missouri.* Duell, Sloan & Pearce, New York, 1941.

Virginia Evening Chronicle (Virginia City, Nevada), August 23, 1900. "Pioneer Journalist Passes." Death of James W. E. Townsend.

Walker, Franklin. *San Francisco's Literary Frontier.* Alfred A. Knopf, New York, 1939.

Wigginton, Eliot, ed. *Foxfire 2.* Anchor Press/Doubleday, Garden City, New York, 1973.

———. *Foxfire 3.* Anchor Press/Doubleday, Garden City, New York, 1975.

County Records

Marion County Circuit Court Records, No. 3516. *State of Missouri* v. *Vincent Hudson,* for murder.

———. No. 3873. *State of Missouri* v. *William P. Owsley,* for murder.

Index

INDEX

INDEX